W9-CUG-488

# ENCYCLOPEDIA OF THE AGE OF IMPERIALISM, 1800–1914

# ENCYCLOPEDIA OF THE AGE OF IMPERIALISM, 1800–1914

*Volume 1*

A–K

*Edited by* **Carl Cavanagh Hodge**

**Greenwood Press**
Westport, Connecticut • London

**Library of Congress Cataloging-in-Publication Data**

Encyclopedia of the age of imperialism, 1800–1914 / edited by Carl Cavanagh Hodge.
    p. cm.
   Includes bibliographical references and index.
   ISBN 978–0–313–33404–7 (set : alk. paper)—ISBN 978–0–313–33406–1 (v.1 : alk.
paper)—ISBN 978–0–313–33407–8 (v.2 : alk. paper)   1. History, Modern—19th
century—Chronology—Encyclopedias.   2. Europe—History—1789–1900—Chronology—
Encyclopedias.   3. Europe—History—1871–1918—Chronology—Encyclopedias.
4. Great powers—History—19th century—Chronology—Encyclopedias.   5. Great
powers—History—20th century—Chronology—Encyclopedias.   I. Hodge,
Carl Cavanagh.
   D358.E45 2008
   909.8103—dc22        2007026483

British Library Cataloguing in Publication Data is available.

Library of Congress Catalog Card Number: 2007026483

ISBN-13: 978–0–313–33404–7 (set)
        978–0–313–33406–1 (vol 1)
        978–0–313–33407–8 (vol 2)

First published in 2008

Greenwood Press, 88 Post Road West, Westport, CT 06881
An imprint of Greenwood Publishing Group, Inc.
www.greenwood.com

Printed in the United States of America

The paper used in this book complies with the
Permanent Paper Standard issued by the National
Information Standards Organization (Z39.48–1984).

10   9   8   7   6   5   4   3   2   1

Every reasonable effort has been made to trace the owners of copyright materials in this book,
but in some instances this has proven impossible. The editor and publisher will be glad to
receive information leading to a more complete acknowledgments in subsequent printings of
the book and in the meantime extend their apologies for any omissions.

To Jane, the best of friends, Easter 2007

# CONTENTS

# LIST OF ENTRIES

ABC Powers
Abd-al-Qādir (1808–1883)
Abensberg, Battle of (1809)
Aborigines
Aboukir Bay, Battle of (1798)
Abyssinia
Achinese War (1873–1907)
Action Française
Act of Union (1801)
Acton, Lord John (1834–1902)
Adams, John (1735–1826)
Adams, John Quincy (1767–1848)
Adams-Onís Treaty (1819)
Adowa, Battle of (1896)
Adrianople, Treaty of (1829)
Aehrenthal, Aloys Lexa von (1854–1912)
Afghanistan
Afghan Wars (1838–1842, 1878–1880)
Africa, Scramble for
Afrikaners
Agadir Crisis (1911)
Aigun, Treaty of (1858)
Aix-la-Chapelle, Congress of (1818)
*Alabama* Dispute (1871–1872)
Alamo, Battle of (1836)
Åland Islands
Alaskan Boundary Dispute (1896–1903)
Alaska Purchase Treaty (1867)
Albania
Albrecht Friedrich Rudolf, Archduke (1817–1895)
Alexander, King of Yugoslavia (1888–1934)
Alexander I, Tsar of Russia (1777–1825)

Alexander II, Tsar of Russia (1818–1881)
Alexander III, Tsar of Russia (1845–1894)
Algeciras Conference (1906)
Algeria
Aliwal, Battle of (1846)
Alsace-Lorraine
American Civil War (1861–1865)
Amiens, Treaty of (1802)
Amundsen, Roald (1872–1928)
Anarchism
Andijan Revolt (1898)
Andrássy, Gyula, Count (1823–1890)
Anglo-American Treaty (1818)
Anglo-American War (1812–1815)
Anglo-Burmese Wars (1824–1826, 1852, 1885)
Anglo-Japanese Alliance (1902, 1905)
Anglo-Nepal War (1814–1816)
Anglo-Russian Convention (1907)
Angola
Annam
Annexation Crisis (1908–1909)
Antarctica
Anti-Corn Law League
Antietam, Battle of (1862)
Arctic
Argentina
Armed Neutrality, League of
Armenia
Armenian Massacres (1894–1896)
Arrah, Siege of (1857)
Arrow War (1856–1860)
Artigas, José Gervasio (1794–1850)

# LIST OF PRIMARY DOCUMENTS

# GUIDE TO RELATED TOPICS

## Acts, Conventions, Treaties, and Understandings

Act of Union (1801)
Adams-Onís Treaty (1819)
Adrianople, Treaty of (1829)
Aigun, Treaty of (1858)
Alaska Purchase Treaty (1867)
Amiens, Treaty of (1802)
Anglo-American Treaty (1818)
Anglo-Russian Convention (1907)
Ausgleich (1867)
Australian Colonies Government Act (1850)
Bassein, Treaty of (1802)
Bates Agreement (1899–1904)
Beijing, Conventions of (1860)
Björkö, Treaty of (1905)
Bond of 1844
Boxer Protocol (1901)
British North America Act (1867)
Burlingame Treaty (1868)
Carlsbad Decrees (1819)
Chaumont, Treaty of (1814)
Clayton-Bulwer Treaty (1850)
Concordat of 1801
Corn Laws (1804, 1815)
Cuban Reciprocity Treaty (1902)
Entente Cordiale (1904)
Foraker Amendment (1899)
Franco-Italian Convention (1902)
Franco-Spanish Agreement (1904)
Frankfurt, Treaty of (1871)
French Restoration (1814)

Geneva Convention (1864)
Guadalupe Hidalgo, Treaty of (1848)
Hay-Bunau-Varilla Treaty (1903)
Hay-Herrán Treaty (1903)
Hay-Pauncefote Treaty (1901)
Heligoland-Zanzibar Treaty (1890)
Inkiar Skelessi, Treaty of (1833)
Irish Land Acts (1870–1909)
Kanagawa, Treaty of (1854)
Kittery Peace (1905)
London Straits Convention (1841)
London, Treaty of (1839)
Louisiana Purchase (1803)
Lunéville, Treaty of (1801)
Mediterranean Agreements (1887)
Military Conversations (1906–1914)
Missouri Compromise (1820)
Münchengrätz Convention (1833)
Nanjing, Treaty of (1842)
Navigation Acts
Paris, Declaration of (1856)
Paris, Treaty of (1815)
Paris, Treaty of (1856)
Paris, Treaty of (1898)
Platt Amendment (1901)
Portsmouth, Treaty of (1905)
Pressburg, Treaty of (1805)
Pretoria, Convention of (1881)
Reinsurance Treaty (1887)
Royal Titles Act (1876)
Rush-Bagot Treaty (1817)
Sand River Convention (1852)
San Stefano, Treaty of (1878)

## Artists, Intellectuals, Inventors, and Explorers

## Asia, the Middle East, the Pacific, and the Polar Regions

Annam
Antarctica
Arctic
Australia
Australian Commonwealth (1900)
Australian-German Relations
Australian-Japanese Relations
Bengal
Burma
Calcutta
Cambodia
Ceylon
China
Cochin China
Dutch East Indies
East India Companies
Far East
Great Game
Hindustan
Hong Kong
Hyderabad
India
India Act (1858)
Indian Mutiny (1857–1858)
Indochina
Itō, Hirobumi (1841–1909)
Japanese Empire
Java
Kashmir
Khalsa
Khiva Khanate
Kiaochow
Korea
Kwang-chow Wan
Laos
Madras
Manchuria
Meiji Restoration (1868–1912)
Nepal
New Guinea
New Zealand
Open Door
Oyama, Iwao (1842–1916)
Persia
Philippines
Port Arthur
Punjab
Raffles, Sir Thomas Stamford (1781–1826)
Russian Far East
Sakhalin
Satsuma Rebellion (1877)

Sepoy
Shanghai
Siam
Siberia
Silk Road
Singapore
Sun Yatsen (1866–1925)
Syria
Taiping Rebellion (1850–1864)
Taisho Democracy
Tatars
Thugs
Tokugawa Shōgunate (1600–1868)
Tonkin
Trans-Siberian Railway
Ts'u Hsi (1835–1908)
Turkestan
Vladivostok
Weihaiwei
Zaibatsu
Z-Flag

## Battles

Abensberg, Battle of (1809)
Aboukir Bay, Battle of (1798)
Adowa, Battle of (1896)
Alamo, Battle of (1836)
Aliwal, Battle of (1846)
Antietam, Battle of (1862)
Arrah, Siege of (1857)
Aspern-Essling, Battle of (1809)
Assaye, Battle of (1803)
Austerlitz, Battle of (1805)
Badli-ke-Serai, Battle of (1857)
Bailén, Battle of (1808)
Balaklava, Battle of (1854)
Beresina, Battles of (1812)
Blood River, Battle of (1838)
Borodino, Battle of (1812)
Buena Vista, Battle of (1847)
Burkersdorf, Battle of (1866)
Caldiero, Second Battle of (1805)
Chancellorsville, Battle of (1863)
Chattanooga, Battle of (1863)
Chickamauga Creek, Battle of (1863)
Colenso, Battle of (1899)
Copenhagen, First Battle of (1801)
Copenhagen, Second Battle of (1807)
Corunna, Battle of (1809)
Custoza, Battles of (1849, 1866)
Delhi, Battle of (1803)
Delhi, Siege of (1857)

## Concepts, Labels, and Slogans

Tirpitz Plan
Treaty Ports
Two-Power Standard
Union
*Weltpolitik*
White Man's Burden

## Conferences and Congresses

Aix-la-Chapelle, Congress of (1818)
Algeciras Conference (1906)
Berlin Conference (1884–1885)
Berlin, Congress of (1878)
Hague Conferences (1899, 1907)
Imperial Conferences
Congress System
Laibach, Congress of (1821)
Troppau, Congress of (1820)
Verona, Congress of (1822)
Vienna, Congress of (1815)

## Crises

Agadir Crisis (1911)
*Alabama* Dispute (1871–1872)
Annexation Crisis (1908–1909)
Armenian Massacres (1894–1896)
Balkan Crises (1875–1878, 1908–1913)
Dogger Bank Incident (1904)
Dreyfus Affair (1894–1906)
Ems Telegram (1870)
Fashoda Incident (1898)
Irish Famine (1845–1850)
July Crisis (1914)
July Monarchy (1830–1848)
July Revolution (1830)
Moroccan Crisis (1905)
October Manifesto (1905)
Oregon Question
Panama Scandal (1892–1893)
Paris Commune (1871)
Perdicaris Affair (1904)
Russian Revolution (1905)
Samoan Crisis
Tampico and Vera Cruz Incidents (1914)
Venezuelan Crisis (1895)

## Empires

British Empire
French Empire
German Empire
Habsburg Empire
Japanese Empire
Ottoman Empire
Portuguese Empire (1415–1808)
Russian Empire
Spanish Empire
United States

## Europe

Åland Islands
Albania
Alsace-Lorraine
Armenia
Austrian Empire
Austria-Hungary
Bavaria
Belgium
Bohemia
Bosnia-Herzegovina
Bosporus
Bulgaria
Caucasus
Central Powers
Confederation of the Rhine (1806–1813)
Crete
Croatia-Slavonia
Cyprus
Danubian Principalities
Dardanelles
Denmark
Finland
German Confederation
Gibraltar
Greece
Hesse-Cassel
Hesse-Darmstadt
Hungary
Iceland
Ireland
Italy
Kiel
Macedonia
Malta
Montenegro
Moscow
Netherlands, Kingdom of the
Norway
North German Confederation (1867–1871)
Novibazar, Sanjak of
Ossetia
Piedmont-Sardinia, Kingdom of
Prussia
Rumania
Saar
Salonica

Wilson, Woodrow (1856–1924)
Witte, Sergei (1849–1915)
Wolseley, Garnet Wolseley, Field Marshal Viscount (1833–1913)
Wood, Leonard (1860–1927)

## Monarchs and Dynasties

Albrecht Friedrich Rudolf, Archduke (1817–1895)
Alexander, King of Yugoslavia (1888–1934)
Alexander I, Tsar of Russia (1777–1825)
Alexander II, Tsar of Russia (1818–1881)
Alexander III, Tsar of Russia
Bonaparte, Louis (1778–1846)
Bonaparte, Louis Napoleon (1808–1873)
Bonaparte, Napoleon (1769–1821)
Bourbon Dynasty (1589–1848)
Bukhara Emirate
Charles, Archduke of Austria (1771–1847)
Charles X, King of France (1757–1836)
Edward VII, King of Great Britain (1841–1910)
Francis Ferdinand, Archduke of Austria (1863–1914)
Francis Joseph, Emperor of Austria (1830–1916)
George III, King of Great Britain (1738–1820)
George IV, King of Great Britain (1762–1830)
George V, King of Great Britain and Emperor of India (1865–1936)
Haakon VII, King of Norway (1872–1957)
Habsburg Dynasty
Hohenzollern Dynasty
Louis XVIII (1755–1824)
Maximilian, Emperor of Mexico (1832–1867)
Mehmet Ali (1769–1848)
Mehmet V, Sultan of Turkey (1844–1918)
Mutsuhito, Emperor of Japan (1852–1912)
Nicholas I, Tsar of Russia (1796–1855)
Nicholas II, Tsar of Russia (1868–1918)
Qing Dynasty (1644–1912)
Victor Emmanuel II (1820–1878)
Victor Emmanuel III (1869–1947)
Victoria, Queen of Great Britain (1819–1901)
Wilhelm I, Kaiser of Germany (1797–1888)
Wilhelm II, Kaiser of Germany (1859–1941)

## Movements

Action Française
Anarchism
Anti-Corn Law League
Black Hand
Bolsheviks
Bonapartism
Communism
Decembrists
Freemasonry
Impressionism
Internationalism
Jadidism
Liberal Imperialists
Liberalism
Mensheviks
Mercantilism
Narodna Odbrana
Navalism
Nihilism
Orientalism
Progressivism
Protectionism
Radicalism
Sinn Féin
Slavism
Social Darwinism
Tariff Reform League
Terrorism
Young Ireland
Young Italy (1831)
Young Turks
Wahhabi/Wahhabism
Zionism

## Soldiers

Blücher, Gebhard von (1742–1819)
Bonaparte, Napoleon (1769–1821)
Boulanger, General Georges-Ernest (1837–1891)
Campbell, Sir Colin, Baron Clyde (1792–1863)
Clausewitz, Carl von (1780–1831)
Falkenhayn, Erich von (1861–1922)
Foch, Ferdinand (1851–1929)
Gneisenau, August Wilhelm von (1760–1831)
Gordon, Charles George (1833–1885)
Grant, Ulysses S. (1822–1885)
Haig, Douglas (1861–1928)
Hindenburg, Paul von Beneckendorff und von (1847–1934)
Jackson, Andrew (1767–1845)
Jellicoe, John Rushworth (1859–1935)
Mackensen, August von (1849–1945)

MacMahon, Patrice Edmé Maurice (1808–1893)

Moltke, Helmuth von (1800–1891)

Moltke, Helmuth Johannes Ludwig von (1848–1916)

Nelson, Horatio (1758–1805)

Roon, Albrecht von (1803–1879)

Scharnhorst, Gerhard Johann von (1755–1813)

Tirpitz, Alfred von (1849–1930)

## Technologies and Inventions

Berlin-Baghdad Railway

*Dreadnought*

Great Exhibition (1851)

Kaiser-Wilhelm-Kanal

Machine Gun

Oil

Panama Canal

Railways

Steamboats/Steamships

Telegraph

Zoological Gardens

## Wars and Conflicts

Achinese War (1873–1907)

Afghan Wars (1838–1842, 1878–1880)

American Civil War (1861–1865)

Andijan Revolt (1898)

Anglo-American War (1812–1815)

Anglo-Burmese Wars (1824–1826, 1852, 1885)

Anglo-Nepal War (1814–1816)

Arrow War (1856–1860)

Ashanti Wars

Australian Frontier Wars (1788–1928)

Austro-Prussian War (1866)

Balkan Wars (1912–1913)

Boer Wars (1880–1881, 1899–1902)

Boxer Insurrection (1900)

Carlist Wars (1833–1840, 1847–1849, 1872–1876)

Crimean War (1853–1856)

Franco-Prussian War (1870–1871)

Indian Wars

Italo-Abyssinian War (1887–1896)

Italo-Turkish War (1911–1912)

Kaffir Wars (1781–1879)

Liberation, War of (1813)

Maji-Maji Rebellion (1905–1907)

Maori Wars (1843–1847, 1863–1870)

Maratha Wars (1775–1782, 1803–1805, 1817–1818)

Matabele Wars (1893–1894, 1896–1897)

Mexican-American War (1846–1848)

Napoleonic Wars (1792–1815)

Opium War (1839–1842)

Peninsular War (1808–1814)

Polish Rebellions

Restoration War (1868–1869)

Russo-Khokandian War (1864–1865)

Russo-Japanese War (1904–1905)

Russo-Swedish War (1808–1809)

Russo-Turkish War (1806–1812)

Russo-Turkish War (1828–1829)

Russo-Turkish War (1877–1878)

Sikh Wars (1845–1846, 1848–1849)

Sino-French War (1883–1885)

Sino-Japanese War (1894–1895)

Sioux Wars (1862, 1876–1877, 1890–1891)

Spanish-American War (1898)

War of the Pacific (1879–1882)

Zulu War (1879)

# PREFACE

"It is a comfortable feeling to know that you stand on your own ground," observes the archdeacon in Trollope's *Last Chronicle of Barset*, "land is about the only thing that can't fly away." A unifying theme to the competition among the Great Powers over the 100 years preceding the outbreak of World War I is that of a constant struggle over territory in Europe and beyond. From Napoleon's Marengo campaign to force Austria out of northern Italy in 1800 to Austria-Hungary's determination in 1914 to punish Serbia for its interference in the Habsburg province of Bosnia-Herzegovina, conflicts over land provide the bookends for an era of sweeping and ultimately explosive change. There is, of course, more than one unifying theme for European and international history between 1800 and 1914. There is the evolution of modern war, the gathering pace of industrialization, the rise of modern nationalism; and the accelerated colonization of non-European peoples through deceit, intimidation, or conquest.

The *Encyclopedia of the Age of Imperialism* was conceived as a jargon-free reference companion for students engaged in the history of the modern world, with special attention to the interconnectedness of these themes. Such a book cannot hope to be exhaustive, but it must at least strive to be comprehensive. The period with which it deals has today such a dense and varied historiography that it would require an author of extraordinary talent or conceit—possibly both—to undertake alone the composition of a reference work that both scholars and educated citizens curious about the past will find reliably useful. The editor of the *Encyclopedia* has instead drawn on the knowledge of more than 60 senior and junior scholars to provide the reader with a selection of entries covering the Great Powers in rise and decline, the wars that attended their fortunes along with the treaties that recorded them, the statesmen and political leaders whose ambitions steered them, the great political and cultural changes that influenced them, and the places and peoples most profoundly affected by them.

A problem peculiar to a work such as this is that it may well succeed in presenting a compendium of facts interesting of themselves without providing a coherent interpretation of their meaning. Aside from its brief Introduction, provided along with a Chronology for putting the reader in temporal context, the *Encyclopedia* is organized around the central assumption that it must emphasize description over interpretation. It attempts through the "See also" cross-references at the end of the text of most entries to highlight the interrelatedness of certain people, places, and events. Equally, the Further Reading listings that end each entry supplement the Select Bibliography found in the back of the book by alerting the reader to the interpretive scholarship available on each entry. The Guide to Related Topics will help readers easily and quickly trace broad and important themes across the *Encyclopedia's* more than 800 entries. The appendix of primary documents is based on the idea that the reader's use of the book can be enriched by exposure to documentary evidence of the thoughts and words of pivotal personalities of the age. Even the determined presentation of objective facts involves a degree of interpretation, to the extent that some facts are deemed more important than others. Documentary evidence, on the other hand, does not fly away.

# ACKNOWLEDGMENTS

It has been a genuine pleasure to be involved in this project, not least of all due to the many scholars with whom I have had the privilege to work. I would like to thank them all for their contributions, large and small, and express to them the hope that my presentation of their work will meet with their approval. I would like further to thank Michael Hermann at Greenwood, both for encouraging me to tackle the project and for indulging my ideas, those of a comparative amateur, on how it ought to be completed. I would lastly like to thank John Wagner for his thorough professionalism and endless patience with me during the completion of the manuscript. The strengths of the *Encyclopedia of the Age of Imperialism* belong to these people. Its weaknesses are my own.

# INTRODUCTION

The Age of Imperialism was a particularly protean period in European and world history beginning with the Napoleonic Wars and ending with outbreak of World War I. In slightly more than a century the matrix of the modern world—visions of independent nationhood contending with notions of international commonwealth, free trade clashing with imperial preference, technological change facilitating both industrial and social revolution and total war—emerged. The recurrent impulse of the period was one of territorial aggrandizement. Derived from the Roman notion of *imperium,* connoting domination brought about through the conquest of one identifiable ethnic group by another, *imperialism* is typically used to refer to *the extension of the power and dominion of one nation over others by military coercion or by political and economic compulsion.*[1] Whereas Europeans governed about a third of the world's land surface in 1800, by 1900 more than 80 percent was under some form of European ascendancy.

Admittedly, the impulse was not particularly new. Leaders of the previous century as dissimilar in temperament and national circumstance as Catherine the Great of Russia and William Pitt the elder of Britain held in common the conviction that states had not only a right but a duty to expand, if necessary at their neighbor's expense. In 1772, Catherine, Frederick the Great of Prussia, and Maria Theresa of Austria partitioned Poland among themselves largely because nothing could stop them. Voltaire, a colossus of the Enlightenment, celebrated the act as a service to humanity.[2] Moreover, by the nineteenth century some the greatest colonial empires built were already in advanced decline. In the sixteenth century, Spain had accumulated vast overseas territories in the first "world empire," yet by 1825 had lost most of it. Portugal's greatest overseas possession, Brazil, was penetrated relatively slowly after 1500 during Lisbon's career as a secondary power with a major role in the Atlantic slave trade and a maritime spice trade stretching from Cape Verde to India and Japan. By 1641, Portugal had lost many of its other overseas possessions to the Dutch. The Netherlands retained many of these into the twentieth century, but the wealth of the Dutch Golden Age of the second half of the seventeenth had by 1800 long since passed. A victim of French conquest and annexation between 1795 and 1814, the Netherlands spent the nineteenth century as an object of Great Power bargains—not the least of which was the secession of Belgium in 1839. By contrast, the Ottoman and Habsburg Empires remained powers to be reckoned with. They governed dozens of subject nationalities right up to the outbreak of World War I in August 1914, although they had known creeping decay as the product of a host of domestic and international factors going back two centuries. The Russo-Turkish War of 1828–1829 and the Austro-Prussian War of 1866 were symptomatic of their eclipse by more robust imperial enterprises.

What distinguished the period between 1800 and 1914 was its enormous consequence for European and global politics in the twentieth century. After 1789, every aspect of the European political and social order, of class, authority, and privilege was challenged by the philosophical ideals and revolutionary upheaval in France, the dominant continental power. And France had yet to recover from the ravages of The Terror before something equally novel succeeded it. If the French Revolution can be called "the single most important event in the entire history of government,"[3] the popular tyranny of Napoleon Bonaparte that signaled an end to its anarchy signaled the birth of the secular religion of nationalism, of mass citizen armies, of war as the science of slaughter—of modern international relations. Bonaparte betrayed the political and civil liberties of 1789. But he also exported the Revolution to the four corners of Europe, redrawing its map and pulling down the edifice of traditional authority wherever his armies marched. Its arbitrary arrests and executions notwithstanding, his regime claimed infinitely fewer lives at home than abroad. Approximately 4 million military and civilian dead are thought to be the cost of European conflict between 1792 and 1814.[4] This figure was itself dwarfed a century later by the return of military conflict among the European powers after more than a half-century of imperial rivalry overseas.

### The Napoleonic Legacy

Napoleonic France's short but extraordinarily dynamic dominion over the European continent, then, was the first chapter in the Age of Imperialism. It began with Bonaparte's innovative response to the conditions created by the Revolution itself, of which he was initially merely a promising soldier. In one form or another the changes wrought by the revolutionary period—the glorification of the expansion of states, the attack on the legitimacy of the territory and social order of the old regime, the extraordinary financial needs of the revolutionary government, and opportunity created by revolutionary flux for the rise of ambitious talent—all spoke to matters of scale and dimension. In the military realm Napoleon did not invent, but rather inherited, modified, and perfected, a form of warfare conceived by Lazare Nicolas Carnot, the minister of war to the revolutionary regime. It was Carnot who applied the *levée en masse* to France's army, an army of now nominally free citizens conscripted to the defense of the republic and the nation to a strength of more than a million men under arms. It was also Carnot who demanded a national force capable of crushing any other by sheer weight of numbers in a war of annihilation rather then maneuver. Lastly, it was Carnot who conscripted the resources of the nation in a planned economy of totalitarian ambition and reversed the eighteenth-century prohibition against armies living off the land into a patriotic duty. Tasked with defending a Jacobin dictatorship fighting for its life and in 1794 spending five times more than its revenue, he could do little else. Yet the success of these armies was neither assured nor probable until they came under the command of the greatest military talent since Alexander.[5]

A graduate of the *École Royale Militaire* as a specialist in artillery, Napoleon launched his career in 1793 in the War of the First Coalition by doing more to capture Toulon from royalist forces than any of the commanders senior to him. Thereafter, his star rose with few interruptions. After proving his loyalty to the regime by raking a Parisian royalist mob with grapeshot, Napoleon secured Carnot's approval of his plan for the invasion of Italy. Under his command the republic then "moved from the defensive to the large-scale offensive and became an expansionist force, determined to roll up the old map of Europe and transform it on principles formed by its own ideology."[6] The Habsburg Empire was the principal victim of Bonaparte's victories in Italy, but these might never have been so consequential had Napoleon not been able to shift roles effortlessly from general to proconsul to diplomat to produce the French puppet Cisalpine and Ligurian Republics and the Treaty of Campo Formio that gave the Austrian Netherlands to France and extended its frontier to the Rhine.

Napoleon's Egyptian campaign was a disaster, but consciousness of that fact was eclipsed by the even greater disaster of the Directory back in France that ultimately occasioned the coup of 18 Brumaire and the true beginning of the Napoleonic era. In Egypt the French army cut down some 10,000 Mamlukes against a loss of only 29 of its own in the Battle of the Pyramids; only days later, however, the British admiral Nelson destroyed most of the French Fleet at Aboukir Bay, better known as the Battle of the Nile, and marooned Napoleon and his men on the wrong side of the Mediterranean. Napoleon scored several victories against large Turkish forces, but then failed to take Acre from a Turkish army under British command. Aside from an appreciation of the value of Egypt—more to the point, the strategic value of a canal there—the campaign did little more in the short term than to make all things Egyptian suddenly fashionable in Paris.[7]

For a coup that was largely bungled, the consequences of the 18 Brumaire were sweeping. A new constitution created a three-member Consulate with Napoleon as First Consul. It also established a Tribunate and a Legislature based on a complex formula of indirect election, yet vested all legislative initiative with the executive. Put to the people in a rigged plebiscite, the document delivered immense power to Napoleon even before the plebiscite of 1802 made him first consul for life. Napoleon's journey to autocracy was completed in May 1804, when the Tribunate proposed to popular approval that he be proclaimed hereditary emperor of the French.[8] The Consulate also produced the 1801 Concordat between the French state and the papacy; the Civil Code, comprehensive reform of the administration of government including the foundation of the prefecture system, an overhaul of the financial system around the creation of the Bank of France, and the establishment of 45 *lycées* assigned the task of education and patriotic indoctrination. The latter goal came easily with Napoleon's first truly great military victory, over the Austrians in the War of the Second Coalition, at the village of Marengo in Piedmont on June 14, 1800.

Between 1800 and 1812, a pattern then set in. It involved a steadily rising level of conflict between Napoleonic France and the serial coalitions arrayed against her on the European continent. It was punctuated by defeats at sea at the hands of the British Royal Navy under Admiral Horatio Nelson, and, with the start of the War of the Fifth Coalition in 1809, increasing British involvement in the continental struggle.

Even more than the name Nelson, Napoleon came to loath that of William Pitt, the implacable Tory whose ministries led British efforts against France in the first three coalitions. The War of the Third Coalition (1805–1806), following a short-lived Anglo-French peace of the Treaty of Amiens, was pivotal to the fate of both nations. It began with the formation of an alliance of Austria, Russia, Sweden, and several of the lesser German states to destroy the French armies in Italy in preparation for an invasion of France itself. Napoleon preempted his enemies by crossing the Rhine with 200,000 men into Bavaria and cutting off, surrounding, and forcing the surrender of an Austrian army of 23,500 at Ulm on October 17, 1805. This dashed the allied plan and laid open Vienna to French occupation. It was followed only four days later by Nelson's destruction of the combined French and Spanish fleets off Cape Trafalgar—19 ships sunk or captured, against none on the British side—thereby securing Britain against French invasion. Napoleon was still digesting this news when word came of a large Russian army marching against him from the north. He moved his own forces to meet the remaining Austrians and their Russian allies to give them battle at Austerlitz on December 2. The result was his greatest victory, a masterpiece of maneuver and deception culminating in a complete rout of numerically superior allied force that ended the Third Coalition with the Treaty of Pressburg. Austerlitz testified to Napoleon's mental grasp of the big picture and understanding of terrain. It also demonstrated a capacity to deploy a large army quickly and the audacity to risk all to divide and annihilate his enemies. A binge of hyperbolic violence involving 73,000 French and more than 90,000 allied troops, Austerlitz established Napoleon's reputation for invincibility. Yet over the long term it was less important than Trafalgar, "the guarantor of Britain's economic prosperity, which allowed her to continue at war and to subsidize her allies at war, while Napoleon ground up and consumed the resources of France and all of Western Europe to feed his military ambitions."[9]

Other great victories followed, but when those ambitions extended from to Spain in 1809 and Russia in 1812, Napoleon exhausted the capacity of his army to prevail against the growing collective strength of his enemies. His bloody victory at Borodino on the march to Moscow, recreated vividly in Tolstoy's *War and Peace*, was the beginning of the end. "The age of cannon-fodder had come," notes one account, "although more than a century was to elapse before it reached its peak of tragic futility in the fields of France and Flanders."[10] Thereafter, the Battle of Leipzig—involving 350,000 Austrian, Swedish, Prussian, Russian, and British troops against 195,000 French and Saxon—was the most decisive single episode in his ultimate defeat. Dramatic thought it was, Waterloo merely ended the Hundred Days with the resounding verdict that there would be no Napoleonic comeback. From Moscow to Leipzig to Waterloo, the tide against it was never truly reversed. In *Les Miserables*, Victor Hugo recorded that "Napoleon had been impeached in heaven and his fall decreed; he was troublesome to God."

Napoleonic France was in substance an experiment in colonialism within Europe. Overseas projects were sporadic, whereas the effort of Napoleon's Continental system to bring all of Europe under economic subordination to France was constant.[11] To the considerable extent that its European colonies were bent to France's military objectives, the empire was also "anti-economic from the ground up, in spirit and essence."[12] The industrialization of certain sectors was accelerated, yet that of others retarded. Ship-building was damaged, and France's overseas trade was destroyed.

In the realm of myth, Napoleon's legacy was gigantic. To French politics, he left a Bonapartist ideal of political leadership that haunted domestic politics into the twentieth century.[13] He also bequeathed to his time an aesthetic astride the classical and romantic, devoting personal attention and national treasure to memorable visual depictions that rooted his regime in the empires of antiquity and projected an intoxicating vision of France's new career of conquest. In 1808, the Italian sculptor, Antonio Canova, made Princess Pauline Bonaparte a half-naked *Venus Victrix* in marble. Painters August-Dominique Ingres and Jacques-Louis David meanwhile provided some of the most effective visual propaganda ever commissioned. David, a revolutionary, friend of Robespierre and leading iconographer of the Terror, was given the title of First Painter invented by Louis XIV and revived by Napoleon. He responded to the compliment "with cringing servility and unparalleled professional skill."[14] His *Napoleon Crossing the Alps* gave us an icon of virile determination. No matter that Napoleon made the journey on the back of a mule, the image of him atop a white stallion "was destined for posterity and thus for eternity."[15] For the painter Delacroix, Napoleon was himself *the* artist of his time, the very spirit of mature Romanticism. There is something to this. David's Napoleon is the one we prefer to remember. It has ever since encouraged us to believe in manifest nonsense about the subliminal virtues of charismatic political leadership to an extent that is routinely reckless and occasionally disastrous.

After Napoleon's final defeat and exile, trade became the trump card for the rapidly industrializing British economy. The "nation of shopkeepers" won prestige for her contribution to Napoleon's defeat and in playing the role of the disinterested mediator of European rivalries at the Congress of Vienna. Britain also added to her overseas possessions Malta, the Ionian Islands, Trinidad. Tobago, St. Lucia, the Cape Colony, and Mauritius. Moreover, Nelson had eliminated French naval rivalry. This fact alone favored the further expansion of British global commerce, insofar as it "greatly reduced the need for direct British political influence abroad and made the pursuit of new markets compatible with the drive for cheap government."[16] The establishment of a new continental balance of power at Vienna and the "Congress system" it inaugurated established a period of comparative peace among the Great Powers that did not begin to unravel until the 1870s. The Pax Britannica was thus a form of restoration, less a European peace made possible by British preponderance than a truce upheld by naval power to the advantage British interests beyond Europe.[17]

A footnote to the period is the Anglo- American War of 1812. In 1815, the very survival of the American republic remained anything but a certainty. Yet in January of that year the commander of the American garrison at New Orleans, General Andrew Jackson, managed to humiliate the most powerful maritime nation on earth in a battle that cost him only 13 men against 2,000 British. The Battle of New Orleans was altogether unnecessary. The Treaty of Ghent ending the War of 1812 had been signed on Christmas Eve of 1814 and the engagement underway before the news had crossed the Atlantic. Still, it established a personal reputation that later took Jackson to the presidency of the United States and confirmed a national reputation for military precociousness.[18] A sense of American potential, certainly, had informed Talleyrand's advice to Napoleon to sell Louisiana to the United States in 1803 at a bargain price. Talleyrand observed that, whatever the memories of their struggle for political independence, Americans remained more English than not.

In the event of renewed conflict with Britain, he counseled, prudence required that France do what it could to keep the United States out of the enemy camp.[19]

## Pax Britannica

In Britain the label *imperialist* had hitherto applied to Napoleonic dominion in Europe. The term *bonapartiste* now gradually replaced it, because it was more precise in capturing the spirit of the French Second Empire's political regime but also because British political and commercial leadership had an interest in investing imperialism with a more wholesome aura. And for good reason. Captive colonial markets made Britain the master of world trade. Although this position fostered a self-righteous and smug national chauvinism, Britain's gradual conversion from mercantilism to free trade meant that the claim that the British Empire was the benefactor of all humankind was not wholly without foundation.[20] London became an exporter of capital and credit, not least of all to the recovering economies of Europe. Among these, Prussia merits special attention. In Germany, Napoleonic domination had eliminated the Holy Roman Empire, erasing 120 sovereign entities dating to the Peace of Westphalia. It had established the puppet-state Confederation of the Rhine, and "served to clear the German stream-bed of economic obstacles just as it did territorially, juridically, and politically."[21] The British loan to Prussia in 1818 represented on the one hand an attempt to export British financial practices along with British capital. On the other, it was integral to the project of beginning the modernization of the Prussian state that ultimately took the lead in welding Germany into a Great Power.

The memory of Napoleon was in part the catalyst for this. Indeed, one history of Germany from 1800 to 1866 submits that "in the beginning there was Napoleon"; it was in the shadow of French occupation that Johann Gotlieb Fichte became the ideological father of modern German nationalism, by virtue of Fourteen Speeches to the German Nation in which he claimed the Germans were an "authentic people" (*Urvolk*) with a mission to carry forward the cultural inheritance of Europe.[22] Carl von Clausewitz, a contemporary of Fichte and a Prussian veteran of the Napoleonic Wars, meanwhile approached the science of war with a studied urgency. This became a general trend. National military academies across Europe placed a new emphasis on the education of a new generation of staff officers and sought to integrate the apparent lessons of recent campaigns into their curricula. The available literature of the military sciences, from Clausewitz's *Vom Kriege* in 1832 to Hamley's *Operations of War* in 1866, increased exponentially.[23] But German officers became far and away the most avid students of the new arts and sciences of military conflict, which was to have profound consequences.

The British outlook between 1815 and 1859 was a mirror image of Prussia's, fundamentally optimistic, and based on a strategic triangle of trade, colonies, and the Royal Navy. The national circumstances of this period, in fact, favored the policy dominance of the first side of the triangle—trade—over the possession of new colonies in large part by virtue of British command of blue waters. The mercantilist tradition gave way to the ideas of Adam Smith and David Ricardo, and later Richard Cobden and John Bright. A free trade policy was the logical product of naval dominance. No country depended more on the expansion of world trade than did Britain with its lead in industrial innovation, need of raw materials, and large merchant marine. British propagation of free trading principles met with skepticism in continental capitals, but it also elicited the enthusiasm of merchants and firms to an extent that the rapid growth of world commerce during the free trade era, roughly 1846 to 1880, merits description as a formative phase in the history of "globalization."[24]

Because this trend benefited Britain above all, British interest in a larger colonial empire and formal control of more overseas territories declined in proportion. Provided that markets and raw materials were open to all, new colonies made little sense, since the costs of their administration and defense were, to use Disraeli's words, "simply 'millstones' around the neck of the British taxpayer."[25] With the accelerating pace of industrialization and the production of goods in excess of anything the domestic market and formal empire could consume, British merchants pushed to open up non-Empire markets in Asia, Brazil, Argentina, the west coast of Africa, Australia, and the coasts of Central and South America. Beyond the overseas colonies that came to Britain at the Congress of Vienna, new territorial acquisitions during this period had specific roles as island entrepôts for commerce and/or strategically located and defensible harbors useful as naval stations. These included in 1819 Singapore at the entrance to the South China Sea; in 1833, the Falkland Islands overlooking access to Cape Horn from the Atlantic; in 1839, Aden at the southern gate of the Red Sea; and in 1841, the port of Hong Kong—along with Lagos, Fiji, Cyprus, Alexandria, Mombasa, Zanzibar, and Wei-hai-wei. While Royal Navy supremacy and receipts from expanding commerce made the acquisition of these strategic points easy and affordable, their possession reinforced British supremacy and economic growth.[26]

The period between 1815 and 1870 is widely regarded as a period of stagnation in imperial competition among the European powers. This generalization is valid when applied to overseas colonization. Yet it is also misleading. The two powers at the frontiers of the Napoleonic Europe yet critical to Bonaparte's ultimate overthrow, Great Britain and tsarist Russia, were in the 1830s deeply involved in a contest of influence over Central Asia, along a frontier of their respective empires stretching from Persia through Afghanistan to Tibet, first referred to by a young British officer, Captain Arthur Connolly, as the "Great Game." The Russo-Persian War of 1828–1829 and the First Afghan War of 1839–1842 were small but significant conflicts testing the territorial limits of British and Russian power. France's colonial adventure in Algeria, meanwhile, began with outright invasion in 1830–1832 partly as the result of the need of a weak monarch, Charles X, to shore up domestic support with a foreign triumph. It is equally true, however, that the French incursion was a response to Ottoman decline. Although the Ottoman Porte still laid claim to northern Africa in 1830, it had been for two decades unable to govern it, and Algeria was an increasingly anarchic place. *The Régiment Étranger*, better known as the French Foreign Legion, saw its first action in Algeria, and the invasion of 1830 was to have an impact on French colonialism and domestic politics beyond World War II.

The Crimean War of 1853–1856 was exhaustively imperial in nature, from the causes of its outbreak to the strategic logic behind the alignment of forces and the prosecution of the conflict itself. Russia provoked the war with its claim to protection of Ottoman Christian minorities in the Holy Land and its demand that Turkey surrender the key to historic Orthodox Christian churches there. But what Tsar Nicholas I sought with this *casus belli* was to exploit the weakening of the Ottoman Empire by carving up its outer provinces in Eastern Europe and securing access to the Mediterranean—precisely what Britain was determined to thwart, even at the cost of propping up Constantinople and allying itself with France. The war itself featured a Janus-like combination of tactics that dated to Napoleon, with changes that presaged the trenches and high-velocity weapons of World War I. It took place appropriately almost halfway between Waterloo in 1815 and Flanders in 1914.[27]

The American Civil War, though not an imperial conflict, followed only five years later and wrought significant changes both to the conduct of warfare and, over the longer term, to the landscape of international affairs. The United States was already an economic giant before the issue of Confederate secession became a shooting affair. Thereafter, the war quickly attained a scale and ferocity that temporarily transformed the latent national power of the United States into the greatest military nation on earth. It mobilized large conscript armies and introduced new technologies ranging from telegraph communications to rotating turrets, torpedoes, mines, and steam-powered commerce raiders. The Union revolutionized the movement of troops and supplies with the use of the railroad. In 1861, the United States already had more miles of it than the rest of the world combined. By the time the Union Army had prevailed, it had also invented the "American way of war" and anticipated the total wars of the twentieth century by mobilizing massive industrial and technological power to utterly crush the Confederacy.[28] But, above all, the American republic had survived. The mobilization of its resources and the centralization of its government had made the United States a Great Power in-waiting. Almost from the moment American independence had been secured, no less a figure of the founding generation than Alexander Hamilton had established a perspective on the future of foreign relations, the central concern of which was how to integrate the infant American economy "into the British world system on the best possible terms."[29] Before and after the Civil War those terms were very advantageous. Not only did the American economy benefit from British investment, but the Pax Britannica and British financial system conditioned the international system in which that economy matured. The end of the Civil War marked "the beginning of a period when the United States moved steadily toward equality."[30]

Another emergent great power of the time, Germany, was a more problematic fit with British international supremacy. The Wars of German Unification, with Austria in 1866 and France in 1870–1871, brought forth under Prussian leadership a new and vigorous power at the center of Europe, the German Empire proclaimed by Kaiser Wilhelm I. In the Franco-Prussian War, German forces used to decisive advantage many of the technologies that had facilitated Union victory in America, above all railroads, and exhibited a similar tendency toward absolute war as the conflict progressed. Indeed, the former Union General, William Sheridan, observed the war from the German headquarters and advised its command that their conduct of the war was possibly not as absolute as it could be. The Union Army had found it necessary, he noted, to inflict suffering on the civilian population of the South to force surrender from the Confederacy.[31] The war was over, in any event, after a scant 180 days of fighting, exhibiting the speed and lethal efficiency of the German forces. In Paris the Second Empire collapsed and the Third Republic was declared.

Although these events were not of themselves enough to give the British government sleepless nights, they had disturbing aspects. The war had been provoked by cynical diplomacy and was a masterpiece of predatory cost-effectiveness. "Probably the most profitable war of the entire nineteenth century," the Treaty of Frankfurt that ended it imposed the immense fine of 5 billion francs on France or "four times the previous year's Prussian defense budget" and handed the province of Alsace-Lorraine to the new German Empire.[32] The officer class of the new German Reich had learned the lessons of Napoleon and Clausewitz perhaps too well, overthrowing the continental balance of power with two impeccably executed limited wars, gaining cheaply bought victories, and "creating unrealizable expectations of future equivalent successes."[33] Britain could live with a new continental power, but how long would its aspirations remain confined to the continent? Not surprisingly, the victory of 1871 also accelerated the militarization of Prussian and German society that Theodore Fontane attacked in his novels. *Vor dem Sturm* is set in the winter of 1812–1813 but was published in 1878. It rails not against Napoleonic conquest but rather against its imprint on Prussia in the form of an arrogant nationalism apparently vindicated by the recent victory over France and rapidly eclipsing traditional Prussian virtues.[34]

### The Scramble

The comparatively quiet period of overseas colonial activity ended abruptly in the 1870s. A classic study of modern Great Power competition within and beyond Europe, in fact, dates the Age of Empire to 1875.[35] After that year there was an increasing awareness of developments that today are often assumed to be phenomena of an only recently inaugurated process of globalization. This featured a new appreciation of the world's dimensions, and therefore its limitations, as the last great exploratory expeditions turned to the Arctic and Antarctic while more hospitable environments were either extensively mapped or rapidly becoming so. A rapid increase in the global population and technological innovations such as railways and telegraphic communications simultaneously made human society demographically larger as it became geographically smaller.[36] A new commercially viable cross-fertilization of cultures was thus made possible. In 1875, Arthur Lazenby Liberty opened a shop at 218A Regent Street in London, which became the home of Art Nouveau in England. Liberty imported silks from the East and later porcelain, ceramics, fans, screens, wallpapers, swords, mats, lacquer ware, lanterns, bronzes, and wall masks from Japan. After Japan banned the wearing of swords in 1876, many Japanese metalworkers diversified into cutlery and kitchenware featuring motifs altogether novel and extraordinarily appealing to English customers.[37]

As appealing as commerce with Japan was, it was commerce with an emerging power the very existence of which signaled the beginning of a period of intensifying imperial competition. The sense of both opportunity and limitation among the European powers in particular prompted a competition that came to focus on the continent of Africa, because it was large, comparatively close, and, above all, defenseless. Whereas in 1875 90 percent of Africa was "dark" only to most Europeans and otherwise under the control of indigenous rulers, by 1912 only small pockets remained free of European military occupation. In 1798, Napoleon's army in Egypt had defeated the Mamlukes with discipline and ruthlessness; after 1875 the industrialized European powers confronted the indigenous peoples of Africa with such superior weaponry that whatever discipline and courage the Ashanti and Zulu brought to the battle was usually irrelevant to the outcome. For Britain, Russia, and the Netherlands, much of the nineteenth century was a continuous effort in expansion—in the latter case actually territorial contraction set against consolidation of its hold on the

Netherlands-Indies. For Belgium, France, Germany, and Italy the 1880s inaugurated an era of frantic colonial acquisition. By 1914, the total land area of all European colonies had doubled. Although Asian possessions were usually the most valuable, European expansion was far and away at its most spectacular in Africa.[38]

The radical change of the continental balance of power wrought by the Franco-Prussian War contributed to the sudden interest in Africa. France had been the leading power in Europe since the Treaty of Westphalia in 1648, but the unification of the German states and the rout of French forces at Sedan put a new nation with an industrial economy, a strong state, and powerful army at the center of Europe.[39] In 1815, France had been returned those parts of its old colonial empire that were of no strategic interest to Britain.[40] After 1871, French foreign policy was therefore troubled most of all by the German question, but French politics was preoccupied with domestic affairs of a highly particularist nature. Even among politicians for whom elementary national honor alone demanded revenge for the amputation of Alsace-Lorraine, there was little agreement about how and when it should be achieved. To others overseas expansion seemed to offer a form of compensation. No single decision or decisive debate decided the French Third Republic for this option, but in acquiring a gigantic colonial empire over the next four decades, France clearly picked prestige over power. Admittedly, this formula is a little too tidy when applied to *revanchists* and imperialists who, like Léon Gambetta, wondered whether France might not be able to recover Alsace-Lorraine from Germany in exchange for colonies. It is nonetheless a valid generalization that the imperialists of the Third Republic attached vast importance to *gloire* and the most visible trappings of France's standing among nations. Gambetta, who was simultaneously one of the Third Republic's most gifted politicians and among its most eccentric personalities, was also typical of his generation of imperialists. He was a great champion of republicanism against royalism, yet in equal part a nationalist who came to view colonialism as a passport to greatness. His instincts on Africa became competitive to the point of recklessness. In the 1880s, his insistence that France should have absolute equality with the British in Egypt precipitated a small crisis with Gladstone's government in London.[41]

The French were not alone in the conviction that prestige in Europe depended on new colonies overseas. In France colonial projects at least enjoyed a measure of parliamentary support. In Belgium they had nothing of the kind, so King Leopold bankrolled Henry Stanley's exploration of the Congo River Basin and its exploitation in the name of Belgium as a personal crusade. That a territory so enormous should be acquired, officially or not, by a country as small as Belgium and until only recently a province of the Netherlands was indeed a spectacular coup. Leopold's adventure has been cited by more than one treatment as the single most important causal episode in the Scramble for Africa. Whatever the verdict as to cause, the Belgian Congo certainly merits major attention in terms of consequences. Leopold sought prestige, but he also sought wealth. The commercial interests he invited to the Congo fell upon it with rapacious glee. The Belgian colonial regime there ultimately acquired the most infamous reputation in all of European colonialism. In the meantime, France's "new empire" in Africa had its Stanley in the person of Pierre de Brazza. Brazza was a patriot aware of, and in large part motivated by, the race with Belgium in the Congo. His ideas for planting the French flag in the Congo got a sympathetic hearing from Gambetta and the most important figure in French colonialism after 1880, Jules Ferry. More than any other single factor, it was due to Brazza's zeal that France secured a foothold in the Congo basin.[42]

There was a certain appropriateness to the fact that Senegal on the west coast of Africa became a key base in the effort to penetrate the African interior and ultimately to link it with Algeria and the Congo to establish French dominion over African territory from the Atlantic to the Nile. Senegal belonged to the Old French Empire predating the Revolution and the Napoleonic Wars, much of which had been stripped away by Britain and returned only in part after 1815. If France were to recover lost ground and compete again in the first rank of powers against a dominant Britain and an assertive Germany, the Atlantic port of Dakar was an open door to limitless possibilities. For the political and commercial leadership of the Third Republic, moreover, there was just possibly an opportunity this time to buttress parliamentary government at home with expansion abroad:

> In reaction against the free trade policies of the Second Empire, the traditional mercantilism of the French people was given free play. France, a late starter in the industrialization of her economic life, was reasonably apprehensive as to her chances of competing on world markets, and to win for nascent French industry a closed market was a natural ambition. Even so hard-headed a statesman as Jules Ferry saw through very rosy spectacles when the economic possibilities of the new empire were in question. Thanks to an empire in which French goods would have preferential right of entry, the industries of the nation and the welfare of the working classes would both be benefited, or so it was believed.[43]

Because France of the 1880s was a comparatively democratic place, political circumspection was important. Where overseas ventures were concerned, seasoned politicians such as Ferry, who was "careful not to come into the open; careful to represent each step in his scheme as the last," were nonetheless hardly unique to France.[44] Among the first British venture capitalists to become aware that in Africa a scramble was on, George Goldie convinced rival British companies in Niger to form the United Africa Company to strengthen his hand in bargaining with Africans but also to meet French competition on the Upper Niger. He then forced the smaller French firms to sell out to him, often by trading at a loss, which ultimately led to French and German recognition of British control of the region at the Berlin Conference of 1884 at which Goldie was an unofficial advisor to the British delegation. Among the attentive critics of British overseas commitments there was a growing recognition that, once the stakes were high enough in terms of access to markets and materials, the adventures of men like Goldie forced resources, decisions, and diplomacy from the highest political level.[45] Consequently, the fiscal burden and political morality of Britain's imperial vocation accounted for a good deal of the partisan division between Disraeli's Conservative Party and Gladstone's Liberals in the 1870s and 1880s, although the imperial enthusiasms of Liberals such as John Dilke and Joseph Chamberlain testified to the limits of partisanship subjected the special rigors of foreign affairs. After all, politicians unexcited by the prospect of governing distant peoples could nevertheless appreciate the importance of overseas resources to a mature industrial society and increasingly democratic political system.

Regardless of their parliamentary majority's composition, successive governments were under pressure to demonstrate the British presence in Africa simply because other powers were busily asserting theirs. Compared to Egypt or South

Africa, the material value to Britain of tropical Africa was trivial. The fact of foreign competition alone, however, recalibrated that value significantly. Hence Britain, the past-master of balance-of-power diplomacy in Europe, instinctively backed the historical claims of Portugal, an old ally of the Napoleonic Wars, to the Congo Delta to counter France's ability to block access to the African interior. While the British commitment to free trade principles championed earlier in the century remained officially intact, moreover, the worry that other great powers might have fewer scruples about protectionism was ever-present. As commercial expansion was slowed by falling export prices and lower rates of growth after 1875, the simultaneous French thrust from Senegal into the African interior—along with later German claims to Cameroon and Togo—"aroused both cupidity and anxiety," among both British representatives in West Africa and the metropolitan center of demand back in London.[46]

German claims became especially worrisome. Germany's victory in the Franco-Prussian War was a change with which Britain could live, as Germany's dominant position on the continent posed no direct problem to Britain's preeminent world status. Also, as the architect of the new German Empire, Chancellor Otto von Bismarck enjoyed unrivalled moral authority among his countrymen and almost unlimited political power over them. Bismarck regarded colonialism as a business for other nations that would hopefully divert enough of their attention and energies away from his plans for Europe where Germany's position was—industrial and military strength notwithstanding—inherently vulnerable. This attitude Bismarck famously summed up to a colonial enthusiast by observing that "your map of Africa is very fine, but my map of Africa is here in Europe. Here is Russia and here is France and here we are in the middle."[47] Yet Bismarck's sobriety was increasingly out of step with the heady nationalist romanticism of his countrymen in the last quarter of the century—a country in which Richard Wagner's *Ring* cycle of operas was given its first full performance in 1876 and Richard Strauss's tone poem, *Ein Heldenleben* continued the tradition of heroic self-dramatization in 1897.

Bismark's change of heart on the colonial issue has attracted attention and disagreement among historians, but a common theme of many explanations is his opportunistic pragmatism in dealing with contending pressures in domestic politics and foreign affairs. By the 1880s, some of Bismarck's conservative supporters held that the acquisition of overseas colonies was fast becoming an economic necessity; others observed that the vision of a colonial empire aroused sufficient popular enthusiasm to be of electoral advantage. Although the Reichstag presented none of the checks to executive authority presented by the British or French parliaments, elections were for Bismarck a measure of national sentiment powerful enough to chasten the critics of his policy. In spite of tariff legislation passed in 1879, Bismarck was advised that a return to protectionism alone was unlikely to revitalize a German industry hungry for new markets unless and until commercial policy were given an entirely new direction. The fortunes of the Social Democratic Party continued to wax in the face of laws prohibiting most of its activities, so that a failure to conjure a convincing answer to the domestic misery caused by overproduction might well realize the worst of Bismarck's fears: domestic instability. Lobbies such as the *Kolonialverein* and the *Gesellschaft für deutsche Kolonisation* defended their imperial enthusiasms, often incoherently, in the language of hard-headed economic calculation one week and in terms of international prestige the next. Academics Gustav

Schmoller and Heinrich von Treitschke warned darkly that colonial policy was of existential importance. Bismarck did not have to take any of their arguments wholly seriously to know that their aggregate nuisance potential had to be addressed. His political instincts told him that, with the appropriate posture, grievances could be mollified and neuroses indulged at home even as powers were balanced abroad. For the moment, he concluded, Germany's posture should be dramatic and vaguely anti-British, cultivating a patriotic press while rewarding France for its part in the Scramble and its waning interest in recovering Alsace-Lorraine.[48] As a consequence, Bismarck declared the official protection of the Reich over Lüderitzland, the founding of German South-West Africa, in April 1884, promptly followed by Togo, and, in February 1885, German East Africa. The first of these gave the British in Cape Colony a new and unwanted German neighbor; the latter placed a Germany colony smack in the path of the Cairo-to-Cape railway envisioned by Cecil Rhodes in the 1890s to connect Egypt and the Mediterranean with Cape.

In the meantime, Bismarck parlayed Germany's colonial coming-out into gains for nationalist parties in the 1884 Reichstag elections and significant diplomatic concessions at the Berlin Conference of 1884–1885. It was at the Berlin Conference that the Scramble began to approximate a partition. After comparing lofty sentiments, the delegates of 13 European countries, with the United States in an observer role, settled in for three-and-a-half months of bargaining that drew or confirmed borders in Africa, including the Belgian Congo. They also declared the Congo and Niger Rivers open to free trade and divided Lower Guinea between France and Germany. They gave Gabon to France and Congo to Belgium and confirmed German claims to Tanganyika and South West Africa along with Britain's claim to Egypt. Bismarck steered clear of challenging British vital interests in the Lower Niger and in return secured free trade access to the Congo Basin. The most important agreement obliged all the signatories to make formal notification, after establishing effective territorial control, of any new protectorates or colonies. Its effect was to force Britain to establish direct control over territories that it had hitherto governed at arm's length.[49] The conference issued a resolution calling for the end of slavery and the slave trade in Africa, but it was oblivious to both the hard interests and the gathering fears of Africans themselves.

Thus Bismarck's brief career in colonial policy, in which the colonies themselves often had a tertiary role, gave German imperialism an improvised character. After Bismarck's dismissal by Wilhelm II in 1890, German imperialism lost his characteristic caution and became progressively more erratic. British Prime Minister Lord Salisbury, who could never be counted among Bismarck's admirers, called his demise "an enormous calamity," rightly guessing that Wilhelm would steer an adventurous course.[50] Although Anglo-German relations in the late 1880s were not without friction, over rights in Samoa and East Africa in particular, the 1890s represented a new stage in Anglo-German antagonism. Prodded by nationalist liberals such as Otto Michaelis in the Reichstag and academics such as Max Weber, Wilhelm embraced *Weltpolitik*, the project of developing Germany from a continental to a world power.[51] Although Wilhelm usually devoted strident rhetoric to taking public umbrage at British imperiousness, few in Britain doubted that Germany could eventually back him up with substance. Too often Wilhelm caused gratuitous offence without gaining anything for Germany. In Africa specifically he had a case against the terms of the Anglo-Congolese Treaty of 1894, but in the instance of the Kruger Telegram he congratulated the Boers of South Africa for defeating the Jameson Raid, which never had London's authority behind it, and mischievously implied that the Boers could count on German support in a future conflict with the British Empire. In 1894, the publication of a classic of British popular imperialism conveyed a sense of darkened horizons and coming struggle:

> Young Rudyard Kipling, the son of an artist who was the curator of an Indian museum, had begun his literary career by imitating the French novel, and had dreamed of becoming an English—or Anglo-Colonial—Maupassant. But soon, as he celebrated the melancholy of the British Tommy on garrison in Asia and hymned the greatness of an empire washed by 'seven seas,' he became by universal consent the unofficial poet laureate of British imperialism. And now he wrote—for children, was it, or for adults?—his *Jungle Book*. He set his hero, the little Mowgli, in the world of beasts, and the beasts taught Mowgli the law of the jungle, which maintains the balance of species at the cost of a never-ending struggle, a truce-less war. Must this struggle, this war, be condemned as evil? Not when it is the law of the world. The spirit of conquest and aggrandizement must not be confused with the spirit of hatred, greed, and delight in doing mischief for its own sake; it is the courage to hazard all risks which gives victory to the better man. A species of Darwinian philosophy expressed in a mythical form was the foundation of a moral code, chaste, brutal, heroic, and childlike.[52]

In the 1890s, this world of beasts was increasingly inhabited by steel monsters, battleships, as the "new navalism" prompted a number of powers—after Britain, France, Germany, Russia, Italy, Japan, the United States—to add to their fleets. Britain's capacity to contain rival sea power inside Europe, unchallenged for most of the century, was being compromised as European and non-European powers were now constructing battle fleets.[53] In the 1880s, Japan had no battleships. Yet in 1894–1895, its growing navy was critical to victory in the Sino-Japanese War, after which the Treaty of Shimonoseki gave Formosa, the Pescadores Islands, and the Liaotung Peninsula to Japan. In 1898, naval power aided the United States to triumph in the Spanish-American War. The peace settlement secured Cuban independence, ended the Spanish Empire in the Americas, and signaled the coming out of the United States as a colonial power by making Puerto Rico, Guam, the Philippines, and Hawaii American possessions. The same year, back in Africa, British and French expeditions met at Fashoda to register conflicting claims to the Upper Nile. This started several months of diplomatic crisis at the end of which the superiority of the Royal Navy and London's apparent willingness to go to war forced Paris to back down.[54]

That willingness, influenced as much by Britain's resolve to demonstrate determination as by its Cape Colonists' greed, ended the Scramble with a bang in the Second Boer War of 1899–1902. For the handful of British leaders who actually sought a fight with the Boers of the Transvaal—above all Alfred Milner, governor of the Cape Colony, backed somewhat reluctantly by Colonial Secretary Joseph Chamberlain—the war was every bit as predatory as the Bismarck's war with France 30 years earlier. But it was clearly not as economical. Where that contest involved two major European powers, the South African war pitted a large expeditionary force from the world's preeminent power against a rag-tag army of Afrikaner farmers in which the latter initially subjected an ill-prepared British army to a series of humiliating defeats. Once a reinforced army under new command had turned the tide and captured Pretoria, the capital of Transvaal, on June 5, 1900, the war appeared to be all but over. Instead, the Boers resorted to guerrilla tactics so effective as to render South Africa ungovernable. The British counterstrategy attacked the very means of the Boers sustenance by destroying their farms and livestock and herding Boer women and children, along with their black African laborers, into internment facilities, referred to for the first time in English as concentration camps. In 1900, Salisbury's government had won reelection in the "khaki lection" partly on the back of jingoist enthusiasm for recent victories in South Africa, but by the time of the Boer surrender in May 1902, the opposition attacked the government's prosecution of the war as barbaric, while the government itself felt mounting humiliation at its apparent inability to extract a Boer surrender.[55]

### Armageddon

Even the great continent of Africa had become a crowded place. By the end of the century, any crisis over African soil or access to it immediately ratcheted up tension within Europe itself. In both Britain and Germany there were advocates of an alliance of the "Anglo-Saxon and Teutonic powers" in this newly dangerous neighborhood. They competed unsuccessfully with the objective facts of conflicting strategic interests between London and Berlin, in particular German naval and imperial ambitions, which, combined with Wilhelm's callow conduct of foreign affairs, ultimately drove Britain into the arms of France.[56] The emergence of Japan and the United States as naval powers posed a challenge to Britain's position in the Western Hemisphere and the Far East. Yet any attempt to meet the challenge by reinforcing Royal Navy squadrons in these theaters was offset by the potential threat to home waters of German naval construction, begun with the Navy Bill of 1898 and bolstered by a supplementary bill in 1900, on the blueprint of the Tirpitz Plan. For decades Britain's sea power had been the fulcrum of the European balance, but, after 1900, British leadership concentrated less on the balance of power than on the maintenance of peace. No nation had less to gain from war.[57]

Named for Admiral Alfred Tirpitz, head of the Reich Navy Office, Germany's plan was to expand the Imperial German navy to 60 battleships in 20 years, a fleet powerful enough to confront the Royal Navy in a decisive engagement in the North Sea. Beyond the stretching of fiscal resources required to answer all of these developments simultaneously, the prospect of German *Weltpolitik* in the form of such a navy in European waters was alone a problem of sufficient strategic magnitude to move Britain to seek a new understanding with France and possibly Russia as well.[58] Additionally it precipitated redeployment and radical reform. Under the direction of First Sea Lord Sir John Fisher, warships from overseas squadrons were moved to the North Sea over the protests of the foreign and colonial offices, while a massive overhaul of the fleet—described, in his Fischer's words, as "Napoleonic in its audacity and Cromwellian in its thoroughness"—confronted Germany with a naval arms race on wholly new terms.[59] The core of the overhaul was in effect to scrap much of the existing Royal Navy and build a new fleet of warships based on the new all-big-gun *Dreadnought.* Because this meant replacing scores of cruisers, sloops, and gunboats that had hitherto shown the Union Jack to African chiefs, pirates, and slavers with large armored ships for a future war against a first-class navy, Fischer's reforms implicitly assumed European waters to be the primary theater of Britain's next conflict.

In April 1904, Pairs and London agreed to the *Entente Cordiale*. It settled fishing and colonial disputes and assigned Egypt to Britain's sphere of influence and Morocco to France. The tilt of the naval reforms then became explicit after the Morocco Crisis of 1905, in which Kaiser Wilhelm declared support for Moroccan independence and Britain backed France at the Algeciras Conference the following year, when the Admiralty began to draw up plans for war against Germany.[60] Republican France had already constructed an alliance with tsarist Russia between 1891 and 1894, based on a mutual apprehension of Germany now strong enough to eclipse all ideological differences between them. At precisely the diplomatic moment of Anglo-French rapprochement, however, Russia was traumatized by defeat in the Russo-Japanese War at sea and in Manchuria, followed by the revolution of 1905 at home. The effect of these simultaneous blows was to make St. Petersburg anxious about the exposure of its vulnerability and London doubly nervous over the continental balance of power.

These neuroses converged in the Anglo-Russian Entente of 1907. The agreement addressed disputes dating to the Great Game by establishing mutual spheres of influence in Central Asia, a British protectorate over Afghanistan and official, if not actual, Chinese control in Tibet. Unsettled questions were papered over, because, as in the case of the *Entente Cordiale*, the overriding priority was a truce on colonial rivalries in anticipation of crisis in Europe. The fact that Britain had, in 1902, already secured a treaty of mutual assistance with Japan to recall the Royal Navy to home waters—a treaty that opened the way for Russo-Japanese War—and yet could obtain an understanding with Russia only five years later testifies to the strength of that priority. The completion of this "Triple Entente" was little short of disaster for Germany. Wilhelm's *Weltpolitik*, on paper no more ambitious than the foreign policy of any other Great Power, had nonetheless "triggered the creation of a power bloc which not only seemed to prevent the flexing of Germany's own industrial and commercial muscle but also to encircle Germany by land to the east and west and by sea to the north."[61] To be sure, Germany was in 1907 encircled by "understandings" rather than alliances, but the structure of the Armageddon of 1914 was already in place.[62]

This turn of events left Germany with the consolation of the secret Triple Alliance, signed by Bismarck with Austria-Hungary and Italy back in 1882 and renewed at five-year intervals. Because Italy had signed a secret nonaggression pact with France in 1902, the alliance was weaker than Germany supposed. It could even be called perilous, because by 1908, the multinational empire of the Habsburgs had become administratively backward, economically sluggish, and strategically vulnerable in the Balkans as a result of the territorial disintegration of the Ottoman Empire.[63] The Young Turk revolution of 1908, launched by a group of army officers calling themselves the Committee on Union and Progress, was intended to revive and modernize Ottoman rule but instead seemed to excite nationalism among the Porte's own subject peoples. Startled by the flux on its southeastern frontier, Austria-Hungary moved to forestall further change, above all the designs of Serbian nationalists, by turning its military occupation of the former Turkish provinces of Bosnia and Herzegovina into outright annexation. The tsar's government interpreted this move as Austrian expansion, expansion that could ultimately endanger Russian warm water access to the Mediterranean through the straits, but ran up against loud and unconditional support for the Austria's claim from Berlin. Thus two great powers recently thwarted in other theaters of imperial competition—Russia in Central Asia by Britain and in Manchuria by Japan, Germany in Morocco by France and then by the Anglo-Russian Entente—had in response redirected their attention to the southeast of the European continent and now glared at each other over the Balkans. Because neither Britain nor France chimed in on Russia's behalf, Berlin thought it had exposed the weaknesses of the Triple Entente.[64] After 1900, however, every attempt by German economic power to expand beyond its traditional markets met with frustration. Even Ottoman territories, a target of German economic ambition symbolized above all by the idea of a Berlin-to-Baghdad Railway, were awash in British and French capital and credit.

Worse still was the state of affairs in the upper reaches of the German government. The German chancellor, Prince Bernhard von Bülow, was in charge of the day-to-day substance of diplomacy and played key roles in both the Moroccan and Bosnian crises. The high command of the army was increasingly fatalistic about the probability and scale of imminent war. Meanwhile Wilhelm, evermore out of touch even with Bülow, precipitated a furor at home and abroad with his interview for the London *Daily Telegraph* in which he opined that England might find herself grateful that Germany possessed a large fleet if they were to find themselves on the same side in the "great debates of the future."[65] That they would not be on the same side became even more apparent in the Second Morocco Crisis in 1911, in which Berlin demanded the French Congo as compensation for France's declaration of a protectorate over Morocco. The appearance of the German gunboat *Panther* in the port of Agadir was supposed to intimidate France and drive a wedge in the *Entente*. Instead it prompted from British Chancellor of the Exchequer, David Lloyd George, the famously bellicose Mansion House speech in which he expressed a British willingness to fight on France's side in the event of war.[66]

In France the public mood turned dark and the argument that the time had come to avenge the humiliation of 1870 more popular. Internationally, the pace of events picked up, as Italy forced the North African territories of Libya and Tripolitania from Turkey and thereby emboldened the members of the newly formed Balkan League of Bulgaria and Serbia, Greece, and Montenegro to challenge the Ottoman hold on the more strategically sensitive terrain of Macedonia. The First and Second Balkan Wars of 1912–1913 thereupon established the local political conditions that led to World War I by fatally wounding Turkey's dominance in the region and, above all, rewarding Serbia's cockiness with additional territory in the Treaty of Bucharest. This moved the Austro-Hungarian foreign minister, Count von Leopold von Berchtold, to consider the multinational empire of the Habsburgs imminently threatened by Serbian irredentism and pan-Slavic nationalism.

In this conviction he was wholly correct. Both the Serbian government and the Black Hand nationalist organization that operated with a strong measure of its connivance rejected Austria's claim to Bosnia-Herzegovina and the very notion of Germanic dominion over the Slavic and Orthodox population in the province. Neither had any intention of conceding Bosnia without a fight. The assassination of the Habsburg heir, Archduke Franz Ferdinand, in the Bosnian capital of Sarajevo in June 1914 reflected the policy of a government in Belgrade, as well as the sentiment of the mad dogs of Serbian nationalism. The critical question centered on what nature of fight Serbia and Austria would hazard. In the latter case in particular it was possibly Austria's unwillingness to act promptly and unilaterally in punishing

Serbia that, more than any other single factor traceable to the behavior of the Great Powers, transformed a local crisis in a general European war.[67] There were nonetheless other factors critically responsible for the fact that an ultimatum delivered by Vienna to the Serbian government on July 23 led by August 4 to a war pitting Austria-Hungary and Germany against the entire Triple Entente of Britain, France, and Russia. Not least among them was the blank check of support issued by Berlin for Vienna's punitive policy in a corner of the Habsburg Empire that in Bismarck's famous appraisal of 1878 was not worth the bones of a single Pomeranian grenadier—an abdication of judgment that over the next four years cost Germany 2.5 million souls.

In the last week of peace Wilhelm's new chancellor, Theobald von Bethmann-Hollweg, in fact concentrated his efforts not on averting a general war but rather on using the threat thereof to deter Russia from backing Serbia. Failing that, the goal was to fight Russia before it was able to complete its crash program of rearmament. If a European war was genuinely inevitable, "the circumstances of July 1914 seemed as propitious for Germany as could reasonably be expected."[68] These circumstances would be optimum, of course, if Russia could be isolated from her Western allies, so to Bethmann's fatalism the foreign office official Gottlieb von Jagow added deception by assuring the British and French ambassadors that Berlin was working for direct talks between Vienna and St. Petersburg without in fact doing anything of the kind.[69] At that time the British foreign secretary, Sir Edward Grey, had proposed a four-power conference on the crisis. Having secured Germany's backing, however, the Austrian government now sought to press its advantage by declaring war on Serbia on July 28 to undercut any attempt at mediation.

In every national capital the rigid requirements of detailed war plans, prudently prepared for the worst-case scenario, overtook last-minute gestures at diplomacy and hastened the very advent of that scenario. Railroads, the same technology that had facilitated European penetration of the African interior, had radically altered the time-space parameters of the mass movement of troops and therefore the potential cost of a single day's delay in the call to arms. Russian partial mobilization against Austria was countered by Austrian and German general mobilization and led to French mobilization on August 2. Only Britain's intentions remained a mystery. In Berlin both Wilhelm and Bethmann nurtured the notion that Britain would remain neutral if France were not actually attacked. It is nonetheless doubtful that a general war would have averted, even if London had openly and energetically contradicted this hope, because both Russia and France would doubtless have been emboldened by a British declaration of belligerence.[70] Germany's violation of Belgian neutrality for operations in northern France, in any event, ended the speculation over the British position at midnight on August 4.

This outcome was never inevitable. In his magisterial treatment of World War I, John Keegan points out that it was at the time thought highly improbable. The accumulation of wealth and proliferation of trade produced during the nineteenth century's high season of European imperialism had created a measure of international cooperation and commercial integration hitherto common only in smaller, regional settings. The worldwide connections of private banks, discount houses, insurance, and commodities markets had by 1900 created interdependency among nations along with the rudimentary apparatus of international governance. South African gold and diamonds, Indian textiles, Canadian wheat, Malayan rubber, and

American manufactured goods found mass markets halfway around the world, and developing national and colonial economies soaked up European investment capital as fast as it could be lent.[71]

Many among the best-educated classes of Europe assumed that major wars had become impossible. The complacency with which they settled into their comfort left them unable to appreciate that their world was in fact a less peaceful place. Competition among the most dynamic national economies for overseas colonies had compromised the principle of free trade and returned wealth production to zero-sum terms. It is unlikely that this in itself would have produced the catastrophe of 1914 were it not for the simultaneous militarization of European society that the Napoleonic era had begun and the Industrial Revolution accelerated. By the time Great Power imperial rivalry returned to the European theater, the diplomatic terrain of the old continent had changed fundamentally. A European war had become, if not a certainty, an eminent probability. European peoples and their subject populations were drawn into conflict that quickly assumed global dimensions and ultimately claimed 15 million lives. The great irony was that in the end, it was not in an Asian or African "place in the sun" but rather in a not-very-coveted corner of the decaying Habsburg Empire that the match was put to the powder.

## Notes

1. S. E. Finer, *The History of Government,* 3 vols. (New York: Oxford University Press, 1997) I, p. 8.

2. David Kaiser, *Politics & War* (Cambridge: Harvard University Press, 2000), p. 209.

3. Finer, III, pp. 1517–1566.

4. Arno J. Mayer, *The Furies: Violence and Terror in the French and Russian Revolutions* (Princeton: Princeton University Press, 2000), pp. 533–606.

5. Finer, III, pp. 1549–1553; Kaiser, pp. 216–218; Michael Howard, *War in European History* (New York: Oxford University Press, 1976), pp. 80–83.

6. Paul Johnson, *Napoleon* (New York: Penguin, 2002), p. 29.

7. Zachary Karabell, *Parting the Desert: The Creation of the Suez Canal* (New York: Random House, 2003), pp. 12–24.

8. Finer, III, pp. 1562–1564.

9. N.A.M. Rodger, The *Command of the Ocean: A Naval History of Britain, 1649–1815* (New York: W. W. Norton, 2004), p. 543.; Paul W. Schroeder, *The Transformation of European Politics, 1763–1848* (New York: Oxford University Press, 1994), p. 384; Robert Goetz, 1805, *Austerlitz: Napoleon and the Destruction of the Third Coalition* (Mechanicsburg: Stackpole Books, 2005).

10. Alan Palmer, *Napoleon in Russia* (London: Robinson, 1997), p. 128.

11. Schroeder, pp. 385–392.

12. Ibid., p. 391.

13. Sudhir Hazareesingh, *The Legend of Napoleon* (London: Granta, 2005), pp. 40–183.

14. Paul Johnson, *The Birth of the Modern: World Society, 1815–1830* (New York: Harper Collins, 1991), pp. 143–145.

15. Anita Brookner, *Romanticism and Its Discontents* (New York: Viking, 2000), p. 18; Hugh Honour, *Neo-classicism* (Harmondsworth: Penguin, 1968).

16. P. J. Cain and A. G. Hopkins, *British Imperialism, 1688–2000* (London: Longman, 2000), p. 99; Schroeder, pp. 383–386.

17. Henry Kissinger, *A World Restored: Metternich, Castlereigh and the Problems of Peace, 1812–1822* (London: Weidenfeld & Nicolson, 1957).

18. Russell Weigley, *The American Way of War: A History of the United States Military Strategy and Policy* (Bloomington: Indiana University Press, 1973), pp. 3–92.

19. Alistair Horne, *The Age of Napoleon* (New York: Modern Library, 2006), p. 59.

20. Niall Ferguson, *The Cash Nexus: Money and Power in the Modern World, 1700–2000* (New York: Basic Books, 2001), pp. 269–272; Lawrence James, *The Rise and Fall of the British Empire* (London: Abacus, 1998), pp. 164–173.

21. Schroeder, p. 387.

22. Thomas Nipperdey, *Deutsche Geschichte, 1800–1866: Bürgerwelt und starker Staat* (Munich: C. H. Beck, 1984), p. 11; Heinrich August Winkler, *Der lange Weg nach Westen*, 2 vols. (Munich: C. H. Beck, 2001), I, pp. 57–58; Finer, III, p. 1546.

23. Howard, pp. 95–96.

24. Paul M. Kennedy, *The Rise and Fall of British Naval Mastery* (New York: Humanity Books, 1998), p. 152; Jürgen Osterhammel and Niels P. Petersson, *Geschichte der Globalisierung: Dimenzionen, Prozesse, Epoche* (Munich: C. H. Beck, 2003), pp. 60–63; Cain and Hopkins, pp. 662–681.

25. Ibid., p. 153.

26. Ibid., pp. 153–155.

27. Trevor Royle, *Crimea: The Great Crimean War, 1854–1856* (New York: Palgrave, 2004).

28. John Keegan, *A History of Warfare* (Toronto: Random House, 1993), pp. 305–306; Paul M. Kennedy, *The Rise and Fall of the Great Powers* (New York: Fontana, 1989). pp. 228–233; Weigley, pp. 128–152.

29. Walter Russell Mead, *Special Providence: American Foreign Policy and How It Changed the World* (New York: Alfred A. Knopf, 2001), p. 38.

30. Ibid, p. 5, p. 82; Richard Franklin Bensel, *Yankee Leviathan: The Origins of Central State Authority in America, 1859–1877* (New York: Cambridge University Press, 1990), pp. 94–239.

31. Michael Howard, *The Franco-Prussian War* (New York: Collier, 1969), p. 380; Geoffrey Wawro, *The Franco-Prussian War: The German Conquest of France in 1870–1871* (New York: Cambridge University Press, 2003).

32. Ferguson, p. 398.

33. Dennis Showalter, *The Wars of German Unification* (London: Arnold, 2004), p. 350.

34. Gordon A. Craig, *Theodore Fontane: Literature and History in the Bismarck Reich* (New York: Oxford University Press, 1999), pp. 161–162.

35. Eric Hobsbawm, *The Age of Empire, 1875–1914* (New York: Vintage, 1989).

36. Ibid., 13–15; Osterhammel and Petersson, pp. 47–70.

37. Victor Arwas, *Art Nouveau: From Macintosh to Liberty, The Birth of a Style* (London: Andreas Papadakis, 2000), pp. 90–91.

38. H. L. Wesseling, *The European Colonial Empires, 1815–1919* (Harlow: Pearson Education, 2004), p. 147.

39. Kennedy, *Rise and Fall of the Great Powers*, pp. 239–241.

40. Denis Brogan, *The Development of Modern France, 1870–1939* (London: Hamish Hamilton, 1967), p. 217.

41. H. L. Wesseling, *Divide and Rule: The Partition of Africa, 1880–1914*, trans. Arnold J. Pomerans (Westport, CT: Praeger, 1996), pp. 11–15; Thomas Pakenham, *The Scramble for Africa: White Man's Conquest of the Dark Continent from 1876–1912* (New York: Harper Collins, 1991), pp. 128–131.

42. Brogan, pp. 243–249.

43. Ibid., p. 218

44. Ibid., p. 231.

45. Pakenham, pp. 183–188.

46. Cain and Hopkins, p. 329.

47. Quoted in Gordon Craig, *Germany, 1866–1945* (New York: Oxford University Press, 1978) pp. 116–117; Fritz Stern, *Gold and Iron: Bismarck, Bleichröder and the Making of the German Empire* (New York: Vintage Books, 1977), pp. 394–435.

48. Ibid., p. 119.

49. Wesseling, *Divide and Rule,* pp. 113–119.

50. Paul M. Kennedy, *The Rise of Anglo-German Antagonism, 1860–1914* (London: George Allen & Unwin, 1980), p. 204.

51. Winkler, II, pp. 266–377.

52. Elie Halévy, *A History of the English People in the Nineteenth Century,* 6 vols., trans. E. I. Watkin (London: Ernest Benn, 1961), V, p. 20–21.

53. Kennedy, *Rise and Fall of British Naval Mastery,* pp. 208–209.

54. Brogan, pp. 323–326; Darrell Bates, *The Fashoda Incident of 1898: Encounter on the Nile* (New York: Oxford University Press, 1984).

55. Byron Farwell, *The Great Anglo-Boer War* (New York: Harper & Row, 1976); Thomas Pakenham, *The Boer War* (New York: Random House, 1979); Gregory Fremont-Barnes, *The Boer War, 1899–1902* (Oxford: Osprey, 2003).

56. Craig, *Germany 1866–1945,* pp. 313–314.

57. William L. Langer, *The Diplomacy of Imperialism: 1890–1902* (New York: Alfred A. Knopf, 1965), pp. 788–789.

58. Kennedy, *The Rise and Fall of British Naval Mastery,* p. 215; Volker R. Berghahn, *Der Tirpitz-Plan: Genesis und Verfall einer innenpolitischen Krisenstrategie unter Wilhelm II* (Düsseldorf: Droste, 1971); H. H. Herwig, *H. H. Luxury Fleet* (Atlantic Highlands: Ashfield Press, 1981).

59. Ibid., p. 217; Nicholas A. Lambert, *Sir John Fisher's Naval Revolution* (Columbia: University of South Carolina Press, 1999).

60. Lambert, pp. 177–182.

61. Hew Strachan, *The First World War: To Arms* (New York: Oxford University Press, 2001), p. 20.

62. Luigi Albertini, *The Origins of the War of 1914,* 3 vols., trans. Isabella M. Massey (New York: Oxford University Press, 1952), I, pp. 118–189.

63. Strachan, pp. 35–41.

64. Ibid., pp. 41–45.

65. Craig, *Germany, 1866–1945,* pp. 323–324; Winkler, II, p. 299.

66. Geoffrey Barraclough, *From Agadir to Armageddon: Anatomy of a Crisis* (London: Weidenfeld & Nicholson, 1982).

67. John Keegan, *The First World War* (London: Hutchinson, 1998), pp. 48–52.

68. Strachan, p. 74.

69. Keegan, *The First World War,* pp. 59–60.

70. Winkler, II, p. 332.

71. Keegan, *The First World War,* pp. 10–18.

# MAPS

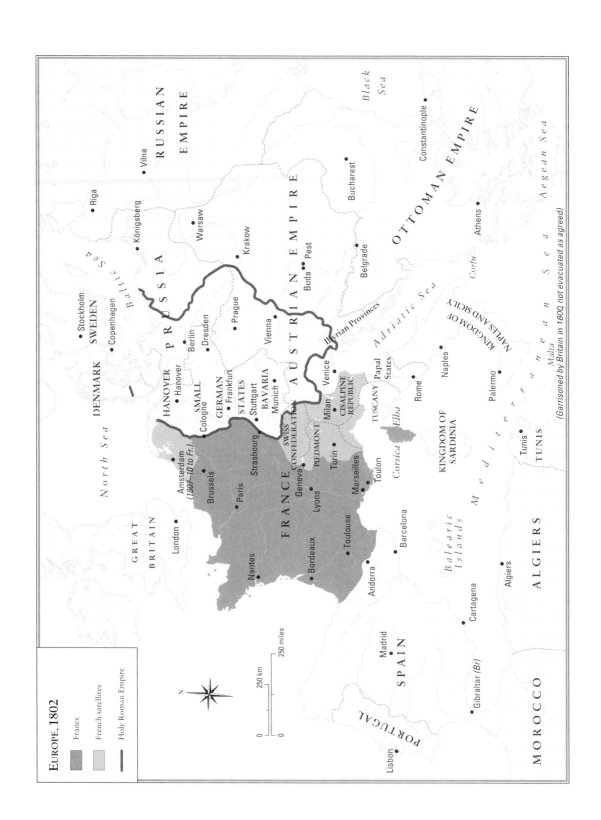

**EUROPE, 1802**

France

French satellites

Holy Roman Empire

250 miles

250 km

GREAT BRITAIN

DENMARK

SWEDEN

PRUSSIA

RUSSIAN EMPIRE

AUSTRIAN EMPIRE

OTTOMAN EMPIRE

FRANCE

SPAIN

PORTUGAL

MOROCCO

ALGIERS

TUNIS

HANOVER

SMALL GERMAN STATES

BAVARIA

SWISS CONFEDERATION

PIEDMONT

KINGDOM OF SARDINIA

CISALPINE REPUBLIC

TUSCANY

Papal States

KINGDOM OF NAPLES AND SICILY

Illyrian Provinces

North Sea

Baltic Sea

Black Sea

Adriatic Sea

Mediterranean Sea

Aegean Sea

Balearic Islands

Corsica

Elba

Malta

Corfu

London

Amsterdam (1807–10 to Fr.)

Brussels

Paris

Nantes

Bordeaux

Toulouse

Lyons

Geneva

Strasbourg

Hanover

Cologne

Berlin

Dresden

Frankfurt

Stuttgart

Munich

Vienna

Prague

Krakow

Buda

Pest

Belgrade

Bucharest

Constantinople

Athens

Warsaw

Königsberg

Vilna

Riga

Stockholm

Copenhagen

Turin

Milan

Venice

Rome

Naples

Palermo

Marseilles

Toulon

Andorra

Barcelona

Cartagena

Madrid

Lisbon

Gibraltar (Br)

Algiers

Tunis

(Garrisoned by Britain in 1800, not evacuated as agreed)

N

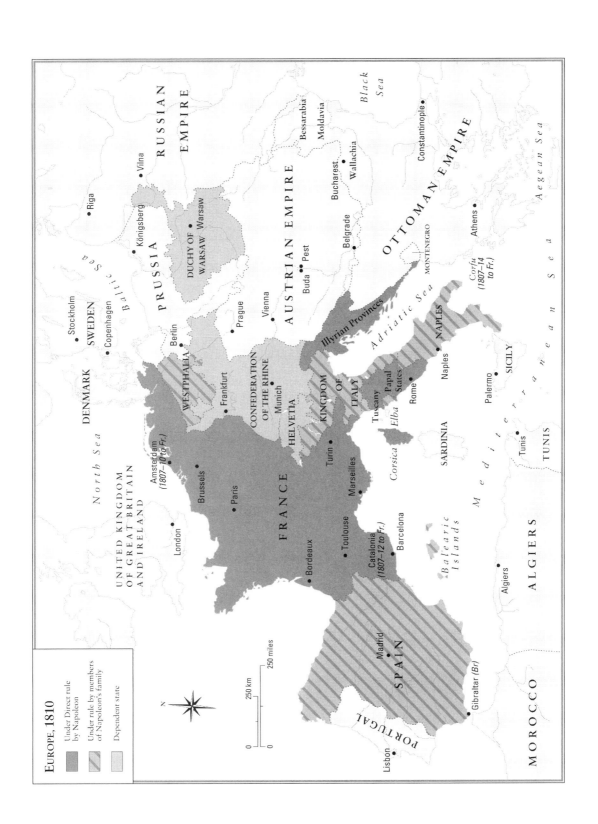

EUROPE, 1810

Under Direct rule
by Napoleon

Under rule by members
of Napoleon's family

Dependent state

N

250 km

250 miles

UNITED KINGDOM
OF GREAT BRITAIN
AND IRELAND

London

North Sea

DENMARK

Copenhagen

Stockholm

SWEDEN

Baltic Sea

Riga

Königsberg

Vilna

RUSSIAN
EMPIRE

PRUSSIA

Berlin

DUCHY OF
WARSAW

Warsaw

Amsterdam
(1807–10 to Fr.)

Brussels

WESTPHALIA

Frankfurt

CONFEDERATION
OF THE RHINE

Munich

Prague

Vienna

AUSTRIAN EMPIRE

Buda

Pest

Belgrade

Bucharest

Bessarabia

Moldavia

Wallachia

Black
Sea

Paris

FRANCE

HELVETIA

KINGDOM
OF
ITALY

Illyrian Provinces

Adriatic Sea

MONTENEGRO

Corfu
(1807–14
to Fr.)

OTTOMAN EMPIRE

Constantinople

Athens

Aegean Sea

Bordeaux

Toulouse

Marseilles

Turin

Tuscany

Papal
States

Rome

Elba

Corsica

SARDINIA

Naples

NAPLES

Palermo

SICILY

Mediterranean Sea

Catalonia
(1807–12 to Fr.)

Barcelona

Balearic
Islands

Tunis

TUNIS

SPAIN

Madrid

PORTUGAL

Lisbon

Gibraltar (Br)

Algiers

ALGIERS

MOROCCO

Europe in 1815 After
the Treaty of Vienna

──── German Confederation

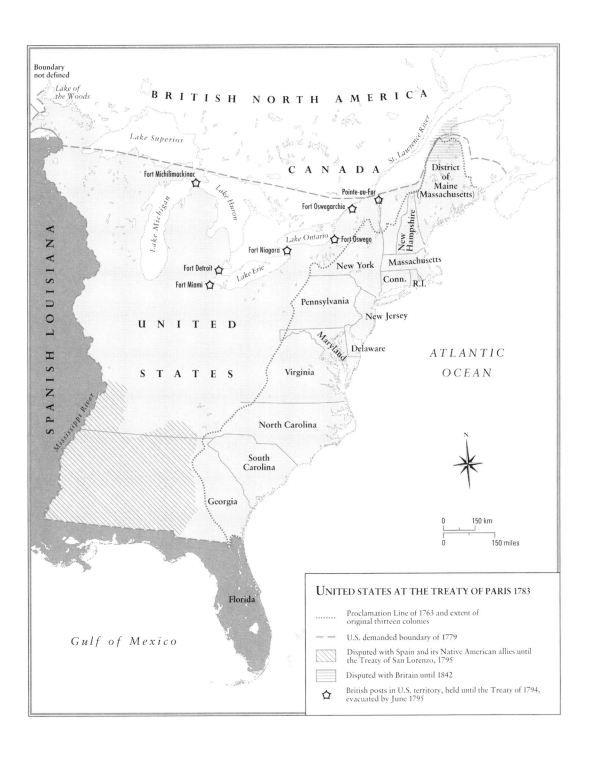

Boundary
not defined

*Lake of
the Woods*

B R I T I S H   N O R T H   A M E R I C A

*Lake Superior*

C A N A D A

*St. Lawrence River*

District
of
Maine
(Massachusetts)

Fort Michilimackinac

*Lake Huron*

Pointe-au-Far

Fort Oswegarchie

*Lake Michigan*

*Lake Ontario* Fort Oswego

Fort Niagara

New
Hampshire

Fort Detroit

*Lake Erie*

New York

Massachusetts

Fort Miami

Conn.

R.I.

Pennsylvania

New Jersey

U N I T E D

Maryland

Delaware

S P A N I S H   L O U I S I A N A

*Mississippi River*

S T A T E S

Virginia

*ATLANTIC
OCEAN*

North Carolina

N

South
Carolina

Georgia

0        150 km

0        150 miles

Florida

*Gulf of Mexico*

**UNITED STATES AT THE TREATY OF PARIS 1783**

......... Proclamation Line of 1763 and extent of
original thirteen colonies

— — —  U.S. demanded boundary of 1779

Disputed with Spain and its Native American allies until
the Treaty of San Lorenzo, 1795

Disputed with Britain until 1842

☆  British posts in U.S. territory, held until the Treaty of 1794,
evacuated by June 1795

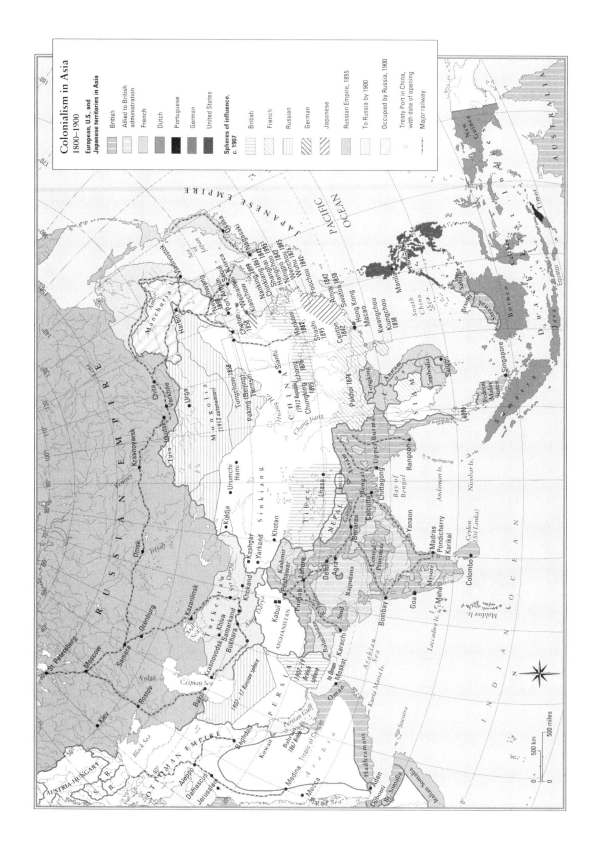

Colonialism in Asia
1800–1900

European, U.S., and
Japanese territories in Asia

British
Allied to British
administration
French
Dutch
Portuguese
German
United States

Spheres of influence,
c. 1907

British
French
Russian
German
Japanese

Russian Empire, 1855
To Russia by 1900
Occupied by Russia, 1900

Treaty Port in China,
with date of opening
Major railway

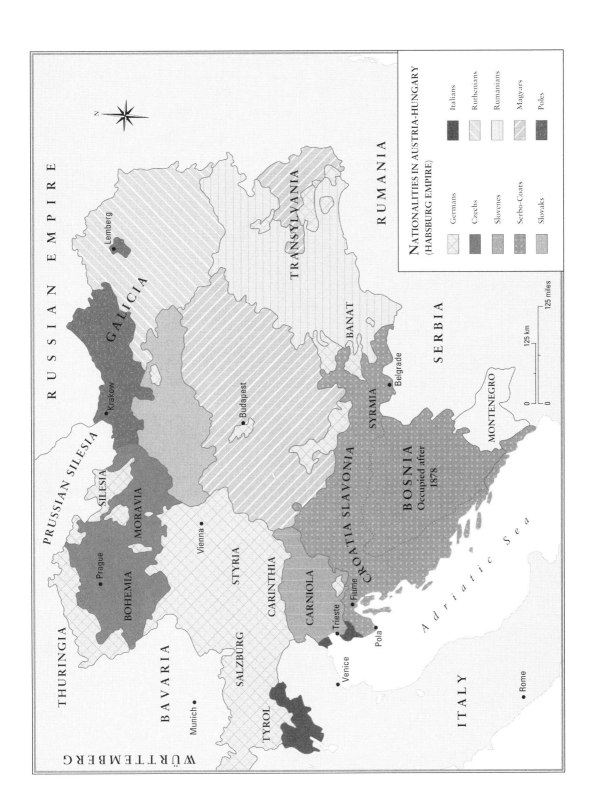

NATIONALITIES IN AUSTRIA-HUNGARY
(HABSBURG EMPIRE)

Germans
Czechs
Slovenes
Serbo-Coats
Slovaks

Italians
Ruthenians
Rumanians
Magyars
Poles

THE BALKANS, 1878–1914

Area of Turkey in Europe before Treaty of Berlin, 1878

Area of Turkey in Europe before the Balkan Wars, 1912–1913

Area ceded by Bulgaria to Romania, 1913

Boundaries before the Balkan Wars

Boundaries after the Balkan Wars

*Dniester*

BESSARABIA

*Pruth*

MOLDAVIA

*Drava*

*Sava*

BANAT

ROMANIA

Belgrade

• Bucharest

BOZNIA
Occupied by
Austria, 1878;
annexed, 1908

• Craiova

*Black
Sea*

Sarajevo
•

SERBIA

*Danube*

HERZEGOVINA

BULGARIA

DALMATIA
(Austria)

MONTENEGRO

• Sofia

*Bosphorus*

• Scutari

*Vardar*

• Adrianople

TURKEY

M A C E D O N I A

THRACE

Constantinople •

Albania created
from former
Turkish territory
1913

*Sea of
Marmara*

ITALY

A L B A N I A

Salonika
•

*Dardanelles*

THESSALY

*Aegean
Sea*

TURKEY

to GREECE 1881

*Ionian
Sea*

G R E E C E

• Smyrna

N

*Ionian Islands*

MOREA

• Athens

*Cyclades*

0        100 km

*Cerigo*

DODECANESE
to Italy, 1912

RHODES

0        100 miles

to Greece, 1913

CRETE

*M e d i t e r r a n e a n    S e a*

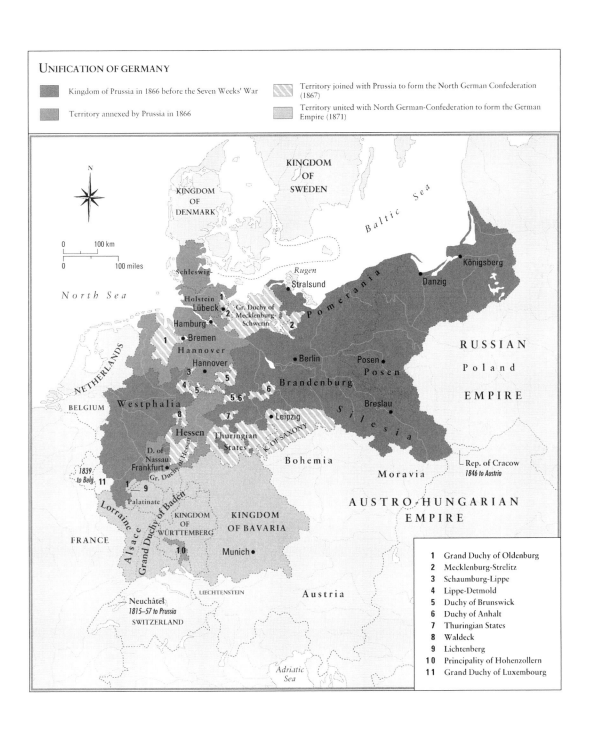

# UNIFICATION OF GERMANY

Kingdom of Prussia in 1866 before the Seven Weeks' War

Territory annexed by Prussia in 1866

Territory joined with Prussia to form the North German Confederation (1867)

Territory united with North German-Confederation to form the German Empire (1871)

N

KINGDOM OF SWEDEN

KINGDOM OF DENMARK

*Baltic Sea*

0    100 km
0    100 miles

*North Sea*

Schleswig-

*Rugen*

Stralsund

Königsberg

Danzig

Holstein   **1**
Lübeck ●
**2** Gr. Duchy of Mecklenburg-Schwerin

*Pomerania*

Hamburg ●
**2**

**1** ● Bremen

Hannover

Hannover

● Berlin

Posen
*Posen*

RUSSIAN

*Poland*

EMPIRE

NETHERLANDS

**3**
**4**  **5**
**5**

**5**
**5.6**  **6**

*Brandenburg*

Breslau

*Silesia*

BELGIUM

Westphalia

**7**

● Leipzig

**8**

Hessen

Thuringian States

K. OF SAXONY

Bohemia

Moravia

Rep. of Cracow
*1846 to Austria*

D. of Nassau
Frankfurt ●

Gr. Duchy of Hesse

*1839 to Belg.*  **11**

**1**  **9**

Palatinate

Grand Duchy of Baden

KINGDOM OF WÜRTTEMBERG

KINGDOM OF BAVARIA

AUSTRO-HUNGARIAN EMPIRE

Lorraine

Alsace

FRANCE

**10**

Munich ●

LIECHTENSTEIN

*Austria*

Neuchâtel
*1815–57 to Prussia*

SWITZERLAND

*Adriatic Sea*

| | |
|---|---|
| **1** | Grand Duchy of Oldenburg |
| **2** | Mecklenburg-Strelitz |
| **3** | Schaumburg-Lippe |
| **4** | Lippe-Detmold |
| **5** | Duchy of Brunswick |
| **6** | Duchy of Anhalt |
| **7** | Thuringian States |
| **8** | Waldeck |
| **9** | Lichtenberg |
| **10** | Principality of Hohenzollern |
| **11** | Grand Duchy of Luxembourg |

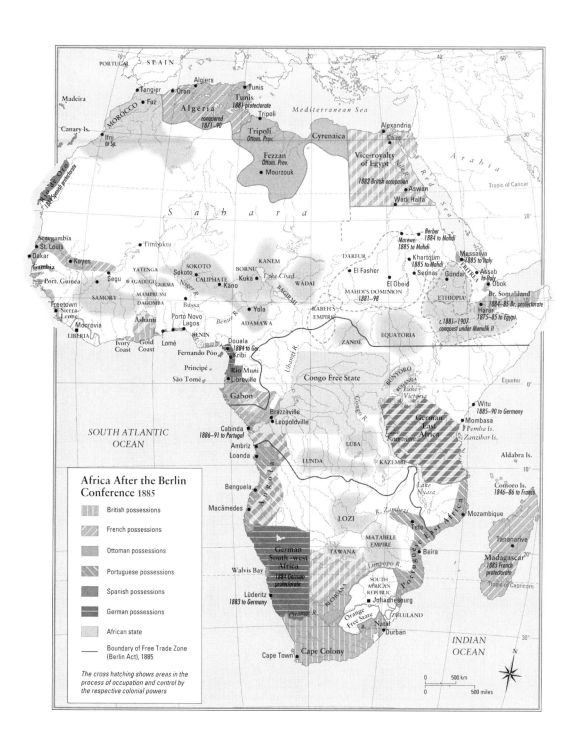

Africa After the Berlin Conference 1885

PORTUGAL SPAIN

Madeira

Canary Is.

MOROCCO

Tangier · Fez
Algiers · Oran
Tunis
Tunis 1881 protectorate
Tripoli
Algeria
conquered
1871–90

Mediterranean Sea

Tripoli
Ottom. Prov.

Cyrenaica

Alexandria
Cairo

Vice-royalty
of Egypt

Arabia

Tropic of Cancer

Ifni
to Sp.

Rio de Oro
1884 Spanish protectorate

Fezzan
Ottom. Prov.

· Mourzouk

1882 British occupation
· Aswan
Wadi Halfa

Red Sea

S a h a r a

20

Senegambia
· St. Louis
· Dakar · Kayes
Gambia
Port. Guinea
Segu
SAMORY
Freetown
Sierra
Leone
Monrovia
LIBERIA

· Timbuktu

SOKOTO
Sokoto
CALIPHATE
Kano
WAGADUGU GURMA
MAMPRUSSI
DAGOMBA
Bussa

Ivory
Coast
Gold
Coast
Lomé

KANEM
BORNU
Kuka
Lake Chad
WADAI
BAGIRMI

DARFUR

· El Fasher

Berber
1884 to Mahdi
Marewe
1885 to Mahdi
Khartoum
1885 to Mahdi
Sennar
El Obeid

Massawa
1885 to Italy
Assab
to Italy
Obok
Gondar

ERITREA

Br. Somaliland

YATENGA

Niger R.

Benue R.

· Yola

MAHDI'S DOMINION
1881–98

ETHIOPIA
1884–85 Br. protectorate
Harar 1875–85 to Egypt
c.1881–1907
conquest under Menelik II

Ashanti
Porto Novo
Lagos
BENIN
Douala
1884 to Ger.
Kribi
Fernando Póo

Principé ·
São Tomé ·

Rio Muni
· Libreville

Gabon

ADAMAWA

RABEH'S
EMPIRE

ZANDE

EQUATORIA

Congo Free State

Ubangi R.

Congo R.

Brazzaville
· Leopoldville

SOUTH ATLANTIC
OCEAN

Cabinda
1886–91 to Portugal
Ambriz
Loanda

LUNDA

LUBA

KAZEMBE

BUNYORO
UGANDA
Lake
Victoria

German
East
Africa

Witu
1885–90 to Germany
· Mombasa
Pemba Is.
Zanzibar Is.

Lake
Tanganyika

Aldabra Is.

Equator

Benguela

Macâmedes

Angola

LOZI

Lake
Nyasa

R. Zambezi

Comoro Is.
1846–86 to France

· Mozambique

Tananarive

Madagascar
1885 French
protectorate

Tropic of Capricorn

German
South-west
Africa
1884 German
protectorate

Walvis Bay

Lüderitz
1883 to Germany

TAWANA

BECHUANA

Orange R.

MATABELE
EMPIRE

Limpopo R.

SOUTH
AFRICAN
REPUBLIC
· Johannesburg

Orange
Free State

Tete

Beira

Portuguese East Africa

Natal

ZULULAND

· Durban

INDIAN
OCEAN

N

Cape Town ·
Cape Colony

British possessions

French possessions

Ottoman possessions

Portuguese possessions

Spanish possessions

German possessions

African state

Boundary of Free Trade Zone
(Berlin Act), 1885

The cross hatching shows areas in the
process of occupation and control by
the respective colonial powers

0    500 km

0    500 miles

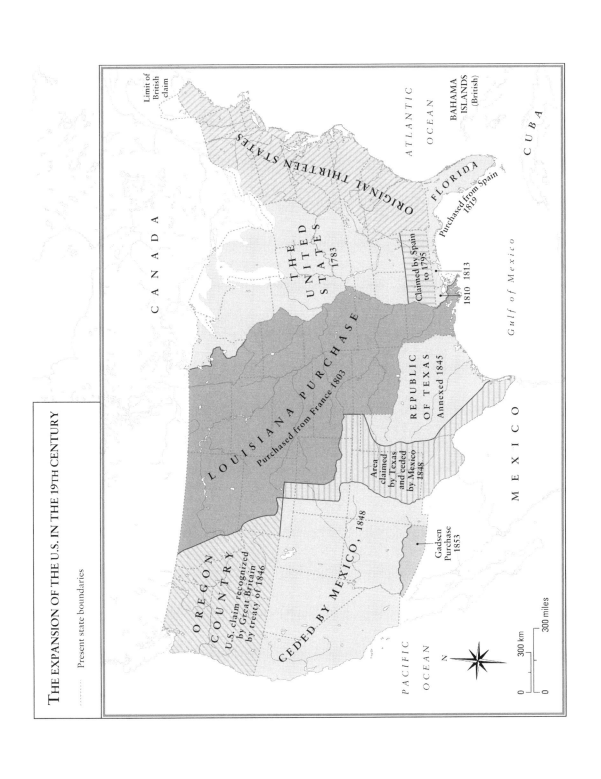

## THE EXPANSION OF THE U.S. IN THE 19TH CENTURY

------- Present state boundaries

CANADA

Limit of British claim

ATLANTIC OCEAN

BAHAMA ISLANDS (British)

CUBA

ORIGINAL THIRTEEN STATES

FLORIDA
Purchased from Spain 1819

THE UNITED STATES 1783

Claimed by Spain to 1795

1810   1813

Gulf of Mexico

LOUISIANA PURCHASE
Purchased from France 1803

REPUBLIC OF TEXAS
Annexed 1845

Area claimed by Texas and ceded by Mexico 1848

OREGON COUNTRY
U.S. claim recognized by Great Britain by treaty of 1846

CEDED BY MEXICO, 1848

MEXICO

Gadsen Purchase 1853

PACIFIC OCEAN

N

0    300 km

0    300 miles

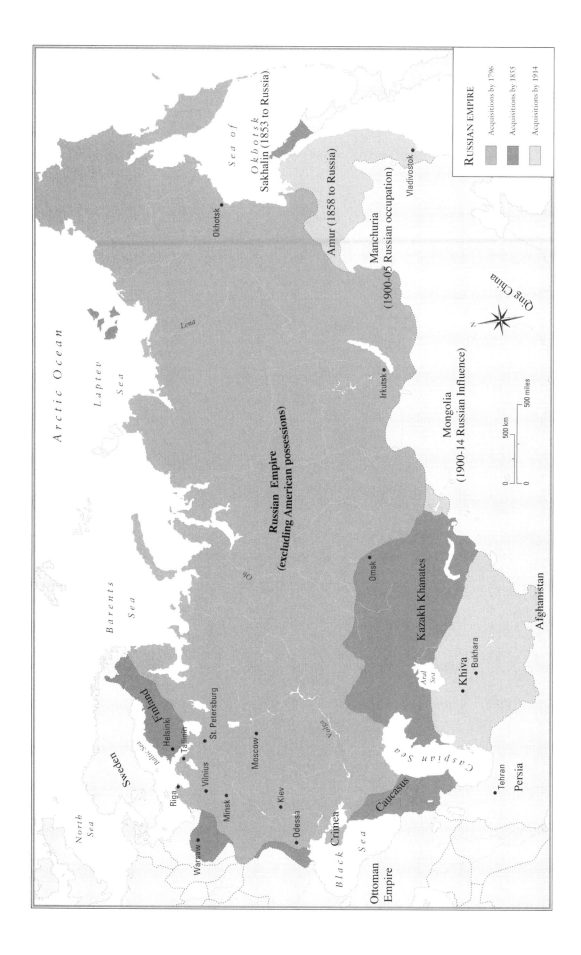

RUSSIAN EMPIRE

Acquisitions by 1796
Acquisitions by 1855
Acquisitions by 1914

Arctic Ocean

Barents Sea

Laptev Sea

Sea of Okhotsk

Sakhalin (1853 to Russia)

Okhotsk

Lena

Amur (1858 to Russia)

Manchuria (1900–05 Russian occupation)

Vladivostok

Russian Empire (excluding American possessions)

Irkutsk

Qing China

Mongolia (1900–14 Russian Influence)

500 km

500 miles

North Sea

Sweden

Baltic Sea

Finland

Helsinki

Tallinn

St. Petersburg

Riga

Vilnius

Minsk

Moscow

Warsaw

Kiev

Odessa

Crimea

Black Sea

Ottoman Empire

Volga

Caucasus

Caspian Sea

Tehran

Persia

Aral Sea

Khiva

Bukhara

Kazakh Khanates

Omsk

Afghanistan

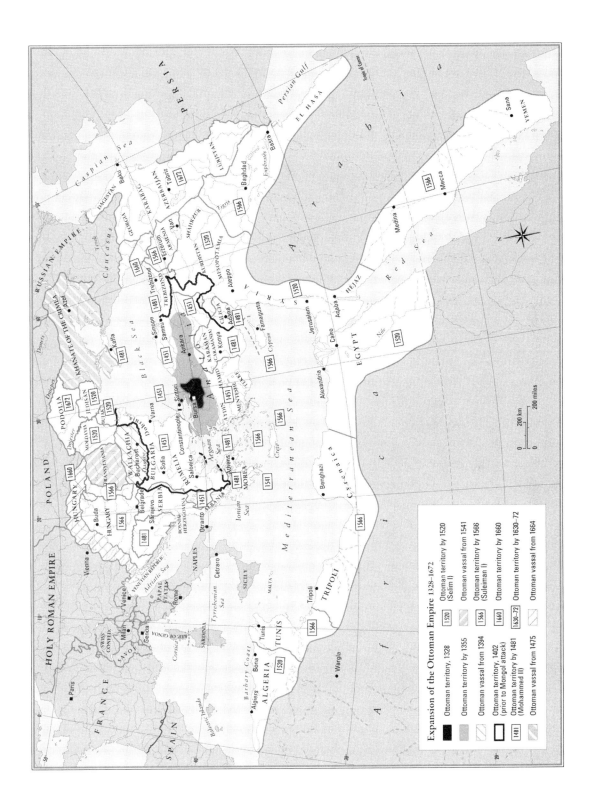

**Expansion of the Ottoman Empire 1328–1672**

| | |
|---|---|
| Ottoman territory, 1328 | Ottoman territory by 1520 (Selim I) |
| Ottoman territory by 1355 | Ottoman vassal from 1541 |
| Ottoman vassal from 1394 | Ottoman territory by 1566 (Suleiman II) |
| Ottoman territory, 1402 (prior to Mongol attack) | Ottoman territory by 1660 |
| Ottoman territory by 1481 (Mohammed II) | Ottoman territory by 1630–72 |
| Ottoman vassal from 1475 | Ottoman vassal from 1664 |

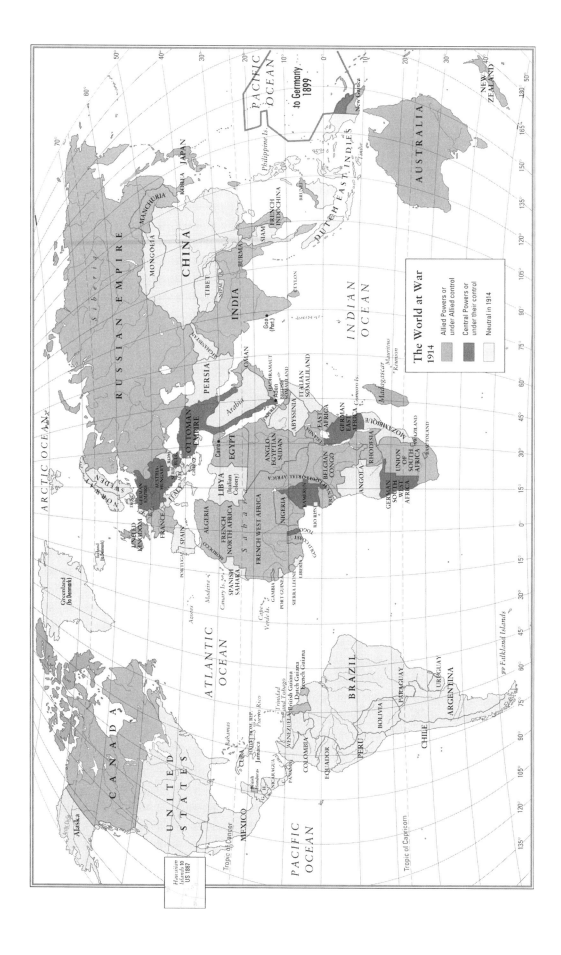

The World at War
1914

Allied Powers or
under Allied control

Central Powers or
under their control

Neutral in 1914

# CHRONOLOGY FOR THE AGE OF IMPERIALISM, 1800–1914

Cross-references to entries in the main entry section are in **boldface.**

## 1. Napoleonic Wars, 1800–1815

1799–1804: The Consulate ends the France's revolutionary period. A dictatorship by Napoleon **Bonaparte** with the formal trappings of a republic is established.

## 1800

May: Napoleon crosses the St. Bernard Pass with 40,000 men.

June 14: Battle of **Marengo,** a great Napoleonic victory brings all fortresses west of the Mincio and south of the Po under French control.

December 3: Battle of **Hohenlinden,** French General Moreau defeats Austrians decisively. Austria sues for peace.

December 16: League of Armed Neutrality formed.

## 1801

February 9: Treaty of **Lunéville** dissolves the Second Coalition and dismantles much of the Holy Roman Empire.

March 23: Tsar Paul I murdered, Alexander I succeeds.

March 29: Treaty of Florence.

April 2: British attack Copenhagen.

July 15: The Concordat establishes a new relationship between the French state and the Catholic Church.

October 8: Treaty of **Paris.**

## 1802

West India docks built in London.

French expeditionary forces arrive in Santo Domingo.

March 27: Treaty of **Amiens** between Britain and France establishes fourteen-month Anglo-French truce.

August 2: Napoleon named Consul for life.

September 11: France annexes Piedmont.

## 1803

Ludwig van Beethoven completes Symphony No. 3, "Eroica."
Henry Schrapnel invents the fragmentation shell.
Battle of Assaye: Arthur Wellesley defeats the Marathas.
April 30: Louisiana purchased by the United States.
May 16: Britain declares war on France.
June 1: Frances seizes Hanover.
June 15: French forces concentrate along English Channel.

## 1804

March: Code Civil established.
May 18: Napoleon Bonaparte becomes Napoleon I, Emperor of the French.
December 2: Napoleon is crowned.
December 14: Spain declares war on Britain.

## 1805

Modern Egypt established, Mehemet Ali is Pasha.
Formation of the Third Coalition: Britain is joined by Austria, Russia, and Sweden in alliance against France and Spain.
May 26: Napoleon crowned king of Italy.
Battle of Elchingen.
October 17: 30,000 Austrians surrender to France at **Ulm.**
October 21: Battle of **Trafalgar,** Nelson's naval victory over a combined French and Spanish fleet.
November 14: Napoleon enters Vienna.
December 2: Battle of **Austerlitz,** Napoleon routs combined Austrian and Russian armies.
December 26: Treaty of **Pressburg** signed between France and Austria.

## 1806

Slave trade to British colonies prohibited.
United States bans importation of slaves.
1806–1812: Russia at war with Turkey
June 12: Confederation of the Rhine organized under French auspices.
August 6: Napoleon formally dissolves the Holy Roman Empire.
August 9: Prussia mobilizes against France.
September 26: Fourth Coalition formed.
October 10: British forces return to the Cape; surrender of Pappendorp.
October 14: Battle of Jena-Auerstädt, Napoleon routs Prussian armies.
October 27: French army occupies Berlin.
November 21: Berlin Decree, Napoleon proclaims a blockade of Britain.

## 1807

Napoleon campaigns in Poland against Russia.
British invasion and occupation of Alexandria.
Britain abolishes slave trade.
February 7–8: Battle of **Eylau,** a bloody but indecisive Franco-Russian engagement.
March 18–May 27: Siege of Danzig
March 25: Abolition of slavery in the British dominions.
June 14: Battle of Friedland, Napoleon defeats the Russian army.

July 7–9: Treaties of **Tilsit,** diplomatic and territorial concessions by Prussia and Russia to France.

September 5–7: Royal Navy bombards Danish fleet at Copenhagen, denying Danish coast to Napoleon's **Continental System.**

November: Portugal refuses to join the **Continental System** and is occupied by French troops, **Peninsular War** begins.

## 1808

Sierra Leone declared a British colony.

1808–1815: Britain releases 6,000 slaves taken at sea in Sierra Leone.

February 2: Occupation of Rome.

March: 100,000 French troops invade Spain.

May: Napoleon ousts Ferdinand VII from Spanish throne and replaces him with his brother, Joseph, precipitating a nationalist uprising.

May 2: Murat represses Madrid uprising.

July 22: Battle of Bailén.

August 21: British forces defeat French at Vimeiro.

September: Congress of Erfurt reinforces Franco-Russian alliance; Napoleon is at the height of his power.

November 30: Battle of Somosierra.

December 13: Madrid falls to French army.

## 1809

British capture French settlements on the Senegal.

The Khoikhoi of South Africa placed under colonial law.

January 8: Austria decides on war.

January 16: French victory in the Battle of **Corunna.** Britain forced to evacuate Spain.

February 21: French forces take Oporto.

April 9: Fifth Coalition formed.

April 10: Austria invades Bavaria.

May 12: Anglo-Portuguese forces under Wellesley recapture Oporto.

July 28: Battle of Talavera slows French invasion of Portugal.

November 19: Battle of Ocaña, Spanish army defeated by French forces.

May 21–22: Battle of **Aspern-Essling,** Napoleon defeated by Austrian forces.

July 5–6: Battle of **Wagram,** Napoleon defeats Austrian forces.

October 14: Treaty of **Schönbrunn,** Austria cedes territory to France and French allies.

## 1810

British capture Guadaloupe.

Revolutions in Buenos Aires and Bogata.

Simon Bolivar emerges as "The Liberator."

Britain seizes Mauritius, Réunion, and French stations in Madagascar.

April 1: Napoleon marries Archduchess Marie Louis of Austria, a union arranged by Metternich.

March 13: King Gustavus IV of Sweden arrested and forced to abdicate, is succeeded by Charles XIII.

July 9: France annexes Holland.

September 17: Treaty of Friederichsham.

## 1811

British occupy Java.

Paraguay and Venezuela declare independence.

1811–1812: British forces drive 20,000 Xhosa from Zuurveld.
March 1: Massacre of the Mamluks in Cairo.
March 5: Massena begins retreat from Portugal.
May 3–5: Battle of Fuentes de Oñoro.
May 16: Battle of Albuera.

## 1812

Outbreak of the **Anglo-American War** of 1812.
Usuman dan Fodio establishes the Sokoto Caliphate.
January: France reoccupies Swedish Pomerania.
January 19: Wellington storms Ciudad Rodrigo.
April: **Treaty of St. Petersburg** signed by Sweden and Russia.
May 28: Treaty of Bucharest signed by Ottoman Empire and Russia.
June: Britain makes peace with Sweden and Russia.
June 20: Sixth Coalition formed.
June 24: French troops cross the Nieman River, Napoleonic invasion of Russia begins.
August 12: Wellington enters Madrid.
August 17–18: Battle of **Smolensk.**
September 7: Battle of **Borodino,** a costly Napoleonic victory.
September 14: French troops occupy **Moscow.**
September 15–17: Burning of Moscow.
October 19: Napoleon begins retreat from Moscow.
November 26–28: Battle of the Beresina.
December 30: Prussian General Yorke concludes Convention of Tauroggen with Russia.

## 1813

Monopoly of the East India Company abolished.
Russia seizes Dagestan.
Austria and Prussia join Russia to push France out of Germany.
February 28: Treaty of Kalisch signed by Prussia and Russia.
March 4: Russians enter Berlin.
March 16: Prussia declares war on France.
March 17–27: Prussians and Russians occupy Hamburg and Dresden.
May 2: Battle of Lutzen.
May 20: Battle of Bautzen.
May 23: Wellington advances into Spain.
June 12: French army evacuates Madrid.
June 21: Wellington victorious at Vitoria.
August 12: Austria declares war on France.
August 26–27: Battle of **Dresden.**
September 9: Treaty of Teplitz agreed by Austria, Prussia, and Russia.
October 16–19: Battle of **Leipzig,** Allied victory forces further French retreat.

## 1814

January 14: Treaty of Kiel, Denmark cedes Norway to Sweden.
February 1: Battle of La Rothière.
March 9: Treaties of **Chaumont** provide for continued Allied struggle against Napoleon.
February 5–March 19: Congress of Châtillon.
March 20: Battle of Arcis-sur-Aube.
March 31: Allies enter Paris.

April 6: Napoleon abdicates.

April 10: Wellington defeats Soult at Toulouse.

May 30: First Treaty of **Paris,** a lenient peace for France restores the Bourbons.

September–June 1915: Congress of **Vienna,** establishes a comprehensive European settlement.

December 24: Treaty of Ghent ends War of 1812.

## 1815

Britain declares control of South African **Cape Colony.**

Slachter's Nek rebellion in the Eastern Cape.

February 26: Napoleon escapes from Elba.

March 1: Napoleon lands at Cannes.

March 3: United States begins naval operations against Algiers.

March 27: Seventh Coalition formed.

June 15: Napoleon crosses into Belgium.

June 16: Battle of **Ligny,** Battle of **Quatre Bras.**

June 18: Battle of **Waterloo,** Anglo-Prussian forces under Wellington inflict final defeat on Napoleon.

June 22: Second abdication of Napoleon.

September 26: Creation of the **Holy Alliance.**

November 20: Second Treaty of **Paris** imposes territorial losses and reparations on France and renews the **Quadruple Alliance** of Austria, Britain, Prussia, and Russia.

## 2. Pax Brittanica, 1815–1870

## 1816

Britain returns Java to the Netherlands.

Intensified Protestant missionary activity in the Eastern Cape.

British bombard **Algiers** and demand that the *dey* end Christian slavery.

Argentine provinces declare independence.

August 27: Anglo-Dutch bombardment of Algiers.

December 22: United States signs peace treaty with Algiers.

## 1817

San Martin defeats Spain at Chacubuco.

Shaka becomes chief of the Zulu Kingdom.

March: British parliament passes *Coercion Acts.*

## 1818

End of Maratha Wars, Raijput States, and Poona under British rule.

Martin defeats Spanish at Maipó.

Chile declares independence.

Canada and United States establish border at 49th parallel.

1818–1819: Xhosa war of resistance defeated.

Wahabis defeated in Arabia.

September: Congress of **Aix-la-Chapelle.**

## 1819

East India Company establishes settlement at Singapore.

1819–1820: Zulus defeat Zwide's Ndwandwe.

August 16: Peterloo Massacre.
September 20: Carlsbad Decrees sanctioned by the Diet of the German Confederation.
October: Prussia begins construction of the German *Zollverein.*
December: British parliament passes the Six Acts.

## 1820

10,000 British settlers land on Eastern Cape.
Tijaniyya Sufi uprising in Oran against Ottoman rule.
1820–1830: Rise of the Basotho Kingdom.
March 3: Missouri Compromise.
October 20: Congress of **Troppau.**

## 1821

San Martin declares Peruvian independence.
Guatemala, Mexico, Panama, and Santo Domingo independent of Spain.
Egyptian governor-general installed in Khartoum.
Sierra Leone, Gold Coast, and Gambia joined as British West Africa.
January–May: Congress of **Laibach.**

## 1822

Brazil independent of Portugal.
English replaces Dutch as the official language of South Africa.
Egyptian forces complete conquest of the Sudan.
Liberia becomes a colony for freed American slaves.
October 20: Congress of **Verona.**

## 1823

Outbreak of the First Anglo-Ashanti War.
December 2: U.S. President James Monroe articulates the **Monroe Doctrine.**

## 1824

Ludwig van Beethoven's Symphony No. 9 premiers in Vienna.
British traders establish post at Port Natal.
January: Outbreak of the First **Anglo-Burmese War.**

## 1825

Bolivia declares independence.
Ndebele become the dominant kingdom of the high veld.

## 1826

Cape Colony extended north to the Orange River.
January 2: British troops storm Melloon, ending First Anglo-Burmese War.

## 1827

*Dey* of Algiers hits French consul with a fly whisk; France demands satisfaction.

## 1828

The Black War in Australia.
**Shaka** assassinated; Dingane becomes king of the Zulu.
July 15: British parliament passes the revised *Corn Law.*

## 1829

**Suttee** is abolished in Bengal.
British Slave Trade Commission takes over Fernando Po.
March–April: *Catholic Emancipation* passes British Parliament.

## 1830

Mysore becomes new British possession in India.
July 5: French expeditionary force occupies **Algiers.**
July 26: French government imposes the July Ordinances.
July 28: Insurgents control much of Paris, the July Revolution.
July 30: **Louis Philippe** proclaimed constitutional monarch of France.

## 1831

Darwin begins voyage in *Beagle.*
March 31: Louis Philippe creates the French Foreign Legion.

## 1832

Black Hawk War and Indian war in the American Midwest.
Britain occupies Falkland Islands.
1832–1834: Attacks on French forces by **Abd al-Qādr.**

## 1833

August 23: Abolition of slavery in the British Empire.

## 1834

Outbreak of the **Carlist War** in Spain.
Angola ignores antislavery laws.
12,000 Xhosa attack Cape Colony outposts.
Dutch slaveholders in Africa Cape protest lack of compensation.
April 22: Quadruple Alliance.

## 1835

Turkish forces land at Tripoli.
1835–1837: Outbreak of the French war against Abd al-Qādr.
Beginning of the **Great Trek** of the Boers to the north and east of the Orange River.

## 1836

Republic of Texas established.
French defeat Abd el-Qādr at Sikka River.

## 1837

Revolts in Upper and Lower Canada.
Lin Zexu, governor of Hunan and Hupeh, orders destruction of opium cargoes.
Treaty of Tafna: France abandons Algerian interior to Abd al-Qādr.

## 1838

Founding of the New Zealand Company.
Governor of Angola removed for slave trafficking.
First **Afghan War** begins.
June 28: Coronation of Victoria I.
February: Zulus massacre Boer Vortrekkers in Natal.
December 16: Battle of **Blood River,** Boers defeat Zulus, establish Republic of Natal.

## 1839

British expedition into Afghanistan.
Quadruple Alliance of Britain, France, Portugal, and Spain defeats Carlists.
Mpande and Boers overthrow Dingane.
November 3: Imperial Commissioner Lin Zexu forces surrender of opium cargo, outbreak
    of the **Opium War.**

## 1840

Abd el-Qādr begins new attacks on French settlers.
Upper and Lower Canada united.
Treaty of Waitangi, Britain claims sovereignty over New Zealand.
Portuguese merchants found port of Mocamedes on Angolan coast.
Britain occupies Chusan and Canton river ports.
December: Start of French campaign against Abd al-Qādr.

## 1841

Britain proclaims sovereignty over Hong Kong.
New Zealand becomes British colony.
July 13: **Straits Convention.**

## 1842

1842–1843: War between Britain and Boers, Britain takes Natal.
August 29: Treaty of **Nanjing** ends the Opium War.
August 9: Britain and United States sign **Webster-Ashburton Treaty.**
September: British force captures Kabul, ending First Anglo-Afghan War.

## 1843

June 17: Outbreak of First **Maori War.**
August 8: Natal becomes a British colony.
December: Basutoland becomes a *de facto* British protectorate.

## 1844

Arab trading post established at Umyanyembe.
French defeat Abd el-Qādr at Isly.
September 10: *Treaty of Tangier* concludes French campaign in Morocco.

## 1845

March 1: United States Congress votes to annex Texas.

John O'Sullivan publishes an article on the **Manifest Destiny** of the United States.

July 7: John Drake Sloat claims Mexican territory in California for the United States.

December 11: Outbreak of the First **Sikh War.**

## 1846

1846–1848: United States at war with Mexico.

1846–1847: Shepstone establishes reserve system in Natal.

March 11: Treaty of Lahore ends First Anglo-Sikh War and makes the Punjab a British protectorate.

April 12: Mexican troops cross the Rio Grande, outbreak of the **Mexican War.**

May 8–9: American victories at Palo Alto and Resaca de la Palma.

May 24: U.S. troops capture Monterey.

June 15: Britain and United States sign **Oregon Treaty.**

## 1847

Slavery abolished throughout French Empire.

February 22–23: Battle of **Buena Vista.**

July 26: Free and Independent Republic of Liberia established.

September 12–13: Battle of Chapultepec.

September 14: U.S. troops capture Mexico City.

December 23: Abd al-Qādr surrenders to France and is imprisoned.

## 1848

Marx and Engels issue *The Communist Manifesto.*

Algeria annexed to France, organized into three departments.

First delegate from Senegal sent to French National Assembly.

February: February Revolution in Paris.

February 2: Treaty of **Guadalupe Hidalgo** ends Mexican War.

March 15: Uprisings in Berlin.

April 20: Outbreak of Second **Sikh War.**

## 1849

France founds Libreville with freed slave settlers.

1849–1852: Influx of British-sponsored settlers to Natal.

April 5: France declares protectorate over French Guinea.

1849–1850: Don Pacifico Affair.

February 22: Battle of **Gujarat** ends Second Anglo-Sikh War; Britain annexes the Punjab.

## 1850

The Kololo of South Africa enter the Angolan slave trade.

1850–1860: Ivory trade fuels gun trade in South Central Africa.

1850–1864: **Taiping** Rebellion.

August: Australian Colonies Government Act.

## 1852

**Sand River** Convention between British and Transvaal Boers.
April 1: Outbreak of Second **Anglo-Burmese** War.
November 21: British troops capture Pegu, ending Second Anglo-Burmese War.

## 1853

Cape Colony constitution establishes an elected parliament.
Hanover, Brunswick, and Oldenburg join the Prussian *Zollverein*.

## 1854

Slave-trading boom in Karka and Shillukland.
Bloemfontein Convention paves way for an Orange Free State.
1854–1884: Rule of Kabaka Mutesa in Buganda.
1854–1861: France revives colonial interests in Senegal.
March 28: Outbreak of **Crimean War.**
November 30: Suez Canal concession granted to Ferdinand de Lesseps.

## 1855

*The Economist* begins publication.
Taiping Rebellion ends.
Paris World's Fair.
1855–1868: Tewodros II begins modern period in Ethiopia.

## 1856

Swahili traders reach Katanga.
July 12: Natal becomes a British colony; civil war in the Zulu kingdom.
October 8: Qing officials search British ship *Arrow*, outbreak of **Arrow War.**

## 1857

British destroy Chinese fleet.
1857–1858: **Indian Mutiny.**
Anglo-French seizure of Canton.

## 1858

East India Company is transferred to the British crown.
Slavery abolished in Russia.
Suez Canal Company established.
Treaty of **Aigun**.
June 26–29: Treaties of **Tientsin.**

## 1859

Spain sends expeditionary force to Morocco.
**Darwin** publishes *The Origin of Species*.
London Missionary Society founded in Inyati Rhodesia.
First indentured Indian labor arrives in Natal.
April 29: Work begins on the Suez Canal.

## 1860

Republic of Lydenburg joins South African Republic.
1860–1890: Expansion of slave trade northward and eastward from Congo Basin.
October 12: Anglo-French occupation of Peking ending **Arrow War.**
November 6: Abraham Lincoln is elected President of the United States.
December 20: South Carolina secedes from the United States.

## 1861

Sikkum campaign.
French expeditions in Mexico.
January 9–26: Mississippi, Florida, Alabama, Georgia, and Louisiana secede from the United States.
April 12–13: Bombardment of Sumter, **American Civil War** begins.
November–December: Trent Affair.

## 1862

Victor **Hugo** publishes *Les Miserables.*
R. J. Gatling invents machine gun.
France acquires the port of Obock from the Sultan of Tarjura.
Anglo-French forces defeat Chinese, Treaty of Peking signed.
September 23: **Bismarck** appointed minister-president of Prussia.
September 30: Bismarck delivers "iron and blood" speech to Prussian parliament.

## 1863

Outbreak of the Second **Maori War.**
Ismael Pasha becomes khedive of Egypt.
Battle of Camerone in Mexico.
1863–1865: France revives territorial expansion west of Sudan.
January 1: Lincoln issues Emancipation Proclamation.
February: Polish uprising in Russian Poland.
February 25: France establishes a protectorate over Porto Novo.
July 1–3: Battle of **Gettysburg.**
July 4: Fall of **Vicksburg.**
June 5: Treaty of Saigon. France acquires control of three southern provinces of **Cochin China.**

## 1864

France takes Cochin China.
Geneva Convention establishes rules for war.
January 16: Austro-Prussian alliance.
February 1: Austrian and Prussian armies invade Schleswig.
October 30: Treaty of Vienna confirms Austrian and Prussian control of Schleswig-Holstein and Lauenburg

## 1865

Richard **Wagner** finishes *Tristan und Isolde.*
1865–1866: War between Orange Free State and Moshoeshoe's Sotho.
January 31: Slavery is abolished in the United States

April 9: Lee surrenders to Grant at Appomattox.
April 14: President Abraham Lincoln is assassinated.
May 26: Last Confederate army surrenders, ending American Civil War.
August: Austro-Prussian *Gastein Convention.*

## 1866

Kaffraria is joined to the Cape Colony.
April 8: Prussian alliance with Italy.
June 6: Prussia protests Austrian policy in Holstein.
June 14: **Austro-Prussian** War begins.
July 3: Prussians defeat Austria at **Königgrätz.**
August 18: Prussian treaty of federation with North German states.
August 23: Treaty of Prague ends Austro-Prussian War.

## 1867

British North America Act establishes Dominion of **Canada.**
Karl **Marx** publishes *Das Kapital.*
British expeditionary mission sent to Ethiopia.
April: Diamonds discovered near Hopetown on the Orange River.
April 16: Constituent Reichstag passes constitution of **North German Confederation.**
April–May: Luxemburg Crisis.

## 1868

Dostoevsky publishes *The Idiot.*
British forces invade Abyssinia.
Sir John Kirk becomes British representative in Zanzibar.
January 1: Hyōgo and Ōsaka opened to foreign trade.
January 3: Inauguration of the **Meiji Restoration** in Japan.
March 12: Britain annexes Basotholand and establishes white government.
April 13: British capture Magdala.
1868–1869: Irish Question.

## 1869

Richard Wagner's *Rheingold* premiers in Munich.
Gustave Flaubert publishes *l'Education sentimentale.*
Red River Rebellion in Canada.
Italian Rubattino Company buys the port of Assab on the Red Sea.
November 17: **Suez Canal** officially opens.

## 3. Period of Intensified Imperial Competition, 1870–1900

## 1870

Richard Wagner's *Die Walküre* premiers in Munich.
Digger's Republic proclaimed at Klipdrift.
Diamonds discovered in the Orange Free State.
1870–1876: Bunganda moves toward Islam, then Christianity.
March 15: Bismarck backs Hohenzollern candidacy for the Spanish throne.
July 13: Bismarck releases **Ems Telegram.**
July 19: France declares war on Prussia. **Franco-Prussian War** begins.
September 1: Battle of **Sedan.** Prussia defeats French army, captures Napoleon III.

## 1871

Giueseppe Verdi's **Aïda** premiers in Cairo.
Town of Kimberley founded as the center of the South African diamond industry.
January 15: Proclamation of the **German Empire** at Versailles. Wilhelm I is Emperor.
February: Provisional peace facilitates German annexation of Alsace Lorraine.
April: Britain annexes Griqualand West diamond region.
April 14: Remodeled constitution amalgamates 25 states in the German Reich.
May 10: Treaty of **Frankfurt.**

## 1872

1872–1874: Egypt occupies Red Sea coast.
Cape Colony granted self-government.

## 1873

Onset of economic recession.
Tolstoy publishes *Anna Karenina*.
General Charles **Gordon** seconded to the khedive of Egypt as governor of Equatoria.
Outbreak of the Second Anglo-Ashanti War.

## 1874

Gordon becomes governor-general of the Sudan.
Japanese occupation of Formosa.

## 1875

United Free Church of Scotland founds mission at Blantrye and Livingstonia.
Slavery and forced labor abolished in Angola.
1875–1878: Egyptian war with Ethiopia.
November 25: Britain purchases 40 percent share in **Suez Canal** from khedive of Egypt.

## 1876

**Victoria** proclaimed Empress of India.
First complete performance of Richard Wagner's *Der Ring des Niebelungen*.
Telephone is invented in the United States.
February: Ethiopian army defeats Egyptian forces.
April 4: Egyptian finances declared insolvent.
September 12: King Leopold of Belgium hosts international conference on Africa.
November 18: Anglo-French controllers appointed to administer Egyptian debt.

## 1877

March 18: Britain annexes Walvis Bay in Southwest Africa.
April 12: Britain annexes Transvaal in violation of the **Sand River Convention.**
April 24: Russia declares war on Turkey.

## 1878

German Africa Society establishes posts between Bagamoyo and Lake Tanganyika.
March 3: Treaty of **San Stefano.**
June 13–July 13: Congress of **Berlin.**
October 7: German-Austrian alliance.

June 18: Alliance of the Three Emperors.
August 15: Nubar Pasha Ministry in Egypt.
November: British army invades Afghanistan, starting Second Anglo-Afghan War.
November 15: Belgium commissions Henry Stanley to establish posts in Congo region.

## 1879

Jesuits establish mission at Bulawayo.
France begins conquest of Umarian Empire.
Afrikaner Bond founded.
Catholic White Fathers arrive in Buganda.
1879–1881: Franco-Italian rivalry in Tunis.
January 12–September 1: British forces invade and defeat **Zulu** Kingdom.

## 1880

France founds Brazzaville and establishes a protectorate.
1880–1900: Christian missionaries penetrate East African interior.
1880–1881: Boers of Transvaal revolt against the British. Barnato Diamond Mining Company founded; De Beers Mining Corporation founded.
Madrid Convention sets status and rights of foreigners in Morocco.
September 1: Battle of **Kandahar,** British defeat Ayub Khan, ending Second Anglo-Afghan War.
December 30: Boers proclaim Republic of South Africa, starting First **Boer War.**

## 1881

France makes first attempt at a Trans-Saharan Railway.
1881–1885: International Association of the Congo established.
1881–1885: Mahdist revolution against Turco-Egyptian power in Sudan.
January 28: Boers defeat British at Laing's Nek.
February 27: Boer's defeat British at Majuba Hill.
April 5: Treaty of Pretoria between Britain and Boers recognizes South African Republic.
April 30: French navy seizes Bizerta.
May 12: Treaty of Barto, *Bey* of Tunis accepts French protectorate.
February 1: Rising of Egyptian officers.
September 9: Second rising of Egyptian officers.

## 1882

Boer expansion into Bechuanaland.
Italian government takes over Assab.
January 8: Anglo-French "Gambetta Note" delivered to Egypt.
May 20: **Triple Alliance** of Germany, Austria, and Italy formed.
June 12: Riots in Alexandria.
July 11: British bombardment of Alexandria.
September 13: British victory at Tel-el-Kebir.
September 15: British occupy Cairo and Suez Canal Zone.

## 1883

French invade Annam and Tonkin.
Marxist party founded in Russia.
Britain defeats Pedi Kingdom.

German settlers come to Southwest Africa.
Convention of Marsa gives France control of Tunisian affairs.
Civil War in Zululand.
April 16: Paul **Kruger** becomes president of South African Republic.
November 5: Battle of Obeid.

# 1884

Germany occupies South-West Africa.
Britain establishes a protectorate around Zeila on the Somali coast.
1884–1885: Berlin West Africa Conference.
January 18: **Gordon** sent to evacuate Khartoum.
April 22: U.S. recognizes International Association of the Congo as a territorial power.

# 1885

Britain establishes Bechuanaland Protectorate.
Outbreak of the Franco-Mandingo Wars.
Anglo-Egyptian forces evacuate Sudan.
Defeat of Second **Riel** rebellion in Canada.
French attempt and fail to take Madagascar.
French defeat in Tonkin topples Ferry government.
January 26: The Mahdi captures Khartoum.
February: German East Africa Company claims protectorate between Umba and Rovuma Rivers.
February 6: Italy establishes a base at Massawa.
April: Belgium establishes Congo Independent State.
April: Anglo-Russian crisis in Afghanistan.
August: Germany establishes protectorate over Witu in Zanzibar.
November: Third **Anglo-Burmese War** lasts 20 days.

# 1886

First meeting of Indian National Congress.
Burma incorporated into British India.
Gold discovered on Witwatersrand.
September: Town of Johannesburg established.

# 1887

First Colonial Conference opens in London.
British East Africa Company secures 50-year lease between Umba and Tanas Rivers.
January 26: Ethiopians defeat Italians at the Battle of Dogali.
February 12: First Mediterranean Agreement.
February 20: Renewal of the **Triple Alliance.**
May 22: Drummond-Wolff Convention.
June 21: Britain annexes **Zululand.**
June 18: Russian-German Treaty.
December 12: Second Mediterranean Agreement.

# 1888

**Wilhelm II** becomes Emperor of Germany.
Matabele accept British protection, Cecil **Rhodes** is granted mining rights.

French conquest of upper Niger completed.
October 29: Treaty of Constantinople.

## 1889

Eiffel Tower opens in Paris.
Britain establishes protectorate over the Shire River region.
Outbreak of the First Franco-Dahomean War.
1889–1913: Menelik II enlarges the Ethiopian Empire.
January 10: French protectorate over Ivory Coast.
May 2: Treaty of Uccialli; Italy confirms claim to protectorate over Ethiopia.
October 18: Muslims faction dominant in Buganda, Christian missionaries expelled.
October 29: British South Africa Company chartered to develop territory north of the Zambezi and west of Mozambique.

## 1890

Alfred Thayer **Mahan** publishes *The Influence of Sea Power upon History*.
French troops capture Umarian city of Segu.
France establishes protectorate over Dahomey.
Rise of Ahmad Bamba's Mouridiyya brotherhood.
Rhodes's British South Africa Company sends settlers into Rhodesia.
Rhodes becomes prime minister of the Cape Colony.
Italian Red Sea possessions become the colony of Eritrea.
1890–1892: Portugal conquers Ovimbundu kingdoms.
June 27: British South Africa Company signs treaty of protection with Barotseland.
July 2: *Brussels Act* calls European power to end slave and arms trade in colonies.
August 1: Sultan of Zanzibar signs antislavery decree.
October: End of First Franco-Dahomean War, France establishes protectorate over Dahomey.
November 4: Britain claims protectorate over Zanzibar.
December: **Lugard** arrives in Buganda with armed force.

## 1891

Pan-German League is formed.
French offensive against Samori.
April 15: Katanga Company established.
May 1: Renewal of Triple Alliance.

## 1892

Intensified Arab and Swahili slave trading in Congo and Tanganyika region.
1892–1893: Ndebele rebellion against British South Africa Company (BSAC).
March 27: Outbreak of Second Franco-Dahomean War.

## 1893

French troops capture Umarian city of Nioro.
Outbreak of the Third Anglo-Ashanti War.
July 15: German military bill increases size of forces.

## 1894

Lugard partitions Buganda among Protestant, Catholic, and Muslim groups.
Britain annexes Pondoland, linking Cape Colony and Natal; expedition against Matabele begins.

January 29: French capture Dahomean King Behanzin, France annexes Dahomey.
May 12: Treaty between Britain and Congo Free State for Cape-to-Cairo railway and telegraph.
August: Glen Grey Act provides for indirect African self-rule.
August 1: Outbreak of **Sino-Japanese War.**
December 27: Franco-Russian exchange of notes on army mobilization.

## 1895

French invade Madagascar.
Outbreak of Fourth Anglo-Ashanti War.
Slave trade abolished in Cameroon.
1895–1899: Anti-Portuguese risings in Mozambique.
1895–1905: Labor migration from Congo due to Belgian work conditions.
January 1: Royal Niger Company proclaims protectorate in Busa and Nikki.
March 25: Italy begins advance into Ethiopia.
April 17: Treaty of **Shimonoseki.**
April 23: Formation of the Far Eastern Triplice.
December 29, 1895–January 2, 1896: Leander Starr **Jameson** raids Johannesburg.

## 1896

C. E. Calwell publishes *Small Wars.*
Marchand expedition sets out.
Matabele revolt defeated.
1896–1898: British reconquest of the Sudan.
January 6: Implicated in the **Jameson Raid,** Cecil Rhodes resigns.
March 1: Ethiopians defeat Italians at Battle of **Adowa.**
January 3: Kaiser sends Kruger Telegram in support of Natal.
September 21: Kitchener takes Dongola.
October 26: Italy and Ethiopia sign Treaty of Addis Ababa, declaring Ethiopia independent.

## 1897

Colonial Conference in London.
Zululand incorporated into Natal Colony.
Shona risings in Rhodesia.
February: Belgian forces reach the Nile, occupy Loda and Wadelai.
April 5: Slavery abolished in Zanzibar.
April 17: War between Greece and Turkey.
July–August: British defeat Mwanga rebellion in Uganda.

## 1898

Britain obtains 99-year lease on Kowloon and New Territories.
Uitlander agitation against South African Republic increases.
January: Anglo-Portuguese operations against Yao.
January 10: Rioting in Havana, Cuba; U.S. sends *U.S.S. Maine.*
February 15: *Maine* destroyed in Havana harbor.
March 28: First German Naval Bill passes Reichstag.
April 8: Battle of Atbara River.
April 15: United States declares war on Spain; **Spanish-American** War begins.
May: French troops occupy Sikasso and capture Samori.
May 1: Battle of **Manila Bay.**
June 29: U.S. Navy captures Guam.

July 3: U.S. Navy destroys Spanish fleet in Cuba.
July 4: U.S. occupies Wake Island.
July 6: U.S. annexes **Hawaii.**
July 10: French forces under Marchand reach Fashoda.
September: End of the Franco-Mangingo Wars.
September 2: Battle of **Omdurman;** British forces defeat Mahdists.
September 6: Filipinos declare independent republic.
September 19: British forces reach Fashoda, occupied by Marchand's French forces, **Fashoda Crisis.**
December 10: United States and Spain sign Treaty of Paris.

## 1899

Portuguese labor law subjects Africans to moral duty to work.
1899–1902: General unrest in German East Africa.
January 23: Aguinaldo elected president of Philippine republic.
February 4: Fighting erupts between U.S. forces and Filipinos in Manila.
February 6: U.S. annexes Guam, Puerto Rico, and the Philippines.
March 11: Britain, Germany, and the United States quarrel over Somoa.
March 21: Anglo-French convention ends Fashoda Crisis.
May 18–July 29: First **Hague Peace Conference.**
May 31–June 5: Bloemfontein Conference.
September 6: U.S. asks European powers and Japan to recognize **Open Door** in China.
September 8: Britain sends 10,000 troops to Natal.
October 9: Kruger Ultimatum.
October 11: Orange Free State joins Transvaal, Second **Boer War** begins.
October 14: Boer siege of Kimberley and Mafeking begins.
November 2: Boer siege of Ladysmith begins.
November 25: Berlin-Baghdad Railway concession.

## 1900

January 1: British protectorate declared over Nigeria; Frederick Lugard is high commissioner.
February 28: Ladysmith relieved by British forces.
March 10: Definitive Anglo-Ugandan treaty.
March 13: Bloemfontein captured by British forces.
May 17: Mafeking relieved by British forces.
May 28: Britain annexes Orange Free State.
May 31: British forces capture Johannesburg.
June 5: British forces capture Pretoria.
June: Second German Naval Bill passes Reichstag.
June 13–August 14: **Boxer Insurrection** in China.
September 1: Britain annexes Transvaal.
September 5: France proclaims protectorate over Chad.
December 14: Secret Franco-Italian over Morocco and Tripoli.

## 4. Collapse of the European Balance of Power, 1901–1914

### 1901

Ugandan Railway opened.
February 10: Boers invade British Cape Colony.
September 26: Kingdom of the Ashanti annexed into the Gold Coast.

## 1902

J. A. **Hobson** publishes *Imperialism.*
January 30: Anglo-Japanese Alliance.
May 15–31: Anglo-Boer peace talks and Treaty of **Vereeniging;** Boer War Ends.
June 28: Renewal of **Triple Alliance** for six years.
November 8: Franco-Spanish agreement on Morocco.

## 1903

Popular agitation in Britain, U.S., and Germany against labor conditions in Congo.
British Royal Niger Company seizes Kano, Sokoto, Burwuri in northern Nigeria.
June: Lord Delamere settles Kenya.
November: Anglo-Russian conversations.

## 1904

February 4: Outbreak of **Russo-Japanese** War.
April 8: Anglo-French *Entente Cordiale* established.
July 4: Tripartite Pact; Britain, France and Italy declare independence of Ethiopia.
October 21: **Dogger Bank Incident.**
October 27–November 23: German-Russian alliance negotiations.

## 1905

1905–1907: **Maji-Maji rebellion** in German East Africa.
March 31: Kaiser Wilhelm I visits Tangier, provoking First **Moroccan Crisis.**
May 17, 25: Britain proposes confidential discussions with France.
May 27: Battle of **Tsushima.**
July 24: **Björkö Treaty.**
August 12: Renewal of Anglo-Japanese Alliance.
September 5: Treaty of Portsmouth.

## 1906

1906–1908: Congo Reform Association exposes labor abuses in Congo.
January 10: Beginning of Anglo-French military and naval conversations.
January 16–April 7: **Algeciras Conference** ends First Moroccan Crisis.
February 10: *H.M.S. Dreadnought* launched.
May: German government decides to widen Kiel Canal.
May: Lagos incorporated into Southern Nigeria.
May 9: Anglo-Belgian agreement on the Congo.

## 1907

Large-scale insurrections in Angola.
Transvaal government passes Asiatic Registration Bill; Mohandas Gandhi begins passive re-
  sistance movement.
May 17: Pact of Cartagena among Britain, France, and Spain.
June15–October 18: Second **Hague Peace Conference.**
July: Russian Japanese Agreement.
July: Renewal the **Triple Alliance** for six years.
August 4: French forces bombard Casablanca.
August 31: **Anglo-Russian Convention.**

## 1908

April 23: Baltic and North Sea Conventions.
July 24: **Young Turk** victory.
September 25: Casablanca Affair.
October 6: Austrian annexation of **Bosnia-Herzegovina.**
October 18: Belgium annexes Congo Free State.
October 28: *Daily Telegraph* Affair.
December 4: London Naval Conference.

## 1909

January: Native court system established in Buganda.
January 12: Austro-Ottoman agreement on Bosnia.
February 9: Franco-German agreement on Morocco.
March 21: German note to Russia urging recognition of Bosnian annexation.
March 31: Serbian note to Austria recognizing Bosnian annexation.
April: Ottoman government recognizes independence of Bulgaria.

## 1910

French Congo renamed French Equatorial Africa.
1910–1914: Young Ethiopians lead program of national modernization.
May 13: Union of South Africa created.

## 1911

June–November: Second **Moroccan Crisis**
July 1: **Agadir** Incident. German gunboat *Panther* visits Moroccan port.
July 15: Germany seeks French Congo in return for abandoning rights in Morocco.
July 21: Lloyd George delivers Mansion House speech.
September 28: Outbreak of Tripolitan War.
November 4: Franco-German agreement on Morocco.

## 1912

South African Native National Congress established.
February 8: Haldane mission to Berlin to seek agreement on colonies and German fleet.
March 8: Publication of a new German Naval Bill.
March 13: Alliance between Bulgaria and Serbia.
April: Italy bombards Dardenelles.
May 4–16: Italians capture Rhodes.
May 29: Alliance between Bulgaria and Greece.
July 16: Naval convention between France and Russia.
October 8: Austro-Russian note to Balkan states.
October 8: Montenegro declares war on Ottoman Empire.
October 18: Outbreak of First **Balkan War.**
October 18: Treaty of Lausanne ends Tripolitan War.
December 3: Armistice of Turkey, Bulgaria, and Serbia.
December 5: Last renewal of Triple Alliance.

## 1913

March 26: Bulgarians capture Adrianople.
April 16: Bulgaria and Ottoman Empire conclude an armistice.

April 22: Montenegrins take Scutari.

May 3: Montenegrins leave Scutari and Serbs Durazzo under threat of war from Austria.

May 30: Treaty of London ending First Balkan War.

June 1: Greece and Serbia ally against Bulgaria.

June 14: Native Land Act establishes territorial segregation in South Africa.

June 29–July 30: Outbreak of Second **Balkan War.**

August 10: Treaty of Bucharest.

September 23: Serbia invades Albania.

September 29: Treaty of Constantinople.

October: Austria demands Serb evacuation of Albania; Serbia complies.

## 1914

January 1: Northern and southern Nigeria are merged; Frederick Lugard is governor-general.

June 15: Britain and Germany resolve Berlin-Baghdad Railway dispute.

June 28: Austrian Archduke **Franz Ferdinand** assassinated in Sarajevo.

July 5: Austrian Count Alexander Hoyos seeks support in Berlin.

July 7: Austrian crown council favors war; Hungarian Count Tisza opposed.

July 14: Second Austrian council wins Tisza to war footing.

July 20–23: French President Poincaré and Prime Minister Viviani visit St. Petersburg.

July 23: Austria delivers ultimatum to Serbia.

July 25: Serbian reply is evasive; Austria mobilizes against Serbia.

July 26: British Foreign Secretary Grey proposes conference; France accepts, Austria declines.

July 27: France makes first preparations for war; British fleet is assembled.

July 28: Austria declares war on Serbia.

July 29: German Chancellor Bethmann-Hollweg urges Austro-Russian negotiations and British neutrality; Tsar agrees to Russian general mobilization.

July 30: Austro-Russian discussions resume.

July 31: Germany proclaims imminent danger of war, demands Russia cease preparations on German frontier; Germany seeks clarification of France's position on a Russo-German war; Germany refuses British demand for respect for Belgian neutrality; Austria begins general mobilization; Germany declares war on Russia.

August 1: France states that it will be guided by its interests, begins mobilization; Germany begins mobilization.

August 2: British cabinet votes to protect French coast from German attack; Germany invades Luxembourg.

August 3: Germany declares war on France, begins invasion of Belgium.

August 4: Britain declares war on Germany.

August 6: Austria declares war on Russia; World War I begins.

# ENCYCLOPEDIA OF THE AGE OF IMPERIALISM, 1800–1914

## ABC Powers

**Argentina, Brazil,** and Chile are referred to collectively as the ABC powers because by 1914 they appeared to have achieved domestic tranquility as independent states and demonstrated a desire to submit boundary disputes to arbitration rather than war. Argentina achieved de facto independence from Spain in 1810; Brazil became a kingdom independent of Portugal in 1815; and Chile won independence from Spain in 1818. In each case independence was furthered by the struggles of Spain and Portugal in the **Peninsular War** in Europe, 1808–1813. In 1898, a boundary quarrel between Argentina and Chile might have resulted in war had the two states not settled it through arbitration. The pacific potential of the ABC powers in their own region and beyond was demonstrated in 1914 when at the Niagara Conference they mediated a settlement in the crisis between the United States and Mexico prompted by American refusal to recognize the Huerta regime in Mexico City and brought to head in the **Tampico Incident.**

FURTHER READING: Barman, Roderick J. *Brazil: The Forging of a Nation, 1798–1852.* Stanford, CA: Stanford University Press, 1988; Collier, Simon, and William F. Sater. *A History of Chile, 1808–1994.* New York: Cambridge University Press, 1996; Lewis, Daniel K. *The History of Argentina.* Westport, CT: Greenwood, 2001.

CARL CAVANAGH HODGE

## Abd al-Aziz ibn Saud

*See* Ibn Saud

## Abd-al-Qādir (1808–1883)

Algerian leader of the Hashim tribe and of the Sufi Qadiriyya fundamentalist Islamic sect who led a *jihad* against French dominion. Two years after the French invasion of **Algeria** in 1830, he united the tribes of Western Algeria and began a campaign of harassment of French forces—commonly referred to as the Abd-al-Qādir Wars (1832–34, 1835–37, 1840–47)—in which he emerged triumphant in a number of small engagements. A charismatic leader of exceptional military and organizational ability, al Qādir became the most formidable enemy of the **French Empire** in Northern Africa.

At the head of a highly mobile army of approximately 10,000 regulars and a larger following of irregulars, he forced France to cede most of the Algerian interior in the Treaty of Tafna in 1837. In 1840, Marshal Thomas Bugeaud de la Piconnerie assumed command of French forces in Algeria and began an offensive against the interior tribes that included the destruction of crops and livestock. Following defeats at Takdempt, Tlemcen, and Smala, al-Qādir retreated to Morocco and raised a new army but was defeated by Piconnerie at the Battle of Isly River in 1844. After a victory at Sidi Brahim he was driven back into Morocco and finally surrendered in December 1847. Although promised the right to emigrate to Alexandria or Syria, al-Qādir was detained in France until 1852 when he was freed by Napoleon III. In 1860, he saved large numbers of Christians from a violent mob of Druze and Maronite fanatics, a deed for which he was awarded the Legion of Honor.

FURTHER READING: Stora, Benjamim. *Algeria: A Short History.* Translated by Jane Marie Todd. Ithaca, NY: Cornell University Press, 2001.

CARL CAVANAGH HODGE

## Abensberg, Battle of (1809)

A Napoleonic victory over Austrian Archduke Charles in Bavaria. The Austrians had seized the initiative in the opening stages of the War of the Fifth Coalition, but Napoleon quickly recovered. He sent Marshal Jean Lannes with a force of 25,000 men supported by two divisions under Marshal Louis Nicolas Davout, three divisions from Bavaria, and 12,000 troops from Württemberg to move against the Austrians. Davout and Marshal André Masséna were stationed on the wings to deliver the final blow.

On April 20, the French forces split the Austrian forces while inflicting heavy causalities. Baron Johann Hiller withdrew toward **Landshut,** where he was pursued by Marshal Jean Lannes. Charles withdrew toward **Eckmühl,** where he outnumbered Davout's forces, with Napoleon in pursuit. Thus, in addition to the Austrian losses of almost 7,000 counting prisoners, Napoleon managed to split the Austrian forces and regain the initiative in the campaign. *See also* Habsburg Empire; Napoleonic Wars.

FURTHER READING: Alexander, R. S. *Napoleon.* London: Arnold, 2001; Chandler, D. G. *The Campaigns of Napoleon.* New York: Macmillan, 1996; Markham, J. David. *Napoleon's Road to Glory: Triumphs, Defeats, and Immortality.* London: Brassey's, 2003.

J. DAVID MARKHAM

## Aborigines

**Australia**'s indigenous peoples, thought to have first migrated to the continent 50,000 years ago. Before the arrival of Europeans in 1788, Aborigines arranged themselves into approximately 500 language and territorial groupings later dubbed "tribes" by white settlers. The Aborigines practiced a hunter-gatherer lifestyle and developed a diverse clan-based, highly ritualized culture that emphasized their links to the land.

By the 1830s, the spread of white settlement in Australia had a devastating impact on the Aboriginal population. Disease, loss of land, and violence decimated the population. Imported illnesses such as smallpox, influenza, and venereal disease were responsible for often deadly epidemics and declining fertility, but competition for land and water took an even larger toll. Aboriginal efforts to resist the systematic expropriation of their land for the creation of settler farms and ranches often led to violent reprisals, leaving the survivors to face discrimination and marginalization on the fringes of white society. By the late nineteenth century official policy toward Aborigines changed into one of protection, segregation, and control, resulting in the twin policies of relocating Aborigines onto reservations and the forced removal of children from their families in an attempt at cultural assimilation. Under the 1902 federal constitution, which created a united Australia, Aborigines were specifically excluded from voting rights and were denied full citizenship—injustices that were rectified only incrementally between the 1960s and 1990s. *See also* Australian Colonies Government Act.

FURTHER READING: Broome, Richard. *Aboriginal Australians: Black Responses to White Dominance, 1788–1994.* 3rd ed. St. Leonards, New South Wales: Allen and Unwin, 2002; McGrath, Ann, ed. *Contested Ground: Australian Aborigines under the British Crown.* St. Leonards, New South Wales: Allen and Unwin, 1995.

KENNETH J. OROSZ

## Aboukir Bay, Battle of (1798)

An Anglo-French naval engagement of the Napoleonic Wars, otherwise known as the Battle of the Nile, fought on August 1, 1798. The French fleet, which had escorted Napoleon's forces to **Egypt,** was caught by a British fleet under Lord Horatio **Nelson** lying at anchor in Aboukir Bay, 20 miles northeast of Alexandria. The French did not expect a battle and so were ill-prepared when Nelson risked shoal waters and failing light to launch an immediate attack. In all 11 of 13 French ships-of-the-line were taken or sunk by a similarly size British fleet.

"Victory is certainly not a name strong enough for such a scene," was Nelson's verdict. The effect of the battle was to leave Bonaparte stranded with his army in Egypt. In the spring of 1799, he was defeated by the Turks in cooperation with a small naval force under Sir Sidney Smith and decided to abandon his Egyptian army and return surreptitiously to France. This marked the end of France's occupation of Egypt. Because the defeat at Aboukir Bay was a naval affair, some of the glamour of the Battle of the Pyramids remained attached to Napoleon. *See also* Napoleonic Wars.

FURTHER READING: Lambert, Andrew D. *Nelson: Britannia's God of War.* London: Faber, 2004; Rodger, N.A.M. *The Command of the Ocean: A Naval History of Britain, 1649–1815.* London: Allan Lane, 2004.

MARK F. PROUDMAN

## Abyssinia

A largely mountainous and desert country in northeast Africa, also known as Ethiopia. Abyssinia was a Christian country associated in the European mind with the mythical Prester John and the Queen of Sheba, and it remained throughout the period of high imperialism the only independent native African state. It was invaded by a British punitive expedition under the command of Lord Robert Napier in 1868 in retaliation for the imprisonment of British diplomats, but the British had no intention of staying, and having liberated their prisoners and sacked the Emperor Theodore's fortress at Magdala, Napier's army marched back to the coast.

Abyssinia was again invaded in 1896, this time by the Italians. They suffered a humiliating defeat at the battle of **Adowa,** on March 1, 1896, which stands alongside the battles of Isandlwana and Little Big Horn as one of the few battlefield defeats of Western forces by native armies in the nineteenth century. Adowa was never avenged, a fact that rankled Italian nationalists until Mussolini's invasion in 1935. *See also* Africa, Scramble for; Italy.

FURTHER READING: Farwell, Byron. *Queen Victoria's Little Wars.* New York: W. W. Norton, 1972.

MARK F. PROUDMAN

## Achinese War (1873–1907)

A protracted but low-level and sporadic conflict waged by the Muslim population of Acheh in northern Sumatra against Dutch rule. Acheh had been an independent sultanate for four centuries before the subjugation of Sumatra by the Netherlands. Rumors of American and Italian interest in Aceh prompted the Dutch to establish firm control. A military expedition to Aceh in 1873 was initially a fiasco, but a second attempt later the same year resulted in January 1874 in the capture of the sultan's fortress. The Achinese continued a guerrilla campaign until 1907 when the region was finally pacified.

FURTHER READING: Robertson, J. B., and J. Spruyt. *A History of Indonesia.* New York: St. Martin's, 1967.

CARL CAVANAGH HODGE

## Action Française

A radical, right-wing, anti-Semitic movement founded in 1898 by Henri Vaugeois at the height of the **Dreyfus Affair.** The Action Française portrayed a bleak, pessimistic picture of contemporary national life, influenced by the fact that France by the end of the nineteenth century was an imperial power in decline. This condition was blamed on Jews, Protestants, and Freemasons, as well as Métèques, a word derived from the Greek that could be vaguely applied to anyone with foreign ancestors. Against all these Charles Maurras (1868–1952), the Action Francaise's principal ideologue, claimed to defend an ancient race in the ancestral homeland of France.

Initially, the movement was neither primarily Royalist nor Catholic. Catholicism was actively promoted, however, as the movement opposed the anticlericalism of the Third Republic. The Royalist tradition experienced a revival among people who believed that the recovery of French greatness depended on a strong and stable government headed by a hereditary, decentralized, antiparliamentary monarchy. Democracy, Maurras maintained, led to internal feuding and should therefore be suppressed through a coup d'état to restore the monarchy. Maurras believed that the solidarity of the nation could be guaranteed by the freedom of multiple centers of control in provinces just as during the days before the French Revolution.

Between 1908 and 1914, Action Française played a major role on the far right of French politics. It experienced a setback in 1926 when Pope Pius XI sought to check the participation of Catholics in the organization, but it remained active alongside the fascist leagues of France during the interwar years. *See also* Anti-Semitism.

FURTHER READING: Sternhell, Zeev. *Neither Right Nor Left: Fascist Ideology in France.* Translated by David Maisel Princeton, NJ: Princeton University Press, 1986; Weber, Eugen Joseph. *Action Française.* Stanford, CA: Stanford University Press, 1962.

NURFADZILAH YAHAYA

## Act of Union (1801)

Passed in 1800 by the administration of **William Pitt** the Younger in reaction to the Irish rebellion of 1798, the Act of Union created a unitary state with a single Parliament on the model of the Scottish union of 1707, from what had been the two formally separate states sharing a single monarch.

If **Ireland** is seen as the first British colony, then the Act of Union represented the only attempt in British history to solve the problem of colonial government by directly absorbing the colony into the metropolitan political system. Although the Union was apparently successful in the short term, many—although by no means all—Irish were never happy with their formally equal, but in many ways subordinate, status in the United Kingdom of Great Britain and Ireland. As Catholic emancipation and the reforms of the nineteenth century enfranchised the Catholic majority in Ireland, pressure for Irish self-government, or Home Rule, grew.

FURTHER READING: Foster, R. F. *Modern Ireland.* London: Allen Lane, 1988.

MARK F. PROUDMAN

## Acton, Lord John (1834–1902)

John Emerich Edward Dalberg, first Lord Acton, was a historian and advocate of political liberty. Dalberg was born on January 10, 1834, in Naples. He assumed the Regius Chair of Modern History at Cambridge University in 1895 and was concerned with the danger to individuals by religious and political persecution. Embodying a liberal view, Acton emphasized progress of freedom through centuries. His universal history outlined relationship between individual liberty and religious virtue. Acton argued that revolution increased freedom, although he did not approve it. His ideas are reflected in *Essays in the History of Liberty, Essays in the Study of Writing and History* and *Essays in Religion, Politics, and Morality.* He was the author of powerful and popular aphorisms such as "it is bad to be oppressed by a minority, but it is worse to be oppressed by a majority," "power tends to corrupt and absolute power corrupts absolutely," and "liberty is the prevention of control by others." He died in 1902 at Tegernsee.

FURTHER READING: Hill, Roland. *Lord Acton.* New Haven, CT: Yale University Press, 2000.

PATIT PABAN MISHRA

## Adams, John (1735–1826)

An American revolutionary leader, a Federalist, and second President of the **United States** (1797–1801). Adams was at the forefront of protests in Britain's American colonies against taxation without representation. In 1774, he was selected by the Massachusetts legislature as one of five delegates to the First Continental Congress and quickly became the leading voice for American independence. During the American Revolution, Adams was dispatched to Europe to secure alliances and financial support for the colonial struggle against Britain. In 1783, he then negotiated, together with John Jay and Benjamin Franklin, the Treaty of Paris, which formally acknowledged the independence of the United States. Adams was appointed the American ambassador to London, where he tried and failed to secure British agreement to open ports to American commerce, to obtain guarantees respecting American navigation and fishing rights, and to achieve the withdrawal of British troops.

In 1793, when war broke out between France and Britain, Washington had insisted that the United States maintain a policy of neutrality. As president, Adams attempted to continue this policy by steering a middle course between the pro-British and pro-French factions at home, but French attacks on American shipping made this difficult. Together with the cynical treatment of American diplomatic envoys by the Directory in the "XYZ Affair," these predations forced Adams into an unofficial Quasi War with France. On April 30, 1798, Adams signed the bill authorizing the creation of a Department of the Navy. Congress also authorized increases in naval power and the use of the navy against French warships and privateers. By September 1799, the United States had deployed three battle squadrons to the Caribbean and the United States was taking its first precocious steps toward becoming a naval power.

Adams also signed the Alien and Sedition Acts of 1798, pushed by the Federalist majority in Congress. The acts were influenced by alarm at the influx of French fugitives from the Terror, as well as from the slave uprisings in the Caribbean and Irish refugees from the Rebellion of 1798. In 1800, Adams lost his bid for reelection to **Thomas Jefferson.** His presidency had been consumed by the Quasi-War, a product of the unique international circumstance and conflicting pressures of the time. Adams believed that the national interest lay in peace through neutrality but rightly concluded that it would require a powerful American fleet to defend it. *See also* British Empire, French Empire.

FURTHER READING: DeConde, Alexander. *The Quasi-War: The Politics and Diplomacy of the Undeclared War with France, 1797–1801.* New York: Charles Scribner's Sons, 1966; Ellis, Joseph J. *Passionate Sage: The Character and Legacy of John Adams.* New York: W. W. Norton, 2001;

McCullough, David. *John Adams.* New York: Touchstone, 2001; Smith, Page. *John Adams.* 2 vols. Garden City, NY: Doubleday, 1962.

CARL CAVANAGH HODGE

## Adams, John Quincy (1767–1848)

John Quincy Adams was the son of **John Adams** and the sixth president of the **United States** (1825–1829). Adams spent almost his entire professional life in public service and politics, as diplomat, senator, secretary of state, president, and member of the House of Representatives. During much of his career, Adams advocated American expansion and strongly supported the concept of **Manifest Destiny,** which claimed the North American continent for the United States as divinely chosen redeemer nation and model to the world.

One of his most important accomplishments as secretary of state during the Monroe-Administration was his negotiation of the Transcontinental Treaty (1819), which obtained east and west Florida from the Spanish Empire and extended the nation's first transcontinental boundary to the Oregon coast in exchange for $5 million and a temporary recognition of Spanish claims to **Texas.** This treaty completed the **Louisiana Purchase,** developed a framework for further expansion, underlined American claims to the Pacific Coast, and thus corresponded with Adams's vision of the United States as a global commercial power.

His second accomplishment was the drafting of the **Monroe Doctrine** (1823). This highly influential statement of foreign policy principles summarized U.S. containment policy in the Western Hemisphere and hinted at a claim to hemispheric hegemony and a superior international role for the United States. The doctrine demanded European abstention from intervention in the Americas and pledged U.S. abstention from entanglements in the Old World. It also reiterated George Washington's warnings against foreign entanglements and underlined the no-transfer principle of adjacent colonial dominions in North America from one European power to another.

Driven by his antislavery views and his concern that further expansion would foster and sustain slave-holding in the United States, Adams led congressional opposition to the annexation of Texas (1836) and the Mexican-American War (1846–1848) in his post-presidential years. *See also* Adams-Onís Treaty.

FURTHER READING: Bemis, Samuel Flagg. *John Quincy Adams and the Foundations of American Foreign Policy.* New York: Alfred E. Knopf, 1949; Weeks, William Earl. *John Quincy Adams and the American Global Empire.* Louisville: University Press of Kentucky, 1992.

FRANK SCHUMACHER

## Adams-Onís Treaty (1819)

Known officially as the *Treaty of Amity, Settlement and Limits, Between Spain and the United States,* the Adams-Onís Treaty arranged for U.S. acquisition of Florida from Spain and settled much of the border between the United States and Spanish holdings. The treaty is also referred to as the Transcontinental Treaty and the Florida Purchase Treaty. Negotiations by Don Luis de Onís, Spanish minister to Washington, and **John Quincy Adams,** U.S. Secretary of State, concluded on February 22, 1819, and the treaty was proclaimed on February 22, 1821.

Spanish-American relations had frayed because of conflicts regarding Spanish Florida and an imprecise boundary between the Louisiana territory and Spanish holdings. Through the treaty, Spain ceded Florida and the United States ceded claims to Texas and agreed to assume up to $5 million in claims by American citizens against Spain. The boundary between Spanish lands and the United States was set, and Spain effectively ceded claims to territory north and west of the boundary, especially Oregon north of California.

As a result, Spain, a declining imperial power, established a temporary buffer, **Texas,** between her territories and the United States; and the **United States,** a rising continental power, achieved a boundary line extending to the Pacific. John Quincy Adams's continental vision had scored a significant diplomatic triumph, bringing an American continental empire closer to reality. *See also* Oregon Question.

FURTHER READING: Miller, Hunter, ed., *Treaties and Other International Acts of the United States of America.* Vol. III. Washington, DC: U.S. Government Printing Office, 1933, pp. 3–18 (text of treaty); 18–64 (related documents and notes); Weeks, William Earl. *John Quincy Adams and American Global Empire.* Lexington: University Press of Kentucky, 1992.

KENNETH J. BLUME

## Adowa, Battle of (1896)

The decisive battle ending the First **Italo-Abyssinian War.** In 1889, **Menelik,** the king of Shoa, an Italian ally and claimant to the Ethiopian throne, signed the Treaty of Uccialli pledging to accept an Italian protectorate in return for substantial amounts of munitions. Menelik achieved the throne and then claimed that the Amharic text of the treaty never required a protectorate. In late 1894, Menelik then indirectly encouraged a native revolt inside **Italy**'s colony of **Eritrea.** The Italians crushed the rebellion and invaded the Ethiopian province of Tigre to force the acceptance of the protectorate. In October 1895, Menelik raised a substantial feudal army and encamped at the city of Adowa. The Italian governor of Eritrea, General Oreste Baratieri, entrenched his mixed metropolitan and colonial force to guard the approach into Eritrea, intent on conducting defensive operations that would slowly dissipate Menelik's army. Rome, however, demanded an offensive victory over a native state and pressured Baratieri into ordering an assault on the city.

The attack started with a nighttime approach-march to the Abyssinian defensive positions. The Italian formation lost its cohesion in the mountainous terrain and was spotted by the Abyssinians, who launched a surprise attack with vastly superior numerical forces. The attack overwhelmed the Italians and defeated them piecemeal. By mid-afternoon they withdrew, leaving 6,000 soldiers dead on the field, 1,428 wounded, 954 missing, and another 1,865 taken prisoner; the Abyssinian loss was 7,000 dead and 10,000 wounded. The loss at Adowa humiliated Italy, led to the fall of the government, halted its expansionism in East Africa, and guaranteed Ethiopia's independence until 1936. *See also* Africa, Scramble for; Omdurman, Battle of.

FURTHER READING: Berkeley, G.F.H. *The Campaign of Adowa and the Rise of Menelik*. London: Archibald Constable, 1902.

FREDERICK H. DOTOLO

## Adrianople, Treaty of (1829)

The peace treaty ending the **Russo-Turkish War** of 1828–1829. The war's proximate cause was the sinking of the Turkish-Egyptian fleet at Navarino in October 1827. The fleet was moored there in support of operations that aimed at suppressing the Greek revolt in the Morea. An allied force of British, French, and Russian naval units had moved into the harbor to pressure the Turks into mediation, but under tense conditions fighting began and resulted in the annihilation of the Turko-Egyptian force. The Turks then repudiated the Convention of Akkerman, an earlier diplomatic agreement with the Russians, which had dealt with a number of outstanding issues between the powers.

Fighting began in April of 1828, and although the Russians initially made little headway, by August 1839, Russian forces were in possession of Adrianople, an ancient Ottoman capital and strategic point within a few days march of Constantinople. The Turks were forced to sue for peace. Negotiations began on September 2, 1839. By September 14, the peace treaty was signed. The Turks recognized Russian territorial gains at the mouth of the Danube, Russian annexation of Georgia and eastern **Armenia,** Russian suzeraintry over Circassia; free and unfettered passage for Russian merchant ships through the Straits, freedom for Russian merchants to conduct trade throughout the **Ottoman Empire,** and renewed acceptance by the Ottomans of the autonomy of Moldova, Wallachia, **Serbia,** and **Greece.** Although Greek autonomy was included in the clauses of the treaty, it was outstanding friction between Russia and Turkey over the Caucasus and the Balkans generally, not the Greek drive for independence, which had caused the war and with which the peace was primarily involved. Although the conquest of Constantinople had perhaps been within Russia's grasp, the Russian court decided at this time that the collapse of the Ottoman Empire was less in her interest than a predominant Russian influence at the Ottoman court in the future. *See also* Eastern Question; Russian Empire.

FURTHER READING: Anderson, M. S. *The Eastern Question 1774–1923*. London: Macmillan, 1966; Hale, William. *Turkish Foreign Policy 1774–2000*. London: Frank Cass, 2000; Jelavich, Barbara. *A Century of Russian Foreign Policy 1814–1914*. Philadelphia: J. B. Lippincott, 1964; Karsh, Efraim, and Inari Karsh. *Empires of the Sand: The Struggle for Mastery in the Middle East 1789–1923*. Cambridge, MA: Harvard University Press, 1999.

ROBERT DAVIS

## Aehrenthal, Aloys Lexa von (1854–1912)

Aloys Lexa von Aehrenthal was an Austro-Hungarian foreign minister. Born in September 1854 in Gross-Skal, Bohemia, Aehrenthal started his career at the foreign service of the Habsburg monarchy in 1877 and served in the Foreign Office and as envoy to Romania. In 1899, he became ambassador to Russia. Seven years later he was appointed as foreign minister, launched a policy of strengthening Austria-Hungary's position in the Balkans, and initiated the unilateral Habsburg annexation of **Bosnia-Herzegovina.** Aehrenthal thereby provoked the **Annexation Crisis** of 1908–1909 as a consequence of which relations with Russia and Serbia were severely strained while Austria-Hungary seemed diplomatically isolated and completely dependent on German support.

Aehrenthal tried to improve relations with Italy and to gain more leeway in international affairs but died of leukemia in February 1912, his visions of stronger Austria-Hungary unfulfilled. It was his successor, Count Berchtold, who had to face the dramatic decline of the security situation in the Balkans in 1912. *See also* Balkan Crises; Habsburg Empire.

FURTHER READING: Albertini, Luigi. *The Origins of the War of 1914.* Translated by Isabella M. Massey. New York: Enigma, 2005.

GUENTHER KRONENBITTER

## Afghanistan

A landlocked, mountainous, and arid country of Central Asia on the northwestern frontier of India. Afghanistan was a principal object in the **Great Game** of imperial rivalry between Great Britain and tsarist Russia. The southward expansion of Russia was deemed by Britain to pose a threat to India, whereas Russia suspected Britain of having designs on the Hindu Kush.

In the mid-eighteenth century the country's tribes were united under a Pathan monarch, Ahmad Shah, and launched a series of plundering raids into India. The Pathans became bogged down in frontier wars with the Sikh kingdom of the Punjab and were also sufficiently divided among themselves to tempt foreign intervention. In the early nineteenth century the thought that Afghan leaders might collaborate with Napoleon aggravated British concern for the security of India. Even after Napoleon's defeat this concern only intensified. And for good reason. In 1837, the Shah of Persia led an expedition, with the support of Russian agents, to lay siege to the city of Herat in western Afghanistan. Although the siege failed a British invasion that opened the first of the **Afghan Wars** followed in 1838. By 1842, the invasion had ended in one of the greatest humiliations of British arms. Continuing Russian pressure southward prompted Britain to adopt a forward policy for Afghanistan with the goal of establishing a defensive line against an invasion of India on the northern heights of the Hindu Kush. The Second Anglo-Afghan War began in 1878 with a second and more successful British invasion and ended in 1880 with assumption of power of the pro-British Abdur Rahman, who remained on the throne until 1901. Britain promised to help Rahman repel foreign invaders but forbade him from conducting diplomatic relations with any other power.

In 1895, Britain and Russia reached an agreement establishing the boundary between Afghanistan and Russia, and in 1907, Russia declared the country outside its sphere of influence, promised to send no agents there, and agreed to consult with Britain on Afghan affairs. Britain agreed not to annex Afghanistan or interfere in its domestic affairs. *See also* British Empire; East India Company; Russian Empire.

FURTHER READING: Bilgrami, Asghar H. *Afghanistan and British India, 1793–1907: A Study in Foreign Relations.* New Delhi: Sterling, 1972; Ewans, Martin. *Afghanistan: A Short History of Its People and Politics.* New York: Harper Perennial, 2002.

CARL CAVANAGH HODGE

## Afghan Wars (1838–1842, 1878–1880)

The Afghan Wars were two nineteenth-century conflicts occasioned by British fears of the threat posed by Russia to British interests in India and the Persian Gulf.

In the first the **East India Company** invaded Afghanistan to return to power the deposed amir, Shah Shuja-ul-Mulk. A British army of 15,000 with 30,000 followers captured Kandahar without resistance and occupied Kabul in August 1839. British forces were unable to control the countryside, however, and this seemingly easy victory turned into a rout when, in 1841, the Afghans struck back and turned the British retreat into a massacre in which 4,500 troops and 12,000 civilians were killed by Afghan raiders and the bitter winter weather of January 1842. A punitive expedition returned to Afghanistan, defeated the Afghans in a series of small engagements, and, in an act of retribution, burned the Great Bazaar in Kabul. Still, the initial purpose of the British campaign was thwarted when Dost Muhammad Khan, a self-proclaimed amir friendly to Russia, returned to power in Kabul shortly after the British army returned to India and reigned for 20 years.

In the Second Afghan War, British forces invaded after Tsar Alexander II annexed the Central Asian Khanates of Bukhara, Khiva and Samarkand to the Russian Empire and Shere Ali, son and heir of Dost Muhammad, renewed the Afghan policy of friendliness toward Russia. The campaign began in November 1878 and quickly chalked a series of victories leading to the capture of Jalalabad and Kandahar early in 1879. Shere Ali died and was succeeded by his son, Yakub Khan, who signed a treaty ceding the Khyber Pass, Kurram, Pishin, and Sibi to Britain and agreed to receive a British agent in Kabul. The peace was shattered almost immediately, however, as the entire British mission was slaughtered by mutinous Afghan soldiers shortly after their arrival in Kabul. A punitive expedition led by General Frederick Roberts took Kabul, and some 100 Afghan deemed responsible for the massacre of the British mission were hanged.

In December 1879, Roberts then beat back an attack by a large Afghan force in the Battle of Sherpur. Abdur Rahman, grandson to Dost Muhammad, then led a new Afghan army equipped with modern Russian rifles into northern Afghanistan. Rather than oppose him, the British offered him the throne. When a rival claimant to throne, Ayub Khan, defeated a British army of 20,000 men in the Battle of Maiwand and forced a retreat to Kandahar, the settlement was imperiled until Roberts marched 10,000 men from Kabul to Kandahar—313 miles in 22 days—and defeated Ayub Khan in the **Battle of Kandahar.** When the victorious British withdrew to India, Ayub Khan seized Kandahar but this time was defeated by Abdur Rahman.

Afghanistan was now within Britain's sphere of influence in Central Asia, but the brutality of the fighting there helped to defeat the government of Disraeli in the British general election of 1880. *See also* Disraeli, Benjamin; Gorchakov, Alexander; Khiva Khanate; Russian Empire.

FURTHER READING: Farwell, Byron. *Queen Victoria's Little Wars.* New York: W. W. Norton, 1972; Heathcote, T. A. *The Afghan Wars, 1839–1919.* Staplehurst, England: Spellmount, 2003; Tanner, Stephen. *Afghanistan: A Military History from Alexander to the Fall of the Taliban.* Karachi: Oxford University Press, 2003.

CARL CAVANAGH HODGE

## Africa, Scramble for

The term *Scramble for Africa* defines a 30-year period stretching from 1884 to 1914 during which European nations abandoned their earlier preference for informal rule and instead engaged in a frenzied race to carve up the continent of Africa and create formal colonial empires there. The process was so rapid and complete that although only 10 percent of Africa was under European control at the start of the scramble, by 1912 the entire continent, with the exceptions of Liberia and Ethiopia, had been devoured.

### Informal Rule

Since the end of the American Revolution, European powers were generally reluctant to take on new colonies, preferring instead to rely on free trade and informal economic control in the belief that it was more profitable, more flexible, and avoided unnecessary foreign entanglements. There were some notable exceptions to this rule—including the expansion of British holdings in **India,** the colonization of **Australia, New Zealand** and French **Indochina,** but none of the exceptions were part of a grand colonial scheme. They were instead haphazard, often ill-thought-out acquisitions triggered by efforts to divert attention from domestic problems in Europe, responses to local conditions in potential colonies, or the result of actions by men on the spot.

In Africa, for example, the French invaded **Algeria** in 1830 in an effort to distract the masses from the deeply unpopular regime of **Charles X.** Elsewhere Louis Faidherbe, the French Governor of **Senegal** from 1854–1865, repeatedly acted on his own authority and, against the wishes of his superiors in Paris, expanded French holdings by deliberately provoking border wars with his Muslim neighbors. British expansion in South Africa, on the other hand, was largely triggered by the **Great Trek** in which the Boers tried unsuccessfully to flee British control as a result of disagreements over native policy and anglicization.

Europeans otherwise contented themselves for most of the nineteenth century with a handful of coastal forts and trading stations inherited from the days of the recently abolished transatlantic slave trade. The combination of disease, punishing terrain, and potential resistance from the indigenous peoples made the prospect of expansion inland difficult, dangerous, and expensive. It was also unnecessary because African middlemen were already bringing everything that European merchants wanted to coastal trading ports for export abroad.

In the 1870s, however, the situation began to change. The steady industrialization of Europe, together with intensified international economic competition, tarnished the allure of **free trade** and led many nations to consider the acquisition of formal colonies as a form of safety net that would guarantee future access to markets and raw materials. Colonies also promised to ensure domestic political stability at home in Europe by distracting the masses from chronically low wages and poor working conditions. For newly unified countries like Italy and Germany, the acquisition of colonies symbolized proof of **Great Power** status. Other nations sought colonies to improve their strategic position, protect foreign investments, or, in the case of France, to acquire additional manpower and raw materials to recover from the Franco-Prussian War. Additional considerations behind the sudden renewed interest in formal colonization included simple Victorian curiosity, **social Darwinism,** the pursuit of profit, and the desire to spread Christianity.

### The Prelude to the Scramble

Although all of Europe was increasingly interested in resuming the creation of formal colonial empires, it took the actions of Leopold II of Belgium to set these pent-up impulses into motion. Chafing under the restrictions imposed by his status as the constitutional monarch of **Belgium,** Leopold opted to make a name and fortune for himself in Africa. Although the privately funded International Congo Society was ostensibly founded in 1878 to explore the Congo River basin and engage in "humanitarian" work, Leopold used it to hire **Henry Morton Stanley** and send him on a secret mission lasting from 1879–1884 to sign treaties with African chieftains granting Leopold political authority and trading rights along the southern bank of the Congo River.

When news of Stanley's activities leaked out, the French, who had possessions in nearby Gabon, sprang into action and sent Savorgnan de **Brazza** to negotiate treaties of their own along the northern bank of the Congo lest Leopold secure a total monopoly on trade in the region. This expedition in turn upset Britain, worried in the wake of its takeover of **Egypt** that France was seeking revenge by trying to secure a monopoly on the Congo River trade. Consequently, in late February 1884, the British government suddenly recognized Portugal's historical claims to the Congo delta in the hopes of ensuring that a friendly power would control access to the lucrative Congo basin.

Although it had yet to be ratified by the British parliament, the Anglo-Portuguese treaty infuriated the rest of Europe, as it settled bilaterally what was thought to be a larger international issue. German chancellor Otto von **Bismarck** promptly seized the opportunity simultaneously, both to steal the diplomatic limelight and to placate France by joining prime minister Jules **Ferry** in demanding that the entire matter be submitted to an international conference open to all interested parties. The need for such a conference was further underscored by Germany's sudden announcements in April and July 1884 that it had established protectorates over southwest Africa, **Cameroon,** and **Togo.** Germany's claims, which were based on paper partitions rather than physical occupation, created a dangerous precedent and raised the possibility that rival nations could claim the same piece of territory or, worse yet, that one country could claim the entire continent. As either situation could lead to a war, it was imperative that a conference be convened to establish ground rules for future colonial acquisitions. During the **Berlin Conference** of 1884–1885 the participants agreed to recognize existing German and Belgian claims, yet insisted that all future efforts to claim territory in Africa had to be officially announced and had to be backed up by actual occupation.

### The Scramble for Territory

Once the ground rules had been set, all of the major European powers engaged in a desperate race to claim African territory. In the Congo, Leopold confined his subsequent expansion to the occupation of areas already claimed on paper before the Berlin Conference. Similarly, in Togo, Cameroon, and southwest Africa, the Germans sought only to make good on their paper partitions by occupying the interior. The rest of the continent, however, was an altogether different matter.

Britain, which had enjoyed informal control over the East African coastline dating back to 1840 as a result of its efforts to end the slave trade and its involvement in the Sultan of **Zanzibar**'s clove plantations, was suddenly forced to formalize its claims in the region as a result of the announcement in February 1885, just days after the Berlin Conference, that Germany had established a new protectorate in East Africa. Thereafter British and German officials raced to sign additional treaties with interior peoples and establish formal occupation of their respective protectorates. This rivalry finally ended in 1890 with the signing of an Anglo-German Treaty.

Eager to establish credentials as a world power, **Italy** followed the British and German lead in trying to create colonies in East Africa. When the French closed the door on their hopes of colonizing **Tunisia** in 1881, the Italians opted instead to transform their existing small protectorate in Somalia into a larger formal empire by intervening in the internal politics of neighboring **Ethiopia.** When Ethiopia resisted, the Italians invaded and but were crushed at the Battle of **Adowa** in 1896. In the resultant peace settlement, Ethiopia nonetheless allowed Italy to retain **Eritrea** and expand its holdings in Somalia. Still, in an effort to ease the sting of their humiliation at Adowa, the Italians began plotting to take over the Ottoman province of **Libya.** They finally got their chance in 1911 when unrest inside the Ottoman Empire created a pretext for a successful invasion and the creation of a new Italian colony.

The principal architect of British expansion in South Africa, meanwhile, was Cecil **Rhodes,** prime minister of the **Cape Colony** and head of the De Beers diamond mine. As an ardent imperialist who thought that Britain was destined to rule most of the world, Rhodes pushed relentlessly to expand South Africa northward with the goal of creating an unbroken band of British African territory united north to south by a Cape-to-Cairo railroad. For the remainder of the nineteenth century, he used his political position and his fortune to bring this plan to fruition. In the process he forcibly annexed a variety of African kingdoms and sought to topple the Boer republic in the **Transvaal** in an effort to both secure control of additional rumored gold fields and to create a single block of British territory. His activities helped trigger the Second **Boer War** (1899–1902), which eventually led to the creation of a South African federation uniting Cape Colony and the Boer Republics under the Union Jack.

In west and central Africa, France, shut out of Egypt, resolved to expand its existing holdings so as to surround and contain nearby British territories. Ideally, the French hoped to continue their expansion all the way across Africa in an effort to seize the headwaters of the Nile and force Britain out of Egypt altogether. Britain initially ignored this threat to concentrate instead on expanding into the interior of **Nigeria** and the **Gold Coast** in search of additional sources of trade goods, but the 1896 expedition by Jean-Baptiste Marchand forced London to reassess French goals. Marchand's plan was to drag a small steamship in pieces from the Congo to the **Sudan** where he and his compatriots would reassemble it before sailing down the Nile claiming everything they saw in the process. Desperate to prevent this, Britain dispatched an army from Egypt to recapture the Sudan, which had fallen under the control of the **Mahdi** and his successors, and keep the source of the Nile out of French hands. Although the French beat them to the tiny riverside village of **Fashoda** in 1898, the British, having arrived with an army and a railroad, forced the French to withdraw, precipitating a diplomatic crisis that was not mended until the establishment of the **Entente Cordiale.** In exchange, Britain signed a 1904 agreement recognizing French claims to **Morocco.**

Although the colonial powers continued to negotiate periodic border adjustments to their newly acquired holdings right up until the outbreak of World War I, by the turn of the century the scramble for Africa had largely given way to the tasks of governing, extracting resources and trying to "uplift" subject African populations. In a bitter twist of irony, the benefits that Europe hoped to realize from these activities were largely destroyed by the onset of war in 1914. *See also* Agadir Crisis; Algeciras Congress; Belgian Congo; British East African Protectorate; British Empire; French Empire; German Empire; German Southwest Africa; Moroccan Crisis; Somaliland; Uganda.

FURTHER READING: Betts, Raymond F., ed. *The "Scramble" for Africa: Causes and Dimensions of Empire.* Boston: D. C. Heath and Co., 1966; Chamberlain, Muriel. *The Scramble for Africa,* 2nd ed. New York: Longman, 1999; Cook, Scott B. *Colonial Encounters in the Age of High Imperialism.* New York: Longman, 1996; Pakenham, Thomas. *The Scramble for Africa: White Man's Conquest of the Dark Continent, 1876 to 1912.* New York: Harper Collins, 1991.

KENNETH J. OROSZ

## Afrikaners

Afrikaners were the descendants of European settlers, mostly of Dutch origin, who established a unique society, culture, and language in southern Africa beginning with their arrival in 1652. In the ensuing half century, they expanded their settlements from the coast as far as 250 miles inland. Within a few years of their arrival on the new continent, they began the importation of slaves. Huguenot refugees from France arrived at the Cape in 1688, followed by Germans and others from largely Protestant European states. The settlers were later known as "Boers," the Dutch word for "farmers," a designation applied to those who left Cape Colony on the **Great Trek** to establish independent republics in the African hinterland. They fought two major conflicts with the British Empire in the Anglo-Boer Wars 1880–81 and 1899–1902, with the result that the Orange Free State and the Transvaal formed parts of the Union of South Africa in 1910. The term *Boer* was replaced in the twentieth century with the term *Afrikaner,* which simply means a person who speaks the Afrikaans language. *See also* Africa, Scramble for.

FURTHER READING: Omer-Cooper, J. D. *A History of Southern Africa.* Oxford: James Currey Publishers, 1997.

GREGORY FREMONT-BARNES

## Agadir Crisis (1911)

A Great Power crisis aggravating the tense atmosphere of European diplomacy leading to World War I. In the early part of the twentieth century, German's leaders viewed their country as increasingly "encircled" following a number of international crises. These fears increased following the Agadir, or Second Moroccan, Crisis of 1911. Specifically, Berlin resented French military intervention in Morocco in 1911, a move that amounted in effect to the establishment of a French protectorate in Morocco and ran counter to the **Algeciras Conference** of 1906 and to the Franco-German agreement on Morocco of 1909. In response to the French "dash for Fez" in the spring of 1911, Germany wanted to assert its status as a Great Power, achieve compensation for France's territorial gains, and possibly weaken the **Entente Cordiale** in the process. State Secretary for Foreign Affairs Alfred von Kiderlen-Wächter acted forcefully and was rewarded with an enthusiastic response in Germany. Germany's military leaders advocated a war, but Berlin instead dispatched the gun-boat *Panther* to the Moroccan port of Agadir to intimidate the French, an event that marked the beginning of the crisis. Berlin demanded the French Congo as compensation for the extension of French influence in Morocco, but France received diplomatic support from Britain so their Germany's action only strengthened rather weakened the links between the Entente partners. This was demonstrated by British Chancellor of the Exchequer, David Lloyd George, in his famous "Mansion House Speech" of July 21, 1911 in which he threatened to fight on France's side against Germany if necessary.

Thus, the crisis produced another German diplomatic defeat despite the fact that Berlin secured a small part of the French Congo as compensation. In Berlin, the defeat resulted in a bellicose anti-French and a particularly anti-British mood. Kiderlen-Wächter did not seek war in 1911, but he was willing to threaten it for diplomatic gains. But in the aftermath of the crisis, demands for a preventive war became widespread. Public enthusiasm for the army became more pronounced, especially as a result of the propaganda work of the German Army League, founded in January 1912. Agadir also had serious international consequences. In France, public mood turned distinctly anti-German. Because Britain and Germany were compensated for French gains in Morocco, Italy decided to annex Libya and Tripolitania in November 1911. Thereafter, enfeebled Turkey became an easy target for the **Balkan League** during the **Balkan Wars** of 1912/13. Italy became a less reliable alliance partner for Germany and Austria-Hungary, while the newly strengthened Serbia and Montenegro posed a more serious threat to the Dual Monarchy. The crisis gave rise to the Anglo-French naval agreement, discussed against the backdrop of the events of 1911 and signed in February 1913. Germany's "encirclement" was fast becoming reality. *See also* German Empire; Gibraltar; Navalism; Ottoman Empire.

FURTHER READING: Barraclough, Geoffrey. *From Agadir to Armageddon: Anatomy of a Crisis.* London: Weidenfeld & Nicholson, 1982; Joll, James, and Martel, Gordon. *The Origins of the First World War*, 3rd ed. London: Longman, 2006; Rich, Norman. *Friedrich von Holstein. Policy and Diplomacy in the Era of Bismarck and Wilhelm II.* 2 vols. Cambridge: Cambridge University Press, 1964.

ANNIKA MOMBAUER

## Aigun, Treaty of (1858)

A Sino-Russian agreement negotiated between eastern Siberia's governor-general, Nikolai Nikolaevich Muravev, and the regional Manchu governor, I-shan.

The treaty ceded to the **Russian Empire** all lands north of the Amur River down to its confluence with the Ussuri River; allowed joint sovereignty by Russia and China over the lands east of the Ussuri; limited travel along the Amur, Ussuri, and Sungari Rivers to these two nations; and provided for trade between nationals living along these rivers.

The treaty was a result of the "Far Eastern Policy" initiated by Russian Foreign Minister Aleksandr Mikhailovich **Gorchakov** in response to Anglo-French incursions into India and China in the 1850s. Muravev was given plenipotentiary powers to expand the empire's borders and in the years leading up to the treaty began settling Cossacks and their families in the Amur River valley despite its being Chinese territory. When Muravev himself dramatically arrived aboard a gunboat at the Manchu garrison of Aigun, Governor I-shan initially refused his demands to sign the ready-made treaty, but several bluff cannonades forced him to change his mind.

The Aigun Treaty was followed within weeks by the Treaty of **Tientsin,** negotiated by Admiral Evfimii Vasilevich Putiatin. Ignorant of Muravev's treaty, Putiatin reproduced much of it in his own, although he also secured greater access to Chinese markets. In November 1860, the Russo-Chinese Convention of Peking confirmed both treaties as well as formalized Russia's annexation of the lands east of the Ussuri River. By such means Russia painlessly expanded its empire by 350,000 square miles—a territorial expansion equal to the size of France and Germany. Off with a bang, the "Far Eastern Policy" later culminated in Russia's humiliation during in **Russo-Japanese War.**

FURTHER READING: March, G. Patrick. *Eastern Destiny: Russia in Asia and the North Pacific.* Westport, CT: Praeger, 1996; Stephan, John J. *The Russian Far East: A History.* Stanford, CA: Stanford University Press, 1994.

ANDREW A. GENTES

## Aix-la-Chapelle, Congress of (1818)

The first post-Vienna meeting of the **Congress System** that governed post-Napoleonic Europe. In 1818, the four Great Powers—Britain, Russia, Austria, and Prussia—met in the first of several meetings to uphold the Congress system, a means of discussing diplomatic problems at periodically held international conferences. The Congress enlarged the **Quadruple Alliance** to include France and ended the occupation of French territory two years earlier than originally agreed. The Congress discussed the question of French reparations owed by the terms of the second Treaty of **Paris,** the issue of Napoleon's security on St. Helena, and reiterated the civil rights of German Jews as agreed at the Congress of **Vienna** three years before. Britain was the first nation to diverge from the united policies of the other powers by rejecting a call by Tsar **Alexander II** for an alliance pledged to guarantee the existing forms of government of the individual European states.

FURTHER READING: Kissinger, Henry. *A World Restored: Metternich, Castlereagh, and the Problem of Peace 1812–1822.* London: Weidenfeld & Nicolson, 2000; Lowe, John. *The Concert of Europe: International Relations, 1814–70.* London: Hodder and Stoughton, 1991.

GREGORY FREMONT-BARNES

## *Alabama* Dispute (1871–1872)

An Anglo-American diplomatic crisis of the **American Civil War** era. During the Civil War, the South focused on disrupting Union trade routes, but once the Confederacy's own ports were blockaded, she needed help from abroad. Although Great Britain was officially neutral, many British merchants continued to do business with the South. The most notorious example was the *Alabama*, built in Liverpool in 1862, which for two years terrorized the seas, confiscating goods and burning ships headed to or from the North. In June 1864, its reign of terror ended when it sank off the coast of France. Subsequently, the United States accused Britain of failing to enforce her laws of neutrality and demanded reparations. The matter was submitted to an international tribunal, but so tense were the negotiations that American newspapers proclaimed the possibility of war. In the resulting Washington Treaty, Britain agreed to pay $15.5 million in damages.

FURTHER READING: Cook, Adrian. "A Lost Opportunity in Anglo-American Relations: The Alabama Claims, 1865–1867." *Australian Journal of Politics and History* 12, 1 (1966): 54–65; Marvel, William. *The Alabama and the Kearsarge.* Chapel Hill: University of North Carolina Press, 1996; Robson, Maureen M. "The Alabama Claims and the Anglo-American Reconciliation, 1865–1871." *Canadian Historical Review* 42, 1 (March 1961): 1–22.

LEE A. FARROW

## Alamo, Battle of (1836)

The most storied battle in the Texan War of Independence, in which 189 and perhaps 250 men led by David Crockett, James Bowie, and William Travis held off Mexican President Antonio López de Santa Anna's vastly superior force of 2,000 soldiers for almost two weeks.

The Alamo was a mission turned fort near San Antonio and blocked Santa Anna's march against the main forces of the Texas provisional government. Its 21 guns and the fervor of its defenders notwithstanding, there was no hope for success without reinforcements, which were repeatedly requested. Colonel William B. Travis arrived with only 30 cavalrymen, and Crockett arrived soon thereafter with a small group of Tennessee Volunteers. It was only a token force against the well-trained and supplied regular Mexican army. Political indecision and poor communication prevented any further aid from being sent. The Mexican heavy artillery was more than sufficient to batter down the Alamo's walls in a siege. Once the walls were rubble, the defenders would have no choice but to surrender. But in the early hours of March 6, Santa Anna launched an attack from four sides, over the objections of his senior commanders. The Mexicans suffered heavily from the Alamo's guns, but superior numbers soon prevailed. It was all over within 90 minutes. A handful of combatant survivors, perhaps including Crockett, were executed, but women and children were allowed to leave in safety.

Its mythology notwithstanding, the Alamo was of little military significance. It did buy some time for the provisional government to form, but, more important, it became a symbol of resistance on par with the Spartan stand at Thermopylae, and "Remember the Alamo" remains an inspiring part of Texan and American lore. *See also* Manifest Destiny; Mexican-American War.

FURTHER READING: Davis, William C. *Lone Star Rising.* New York: Free Press, 2004.

J. DAVID MARKHAM

## Åland Islands

A stepping-stone cluster of islands stretching between the coasts of Sweden and **Finland** and marking the boundary between the Baltic Sea to the south and the Gulf of Bothnia to the north. The islands were given to Russia, along with Finland, by the Treaty of Frederikshavn concluding the **Russo-Swedish War** in 1809, a tertiary conflict of the **Napoleonic Wars.** When the Treaty of Tilsit made allies of France and Russia, the allies demanded that Sweden abandon membership in the Fourth Coalition and join them in making war against Britain. Sweden's refusal precipitated the war with Russia in which the islands and Finland, Swedish since the twelfth century, were lost. The islands were then made officially neutral and demilitarized as part the diplomatic settlement of the **Crimean War** for the purpose of protecting Sweden from Russian aggression. *See also* Russian Empire.

FURTHER READING: Andersson, Ingvar. *A History of Sweden.* London: Weidenfield and Nicolson, 1956.

CARL CAVANAGH HODGE

## Alaskan Boundary Dispute (1896–1903)

A Canadian-American dispute arising from the discovery of gold in the Klondike region in August 1896. The Canadian government unearthed the Anglo-Russian treaty of 1825, upon which the Russian-American Treaty of 1867 was based, to support its claim to a boundary that enabled **Canada** to keep a strip of land in the so-called Alaskan panhandle, thus cutting it off from the rest of Alaska. The main motivation on the Canadian side was to facilitate access by sea to the gold sites. A temporary agreement was reached in 1899 and passions cooled off until this *modus vivendi* was questioned three years later. In March 1902, American President Theodore **Roosevelt,** who regarded the Canadian claim as unfair and fraudulent, had troops sent to the disputed territory—the Lynn Canal—in southern Alaska. A convention—the Hay-Herbert Treaty—reluctantly negotiated in 1903 provided that "six impartial jurists of repute," three for each party, would meet and settle the issue by a majority vote. For Roosevelt, this arrangement was simply meant to help Canadian and British leaders save face, for it was out of the question to yield any territory whatsoever. The Canadians were angered by his choice of fake jurists, who could not possibly be impartial in view of their connection with the Roosevelt Administration, but the British government was unwilling to antagonize the United States.

The Alaskan Boundary Tribunal that sat in London from September 3 to October 20, 1903, vindicated the American position. The two Canadian members voted as expected, but Lord Chief Justice Alverstone sided with the three Americans, to Roosevelt's intense satisfaction. In so doing, he did not so much heed the Rough Rider's waving of the Big Stick as he chose to incur the Canadians' wrath for the sake of his own country's policy of friendship with the United States. Despite occasional bickering, the late nineteenth century had been an era of Anglo-American rapprochement. To Roosevelt, who admired the British Empire and believed in the civilizing mission of "the English-speaking race," an Anglo-Saxon entente was a valuable asset in world politics in an age of imperial rivalries, and many Englishmen shared his views, which accounted for British moderation in the dispute. *See also* Manifest Destiny.

FURTHER READING: Beale, Howard K. *Theodore Roosevelt and the Rise of America to World Power.* Baltimore: The Johns Hopkins University Press Paperbacks, 1984; Campbell, Charles S., Jr. *Anglo-American Understanding, 1898–1903.* Baltimore: The Johns Hopkins Press, 1957; Marks, Frederick W., III. *Velvet on Iron: The Diplomacy of Theodore Roosevelt.* Lincoln: University of Nebraska Press, 1979; Tansill, Charles C. *Canadian-American Relations, 1875–1911.* New Haven, CT: Yale University Press, 1943; Tilchin, William N. *Theodore Roosevelt and the British Empire: A Study in Presidential Statecraft.* New York: St. Martin's Press, 1997.

SERGE RICARD

## Alaska Purchase Treaty (1867)

A treaty transferring Alaska, a Russian possession in North America, to the United States. Negotiations between Secretary of State William H. Seward and Russian Minister Edouard de Stoeckl concluded on March 30; the U.S. Senate ratified the treaty on April 9; and President Andrew Johnson proclaimed it on June 29, 1867. Russia had begun to see its North American holdings as political and financial liabilities and approached the United States before the Civil War, but only after the war could Washington take advantage of the offer.

The treaty provided for Russian cession of the territory in exchange for $7.2 million, a deal ridiculed in the United States as "Seward's Folly." The property of the "Greek Oriental Church" was to be protected, and inhabitants could return to Russia within three years. Those who remained would enjoy the "rights, advantages, and immunities of citizens of the United States." Alaska was the nation's final continental acquisition and symbolic of its **manifest destiny** to expand. The purchase addressed concerns over Russia's North American presence but left issues of government and citizenship unresolved, as the treaty did not specify that the territory was slated for statehood. A domestic corruption scandal over congressional funding for the purchase blunted the expansionist drive for 30 years. *See also* Russian Empire; Appendix: Words and Deeds, Document No.3.

FURTHER READING: Bevans, Charles I. *Treaties and Other International Agreements of the United States of America 1776–1949.* Vol. 11. Washington, DC: Government Printing Office, 1974, pp. 1216–1219; Jensen, Ronald J. *The Alaska Purchase and Russian-American Relations.* Seattle: University of Washington Press, 1975.

KENNETH J. BLUME

## Albania

A mountainous Balkan country that was part of the **Ottoman Empire** for more than 450 years. During Ottoman rule, however, Albanian chiefs controlled most local matters and the people were converted to Islam. But after the 1780s, Albania came under the control of Ali Pasha of Jannina.

Taking the lead from its neighbors, an Albanian nationalist movement evolved, taking as its rallying cry "the religion of Albanians is Albanianism!" In 1878, a group of Albanian leaders organized the League of Pizren, which called for self-government within the Ottoman Empire and initiated the development of the native language, literature, education, and a new alphabet. The movement remained active but was less noticeable than neighboring nationalist movements until in November 1908 an Albanian national congress representing Muslims, Catholics, and Orthodox met at Monastir and, although it supported the **Young Turks,** led a revolt in 1910.

The Habsburg government stimulated the nationalist movement by subsidizing schools and newspapers, because an independent Albania was the best way of preventing Serbia from obtaining a foothold on the Adriatic coast. Both Germany and Britain seconded this policy. At the London Conference of Great Power ambassadors in December 1912, it was therefore agreed to establish an independent Albania. But the frontiers became an issue of dispute, as Austria-Hungary, Germany, and Italy wanted Albania to be as large as possible and to include Scutari. Russia, and France, and to a lesser extent Britain, believed the area to be disputed and that Serbia and Greece should also receive parts of it. Nothing was decided. During the Second **Balkan War** Albania was again a battleground, with Montenegrin forces capturing Scutari. Heavy pressure from the powers and Austro-Hungarian threats of military action forced the Montenegrins to relinquish claims to it.

In July 1913, Austria-Hungary and the Albanian nationalists achieved an independent state. Russia deprived it of some Albanian villages, which went to Serbia, and Greece was also deprived of some Orthodox areas included in southern Albania. The powers agreed to guarantee Albania's neutrality. A German army officer, the nephew of "Carmen Sylvia" Romania's Queen, Prince William of Wied, was chosen to rule. But civil war and a lack of European Power support made his position untenable, and aid ceased during World War I. A successful rebellion in September 1914, under Essad Pasha, an Ottoman commander, forced William to flee. Essad then governed dictatorially and maintained himself, with Italian aid, until the Austrians defeated him in 1916. In 1920, a national legislative assembly met in Tirana and within month a government formed, but Albania's frontiers were not fixed until 1926. *See also* Eastern Question; Habsburg Empire.

FURTHER READING: Pollo, Stefanaq, and Arben Pluto. *The History of Albania: From Its Origins to the Present Day.* London: Routledge & Kegan Paul, 1981; Skendi, Stavro. *The Albanian National Awakening, 1878–1912.* Princeton, NJ: Princeton University Press, 1967; Vickers, Miranda. *The Albanians: A Modern History.* London: I. B. Tauris, 1999.

ANDREKOS VARNAVA

## Albrecht Friedrich Rudolf, Archduke (1817–1895)

Austrian military commander born in Vienna in August 1817. Albrecht was the son of Archduke Charles, who had defeated Napoleon in the Battle of **Aspern-Essling** in 1809. In the wake of the revolution of 1848–49, Albrecht got involved in politics, serving as governor of Hungary and becoming the leading ultraconservative among the Habsburgs. In the war of 1866, he commanded the Austrian army on the Italian theater and defeated the Italians at Custoza. After the war, the victorious field commander became supreme commander of the army and general inspector. He cooperated closely with Count Friedrich **Beck-Rzikowsky,** the chief of the general staff since 1881. Struggling relentlessly against both liberal and nationalist tendencies in the military, as well as political and dynastic elites of the Habsburg monarchy, Albrecht usually favored a cautious foreign policy. He died in Arco in February 1895. *See also* Austro-Prussian War; Habsburg Empire.

FURTHER READING: Wawro, Geoffrey. *The Austro-Prussian War: Austria's War with Prussia and Italy in 1866.* New York: Cambridge University Press, 1996.

GUENTHER KRONENBITTER

### Alexander, King of Yugoslavia (1888–1934)

A member of the Karaddjordjevic family, Alexander was Prince Regent of **Serbia** and, after 1921, king of Yugoslavia. Alexander was the son of King Peter whose authority he largely replaced in June 1914 because of the king's failing health. During World War I, Alexander served as Serbia's nominal supreme commander, in which capacity he accompanied Serbian forces in their retreat through Albania in 1915. He became King of the United Kingdom of the Serbs, Croats, and Slovenes after 1918 and of Yugoslavia after 1929, at which time he suspended the constitution and ruled as a dictator. On October 9, 1934, Alexander was assassinated by a Macedonian nationalist in Marseilles. *See also* Habsburg Empire.

FURTHER READING: Jelavich, Barbara. *Russia's Balkan Entanglements, 1806–1914.* New York: Cambridge University Press, 1991.

MARTIN MOLL

### Alexander I, Tsar of Russia (1777–1825)

Alexander I was tsar of Russia from 1801 to 1825. After succeeding his father, Paul I, Alexander soon became alarmed at Napoleonic expansion and was instrumental in establishing the Third Coalition against France in 1805. When his forces were decisively defeated at **Austerlitz,** Alexander withdrew to Poland, where in the following year, in alliance with Prussia, he continued operations until the spring of 1807. After his army's defeat at Friedland in 1807, he met Napoleon at **Tilsit** and came to an arrangement with the French emperor by which the tsar agreed to join the Continental System, so prohibiting all trade between Russia and Britain. Within a few years, however, Franco-Russian relations broke down. Realizing that his alliance with France was detrimental to Russia's economy, angered by the failure of Napoleon to support Russia's interests in Turkey and Sweden, and concerned about the proximity of Napoleon's Polish satellite state, the Duchy of Warsaw, Alexander found himself again at war with France. Prodded by Napoleon's disastrous invasion in 1812, Alexander played a key role in the ultimate defeat of France and the re-establishment of the balance of power in Europe through the political restructuring of the Continent agreed at the Congress of Vienna in 1815. *See also* Alexander II; Napoleonic Wars; Nicholas I; Russian Empire.

FURTHER READING: Dziewanowski, M. K. *Alexander I: Russia's Mysterious Tsar.* New York: Hippocrene Books, 1990; Hartley, Janet. *Alexander I.* London: Longman, 1994; Klimenko, Michael. *Tsar Alexander I: Portrait of an Autocrat.* Tenafly, NJ: Hermitage Publishers, 2002; Palmer, Alan. *Alexander I: Tsar of War and Peace.* London: Weidenfeld & Nicolson, 1974.

GREGORY FREMONT-BARNES

## Alexander II, Tsar of Russia (1818–1881)

Alexander II was tsar of Russia from 1855 to 1881, coming to the throne in the midst of Russia's unsuccessful involvement in the **Crimean War.** Alexander occupied himself mostly with domestic affairs, and his reign became known as the Era of the Great Reforms. He carried out the emancipation of the Russian serfs in 1861 as the first step in a series of reforms designed to modernize Russia. His Zemstvo Reform of 1864 created an elected unit of local administration, the *zemstvo.* Alexander also created an independent judiciary and approved the introduction of universal manhood conscription for the Russian army in 1874. In the realm of imperial expansion, Alexander approved the military conquest of the Central Asian Khanates of Kokand, **Bukhara,** and **Khiva** during the 1860s and 1870s and efforts to extend Russian influence in **Afghanistan.** Kokand was annexed into the tsarist empire while the other two khanates were reduced to the status of Russian protectorates. Alexander oversaw the **Russo-Turkish War** of 1877–1878, which resulted in Russian territorial gains in the Caucasus and the creation of a Principality of **Bulgaria** under Russian influence.

His reforming activities raised expectations for still greater reforms, but his maintenance of tsarist autocracy led to disappointment. Many student radicals joined revolutionary movements to generate a peasant uprising to overthrow Alexander. When this movement failed in 1874–1875, some revolutionaries trained their sights on the tsar himself. One of these groups, the Peoples' Will, succeeded in assassinating him in 1881. *See also* Great Game; Ottoman Empire; San Stefano, Treaty of.

FURTHER READING: Lincoln, W. Bruce. *The Great Reforms: Autocracy, Bureaucracy, and the Politics of Change in Imperial* Russia. DeKalb: Northern Illinois University Press, 1990; Lincoln, W. Bruce. *The Romanovs: Autocrats of All the Russias.* Reprint ed. New York: Anchor, 1983; Mosse, W. *Alexander II and the Modernization of Russia.* London: I. B. Tauris and Company, Ltd., 1995.

JONATHAN GRANT

## Alexander III, Tsar of Russia (1845–1894)

In contrast to his father, **Alexander II,** Alexander III was a reactionary autocrat in domestic affairs yet instinctively cautious in his diplomacy. Recoiling from the assassination of his father, Alexander adhered to a policy of political repression throughout his reign, employing secret police against real and imagined enemies, intensifying the "Russification" of the subject nationalities of the **Russian Empire,** and allowing pogroms against Russia's Jews. He had the utmost confidence in the judgment of Konstantin **Pobedonostsev,** his chief policy advisor and Procurator of the Holy Synod, and the competence of Vyacheslav von Plehve, his director of police and later minister of the interior. The Jews in particular suffered horribly under the "Temporary Rules" imposed in May 1882 and the increasingly violent waves of popular anti-Semitism that climaxed in the Kishinev Massacre of 1903. In the interim, Alexander issued a decree in 1890, according to which all Jews in the Russian interior were to migrate to the western provinces, where they were forbidden either to own or lease land or take up liberal professions. Meanwhile, genuine political enemies of the regime were forced to become more secretive and to form alliances of convenience across rival groups.

Alexander sought to avoid international conflict. After 1890, he was so alarmed by the course of German foreign policy that he abandoned the tradition of the *Dreikaiserbund* and gravitated toward an understanding with France that in 1894 culminated secretly in the Franco-Russian Alliance only months before Alexander's death. Alexander also promoted the development of the **Russian Far East** and authorized construction of the **Trans-Siberian Railway.** His reign was therefore a period of expansion and diplomatic realignment abroad accompanied by repression and rising political tensions at home, which led, in the reign of his son **Nicholas II,** to the revolutionary upheavals of 1905. *See also* Witte, Sergei.

FURTHER READING: Geyer, Dietrich. *Russian Imperialism: The Interaction of Domestic and Foreign Policy, 1860–1914.* New York: Berg, 1987; Seton-Watson, Hugh. *The Russian Empire, 1801–1917.* Oxford: Clarendon Press, 1967; Whelan, Heide W. *Alexander III & the State Council: Bureaucracy & Counter-reform in Late Imperial Russia.* New Brunswick, NJ: Rutgers University Press, 1982.

CARL CAVANAGH HODGE

## Algeciras Conference (1906)

The Algeciras Conference was an international conference convened to resolve the First Moroccan Crisis of 1905; it was held at the Spanish port of Algeciras from January 16 to April 7, 1906. Germany had insisted on a conference to resolve its dispute with France over Morocco but found itself isolated at the conference, with support only from Austria-Hungary. Although the conference confirmed Moroccan independence under a Sultan, it granted France and Spain the right to police the country under a Swiss inspector-general and gave France economic control over Morocco. This amounted to a diplomatic defeat for Germany, leading to the resignation of Friedrich von Holstein from the Foreign Office. There could now be no talk of a Franco-German reconciliation. The **Entente Cordiale** between France and Britain was therefore strengthened by Germany's diplomatic blunder. In 1911, Germany provoked a further confrontation over Morocco in the **Agadir Crisis,** arguing that France had breached the Algeciras agreement. *See also* German Empire, Wilhelm II.

FURTHER READING: Anderson, Eugene N. *The First Moroccan Crisis, 1904–1906.* Handen, CT: Archon Books, 1966; Martel, Gordon. *The Origins of the First World War.* 3rd ed. London: Longman, 2003.

ANNIKA MOMBAUER

## Algeria

By the mid-nineteenth century, Algeria was a uniquely significant Northern African territory of the **French Empire.** After centuries as both the westernmost province of the Ottoman Empire and a base for the Barbary pirates, Algeria was invaded and colonized by the French in 1830 as part of **Charles X**'s efforts to preserve his throne after his attempts to restore autocratic royal power in France triggered widespread discontent. Although Charles lost his throne in the July Revolution of 1830, his successors opted to retain Algeria and spent the next several decades conquering the interior in the hopes of establishing a settlement colony that could also serve as a source of labor and food imports. The French presence was bitterly opposed by the Algerian forces under **Abd-al-Qādir** who quickly launched a fierce **guerilla** war to drive out the invaders. France in turn retaliated by confiscating land, engaging in collective reprisals, and embracing a scorched earth policy of destroying crops and livestock. General Thomas-Robert Bugeaud, with the aid of over 100,000 French troops, eventually succeeded in conquering and pacifying the bulk of Algeria in 1847, but smaller French military operations continued in the interior zones until the early twentieth century.

As the army worked to pacify the interior, French settlers, also known as *colons* or *pieds noirs,* poured into Algeria's urban and coastal areas in search of cheap land and business opportunities. Throughout the nineteenth century, the ranks of free settlers were also swelled by political prisoners deported after the Revolution of 1848 and the Paris Commune of 1870, as well as immigrants from Spain, Italy, and the nearby British colony of Malta. The size of the European settler community, which eventually reached 10 percent of the total Algerian population, meant that it exerted substantial political influence in Paris. the settlers enjoyed voting rights, owned most farms and businesses, and controlled the local administration, and the Algerian masses were rendered second-class citizens. In addition to facing chronic unemployment, poverty, and limited prospects for education, unless they abandoned their traditional culture and religion, Algerians were also denied voting rights and were subject to the *indigénat,* an arbitrary legal policy that allowed colonial administrators to impose summary fines and jail terms for a wide range of alleged offenses. The end result of these policies was lingering resentment that led to the rise of Algerian nationalism in the aftermath of the twentieth century's two World Wars. *See also* French Foreign Legion; *Jihad;* Ottoman Empire.

FURTHER READING: Ageron, Charles Robert. *Modern Algeria: A History from 1830 to the Present.* Trenton, NJ: Africa World Press, 1991; Bennoune, Mahfoud. *The Making of Contemporary Algeria, 1830–1987: Colonial Upheavals and Post-independence Development.* 2nd ed. Cambridge: Cambridge University Press, 2002; Stora, Benjamin. *Algeria 1830–2000: A Short History.* Ithaca, NY: Cornell University Press, 2001.

KENNETH J. OROSZ

## Aliwal, Battle of (1846)

A decisive British victory in the First **Sikh War.** The British and the Sikhs met at an open field near the village of Aliwal on the south bank of the Sutlej River on January 28, 1846. Although on the losing side at **Ferozeshah,** most in the Sikh army blamed that defeat on the leadership and felt confident that they were superior to the British army. The Sikh army of about 13,000 had its back to the Sutlej, while the British army of 10,000, led by General Sir Harry Smith, marched down from a ridge to attack. The Sikhs fired from 700 yards. From the ridge, Smith could see the Sikh weakness and ordered the village of Aliwal, on the Sikh left flank, to be taken. The Sikhs formed squares but these were broken. Fighting was vicious. The Sikhs sought cover behind the banks of the Sutlej but were dispersed by artillery fire and a battalion of **sepoys.** It was a complete route for the British, who suffered only 500 casualties to the Sikhs' 3,000. The loss of men and material was high, but what was perhaps more devastating to the Sikh army was the loss of morale as a result of the defeat. *See also* British Empire; India.

FURTHER READING: Bruce, George. *Six Battles for India: The Anglo-Sikh Wars, 1845–6, 1848–9.* London: Arthur Barker, 1969; Cook, Hugh. *The Sikh Wars: The British Army in the Punjab, 1845–1849.* London: Leo Cooper, 1975; Crawford, E. R. "The Sikh Wars, 1845–9." In Brian Bond, ed. *Victorian Military Campaigns.* New York: Frederick A. Praeger Publishers, 1967; Farwell, Byron. *Queen Victoria's Little Wars.* New York: W. W. Norton & Co., 1972.

DAVID TURPIE

## Alsace-Lorraine

A region of present-day northeastern France and a principal territorial gain of the Second German Reich in the **Treaty of Frankfurt** in 1871 after the Prussian victory in the **Franco-Prussian War.** Its acquisition was in many respects a central goal of the wars of German unification, in part because the south German states cited it as justification for their armies' treatment as equals in the German national mission despite their military status as very junior partners with Prussia, but also because it symbolized to German nationalists the correction of what they considered a great injustice. Alsace was taken by France in 1648 as a prize of victory in the Thirty Years War. Lorraine had been part of the Holy Roman Empire since the ninth century but had been appropriated by France on a piecemeal basis in the sixteenth and seventeenth centuries. Bismarck justified the annexation of the region on the basis of the Germanic dialect and culture of the local population, but the region also included predominantly French-speaking areas for the military expedience of defensible borders. Under the Second Reich the region was governed directly from Berlin as the *Reichsland* of Elsaß-Lothringen. After 1871, the recovery of Alsace-Lorraine immediately became the focus both of French nationalists and war planners. Its retention by Germany, not surprisingly, figured prominently in the **Schlieffen Plan.** *See also* Bismarck, Otto von; German Empire.

FURTHER READING: Blumenthal, Daniel. *Alsace-Lorraine.* New York: G. P. Putnam's, 1917; Hazen, Charles Downer. *Alsace-Lorraine under German Rule.* Freeport: Books for Libraries Press,

1971; Wawro, Geoffrey. *The Franco-Prussian War: The German Conquest of France in 1870–1871.* New York: Cambridge University Press, 2003.

CARL CAVANAGH HODGE

## American Civil War (1861–1865)

The American Civil War was fought between the military forces of the Federal Government of the **United States** against those of the Confederate States of American, made up of 11 states who announced their secession from the Union in early 1861. The respective parties are often referred to as the Union or the "North," and the Confederacy or the "South." More than 600,000 American soldiers lost their lives, more than half from the effects of disease, during the conflict, which involved more than 3 million personnel. After four years of bloodshed, the Union of the United States of America was preserved and slavery was abolished. Northern victory also inaugurated a trying period of Reconstruction and marked a key staging post in the development of the nation.

The events leading to the outbreak of the war in 1861 centered on the issue of slavery as the United States continued to expand westward across the North American continent, bringing more states into the Union. Since the very inception of the American republic, and before, slavery had existed across vast tracks of the South and was integral to the plantation economies of the region. In the face of the abolitionist movement in the North and the demise of slavery in Europe, Southerners became increasingly concerned that their way of life was under threat. Led by South Carolina, the southern states were prompted to secede by the threat they perceived from the election in 1861 of Abraham Lincoln to the presidency. Lincoln, leader of the Republican Party from Illinois, held firmly antislavery views but did not promise federal laws preventing slavery. Instead, he and his supporters argued that slavery should not be permitted in those territories to the west seeking to become states and join the Union. The Republican Party had emerged in the 1850s with a dedicated antislavery agenda, and, for many in the South, the Republican victory in the 1860 presidential election was the final straw. Thus in February 1861, before Lincoln had assumed office, the states of South Carolina, Mississippi, Louisiana, Florida, Alabama, Georgia, and Texas seceded and formed the Confederate States of America; they had adopted a constitution and were led by their own president, Jefferson Davis. The states of Tennessee, North Carolina, Arkansas, and Virginia joined them in April and May. Despite efforts at conciliation conflict followed, not over the issue of slavery itself but over the preservation of the Union against southern secessionism. Lincoln's presidential inaugural address stated that the "Constitution of the Union of these States is perpetual" and therefore could not be dissolved unless all the parties agreed.

The slavery issue nonetheless continued to be important to the progress of the war. Lincoln addressed the dilemma in two parts, by issuing the Emancipation Proclamation in September 1862, and publishing the final version on 1 January 1863, at which point it came into force. The proclamation did not abolish slavery; the Thirteenth Amendment to the Constitution of the United States in December 1865 did that. Rather, it stated that those slaves in the Confederacy were henceforth freemen. Given that the proclamation was a presidential decree and not a law, considerable debate remains as to Lincoln's motivations. Although the impact of the abolitionist movement undoubtedly played a role, Lincoln justified his decision as a war measure. The proclamation, he argued, would enable the North to win the war to preserve the Union by undermining the South. Further, the measure enabled African Americans to be recruited into the Union forces and thus swelled the pool of men fighting for the North by almost 200,000 by the end of the war, far in advance of the Confederacy arming their slaves, which took place only in the final months of the war.

The military prosecution of the war began in the spring of 1861 at Fort Sumter near Charlestown, South Carolina, and was to continue for the next four years to devastating effect. Those years marked the beginning of the industrialization of warfare through the use of the **telegraph,** the **railways,** and the **machine gun** and are seen as part of a movement toward "total war" involving the whole of society and not just the military. The total number of engagements during the war is estimated at more than 10,000, ranging from small unit activity to the set piece battles at **Gettysburg** and Jamestown. The Confederacy won many of the war's battles at the tactical level but was unable to translate these into strategic victory. As the war wore on, the North's population and industrial capacity led to the South's eventual defeat.

The maritime environment played host to some of the most significant engagements of the war, particularly in the sense of the danger of the war escalating and drawing in the European powers. The Union's strategy was to use a blockade and starve the Confederacy of essential war supplies. British businessmen in particular, whose cotton industry was injured by the war in the first instance, constructed a fleet of small ships known as blockade runners to supply the South. Their occasional interception by Union forces ran the risk of British reprisals, but Union forces were careful to return the British crews unharmed after confiscating any contraband.

On land, the battles were particularly bloody. The Battle of Gettysburg at the beginning of July 1863 cost the lives of more than 50,000 Americans in just three days. The battle is often seen as a turning point in the war, as the Union Army repelled the invasion of the North by the skilled Confederate General, Robert E. Lee. Up to this point, Lee had enjoyed successes over Union forces at the Second Battle of Bull Run, Fredericksburg, and Chancellorsville. Lee referred to Chancellorsville as "the perfect battle," because of his skill in maneuvering his forces to outwit the numerically stronger opposition. The leading general on the Union side was Ulysses S. Grant, later the 18th President of the United States, who became General in Chief at the beginning of 1864 after his capture of **Vicksburg** on July 4, 1863. Grant followed a policy of attrition in campaigning against the South during 1864, which led to massive casualties on both sides. Crucially, Lincoln supported Grant's approach and reinforced his armies. At the end of 1864, the Confederacy's prospects for victory were negligible. In April 1865, Grant's forces broke through the South's defensive lines surrounding Richmond, capturing the Confederate capital and forcing Lee to flee to the West. Lee, realizing his untenable predicament, surrendered to Grant on April 9, 1945. Grant allowed Lee to retain his cavalry sword and horse as a sign of his respect. The rest of the Confederate forces followed suit and the war was over.

In the immediate aftermath of the cessation of hostilities, the nation was rocked by the assassination of President Lincoln on April 14, 1865. The president was shot at close range by the well-known actor and Confederate sympathizer, John Wilkes Booth, while attending a performance at Ford's Theater on Good Friday. He died the next morning without regaining consciousness. The political impact of Lincoln's death was to rally support for the Thirteenth Amendment and the spirit of reconciliation. Lincoln had operated skillfully in maintaining the support of the border states, Democrats who supported the war, the still relatively new Republican Party, and the emancipated slaves, as well as preventing international recognition of the Confederacy by Britain or France. After Lincoln's burial in Illinois, Jefferson Davis was captured and spent two years in a federal jail; however, he was never tried, and when he died in 1889 his funeral in Richmond was attended by thousands of supporters.

More broadly, the impact of the American Civil War was felt in a number of fields. Thousands had died, families had been torn apart, and the economy of the South was ravaged. Nonetheless, the Union had been preserved and the issue of slavery settled, although discrimination against African Americans persisted through the Reconstruction period, and their civil rights continued to be an issue until the mid-1960s. *See also* Antietam, Battle of.

FURTHER READING: Foote, Shelby. *The Civil War: A Narrative.* 3 vols. New York: Vintage, 1986; Gallager, Gary, W., Steven D. Engle, Robert K. Krick, and Joseph T Glatthaar. *The American Civil War—This Mighty Scourge of War.* Oxford: Osprey, 2003; McPherson, James M. *Ordeal by Fire: The Civil War and Reconstruction.* Boston: McGraw-Hill, 2000; Sears, Stephen W. *Gettysburg.* Boston: Houghton Mifflin, 2003.

J. SIMON ROFE

## American Indian Wars

*See* Indian Wars

## Amiens, Treaty of (1802)

A treaty of peace concluded between Britain and France on March 25, 1802, bringing an end to the series of conflicts known as the French Revolutionary Wars. The terms of the treaty were more favorable toward France. France agreed to restore the Kingdom of the Two Sicilies (Naples) and the Papal States to their legitimate rulers but was able to retain Nice, Savoy, Piedmont, and the German territories taken on the left bank of the Rhine since 1792. Britain agreed to restore the Cape Colony in southern Africa to Holland, a French ally; Malta to the Knights of St. John, from whom Napoleon had seized the island in 1798; Tobago to Spain, another French ally; Martinique to France; and Demerara, Berbice, and Curaçao to the Dutch. In return, Britain retained only the former Spanish colony of Trinidad in the West Indies and the former Dutch possession of Ceylon in the Indian Ocean. The French made vague promises to restore or compensate the Kings of Piedmont and the Netherlands and gave general assurances that previous treaties with continental powers would be honored. Both sides viewed the peace as little more than a truce, and war resumed only 14 months later. *See also* Bonaparte, Napoleon; Pitt, William.

FURTHER READING: Grainger, John D. *The Amiens Truce: Britain and Bonaparte, 1801–1803.* Rochester, NY: Boydell Press, 2004.

GREGORY FREMONT-BARNES

## Amundsen, Roald (1872–1928)

Norwegian polar explorer who participated in several expeditions to both the **Arctic** and to **Antarctica.** Amundsen sailed through the North West passage between Canada and Greenland in 1903. As a result of more thorough planning and better use of sled dogs, Amundsen then beat the British explorer, Captain Robert F. Scott, in their 1910–1912 race to become the first man to reach the South Pole. Amundsen also made the first undisputed conquest of the North Pole in 1926. He disappeared in the Arctic in an attempt to rescue the Italian explorer Umberto Nobile in 1928.

FURTHER READING: Huntford, Roland. *Scott and Amundsen: The Last Place of Earth.* New York: Modern Library, 1999.

FRODE LINDGJERDET

## Anarchism

A radical libertarian theory that attained political popularity in the nineteenth century. Derived from the Greek words αν ("without") and αρχία ("rulers"), anarchism connotes a system of thought and action based on the belief that government is not only unnecessary, but also detrimental. The term *anarchist* was first used by the French Pierre-Joseph Proudhon (1808–1865), the first declared anarchist and a precursor of mutualism, in *What Is Property? Or, an Inquiry into the Principle of Right of Government,* published in 1840, in which he made the famous statement that "property is theft."

Whereas in the first half of the nineteenth century anarchist thought gravitated around individualism, in the second half anarchist theory turned towards collectivism, mainly under the influence of Russian anarchist philosopher Mikhail Bakunin (1814–1876), founder of the Social Democratic Alliance in 1869 and considered one of the "fathers of anarchism." In *The Red Association* (1870) he stated that, "Political Freedom without economic equality is a pretense, a fraud, a lie." Karl **Marx** regarded Bakunin as a "sentimental idealist." Anarchist communism also emerged under the initiative of Peter Kropotkin (1842–1921), a Russian prince known as the "Anarchist Prince." Both Bakunin and Kropotkin participated in the International Workingmen's Association, also known as the First International, an organization initially made up of British trade unionists, French socialists, Italian republicans, and anarchists. The Association was founded in 1864 in London and was led by Karl Marx. In 1872, at the Hague Congress, due to a dispute between Marx and Bakunin, the "Bakuninist" anarchists were expelled from the association. This was the origin of the perpetual conflict between Marxists and anarchists.

Anarcho-syndicalism, a variation of libertarian communism, was developed late in the nineteenth century. The general strike was regarded as a main strategy in the pursuit of the anarchist revolution and influenced political life in the United States through the activities of the early labor unions, themselves influenced by anarchist immigrants from Central or Eastern Europe. Although political violence was generally regarded as a necessary revolutionary practice, many anarchists thought riots, bombings, assassinations, and even insurrections were ineffective. Particularly noteworthy is nonviolent Christian anarchism, such as professed by the Russian writer Leo Tolstoy. Anarchist leaders, such as Bakunin and the Italian Errico Malatesta (1852–1932), by contrast considered violence indispensable. William **McKinley,** the 25th president of the United States, was shot in Buffalo, New York, on September 6, 1901, by Leon Czolgosz, a registered Republican who claimed to have been influenced by the writings of Emma Goldman (1869–1940), a prominent anarcho-communist and feminist born in Lithuania. *See also* Marx, Karl.

FURTHER READING: Ward, Colin. *Anarchism: A Very Short Introduction.* Oxford: Oxford University Press, 2004; Wolff, Robert Paul. *In Defense of Anarchism.* Berkeley: University of California Press, 1998.

GEORGIA TRES

## Andijan Revolt (1898)

A major revolt of Islamic peoples against Russian rule in 1898 in the eastern Uzbek city of Andijan on the upper Syr Darya River. The rebellion was planned and led by the Naqshbandi Sufi leader Madali Ishan. It was unsuccessful. Madali Ishan led approximately 2,000 followers in an attack on the Russian barracks, an action he envisioned as part of a *ghazawat* or ***jihad*** against the Russian imperial administration in **Turkestan.** His followers were not well armed, carrying only cudgels and knives against Russian firearms. The attack resulted in the deaths of 22 Russians and 11 rebels before being defeated. In all, 24 rebels were later hanged and over 300 were sent to Siberia. The revolt caused serious concerns for the Russians and forced them to reexamine their administration in the Ferghana Valley. Andijan had been annexed by the Khokand khanate state in the middle of the eighteenth century and was taken by the Russians in 1876. *See also* Great Game; Russian Empire.

FURTHER READING: Manz, Beatrice Forbes. "Central Asian Uprisings in the Nineteenth Century: Ferghana Under the Russians." *The Russian Review* 46 (1987): 267–81.

SCOTT C. BAILEY

## Andrássy, Gyula, Count (1823–1890)

Hungarian prime minister and Habsburg foreign minister. Andrássy was born March 1823 in Kassa to a distinguished Magyar family, became a member of parliament in 1847, and joined the Hungarian independence movement led by Lajos Kossuth. He served as a commander with the Hungarian troops in the war of independence in 1848–49. As a consequence of the Hungarian defeat he was forced to flee the country but was permitted to return in 1857. He became one the preeminent Hungarian politicians that negotiated the **Ausgleich** of 1867, which settled Hungary's semiautonomous position within the Habsburg Empire. Andrássy was the leader of the liberals and prime minister of Hungary from 1867 to 1871, when he was appointed foreign minister of the Habsburg monarchy, a position he held until 1879. His "Andrássy Note" of December 1875 influenced the Congress of Berlin in 1878. He pushed for the occupation of **Bosnia-Herzegovina** in the aftermath of the **Russo-Turkish War.** Just before he resigned in October 1879, Andrássy signed the Dual Alliance treaty with Germany. He died in February 1890 in Istria. *See also* Balkan Crisis; Berlin, Congress of; Eastern Question; Habsburg Empire; Ottoman Empire.

FURTHER READING: Bagdasarian, Nicholas Der. *The Austro-German Rapprochement, 1870–1879.* Rutherford, NJ: Fairleigh Dickinson University Press, 1976; Harris, David. *A Diplomatic History of the Balkan Crisis, 1875–1878.* Hamden, CT: Archon Books, 1969.

GUENTHER KRONENBITTER

## Anglo-American Treaty (1818)

A treaty addressing three issues in Anglo-American relations: Atlantic fisheries, the northern boundary, and the Oregon territory. It was signed October 20, 1818 and proclaimed on January 30, 1819. American fishing rights within Canadian territorial waters, granted in the Treaty of Paris of 1783, had come into question after the War of 1812. In addition, the 1783 treaty contained ambiguities regarding the Canadian-American boundary.

As a result of the 1818 treaty, Americans gained the right to take and dry fish on the uninhabited coasts of Newfoundland and southern Labrador. The treaty also identified a line from the Lake of the Woods, along the 49th Parallel west to the Rocky Mountains, as the northern border of the United States, adding thousands of square miles to American territory. Finally, the two nations arranged a temporary *modus vivendi*—a compromise "joint occupation" of the vast Oregon territory.

A diplomatic triumph for the United States, the agreement represented another step toward better Anglo-American and Canadian-American relations and settled most outstanding Anglo-American controversies except for the West Indies trade issue. *See also* Anglo-American War.

FURTHER READING: Campbell, Charles S., Jr. *From Revolution to Rapprochement: The United States and Great Britain, 1783–1900.* New York: John Wiley, 1974; Miller, Hunter, ed. *Treaties and Other International Acts of the United States of America.* Vol. II. Washington, DC: U.S. Government Printing Office, 1931, pp. 658–62.

KENNETH J. BLUME

## Anglo-American War (1812–1815)

Commonly known as the War of 1812, this conflict was triggered by a long series of outstanding grievances between Britain and the United States, which were largely connected with the former's contemporaneous war against Napoleonic France. From the American perspective, Britain's insatiable demand for sailors to man the Royal Navy had for years led to the impressment of American seamen. Further, American neutral vessels attempting to trade with the European continent—largely controlled by Britain's rival, France—had led British vessels to seize such ships on the dubious basis that their cargoes fell under the loose British definition of contraband. American motives were not, however, entirely blameless. Many in the United States sought expansion into British **Canada** and refused to allow the repatriation of Royal Navy sailors who had deserted and enlisted aboard American merchant vessels with papers claiming American citizenship.

War commenced in June 1812 when a small American militia force of 2,500 men under General William Hull briefly crossed the Canadian border and were held back by an equally small British force. Hull then withdrew to Detroit. A British and Indian force then crossed the frontier, took Fort Dearborn (now Chicago) on August 15, and captured Hull's force. The Americans launched a second invasion of Canada but in October were defeated along the Niagara River at Queenston Heights. Approximately 1,600 American troops captured and set fire to York (now Toronto) in April 1813, but these forces under General Pike were later driven off at Stony Creek on June 6.

In the autumn, General William Henry Harrison crossed Lake Erie with 7,000 American troops, in the wake of the defeat of an opposing naval flotilla on September 10, and forced British General Proctor from Detroit on September 29. In the follow-up action at the Thames River on October 5, Proctor was again defeated. Meanwhile, with the British having failed in their amphibious attack in May on Sackett's Harbor on Lake Ontario, the Americans launched a new offensive under General James Wilkinson, who hoped to take Montreal. This attempt, and attacks elsewhere, failed, and at year's end the British captured Fort Niagara.

From the opening of hostilities, the Royal Navy had continued its blockade of the American coastline, causing economic disruption, especially in New England, which had never supported the war. In the summer of 1814, a new American commander, General Jacob Brown, launched another incursion toward Niagara, which took Fort Erie and defeated the British at Chippewa on July 5. At Lundy's Lane on July 25, both sides fought to a standstill before the Americans finally withdrew.

By this time the war in Europe had ended, and British reinforcements began arriving, the majority in the form of an expedition to Chesapeake Bay. General Robert Ross defeated American militia at Bladensburg on August 24, entered Washington the next day, burned its public buildings, and then withdrew, although he failed to take Baltimore near which he was himself killed. At about the same time, a British thrust down Lake Champlain by General George Prevost failed as a result of an American naval victory at Plattsburg on September 11.

At sea, the tiny American navy, consisting of nothing larger than frigates, acquitted itself remarkably well but was unable to loosen the enemy blockade or prevent amphibious landings, at least not one consisting of 14,000 Peninsular veterans under General Pakenham, which landed in the Mississippi delta on December 13. Neither side was aware that a treaty of peace was concluded at in Belgium on Christmas Eve, and when Pakenham's forces needlessly confronted those under Andrew **Jackson** near New Orleans on January 8, 1815, they were disastrously repulsed. The war ended as a stalemate, with the territorial situation virtually unchanged and, with the Napoleonic Wars over, impressment was now a dead issue. *See also* Napoleonic Wars; Royal Navy.

FURTHER READING: Borneman, Walter. *1812: The War That Forged a Nation.* London: Harper Collins, 2004; Hickey, Donald R. *The War of 1812: A Forgotten Conflict.* Urbana: University of Illinois Press, 1989; Hitsman, J. Mackay. *The Incredible War of 1812: A Military History.* Toronto: University of Toronto Press, 1965; Stagg, J.C.A. *Mr. Madison's War: Politics, Diplomacy, and Warfare in the Early American Republic, 1783–1830.* Princeton, NJ: Princeton University Press, 1983; Wait, Eugene M. *America and the War of 1812.* Commack, NY: Kroshka Books, 1999.

GREGORY FREMONT-BARNES

## Anglo-Burmese Wars (1824–1826, 1852, 1885)

Three short campaigns to extend British control over Burma as part of the larger British imperial regime in **India.** The first was launched in response to disputes along the border between Manipur and south-central Assam. In May 1824, an Anglo-Indian army of 11, 500 landed in Upper Burma and captured Rangoon. Following a series of lesser engagements, the Burmese gained a truce in December 1825 that was promptly broken by the British and the offensive resumed until Burmese resistance collapsed in January 1826. In the Treaty of Yandaboo, the Burmese ceded Arakan, Assam, Manipur, and the coast of Tenasserim to Britain.

The second began with British naval action against Martaban, ostensibly to punish the Burmese for levying a fine on two British ships, followed by a British declaration of war on April 1, 1852, and the capture of Bassein, Pegu, and Rangoon. Lord **Dalhousie,** governor general of India, then annexed Pegu Province of Lower Burma to India. This second Burmese defeat was accompanied by the ouster of the Burmes King Pagan Min and his replacement with Mindon Min, who acknowledged British authority in Pegu.

The third conflict was influenced by British anxiety over possible French penetration of Upper Burma and by King Thibaw Min's attempt to assert a measure of independence by favoring a French teak company over its British rival and agreeing to have a French contractor build a railway from Mandalay to India. It was more directly provoked when Thibaw fined the Bombay-Burmah Trading Company for illegally exporting teak from Upper Burma. The **East India Company** issued an ultimatum on October 22, 1885. When it was rejected a British expedition of 10,000 with 3,000 native auxiliaries began an offensive up the Irrawaddy River and ended the war in just 20 days. In 1886, Upper and Lower were merged into one Indian province. Nonetheless, the British dealt with sporadic guerrilla resistance in Burma for the remainder of the century. *See also* British Empire.

FURTHER READING: Aung, Maung Htin. *A History of Burma.* New York: Columbia University Press, 1967. Farwell, Byron. *Queen Victoria's Little Wars.* New York: W. W. Norton, 1972; Thant Myint-U, *The Making of Modern Burma.* New York: Cambridge University Press, 2001.

CARL CAVANAGH HODGE

## Anglo-German Treaty

*See* Heligoland-Zanzibar Treaty

## Anglo-Japanese Alliance (1902, 1905)

A mutual assistance pact signed in London on January 30, 1902 by British Foreign Secretary Lord Lansdowne and the Japanese minister, Hayashi Tadasu, and aimed ostensibly at Russian expansionism in Asia. For Britain the treaty marked the end of "splendid isolation" and enabled it to secure an ally in Asia to contain Russian ambitions and to safeguard British commercial interests in China. The alliance had the additional benefit of freeing Britain to withdraw Royal Navy squadrons from the China Station to home waters to counter Kaiser **Wilhelm II**'s naval building program. For Japan, the alliance was key to their being recognized as a regional power, if not yet a Great Power, and allowed it to challenge Russia's occupation of **Manchuria** and its designs on **Korea,** culminating in the **Russo-Japanese War** (1904–05). The alliance was renewed in 1905 and again in 1911 and expired in 1921. *See also* Japanese Empire; Russian Empire; Sino-Japanese War.

FURTHER READING: Nish, Ian H. *The Anglo-Japanese Alliance: The Diplomacy of Two Island Empires, 1894–1907*. London: Athlone Press, 1966; O'Brien, Philips, ed. *The Anglo-Japanese Alliance*. New York: Routledge, 2004.

ADRIAN U-JIN ANG

## Anglo-Nepal War (1814–1816)

A conflict between the British **East India Company** and the Gurkhas, also spelled Gorkha, the ruling ethnic group of **Nepal,** and sometimes referred to as the Gurkha War. In the last decade of the eighteenth century, the Gorkha Kingdom, after establishing its sway over Nepal, began to expand in Terai and Uttaranchal regions. This brought it in conflict with East India Company, the paramount power of the subcontinent. The war started in November 1814, when the Company launched four columns into Nepal. Major-General David Ochterlony's column from Ludhiana and Major-General Robert Rollo Gillespie's contingent from Saharanpur attempted to encircle the Gurkha Army. Meanwhile Marley and John Wood's columns from Patna and Gorakhpur advanced toward the Gurkha capital Kathmandu. Marley and Wood's column were unsuccessful and had to turn back. Between November 1814 and January 1815, Wood's contingent was held up at Gorakhpur because of the lack of transport, supplies, and fear of the Gurkhas. Gillespie was ordered to occupy Dehra Dun and besiege Jaithak. On October 31, 1814, Gillespie died during the assault on the fort of Nalapani, situated five miles from Dehra and garrisoned by 600 soldiers under Balabhadra Singh. The company's infantry, operating in line formation and practicing volley firing, did not prove to be suitable in hilly terrain covered with forest. Also, the **sepoys** of the Bengal Army had no training in mountain warfare.

The Gurkha defense system was based on a series of hill forts and stockades. From the stockades constructed of wood and stones amidst the slopes of hills, the Gurkhas, under Amar Singh Thapa and Ranjor Singh Thapa, obstructed the passage of company soldiers. Most of the forts were constructed on the spurs of the hills, which could be reached only through narrow, winding, steep rocky paths. Artillery support for blasting the stockades and the hill forts was not easily available. In the roadless Himalayan terrain, the British found it almost impossible to bring the heavy guns drawn by bullocks and elephants into action. Streams, jungles, and mountains obstructed the deployment of even gallopers' guns drawn by horses. Because of the lack of flat plains, there was no room for the company's cavalry to deploy and maneuver. So the company recruited 4,000 irregular Rohilla infantry armed with matchlocks from Rohilkhand. The British used the Rohilla light infantry as skirmishers and sharpshooters. They were encouraged to use their initiative to take aimed shots at the enemy soldiers.

The mobilization of enormous military and financial assets by the company enabled it to gain some success. By February 1815, the company had deployed 19,000 British troops and 30,000 sepoys. For supplying the troops in the hill, 75,000 porters were employed for seven months. Between October 1814 and April 30, 1815, the commissariat paid 392,410 rupees as wages to the coolies. Ochterlony's occupation of the Malaun hill fort in May 1815, and his victory at Makwanpur in February 1816, forced the Kathmandu government to sue for peace. The company's battle casualties were 3,000 and another 2,000 were lost as a result of sickness and desertion. At the conclusion of the war the company and the Gurkha Kingdom signed the Treaty of Saguli. Under the terms of the treaty, the Gurkha Kingdom retained its autonomy in internal administration; however, the Company acquired the right to conduct Nepal's foreign policy. Moreover, the company annexed Kumaun, Garhwal, Terai, and Dooars regions from the Gurkha Kingdom. In the course of the war, the British officers were impressed by the Gurkha soldiers' ability to take advantage of the terrain to ambush the company's infantry marching in rigid formation. Hence, after 1816 the Company raised several Gurkha infantry battalions from the Magars and Gurung tribes of central Nepal.

FURTHER READING: Great Britain, Ministry of Defence. *Nepal and the Gurkhas.* London: HMSO, 1965; Tuker, Francis Ivan Simms. *Gorkha: The Story of the Gurkhas of Nepal.* London: Constable, 1957.

KAUSHIK ROY

## Anglo-Russian Convention (1907)

An agreement signed by Great Britain and Russia on August 31, 1907, which effectively ended the nineteenth-century **Great Game** and the ceaseless territorial and diplomatic squabbles associated with it. By its terms, both Britain and Russia agreed to relinquish any hopes of invading or conquering Afghanistan; however, Britain was allowed some control over political matters within Afghanistan. Persia was placed under a similar situation, with both Russian and British spheres of influence. Tibet was relinquished to Chinese control, but Britain was allowed to continue trade with the Tibetans and Russian Buddhists were allowed continued access to the Dalai Lhama.

The agreement additionally solidified the creation of a **Triple Entente** among France, Great Britain, and Russia to counter the earlier creation of the **Triple Alliance,** consisting of Austria-Hungary, Germany, and Italy. The tsarist state was greatly weakened in the years immediately before the Anglo-Russian agreement. Russia first suffered a humiliating and crushing defeat to the Japanese in the **Russo-Japanese War** of 1904–1905. This military disaster led to domestic political upheaval. The 1905 revolution happened amidst the background of widespread discontent among workers, peasants, and minority nationalities in Russia and laid bare persistent problems in the Russian Empire of political instability and widely varying degrees of support for and opposition to the tsarist government. This would eventually lead to the overthrow of the tsarist regime and its eventual replacement by the Bolshevik Communist leadership in the revolution of 1917. For Britain, the 1907 agreement happened as the British Empire was reaching the pinnacle of its influence, only to face its ultimate test in World War I. *See also* Afghan Wars; British Empire; Russian Empire.

FURTHER READING: Churchill, Rogers Platt. *The Anglo-Russian Convention of 1907.* Cedar Rapids, IA: The Torch Press, 1939; Kazemzadeh, Firuz. *Russia and Britain in Persia, 1864–1914.* New Haven, CT: Yale University Press, 1968.

SCOTT C. BAILEY

## Angola

A southwest African country subject to Portuguese penetration in the sixteeneth century. Together with the Imbangala, an indigenous people of the interior, the Portuguese used Angola principally as a source of slaves for transport to Brazil. Only the intensified colonization of the continent during the **Scramble for Africa** motivated Portugal to move inland with a settler policy crafted to keep Angola from other European powers. Although Lisbon aspired to an empire in southern Africa stretching from Angola on the Atlantic Coast to Mozambique on the Indian Ocean, the British establishment of Bechuanaland in 1885 and the subsequent extension of the charter of the British South Africa Company to territory north of the Zambezi River in 1889 prevented this. *See also* Slave Trade.

FURTHER READING: Clarence-Smith, W.G. *The Third Portuguese Empire, 1825–1975.* Manchester: Manchester University Press, 1985.

CARL CAVANAGH HODGE

## Annam

A Viet kingdom on the east coast of Indochina, Annam was given its name, "the pacified south," in the seventh century by the Tang Chinese. Louis XVI of France secured a treaty with the Annamite Emperor Gia Long in 1787, marking the beginning of gathering French ambition in Indochina. In the mid-nineteenth century, concern over the British presence in Hong Kong and Singapore and American influence in Japan moved French governments to view Annam as the base for an expanded role in Asia. In three French Indochina Wars—1858–63, 1873–74, 1881–85—Annam, along with Laos, Cambodia, Tonkin, and Cochin China, was ultimately made a French protectorate by the Treaty of Tientsin, although the region was not fully pacified until the 1890s. *See also* French Empire.

FURTHER READING: Chapius, Oscar. *The Last Emperors of Vietnam: From Tu Duc to Bao Dai.* Westport, CT: Greenwood Press, 2000.

CARL CAVANAGH HODGE

### Annexation Crisis (1908–1909)

A diplomatic crisis occasioned by Austria-Hungary's formal annexation of the Turkish provinces of Bosnia and Herzogovina that heightened Great Power tensions in the decade before the outbreak of World War I. The Congress of Berlin in 1878 authorized Austria-Hungary to occupy and administer **Bosnia-Herzegovina,** but officially the territory remained part of the **Ottoman Empire.** Supervised by a department within the common ministry of finance in Vienna, the administration was run by Austro-Hungarian civil servants and officers. Because of its special legal status, Bosnia-Herzegovina had neither a parliament nor a constitution.

A reinvigorated Ottoman Empire might have challenged Austria-Hungary's control over Bosnia-Herzegovina, but in July 1908, the **Young Turks** revolution led to a constitution and political reforms of the Ottoman polity. The Habsburg monarchy's foreign minister, Aloys Lexa von **Aehrenthal**, decided to annex Bosnia-Herzegovina, and, to avoid Russian resistance to the move, he met the Tsar's foreign minister Aleksandr **Izvolsky** in September 1908 in Moravia. As a price, Isvolsky received Aehrenthal's pledge of support for Russia's attempt to open the Straits to Russian warships. Izwolsky nevertheless seemed to be surprised when Aehrenthal acted swiftly and had the annexation announced October7, 1908. That Ferdinand I, Bulgaria's ruler, cut the legal ties to the Ottoman Empire and declared himself Tsar of Bulgaria, led to further Russian misgivings over renewed flux in the Balkans. Meanwhile, fierce protests against the unilateral annexation in the Ottoman Empire and in Serbia further aggravated the situation. The boycott of Austro-Hungarian goods in the Ottoman Empire proved to be less harmful to the Habsburg monarchy than Russian support for Serbia's claims that Austria-Hungary should leave Bosnia-Herzegovina with its South Slavic population.

Assisted by her allies Britain and France, Russia backed Serbia's propaganda campaign and saber rattling. Because Germany stood firmly by Austria-Hungary and threatened to intervene in case of an armed clash between Russia and the Habsburg monarchy, the tsar's government was forced to back down. Without Russian support, Serbia was forced to give in to an Austro-Hungarian ultimatum in March 1909. The Ottoman Porte was mollified by financial compensations from Austria-Hungary and the Habsburg monarchy's evacuation of its troops from the Sanjak of Novipazar. As result, Aehrenthal got away with the risky unilateralist annexation, but only at the price of increased diplomatic isolation of his government. Deeply felt Russian and Serbian hostility toward Austria-Hungary became an important feature of European politics yet to be reckoned with. To Britain and France, the Habsburg monarchy seemed to be completely dependent on Germany, a perception shared by observers in Austria-Hungary and Berlin. Finally, the annexation did little to stabilize Habsburg control over Bosnia-Herzegovina, although it made it possible to proclaim a constitutional statute and to establish a parliament in Sarajevo, while the diplomatic tensions over it prefigured the fatal crisis of August 1914. *See also* Balkan Crisis; Eastern Question; Pan-Slavism; Russian Empire.

FURTHER READING: Bridge, F. R. *From Sadowa to Sarajevo: The Foreign Policy of Austria-Hungary 1866–1914*. London: Routledge & Kegan Paul, 1972; Herrmann, David G. *The Arming of Europe and the Making of the First World War*. Princeton, NJ: Princeton University Press, 1997; Lieven, D.C.B. *Russia and the Origins of the First World War*. New York: St. Martin's, 1983.

GUENTHER KRONENBITTER

## Antarctica

The continent of Antarctica at the southern pole of the earth is last part of the globe to be conquered by humans. The earliest recorded sighting of the continent was made in 1820, as both British naval officers Edward Bransfield and William Smith, as well as American whaler Nathaniel Palmer reported spotting the continent that year. The Russian navigator Fabian von Bellingshausen circumnavigated Antarctica in an expedition from 1819 to 1821, and an American seal hunter became the first to set his feet on the main land in 1821. Antarctica was recognized as a continent in 1840, and several American, German, British, and French expeditions visited in the latter half of the nineteenth century.

Venturing deep into the interior of the continent demanded not only physical strength and endurance, but also know-how in logistics and practical solutions. Ernest Shackleton managed to get within 156 km of the South Pole in an expedition from 1907–1909, when he had to return because he had run out of supplies. In 1910, a race to be the first to reach the South Pole commenced between British naval officer Robert F. Scott and Norwegian explorer, Roald **Amundsen.** Scott had led previous expeditions into the Antarctica, and Roald Amundsen had led many expeditions in the Arctic. Scott, relying on horses and primitive snowmobiles, lost to the better prepared Amundsen, who used dog sledges and skis. Amundsen reached the South Pole on December 14, 1911, and Scott on January 18. Scott and his crew succumbed to the cold and exhaustion from pulling their sledges, while Amundsen returned safely.

As in the Arctic, the hunt for sea mammals such as seal and whale for the purpose of cooking their blubber into **oil** was the main economic motive behind expansion into the Antarctica. Better harpoons and bigger ships had expanded the range of the whalers from around 1860. The populations of Arctic sea mammals were being exhausted, but improved techniques also brought the Antarctica within range and navigators reported large concentrations of these creatures there. In the 1820s and 1830s, South Orkney, South Shetland, Falkland Islands, South Sandwich Islands and South Georgia were annexed by Great Britain. These became important base areas for Antarctic whaling and also a bridgehead for further British land claims on Antarctica proper.

Norway started to fear that British expansion would block its own whaling operations in the area, and it is in this light the previously mentioned race must be seen, as discoveries were means for legitimating land claims. Yet expeditions were undoubtedly also motivated out of adventurism, scientific fervor, and desire for personal glory. Despite the introduction of factory ships, whaling still required land bases not too far from the hunting grounds. Without the presence of any indigenous peoples, it would seem that imperial competition in the Antarctic was a harmless version of a phenomena that killed and enslaved millions elsewhere on the globe.

FURTHER READING: Headland, Robert. *Chronological List of Antarctic Expeditions and Related Historical Events.* Cambridge: Cambridge University Press, 1989; Riste, Olav. *Norway's Foreign Relations – A History.* Oslo: Universitetsforlaget, 2001, pp. 69–137; *Web Site:* Southpole.com < http://www.south-pole.com/>.

FRODE LINDGJERDET

## Anti-Corn Law League

A pressure group that agitated for the repeal of the tariffs protecting expensive British-grown grain from foreign competition. The growing popularity of laissez-faire economic principles opposed to government intervention in the marketplace, undermined the policy of protecting the higher price of domestically grown grain against cheaper imported grain.

In 1838, Richard **Cobden** helped organize the Anti-Corn Law League as a local Manchester society and, in 1839, as a national society. It had only one formal demand—the repeal of the Corn Laws—but in practice challenged the political position of the landlord elite that collected rents from wheat farmers. In addition, some league supporters believed that **free trade** would enhance the prospects for peace among the European powers, and others expected that it would enable manufacturers to pay their workers lower wages because repealing tariffs would lower the cost of living. At the time, bread was a major part of a working-class diet and not simply a symbol of food in general. With the help of John Bright's oratory, the league conducted a propaganda campaign against the "bread tax." A small loaf of bread—all that workers could afford under a system of tariffs—was contrasted with the big loaf that would feed workers and their families under a system of free trade.

The League regarded the **Conservative Party,** dominated by landlords, as its enemy. Beginning in 1841, it intervened in constituency elections to fight protectionist candidates. Ironically, it was the Conservative prime minister, Sir Robert **Peel,** who was responsible for the repeal of the Corn Laws in 1846. The immediate cause was the emergency created by the potato famine in Ireland. Repeal symbolized the triumph of free trade principles, the recognition that Britain could not feed itself, and the shrinking role of agriculture in a predominantly manufacturing economy. It was not until 1903 that a major politician, Joseph **Chamberlain,** dared propose new food taxes. Repeal disrupted the British party system. Peel split his largely agricultural party by repealing the Corn Laws. Some of his Peelite followers, notably William **Gladstone,** eventually joined the rival **Liberal Party.** Although the repeal of the Corn Laws owed more to Peel than to the Anti-Corn Law League, later pressure groups often modeled themselves on the league, its organizational structure and strategies. *See also* Imperial Preference; Liberal Imperialists.

FURTHER READING: McCord, Norman. *The Anti-Corn Law League: 1838–1846.* London: George Allen and Unwin, 1958.

DAVID M. FAHEY

## Antietam, Battle of (1862)

The Battle of Antietam was the bloodiest single day of fighting during the **American Civil War.** Having removed the northern threat to Richmond and defeated a Union army at the Second Battle of Bull Run, Robert E. Lee marched his Confederate Army of Northern Virginia northward into Maryland. Lee crossed the Potomac River on September 4, 1862, threatening Washington and forcing President Lincoln to recall George McClellan to command the Union Army of the Potomac.

The two armies met east of the small town of Sharpsburg along the banks of Antietam Creek, Lee's army with its back to the Potomac. On the morning of September 17, McClellan launched a vicious attack against Lee's left. The battle gradually shifted south as McClellan tried to breach Lee's center. In the afternoon, McClellan attacked the rebel right wing at Burnside's Bridge. Several times during the day Lee appeared to be on the verge of cracking. Only the timely arrival of A. P. Hill's division from Harper's Ferry enabled Lee to hold his lines.

That night, McClellan rejected calls from his subordinates for a renewed assault the next day. Instead, he allowed the defeated Lee to retreat uncontested across the Potomac to the safety of Virginia, a decision that led to McClellan's removal from command. In spite of the rebel escape, Lincoln used the Union victory to issue his Emancipation Proclamation.

FURTHER READING: Sears, Stephen W. *Landscape Turned Red: The Battle of Antietam.* Boston: Houghton Mifflin, 1983.

THOMAS D. VEVE

## Arctic

In strict geographic terms, the island, ice shelves and Eurasian and North American land mass north of the Polar Circle. Under the influence of strong national sentiments in the nineteenth century, the area became subject to daring expeditions and intense exploitation of natural resources. In 1596, the Spitzbergen Archipelago (Svalbard) had been discovered by the Dutch navigator Wilhelm Barents. This set off an intensive hunt of seals and whales for their blubber, which was cooked into oil, providing the most important liquid fuel and lubricants in mechanical devices in an age before drilling for fossil fuels. Basque, English, Norwegian-Danish, American, French and Dutch soon exploited sea mammals from Novaja Semlja in the East, to Newfoundland in the West. When onboard refinement techniques were developed, shore facilities in Svalbard were abandoned. Ashore, Russian hunters took over, but Norwegians replaced these around 1850. By the 1890s, whale, seal, and polar bear had become scarce and many hunters turned their eyes to the Antarctic.

During the nineteenth century, nationalist and imperialist political forces among the European powers meant that scientific expeditions and economic activity increasingly took the form of territorial quest. **Norway** became independent from **Sweden** in 1905 and was enflamed by nationalist sentiment. Experienced in navigating the icy water and possessing the closest all year ice-free ports, the Norwegians brought certain advantages to the competition. Frenetic activity from Norwegian explorers was followed by several land claims, some more successful than others. Around 1830, Denmark had consolidated its rule over Greenland, which was acquired by the Danish Crown through dynastic means in 1380.

A recurring theme in Arctic exploration was the search for new sea lanes. Barents had sought a passage northeast to India. Swedish discoverer, A. E. Nordenskiöld finally succeeded in navigating around the Asian landmass to the North in 1878–1879. The age of discoveries saw similar attempts to find a Northwest Passage, some of the first made by John Cabot in 1497–1498. In 1850, Robert McLure managed to pass through, but had to make the last 300 kilometers with dog sledge over the frozen Artic Sea. In 1903–1906, Norwegian explorer Roald **Amundsen** managed to sail its whole length. Vitus Bering, a Danish navigator in Russian service, discovered Alaska in 1728, and Russia established a colony on Kodiak Island in 1748. Alaska was subsequently bought by the United States and became a territory in 1912 and the 49th state in 1959. Parts of the Canadian North Western Territories were charted by Henry Hudson (1550–1611), and the **Hudson's Bay Company** was given extensive privileges there by the British in 1670. It gained monopoly on trade in the whole area after merging with the North-Western Company in 1821. The Dominion of **Canada** bought the Territory from the Company in 1868–1870, of which the Yukon became a separate Territory in 1898. Toward the end of the nineteenth century, rich mineral deposits were found in Arctic America that also set off the 1897–1898 Klondike gold rush.

The Arctic region was home to a number of nomadic hunter-gatherers and reindeer herders. As modern states consolidated their sovereignty and administration across the Arctic during the nineteenth century, the Samí, Siberian peoples, Native Americans, and Inuit experienced the end of traditional religion, language, culture, and ways of life. *See also* Russian Empire; United States.

FURTHER READING: Kenney, Gerard I. *Ships of Wood and Men of Iron: A Norwegian-Canadian Saga of Exploration in the High Arctic*. Regina: Canadian Plains Research Center, 2004; Riste, Olav. *Norway's Foreign Relations*. Oslo: Universitetsforlaget, 2001; Warrick, Karen Clemens. *The Perilous Search for the Fabled Northwest Passage in American History*. Berkeley Heights, NJ: Enslow, 2004.

FRODE LINDGJERDET

## Argentina

In 1800, Argentina was part of the recently created Viceroyalty of the Río de la Plata. Buenos Aires served as the capital of this administrative section of Spanish America that the Crown split off from Viceroyalty of Lima. Its bureaucracy supervised the mining regions of Upper Peru (Bolivia), **Paraguay,** and the *Banda Oriental* (**Uruguay**). The expansion of ranching led to the rapid growth of Buenos Aires and its merchant elite in the decades leading up to 1800. Exports generated profits, but the local merchants increasingly resented commercial regulations that limited their ability to trade freely with ships from countries other than Spain. Mariano Moreno, who emerged as a spokesperson for the commercial agents and ranchers of Buenos Aires, expressed these sentiments in his petition of 1810, *Representación de los hacendados y labradores.*

Events had put the viceroyalty's ties to Spain under strain. In 1806, an invasion force under the leadership of Sir Home Riggs Popham, invaded Argentina after successfully claiming South Africa, the South Georgian Islands, and the Falkland Islands for Great Britain. The Spanish viceroy and his supporters abandoned Buenos Aires and left the town largely defenseless. Initially, the British expeditionary force was allowed to camp in the city. Civic leaders, however, soon recruited a militia and organized a surprise attack against the British forces, which retreated from Buenos Aires to their ships. Reinforcements arrived and a second battle for Buenos Aires took place in 1807. The Argentine militia, reinforced by troops from Paraguay and the interior, defeated the British a second time. This victory gave the citizens of Buenos Aires a sense of autonomy that brought Argentina's colonial relationship with Spain into question.

Napoleon's invasion of Spain forced the issue more directly. The abdication of King Charles IV and the nomination of Joseph Bonaparte as Spain's puppet king led city and town councils throughout Spanish America to take up the issue of independence. At first, the citizens of Buenos Aires declared their loyalty to Spain. But in 1810, with French forces still occupying most of Iberia, the city council in Buenos Aires declared itself as the capital of the newly independent United Provinces of the Río de la Plata. Buenos Aires rapidly lost its authority over the interior regions of the viceroyalty. Paraguay defeated an invasion from Buenos Aires in 1811 and declared its own independence. Uruguay initially became a stronghold for Loyalists, but then briefly gained its own independence thanks to a local militia under the command of José Gervasio **Artigas** in 1812. Spanish troops occupied Upper Peru and threatened an invasion of Argentina in 1814.

Political conflicts and military failures plagued Argentina until the government in Buenos Aires gave José de **San Martín** command of its armies. His invasion of Chile in 1817, followed by his invasion of Peru in 1821, guaranteed Argentina's independence. The United Provinces soon collapsed and Argentina splintered into a federation of provinces under the rule of local military strongmen, or *caudillos*. After 1825 the province of Buenos Aires emerged as the leading component of this federation thanks to the policies of dictator Juan Manuel de **Rosas.** Rosas used diplomacy, threats, and occasionally military force to monopolize foreign trade in Argentina for the merchants and ranchers of his province. This led to conflict not only with other caudillos but with Great Britain and France who sent naval detachments to the area during the 1830s and the 1840s in an effort to keep trade with the interior provinces open.

Rosas fell from power in 1852. The formation of the Argentine Confederation, which grew much more powerful and centralized after 1860, coincided with Argentina's export-led development. First wool, then beef, and finally grains helped Argentina's merchants and landowners form into a rich and powerful elite. This era was also one of informal empire, as a result of the dominance of British capital and companies in the funding and expansion of Argentina's economic infrastructure. The close linkages that developed between Argentina's rural industries and the British market helped fund what many viewed as Argentina's "Golden Age," from 1880 to 1910. *See also* ABC Powers; British Empire; Peninsular War; Spanish-American War; Spanish Empire.

FURTHER READING: Gravil, Roger. *The Anglo-Argentine Connection, 1900–1939.* Boulder: Westview Press, 1985; Lynch, John. *Argentine Dictator: Juan Manuel de Rosas.* New York: Oxford University Press, 1981; Lynch, John. *The Spanish American Revolutions 1808–1826.* New York: W. W. Norton, 1986; Sábato, Hilda. *Agrarian Capitalism and the World Market: Buenos Aires in the Pastoral Age, 1840–1890.* Albuquerque: University of New Mexico Press, 1990.

DANIEL K. LEWIS

## Armed Neutrality, League of

An essentially anti-British and Russian-instigated alliance of Russia, Denmark, Sweden, and, at one point, Prussia, designed to protect the members' shipping against British search and seizure. The league was initially formed during the American War of Independence to protect neutral shipping against the predations of the Royal Navy. In 1801, Britain went to war with a resurrected league during the Napoleonic Wars, and on April 2 of that year it attacked Copenhagen, successfully destroying the Danish fleet. The British victory at Copenhagen led the Danes to accept an armistice. The assassination of Tsar Paul of Russia, whose anti-British animus had been behind the league, led to an Anglo-Russian peace being signed in July 1801, with the other league powers following by the end of the year. The league did little to secure neutral rights, as was demonstrated a decade later by the **Anglo-American War** of 1812, fought over many similar issues. *See also* Napoleonic Wars; Royal Navy.

FURTHER READING: Feldbæk, Ole. *Denmark and the Armed Neutrality, 1800–1801.* Copenhagen: Akademisk Forlag, 1980.

MARK F. PROUDMAN

## Armenia

A Caucasian territory on the northeastern border of modern Turkey that in the sixteenth century was divided between the Ottoman Empire and Safavid Persia. In 1828, the Persians ceded the northern part of Armenia to Russia. In the late nineteenth century nationalist movements emerged in both Ottoman and Russian Armenia. The Russian imperial regime was less overbearing than that of the Ottoman Turks, who, in 1894–96 and again during World War I, waged a campaign of genocide against the Armenians in their half of the territory. The Treaty of **San Stefano** temporarily placed Armenia under Russian protection, but the Congress of **Berlin** subsequently reversed the decision. *See also* Armenian Massacres; Ottoman Empire; Russian Empire.

FURTHER READING: Adshead, S.A.M. *Central Asia in World History.* New York: St. Martin's, 1994.

CARL CAVANAGH HODGE

## Armenian Massacres (1894–1896)

The first wave of genocidal massacres of Armenians by the Ottoman Turks. At the end of the nineteenth century, Armenians were the largest Christian minority in the Anatolian region of the **Ottoman Empire.** In the 1890s, Sultan Abdul Hamid II ordered a series of massacres that resulted in the rapes and brutal deaths of about 200,000 Armenians. The United States responded with humanitarian relief that involved the combined efforts of individuals like Clara Barton, Julia Ward Howe, and John D. Rockefeller and organizations like the Red Cross. The Europeans powers also condemned the atrocities, setting up an investigatory commission and appealing for reforms, but the Ottoman Empire was never really held accountable. Consequently, the Hamidian massacres delivered the unfortunate message that large-scale murder could be committed with impunity, thus paving the way for the Armenian Genocide of 1915. *See also* Gladstone, W. E.; Appendix: Words and Deeds, Document No.11.

FURTHER READING: Balakian, Peter. *The Burning Tigris: The Armenian Genocide and America's Response.* New York: Harper Collins Publishers, 2003; Morgenthau, Henry. *Ambassador Morganthau's Story.* Preface by Robert Jay Lifton, introduction by Roger Smith, afterword by Henry Morganthau III. Edited by P. Balakian. Detroit: Wayne State University Press, 2003.

LEE A. FARROW

## Arrah, Siege of (1857)

An incident of the **Indian Mutiny.** The town of Arrah was situated 25 miles west of Dinapur in Bihar. On July 26, 1857, about 18 Europeans and 50 loyal Sikhs took refuge in the fort of Arrah. The fort was originally a billiard room that was bricked for defense. The next day, the insurgents—mostly armed retainers and peasants—led by a zamindar named Kunwar Singh laid siege to the fort. Because the rebels lacked artillery, they could not demolish the fort. From the cover of the walls and the trees, the rebels opened musketry fire against the fort. On July 29, Kunwar's men in the suburbs of Arrah ambushed a relieving force of 450 men that had marched from Dinapur. On August 2, another relieving force under Major Vincent Eyre defeated Kunwar's levies at the Battle of Gujrajganj. Kunwar retreated to Jagadishpur and Arrah was relieved next day. *See also* British Empire.

FURTHER READING: James, Lawrence. *Raj: The Making and Unmaking of British India.* New York: St. Martin's Griffin, 1997.

KAUSHIK ROY

## Arrow War (1856–1860)

Also known at the Second **Opium War,** the Arrow War was a conflict of Britain and France against China. Although China was forced to concede many of its territorial and sovereignty rights in the years following the First Opium War, the Western imperial powers also had to face rising antiforeign sentiment, as many Chinese believed that uncultured barbarians should be excluded from the Middle Kingdom.

On October 8, 1856, in this tense atmosphere in Guangzhou, Chinese policemen boarded the *Arrow,* a Chinese ship registered in Hong Kong under a British flag, and arrested 12 crewmen accused of smuggling and piracy. The British flag was reportedly torn during the struggle. The incident was immediately seized upon by Harry Parkes (1828–1885), the British consul in Guangzhou who wanted to legalize the opium and expand trade in China yet was frustrated by Cantonese opposition. Parkes demanded that the Qing Government release the *Arrow*'s crew and apologize for the insult to the British flag. When Ye Mingchen (1807–1859), the Viceroy of Liangguang, released the Chinese crewmen but refused to apologize, Parkes had a fleet bombard Guangzhou. The British parliament sent an expedition under James

Bruce (1811–1863), the Earl of **Elgin,** to defend its honor. Meanwhile, France also dispatched its fleet under Baron Gros (1793–1870) to China. On the pretext of retaliating for the murder of a French missionary in the Guangxi Province. The Anglo-French force fought its way to Guangzhou and captured Ye Mingchen by the end of 1857. When local officials still did not produce the results the Western powers demanded, the joint fleet moved northwards along the Chinese coast and captured the Daku (Taku) fort outside Tianjin (Tientsin) in March 1858. In the meantime Russia and the United States sent representatives to Beijing for diplomatic maneuvering.

The Qing government had no choice but to comply with the Anglo-French terms, which included the payment of indemnities, the residence of foreign diplomats in Beijing, the right of foreigners to travel in China's interior, the opening of the Yangtze River to foreign navigation, the permission for Christian missionaries to propagate their faith, the legalization of opium importation and the coolie trade, and the opening of 10 new ports to foreign trade and residence. As "neutral" mediators, the Russian and American diplomats secured similar privileges to those gained by Britain and France. In June 1858, the Chinese government reached separate Tianjin (**Tientsin)** treaties with the four Western powers.

A year later Elgin was dispatched to China to exchange the ratifications. He demanded exchanging the treaty in Beijing rather than in Shanghai as the Chinese wanted. Ignoring warnings he sailed north and ran into a blockade at Daku, where his convoy suffered many casualties and four British gunboats were sunk by the Chinese. In 1860, the British sent 10,500 troops and 41 warships, again under Elgin, along with 6,300 French soldiers and more than 60 French ships for the purpose of retaliation. The Chinese imperial army under the command of Mongol Prince Senggerinchin (1811–1865) was quickly defeated. The allied force entered Beijing and looted the Forbidden City and the Summer Palace in October 1860. Emperor Xianfeng fled to Chengde, and his younger brother, Prince Gong Qinwang, was appointed imperial commissioner in charge of negotiation. Nonetheless, when the chief British negotiator was seized while under a flag of truce and some of his people were executed by the Chinese, Elgin took personal revenge against the emperor by burning the Summer Palace, the royal retreat of Yuanmingyuan in northwest Beijing. Faced with the arrival of winter and short of ammunition, the Anglo-French force had to seek a quick settlement and withdraw. The Conventions of **Beijing** were promptly reached, ending a war of four years and resulting in further Chinese concessions. *See also* Boxer Insurrection.

FURTHER READING: Hurd, Douglas. *The Arrow War: An Anglo-Chinese Confusion, 1856–1860.* New York: Macmillan, 1968; Wong, J. Y. *Deadly Dreams: Opium, Imperialism, and the Arrow War in China.* New York: Cambridge University Press, 1998.

WENXIAN ZHANG

## Artigas, José Gervasio (1794–1850)

A rebel leader who emerged as the most successful military commander in Uruguay after 1810. Artigas was part of the landowning elite in a territory claimed by both Spanish and Portuguese colonial authorities. He gained experience in the *Blandegues,* a militia cavalry that countered Native American raids and smugglers.

He initially sided with the independence movement launched in Buenos Aires, but by 1811, he pushed Montevideo and Uruguay in a more radical direction.

Promising independence, democracy, and land distribution to the poor of all races, Artigas built a large popular base. His initial victories helped *caudillos,* local military leaders, gain control of neighboring provinces. Isolation and a large-scale invasion of Portuguese troops from Brazil in 1816 led to a series of defeats. Fleeing north, he continued to fight as his troops dwindled in number. A final defeat at the Battle of Avalos forced him into exile in Paraguay.

FURTHER READING: Steet, John. *Artigas and the Emancipation of Uruguay.* Cambridge: Cambridge University Press, 1959.

DANIEL K. LEWIS

## Ashanti Wars

A series of four nineteenth-century Anglo-Ashanti conflicts in West Africa. The Ashanti essentially won the first two wars, the British the last two.

In 1821, the West African coastal forts, originally established for slaving, were taken by the British government from the disbanded Royal African Company, and for the next half-century were used against the slave trade and to support mercantile interests in the region. Although the explorer Thomas Bowditch had signed a treaty of cooperation on behalf of the African Company with the Ashanti in 1818, in 1823 the Ashanti moved against Cape Coast Castle in retaliation for British protection of their enemies, the Fante. In January 1824, a small forward party of British troops and African troops in British service was completely overwhelmed by the Ashanti. Its leader, the Governor of Cape Coast Castle, Lieutenant Colonel Sir Charles Macarthy, was killed and his head taken as a trophy by the victorious Ashanti.

This episode led the government to let a committee of merchants take control of Cape Coast Castle. One of their employees, Captain George McLean, negotiated an agreement with the Ashanti whereby the regions near the coast fell under British protection and the British recognized Ashanti rights in the interior. What has been called the McLean system then broke down over British efforts to suppress the slave trade. An unauthorized expedition into the interior at the initiative of the local governor in 1863–1864 led to massive loss of life from disease. The disaster led a committee of the House of Commons to suggest that the Gold Coast be abandoned. The suggestion, however, was never acted on.

In 1873, disputes over slavery and fugitives aggravated by the British acquisition of additional territory in the region from the Dutch led to an Ashanti invasion of British-protected territory. This time an expedition was sent from England under the command of Sir Garnet **Wolseley,** "the very model of a modern major general," who had the wisdom to fight his campaign during the dry and hence healthier season. Wolseley defeated the Ashanti army and burned Kumasi to the ground. A treaty in 1874 extracted an indemnity.

Failure to pay the indemnity of 1874 and the ever-recurring issue of slavery led to a renewed British expedition against Kumasi in 1895–1896, this time rapidly successful. A subsequent unsuccessful rebellion by a number of Ashanti chiefs in 1900 led to the 1901 declaration of a British protectorate over the territory of the Ashanti. *See also* Africa, Scramble for; Slavery.

FURTHER READING: Baden-Powell, R.S.S. *The Downfall of Prempeh.* London: Methuen, 1896; Kochanski, Halik. *Sir Garnet Wolseley: A Victorian Hero.* London: Hambledon, 1999; Lloyd, Alan. *The Drums of Kumasi: The Story of the Ashanti Wars.* London: Longmans, 1964.

MARK F. PROUDMAN

## Aspern-Essling, Battle of (1809)

The first defeat of a Napoleonic army, inflicted by the Austrian army under Archduke Charles near Vienna on May 21 and 22, 1809. Having defeated the Austrians in Bavaria, Napoleon marched down the Danube to capture Vienna on May 12. A failed attempt to seize the northern end of the destroyed Danube bridge at Schwarze Lackenau on the next day prompted Napoleon to order the construction of an improvised bridge into the Lobau, a large island downstream of Vienna, and then across a narrow river arm to the north riverbank, where French forces were steadily reinforced on May 20.

The Austrians had marched through Bohemia to the Marchfeld plain on the north side of the river and prepared to advance that afternoon, thinking that the French would again try to reach the old bridgehead. Consequently, their attack was off-balance: three Korps marched from the west and just one Korps in two columns from the east, with cavalry screening the center. About 1 P.M. Napoleon began the battle with 24,000 men against 99,000 Austrians. The breaking of the fragile bridge by boats and trees thrown into the river by Austrian engineers upstream hampered French reinforcements from crossing throughout the battle. That afternoon saw a series of unsuccessful Austrian assaults on Aspern village, which was held by Marshal Masséna anchoring the French left flank; in the center, French cavalry made several attempts to split the Austrian army by charging the weak screen. It was 9 P.M. before the first Austrian assaults were made on Essling, defended by Marshal Lannes and anchoring the French right, but Feldmarschalleutnant Rosenberg's IV Korps made little progress.

During the night, French forces were increased to 71,000. In the early morning, Napoleon prepared to attempt to break the Austrian center, now reinforced by II Korps. Both Aspern and Essling were fiercely contested until the French secured both by 7 A.M. At that point Lannes' 2 Corps began its advance against the Austrian center but was soon bogged down under intense Austrian artillery fire. Attempts by French cavalry to break through were beaten off by steady Austrian infantry masses (closed-up columns). French artillery briefly smashed a hole in the Austrian line, as Infantry Regiment 15's masses broke up, but Archduke Charles rode forward to restore order, while the Reserve Grenadiers plugged the gap. After two hours, Lannes lost momentum, while another breach in the bridge prevented Marshal Davout's 3 Corps from crossing. By noon, the French were back behind the Aspern-Essling Road.

A series of Austrian assaults on Aspern set the whole village alight. Despite the intervention of French Guard infantry, the village was finally taken by 1 P.M. Archduke Charles then turned his attention to Essling and threw in four Grenadier battalions to help Rosenberg's Korps. Two hours later, Essling, too, except for its stone granary, had been secured, while in the center, a massive Austrian artillery barrage with 200 guns blasted Napoleon's army. Nevertheless, General Boudet led some Young Guard battalions into Essling to retake the village and thereby threaten the Austrian right wing. By 4 P.M., both sides fell back some distance, having sustained heavy casualties, and the battle was reduced to artillery exchanges. The French retreated to their base in the Löbau. The Austrians had suffered about 20,000 casualties compared with 23,000 French. Napoleon would try again at the Battle of **Wagram** six weeks later. *See also* Napoleonic Wars.

FURTHER READING: Arnold, J. *Napoleon Conquers Austria*. Westport, CT: Praeger, 1995; Castle, I. *Aspern & Wagram 1809*. Oxford: Osprey, 1996; Wöber, F. *Schlacht bei Aspern 1809*. Vienna: Wöber, 1992.

DAVID HOLLINS

## Asquith, Herbert Henry, Earl of Oxford and Asquith (1852–1928)

British prime minister from 1908 to 1916. Asquith entered politics on the radical wing of the **Liberal Party,** but in 1914 it was he who took the decision to lead Britain into World War I.

Asquith won a scholarship to Balliol College, Oxford, in 1870, went on to a career at the bar, and came to some prominence as a strongly Liberal voice in the columns of the *Spectator* and the *Economist*. Asquith was first elected to the Commons as a Gladstonian Liberal and supporter of Irish **Home Rule** in 1886, and his intellect and his forensic debating skills assured his rapid rise to prominence. He became Home Secretary in William **Gladstone's** fourth government of 1892.

Asquith was one of the most prominent of the so-called Liberal imperialists of the 1890s. Along with R. B. **Haldane** and Sir Edward **Grey,** he supported an assertive British foreign policy, in part because he saw the traditional radical suspicion of the Empire as impractical. Asquith and the Liberal imperialists supported the Tory government during the **Boer War** of 1899–1902. Asquith did much, however, to make the case for **free trade** against the former radical Joseph **Chamberlain's** 1903 proposals for tariff reform on imperial lines.

After the resignation of A. J. **Balfour's** Tories in 1905, Asquith became Chancellor of the Exchequer in the government of Sir Henry **Campbell-Bannerman** and succeeded him as prime minister in 1908. It was under Asquith's premiership that David **Lloyd George's** "peoples' budgets," including old age pensions and higher direct taxation, were pushed through Parliament against the opposition of the House of Lords. Having won two elections in 1910, Asquith's government enacted the Parliament Act of 1911, limiting the powers of Lords, with the aid of a commitment from the new King George V to create peers if necessary to force the bill through the upper house.

Asquith's pre-1914 premiership was marked by extensive social conflict, including the suffragette movement, militant trade unionism, and Irish unrest. Nevertheless, his government's most significant decision was to take Britain to war in August 1914. The German violation of Belgian neutrality—guaranteed by the Treaty of **London** of 1839, the famous "scrap of paper"—was the legal *causus belli*; but it also caused great moral offence among the Liberal caucus, ensuring that Asquith was able to lead his otherwise antimilitarist cabinet and party to war with few defections. Asquith served as prime minister until 1916, when he was replaced by Lloyd George. *See also* July Crisis.

FURTHER READING: Jenkins, Roy. *Asquith.* London: Collins, 1964; Matthew, H.C.G. *The Liberal Imperialists.* Oxford: University Press, 1973; Spender, J. A. *The Life and Letters of Herbert Henry Asquith.* 2 vols. London: Hutchinson, 1932.

MARK F. PROUDMAN

## Assaye, Battle of (1803)

The fiercest encounter of the Second Anglo-Maratha War, 1803–1805. On September 24, 1803, the Maratha and the **East India Company**'s forces clashed at Assaye. Sir Arthur Wellesley, later the Duke of **Wellington**, deployed 6,900 cavalry and 4,000 infantry 34 guns. After crossing the stream Kaitna, Wellesley deployed his infantry into two lines. When the company's infantry was 400 yards from the village of Assaye, Maratha artillery and seven infantry battalions deployed at this village opened up and caused great carnage among Wellesley's troops. Wellesley launched a frontal bayonet charge and his infantry was able to capture Assaye. The Marathas withdrew to Ajanta Ghat leaving behind 2,000 dead and 98 guns. Casualties among the company's forces numbered 428 killed and 1,138 wounded. *See also* India.

FURTHER READING: Keay, John. *The Honourable Company: A History of the East India Company.* New York: Macmillan, 1994.

KAUSHIK ROY

## Association Internationale Africaine

The first of three organizations founded by King Léopold II of **Belgium** ostensibly to enhance international scientific and philanthropic cooperation in opening up the interior of Central Africa. The organization was founded at the Brussels Conference of 1876 and was intended to facilitate the sharing of newly acquired knowledge of the African interior among the colonizing powers. It failed to overcome either the fundamentally competitive relationship among the members or the corruption of Belgium's own imperial project in the Congo. It was supplemented in 1878 by the Comité d'Études du Haut-Congo and by the Association Internationale du Congo in 1881–85. The latter broke up over imperial rivalries and ultimately resulted in the **Berlin Conference** of 1884–85, which established rules and a semblance of order to the **Scramble for Africa.**

FURTHER READING: Hochschild, Adam. *King Leopold's Ghost: A Story of Greed, Terror and Heroism in Colonial Africa.* Boston: Houghton Mifflin, 1998.

CARL CAVANAGH HODGE

## Atatürk

*See* Kemal, Mustapha

## Atlanta Campaign (1864)

A late and critical campaign in the western theater of the American Civil War. The campaign for Atlanta began on Rocky Face Ridge at Dalton, Georgia, on May 5, 1864 and ended with the fall of Atlanta on September 1, 1864. General William Tecumseh Sherman commanded the Union Army, a total force of 110,000 soldiers and 250 guns. Defending Dalton was the Army of Tennessee commanded by General Joseph E. Johnston. Confederate total strength was 73,000 men.

In May, Sherman moved south from Chattanooga, Tennessee, to near Dalton, Georgia, where the Confederates had fortified the north and south sections of Rocky Face Ridge cut by Mill Creek at Buzzards' Roost Gap. Mill Creek had been damned to form a lake in the floor of the gap to protect Dalton. Blocked by the defenses Sherman moved through the mountains to flank Johnston. The outnumbered Confederates were flanked time after time. New battles of varying intensity were fought at Dug Gap, Resaca, Rome Crossroads, Cassville, New Hope Church, Pickett's Mill, Dallas, Kolb's Farm, Lost Mountain Line, Kennesaw Mountain, Smyrna Line, and Chattahoochee River Line, as Johnston was forced southward.

On July 17, Confederate President Jefferson Davis replaced Johnston with General John Bell Hood. His attacks at Peachtree Creek, Atlanta, Ezra Church, Utoy Creek, and Jonesboro failed to stop the Union advance. Atlanta's capture ensured President Abraham **Lincoln**'s reelection. General Sherman's use of the **railways** and his scorched earth policy were noted by Helmuth von **Moltke** and others. On November 15, after burning Atlanta, Sherman's army began a 300-mile "March to the Sea." A 50-mile wide swath across Georgia was deliberately ravaged to crush civilian morale. Savannah was captured on Christmas Day 1864.

FURTHER READING: Cox, Jacob D. *Sherman's Battle for Atlanta*. New York: Da Capo Press, [1882] 1994; Scaife, William R. *The Campaign for Atlanta*. Atlanta: William Scaife, 1993.

ANDREW JACKSON WASKEY

## Ausgleich (1867)

The diplomatic compromise that converted the Austrian Empire into the Dual Monarchy of **Austria-Hungary.** Traditionally, the Hungarian parts of the Habsburg monarchy enjoyed a high degree of autonomy, but in the aftermath of their defeat in the war of independence, 1849, Hungarians saw many of their privileges being revoked. Because of the weakened international position of the Habsburg monarchy since 1859, constitutional reform and a new legal status of Hungary had to be negotiated. In February 1867, the Ausgleich between the Hungarian opposition and the Austrian Emperor Francis Joseph I transformed the monarchy. According to this agreement, the kingdom of Hungary would have its own government and parliament in Budapest and accept Francis Joseph and his heirs as kings. The agreement was approved by the Hungarian diet and laid down in Law XII of 1867. The monarch as King of Hungary and Emperor of **Austria;** the common ministries of foreign affairs, war, and finance; and the regular meetings of delegations from both parliaments formed institutional bonds between Austria and Hungary. There was also a common Austro-Hungarian army and navy. The customs union and a sharing of accounts had to be revised every 10 years. *See also* Habsburg Empire.

FURTHER READING: Kann, Robert A. *A History of the Habsburg Empire, 1526–1918*. Berkeley: University of California Press, 1974; Macartney, C. A. *The Habsburg Empire, 1790–1918*. London: Weidenfeld and Nicolson, 1971.

GUENTHER KRONENBITTER

### Austerlitz, Battle of (1805)

The decisive battle of the War of the Third Coalition, and widely regarded as Napoleon's greatest tactical success. Austerlitz was fought on December 2, 1805 in Moravia, in the Austrian Empire, between approximately 70,000 French with 139 guns and 85,000 Allies (60,000 Russians and 25,000 Austrians) with 278 guns. Having surrounded and captured an Austrian army near Ulm six weeks earlier and taken Vienna, Napoleon proceeded northward to a position near Brunn. There he sought to draw the Allied army into a trap by feigning weakness; he first occupied, and then conceded, the high ground on the Pratzen plateau. With Tsar **Alexander I** of Russia and Emperor Francis II of Austria attached to his headquarters, the Russian general Mikhail Kutusov commanded a numerically superior Allied army, with which he occupied the heights unchallenged.

Ignorant that Napoleon had deliberately overextended his right flank and concealed some of his troops, Kutusov opened the battle with a flanking movement in an effort to cut French communications with Vienna. When a French corps under Marshal Davout arrived, Napoleon's position stabilized, prompting Kutusov to throw yet more troops into the fray. On the French left, Marshals Lannes and Murat enjoyed considerable success, driving back the Allied assaults before moving to the offensive themselves and pushing their opponents eastward. Seeing this development, and aware that the shift of Allied troops south across the Heights of Pratzen left that weakened, Napoleon threw in Marshal Soult's corps to seize the heights. The Russians counter-attacked with their Imperial Guard, against which the French sent their own elite formation, with the former unable to retake the lost ground. The French made still further gains, in the process dividing the Allied army in half and piercing their lines. Soult thereupon struck the Allied rear, already committed to the fighting against Davout. Finding themselves surrounded, the Allies fled across the nearby frozen lakes, where many drowned when the ice broke under French artillery fire.

Austerlitz constituted a crushing French victory. A third of the Allied army was rendered out of action, with 16,000 killed and wounded and perhaps 11,000 taken prisoner, plus a loss of 180 cannon. The French lost 1,300 killed and 7,000 wounded, plus 500 taken into captivity. Unable to prosecute the war further, the Austrians concluded a treaty of peace at **Pressburg** on December 23, thus confirming their withdrawal from the Third Coalition. The Russians, incapable of bearing the sole burden of the fighting, withdrew east into Poland. *See also* Napoleonic Wars; Ulm, Capitulation at.

FURTHER READING: Bowden, Scott. *Napoleon and Austerlitz*. Chicago: The Emperor's Press, 1997; Castle, Ian. *Austerlitz 1805: The Fate of Empires*. Oxford: Osprey, 2002; Castle, Ian. *Austerlitz and the Eagles of Europe*. London: Leo Cooper, 2005; Duffy, Christopher. *Austerlitz 1805*. London: Seeley Service, 1977; Goetz, Robert. *1805—Austerlitz: Napoleon and the Destruction of the Third Coalition*. London: Greenhill Books, 2005.

GREGORY FREMONT-BARNES

## Australia

Originally *Terra Australis Incognita,* or the unknown southern continent, Australia was first claimed for Britain by Captain James Cook on August 22, 1770. Although the Dutch navigator Tasman had first explored what is now Tasmania in the seventeenth century, and the French were active in eighteenth century Pacific exploration, the British claim to Australia and many adjacent islands was within a short number of decades widely accepted. The lack of competition from other Western powers and weakness of the Australian Aborigines made Australia a land more or less available for the taking: it became the prototypical colony of British settlement, a fact exemplified by the title of Edward Gibbon Wakefield's treatise on the theory of settlement, *A Letter from Sydney.*

Facing overcrowded prisons, a dispossessed American loyalist population, and having lost in the war of American independence the ability to transport convicted felons there, the administration of **Pitt** the Younger was determined to establish a penal colony in Australia. The first colony of transported felons sailed from Portsmouth under Captain Arthur Phillip, RN, arriving at Botany Bay in New South Wales. Phillip selected the site of what is now Sydney for its qualities as an anchorage, and landed his small fleet there on January 26, 1788, now remembered as Australia Day, naming the place after Lord Sydney, then Home Secretary.

Cook named his discovery New South Wales, and Britain claimed the entire coast inland to the 135th meridian, although the geography of that coast was poorly understood at the time. In 1829, Britain also laid claim to Western Australia. In the course of the nineteenth century, as exploration and settlement proceeded, regions were separated from New South Wales, to create the colonies of Van Dieman's land in 1825, South Australia in 1836, Victoria in 1851, and Queensland on the northeastern coast in 1859.

The first free settlers arrived in 1793. Tensions between free settlers, convicts, and freed convicts who had served out their sentences, and the military and official establishments charged with guarding the convicts shortly became the central feature of New South Wales politics. Popular resentment at the transportation system long characterized Australian attitudes to the mother country, and after much agitation it was abolished in New South Wales in 1854. In Western Australia, however, the local authorities welcomed convict labor, and from 1850 until the British abolished transportation altogether in 1868 that colony was a willing participant in a system decried elsewhere on the continent.

Sheep were grazed in Australia from the early years of the nineteenth century, but it was only in the 1820s that significant quantities of high quality Australian wool were imported into Britain. By 1850, Australia had displaced European suppliers from the British wool trade. The economic incentives of the wool trade ensured that Australia soon filled with sheep. Although the colonial authorities were determined to keep settlement within official boundaries, so-called "squatters" moved outside the settled region in search of good grazing land. Although the term originally referred to small holders who simply took possession of unoccupied land, it soon came to refer to well-capitalized who took large numbers of sheep into the interior and established *de facto* but formally illegal claims to large tracts of grazing land. The state was compelled to recognize the legal status of the colonies' economic mainstay, and regularize the position of the squatters.

Gold was discovered in Victoria in 1851, and the discovery produced a rapid influx of miners and speculators, which led to some disorder, notably the Ballarat riots of 1854, rapidly put down by the authorities. Gold diggings and other mineral exploration contributed to the inflow of settlers, and hence indirectly to the building of railways and to the establishment in 1852 of a regular steamship service to Britain. By the 1870s, Australia attracted large amounts of British capital and a consequent railway boom. Victoria introduced protectionist legislation in the 1860s, and even under the united Commonwealth formed in 1901, protectionist feeling remained strong.

Australians were often enthusiastic imperialists. They feared the expansion of other European powers in the Pacific, and attempted to implement an exclusionary Monroe-type doctrine in their region. There was a movement for the annexation of Fiji, and in 1882 the colony of Queensland annexed New Guinea, an act rapidly disallowed by the colonial office on the grounds that questions of international import were to be decided in London. On several occasions during the nineteenth century, Australia offered the mother country military forces to serve in imperial wars, and the several colonies sent a total of 16,000 men to serve in the Boer War of 1899–1902.

The idea of an Australian federation had first been mooted by Earl **Grey** in the 1840s, but ran into many local objections, particularly with respect to fiscal policy, and even a movement for free trade among the various colonies could make little headway. A national convention to design a federal constitution met beginning in 1891 under the chairmanship of Sir Henry Parkes. Extended disputes as to the form and powers of the new federation ensued. A further convention in 1897–1898 completed the task of writing a constitution that provided for a House of Representatives and a Senate, and reserved to the states all powers not explicitly conferred on the federation. Chief among the latter were control of interstate and foreign commerce. The six Australian colonies and the Northern territory were united under a federal government as the Commonwealth of Australia on January 1, 1901, by an act of the Imperial Parliament. *See also* British Empire; Japanese Empire.

FURTHER READING: Bolton, Geoffrey, ed. *The Oxford History of Australia.* Melbourne: Oxford University Press, 1996; Hughes, Robert. *The Fatal Shore.* New York: Vintage, 1988; Walker, David. *Anxious Nation: Australia and the Rise of Asia, 1850–1939.* St. Lucia: University of Queensland Press, 1999.

MARK F. PROUDMAN

## Australian Colonies Government Act (1850)

Passed by the British Parliament at the initiative of the Colonial Secretary (the third) **Earl Grey,** this act began a process of constitutional legislation in the Australian colonies that resulted by 1853 in the effective adoption of responsible government in New South Wales, Victoria, South Australia, and Van Diemen's Land, now Tasmania.

Although the act reserved control of waste or unsettled lands to the Crown and provided for revenues from them to pay Crown appointees independently of legislative control, it also called for the addition of elected members to colonial legislative councils. In short order, the British government gave up its claim to control waste lands and the colonial legislatures elected under the terms of the Act of 1850 enacted constitutional measures of their own which had the intended effect of rendering colonial executives responsible to the elected members of colonial legislatures. As the British government had conceded in principle the desirability of local self-government, it shortly conceded the reality.

FURTHER READING: Clark, C.M.L. *A Short History of Australia.* New York: New American Library, 1963; Crowley, F. K. *Australia's Western Third.* New York: St. Martin's, 1960; Robson, L. L. *A Short History of Tasmania.* Melbourne: Oxford University Press, 1985.

MARK F. PROUDMAN

## Australian Commonwealth (1900)

Passed by the British Parliament under the auspices of the then-Colonial Secretary Joseph **Chamberlain,** the Australian Commonwealth established a federal government for Australia, creating a British Dominion on the Canadian model. It provided for a lower House of Representatives elected by population, a Senate with equal representation for each state as an upper house, and a ministry responsible to the lower house, on traditional British lines. There was full adult suffrage. A governor-general resident in Australia represented the sovereign. To ensure passage of the constitution within the various prefederation Australian colonies, powers not specifically allocated to the federal government were reserved to the states. *See also* Canada.

FURTHER READING: Bolton, Geoffrey, ed. *The Oxford History of Australia.* Melbourne: Oxford University Press, 1996; Robson, L. L. *A Short History of Tasmania.* Melbourne: Oxford University Press, 1985.

MARK F. PROUDMAN

## Australian Frontier Wars (1788–1928)

A series of frontier wars waged by Australian **Aborigines** against British settlers, soldiers, and police from the late eighteenth to the early twentieth century for control of what is now Australia.

British authorities did not recognize these conflicts as war, as to do so would undermine the basis on which the British had occupied Australia. The British did not acknowledge aboriginal land ownership when they established the colony of New South Wales at Sydney in 1788. Unlike other British colonies, no treaties were signed with indigenous peoples. The British government claimed that all Australian Aborigines had automatically become British subjects and therefore any aboriginal armed attack was defined as criminal rather than warlike activity. As the Colonial Secretary, Lord Glenelg, told Sir Richard Bourke, Governor of New South Wales, in

1837 that "To regard them as Aliens with whom a War can exist, and against whom H[er] M[ajesty]'s Troops may exercise belligerent right, is to deny them that protection to which they derive the highest possible claim from the Sovereignty which has been assumed over the whole of their Ancient Possession."

Australian Aborigines fought on the frontier using a combination of traditional warfare and new tactics developed to deal with the new enemy. Aborigines spoke about 250 different languages, and these nations were further divided into smaller autonomous groups sharing kinship or a connection to a particular area of land. Aborigines did not have chiefs or hierarchical structures of government. Instead, decisions were made by a consensus of the elder men. For this reason, Aborigines found it hard to unite against the British and generally each group fought the invader on their own. Warriors used traditional tactics of raiding and ambush and also learned to attack crops, sheep, and cattle and to burn fences and farmhouses. In some areas where the terrain assisted this style of warfare, Aborigines were able to temporarily hold back the settlers. They retained their traditional weapons of spears and clubs and made little use of firearms. The British, as the sole colonizing power in Australia, were in a position to prevent firearms passing across the frontier, but equally the spear was a symbol of manhood in some aboriginal groups, and they may have thought it inconceivable to fight with another weapon.

On the British side, warfare was carried out by soldiers, mounted police, and settlers. Although New South Wales and Van Diemen's Land (present-day Tasmania) remained mainly convict colonies, governors were unwilling to distribute firearms among the civilian population and sent detachments of soldiers to the frontier to fight the Aborigines when required. These operations were defined as "aid to the civil power" rather than warfare. Martial law was declared in New South Wales in 1824 and in Van Diemen's Land from 1828 to 1831 to provide legal protection for any soldier who killed an Aborigine. The last major British army deployment to the frontier took place in New South Wales in 1838. Therafter , settlers and police took over the fight.

The defining factor in the British success on the Australian frontier was not firearms but horses. These gave the extra mobility, both in range and speed, that was necessary to pursue and attack aboriginal raiding parties. The New South Wales Mounted Police was established in 1825. At first this consisted of soldiers mounted at the colonial government's expense, but at the War Office's insistence, it became a civilian force from 1838. Aborigines were also recruited for native police forces. Under the command of white officers, and deployed against Aborigines to whom they had no kin relationship, the Queensland native police in particular became notorious for its brutality.

Settlers did the bulk of the fighting on the British side on the Australian frontier. They defended their farms from aboriginal attacks and carried out punitive raids on aboriginal campsites. These actions were veiled in secrecy for fear of prosecution for murder. As the Victorian farmer George Faithfull wrote about his district in the 1840s, "People formed themselves into bands of alliance and allegiance to each other, and it was then the destruction of the natives really did take place." In the end, colonial authorities arrested and tried only a tiny number of settlers for murdering Aborigines. Fewer still were convicted and punished.

The Australian frontier was not universally violent. In some areas, especially coastal regions, there was little armed conflict as Aborigines and settlers found ways to share economic resources and coexist. Where fighting did take place, Aborigines fought in small groups against the British colonizers, so although the numbers of casualties may have been small, the casualty rate was proportionally high and devastated aboriginal groups. Although the fighting on the Australian frontier was small scale, it conformed to Clausewitz's classic definition of war as "an act of force to compel our enemy to do our will."

The first frontier war in Australia was fought for control of the Hawkesbury River west of Sydney between 1795 and 1816. The Darug people destroyed settlers' maize crops and burned their farmhouses. Resistance ended once a British army expedition scoured the river valley and killed 14 Aborigines during a nighttime raid on a campsite. When the British crossed the Blue Mountains onto the inland plains, the Wiradjuri people killed cattle and convict stockmen. The Wiradjuri campaign forced the New South Wales Governor to declare martial law and led to the creation of mounted police units. In 1826, Lieutenant Nathaniel Lowe was charged with ordering the shooting of an aboriginal prisoner while serving with the mounted police. His fellow officers, however, quickly acquitted him when he came to trial.

Van Diemen's Land saw sustained frontier warfare from 1826 to 1831. Governor George Arthur mobilized 10 percent of the male civilian population along with soldiers and police in 1830 and had them march across the settled districts to clear these areas from Aborigines in an operation that became known as the "Black Line." The operation failed to capture many Aborigines, but its scale disheartened the raiding parties, and gradually each group came in and agreed to leave their land for the Flinders Island reservation.

From the late 1830s, settlers and their sheep and cattle spread rapidly onto aboriginal land, bringing conflict throughout inland eastern Australia. In what is now Victoria, aboriginal warriors deliberately dislocated the legs of hundreds of sheep so that they would be useless for pastoralists. In what is now Queensland, there were about 10 cases in which settlers probably poisoned Aborigines with flour laced with arsenic or strychnine. In the 1880s, fighting flared in western Queensland and the north of western Australia. The Kalkadoon were defeated in 1884 when they foolishly abandoned their raiding tactics after six years of success and openly attacked settlers at Battle Mountain, near Kajabbi in Queensland. In western Australia, one pastoral company claimed it lost 7,000 sheep to Aborigines in 1888 alone. Fighting continued in the Northern Territory at a sporadic level into the twentieth century. When a Walpiri man killed a white miner at Coniston, the local police officer mounted a punitive expedition and killed at least 31 Aborigines. An action that once had been condoned was now finally criticized, and there was an official inquiry into the massacre.

The frontier wars remain a controversial part of Australian history. According to Ernest Scott, the first great Australian historian, there had not been any frontier conflict at all. He wrote in 1910 that "Australia is the only considerable portion of the world which has enjoyed the blessed record of unruffled peace." In the 1970s, this view was revised as historians began examining official and private records and found example after example of frontier warfare. At the beginning of the twenty-first century, Keith Windschuttle led a conservative critique of most that has been written about frontier conflict, arguing that other historians had exaggerated the level of violence and the number of casualties. A second dispute revolves around whether "genocide" was perpetrated on the Australian frontier. There is no instance of government authorities ordering the extermination of Aborigines, so this argument considers whether there is evidence of individuals and small groups showing the intent and having the means to commit genocide. Both debates are certain to continue for some time. *See also* Canada, South Africa.

FURTHER READING: Attwood, Bain. *Telling the Truth about Aboriginal History*. Sydney: Allen & Unwin, 2005; Broome, Richard. "The Struggle for Australia: Aboriginal-European Warfare, 1770–1930." In M. McKernan and M. Browne, eds. *Australia: Two Centuries of War and Peace.* Canberra: Australian War Memorial in association with Allen & Unwin, 1988; Connor, John. *The Australian Frontier Wars, 1788–1838.* Sydney: University of New South Wales Press, 2002; Moses, A. Dirk, ed. *Genocide and Settler Society: Frontier Violence and Stolen Indigenous Children in Australian History.* New York and Oxford: Berghahn Books, 2005; Reynolds, Henry. *The Other Side of the Frontier: Aboriginal Resistance to the European Invasion of Australia.* Ringwood, Victoria: Penguin, 1982; Reynolds, Henry. *An Indelible Stain? The Question of Genocide in Australia's History.* Ringwood, Victoria: Penguin, 2001; Windschuttle, Keith. *The Fabrication of Aboriginal History.* Sydney: Macleay Press, 2002.

JOHN CONNOR

## Australian-German Relations

The German annexation of part of **New Guinea** in 1884 led to a minor rift between the Australian colonies and the British Government. Since the 1870s, Australians had perceived all nearby Pacific Islands as their sphere of influence and wanted the region under the British flag. In 1874, the Queensland, New South Wales, and South Australian governments asked Britain to annex Fiji, and the British met this request. The next year, the three colonies made a similar call in relation to the eastern half of New Guinea, the western half being under Dutch control, but the British refused to comply on the grounds that the cost of administering the colony outweighed any economic benefit. In 1879, the Queensland government claimed the islands in the Torres Strait between Australia and New Guinea. In 1883, in light of rumors of German interest in New Guinea, Queensland annexed the eastern half of the island. The British Government refused to recognize the colonial government's action. The next year, the Germany annexed the northeast section of New Guinea. Embarrassed, the British Government then hurriedly claimed the remaining southeastern area, with the costs of administering the colony shared between the British, Queensland, New South Wales, and Victorian governments.

Germany created a colonial empire in the Asia-Pacific and developed a network of radio and coaling stations for the German East Asiatic Squadron based at Tsingtao, now Qingdao, China. German naval war plans called for the East Asiatic Squadron to attack British merchant shipping around Australia and elsewhere in the region. Australian and New Zealand military planning for a war with Germany began during the First **Balkan War** of 1912. It was decided that, in the event of war, Australia would occupy German New Guinea and New Zealand would take Samoa. This plan was followed on the outbreak of war in 1914. *See also* British Empire; German Empire; Navalism.

FURTHER READING: Hiery, Herman J. *The Neglected War: The German South Pacific and the Influence of World War I.* Honolulu: University of Hawaii Press, 1995; Overlack, Peter. "Australasia and Germany: Challenge and Response before 1914." In David Stevens, ed. *Maritime Power in the Twentieth Century: The Australian Experience.* Sydney: Allen & Unwin, 1998.

JOHN CONNOR

## Australian-Japanese Relations

Although Australia was part of the British Empire, and Japan had signed a treaty of alliance with Britain in 1902, these two nations had a strained relationship in the period immediately before the World War I. Japan considered the Australian policy of immigration restriction toward Asians as an affront, and Australians viewed the rise of Japanese military power with apprehension after its victory in the **Russo-Japanese War** of 1904–1905 and annexation of **Korea** in 1910. The popular fear of a Japanese invasion of Australia manifested itself in the 1908 play, *White Australia—or the Empty North,* the 1909 novel, *The Australian Crisis,* and the 1913 film *Australia Calls,* which included scenes of Australian cities being bombed by aircraft of an unspecified Asian nation. It also led the Australian government to introduce compulsory military training and establish the Royal Australian Navy and Australian Flying Corps. These anxieties, however, did not prevent the development of economic ties. The Japanese had imported Australian coal since the 1860s, and Japanese divers had played a vital role in the Australian pearling industry at Broome in Western Australia and Thursday Island in Queensland since the 1880s. With the outbreak of World War I in 1914, Australia and Japan fought on the same side against Germany and the first convoy of Australian and New Zealand troops was escorted by the Japanese cruiser *Ibuki. See also* Japanese Empire.

FURTHER READING: Frei, Henry P. *Japan's Southward Advance and Australia: From the Sixteenth Century to World War II.* Melbourne: Melbourne University Press, 1991; Meaney, Neville. *The Search for Security in the Pacific, 1901–14.* Sydney: Sydney University Press, 1976.

JOHN CONNOR

## Austria-Hungary

The state of Austria-Hungary was the product of the 1867 **Ausgleich** between the Hungarian opposition and the Austrian Emperor Francis Joseph I. According to this agreement, which transformed the constitutional framework of the Habsburg monarchy, the kingdom of Hungary would have its own government and parliament in Budapest, and accepted Francis Joseph and his heirs as kings. The rest of the Habsburg monarchy, officially named the "kingdoms and lands represented in the Reichsrat," the parliament in Vienna, was usually called Austria. The monarch as king of Hungary and emperor of Austria; the common ministries of foreign affairs, war, and finance; and the regular meetings of delegations from both parliaments formed institutional bonds between Austria and Hungary. There was also a common Austro-Hungarian army and a common Austro-Hungarian navy. From 1867 to 1918, "Austria-Hungary" was the official name of the Habsburg monarchy.

Because of its status as a union of two states, Austria-Hungary was also called the "Dual Monarchy." *See also* Austrian Empire; Habsburg Empire.

FURTHER READING: Good, David F. *The Economic Rise of the Habsburg Empire, 1750–1914.* Berkeley: University of California Press, 1984.

GUENTHER KRONENBITTER

## Austrian Empire

The *Kaisertum Österreich* was proclaimed on August 11, 1804, by the Holy Roman Emperor Francis II. This was done as a reaction to the gradual dismantlement and possible dissolution of the Holy Roman Empire and the self-coronation of Napoleon Bonaparte as Emperor of the French. Under pressure from Napoleon and the Confederation of the Rhine created by him, Francis dissolved *de facto* the Holy Roman Empire on August 6, 1806. The hereditary Austrian Empire encompassed all of the Habsburg's territories until 1867, when the **Ausgleich** transformed the Habsburg Empire into Austria-Hungary, the union of the Kingdom of Hungary (and the Kingdom of Croatia-Slavonia), and the other kingdoms and lands under Habsburg rule. *See also* Austria-Hungary; Habsburg Empire; Napoleonic Wars.

FURTHER READING: Kann, Robert A. *A History of the Habsburg Empire, 1526–1918.* Berkeley: University of California Press, 1974; Macartney, C. A. *The Habsburg Empire, 1790–1918.* London: Weidenfeld and Nicolson, 1971.

GUENTHER KRONENBITTER

## Austro-Prussian War (1866)

Also known as the Seven Weeks' War, the Austro-Prussian War was a short although pivotal episode in the wars of German unification. German Chancellor Otto von **Bismarck** sought the conflict in order to annex the northern states of the **German Confederation** and also to expel Austrian influence from southern Germany. After the defeat of Denmark in the Schleswig-Holstein War, Prussia and Austria quarreled over newly acquired territory until a Prussian army under Edwin Hans Karl von Manteuffel forced a weaker Austrian force out of Holstein. On June 14, Austria, Bavaria, Saxony, Hanover, and several smaller German states declared war. After securing the neutrality of France and a secret alliance with Italy (Piedmont-Sardinia), Bismarck ordered Prussian forces under Helmuth von **Moltke** to the offensive.

Austria possessed an army of some 320,000 men, yet could field only 240,000 against Prussia's 254,000 because of the need to fight Italy simultaneously. The Austrian army was at the time widely considered to be superior, but the very reverse was demonstrated when the better trained and better equipped Prussian army demolished the Austrians at **Königgrätz.** Prussia was further advantaged by two other factors. Most of the Austrian officers spoke only German, whereas many of their troops spoke one or the other of the several languages of the multinational Habsburg Empire. The Austrians were also outclassed in their mobilization effort, as Prussia had superior **railway** and **telegraph** systems. The fighting was made brief by these factors, as well as by Bismarck's restraint of Prussian generals, who wanted to invade Austria, and his insistence on a magnanimous peace. On August 23, the Treaty of Prague stripped Austria of no territory save Ventia, which went to Italy. The south German states that had been in Vienna's sphere of influence, however, now quickly came into Prussia's orbit by way of secret agreements; meanwhile, Frankfurt, Hanover, Hesse-Cassel, Hesse-Nassau, and Schleswig-Holstein were annexed to Prussia.

In one stroke, Prussia became the unrivaled leader of the German states. The **Franco-Prussian War** and an even more spectacular demonstration of Prussian military professionalism made it the dominant power on the European continent. *See also* German Empire; Habsburg Empire.

FURTHER READING: Showalter, Dennis. *The Wars of German Unification.* London: Hodder Arnold, 2004; Wawro, Geoffrey. *The Austro-Prussian War.* New York: Cambridge University Press, 1996.

CARL CAVANAGH HODGE

# B

## Badli-ke-Serai, Battle of (1857)

A late engagement of the **Indian Mutiny.** On June 8 the rebels offered battle at Badli-ke-Serai, halfway between Alipur and Delhi, taking up a defensive position on both sides of the main road to Delhi. Their right was anchored at a walled village protected by a swamp where they deployed large number of infantry. The left of the rebel line was protected by a sandbag battery made up of four heavy guns and an eight-inch mortar. *Nullahs,* sharp and narrow gullies, intersected the ground on both sides of the rebel line's flanks. About a mile from the rebel's left wing ran the Western Jamuna Canal. The British 75th Foot charged at the enemy's guns and suffered 62 casualties. Brigadier Hope Grant, with 10 horse artillery guns, 3 squadrons of the 9th Lancers, and 50 Jhind *sowars* turned the enemy's left flank. The rebels then retired to Delhi, leaving their guns and prepared to withstand a long siege.

FURTHER READING: Embree, Ainslie T. *1857 in India: Mutiny or War of Independence?* Boston: Heath, 1963; Farwell, Byron. *Queen Victoria's Little Wars.* New York: W. W. Norton, 1972.

KAUSHIK ROY

## Bagehot, Walter (1826–1877)

British journalist, economist, political scientist, and editor of *The Economist* from 1860 to his death. Although Bagehot failed to win election to the British parliament three times, he was influential in mid-nineteenth-century England because of his writings and personal connections. Born into a Unitarian banking family in Langport, Somerset, he initially attended Bristol College and in 1842, at the age of 16, he began his degree studies at University College London. He studied and initially practiced law but soon moved into the family business of banking. He always wrote copiously, however, particularly for the *National Review,* and from 1860 edited his father-in-law James Wilson's paper, *The Economist.*

Bagehot is best known for *The English Constitution,* in which he analyzed the major institutions of British government. He split the functions of government into "dignified" and "efficient" parts. The dignified institutions, the monarchy and the House of Lords, were important because they distracted the attention of the uneducated masses, about whom Bagehot was uniformly scathing, and hence bolstered the legitimacy of the system. The efficient institutions, primarily the House of Commons, were important because they appointed the cabinet, which in fact wielded most real power, a fact obscured by the noticeable dignified aspects of the constitution. Written at a time when electoral reform was being hotly debated, Bagehot disapproved of democracy, as he felt it would give the upper hand to the uneducated masses.

Bagehot had many interests. Another significant work, *Physics and Politics,* was translated into seven languages and had already reached its fifth French edition by 1885. Subtitled "Thoughts on the Application of the Principles of 'Natural Selection' and 'Inheritance' to Political Society," it was a broad attempt to apply Darwinian ideas to politics. The book described the historical evolution of social groups into nations, and sought to explain why European nations alone were truly progressive. Bagehot argued that these nations had evolved primarily by succeeding in conflicts with other groups. For many political scientists and military strategists, ideas such as these justified overseas expansion during the later nineteenth century. Thus, in common with other nineteenth-century British thinkers, Bagehot's writings helped to bolster the notion idea of European superiority and of English exceptionalism.

FURTHER READING: St John-Stevas, N., ed. *The Collected Works of Walter Bagehot.* 15 vols. London: The Economist, 1986.

PAUL LAWRENCE

## Bailén, Battle of (1808)

The Battle of Bailén (or Baylen) was a small but significant engagement of the **Peninsular War** that shattered the myth of Napoleonic invincibility. A French army of 22,250 men under the leadership of General Pierre Dupont de l'Étang conducting a campaign of pacification in Andalusia was attacked and routed by a Spanish force of 29,770 men commanded by Francisco Castaños. Although there was clear incompetence on both sides, the more spectacular instances came form Dupont and his subordinates, with the result that 17,635 French soldiers ultimately surrendered to the Spanish. An offer of safe conduct back to France was promptly violated, as the French troops were denied repatriation, confined on prison ships in Cádiz harbor, and eventually left on Balearic Island to starve to death. Dupont, who had shown ability at Austerlitz, was operating for the first time in independent command and had begun the campaign in the hope of winning a marshal's baton. Instead, he was disgraced and imprisoned for six years. *See also* Napoleonic Wars.

FURTHER READING: Esdaile, Charles. *The Penninsular War, A New History.* London: Allen Lane, 2002.

CARL CAVANAGH HODGE

## Bakunin, Mikhail (1814–1876)

Mikhail Bakunin was a Russian intellectual known for his political philosophy of anarchism. The eldest son of a wealthy Russian landowner, Bakunin was fluent in

French, educated in the standard subjects and the classic works of European literature, and, as a young man, attended the Artillery Cadet School in St. Petersburg. He first began to read the German philosophers seriously in 1833–1834 and by 1835 had joined an intellectual circle in Moscow named for its head Nikolai Stankevich. Here Bakunin found his place. Steeped in the writings of the German philosophers such as Johann **Fichte** and G.W.F. **Hegel,** he began to formulate his own philosophy. He believed that to achieve inner harmony one had to abandon the old self, reject materialism, and live a life of self-denial. Complete freedom could be achieved only through complete destruction of the current repressive regime; there was no utility in gradual change within the system. He did not promote an individualistic rebellion against society; on the contrary, he had a strong faith in humanity's innate collectivism.

His anarchism was based on a sharp opposition between "society" and "state," the state being an alien power that, tied to the institution of private property, killed the natural social instincts in humans. Bakunin became a recognized leader of the anarchist movement and the main antagonist of Karl **Marx** in the First International. His emphasis on the Russian peasantry as the source of all revolutionary energy came in direct conflict with Marx's focus on the industrial working class. Moreover, he criticized Marx's theories as proposing yet another form of tyranny, that of the educated over the uneducated workers. Bakunin's theories were very influential; his belief in the revolutionary instincts of the peasant inspired the great "go to the people" movement in Russia in 1874. *See also* Anarchism; Russian Empire.

FURTHER READING: Carr, Edward Hallett. *Michael Bakunin.* New York: Vintage Books, 1975; Joll, James. *The Anarchists.* 2nd ed. Cambridge, MA: Harvard University Press, 1980; Kelly, Aileen. *Mikhail Bakunin: A Study in the Psychology and Politics of Utopianism.* New Haven, CT: Yale University Press, 1987.

LEE A. FARROW

## Balaklava, Battle of (1854)

Fought on October 25, 1854, Balaklava was one of several major battles of the **Crimean War** (1854–56). With British and French forces besieging the principal Black Sea port of Sevastopol, the Russian General Menshikov sought to drive a wedge between Allied forces and the British base at Balaklava. Russian troops managed to seize some Turkish redoubts and guns on a height known as the Vorontsov Ridge, which commanded the Balaklava-Sevastopol road; but, when Menshikov's cavalry attempted to exploit this success, they were repulsed by the British Heavy Brigade and by a regiment of Highland infantry. The most noteworthy episode of the battle concerns the epic charge of the Light Brigade, accidentally launched to its destruction down a valley with enemy artillery to its front and infantry deployed on the heights on both flanks. Although it managed to silence the Russian guns, the Light Brigade suffered horrific losses, thus ceasing to be operationally effective for the remainder of the war. The Light Brigade's sacrifice, immortalized in a poem by Alfred, Lord Tennyson that has since been memorized by generations of school children, was tactically inconsequential. Nevertheless, the Russian attempt to disrupt the siege and capture the British supply base failed, thus enabling the Allies to continue operations as before.

FURTHER READING: Adkin, Mark. *The Charge: The Real Reason Why the Light Brigade Was Lost.* London: Leo Cooper, 1996; Barthorp, Michael. *Heroes of the Crimea: Balaclava and Inkerman.* London: Blandford, 1991; Brighton, Terry. *Hell Riders: The True Story of the Charge of the Light Brigade.* London: Henry Holt & Co., 2004; Sweetman, John. *Balaclava 1854: The Charge of the Light Brigade.* London: Greenwood Publishing, 2005; Woodham-Smith, Cecil. *The Reason Why.* London: Penguin, 1991.

GREGORY FREMONT-BARNES

## Balance of Power

A term with several meanings, most widely associated with the principle whereby military and political power is so distributed among nations that no one state wields overwhelming power with which to dominant the others. A state of equilibrium can be produced by ensuring that any threat of predominance by a single country or alliance is counterbalanced by the existence or creation of a group of nations of approximately equal power. In the case of the **Great Powers** of Europe up to 1914, the concept was generally applied across the Continent, although a balance could be—and continues to be—applied to a region. Statesmen and rulers in the eighteenth and nineteenth centuries were acutely aware that any nation that sought to overthrow the existing political balance constituted a menace to peace and stability, although the growing power of one's neighbor need not necessarily portend imminent conflict. Nevertheless, coalitions were frequently formed—usually after fighting began—precisely to redress the imbalance created by the overweening power of a nation seeking to revise the political situation in Europe. The cases of Louis XIV and Napoleon serve as prime examples of this, as do Imperial and Nazi Germany in the twentieth century. Moral issues seldom arose; when mutual advantage demanded it, Christian states cooperated with Muslim Turkey, Protestant states aligned themselves with Catholic ones, and democracies worked with autocracies.

The maintenance of the balance of power generally aids in the preservation of sovereignty and the avoidance of conflict, but its principal purpose is not the maintenance of peace, but rather the survival of the strongest powers, often at the expense of weaker ones. Those favoring equilibrium of this kind do so through a conservative instinct for the political and military status quo, with the preservation of international order the primary function over considerations of justice, civil rights, or national self-determination. Hence, those who in 1815 convened at the Congress of Vienna and parceled out German, Polish, and Italian territory to the contending Great Powers did so with little or no interest in satisfying the nationalist aspirations of the various ethnic peoples of Europe. Borders shifted on the basis of political and strategic expediency; language and culture seldom influenced decisions of statecraft until the mid-nineteenth century. *See also* Entente Cordiale; Vienna, Congress of; Napoleonic Wars; Strategy.

FURTHER READING: Gullick, Edward. *Europe's Classical Balance of Power: A Case History of the Theory and Practice of One of the Great Concepts of European Statecraft.* Ithaca, NY: Cornell University Press, 1955; Kissinger, Henry. *A World Restored: Metternich, Castlereagh and the Problems of Peace, 1812–1822.* London: Weidenfeld & Nicolson, 1957; Schroeder, Paul W. *The Transformation of European Politics, 1763–1848.* Oxford: Clarendon, 1994.

GREGORY FREMONT-BARNES

## Balfour, Arthur J. (1848–1930)

Arthur J. Balfour, First Earl Balfour of Wittinghame, was Prime Minister of Great Britain from 1902 to 1905 in succession to his uncle Lord **Salisbury,** and later Foreign Secretary under David **Lloyd George** from 1916 to 1919.

Known for his air of aristocratic languor, Balfour was a skilled Commons debater, and also a noted philosopher. Briefly associated with the populist Tory "fourth party" in the early 1880s, he joined Salisbury's cabinet in 1886. In 1887, he was given the demanding job of Irish Secretary, where his stern law-and-order Unionism earned him the sobriquet "bloody Balfour." In 1891, he became leader in the Commons as First Lord of the Treasury—the Prime Minister being in the Lords—a role in which he continued when the Tories were in office until he succeeded to the Premiership in 1902.

Balfour's premiership is primarily memorable for divisions within the Unionist party, chiefly over imperial tariff policy. Following the massive Liberal victory of December 1905, he led the Conservative opposition until 1911, and against his own party's diehards, favored a compromise over the Parliament Act of that year.

During World War I, Balfour joined Liberal Prime Minister H. H. **Asquith**'s coalition ministry of 1915 as First Lord of the Admiralty, after the departure of Winston Churchill as a result of the Dardanelles disaster. He moved to the Foreign Office when his old adversary Lloyd George became Premier in December 1916. As Foreign Secretary he did much to solidify U.S. support for the allied war effort, but he is chiefly remembered for the Balfour Declaration of 1917, which expressed approval for the idea of Jewish homeland in Palestine, as a means of attracting Jewish support for the western side in the war. He played a role secondary to Lloyd George at the Paris peace conference of 1919.

At the Imperial conference of 1926, Balfour negotiated with the settlement Dominions the agreement formalized in the Statute of Westminster of 1931, by which the independent Dominion governments were recognized as governments of the Crown equal in status to that at Westminster. The Statute of Westminster marked the final transformation so far as the settler states were concerned of the British Empire into the British Commonwealth of Nations. *See also* Conservative Party; Ireland.

FURTHER READING: Dugdale, B.E.C. *Arthur James Balfour, First Earl Balfour.* 2 vols. London: Hutchinson, 1936; Rasor, E. L. *Arthur James Balfour: Historiography and Annotated Bibliography.* Westport, CT: Greenwood, 1998.

MARK F. PROUDMAN

## Balkan Crises (1875–1878, 1908–1913)

A series of ethnic conflicts in southeastern Europe intertwined with imperialist aspirations of the great powers directly involved, that is, Austria-Hungary, Russia, and the Ottoman Empire, plus those indirectly implicated, that is, Great Britain, Germany, France, and Italy, which led to the outbreak of World War I in 1914. Under the impact of national movements all over Europe since the mid-nineteenth century, Southern Slavs became politically sensitive to the ethnic, religious, and cultural nature of Ottoman Muslim rule. Nationalists believed that a national government would better suit their Slavic identity than a multiethnic empire, and they were also convinced that the European Great Powers would support their struggle for independence.

The first Balkan crisis began with an anti-Ottoman uprising in the province of **Bosnia-Herzegovina** in July 1875. At first a peasant revolt against Ottoman taxation, Serbs, and Croats ultimately demanded outright freedom. Although there were several revolts in the Balkans in the first half of the nineteenth century—such as the Serbian uprising of 1804–1810, the Greek war of independence from 1821 to 1830, and the rebellions in Montenegro in the 1850s—from the 1860s onward national protest seized broad masses of illiterate rural, non-Turkic population. The European powers feared insoluble ethnic conflicts and aimed at a preservation of the Ottoman Empire. They also appreciated that the situation in the Balkans could trigger a larger war among them like the **Crimean War** of 1853–56. At first, no European power sought to interfere in the Bosnian conflict, but when Serbia threatened to declare war on the Ottomans in order to support Bosnian Serbs, Austria-Hungary feared a territorial expansion of Serbia in the region.

This fear was not far-fetched. A Serbian minority lived in the southern regions of Hungary, and there was the danger that irredentism could spread from the Balkans to Hungary and expose the Austro-Hungarian monarchy to the same fate of progressive disintegration as the Ottoman Empire. Austria-Hungary therefore began consultations on the Bosnian question with Germany and Russia, the other members of the Three Emperors' League. In the summer of 1876, the situation escalated when Serbia declared war on the Porte on June 30 and was joined by Montenegro on July 2. Great Britain feared military intervention of Russia on the Serbian side. At the international conference in Constantinople in December 1876, a truce was negotiated between Serbia and the Ottomans, but the Porte rejected a Great Power demand for inner reforms. In April 1877, Russia declared war on the Ottoman Empire, beginning the **Russo-Turkish War** of 1877–78 in which Romania and Serbia became Russian allies. The war ended with the Treaty of **San Stefano** in February 1878. The Ottomans were forced to guarantee the autonomy of the Bulgarian principality, independence of Montenegro, Serbia, and Romania, and cede self-administration to Bosnia and Herzegovina.

This provoked the resistance of Great Britain and Austria-Hungary. German chancellor Bismarck mediated between Great Britain, Austria-Hungary, and Russia to prevent a major war in the Balkans. The Treaty of Berlin, concluded in July 1878, approved the state independence of Serbia, Montenegro and Romania yet failed to define clearly the new borders in the Balkans, thereby fuelling further armed conflicts over the territorial question that culminated in the Austrian annexation of Bosnia and Herzegovina in October 1908. This in turn aggravated Austro-Serbian animosity and Austro-Russian antagonism. Three years later Serbia, Bulgaria, Montenegro, and Greece founded the **Balkan League** that declared war on the Ottoman Empire in the First **Balkan War** and the Porte from the Balkan territory in 1913. Internal strife among the allies over the territorial division then brought on the Second Balkan War in 1913. Bulgaria had to give up her dream of a leading power in the Balkans, while Macedonia was divided between Serbia and Greece. *See also* Balkan League; Balkan Wars; Bismarck, Otto von; Ottoman Empire; Russian Empire.

FURTHER READING: Albertini, Luigi. *The Origins of the War of 1914*. 3 vols. Translated by Isabella M. Massey. New York: Oxford University Press, 1952; Glenny, Misha. *The Balkans 1804–1999: Nationalism, War and the Great Powers*. London: Granta Books, 1999; Lieven, D.C.B. *Russia and the Origins of the First World War*. New York: St. Martin's, 1983.

EVA-MARIA STOLBERG

## Balkan League (1912)

An alliance of Serbia, Montenegro, Greece, and Bulgaria against the Ottoman Empire during the First Balkan War. Eleutherios Venizelos, the prime minister of Greece, had pushed for an alliance with Bulgaria early in 1911 to protect oppressed Christian subjects of Ottoman rule in Macedonia. Bulgaria thought Greece was too weak and too close to war with the Porte over Crete. But the weakness of the Ottomans in the Italo-Turkish War resulted in the Balkan states putting aside differences to tackle their irredentist ambitions. In March 1912, a secret bilateral defensive alliance was signed between Serbia and Bulgaria, which a military contract in May expanded. Athens then signed a military alliance with Sofia, and Sofia signed a similar one with Montenegro. Thus Balkan states formed a network of alliances against Constantinople.

The Great Powers immediately saw a threat to their interests. France feared Russian domination of the Balkans and with Austria-Hungary, itself unwilling to see an expanded Serbia on its southern border, rallied the other powers to caution the Balkan states against a change in the balance of power. But the Balkan League felt strong enough to challenge the Ottoman Empire militarily. On October 8, 1912, Montenegro was the first state to declare war. After issuing an ultimatum to the Porte on October 13, the other three states declared war four days later. The combined Balkan armies effectively destroyed Ottoman power in Europe and carved up Macedonia. But the alliance did not hold. After the successful conclusion of the First Balkan War, differences over the partition of Macedonia surfaced. Bulgaria's jealousy of Serbia and Greece tore the League apart and led to the Second Balkan War. *See also* Balance of Power; Balkan Crises; Balkan Wars; Ottoman Empire.

FURTHER READING: Gerolymatos, André. *The Balkan Wars: Conquest, Revolution, and Retribution from the Ottoman Era to the Twentieth Century and Beyond*. New York: Basic Books, 2002; Glenny, Misha. *The Balkans: Nationalism, War, and the Great Powers, 1804–1999*. New York: Viking, 2000; Mazower, Mark. *The Balkans: A Short History*. New York: Modern Library, 2000.

ANDREKOS VARNAVA

## Balkan Wars (1912–1913)

Two wars fought principally over control of the Ottoman provinces in Macedonia and Thrace. The first, from October 1912 to May 1913, brought the states of the Balkan League, Bulgaria, Serbia, Greece, and Montenegro, together into a military alliance against the Ottoman Empire with the goal of driving the Turks from Europe. In fall of 1911, Serbia and Bulgaria had first exchanged proposals and in March 1912 signed an agreement recognizing Bulgarian interest in Thrace and southern Macedonia and Serb interest in Kosovo and Albania but with no agreement on the final terms of partition of Macedonia. Taking advantage of Turkish weakness caused by the **Italo-Turkish War** of 1911–1912, Montenegro started the First Balkan War on October 8, 1912, and the other Balkan states jumped in. Bulgarian forces won a victory at Kirk-Kilisse in Thrace and the Serbs at Kumanovo in Macedonia, while Greece captured Salonika. Bulgarian forces reached the outskirts of Constantinople. The first war ended with the Treaty of London on May 30, 1913 under the terms that the Turks gave up all their European possessions west of the Enos-Media line. To block Serbia from reaching the sea coast, **Austria-Hungary** and Italy insisted that an independent Albanian state be created out of the lost Ottoman territory.

These demands seriously limited the anticipated gains of Serbia and Greece, and consequently both states sought territorial compensation in Macedonia. Conflicting claims over Macedonia led to a second conflict between Bulgaria on one hand and Serbia and Greece on the other. Feeling deprived of most of the fruits of the war, Bulgaria attacked Serbia and Greece on June 29–30, 1913, starting the Second Balkan War. Montenegro immediately allied with the Serbs while Romania and the Ottomans also entered the fray against Bulgaria. Forced to fight on all sides, Bulgaria was defeated and the war ended with the Treaty of Bucharest on August 10, 1913, which confirmed Serbian and Greek gains in Macedonia, brought Crete and part of Epirus under Greek control, gave southern Dobrudja to Romania, and granted Bulgaria only a thin slice of Macedonia and a bit of the Aegean coastline. By the terms of the Treaty of Constantinople in October 1913 Bulgarian-Turkish hostilities ended with most of Eastern Thrace, including the city of Adrianople, reverting back to Turkish control. Serbia doubled in size, gaining the Kosovo region with its large Albanian Muslim population. *See also* Balkan League; Ottoman Empire; Russian Empire; Serbia.

FURTHER READING: Erickson, Edward J. *Defeat in Detail: The Ottoman Army in the Balkans, 1912–1913.* Westport: Praeger, 2003; Hall, Richard C. *The Balkan Wars, 1912–1913: Prelude to the First World War.* London: Routledge, 2000; Schurman, Jacob Gould. *The Balkan Wars, 1912–1913.* New York: Cosimo Classics, 2005.

JONATHAN GRANT

## Barbary States

Four states of Northern Africa—**Morocco,** Algiers, Tunis, and Tripoli—that plundered seaborne commerce for centuries. With the exception of Morocco, they were nominally part of the **Ottoman Empire.** Surviving by blackmail, they received great sums of money, ships, and arms yearly from foreign powers in return for allowing the foreigners to trade in African ports and sail unmolested through the Barbary waters. They demanded tribute money, seized ships, and held crews for ransom or sold them into slavery.

By the end of the eighteenth century, the effectiveness of Tripoli's corsairs had long since deteriorated, but their reputation alone was enough to prompt European maritime states to pay the tribute extorted by the *pasha* to ensure safe passage of their shipping through Tripolitan waters. American merchant ships, no longer covered by British protection, were seized by Barbary pirates in the years after American Independence, and American crews were enslaved. In 1799, the United States agreed to pay $18,000 a year in return for a promise that Tripoli-based corsairs would not molest American ships. Similar agreements were made at the time with the rulers of Morocco, Algiers, and Tunis.

In May 1801, however, the United States refused to succumb to the increasing demands of the pasha of Tripoli; in return, the pasha declared war. The United States sent naval squadrons into the Mediterranean under the leadership of Commodores Richard Dale and Edward Preble. The navy blockaded the enemy coast, bombarded his shore fortresses, and engaged in close gunboat actions. In June 1805, a peace settlement was negotiated, thus ending officially the Tripolitan War.

After the War of 1812, two American naval squadrons returned to the Mediterranean. Diplomacy backed by resolute force soon brought the rulers of Barbary to terms. Commodore Decatur obtained treaties that eliminated the American tribute. In the years immediately after the Napoleonic Wars the European powers forced an end to piracy and the payment of tribute in the Barbary States. Algiers capitulated to the French on July 5, 1830, the *Dey* (ruler) went into exile and the Ottoman **janissaries** were shipped back to Constantinople. Following the French conquest of Algiers, Tunis and Tripoli proclaimed at once an end to Christian slavery and corsair activities. They preserved a fictitious independence until they became respectively in 1881 and in 1911 a French protectorate and an Italian colony. *See also* Algeria.

FURTHER READING: Fisher, Godfrey. *Barbary Legend: War, Trade, and Piracy in North Africa.* Westport, CT: Greenwood Press, 1974; Lane Poole, Stanley with the collaboration of J. D. Jerrold Kelly. *The Barbary Corsairs.* Westport, CT: Negro Universities Press, 1970.

MOSHE TERDMAN

## Bashi-Bazouks

Irregular Ottoman cavalrymen noted for their horsemanship, lack of discipline, and cruelty. Sometimes referred to as the "Spahis of the Orient," they were usually Albanians, Circassians, or Kurds. The Anglo-French forces sought to employ them during the Crimean War but had little success in developing military discipline among them. In 1876, bashi-bazouks massacred 12,000 Christians in putting down a revolt against Ottoman rule. The "Bulgarian atrocities" provoked international outrage, particularly among pan-Slavists in Russia and in Britain in the attacks of William Gladstone against the government of Benjamin Disraeli for its support of Turkey. *See also* Bulgaria; Eastern Question; Pan-Slavism.

FURTHER READING: Goodwin, Jason. *Lords of the Horizons: A History of the Ottoman Empire.* London: Chatto & Windus, 1998.

CARL CAVANAGH HODGE

## Bassein, Treaty of (1802)

A transitional treaty, signed December1, 1802, between the British **East India Company** and the Maratha of **India.** The Maratha Confederacy was composed of four chiefs, namely Sindia, Gaekwad, Bhonsle, and Holkar, under the leadership of the *Peshwa* (prime minister). In 1802, Jaswant Rao Holkar occupied Poona. The

*Peshwa* fled to Bombay and in October 1802 signed the Treaty of Bassein with the East India Company. Under the terms of this treaty, the *Peshwa* became a subordinate ally of the company and a force of 6, 000 British troops was to be stationed with him. The treaty challenged by Sindia, Bhonsle, and Holkar, which resulted in the Second Anglo-Maratha War in 1803.

FURTHER READING: Keay, John. *The Honourable Company.* London: Harper Collins, 1991.

KAUSHIK ROY

## Basutoland

Basutoland, a mountainous area of South Africa conforming to the borders of present-day Lesotho, is the home of the Basotho people. Moshweshwe I created the Basotho nation from various remnant tribes of the early nineteenth century *Lifaqane.* The Boers attempted to engage the Basotho against British encroachment, but the Basotho correctly gauged the balance of power in South Africa and sought the protection of the British Crown, receiving it from **Victoria** I in 1868. Over Basotho objections, the British handed Basutoland over to the **Cape Colony** in 1871. When fighting broke out with the Xhosa in 1877, the Cape Colony attempted to disarm all Africans, including allies of the British.

A war erupted when the Basotho refused to surrender their firearms. Skilled in the use of guns, horses, and guerrilla tactics, the Basotho gave as good as they got against the Cape Colony's poorly trained constabulary forces. Britain resumed direct responsibility and the "Gun War" ended in negotiations with the Basotho keeping their arms. After 1884, Basutoland was governed by **indirect rule,** and, in1910, a Basutoland council of 99 appointed Basothos was officially established as an advisory council. *See also* Africa, Scramble for; Boer Wars.

FURTHER READING: Sanders, Peter. *Moshoeshoe, Chief of the Sotho.* London: Heinemann, 1975.

CARL CAVANAGH HODGE

## Bates Agreement (1899–1904)

An agreement negotiated between **United States** Brigadier General John C. Bates and the Sultan of Sulu, Jamal-ul Kiram II, on August 20, 1899, governing U.S. and Moro relations between 1899 and 1904. According to the agreement, the Sultan and his principal *datos* (local chieftains) recognized American sovereignty over the Moro, the Spanish and American name for the Muslim inhabitants of the Philippines, Provinces of Mindanao, and the Sulu Archipelago in exchange for American recognition of the Sultan's jurisdiction over intra-Moro affairs. Initially designed to placate the Moros and keep them from joining the **Philippine** Insurrection against American rule, the Bates Agreement was abrogated by President Theodore **Roosevelt** on March 2, 1904 because of the Sultan's inability to maintain order and the American desire to curb Moro practices such as slavery, blood feuds, and polygamy. American intervention to curb these local customs led to Moro resistance and to the launch of the Moro Punitive Expeditions. *See also* Spanish-American War; Wood, Leonard.

FURTHER READING: Gowing, Peter. "Mandate in Moroland: The American Government of Muslim Filipinos, 1899–1920." D.S.S. dissertation, Syracuse University, 1968; Jornacion, George W. "The Time of Eagles: United States Army Officers and the Pacification of the Philippine Moros, 1899–1913." Ph.D. dissertation, University of Maine, 1973; Thompson, Wayne Wray. "Governors of the Moro Province: Wood, Bliss, and Pershing in the Southern Philippines, 1903–1913." Ph.D. dissertation, University of California—San Diego, 1975.

JAMES PRUITT

## "Battle of the Nations"

*See* Leipzig, Battle of

## Bavaria

The largest of the South German states incorporated into the German Empire in 1871. An independent duchy under the Holy Roman Empire and a German Electorate after 1623, Bavaria became an independent kingdom in 1806 within the Confederation of the Rhine under Napoleon and a member of the **German Confederation** after the Congress of **Vienna.** Bavaria sought and secured a high degree of autonomy by balancing the rivalry of Austria and Prussia, but nevertheless joined the *Zollverein* in 1834 along with Württemberg, Saxony and Thuringia. This pulled Bavaria somewhat more into the Prussian orbit. Dread of Prussian hegemony shunted Bavaria into alliance with Austria in the Seven Weeks' War of 1866.

After Austria's defeat Bavarian particularism remained resilient enough that Prussian commanders such as Helmuth von **Moltke** hesitated at the thought of linking the fortunes Protestant Prussia with Catholic Bavaria. German Chancellor Otto von **Bismarck,** however, handled peace negotiations with Bavaria delicately. He succeeded first in isolating and then, at the very moment of expiration of the German Confederation, managed to include it in the strongest union of northern and southern German states that had hitherto existed. This union was made stronger still by France's strident reaction to German unification and the subsequent participation of Bavaria, now in league with Prussia, in **Franco-Prussian War** of 1870. The triumph of arms in which Bavarian troops shared enabled German patriotism to overcome distrust of Prussia, so that under the terms of the Treaty of **Frankfurt,** Bavaria and the other South German states joined the Second Reich.

FURTHER READING: Henderson; W. O. *The Zollverein.* Chicago: Quadrangle, 1962; Mattern, Johannes. *Bavaria and the Reich.* Baltimore: The Johns Hopkins University Press, 1923; Showwalter, Dennis. *The Wars of German Unification.* London: Hodder Arnold, 2004.

CARL CAVANAGH HODGE

## Bechuanaland

The British name for Botswana, a land-locked territory of southern Africa dominated by the Kalahari Desert and home of the indigenous Tswana people, whom the British called the Bechuana. The Great Trek of the Boer settlers northward put the Tswana at risk of losing their land, but when the Boers declared a

**protectorate** over the region the British forced the Boers out in 1885. Cecil **Rhodes** secured a royal charter for the British South Africa Company in Bechuanaland in 1889, and in 1891 London declared the Bechuanaland Protectorate under the jurisdiction of the high commissioner for South Africa. The various Tswana tribes applied to London for the recovery of their autonomy, and the five major tribes were granted reserves within which they governed themselves while paying taxes to Britain for protection.

FURTHER READING: Were, Gideon S. *A History of South Africa.* London: Evans Brothers, 1982.

CARL CAVANAGH HODGE

## Baylen, Battle of

*See* Bailén, Battle of

## Beck-Rzikowsky, Friedrich (1830–1920)

An Austrian military reformer, Count Friedrich Beck-Rzikowsky was born in March 1830 in Freiburg in southwestern Germany. He joined the Austrian army in 1846 and became the aide-de-champ (Generaladjutant) of Emperor **Francis Joseph** I and the head of the Emperor's military chancellery. Beck won the trust and friendship of Frances Joseph. From 1881 to 1906, he served as Chief of the Austro-Hungarian general staff and laid the foundations for a more professional general staff officer corps, modernized war preparations, and planning procedures. With his opposite numbers in Berlin, Helmut von **Moltke** and Waldersee, Beck set up a plan for offensive coalition warfare in the East in the 1880s, but under Waldersee's successor, **Schlieffen,** Germany's commitment to a joint campaign against Russia was withdrawn. Beck was able to initiate the construction of new strategic **railways** in the Northeast, but by the late 1880s, with troop numbers stagnant, Austria-Hungary was falling behind her military rivals and allies. The heir to the throne, Archduke **Francis Ferdinand,** called for Beck's resignation, because the septuagenarian general seemed to be an unsuitable choice for military leadership. Beck became commander of one of the Emperor's Guards, a strictly ceremonial post. He died in Vienna in February 1920. *See also* Habsburg Empire

FURTHER READING: Lackey, Scott W. *The Rebirth of the Habsburg Army: Friedrich Beck and the Rise of the General Staff.* Westport, CT: Greenwood, 1995.

GUENTHER KRONENBITTER

## Beijing, Conventions of (1860)

The capstone of the "treaty system" imposed on China by the British Empire. After the dreadful defeat of the **Arrow War,** the Chinese government was forced to enter the Conventions of Beijing with Britain and France. On October 24, 1860, China signed the Convention of "Peace and Friendship" with Britain in Beijing, and with France the next day. Following the advice of the Russian negotiator, Nikolay

Ignatyev, who acted as mediator in securing the evacuation of the invaders from Beijing, Prince Gong exchanged ratification of the Tianjin Treaties of 1858, increased the Chinese indemnities to Britain and France, and added other concessions, including the Kowloon Peninsula in southern China to Britain, and the French demand for Catholic missions to hold property in the interior China. China also agreed to grant foreign powers to station diplomats in Beijing.

Tianjin was opened as a treaty port, and the opium importation was legalized. As the American and Russian negotiators had already exchanged the ratification of Tianjin Treaties in 1859, the 1858–1860 treaties extended the foreign privileges granted after the first **Opium War** and strengthened the developments in the treaty-port system. The Conventions of Beijing further opened the **Qing Dynasty** to Western contact. Not only was the Chinese imperial court forced to further concede its territorial and sovereignty rights, but more importantly the dominant Confucian values of the Chinese feudal society were seriously challenged. The right to disseminate Christianity threatened the backbone of the dynastic rule, and the permanent residence of foreign diplomats in Beijing signified an end to the long-established tributary relationship between China and other countries. As a reward for Russian's mediatory work, the Sino-Russian Treaty of Beijing was also reached, which confirmed the Treaty of **Aigun** and ceded to Russia the territory between the Ussuri River and the sea. In brief, the Conventions of Beijing enlarged the scope of the foreign privileges that British initially obtained, and the Chinese Empire skidded further down a disastrous path to its semicolonial status during the late nineteenth century. *See also* Boxer Insurrection; British Empire.

FURTHER READING: Wong, J. Y. *Deadly Dreams: Opium, Imperialism, and the Arrow War in China* New York: Cambridge University Press, 1998.

WENXIAN ZHANG

## Belgian Congo

A enormous territory of the sub-Saharan African interior conforming to the shape of the Congo River Basin and a Belgian colony from 1908 to 1960. It had hitherto been under the personal rule of the Belgian King, Leopold II (1835–1909), as the Congo Free State. Leopold had long wanted a colony for Belgium, but the country's politicians preferred to concentrate on the domestic economy. Leopold established independently the Association Internationale du Congo, ostensibly a benevolent organization but in fact a vehicle through which Leopold, the *Association*'s sole shareholder, could enrich himself. Leopold focused his ambitions on the Congo River basin, a region largely unexplored by Europeans, and in 1879 independently financed Henry **Stanley,** the American-born British explorer, to undertake a philanthropic and scientific mission that for Leopold and his associates was nonetheless a colonial and commercial venture.

Stanley had gained international fame the previous year by finding the British explorer and missionary Dr. David Livingstone, who had set out to find the source of the Nile and disappeared. Stanley established way-stations and hospitals in the region to stake Leopold's claim, signed treaties on Leopold's behalf with local leaders, and helped open up the river basin to outside trade. In 1884, Leopold's claims to the region were recognized by his European peers at the **Berlin Conference** on West Africa and Congo. The Conference declared the new Congo Free State an international **free trade** zone. In 1885, Leopold proclaimed himself sovereign of the Congo Free State and in 1888 organized the many African mercenaries in his pay into the Force Publique, the colony's army. Leopold subsequently tried to extend his influence into **Sudan,** striking a secret Congo treaty with the British, which would have granted the latter their long-wished-for Cape-to-Cairo line. French and German protests, however, squashed the treaty.

Under Leopold's rule, the Congo Free State combated the Arab **slave trade** in eastern Congo. Such humanitarianism was undercut, however, by Leopold's alliance with Tippu Tip, the Zanzibari slave trader who was the *de facto* ruler of the eastern Congo. Belgian businessmen, colonial officers, and foreign traders also exploited the colony for its rich natural resources, including lumber, ivory, and especially rubber. Rubber was needed for new industrial products like tires and cable insulation. To meet the demand, Belgian companies put horrendous pressures on their Congolese employees. Congolese rubber harvesters who failed to meet quotas had their hands chopped off, a practice that, combined with disease and poor living conditions, caused millions of deaths. Leopold's "personal rule" was among the most violent and tragic manifestations of European colonial rule.

By 1900, international protest against these atrocities increased, led by British activists like E. D. Morel and Sir Roger Casement. The latter's fact-finding mission to the Congo, where he met with indigenous opponents of Leopold, publicized the abuses for the international press and inspired a campaign for Leopold's ouster. In 1908, bowing to international pressure, Leopold transferred authority of the Congo Free State to the Belgian government, whereby it became the Belgian Congo. The Belgian Congo was governed as a formal colony, with a colonial governor responsible to the King of **Belgium.** Christian missionaries directed indigenous education. The Belgian Congo gained its independence in 1960, immediately followed by five years of war.

Joseph Conrad's famous novel *Heart of Darkness,* published in 1902, was inspired by his work as a steamer captain on the Congo. Mr. Kurtz, the European "corrupted" by "going native," is based in part on Arthur Hodister, a British ivory trader who was murdered in the Congo in 1892. *Heart of Darkness* portrays both the growing ambivalence with which some Europeans began to view imperialism by the early twentieth century and the racial prejudices that continued to determine relations between Europeans and Africans. *See also* Africa, Scramble for.

FURTHER READING: Gann, L. H., and Peter Duigen. *The Rulers of Belgian Africa 1884–1914.* Princeton, NJ: Princeton University Press, 1979; Hochschild, Adam. *King Leopold's Ghost.* New York: Houghton Mifflin, 1998.

DANIEL GORMAN

## Belgium

A country the size of the state of Maryland situated in northwest Europe and surrounded by the Netherlands, Germany, Luxembourg, France, and the North Sea. It was an advanced industrial economy and secondary imperial power by the late nineteenth century.

Before the French Revolutionary Wars, Belgium had been known as Austrian Netherlands since 1714 when Austria took possession of the Spanish Netherlands. Nominally ruled by the Hapsburg monarchy from Vienna, it enjoyed considerable autonomy until 1789, when the Austrian emperor attempted to centralize and consolidate his authority in the region. Upset with the loss of autonomy, and influenced by the events in neighboring France, the Belgians revolted and in 1790 declared their independence as the United States of Belgium. The Austrians quickly regained control, but soon found themselves at war with the revolutionary regime in France.

The next three years were chaotic and destructive, as the French conquered the country in a self-described "liberation" by 1792 and enthusiastically imported their revolutionary measures, complete with liberal use of the guillotine and widespread confiscations of church and noble property. The Austrians reconquered the country in 1793, but the French were back the next year. Between the French revolutionary predations and the tendencies of armies during this period to live off the land, Belgium was devastated. In 1795, France formally annexed the region, and for the next 20 years it was officially French. The Revolutionary government nevertheless treated Belgium as a colony to be plundered. Under Napoleon, conditions were eased, at least for French-speaking Belgians, and the country was accepted into the **French Empire.**

After the fall of Napoleon, the European map was redrawn by the victors at the Congress of **Vienna.** One of Britain's major concerns at the Congress was for a power occupying the southern Netherlands that could defend it against what the British assumed would be inevitable expansionist pressure from France. After much discussion and haggling, the parties agreed that Belgium would be handed to the Netherlands. Given the conservative, Great Power preoccupation of the Congress with the European balance of power, little attention was given to what the Belgians themselves thought should happen. The reunified Low Countries were ruled by William I, of the intensely Calvinist Orange family that had ruled as *Stadtholder* in the Dutch Republic. It was supposed to be a joint kingdom, with dual capitals in The Hague and Brussels. William, however, became increasingly authoritarian and was insensitive to his Belgian subjects. His declaration of Dutch as the sole official language upset the French-speaking Walloons, and his attempts to impose the teaching of Calvinist doctrine in the schools offended both French and Dutch-speaking Catholics. Economic issues also played a role, as the Dutch tariff policies favored the northern provinces at the expense of the Belgians. In short, the Belgians and, in particular, the Francophone Walloons felt increasingly threatened.

In 1830, the July Revolution in France brought matters to a head in Belgium. On August 25, the citizens of Brussels rioted, spurred on by the performance of an allegorical opera dealing with revolt and patriotism. The King's son, William II, who resided in Brussels as the crown's representative, was convinced that the only solution to the growing crisis was an administrative separation of north and south. His father, however, rejected the plan, and an army was sent into Brussels to retake control. The operation failed. After intense street fighting from September 23 to 26, a provisional government was declared; and on October 4 a declaration of independence was issued. In November 1830, a National Congress assembled in Brussels, and on February 7, 1831, a constitution was proclaimed. In what became known as the "Ten Days' Campaign," on August 2, 1831, a second Dutch effort to recapture the south began. It was initially successful, winning two quick victories against the Belgians. The attack ground to a halt on August 12, however, and the offensive was called off when a French army appeared to protect the Belgians.

International conditions at the time favored the Belgian cause. The British foreign secretary, Lord **Palmerston,** sought advantageous commercial conditions for British interests on the continent and therefore supported Belgian freedom. Either of two continental powers, France or Russia, might have posed a danger to cooperation in a peaceful resolution, but neither was in a position to run risks. The government of Louis Phillippe was, in 1830, dealing with political turmoil at home, even as a large part of its army was tied down in **Algeria.** Russia, on the other hand, was suddenly facing the **Polish Rebellions.** As a consequence, an international agreement was reached in London on December 20, 1830, recognizing the independence of Belgium. The conflict sputtered on for another eight years, until the powers imposed a peace on the parties in the Treaty of **London,** signed on April 19, 1839. The treaty recognized Belgian independence, with borders roughly similar to those today. More important, it also recognized Belgian neutrality—a neutrality recognized by all of the signatories, including Prussia, Austria, France, Britain, and the Netherlands. This commitment to neutrality would be crucial to the entry of Britain in World War I, some 75 years later.

In the meantime, the Belgians elected Leopold Georg Christian Friedrich of Saxe-Coburg, a German nobleman who was an advisor to his niece, Queen Victoria, as "King of the Belgians" in 1831. Leopold had earlier turned down the job of King of Greece. Belgian independence meant a complete reversal of roles between the Flemish and the Walloons. French became the dominant language, even in the north, and the Walloons the dominant group. Despite being a majority, the Flemish, mostly farmers and factory workers, were considered second-class citizens.

Under the rule of Leopold I and his son, Leopold II, Belgium prospered. Its industrialization was so successful that, by the eve of World War I, Belgium was, by some measures, the fourth strongest economic power in the world. The increasingly prosperous small nation was not a big enough stage for Leopold II, however. He hungered for an empire. Conventional wisdom during the mid-nineteenth century held that industrial powers needed captive colonial markets to provide a source of raw materials, as well as to "soak up" its surplus goods and perhaps also its excess population. Leopold was also driven by personal demons—obsessions with trade, profit, power, and an empire.

From the early 1860s, Leopold lobbied the Belgian parliament and people relentlessly to push the country into an imperial acquisition. Hardly anyone was interested. Eventually, he realized any colonial ambitions would have to be achieved with a private colony owned by him personally. He expanded his efforts to the European scientific and philanthropic community. He hosted conferences and formed international committees on the "plight" of the natives of Africa. These included the Geographical Conference of 1876, the Association Internationale Africaine in 1876, the Committee to Study the Upper Congo in 1878, and the International Association of the Congo of 1883, all studded with leading scientists and nobles. Always, he cloaked his efforts in the language of scientific discovery and philanthropy.

Leopold's breakthrough came in 1878, with his meeting of Henry Morgan Stanley, the American who famously "found" the missionary David Livingston. The next year, Leopold funded an "exploratory" expedition by Stanley of the Congo River in central Africa. The expedition's real purpose was to begin the establishment of

Leopold's personal empire. Leopold and Stanley's efforts were ratified by the international community at the **Berlin Conference** of 1884–1885, which recognized Leopold as sovereign of the Congo Free State. Leopold's personal empire, more in the nature of a proto-multinational corporation than a national colony, had little or no effect on Belgium. Leopold obtained a loan from the Belgian parliament in 1889, ostensibly for philanthropic work in his free state, but in fact used to fund the startup of commercial exploitation. Eventually, the brutal nature of Belgian rule in the Congo became known, and international public pressure forced the Belgian parliament to take over administration of the colony in 1908. The Belgian colonial administration was considerably less brutal than that of the Congo Free State, but no less paternalistic. Political administration fell under the total and direct control of the mother country, with no indigenous democratic institutions and almost no participation of any kind by the native population. The **Belgian Congo** thus earned a special place of infamy in the history of European colonialism.

In the years since independence and the declaration of neutrality in 1839, the Belgians scrupulously adhered to its provisions. The army spent considerable resources building a series of fortifications around major cities throughout the country, but Belgium made no effort to ally itself with any of the Great Powers surrounding it. In each of the abortive crises in the years before the outbreak of the war, the Belgian government made it clear to all of its neighbors that it would resist any incursion across its borders, whether hostile or "supportive." This was not enough to ensure Belgian security. World War I began with the German invasion of Belgium in an attempt to outflank the French army at the Franco-German border to the south. Officially, Britain went to war with Germany over the violation of Belgian neutrality but was not able to provide timely aid. The Belgians resisted stoutly but were rapidly overcome by the surprise and strength of the German army. Within weeks, the Germans had occupied all but a few square miles in the far west. They spent the next four years terrorizing and starving the civilian population, and pillaging the country of its economic resources. "The Rape of Belgium" became the symbol in the Western democracies, and especially the United States, of German barbarism. *See also* Africa, Scramble for; Habsburg Empire; Napoleonic Wars; Netherlands.

FURTHER READING: Blom, J.C.H., and Emiel Lamberts, eds. *History of the Low Countries.* Translated by James C. Kennedy. New York: Berghahn Books, 2006; Hayes, Carlton J. H. *A Political and Social History of Modern Europe.* New York: Macmillan, 1926; Hochschild, Adam, *King Leopold's Ghost.* New York: Houghton Mifflin, 1998; Schama, Simon. *Patriots and Liberators: Revolution in the Netherlands, 1780–1813.* New York: Alfred A. Knopf, 1977; Schroeder, Paul W. *The Transformation of European Politics, 1763–1848.* Oxford: Clarendon, 1994; Taylor, A.J.P. *The Struggle for Mastery in Europe, 1848–1918.* Oxford: Clarendon, 1954; Zuckerman, Larry. *The Rape of Belgium.* New York: New York University Press, 2004.

JOSEPH ADAMCZYK

## Belle Époque

The term *belle époque* refers to the period between 1880 and the start of World War I in 1914 in Europe, and above all in France. The period defined a cultural revolution characterized by a sense of optimism and creative enthusiasm. Paris flourished as a center of art, literature, and fashion. The artistic scene flourished, and the pleasures of life were pursued with conspicuous vigor. The era also witnessed the spectacular popularity of café-concerts and music halls, as well as expositions. The restaurants and cabarets of the Montmartre neighborhood in Paris attracted intellectuals and avant-garde artists converged; the music halls and café-concerts exhibited a new form of theatre free of conventional artistic constraints, not subject to strict social control, and thus accessible to many different social classes. Bourgeois norms were shed. The arts had been "democratized" and were no longer the privilege of the wealthy.

Mass production and new technologies were also on the rise, catering to a larger consuming public of various social strata. Featured in the contemporary novels of Émile Zola, such as *Le Bonheur des Dames,* departmental stores were filled with a huge variety items on display for sale and managed to attract throngs of people through innovative displays of products. The use of new technology was nowhere more prominent than in the development of the underground metropolitan network. The Paris Metro revolutionized urban travel, symbolized progress, and contributed to social optimism. Expositions, too, added to the aura of luxury and abundance. In 1900, the Great Universal Exposition attracted 51 million visitors to Paris to products using new technologies and to marvel at structures such as the Eiffel Tower and the Gare D'Orsay. There were also exhibits from overseas colonies considered exotic by the people of the metropole, including a **human zoo.**

FURTHER READING: Rearick, Charles. *Pleasures of the Belle Epoque.* New Haven, CT: Yale University Press, 1985; Sternau, Susan A. *Art Nouveau: Spirit of the Belle Epoque.* New York: Smithmark, 2005; Tuchman, Barbara. *The Proud Tower: A Portrait of the World Before the War, 1890–1914.* New York: Ballantine, 1996.

NURFADZILAH YAHAYA

## Bengal

Bengal was a large region in northeastern India and an object of British colonial interest since 1633. After coming under the control of the **East India Company** during the eighteenth century, Bengal served as the springboard for the British conquest of the entire Indian subcontinent. Long before the heyday of British rule in India, the East India Company in Bengal operated as a state within a state whose predatory entrepreneurship produced overnight fortunes from ventures in salt, opium, tobacco, timber, and boat-building and made it scandalous with Parliament back in Britain. Divided by Lord Curzon in 1905, over nationalist protests that resulted both in a nationalist boycott of British goods and the founding of the Muslim league, Bengal was reunified in 1911. *See also* India.

FURTHER READING: James, Lawrence. *Raj: The Making and Unmaking of British India.* New York: St. Martin's, 1997.

CARL CAVANAGH HODGE

## Bentham, Jeremy (1748–1832)

One of the most influential philosophers and legal theorists of the modern age. Against the traditionalist account of English law formulated by William Blackstone,

Bentham advanced the principle that law should aim to maximize "utility," which he defined as human happiness, according to a directly hedonist and indeed reductionist account of happiness as pleasure. It was Bentham's rationalist revolt against the prescriptivism of earlier legal and social theorists that was most influential. A method of reasoning that attempted to derive sound social policy from some stated root principle, from which all else was held to follow, was characteristic of Bentham and his followers among the so-called philosophic radicals. The radicalism of Bentham and his followers was a powerful weapon against the often rococo absurdities of the ancient constitution and its associated class structure. But it also led to the kind of dogmatic insistence on principle over evidence that **Macaulay** attacked in James Mill's *Essay on Government* and ultimately depended on an unrealistic optimism about the ability of reason to prescribe social arrangements.

That dogmatic optimism was in evidence in Bentham's letter to the French Assembly of 1793, "Emancipate Your Colonies!," which argued on economic grounds against **imperialism,** and which clearly presumed that a democratic assembly would be swayed by a well-formulated rational argument. Obviously Bentham's advice on colonies was taken neither in Paris nor in London; he later argued that colonies were retained as sources of employment, emoluments, and ideological justification for the ruling class and its institutions, a line of argument that became a fixture of subsequent anti-imperialism. Bentham's rationalism, his humanism—social arrangements existed to further secular human happiness—and his disdain for traditional and prescriptive arguments were central to later arguments about empire, and indeed most other political subjects. *See also* Liberalism.

FURTHER READING: Bentham, Jeremy. *Rights, Representation and Reform.* Edited by Philip Schofield, Catherine Pease-Watkin, and Cyprian Blamires. Oxford: Clarendon Press, 2002; Bowring, John, ed. *The Collected Works of Jeremy Bentham.* Edinburgh: W. Tait, 1843; Dinwiddie, John. *Bentham.* New York: Oxford University Press, 1989.

MARK F. PROUDMAN

## Bentinck, Lord William (1774–1839)

Governor General of **India** from 1828 to 1835, Lord William Bentinck was the second son of the Duke of Portland, leader of the so-called Portland Whigs and effectively Prime Minster in the Ministry of the All the Talents (1807–1809). As a young man, he was commissioned in the army, and was in and out of Parliament for a family-controlled seat between 1796 and 1826. Family influence saw him appointed Governor of **Madras** from 1803 to 1807.

On his return from India, Bentinck commanded a brigade with credit under Sir John Moore at **Corunna.** Appointed ambassador to Sicily in 1811, he became an enthusiast for Italian nationalism, in line with his inherited Whig principles, eventually being recalled in 1815 under Austrian pressure. Appointed Governor General of India by his old ally **Canning,** Bentinck served from 1828–1835. In India, he focused on reducing expenditure and enhancing revenues. He abolished suttee and waged war against the thugs. He also made English the official language of government and was lauded by Macaulay for having aimed to "elevate the intellectual and moral character of the nations committed to his charge." *See also* British Empire; Napoleonic Wars; Suttee; Thugs.

FURTHER READING: Boulger, Demetrius C. *Lord William Bentinck.* Oxford: Clarendon, 1897.

MARK F. PROUDMAN

## Beresina, Battles of (1812)

A series of bloody Franco-Russian engagements fought during Napoleon's retreat from Moscow in 1812. French forces were down to about 50,000 men and were pursued by Kutuzov and Wittgenstein's combined 80,000 men to the north and Tshitshagov's 34,000 men to the south. Worse, the Beresina River had thawed and was impassable.

Diversionary tactics by Oudinot, however, kept Tshitshagov at bay and Kutuzov delayed his pursuit. Engineers worked through the night of the November 25 to build two bridges. The French began to cross and Tshitshagov's realization of the situation on November 26 was too late. Against all odds, by the end of November 28, the French army was across the river. Perhaps 30,000 noncombatants died, many trying to get across in a panic as the bridges were destroyed, or killed by Cossacks in the aftermath. The French lost perhaps 25,000 men, the Russians 10,000. But what was left of the *Grande Armée* was able to continue marching to Poland. *See also* Napoleonic Wars.

FURTHER READING: Palmer, Alan. *Napoleon in Russia.* London: Robinson, 1997.

J. DAVID MARKHAM

## Berlin-Baghdad Railway

An Ottoman-German initiative to construct a continuous rail link between the German capital and Baghdad, securing for Germany access to the Persian Gulf and the Ottoman Empire a modern transportation infrastructure. In 1888, the Ottoman government granted a syndicate of German banks a concession to build a rail link from Constantinople, where the extant Oriental Railway terminated, to Angora. The link was extended to Konia in 1896. In 1903, The Baghdad Railway Company, a German-financed Ottoman organization, was commissioned to extend the line to Baghdad. The railway would strengthen Germany's empire, allowing her to send troops quickly to her African colonies, and enable her to bypass the **Suez Canal,** potentially threatening Britain's primacy in the Mediterranean and India. The project therefore contributed to the heightened international tension that eventually caused war in 1914. It was never completed, and the victorious imperial powers split among themselves the built sections after World War I. *See also* German Empire; Ottoman Empire; Railways.

FURTHER READING: Berghahn, V. R. *Germany and the Approach of War in 1914.* London: Macmillan, 1993; Macfie, A. L. *The End of the Ottoman Empire.* London: Longman, 1998.

DANIEL GORMAN

## Berlin Conference (1884–1885)

A congress hosted in the German capital from November 1884 to February 1885 by Chancellor Otto von **Bismarck** to attenuate growing imperial rivalries caused by what historians now term the "new imperialism." This process, which began in about 1870 and was at its most intense between 1880 and 1900, saw European powers engage in a rapid process of overseas colonization, seeking economic gain, national prestige, and the universalization of European values. The most intense part of this process was the Scramble for Africa, in which European powers carved up the African continent into colonies. The scramble led to several disputes over territory and threatened to cause a European war. The Berlin Conference was called to create rules for continued colonization in Africa. Bismarck also hoped to negotiate a greater imperial role for Germany.

The conference was attended by all of the major European powers, the Ottoman Empire, and the United States. There were no representatives from Africa itself, reflecting a paternalistic view of indigenous peoples common at that time. The conference had two significant outcomes. The first was to recognize "spheres of influence" in Africa, requiring colonial powers to establish administrative and defense capabilities in a region before it could be effectively claimed. This provision recognized the claims of King Leopold II of **Belgium** to the Congo River basin, creating The Congo Free State. Leopold subsequently exploited his position by allowing indigenous peoples to be used as forced labor extracting resources like ivory and rubber. During the next 20 years, people perished from mass killings, disease, and starvation under the brutal oversight of Belgian and international masters. Appalling atrocities were ordered by white officers and carried out by black soldiers. The creation of what was in effect an international free trade zone prioritized the rights of European traders over indigenous peoples, and encouraged many European nations to establish chartered companies to do business in Africa. Closely linked was the Conference's second major provision, the establishment of international freedom of navigation on Africa's waterways.

Alongside Leopold, Germany was the main beneficiary of the Conference, subsequently establishing African colonies in South-West Africa (present-day Namibia), Togoland and Cameroon in West Africa, and **German East Africa** (present-day Tanzania). The meeting also ensured continued Anglo-French rivalries in Africa, a rivalry that almost led to war in 1898 over the Fashoda Crisis in southern Sudan. Germany's later colonial interest in Morocco almost led to war on two separate occasions in 1903 and in 1907. By establishing rules for Africa, the Berlin Conference helped prevent a European war over Africa in the short term. In the long term, it arguably heightened the international tensions that eventually caused war in 1914, a war in which many Africans fought and died. *See also* Africa, Scramble for; Fashoda Incident; German Empire; Morocco Crises.

FURTHER READING: Förster, Stig; Mommsen,Wolfgang J., and Ronald Edward Robinson, eds. *Bismarck, Europe, and Africa: The Berlin Africa Conference 1884–1885 and the Onset of Partition.* London: Oxford University Press, 1988; Pakenham, Thomas. *The Scramble for Africa: White Man's Conquest of the Dark Continent from 1876 to 1912.* New York: Random House, 1991.

DANIEL GORMAN

## Berlin, Congress of (1878)

A meeting called by German Chancellor Otto von **Bismarck** to revise the Treaty of **San Stefano,** the 1878 Berlin conference as the first large international conference of the era of new imperialism. In the aftermath of the Ottoman Empire's defeat by Russia in 1878, the treaty provided for a new order in European and Asiatic Turkey. Serbia, Montenegro, and Romania were extended and a new state, Bulgaria, was to emerge out of the Ottoman provinces north and south of the Balkan Mountains from the Danube to the Aegean and from the Albanian mountains to the Black Sea. Britain and Austria-Hungary agreed that the changes to European Turkey would damage their economic and strategic interests and give a preponderant power to Russia. The Treaty of **Paris** had established that matters pertaining to the Ottoman Empire's integrity was for the joint cognizance of all the European powers, and so the Concert of Europe met to decide its fate.

Representatives of the European Powers and the Ottoman Empire met in the Radziwill Palace, Berlin, on June 13, 1878 under Bismarck's chairmanship. But the British Prime Minister Benjamin **Disraeli** and Lord Salisbury, his Foreign Secretary, had already determined the new balance of power in secret conventions. The convention with Russia was signed on May 30, and in it Britain allowed Russia to retain southern Bessarabia from the Ottoman vassal State of Romania, and Kars, Ardahan, and Batum on the Asian side of the Black Sea. In exchange, Russia agreed to reduce the size of Bulgaria.

In Asia, Disraeli worried about the Russians establishing a foothold in Armenia and moving across Mesopotamia to the Persian Gulf and beyond to India. Britain agreed to Russia retaining Kars, Ardahan, and Batum only after deciding to acquire a base—as it turned out, Disraeli selected Cyprus—in which to station an army to launch against any future Russian incursions against Ottoman Asia. Although the policy of territorial aggrandizement had been muted in 1876 against a weak Porte, it was now linked to maintaining the order established by the Anglo-Russian Convention.

Although the strategic order had been determined by the British, Russian, and Ottoman governments, the delegates at Berlin had a number of other questions to determine. The Congress, which lasted from June 13 to July 13, decided that Serbia, Montenegro, and Romania would be completely independent. Bulgaria became a self-governing principality, subject to the Porte, under Alexander of Battenberg. Not to be outdone, Austria-Hungary was assigned the occupation and administration of the volatile Ottoman province of **Bosnia-Herzegovina.** The British government offered leave to its French and Italian counterparts to pursue their ambitions in Tunis and Tripoli, an offer the French took up within four years, and the Italians in 1911. *See also* Crimean War; Eastern Question; Great Game.

FURTHER READING: Medlicott, W. N. *The Congress of Berlin and After.* Hamden, CT: Archon, 1963; Taylor, A.J.P. *The Struggle for Mastery in Europe. 1848–1918.* Oxford: Clarendon, 1954.

ANDREKOS VARNAVA

## Berlin, Treaty of

*See* Berlin, Congress of

## Bethmann-Hollweg, Theobald von (1856–1921)

Chancellor of Germany from 1909 to 1917, Theobald von Bethmann-Hollweg was born in Hohenfinow, Brandenburg. He studied law in Strasbourg, Leipzig, and Berlin before embarking on a career in the civil service. In 1905, he was appointed Prussian Minister of the Interior and in 1907 to the head of the Imperial Office of the Interior. Finally, he rose to the chancellory upon Berrnhard von **Bülow's** resignation in July 1909.

Bethmann was essentially a well-meaning, able, and industrious bureaucrat. By the German standards of his time, he was a political moderate who was unable to cope effectively with the domestic political pressures exerted by the socialist left and the nationalist and reactionary right. Over strenuous conservative opposition to broader reform, he managed to engineer a constitution for **Alsace-Lorraine** that raised its status to that of a *Reichsland*. In foreign policy he sought détente with Britain. Although unable to halt or slow the Anglo-German naval arms race largely as a result of ferocious opposition from **Tirpitz,** he managed to recover some lost diplomatic capital after the **Agadir Crisis** to work with the British foreign secretary, Sir Edward **Grey,** to lower tensions over the **Balkan Crises** of 1912–1913. After the assassination of Archduke Franz Ferdinand, he initially was among those urging a tough Austrian stand against Serbia but then gestured in support of Grey's late efforts to mediate a settlement. When Britain ultimately declared war on Germany over the latter's violation of Belgian neutrality, Bethmann made himself infamous for referring to the 1839 Treaty of **London** as a "scrap of paper." *See also* German Empire; Wilhelm II.

FURTHER READING: Craig, Gordon A. *Germany, 1866–1945.* New York: Oxford University Press, 1978.

CARL CAVANAGH HODGE

## Bismarck, Otto Eduard Leopold von (1815–1898)

Known as the "Iron Chancellor," Otto von Bismarck was a European statesman, the architect of German unification, and the first Chancellor of the German Empire. Born into a conservative **Junker** family from Pomerania, Bismarck went on to study law before entering the Prussian civil service in the aftermath of the Revolution of 1848. From 1851 to 1859, he served as chief Prussian delegate to the Frankfurt Diet where he frequently clashed with his Austrian counterparts over federal policy and their leadership of the **German Confederation.** Bismarck distinguished himself as an able diplomat during stints as Prussian ambassador to Russia, 1859–1862, and France in 1862, before being appointed Prussian Chancellor in 1862 as part of an effort to break a parliamentary crisis over army reforms.

Soon after his appointment as chancellor, Bismarck orchestrated German unification under Prussian leadership via the **Austro-Prussian** and **Franco-Prussian** Wars, in 1866 and 1870–1871. The **German Empire** was officially created in January 1871 with the coronation of **Wilhelm I** as Kaiser. Thereafter, Bismarck assumed a dual role as Prussian and Imperial Chancellor and committed his political career to safeguarding the newly unified German state. As part of this process, he not only created and controlled a complex alliance system aimed at preserving the **balance of power** in

Europe, but also oversaw a series of domestic social welfare reforms designed to ease the sting of rapid industrialization and ensure continued Prussian dominance.

Although earlier in his career Bismarck had been a vocal opponent of colonialism, arguing that colonies would generate unnecessary political dangers and expense, in the mid-1880s, he oversaw the creation of a German colonial Empire. The reason for the sudden reversal of his anticolonial policy remains the subject of historical debate, with explanations ranging from a simple change of heart, a calculated response to domestic political pressures, or the desire for Germany to keep pace with other great nations in Europe. The combination of Belgian activities in the Congo and growing pressure from German colonial interest groups convinced Bismarck to play host to the Conference of **Berlin** in 1884–1885, which sought to guarantee free trade in the Congo River basin and laid ground rules for the partition of Africa. In the mid-1880s, Germany quickly acquired colonies in **Cameroon, Togo** (now parts of Ghana and Togo), **German East Africa** (now Rwanda, Burundi and Tanzania), **German Southwest Africa** (now Namibia), **New Guinea,** and various Pacific Islands.

Despite years of loyal and effective service, starting in 1888, Bismarck began quarreling with the brash, ambitious, and egotistical new Kaiser **Wilhelm II.** In 1890, he resigned and spent the remainder of his life working on his memoirs and engaging in vocal criticism of the Kaiser and his government. *See also* Africa, Scramble for; Caprivi, Georg Leo von; Ems Telegram; Frankfurt, Treaty of; Koniggrätz, Battle of; Kulturkampf; NorthGerman Confederation; Schleswig-Holstein; Weltpolitik.

FURTHER READING: Crankshaw, Edward. *Bismarck.* New York: Viking Press, 1981; Feuchtwanger, E. J. *Bismarck.* New York: Routledge, 2002; Förster, Stig, Wolfgang J. Mommsen, and Ronald Edward Robinson, eds. *Bismarck, Europe, and Africa: the Berlin Africa Conference 1884–1885 and the Onset of Partition.* Oxford: Oxford University Press, 1988; Waller, Bruce. *Bismarck.* Oxford: Blackwell 1997; Wehler, Hans Ulrich. *The German Empire, 1871–1918.* New York: Berg Publishers, 1997; Williamson, D. G. *Bismarck and Germany, 1862–1890.* New York: Longman, 1998.

KENNETH J. OROSZ

### Björkö, Treaty of (1905)

An abortive Russo-German pact. Against the background of the **Russo-Japanese** War and the First **Moroccan Crisis** in 1905, Germany attempted to split Russia from its alliance partner France. Kaiser **Wilhelm II** met the Russian Tsar Nicholas II at Björkö off the southern coast of Finland on July 24, 1905 and convinced him to agree to a defensive alliance with Germany, which seemed to give Germany the upper hand internationally after the quashing of French ambitions in Morocco. The meeting was a result of the German Kaiser's attempt at personal rule, and he prided himself on his achievement. The treaty would have freed Germany of the threat of a war on two fronts. Nicholas's advisors soon counseled against the agreement, however, because it would upset the European balance of power and make Russia dependent on Germany. The treaty was rejected in favor of Russia's alliance with France in November 1905, leading to a deterioration of relations between Germany and Russia. Although often dismissed as a non-event by historians, Wilhelm II was correct in his estimation of the treaty's potential importance. If successful, the European balance of power could have been significantly altered and ultimately war might have been avoided.

FURTHER READING: McLean, Roderick R. "Dreams of a German Europe: Wilhelm II and the Treaty of Björkö of 1909." In Mombauer, Annika and Deist, Wilhelm, eds. *The Kaiser: New Research on Wilhelm II's Role in Imperial Germany.* Cambridge: Cambridge University Press, 2003, pp. 119–142.

ANNIKA MOMBAUER

## Black Hand

"Black Hand" (in Serbo-Croatian *Crna Ruka*) was the byname of the secret Serbian organization Union or Death *(Ujedinjenje Ili Smrt).* In the early twentieth century, radical nationalist societies operated in **Serbia** and tried to undermine the Habsburg regime in **Bosnia-Herzegovina.** The Black Hand was founded in 1911 by extremists. Most of them were officers in the Serbian army and involved in the regicide of 1903, like the Black Hand's leader Colonel Dragutin Dimitrijevic, head of the intelligence service of the Serbian army. Dimitrijevic (his *nom du guerre* was "Apis") supported the terrorist group that assassinated Austria-Hungary's heir to the throne, **Francis Ferdinand,** and his wife on June 28, 1914, in Sarajevo. In the aftermath of a power struggle within the Serbian government in exile, the leaders of the Black Hand were sentenced to death or imprisonment in a trial in Saloniki in 1917.

FURTHER READING: Cox, John K. *The History of Serbia.* Westport, CT: Greenwood, 2002; Stavrianos, Leften. *The Balkans since 1453.* New York: Rinehart, 1958; Strachan, Hew. *The First World War.* New York: Oxford University Press, 2001.

GUENTHER KRONENBITTER

## Blood River, Battle of (1838)

An engagement between the Boers and the **Zulu** during the former group's **Great Trek,** the Battle of Blood River was fought on December 16, 1838, along the banks of the Blood River in Natal in southern Africa. The Boers, led by Andreas Pretorius, encountered a force of 10,000 Zulu under Dingaan. The battle, in which 3,000 Zulu died with no losses on the Boer side, was a reckoning for the Bloukrans Massacre (February 17, 1838) in which a Zulu force had attacked a Boer laager and killed 41 men, 56 women, and 97 children in violation of a pact in which Dingaan had agreed to permit a Boer settlement in northern Natal. *See also* Afrikaners.

FURTHER READING: Davenport, T.R.H., and Christopher Saunders. *South Africa: A Modern History.* New York: St. Martins, 2000; Harrison, David. *The White Tribe of South Africa.* Los Angeles: University of California Press, 1982; Morris, Donald R. *The Washing of the Spears.* London: Cape, 1966.

CARL CAVANAGH HODGE

## Blücher, Gebhard von (1742–1819)

The most famous Prussian general of the **Napoleonic Wars,** Gebhard von Blücher was a prominent member of the "war party," which sought conflict with France in 1806. He served as a cavalry commander in the disastrous campaign of that year, and carried on resistance until forced to surrender at Ratkau in November. The previous month most of the Prussian Army had been decisively defeated at the twin battles of **Jena** and Auerstädt (October 14) and then relentlessly pursued by Napoleon's forces.

Virulently opposed to cooperation with the French after the occupation of his country, Blücher condemned Prussian participation in Napoleon's invasion of Russia in 1812. He played a prominent part in the "War of German Liberation" of 1813 and in France the next year, during which he commanded a Prussian army that he had helped modernize in the difficult years after 1806.

Although never distinguished as a tactician, Blücher was determined and energetic, and by fulfilling his promise to come to Wellington's aid at **Waterloo,** he was instrumental in ensuring Allied victory and Napoleon's final downfall.

FURTHER READING: Craig, Gordon A. *The Politics of the Prussian Army: 1640–1945.* London: Oxford University Press, 1964; Dupuy, Colonel T. N. *A Genius for War: The German Army and General Staff, 1807–1945.* Fairfax: Hero Books, 1984; Gneisenau, August Wilhelm. *The Life and Campaigns of Field-Marshal Prince Blücher.* London: Constable, 1996; Henderson, Ernest F. *Blücher and the Uprising of Prussia against Napoleon.* New York: G. P. Putnam's Sons, 1911; Hofschröer, Peter. *1815: The German Victory: From Waterloo to the Fall of Napoleon.* London: Greenhill Books, 1999; Paret, Peter. *Yorck and the Era of Prussian Reform: 1807–1815.* Princeton, NJ: Princeton University Press, 1966; Parkinson, Roger. *The Hussar General: The Life of Blücher, Man of Waterloo.* London: Peter Davies Ltd., 1975; Rosinski, Herbert. *The German Army.* New York: Frederick A. Praeger, 1966.

GREGORY FREMONT-BARNES

## Boer Wars (1880–1881, 1899–1902)

Two conflicts waged by Dutch settlers in resistance to the expansion of the British Empire in South Africa. Dutch settlers, later known as "Boers," established farms in southern Africa beginning in the seventeenth century, gradually expanding north into the hinterland, pressing against lands held by indigenous African tribes. Dutch rule ended, however, when in 1795, Britain seized Cape Colony during the French Revolutionary Wars, and at the general European peace of 1815, the colony became a permanent British imperial possession. From the 1830s, many Boers ventured north to establish independent communities that would later become the republics of the Transvaal and the **Orange Free State,** both of which shared borders with the British possessions of **Cape Colony** and Natal.

The source of the wars principally lay with the desire for British expansion into Boer lands, not least after the discovery of gold and diamonds. After the Transvaal was proclaimed in December 1880, conflict arose in what subsequently became known as the Transvaal Revolt or First Anglo-Boer War. Two thousand Boers invaded Natal and defeated a British force of 1,400 under General George Colley at Laing's Nek on January 28, 1881. The decisive encounter took place at Majuba Hill on February 27, when Colley, occupying a hill in the Drakensberg Mountains with a contingent of 550 men, lost 20 percent of his force, himself numbering among the dead. The British government had no desire to pursue the conflict further and on April 5, 1881 concluded the Treaty of **Pretoria,** which granted independence to the Transvaal, of which Paul **Kruger** became president.

The discovery of gold in the Witwatersrand in 1886 increased British interest in the area and led directly to the annexation of Zululand, part of a strategy to isolate the Transvaal from access to the sea. Internally, both Boer republics welcomed foreigners (known as Uitlanders) seeking work in the goldfields, but in the diamond industry and in various urban services, the Boers often resented what they perceived as a growing trend of immorality and licentiousness that permeated their strict, largely rural, Calvinist society. On the other hand, immigrants, most of whom came from Britain, resented the disproportionate share of taxation that fell on their shoulders and campaigned for a share in the political life of the country.

Both Boer republics made large purchases of foreign weapons in 1899, and when Cape authorities refused to conform to an ultimatum from Pretoria to withdraw troops from the borders, hostilities opened in October, with the Boers assuming the offensive. On October 13, General Piet Cronjé laid siege to **Mafeking,** where Colonel Robert Baden-Powell, the future founder of the Boy Scout movement, made superb use of limited resources to establish a determined and successful defense. At the same time, forces from the Orange Free State invested Kimberley on October 15, while the main Boer blow fell on General Sir George White at Talana Hill and Nicholson's Nek later that month, forcing White's troops to take refuge in Ladysmith. In an effort to relieve the three towns, General Sir Redvers Buller divided his forces, a strategy that led to failure in all cases.

At the Modder River on November 28, General Lord Methuen, commanding a column of 10,000 men, seeking to relieve Kimberley, found his progress blocked by 7,000 Boers under Cronjé and Jacobus de la Rey. After losing almost 500 killed and wounded, Methuen succeeded in driving through the Boer lines, but his exhausted troops required rest, and no pursuit was possible. The British army was slow to appreciate three fundamental lessons: first, it was nearly impossible to inflict anything beyond negligible losses on Boer defenders occupying entrenched positions; second, smokeless, repeating rifles, fired from concealed positions, rendered frontal attacks costly, nearly supportable affairs; and third, since all Boer forces were mounted—even if, through force of numbers, they were eventually driven off—they could simply vanish into the veldt, reform, and fight again on another occasion. The British army could not, at least initially, offer an adequate answer to such tactics, for it possessed paltry numbers of mounted forces, and was obliged to rely heavily on Cape yeomanry units. Until the arrival of mounted reinforcements, therefore, British troops were forced to cover vast areas of enemy territory on foot, with little or no opportunity of pursuit even when success on the battlefield invited it.

Despite growing numbers of reinforcements, the British continued to find themselves bested by opponents both more determined than themselves and with considerable more knowledge of the ground. At Stormberg, on December 10, a British force under General Sir William Gatacre lost heavily in an ambush; the same day, at Magersfontein, 8,000 Boers under Cronjé entrenched themselves on a hill overlooking the Modder River and inflicted heavy casualties on Methuen's force, which not only unwisely attacked frontally in heavy rain, but without extending into open order. The third British disaster of what became known as Black Week took place at **Colenso** on December 15, when 21,000 men under Buller, seeking to relieve Ladysmith, crossed the Tugela River and attempted to turn the flank of General Louis **Botha,** in command of 6,000 Orange Free State troops. The Boers, dug in as usual, easily drove off their adversaries, whose flank attack became encumbered by broken ground. Buller suffered about 150 killed and 800 wounded, together with more than 200 men and 11 guns captured.

Disillusioned with this string of defeats, Buller advocated surrendering Lady-smith, a view that led to his being relieved of senior command. His replacement, Field Marshal Viscount Roberts, had extensive experience of colonial warfare, and from January 1900 he and his chief of staff, Viscount Kitchener, began a massive program of army reorganization, in recognition of the need to raise a sizable force of mounted infantry and cavalry. Buller, meanwhile, remained in the field, only to be repulsed at the Tugela in the course of two separate attacks: first, at Spion Kop on January 23, and then at Vaal Kranz on February 5. The British lost about 400 killed and 1,400 wounded; Boer casualties, as usual, were disproportionately small, with only 100 killed and wounded. Nevertheless, General Sir John French managed to relieve Kimberley on February 15, and on the same day, Roberts, with a column of 30,000 men, skirted Cronjé's left flank at Magersfontein, obliging the Boers to withdraw lest their communications be cut off. At Paardeberg on February 18, Cronjé found his retreat across the Modder River opposed by French, who arrived from Kimberley. Owing to illness, French handed command to Kitchener, whose unimaginative frontal attack predictably failed against the Boers' prepared positions, leaving some 300 British dead and 900 wounded.

Fortunes were soon to change, however. On recovering, Robert resumed command and encircled Cronjé's position at Paardeberg, shelling the Boers with impunity while expecting an attempted breakout that never came. After an eight-day siege, the Boers, burdened with many wounded and out of food, surrendered on February 27. Almost simultaneously, the British enjoyed successes in other theaters. Buller, positioned along the Tugela in his third effort to relieve Ladysmith, managed to dislodge the Boers from their positions around the town and reached the garrison on February 28.

For the next six months Roberts, finally benefiting from the arrival of large numbers of reinforcements, was able to make good use of the railways to move troops and supplies considerable distances through enemy territory. Accordingly, on March 13, he took Bloemfontein, the capital of the Orange Free State, which was annexed by the Empire on March 24. In Natal, Buller defeated the Boers at Glencoe and Dundee on May 15, and two days later a fast-moving column of cavalry and mounted infantry under General Bryan Mahon relieved Mafeking after a seven-month ordeal. Thereafter, Roberts was free to invade the Transvaal, taking Johannesburg on May 31, and then the capital, Pretoria, on June 5, before uniting his forces with Buller's at Vlakfontein on July 4. The Transvaal was annexed as an imperial possession on September 3, and two months later, with the fighting apparently over, Roberts was recalled, to be posted to India.

Yet the war was far from over. The capture of the Boer capitals merely marked the end of the conventional phase of the fighting. Indeed, substantial numbers of Boers still remained in the field and a new, more fluid, **guerrilla** phase replaced the more static form of warfare that had hitherto characterized the war. In short, Kitchener found himself faced with the unenviable task of pursuing highly mobile enemy units across the vast South African veldt. For the next 18 months, small groups of Boers harassed British outposts and conducted raids, which Kitchener sought to oppose by implementing a harsh new "scorched earth" policy, which amounted to the wholesale burning of enemy crops and farmhouses and the driving off or slaughter of tens of thousands of Boer livestock. Most controversial of all, Kitchener ordered his troops to round up and imprison Boer women and children in **concentration camps,** both to prevent them from aiding their menfolk in the field, and to weaken the fighting spirit of enemy combatants. Further, British troops laid lengthy cordons of barbed wire and built blockhouses stretching across the country in an effort to curtail enemy movement and communication. Eventually, Boer resistance collapsed, but not before more than 20,000 civilian internees had died of disease and (albeit unintentional) malnutrition while in British custody. In military terms, the war cost British and Imperial forces approximately 6,000 killed and 16,000 wounded, compared to upwards of 7,000 Boers.

By the Treaty of **Vereeniging,** concluded on May 31, 1902, the Boers recognized British sovereignty over their two conquered republics, and the British offered substantial financial compensation for the destruction of Boer farms. In one of the great ironies of a war, the absorption of the republics into the British Empire rapidly led to the establishment in 1910 of the Republic of South Africa which, although it included the large English-speaking populations of Cape Colony and Natal, emerged with an Afrikaner majority, thus effectively placing an erstwhile people in control of what amounted to a single—and massively enlarged—new Boer-dominated republic.

Apart from such far-reaching political consequences, the conflict exposed great deficiencies in the war-making capacity even of the world's largest empire, as a consequence of which substantial army reforms took place in the ensuing years. The conflict also highlighted the problem of troop shortages. In more than two and half years of fighting, Britain found its manpower resources stretched to the limit, thus requiring, for the first time, the deployment of Australian, New Zealand, and Canadian troops for service to the Mother country in a far-flung land. Almost half a million men would eventually be required to subdue the Boer republics, which together could scarcely field more than 40,000 men at any one time. *See also* Africa, Scramble for; Afrikaners; British Empire.

FURTHER READING: Farwell, Byron. *The Great-Anglo-Boer War.* New York: Norton, 1990; Fremont-Barnes, Gregory. *The Boer War, 1899–1902.* Oxford: Osprey, 2003; Jackson, Tabitha. *The Boer War.* London: Channel 4 Books, 1999; Surridge, Keith, and Denis Judd. *The Boer War.* London: John Murray, 2002.

GREGORY FREMONT-BARNES

## Bohemia

Bohemia, a kingdom of east-central Europe occupying roughly the western two-thirds of the current Czech Republic, lost its political independence in the seventeenth century during the Thirty Years War. In the revolution of 1848, an uprising in Prague, the capital, against Habsburg rule was crushed by troops loyal to the crown. In the nineteenth century, Bohemia became the industrial heartland of the **Habsburg Empire.** Unlike Hungary in the **Ausgleich** of 1867, Bohemia did not win a privileged position in the political system of the Habsburg monarchy. One of Austria's crown lands, Bohemia nevertheless played a prominent role in **Austria-Hungary's** domestic politics. The Czech majority of the population and the strong and influential German minority were involved in a long drawn out nationality conflict for supremacy. In 1897, it culminated in riots and chaos in the German-speaking parts of Austria, when protests escalated against prime minister Count Badeni's attempt to put Czech on equal footing with German in public services. *See also* German Confederation; Vienna, Congress of.

FURTHER READING: Kann, Robert A. *The Multinational Empire: Nationalism and National Reform in the Habsburg Monarchy, 1848–1918*. 2 vols. New York: Octagon Books, 1964; Macartney, C. A. *The Habsburg Empire, 1790–1918*. London: Weidenfield & Nicolson, 1968.

GUENTHER KRONENBITTER

### Bolívar, Simón (1783–1830)

Known as *El Libertador*, Simón Bolívar is regarded as the leader of the struggle for independence from Spain in most of Latin America, having liberated Venezuela, Colombia, Ecuador, Peru, Panama, and Bolivia. Bolivar is today celebrated as a national hero throughout most of Latin America.

Born on July 24, 1783 in Caracas, Venezuela, to an aristocratic family, in 1799 Bolívar went to Spain to complete his education and became an ardent admirer of Napoleon **Bonaparte.** In 1802 he married the Spaniard María Teresa Rodríguez del Toro y Alaysa, and in 1803 they went to Caracas where she soon died of yellow fever. Bolívar never remarried. In 1804, he returned to Spain and in 1807 went back to Caracas. In 1808, when Napoleon made his brother Joseph king of Spain and its territories, juntas were formed throughout the Spanish-American colonies, initially in support of the deposed King Ferdinand VII but eventually as the forces of independence. The Caracas junta, in which Bolívar participated, declared its independence in 1810. He was sent to Great Britain as a diplomat. In 1811, the junta leader, Francisco de **Miranda,** assumed dictatorial powers and Bolívar returned to Caracas. When the Spanish attacked in 1812, Miranda surrendered and attempted to escape. Bolívar and others, regarding this surrender as treason, handed him over to the Spanish.

Bolívar fled to Cartagena de las Indias, in the Viceroyalty of New Granada, mostly present-day Colombia. There he wrote the *Cartagena Manifesto*, calling for Latin Americans to unite to form a republic and fight Spain. In 1813, he obtained a military command in the invasion of Venezuela, which took place on May 14, marking the beginning of the Admirable Campaign. He entered Caracas on August 6 and proclaimed the Second Venezuelan Republic, which fell the next year as a result of the royalist rebellion led by José Tomás Boves. Bolívar returned to Nueva Granada where he took part in the republican struggle for independence, but political and military rivalries forced him to flee to Jamaica in 1815. In 1816, with help from the Haitian President Alexandre Pétion, Bolívar went back to Venezuela and took over the city of Angostura, now Ciudad Bolívar. In 1819, the Colombian territory was liberated and in 1821 the federation of Gran Colombia was created, covering the territory of what was to later become Colombia, Venezuela, Ecuador, and Panama. Bolívar was named president. In 1822, in agreement with the Argentinean General José de **San Martín,** the official Protector of Peruvian Freedom, Bolívar took over the task of completely liberating Peru, which was accomplished on August 6, 1824. On the same day the next year, the Republic of Bolivia was created in his honor, for which he wrote a constitution. Internal political dissension moved Bolívar to declare himself dictator in 1828 as a temporary measure, but this only aggravated the situation and led to a failed assassination attempt later that year. Bolívar resigned on April 27, 1830, and died of tuberculosis several months later on December 17, in Santa Marta, Colombia. *See also* ABC Powers; Spanish Empire.

FURTHER READING: Bushnell, David. *Simón Bolívar: Liberation and Disappointment*. New York: Longman, 2003.

GEORGIA TRES

## Bolsheviks

The group of Marxist revolutionaries who carried out the Russian Revolution of October 1917 under the leadership of Vladimir **Lenin.** The group originated in a larger organization of Marxists called the Russian Social Democratic Worker's Party, founded in Minsk in 1898. Lenin began to influence the direction of the movement as he spoke out against what he believed were the liberal tendencies of some Marxists who focused on short-term economic gains for the workers over political aims. Over the next five years, Lenin became well known for his more radical ideas about the possibility of a revolution in Russia, most significantly with the publication of *What Is to be Done?* in which he argued that an effective organization had to be led by a small group of professional revolutionaries who would help the working class develop a political consciousness. These ideas became central to the power struggle within the Social Democratic Party, splitting the party into two factions in 1903.

Lenin, on one side, stressed that the revolutionary party should be secret, disciplined, and set up in a strict hierarchical organization; the other major faction in the Social Democrats, led by Julius Martov, favored a broad conception of the party, open to all who accepted Marx's principles. It was during these disputes that the names emerged: Bolshevik (from the Russian, *bol'she*, meaning larger) and Menshevik (from *men'she*, or smaller). Lenin very cleverly seized the opportunity of a momentary voting majority to call his group the Bolsheviks. Although standard Marxism called for a long interval between the first, bourgeois revolution and the second, socialist revolution, Lenin and his supporters—among them Lev **Trotsky,** Grigorii Zinoviev, and Lev Kamenev—argued in favor of pushing rapidly forward with plans for revolution. Consequently, in the fall of 1917, it was the Bolsheviks who took advantage of the instability of the Provisional Government to stage a coup d'état and establish the new communist regime. *See also* Russian Empire; Nicholas II.

FURTHER READING: Figes, Orlando. *A People's Tragedy: The Russian Revolution, 1891–1924*. New York: Penguin, 1996; Haimson, Leopold. *The Russian Marxists and the Origins of Bolshevism*. Boston: Beacon Press, 1955; Theen, Rolf. *Lenin: Genesis and Development of a Revolutionary*. Princeton, NJ: Princeton University Press, 1973.

LEE A. FARROW

## Bonaparte, Joseph (1768–1844)

Napoleon **Bonaparte**'s eldest brother, best known for his time as king of Spain (1808–1813) during the French occupation of the Iberian Peninsula. Joseph was never accepted by his new subjects, failed to control more than a fraction of the country, and remained largely impotent and strongly influenced by Napoleon, who sent him directives from Paris or from campaign headquarters. Joseph made increasingly urgent and largely futile requests for the social and political reform of his kingdom, and in spite of his several attempts to abdicate, remained on the throne.

He had no aptitude for military affairs, and after his disastrous defeat at the hands of the Duke of **Wellington** at the Battle of Vitoria on June 21, 1813, was forced to flee Spain. During the Allied invasion of France in 1814, Joseph, put in command of Paris, authorized Marshal Marmont to enter into a truce, as a result of which the capital was surrendered. After Waterloo, Joseph went to live under an assumed name in America until 1839, when he retired to Florence and died there five years later.

FURTHER READING: Glover, Michael. *The Legacy of Glory: The Bonaparte Kingdom of Spain, 1808–13.* New York: Scribner 1971; Ross, Michael, *Reluctant King: Joseph Bonaparte, King of the Two Sicilies and Spain.* New York: Mason/Charter, 1977.

GREGORY FREMONT-BARNES

## Bonaparte, Louis (1778–1846)

Napoleon **Bonaparte**'s third brother, Louis, served as an aide-de-camp to his more famous sibling during the 1796–1797 campaigns in Italy, where he was present at Arcola, Rivoli, and at the siege of Mantua. He served in the cavalry in 1799, became a brigadier general in 1803, and a general of division the next year. In September 1806, Louis was given command of all forces in Holland, and on September 24, 1806 he was crowned king of that country. In 1809, he led Dutch troops against the British landings on Walcheren Island. Friction arose between Louis and Napoleon over the latter's Continental System, which was causing severe economic hardship for the Dutch, and which Louis refused to enforce. In July 1810, Louis abdicated and never held a senior position thereafter.

FURTHER READING: Broers, Michael. *Europe under Napoleon, 1799–1815.* London: Arnold, 1996; Connelly, Owen. *Napoleon's Satellite Kingdoms.* New York: Free Press, 1966.

GREGORY FREMONT-BARNES

## Bonaparte, Louis Napoleon (1808–1873)

Nephew of Napoleon **Bonaparte** and himself the Emperor of the French as Napoleon III (1852–1870). Known popularly as Louis-Napoleon, he attempted to seize power in 1836 and 1840 before being elected president of the Second Republic in 1848. Three years later, however, he seized more power for the presidency in a coup and a year after that inaugurated the Second Empire by accepting the imperial title on December 2, the anniversary of his uncle's self-coronation. He allied France with Britain in the **Crimean War** and began France's colonial penetration of **Indochina** in 1857, but he then stumbled badly in 1861 with a foolish scheme to establish a French-dominated empire in Mexico that provoked both Mexican resistance and the threat of American intervention. Thereafter his defeats were confined to Europe but were highly significant.

Otto von **Bismarck** outmaneuvered him diplomatically in the Austro-Prussian War of 1866 and then provoked him into the Franco-Prussian in 1870–1871. Compounding France's defeat, he was captured at Sedan and imprisoned in Germany before spending the last to years of his life in exile in England. The Napoleonic line ended, when his only son died in the British army fighting the **Zulu.** *See also* Bonapartism.

FURTHER READING: Echard, William E. *Napoleon III and the Concert of Europe*. Baton Rogue: Louisiana State University, 1983; Hazareesingh, Sudhir. *The Legend of Napoleon*. London: Granta, 2004; Smith, W.H.C. *Napoleon III*. New York: St. Martin's, 1973.

CARL CAVANAGH HODGE

## Bonaparte, Napoleon (1769–1821)

Emperor of the French as Napoleon I, Napoleon Bonaparte (Napoleone di Buonaparte) was a military genius, law giver, and despot born in Ajaccio, Corsica, on August 15, 1769, to Carlo Bonaparte (1746–1785), a lawyer and Marie-Letizia Bonaparte (1750–1835). He graduated as a second lieutenant and artillery specialist from Parisian *École Royale Militaire* and in 1793 was dispatched by the French Revolutionary government to Toulon where he distinguished himself in the siege, a feat that earned him a national reputation. His fortunes were for the time being tied with the course of the Revolution, so on October 5, 1795, Napoleon suppressed the counter-revolutionary forces of the 13 Vendemiaire and saved the Revolutionary Government of Paris. He had become a national hero and was made the commander-in-chief of the French army in Italy in 1796.

Napoleon swept across northern Italy and marched southward through Milan. The Papal States were defeated, whereupon Napoleon ignored the Directory's order to march on Rome and instead took his army into Austria. As a result of his Italian campaign, Nice and Savoy were annexed to France; and Napoleon forged Bologna, Ferrara, Modena, and Reggio into the Cispadane Republic, a French puppet state. When the towns of Lombardy formed the Transpadane Republic, Napoleon then merged the two into the Cisapline Republic. He overthrew the oligarchy of Genoa and set up a Ligurian Republic and forced a surrender from Venice that ended 1,000 years of independence. His pressure on Austria meanwhile produced the Treaty of Campo Formio in October 1797, according to which the Habsburgs recognized the new French protectorates, ceded the Austrian Netherlands and Ionian Islands to France, and secretly agreed to the expansion of France's border to the banks of the Rhine.

The next year he was off to distant Egypt, a province of the **Ottoman Empire,** seeking to further French trade, build a **Suez Canal,** and undermine British rule in India. Within three weeks he demolished the Mamluk army and with it centuries of Mamkuk dominance in Egypt, but the grandiose plan was cut short by destruction of the French fleet in the Battle of **Aboukir Bay** by the British Vice Admiral Horatio **Nelson.** With the War of the Second Coalition threatening France with invasion, Napoleon returned home in October 1799 and ceased power from the Directorate in the coup d'etat of 18 Brumaire (November 9, 1799).

Napoleon's rule as First Consul (1799–1804) brought a strong government in France backed by far-reaching reforms. The rift between the French state and the Papacy was ended in the **Concordat of 1801**. The Civil Code of March 1804 (renamed the Code Napoleon) addressed questions of personal status and property; individual liberty, equality before law, and arrest with due procedure of law was guaranteed. The progressive spirit of the Code was marked by protection of religious minorities. His most positive legacy, the Code was widely followed all over world. The administration of government was highly centralized and constructed around the prefecture system. The financial administration was overhauled with the creation of the Bank of France in 1800 with the power of issuing bank notes after two years, and industrial ventures were encouraged. The chief purpose of education, according to Napoleon, was to groom the gifted into capable administrators for the service of the state, so he established 45 *lyceees* or high schools with emphasis on patriotic indoctrination. The cohesion of the nation sought by the reforms was backed by military triumphs, which gave Napoleon popular support. So there could be no doubt about such support, he was in 1802 made First Consul for life by a rigged plebiscite.

While Napoleon consolidated his hold on power, he offered peace to Britain. The government of William **Pitt** rejected the offer, and the Consulate was marked by further conquests and territorial aggrandizement. Northern Italy was conquered by defeating the Austrians in the battle of **Marengo** in June 1800. After Napoleon finally destroyed the main Austrian army at **Hohenlinden** the following December, the Peace of **Lunéville** of 1801 secured for France the left bank of the Rhine. In 1802, with Pitt out of office, Napoleon secured the Treaty of **Amiens** with Britain and a breather to concentrate on his domestic reforms and restore the French colonial Empire. He obtained Louisiana from Spain but because of American opposition sold it to the United States for $15 million. His attempt to establish French authority in Australia and India also failed.

On December 2, 1804, Napoleon crowned himself Emperor of the French in the cathedral of Notre Dame de Paris in the in presence of Pope Pius VII. The revolution that had established a republic ended in an empire. The reforms of Napoleon that were implemented in the conquered territories of France had nonetheless disturbed the European social order as Napoleon's ambition menaced its monarchies. War returned to Europe. In May 1804, Pitt returned to power in Britain and set about forming a Third Coalition to defeat Napoleon. The Emperor seized the initiative, however, by reorganizing his forces, renaming them the Grande Armée and moving quickly into Italy and Southern Germany. At **Ulm** he captured 33,000 Austrians with minimal fighting and then scored his most impressive victory at the battle of **Austerlitz** in December 1805 by routing the combined armies of Austria and Russia. Austria sought peace, and the Treaty of **Pressburg** recognized Napoleon's Italian claims. Napoleon further strengthened his position by matrimonial alliances in principalities of southern Germany. The Bourbons were ousted from Naples and Napoleon installed his brother Joseph **Bonaparte** (1768–1844) as the king. The only thorn was Britain, whose navy under Nelson's command shattered the combined fleets of France and Spain off Cape **Trafalgar** in October 1805, ending the chances of a French invasion of Britain. "Wherever wood can swim," he later observed, "there I am sure to find this flag of England."

Having disposed of Austria, Napoleon completely redrew the map of Germany by eliminating 120 sovereign entities dating to and beyond the Peace of Westphalia, dissolving the Holy Roman Empire, and establishing a French protectorate in the **Confederation of the Rhine.** When Prussia then joined Pitt's alliance in October 1806, the War of the Fourth Coalition brought Napoleon to the apex of his military career. He defeated the Prussian army at **Jena** and Auerstädt, occupied Berlin and fought a bloody but inconclusive battle with the Russian army at **Eylau** before smashing it decisively at Friedland. Napoleon now wanted to punish the "nation of shopkeepers" with a trade boycott. With the French army in Berlin, the Emperor issued a decree from there on November 21, 1806 forbidding trade with Britain by France and her allies. Britain was to be in a state of blockade and commerce with her was banned. Britain retaliated by the Orders in Council declaring ports of France and her allies to be in a state of blockade. The naval supremacy of Britain resulted in failure of the Continental System, although trade embargos caused hardship for Europe including France and Britain. The hope of the Emperor that English industry would be devastated did not occur. Russia's defeat at Friedland forced Tsar **Alexander I** to negotiate a spheres of influence arrangement. On July 7, 1807, the Treaty of **Tilsit** made Russia observe the Continental system of trade embargo and recognize the Confederation of the Rhine.

Almost the whole of Europe was under domination of the Napoleonic Empire. Austria, Prussia, and Russia were captive allies after their defeats in war, and the satellites of France were ruled by relatives of Napoleon. At the core was the French Empire and territories acquired since the Revolution. The frontiers of France included Belgium and the Netherlands, Germany west of the Rhine river and along the North Sea, the Duchy of Warsaw, Italy, and the Illyrian provinces. From 1807 onwards, the grandiose plan of conquest, unbridled ambition, and desire for mastery over Europe led to draining of resources of France and the downfall of the Emperor himself. The desire to impose the Continental system on Portugal, an ally of Britain, led to the **Peninsular War,** and it was the "Spanish ulcer" that began Napoleon's ruin. The British Commander Arthur Wellesley (1769–1852), the future Duke of **Wellington,** defeated the French at Rorica and Vimiero. The Convention of Cintra of August 1808 secured for the British a base of operation in Portugal. It angered Napoleon, who invaded Spain and made his brother, Joseph, king. Although Spain was defeated in December 1808 at Madrid, the irreconcilable Spanish people fought Napoleon using **guerrilla** tactics. The long Peninsular war continued with 300,000 troops of Napoleon. Wellington defeated Joseph at the Battle of Vittoria in June 1813 and marched toward southern France.

There were reports of sedition in Paris and the Emperor returned to Paris to settle the matter. Meanwhile, Austria was rearming itself and in 1809 liked its chances enough to declare war against France. After an Austrian victory at **Aspern-Essling,** Napoleon triumphed decisively at the Battle of **Wagram** in July 1809. Russia was getting jittery. The tsar did not abide by the Continental System as agreed at Tilsit, as it was detrimental to Russian trade. With 675,000 troops, the *Grande Armée* crossed the Nieman in June 1812 and marched toward Moscow and opened Napoleon's invasion of Russia. He took Smolensk and in September won a costly victory in the savage Battle of **Borodino** before slogging on to Moscow. Napoleon remained in the burning city for five weeks, but Alexander I did not surrender. The retreat was devastating for the *Grande Armée,* owing to bitter cold, lack of supplies, and the scorched earth policy of the Russians combined with harassing attacks by partisans and Cossacks. Napoleon left 300,000 dead in Russia.

As Wellington was meanwhile chewing up Napoleon's Spanish army, the prestige of the Emperor hit its nadir. Europe was united against Napoleon in the final, Sixth Coalition. In the Battle of **Leipzig** of October 1813, Napoleon suffered his most humiliating defeat. He did not accept the offer of peace and was defeated finally at Arcis-sur-Aub. Paris fell to the invading army in March 1814 and Napoleon abdicated. There was a Bourbon restoration and Louis XVIII (1755–1824), a younger brother of Louis XVI (reigned 1774–1792), became the king of France. Napoleon gave up claims to the throne. He was exiled to the island of Elba with an annual provision of 180,000 pounds. But that was not the end of Napoleon and while the Congress of Vienna was redrawing the map of Europe, he landed near Cannes and entered Paris in March 1815.

The Fifth Regiment sent by the new king to interdict Napoleon joined the Emperor with a cry of *Vive L'Empereur.* Napoleon promised a genuine liberal regime and within three months raised an army of 140,000 soldiers and 200,000 reserves. His old foes arrayed against him soon and his Second Empire lasted for only 100 days only. The final blow came at the battle of **Waterloo** near Brussels from a British army led by Wellington and a smaller Russian force commanded by **Blücher.** After surrendering formally on board the HMS *Bellerophon,* Napoleon was sent to the British island of St. Helena in the south Atlantic Ocean and died there on May 5, 1821. Napoleon was no more, but his legacy remained. He was responsible for doing away with vestiges of feudal order in many parts of Europe. The centralized rule in Italy and Germany laid the foundation for unification of both. For the French, he remained a national hero of mythical attraction, but for his enemies, he was a tyrant and power-hungry conqueror. His ambition and arrogance caused his downfall. Napoleon was an "enlightened" despot, combining liberal ideals and with authoritarian rule, who temporarily restored order to revolutionary France and national pride to the French. Bonapartism and the Napoleonic legend remained. *See also* Bonapartism; French Empire; Napoleonic Wars.

FURTHER READING: Alexander, R. S. *Napoleon.* London: Arnold, 2001; Asprey, Robert B. *The Rise of Napoleon Bonaparte.* New York: Basic Books, 2000; Chandler, D. G. *The Campaigns of Napoleon.* New York: Macmillan, 1996; Dwyer, P., ed. *Napoleon and Europe.* London: Longman, 2001; Ellis, Geoffrey. *Napoleon's Continental Blockade.* Oxford: Clarendon Press, 1981; Englund, S. *Napoleon. A Political Life.* New York: Scribner, 2004; Furet, François. *The French Revolution, 1770–1815.* Cambridge: Basil Blackwell, 1996; Grab, A. *Napoleon and the Transformation of Europe.* New York: Palgrave Macmillan, 2003; Heckscher, Eli F. *The Continental System: An Economic Interpretation.* Oxford: Clarendon Press, 1922; Jones. P. P., ed. *An Intimate Account of the Years of Supremacy 1800–1804.* San Francisco: Random House, 1992; Markham, J. D. *Napoleon's Road to Glory: Triumphs, Defeats and Immortality.* London: Brassey's, 2000; Markham, J. D. *Imperial Glory: The Bulletins of Napoleon's Grandee Armee 1805–1814.* London: Greenhill Books, 2003; McLynn, Frank. *Napoleon.* London: Pimlico, 1998; Melvin, Frank E. *Napoleon's Navigation System.* Brooklyn, New York: AMS Press Inc., 1970.

PATIT PABAN MISHRA

## Bonapartism

An ideological tradition of nineteenth-century France based on the perpetuation of the ideas and the mythical national status of Napoleon I. Bonapartism attempted simultaneously to represent national glory, preserve the achievements of the Revolution, and to affirm the principle of authority. Influenced by the memory of the murderous anarchy of the Terror, it nonetheless sought to square democracy with order by offering leadership to appeal to the whole nation, as opposed to political parties and parliamentary factions who sought power for their own benefit. Bonapartists therefore often advocated the abolition of class and privilege, whether or not they meant it, and promoted a social order based on the equality of all men and social mobility open to talent and ambition.

The Bonapartist ideal was of a charismatic leader capable of unifying the nation by force of personality. Because such leadership was in short supply, Bonapartists adapted to party politics. They became synonymous in the eyes of their opponents with populist authoritarianism, hatred of the Bourbon restoration, the corruption and deceit of Louis Napoleon, and the mischievous use of plebiscites in reactionary causes.

FURTHER READING: Fisher, H.A.L. *Bonapartism* Oxford: Clarendon 1908; Hazareesingh, Sudhir. *The Legend of Napoleon.* London: Granta, 2004; Zeldin, Theordore. *France 1848–1945: Politics and Anger.* New York: Oxford University Press, 1979.

CARL CAVANAGH HODGE

## Bond of 1844

A treaty, signed on March 6, 1844, by the King of Denkera and seven Fanti and Assin chiefs, acknowledging British "power and jurisdiction" over their respective territories on the **Gold Coast.** By the end of the year, the rulers of a dozen more coastal polities had signed the agreement, which banned human sacrifice and other customs and recognized the judicial authority of British officials. The treaty stood as the basic charter of British rule on the Gold Coast until it was superseded by the formation of Crown Colony of the Gold Coast and Lagos in 1874.

In the early 1840s, British authority was officially limited to the coastal forts inhabited by British merchants. Nonetheless, British officials wielded a considerable degree of informal influence within a loosely defined protectorate and were periodically called on to intervene in legal and political disputes. During the tenure of George Maclean from 1830 to 1844, the frequency and scope of such actions grew inexorably despite the formal limits of British jurisdiction. In 1842, the informal and irregular nature of British legal proceedings on the Gold Coast was criticized by a committee of the House of Commons. One result of the inquiry was the passage of new legislation clarifying the legal foundation for British jurisdiction and requiring the formal consent of the various African states.

In this context, it is clear that the Bond of 1844 was not intended to expand British jurisdiction, but simply to document its existing extent. As intellectuals like James Africanus Horton understood, the signatories to the Bond "submitted themselves to the British Government, not as subjects, but as independent nations." In practice, the Bond provided a license for the continued expansion of British authority over the next three decades in ways that went well beyond the actual terms of the agreement. That the Bond was ultimately superseded by a unilateral proclamation of British authority in 1874 rather than another consensual agreement was no accident but rather a reflection of the altered balance of power on the Gold Coast. *See also* Africa, Scramble for; British Empire; Indirect Rule.

FURTHER READING: Fage, J. D. *Ghana: A Historical Interpretation.* Madison: University of Wisconsin Press, 1959.

SCOTT ANDERSON

## Borodino, Battle of (1812)

A bloody and critical battle of the **Napoleonic Wars** fought between French and Russian troops on Russian soil. As Napoleon **Bonaparte**'s forces moved across the European continent, Russian Tsar **Alexander I** formed an alliance with Britain, Austria, and Prussia, the Sixth Coalition, in an attempt to check French expansion. These alliances fluctuated, however, with each French victory. Such was the situation with Russia. Napoleon's powerful war machine inflicted significant military defeats on Russia in 1805 and 1807, forcing Russia to sign the Treaty of **Tilsit** and maintain peaceful relations with France from 1807 to 1812. During this period, Russia was part of Napoleon's Continental System, a reluctant collaboration of subjugated or conquered European nations who, through various trade embargos, were supposed to help Napoleon bring England to its knees. Russia's participation in this system, however, was a product only of Napoleon's military power, not common interests, as Russia had a long trade relationship with England. Alexander was also concerned when Napoleon won Prussia's Polish holdings and created a French-dominated state called the Grand Duchy of Warsaw. Finally, Napoleon's ambitions in the Mediterranean conflicted with Russia's interest in controlling Constantinople and the Turkish Straits.

When it became apparent that Alexander would no longer cooperate, Napoleon decided to invade Russia. He amassed an army of 600,000 men, 200,000 animals, and 20,000 vehicles and entered Russia in late June 1812. The Russians retreated eastward, avoiding battle and drawing the French further into Russia. As they retreated they destroyed everything, leaving nothing of use for the French army. Finally in September, the Russians took their stand at Borodino, under the leadership of Field Marshal Mikhail Kutuzov. Although the battle lasted only one day, both sides suffered devastating losses. The Russians lost more than 40,000 men, about one-third of its strength; although Napoleon's forces won the battle, they lost about half their men yet failed to destroy the Russian army. Exhausted and with severely overextended supply lines, they proceeded to Moscow where they waited a month for Alexander's surrender. When this failed to occur, Napoleon chose to withdraw rather than face the Russian winter. His army, by this point only 30,000 strong, crossed the Russian border in December. The failure of the Russian invasion was a devastating defeat for Napoleon. Napoleon's invasion and Borodino are the backdrop to Leo Tolstoy's novel, *War and Peace*, in which it is described as "a continuous slaughter which could be of no avail either to the French or the Russians." *See also* Russian Empire.

FURTHER READING: Caulaincourt, Armand Augustin Louis. *With Napoleon in Russia: The Memoirs of General de Caulaincourt, Duke of Vincence*. Edited by George Libaire. New York: W. Morrow and Company, 1935; McConnell, Allen. *Tsar Alexander I: Paternalistic Reformer*. New York: Crowell, 1970; Palmer, Alan. *Napoleon in Russia*. London: André Deutsch, 1967; Riehn, Richard K. *Napoleon's Russian Campaign*. New York: McGraw-Hill, 1990; Walter, Jakob. *The Diary of a Napoleonic Foot Soldier*. Edited by Marc Raeff. New York: Doubleday, 1991.

LEE A. FARROW

## Boshin War

*See* Restoration War

## Bosnia-Herzegovina

A southeast European province of the **Ottoman Empire** from 1463 to 1878. Unusual for most Ottoman provinces on the Balkan Peninsula, Bosnia-Herzegovina was home to a large community of Slav Muslims, living alongside Catholic Croats and Orthodox Serbs. In 1878, after the Congress of **Berlin,** Austria-Hungary occupied Bosnia-Herzegovina. Armed resistance against Habsburg rule was crushed by military force. Supervised by a special department within the common ministry of finance, the administration was run by Austro-Hungarian civil servants and officers. The annexation of Bosnia-Herzegovina in 1908 caused an international crisis and outraged Serbian and Yugoslav nationalists who wanted to unite the province with **Serbia.** At least partly successful in modernizing the province, Austria-Hungary's policy in Bosnia-Herzegovina failed to effectively counter Great Serbian or Yugoslav propaganda campaigns. One of the groups striving to free Bosnia-Herzegovina from Habsburg rule, Young Bosnia (Mlada Bosna), managed to assassinate Francis Ferdinand, the Austro-Hungarian heir apparent in the Bosnian capital, Sarajevo, on June 28, 1914. Austria-Hungary perceived this as a legitimate cause to wage war on Serbia that had harbored anti-Habsburg organizations. *See also* Black Hand; Habsburg Empire.

FURTHER READING: Malcom, Noel. *Bosnia, A Short History.* New York: New York University Press, 1994.

GUENTHER KRONENBITTER

## Bosporus

A strait connecting the Sea of Marmara with the Black Sea, 20 miles long and less than 3 miles across at its widest. Bosporus literally means "ox ford" and is traditionally connected with the legendary figure of Io, who in the form of a heifer crossed the Thracian Bosporus in her wanderings. Byzantine emperors and Ottoman sultans constructed fortifications along its shores because of its proximity to Constantinople. With the growing influence of the European powers in the nineteenth century, rules were codified to govern the transit of vessels through the strait.

The Treaty of Kuchuk Kainarji in 1774 and the Treaty of **Inkiar Skelessi** in 1833 gave the Russian government the right to navigate freely in Ottoman waters through the Bosporus, but its strategic value made it a central issue of the Straits Question, and the second treaty was reversed by the **London Straits Convention** in 1841. *See also* Eastern Question; Mehmet Ali; Ottoman Empire; Russian Empire.

FURTHER READING: Anderson, M. S. *The Eastern Question 1774–1923.* London: Macmillan, 1966; Jelavich, Barbara. *A Century of Russian Foreign Policy 1814–1914.* Philadelphia: J. B. Lippincott, 1964; Karsh, Efraim, and Inari Karsh, *Empires of the Sand: The Struggle for Mastery in the Middle East 1789–1923.* Cambridge, MA: Harvard University Press, 1999.

ANDREKOS VARNAVA

## Botha, Louis (1862–1919)

A Boer general and statesman, Louis Botha was a political moderate who was elected to the parliament (*Volksraad*) of the Transvaal. He opposed war with Great

Britain yet joined the Transvaal army when war came and ultimately became commander-in-chief of the Boer forces in the Second **Boer War** (1899–1902). He was initially second in command and later in charge of the Boer forces at Ladysmith, was largely responsible for Boer successes at **Colenso,** Spion Kop, and Val Kranz, and then led an 18-month **guerrilla** campaign when the war turned in Britain's favor.

When the Boer cause was lost, Botha proved as able a negotiator as a soldier. He attended the peace conference and signed the Treaty of **Vereeniging.** After becoming premier of the Transvaal in 1907, he represented the new British possession at Imperial Conferences and promoted reconciliation between Boers and the British in the Cape Colony. A loyal British subject, he became the first premier of the South African Union in 1910, put down a pro-German Boer rebellion in 1914, and then led Empire troops to victory in German Southwest Africa in 1915. *See also* Afrikaner; South Africa.

FURTHER READING: Packenham, Thomas. *The Boer War.* New York: Random House, 1979; Spencer, Harold. *General Botha: The Career and the Man.* New York: Houghton Mifflin, 1916.

CARL CAVANAGH HODGE

## Boulanger, General Georges-Ernest (1837–1891)

French soldier and failed political adventurer, Georges-Ernest Boulanger served in Algeria, Cochin China, and in the Franco-Prussian War. He entered politics in 1884. Initially a protégé of the Radical Party under Georges **Clemençeau,** he was made War Minister in 1886, a post in which he introduced many needed reforms to the French military. When the government fell, Boulanger was relegated to a provincial command and quickly became unhinged. Frantic to recover his position, he now flirted with anti-Republican forces—ranging from disenchanted Radicals to Bonapartistes and royalists—that sought a more authoritarian system. He agitated for the return of Alsace-Lorraine and campaigned for a revision of the constitution. By 1889, he was momentarily so popular that many feared he would attempt a *coup.* Threatened with arrest, however, Boulanger fled the country and was later condemned *in absentia* for treason. He lived for two years in Belgian exile before shooting himself over the grave of his mistress in 1891.

FURTHER READING: Seager, Frederic H. *The Boulanger Affair.* Ithaca, NY: Cornell University Press, 1969.

CARL CAVANAGH HODGE

## Bourbon Dynasty (1589–1848)

The ruling dynasty of France from 1589 until the proclamation of the First Republic in 1792 and the execution of Louis XVI on January 21, 1793. Upon the abdication of Napoleon **Bonaparte** on April 11, 1814, the Bourbons were restored to the French throne in the person of Louis XVIII, brother of Louis XVI. Forced to flee when Napoleon returned from exile, Louis XVIII was again returned to the throne after Napoleon's final defeat at Waterloo. In 1830, the reactionary Bourbon Charles X was toppled in favor of the Duke of Orleans, Louis-Philippe, and the establishment of the "July Monarchy," which lasted until 1848 and the proclamation of the Second Republic.

FURTHER READING: Cobban, Alfred. *A History of Modern France.* 3 vols. New York: Braziller, 1965; Grant, A. J. *The French Monarchy, 1483–1789.* New York: H. Fertig, 1970; Roche, Daniel. *France in the Enlightenment.* Cambridge, MA: Harvard University Press, 1998.

CARL CAVANAGH HODGE

## Boxer Insurrection (1900)

A short conflict arising out of antiforeign sentiment in China as a result of many factors, including the rapid development of European trade and the acquisition by various European powers of important Chinese port cities: **Kiaochow** by Germany in 1897, Port Arthur by Russia, and Wei-hai-wei by Britain in 1898. The Chinese government connived with young Chinese associated with a fanatical secret society known as The Society of the Righteous Harmonious Fists, popularly known as "Boxers," who also received active support from the Dowager Empress Tzu His. While professing a powerlessness to influence matters, she actually incited them. Intensifying violence on a wide scale was directed against converts to Christianity, **missionaries,** and laborers and foreign managers on foreign-controlled railways. Responding to such threats to their own nationals, various European powers, together with the United States and Japan, dispatched troops to China to protect their citizens and to reassert what they claimed to be their commercial and property rights.

Beginning in June 1900, foreign warships began assembling off Tientsin, from which they detached a military contingent of about 500 troops from various nations with orders to proceed to Beijing and guard the foreign legations. Shortly thereafter Vice-Admiral Sir Edward Seymour, commander of the British naval forces in China, landed a force of 2,000 Royal Marines and sailors, who were repulsed by a Chinese force of overwhelming strength at Tang Ts'u. After suffering 300 casualties, the force returned to the ships. On June 17 the allies seized the Taku Forts, which guarded the river up to Tientsin. Meanwhile at Peking, the Boxers murdered the German Minister, massacred thousands of Christians, and laid siege to the foreign legations.

From Taku, a force of Russians, French, British, Germans, Americans, and Japanese were dispatched to the legations' relief. The allied force, reinforced to 5,000, successfully stormed Tientsin on July 23, and by early August numbered 18,000 men. The allies then advanced on Peking, driving off a Boxer force at Yang T'sun on August 5–6, and reached the walls of the capital on the August 13. The troops stormed the walls and gates the next day and relieved the combined legations, which had narrowly survived incessant Boxer attacks. On August 15, American artillery broke down the gates of the Imperial Palace, which, however, in deference to the Emperor, was not occupied until August 28. After Russian forces occupied Manchuria in September, the Dowager Empress accepted all allied demands on December 26. Boxers and suspected Boxers were executed, often by decapitation; German and Russian troops in particular engaged in mass reprisals. According to the **Boxer Protocol,** signed by 12 nations on September 12 1901, China was forced to pay a heavy indemnity of more than $335 million at the 1900 rate of exchange and to submit to other humiliations. *See also* Arrow War; Opium Wars; Qing Dynasty; Sino-Japanese War.

FURTHER READING: Elliott, Jane. *Some Did It for Civilization, Some Did It for Their Country: A Revised View of the Boxer War.* Hong Kong: The Chinese University Press, 2002; Harrington,

Peter. *Peking 1900: The Boxer Rebellion.* London: Greenwood, 2005; Preston, Diana. *A Brief History of the Boxer Rebellion.* London: Constable and Robinson, 2000; Preston, Diana. *Besieged in Peking: The Story of the 1900 Boxer Rising.* London: Constable 1999.

GREGORY FREMONT-BARNES

## Boxer Protocol (1901)

After the allied forces marched into Beijing and crushed the **Boxer Insurrection** in 1900, the Empress Dowager and the imperial court fled to Xian and summoned Viceroy Li Hongzhang (1823–1901) to be in charge of negotiations with the foreign powers. Meanwhile, motivated by a desire to protect its own commercial interests in China, the United States reiterated its **Open Door** policy, insisting on the preservation of the territorial and administrative entity of China, a position eventually consented to by Britain, Germany, Japan, and Russia. Therefore after extensive discussions, partition of China was avoided by mutual restraint among the imperial powers, and a protocol was finally signed on September 7, 1901 by Li, acting for the Qing court, and the plenipotentiaries of 11 countries, officially ending the hostilities and providing for reparations to be made to the foreign powers.

The indemnity included 450 million taels, the equivalent of $335 million, to be paid over the next 40 years, an amount so outrageously excessive that both the United States and Britain volunteered to rechannel some of the money to finance the education of Chinese students abroad. In addition to formal apologies, the Boxer Protocol also specified the execution of 10 high-ranking Chinese officials and the punishment of 100 others, as well as suspension of civic examinations in 45 cities to penalize the gentry class who sympathized with the rebels. Moreover, the settlement demanded the expansion of the Legation Quarter in Beijing, to be fortified and permanently garrisoned, and the destruction of forts and occupation of railway posts to ensure foreign access to Beijing from the sea. In sum, the defeat of the Boxer uprising was a complete humiliation to the Chinese government, and the Boxer Protocol made an independent China a mere fiction. With mounting nationalistic sentiment, the once mighty **Qing** Empire was well on its course of final collapse.

FURTHER READING: Buck, David. *Recent Chinese Studies of the Boxer Movement.* New York: M. E. Sharpe, 1987; Esherick, Joseph. *The Origins of the Boxer Uprising.* Berkeley: University of California Press, 1987; Preston, Diana. *The Boxer Rebellion: China's War on Foreigners, 1900.* London: Robinson, 2002.

WENXIAN ZHANG

## Brandenburg-Prussia

*See* Prussia

## Brazil

Brazil, a country of some 3.3 million square miles on the eastern coast of South America, is by far the largest country on the continent. In the sixteenth century, the first Europeans settled in the land now known as Brazil, the Dutch in the northeast and the Portuguese in the southeast. Archaeological evidence is accumulating that indicates that a thriving, advanced civilization in the Amazon collapsed at the approximate time of the European arrival, possibly because of pandemic disease.

By the nineteenth century, the Portuguese had expelled the Dutch and established a slave-based economy along the coast, focusing on farming and mining. In 1808, the Portuguese royal family, escaping from Napoleon **Bonaparte**'s invasion of Portugal, established Brazil's capital, Rio d Janeiro, as capital of the **Portuguese Empire.** When Napoleon was defeated, the family returned to Lisbon, leaving the Crown Prince, Pedro, as regent for Brazil. The **Peninsular War** opened Brazil to trade when Britain demanded trading access as the price of its support for Portuguese independence. In 1821, when Portugal attempted to tighten control over Brazil, Pedro, urged on by the Luso-Brazilians, Brazilians of European ancestry, declared Brazilian independence and became Pedro I of the Empire of Brazil.

The independent Brazil fought several border conflicts in the nineteenth century, notably with Argentina over Uruguay—after a compromise peace established an independent Uruguay in whose politics both sides meddled freely—and Paraguay. The Paraguayan War in the late 1860s was started when the Paraguayan dictator, Francisco Solano Lopez, simultaneously declared war on Argentina, Uruguay, and Brazil. Paraguay was crushed, and the Brazilians and Argentineans between them claimed about 25 of the country's territory.

Throughout the nineteenth and twentieth centuries, the other South American countries generally mistrusted Brazil's expansionist tendencies, which included interventions in the governments of its neighbors, notably Uruguay, Paraguay, and Bolivia, and the occasional outright land grab. The best example of a land grab is the Brazilian State of Acre. The region, a nominally Bolivian province in the upper Amazon, was experiencing a rubber boom in the 1890s as Brazilian settlers and entrepreneurs flooded the region. In 1899, a Brazilian journalist denounced a nonexistent agreement between the United States and Bolivia to reclaim the region, and set himself up as *presidente* of the Independent State of Acre. By 1904, the Brazilian military had marched in to restore order, and the state was annexed.

Until the late nineteenth century, most of the interior of Brazil was unexplored, and almost all of the population was located along the Atlantic Coast or in isolated settlements such as Acre. Nevertheless, the Indians suffered from the occasional slaving raids—slave trading was banned in 1850, but slavery was not completely abolished until 1888—and epidemics. In 1890, the first serious governmental effort to open up the interior was begun under Cândido Mariano da Silva Rondon, a military officer. Under his command during the next 20 years, thousands of miles of **telegraph** lines were laid linking the wilderness to the central government. Rondon considered himself a champion of the Indians—his motto was "Die if need be, but never kill"—but the government's efforts weren't to preserve them but to peacefully assimilate them.

The Indian Protective Services (SPI), set up in 1910, was officially charged with protection of the Indians. The SPI and its successor organization, the National Indian Foundation, conducted a highly paternalistic campaign to find the Indians and "aid" them, which meant bribing them onto *de-facto* reservations and making them dependent on handouts from the government. In taking this path, the government often found itself in conflict against the mining companies, railroads, and farmers, who often favored extermination, or at least expulsion. *See also* ABC Powers; Tampico Incident.

FURTHER READING: Barman, Roderick. *Brazil, The Forging of a Nation, 1798–1852.* Stanford, CA: Stanford University Press, 1988; Rabben, Linda. *Brazil's Indians and the Onslaught of Civilization: Yanomani and the Kayapo.* Seattle: University of Washington Press, 2004; Smith, Joseph. *A History of Brazil.* New York: Longman, 2002.

JOSEPH ADAMCZYK

### Brazza, Pierre Paul Francois Camille Savorgnan de (1852–1905)

A Franco-Italian naval officer, explorer, and colonial official in Equatorial Africa. Although born into an Italian noble family, he enrolled in the French naval academy in Brest and became a French citizen in 1874. Because of the success of his 1874–1878 exploration of the Gabon and Ogoue Rivers, in 1879 the French government sent de Brazza on a mission to thwart Belgian efforts, led by Henry Morton **Stanley,** to annex the entire Congo River basin. Over the next three years, de Brazza explored portions of the Upper Congo and established a French protectorate centered around the newly created settlement of Brazzaville. After a brief return to France, he served as Governor-General of the French Congo from 1886 to 1897. De Brazza died in Dakar, Senegal in 1905 shortly after completing an investigation into allegations of African exploitation commissioned by the French government. *See also* Africa, Scramble for; Belgian Congo; French Empire.

FURTHER READING: Carbonnier, Jeanne. *Congo Explorer, Pierre Savorgnan de Brazza, 1852–1905.* New York: Scribner, 1960; West, Richard. *Brazza of the Congo: European Exploration and Exploitation in French Equatorial Africa.* London: Cape, 1972.

KENNETH J. OROSZ

### Briand, Aristide (1862–1932)

A French politician and statesman, Aristide Briand started his career in the French Socialist Party, associating himself with the most advanced movements. In 1894, Briand persuaded the trade unions to adopt general strike as a political weapon. Appointed premier in 1909, Briand alienated himself from his socialist colleagues by breaking up a railway strike by conscripting its leaders into the army. Since October 1915, Briand headed a coalition cabinet. His failed attempts to establish control over the army brought his government down. Briand returned to power in 1921.

FURTHER READING: Thomson, Valentine. *Briand: Man of Peace.* New York: Covici-Friede, 1930.

MARTIN MOLL

### British Columbia

The westernmost province of **Canada,** initially an object of European interest when Juan Perez Herdandez explored the Pacific Coast of North America for Spain in 1774. British and Russian traders also became active on the coast in the late eighteenth century, and British interests, in the form of the North West Company and the Hudson's Bay Company, became dominant in the early nineteenth century—

especially after the two companies merged into the Bay Company in 1821, and the new company established a dominant position in the lucrative fur trade west of the Rocky Mountains. Britain's position on the west coast of North America, however, was contested by the arrival of American settlers and commerce in the Oregon Territory in the 1830s. The loss of Oregon to the United States confined the **Hudson's Bay Company** to the northern half of its Pacific territory, and in 1849 Vancouver Island was made a British crown colony.

In response to an influx of American miners during the gold rush of the late 1850s, London sought to preserve British authority by creating the mainland colony of British Columbia in 1858. The Vancouver and mainland colonies were joined in 1866, but British Columbia considered annexation to the **United States** until its was persuaded to join the new Dominion of the Canada Confederation in 1871 by the promise of the construction of a transcontinental railway within two years. In any event, the Canadian Pacific Railway did not link British Columbia to Montreal in the eastern province of Quebec until 1886. *See also* Manifest Destiny.

FURTHER READING: Galbraith, John S. *The Hudson's Bay Company as and Imperial Factor, 1821–1869.* Berkeley: University of California Press, 1957; Rich, E. E. *Hudson's Bay Company, 1670–1870.* New York: Macmillan, 1960; Robinson, J. Lewis. *British Columbia.* Toronto: University of Toronto Press, 1973.

CARL CAVANAGH HODGE

## British East African Protectorate

The territory that became Kenya colony in 1920. British East Africa was originally acquired by the Imperial British East Africa Company (IBEAC), a chartered company under the control of the self-made shipping magnate Sir William Mackinnon. The IBEAC was chartered in 1888, with many prominent Britons, including Sir T. F. Buxton of the Aborigines' Protection Society among its shareholders. It promised to abolish **slavery** and establish **free trade** within its territories; Mackinnon himself told shareholders to expect their returns in philanthropy.

The East Africa Company secured a coastal territory around the port of Mombasa, and attempted to build a **railway** inland to Lake Victoria. Lord **Salisbury** proposed to subsidize the railway on the grounds that it would solidify Britain's control of the headwaters of the Nile and assist in putting down slavery, but Parliament would not go along. The company rapidly ran out of money and had to go back to its shareholders for additional funds on several occasions. It sold its claims in East Africa to the British government in 1895. A railway from Mombasa to Uganda—often then called Buganda—was begun in 1895 and completed in 1902. The railway was built in large part by Indian labor. The opening up of the fertile and temperate regions of what became Kenya attracted British immigrants looking for farmland, leading many to describe British East Africa as "a white man's country." Racial tensions between white immigrants, Africans moved off the land and compelled to work for wages by taxes designed to that end, and Indians demanding equal status with whites characterized politics in the protectorate and eventually led to its reconstitution as Kenya. *See also* Africa, Scramble for; British Empire.

FURTHER READING: Galbraith, John S. *Mackinnon and East Africa, 1878–1895*. Cambridge: Cambridge University Press, 1972.

MARK F. PROUDMAN

## British Empire

The British Empire was the archetypical colonial empire, the empire to which other aspiring empires often looked as a model. The British Empire was for both imperialists and anti-imperialists the epitome of a modern empire. It was at its height the largest of the colonial empires, in some ways the most successful, and certainly the most influential. The United States grew out of British imperial history, and Americans argue at length and in English about such topics as free trade, constitutional rights, and the proper place of religion in society, all issues inextricably linked to the history of the British Empire. And yet a legal pedant could argue that the British Empire never existed. With the possible exception of the British crown itself, there was never a unified legal structure or institution called "The British Empire," and the late Victorian idea of institutionalizing the empire was, in the inimitable words of Robert Gascoyne-Cecil, Lord **Salisbury,** a project better suited to peroration than to argument.

The empire covered at its height a quarter of the earth's surface and included a similar proportion of its population. And yet, for most of the last 500 years, it consisted of a motley collection of islands, ports, and hinterlands. The empire was at the height of its power in the late nineteenth century and reached its greatest territorial extent in the wake of World War I. But as little as a century earlier, Britain's possessions in **India** had been half the size, most of **Australia** was unsettled, and claims to what became **Canada** had been uncertain. As Edmund Burke wrote in the eighteenth century, "the settlement of our colonies was never pursued upon any regular plan; but they were formed, flourished and grew as accidents, the nature of the climate, or the dispositions of private men, happened to operate." Or, one might add, they rebelled, fell away, or failed to flourish for similar contingent reasons.

### British Seaborne Trade

The British Empire was always a seaborne empire; however, the earliest seaborne empires were those of **Portugal** and **Spain.** English seaborne trade in the fifteenth century largely looked eastward to the Baltic and the Hanseatic League of northern Germany, and the domestic instability during the Wars of the Roses of the fifteenth century and the Reformation of the sixteenth century militated against hazardous or expensive overseas voyages. John Cabot, or Caboto, a Genoese living in Bristol, made a westward voyage to **Newfoundland** in 1497, but was lost at sea in a subsequent venture. The Newfoundland fishery was widely known and exploited at the time by the Portuguese, the French, and the Basques, as much as by the English.

The **slave trade** had its origins in mid-sixteenth-century gold-trading voyages to the **Guinea** coast of West Africa by Sir John Hawkins and many others. Hawkins initially obtained African slaves by means of piracy on Portuguese slave traders, but then moved to trading directly with African chiefs. He then sold slaves in the Spanish dominions in America, which was like slavery an illegal activity, at least under Spanish law. The Elizabethan adventurer Francis Drake continued the tradition of interloping among the Spanish Caribbean colonies and preying on Spanish trade.

During his famous circumnavigation of 1577, a feat not repeated by an English sailor until George Anson's voyage of the 1740s, Drake plundered Spanish shipping. To an extent, the English war on Spanish trade in the era of the Spanish Armada of 1588 was a war of self-defense. In this period, piracy, slave trading, commerce-raiding, and naval warfare were not distinct. Most enterprises involved a combination of private and royal vessels, and both crown and merchant hoped for a windfall. There was little idea of securing permanent colonies until the end of the century.

In the sixteenth century, maritime trade was usually pursued through joint-stock companies, in which a number of merchants pooled resources under a royal charter. The **East India Company** was formed on the pattern of other trading enterprises of the time, such as the Levant and Muscovy Companies. The intent was to pool capital and share risk among a number of traders rather than to colonize or conquer the country into which they traded. The Levant Company secured extraterritorial privileges from the Porte (the Turkish government) in 1583, but it had no thought of conquest; likewise the Muscovy Company of 1555 aimed only to trade with the Russia of Ivan the Terrible.

The East India Company was founded on a similar pattern in 1600. During its first century and a half of existence, it made no extensive territorial acquisitions, limiting itself to trading forts and surrounding territories. In India, these included Fort St. George, later **Madras,** and Bombay, acquired from the Portuguese in 1660. The East India Company was not without competition, chiefly from the French, the Dutch, and, in early years, the Portuguese, as well as from English "interlopers," violating the company's monopoly of trade with India. Disorder created by the breakdown of the Mogul Empire in the eighteenth century and consequent opportunities for plunder and mercenary warfare drew the East India Company and its army deeper into Indian politics. The company made significant conquests in southern India, but its most notable conquest was **Bengal,** with Robert Clive's victory at the battle of Plassey in 1757. At that point, the company became a large Indian landowner.

### Colonial Wars

Wars in India customarily reflected, and at points anticipated, those in Europe. Between the Glorious Revolution of 1688 and the consequent wars with Louis XIV's France and the end of the **Napoleonic Wars** over a century later in 1815, Britain and France were at war almost every other decade, and these wars provided both the motivation and the opportunity for imperial expansion in India and elsewhere. The late eighteenth and early nineteenth centuries saw the rapid expansion of Britain's territorial holdings in India. The decline of the Mogul Empire, traditionally a British ally, led the British to assume many of the functions of government and of territorial sovereignty, once performed by that empire. At the same time as the East India Company's power was expanding in India, the company and its growing wealth became the subject of controversy in England. The India Bill of 1784 imposed a London-based Board of Control on the Company, and successive bills further regulated its conduct, restricting its role to that of administering, rather than trading in, India. By the nineteenth century, a widespread view had developed that rule by a chartered company was anachronistic. An 1857 rebellion by **sepoys**— native Indians in the Company's army—was put down only with great bloodshed. It led to the end of company rule in 1858 and the creation of an Indian government responsible to a Secretary of State in London. Since the time of Clive, British rule in India had expanded to encompass the entire subcontinent. The Royal Titles Act of 1876 created Queen **Victoria** Empress of India, marking the new and larger place that India, and the empire as a whole, occupied in the British imagination. The vice-royalty of George Curzon, Lord **Curzon,** and the imperial Durbar at the accession of Edward VII in 1901, marked the height of British prestige in India.

The Seven Years' War (1756–1763) took place in Europe, in India, and at sea; but its most notable result was in North America, where the French colony at **Québec** was conquered by a British expeditionary force, giving Britain an exclusive claim to North America north of Florida. The first English attempt to colonize the mainland of North America was Sir Walter Raleigh's failed settlement at Roanoke, Virginia, in the 1580s. Two further colonies were founded in 1607, one that survived at James-town, Virginia, and another failed colony at Plymouth, Massachusetts. Numerous other small colonies, usually of a single ship's company of settlers, were established in this period throughout the Americas; there was no sense that those in the future United States were in any way special. The famous arrival of the *Mayflower* in New England in 1620 opened the way to more extensive settlement by English Puritans. By the end of the century, there were substantial cities at Boston, Philadelphia, and New York, the latter taken from the Dutch in 1664. Britain also acquired signifi-cant holdings in the Caribbean and small toeholds in South and Central America. **Jamaica** was taken from the Spanish in 1660, and became a rich sugar colony worked by slave labor. By the end of the eighteenth century, Jamaica and related Caribbean sugar islands were among the richest imperial holdings, and the influence of the planter class in London was considerable.

By the mid-eighteenth century, the British-American colonies had 10 times the population of New France, but they were still hemmed in behind the substantial barrier of the Alleghenies. The British conquest of New France removed the threat from the French and their native allies, but it also removed the apparent need for British forces. The British demand that Americans pay taxes to help pay the costs of their own defense led to the American rebellion and subsequent declaration of independence in 1776. In the American Revolutionary War (1775–1783), Britain lost most of its American empire, but retained its colonies in Canada. Historians of the eighteenth century have been inclined to speak of a first British Empire lasting until 1783, and a second British Empire rising afterward. This makes sense in the American context, but not in India, where British power, or rather the power of the East India Company and its traders and soldiers, continued to grow steadily despite its setback in the Americas. Ten years after the conclusion of the War of American Independence, war with France broke out again, and the war would last, with the slight interruption of the 1802–1803 Peace of Amiens, until 1815. During the wars of the French Revolution and Empire, the foundations of the so-called second Brit-ish Empire were laid. That empire consisted of dependent territories throughout the littorals of Asia and Africa, and settler colonies—the future **Dominions**—in Aus-tralia, **New Zealand,** Canada, and **South Africa.**

### Britain in the Scramble for Africa

Britain's original holdings in Africa were acquired to support the slave trade. The Royal African Company was founded in 1672 to exploit the West African slave trade on a more systematic basis than had the buccaneers of the previous century. At the conclusion of the War of the Spanish Succession (1702–1713), Britain retained **Gibraltar** and **Nova Scotia,** and won the right to sell African slaves in Spanish America, an enormous market. Forts, notably Cape Coast Castle, were acquired along the West African coast. After the abolition of the slave trade in 1807 and of slavery itself in the British Empire in 1833, these bases were used by the **Royal Navy** in its long campaign to suppress the slave trade. The colony of **Sierra Leone** was established in 1787 to settle liberated slaves and North Americans of African origin, in the optimistic but never realized hope that other trades would displace the slave trade and bring peace and prosperity to Africa. With the decline of the slave trade, Britain's bases in the region became increasingly less necessary, and it was even proposed in the 1860s to abandon them entirely. Substantial territorial holdings were only acquired in tropical Africa in the 1870s and 1880s, when imperial competition with other powers became acute. Although Mungo Park's explorations of the Niger River in the 1790s had significantly expanded knowledge of that region's interior, and trade to the "oil rivers"—the oil being palm oil—expanded throughout the century, it was not until the end of the century that Sir George Goldie's Royal Niger Company began to assert territorial control in the area; it was only in 1899 that the colony of **Nigeria** was formally brought under British rule. British expansion in East Africa followed a similar pattern, with explorers such as David **Livingston,** Richard **Burton,** and John Speke leading the way, a chartered company professing philanthropic purposes following him, and the formal declarations of East African **protectorates** occurring only in 1895.

The British acquired Cape Colony in South Africa in 1795, during the wars of the French Revolution. Although the colony was briefly returned to the Dutch at the Peace of **Amiens** in 1802, the British retained the Cape at the peace of 1815. This colony presented the British with a number of difficulties, including a disaffected Dutch Creole (or Afrikaner or Boer) population and poorly defined frontiers confronting numerous African tribes. The eastern boundaries of the Cape Colony saw in the nineteenth century by one authoritative count nine frontier wars, or "**Kaffir Wars,**" in the language of the time, in most of which British frontiers advanced in the hope of pacification. Afrikaners discontented with British rule and specifically with the abolition of slavery migrated into the interior, the most significant movement, the **Great Trek,** beginning in 1837. Rapidly coming into conflict with the **Zulu,** the Afrikaners founded independent republics, the most prominent of which were the **Transvaal** and the **Orange Free State,** which were conditionally recognized by Britain in 1852 and 1854, respectively. British traders had in the meantime arrived at the port that became Durban, and the colony of **Natal** was annexed by the empire in 1843, creating another set of frontiers with both Africans and Afrikaners. The discovery of diamonds in the northeast Cape led to the annexation of the area in 1873, the cause of a diplomatic dispute between Britain and the Orange Free State. Further trouble with the Afrikaners resulted from the annexation of the Transvaal in 1877. Two years later, the Zulus, no longer threatened by the Boers, became a threat to the small British colony at Natal. The 1879 Zulu war resulted in a bloody British defeat at **Isandhlwana** before the British finally broke Zulu military power. A Boer rebellion in the Transvaal led to another British defeat at Majuba Hill in 1881 and the restoration of conditional sovereignty to the Transvaal. Gold was discovered in the Rand region of the Transvaal in 1886, leading to an influx of primarily British miners. Disputes about their legal status, combined with ambiguities about the status of the Transvaal and a determination on the part of some British imperialists, including Joseph **Chamberlain** and Alfred **Milner,** to force the Boer republics into a union with the British colonies, led to the outbreak of the South African War, or Anglo-Boer War, of 1899–1902. After a series of initial defeats, the British were able to occupy the Transvaal and the Orange Free State, but it took another two years of **guerilla** warfare to suppress the Boers entirely. South Africa became a self-governing dominion in 1910. One condition of the Boer surrender, however, was the provision that Africans would not be enfranchised before the grant of responsible government, with the result that the Boer majority among the white South African minority was able to impose the apartheid regime of the twentieth century.

British expansion north from South Africa resulted in considerable holdings in southern Africa. Concern about the incursions of other powers, chiefly Germany, and the idea that large and prosperous colonies might be founded in central Africa, led in 1885 to an expedition into what is now Botswana, for the purpose of preserving control of the route north. In 1889, The ambitious diamond magnate Cecil **Rhodes** obtained a charter for his **British South Africa Company,** which established a colony in Rhodesia in 1890, and shortly thereafter fought and won two brief wars with the **Matabele,** a tribe related to the Zulu. Rhodesia included not only the current Zimbabwe but also the mineral-rich territory of northern Rhodesia, now Zambia. In 1915, during World War I, a South African expedition conquered **German Southwest Africa,** resulting in a British-dominated southern Africa.

In the Mediterranean, British trade and the need for protection from pirates dated to the sixteenth century. Britain established an unsuccessful colony at Tangier in the seventeenth century. Gibraltar, seized during the War of the Spanish Succession in the early eighteenth century, was kept as a permanent base afterward. During the French wars of the eighteenth century, Britain at points held the islands of Minorca and Corsica. Malta, seized in 1800, was retained after the Napoleonic Wars, as, for a generation, were the Ionian Islands. Britain acquired Cyprus from Turkey in 1878, for use as a military and naval base directed at Russia and at the protection of the route to India. The Mediterranean had assumed increasing importance as the route to India after the opening of the **Suez Canal** in 1869; although the canal was built with French capital, most of the ships using it were British.

In 1882, British troops occupied **Egypt,** nominally a vassal of the Ottoman Empire, as the result of a nationalist rebellion against the Khedive and of fears that the rebels would renege on Egypt's substantial foreign debts and endanger the route to India. At the time, the objective of the government of Prime Minister William **Gladstone** was only a temporary occupation to restore order; as it was, Britain and British officials, most notably Evelyn Baring, Lord **Cromer,** became increasingly implicated in ruling Egypt. The occupation of Egypt resulted in Britain being sucked into war in the Sudan, where the Egyptian government had claims. General Charles **Gordon,** sent to evacuate the province, was killed at Khartoum in 1885, creating outrage in Britain, and leading ultimately to the 1898 conquest of the Sudan. A protectorate was declared over Egypt when Britain went to war with Turkey in 1914. It was a result of war with Turkey that Britain allied itself with Arab nationalists, most famously as a result of the adventures of T. E. Lawrence (Lawrence of Arabia) and acquired the rest of its short-lived empire in the Middle East, including Palestine, Iraq, and Transjordan. Britain had long had interests in the Persian Gulf, largely as a result of trade between that region and India. In the early years of the century, competition with Russia for influence in Persia led to a 1907 agreement on spheres of influence; the subsequent discovery of large oil deposits led to the formation of the Anglo-Iranian Oil Company to provide fuel for the Royal Navy. British influence in Persia or Iran lasted until the nationalization of British oil interests in 1951.

### Imperial Governance

Historians of the later nineteenth and twentieth centuries—the age of self-conscious, programmatic **imperialism**—have also tended to divide the empire into two, in this case the dependent or autocratically ruled Colonial Office empire on the one hand, and the self-governing dominions or **Commonwealth** on the other. This division also has its uses, but it tends to apply primarily to the Victorian empire and its twentieth-century successor. In the first two-thirds of the nineteenth century, the Colonial Office concerned itself primarily with the emigrant colonies, but toward the end of that century those colonies were in most cases self-governing, and Colonial Office attention was directed toward the management of colonies not merely under British sovereignty but under British rule. Defenders of the British Empire have often emphasized its liberal character, and in so doing have directed attention to the emigrant colonies, or Dominions as they became. **Responsible government,** which meant colonial government in which a colonial ministry was responsible to the legislature and the London-appointed governor was bound to accept the advice of the ministry, was introduced by stages in Canada, but it is generally reckoned to have been permanently established in 1848. Shortly thereafter, responsible government was extended to most of the Australian colonies in 1853, and became effective in New Zealand in 1856. It was granted, under a property franchise that largely but not completely excluded Africans, to the Cape Colony in 1872. The liberal institutions established throughout the settler Dominions customarily excluded natives. However, they created a series of pro-British white Dominions that contributed materially to the empire's strength during the world wars.

**Ireland** has been viewed by some historians as England's first colony. The Norman kings had claimed the island in the twelfth century but did not succeed in imposing direct authority beyond the pale of Dublin. Schemes of "plantation," in the language of the time, under Elizabeth I in the late sixteenth century offered incentives for English settlers to colonize Ireland, the aim being to create populations loyal to the English crown. By the end of the seventeenth century, most of Ireland was in Protestant English hands. The Irish parliament set up in 1782 was abolished by William **Pitt**'s **Act of Union,** which brought Ireland into a legislative union with England, Wales, and Scotland, the aim being to prevent further Irish rebellions by assimilating the Irish into the British state. The policy was hindered by the fact that most Irish, even those few meeting the property qualifications for the franchise, were Catholic. The Catholic Emancipation of 1829 followed by the successive reforms bills of the nineteenth century enfranchised increasing numbers of Irishmen and led to a rising demand for **Home Rule.** In 1886, the Gladstone government proposed to meet this demand, thereby splitting the **Liberal Party** and putting the **Conservative Party,** or Unionists, in power for most of the next 20 years. The idea of separate status for Ireland was an affront to the legal egalitarianism of many Liberals; to the Conservatives, breaking up the union presaged the fragmentation of the empire that they wished to unite. Ireland was granted Dominion status in 1922 as a result of civil war, a process notably divergent from the gradual assumption of self-government in the other Dominions. Although British contemporaries saw Ireland as a poor and disorderly part of Britain, in the eyes of Irish nationalists and many current scholars it was in fact not merely the first colony conquered but the firs to obtain independence.

The most powerful and influential successor state to the British Empire is of course the **United States.** American nationalism originally defined itself against the empire, although at the same time, it derived many of its core characteristics, including its hostility to the state and to centralized authority, from the British constitutional tradition. The **Anglo-American War** of 1812 heightened anti-British opinion in the United States. In the same period, however, Anglo-American trade and cultural links grew rapidly, trade having rapidly doubled its pre-War of Independence volume after the peace of 1783. Anglo-American tensions bubbled to the surface throughout the nineteenth century, but neither country had an interest in war. The seizure of Confederate representatives from a British ship almost led to war between Britain and the Union during the American Civil War in the 1860s, but the United States backed down. In the 1890s, Britain gave way as a result of Anglo-American tensions in British Guyana and **Panama.** Throughout the era of imperialism, Anglo-American trade grew, and Britain became the largest investor in the United States. Anglo-American ties reached their closest point during World War II, but the United States in this era had a profoundly ambivalent attitude to the British Empire, being in theory anti-imperialist but at the same time needing a strong ally.

### The Legacy of British Imperialism

Explanations of the extent and influence of the British Empire have run the gamut from celebrations of the maritime genius of the British people, of the far-sightedness of English statesman, and of the adaptability of the British constitution, to denunciations of the imperialist and irresistible character of capitalism. All have an element of truth. The island nation did have the material basis and the ships and sailors to eventually best the Dutch, Spanish, and French. After the disasters of the American War of Independence, British statesman had the foresight never again to tax a colony, and never for long to deny self-government to a British population. Imperial possessions, notably the "sugar islands" of the Caribbean and the trading forts of India, contributed materially to British wealth in the eighteenth century, and, it has been argued, enabled the Industrial Revolution. The strength of the British domestic economy allowed Britain to dominate world trade and provided both the material basis for the rapid expansion of the nineteenth century and the motivations for the acquisition of many imperial territories. The "man on the spot," in the Victorian phrase, had much to do with many imperial acquisitions, from the Indian conquests of Clive and Lawrence to the later African acquisitions of Rhodes. The self-conscious imperialism of the late nineteenth century, characterized by systematic programs of imperial expansion and rationalization, lasted for only a generation and, although it created pressures for expansion in Africa, was not responsible for creating any of the main imperial holdings. As David Lloyd George said, with characteristic cynicism, "the British empire has done very well out of side-shows," an observation that is both true and provocative of the further question of how and why divergent events and motivations led to the acquisition of the largest and arguably most influential empire the world has ever seen.

The decline of empire is susceptible to the same variety of explanations. Economic growth created an Indian and an African middle class able to confront the

British on their own terms. The Indian National Congress, founded in 1885, was closely linked to the Fabian society in England, and was able to make effective use of anti-imperial ideologies created by British liberals such as J. A. **Hobson.** The decline of British economic power after, and in part as a result of, the world wars undermined Britain's ability to maintain a large empire, and the unprofitability of large parts of that empire reduced the incentives to resist its decline. The myth of Britain's liberal empire—containing, like most myths, an element of truth—and the precedent of the gradual evolution of the settlement Dominions to full self-government undermined the justifications for imperial rule, and provided a path from empire to Commonwealth. Britain fought colonial campaigns in Kenya, Cyprus, and Malaya, but none were as bloody and traumatic as those of the French or Portuguese empires. The one attempt that Britain made to reverse imperial decline by military means, the Suez intervention of 1956, lasted 24 hours and split the British political nation.

The historiography of the British Empire is enormous. No focus or approach has been ignored. Older histories spoke of great men and the acquisition of enormous wealth. More recent histories have also addressed topics of current concern, such as the relation of masculinity to imperial conquest and of discourses of race and alterity to the justifications of empire. The evolving, and it must be said rapidly expanding, state of British imperial historiography is perhaps best captured by the two great multivolume histories produced by England's ancient universities: The *Cambridge History of the British Empire,* in eight volumes, is a comprehensive survey of the acquisition and rule of the British Empire. Published from 1929 forward, it is quite Whiggish in its emphasis on the export of British constitutional practices yet is an invaluable reference work, based as it is on primary sources, full of names and dates, facts, and details. The more recent *Oxford History of the British Empire,* in six volumes from 1998, is more postcolonial in its sensibilities, more diverse in its topics, and concerned to leave out no perspective. So much has been published that its survey necessarily becomes less historical than historiographical, and it is irreplaceable as a survey of current scholarship. Various short surveys of the world the British made, and the process by which they made it, are listed in the Further Reading section. *See also* Disraeli, Benjamin; Fashoda; Navalism; Nelson, Horatio; Wellesley, Arthur, Duke of Wellington; White Man's Burden.

FURTHER READING: Benians, E. A. et al., eds. *Cambridge History of the British Empire.* 8 vols. Cambridge: Cambridge University Press, 1929–59; Black, Jeremy. *The British Seaborne Empire.* New Haven, CT: Yale University Press, 2004; Cain, P. J., and A. G. Hopkins. *British Imperialism, 1688–2000.* London: Longman, 1993. Ferguson, Niall. *Empire.* New York: Basic Books, 2003; James, Lawrence. *The Rise and Fall of the British Empire.* London: Abacus, 2001; Louis, William Roger, ed. *Oxford History of the British Empire.* 6 vols. Oxford: University Press, 1998; Marshall, P. J. *The Cambridge Illustrated History of the British Empire.* Cambridge: Cambridge University Press, 1996; Porter, Bernard. *The Lion's Share: A Short History of British Imperialism 1850–2004.* New York: Longman, 2004.

MARK F. PROUDMAN

## British North America Act (1867)

An act of the British Parliament creating the federal state since known as Canada. It united the separate colonies of Canada, Nova Scotia, and New Brunswick into a federal Dominion of Canada while simultaneously dividing the old colony of united Canada into the provinces of Ontario and Quebec. The capital of the Dominion was established at Ottawa.

The topic of a union of the British colonies in North America had been debated on and off since the War of 1812. In the 1850s, the idea was intermittently discussed, and the prospect of an intercolonial **railway** bringing the trade of the Canadas to maritime ports was raised. With the encouragement of the British government, of events south of the border during the **American Civil War,** and of financial interests looking to make the Canadian railway system at last a paying proposition, meetings of representatives from the three maritime provinces (Nova Scotia, New Brunswick, and Prince Edward Island) and from the Canadian legislature were held at Charlottetown and then at Quebec in 1864. It was agreed that a federal union would be formed, with a parliament consisting of a lower house elected by population and an upper house in which each section (Upper Canada, Lower Canada, and the Maritimes) would be represented equally.

The Canadian legislature, representing both Lower Canada (Quebec) and Upper Canada (Ontario), passed a resolution in favor of Confederation in 1865. The scheme, however, met opposition in Nova Scotia and Prince Edward Island, the latter of which did not join confederation until 1873. New Brunswick, prompted by the 1865 U.S. abrogation of the reciprocity (essentially free trade) treaty of 1854, endorsed it. At the initiative of the British government, a meeting was held in London in December 1866 to finalize the terms of the new union. That meeting, under the chairmanship of Sir John A. **Macdonald** and Lord Carnarvon, Colonial Secretary under **Disraeli,** agreed the terms of a bill to be presented in the imperial parliament. It was suggested that the new federation be termed a "dominion," reference being made to Psalm 72, "he shall have dominion also from sea to sea": transcontinental aspirations guided the confederative project from the beginning.

The British North America (BNA) bill appeared, from the British point of view, to solve a number of potential embarrassing problems. After the Fenian raids of 1866, it unified for the common defense a disparate set of militarily indefensible colonies, it provided further for the expenses of Canadian government to be met by the Canadian taxpayer, and it raised the hope that British-financed railways might become solvent. In short order, the last significant British garrisons were withdrawn from Canada.

The BNA bill received its second reading in the House of Commons on February 28, 1867, passing without a division, after which the House filled up for a debate on a dog duty. The BNA Act received royal assent on 29 March 1867, the Dominion officially coming into existence on 1 July 1867, a date for many years celebrated as Dominion Day, but now known as Canada Day. *See also* British Empire; Manifest Destiny; United States.

FURTHER READING: Ged Martin. *Britain and the Origins of Canadian Confederation.* London: McMillan, 1995.

MARK F. PROUDMAN

## British South Africa Company

A venture controlled by Cecil **Rhodes** and chartered by Lord **Salisbury's** Conservative government in 1889. Rhodes' aim was to take control of a large expanse of

African territory up to and including the area of the Zambezi, largely for mineral exploration. The government's aim was to place the area under British suzerainty, excluding such competitors as the Germans and the Portuguese, without incurring the costs of ruling it or the need to ask Parliament for money. The British South Africa Company was one of a number of such chartered companies—companies holding semi-sovereign power over a territory—created in the final two decades of the nineteenth century for similar reasons, other examples being the Royal Niger Company and the Imperial British East Africa Company. Rhodes's South Africa Company became the best-known, and certainly the most notorious, nineteenth-century chartered company, although it never made the fortune anticipated by its shareholders.

Advocates of chartered companies looked back to the conquest of India by the **East India Company;** anti-imperialists often drew a similar parallel. It was in deference to Victorian opinion that the company's charter promised **free trade** and the abolition of slavery within its territories. The British South Africa Company took over the so-called Rudd concession, a mining concession obtained from the Matabele (or Ndebele) king Lobengula under arguably fraudulent terms, as its main asset. It was under the auspices of the company that the Rhodesian "pioneer column" moved into what became Rhodesia in 1890, establishing Fort Salisbury (now Harare.) As formally a sovereign power in its own right, the British South Africa Company had its own armed force, the British South Africa Company Police. The Company's Police fought and won, with support from other British forces, the **Matabele Wars** of 1893 and 1896 against the forces of Lobengula, who had rapidly come to regret his concession. They were also used by L. S. Jameson, a prominent associate of Rhodes, in his abortive 1896 **Jameson Raid.** Although the company had a great deal to do with the expansion of British power into southern and central Africa—Rhodes' "great dream of the north"—and with subsequent "Cape to Cairo" schemes, it rapidly became unpopular with the settlers living under its rule. Its shares oscillated wildly on the London exchange, leading to justified charges that they were being manipulated and giving a fillip to the credibility of theories of capitalist imperialism, but it did not pay a dividend until 1924, the year after the white settlers of Rhodesia had been granted **responsible government** and the company's rule terminated. *See also* Africa, Scramble for; Boer Wars; British Empire.

FURTHER READING: Pakenham, Thomas. *The Boer War.* New York: Avon Books, 1992; Rotberg, Robert. *The Founder: Cecil Rhodes and the Pursuit of Power.* New York: Oxford University Press, 1988; Wheatcroft, Geoffrey. *The Randlaords.* New York: Atheneum, 1985.

MARK F. PROUDMAN

## Buena Vista, Battle of (1847)

An important engagement of the **Mexican-American War** (1846–1848). After the conquest of its northern provinces failed to compel the Mexican government to accept American territorial demands, U.S. President James K. Polk, in late 1846, ordered the capture of Mexico City itself. The campaign's commander, General Winfield Scott, out of necessity drew units from General Zachary Taylor's Army of Occupation at Monterrey. Losing half his troops and most of his regulars, Taylor was left with a depleted army of largely inexperienced volunteers.

At San Luis Potosi, Mexican General Antonia Lopez de Santa Anna learned of Taylor's weakened status through a captured dispatch and quick-marched 15,000 men northward across 250 miles of barren country in February 1847. Taylor, expecting Santa Anna to move southward against Scott, was completely unprepared for the onslaught. Belatedly alerted to the danger on February 21, Taylor hastily concentrated his 4,800 effectives at Angostura Pass near Hacienda Buena Vista. Mountain spurs and steep gullies made "the Narrows" ideally suited to the defense.

Santa Anna struck on February 22, 1847. Wave after wave of Mexican infantry and cavalry constantly threatened to envelop the American position in two days of hard fighting. Outnumbered three to one, Taylor refused to panic, skillfully maneuvering his units from one threatened point to another. His conspicuous presence on the battlefield also inspired his men, who repeatedly rallied to repair gaping holes in the American lines. Taylor's artillery also proved decisive, shifting rapidly to fill the breeches and providing rallying points for the often panic-stricken volunteers. Firing spherical case shot and canister, American batteries first blunted and then smashed successive columns of attackers.

Santa Anna withdrew in defeat on February 23, his army having suffered 2,100 casualties. American losses exceeded 660 killed, missing, and wounded. Although stunning, Taylor's victory at Buena Vista failed to advance President Polk's strategic objectives and Mexican capitulation remained elusive. *See also* Manifest Destiny; United States.

FURTHER READING: Bauer, K. Jack. *The Mexican War, 1846–1848.* Lincoln: University of Nebraska Press, 1992; Eisenhower, John S. D. *So Far from God: The U.S. War with Mexico, 1846–1848.* New York: Random House, 1989; McCaffrey, James M. *Army of Manifest Destiny: The American Soldier in the Mexican War, 1846–1848.* New York: New York University Press, 1992; Smith, Justin H. *The War with Mexico.* 2 vols. Gloucester, MA: Peter Smith, 1963.

DAVID R. SNYDER

## Bukhara Emirate

One of the substantial Islamic states of Central Eurasia during the age of Russian imperialism. The Bukharan Emirate's capital, the city of Bukhara, was a very old city that had long been a center of Islamic cultural and intellectual achievement. The emirate was a major political contender and ally of Russia during the late-nineteenth and early-twentieth centuries. It was ruled according to Islamic law and under the leadership of an emir. In 1868, Bukhara formally recognized the superiority of the Russian Empire and, in 1873, was made a Russian protectorate but maintained its sovereignty until Bolshevik conquest in 1920. The last emir of Bukhara was Emir Muhammad Alim **Khan,** who continued the legacy of traditional Islamic rule. From 1800 until 1920, Bukhara was formally led by the Mangit dynasty, who took over rule from the Chinggisid rulers in the middle of the eighteenth century. *See also* Great Game; Russian Empire.

FURTHER READING: Holdsworth, Mary. *Turkestan in the Nineteenth Century: A Brief History of the Khanates of Bukhara, Kokand and Khiva.* Oxford: St. Anthony's College (Oxford) Soviet Affairs Study Group, 1959.

SCOTT C. BAILEY

## Bulgaria

Since 1396, a European province of the Ottoman Empire. In 1870, the Porte (Ottoman government) permitted the establishment of a branch of the Orthodox Church, the Exarchate, for Christian subjects in Bulgaria. The Exarchate then nurtured a Bulgarian nationalist movement and was encouraged in the enterprise by the Russian government, as well as by Pan-Slavist organizations. The brutal repression of Bulgarian nationalism in 1875–1876 provoked international outrage, the most articulate of which was William Gladstone's protest of the "Bulgarian Horrors" and of the British Conservative government of Benjamin Disraeli for its alliance with Turkey, but the most important of which was the **Russo-Turkish War** of 1877–1878. The outcome of the latter led to Ottoman acceptance of Bulgarian autonomy in the Treaty of **San Stefano.**

The Treaty of **Berlin** then limited Bulgarian autonomy to the territory north of Sofia and made southern Bulgaria the separate Ottoman province of Eastern Roumelia. Having won its freedom, Bulgaria promptly became an obstreperous nuisance to the Great Powers by expanding into Eastern Roumelia and inflicting a military defeat on **Serbia.** This made Bulgaria the largest of the new Slav states in the Balkans, a position it improved in the First Balkan War and then frittered away in the Second. *See also* Balkan Wars; Eastern Question; Ottoman Empire; Russian Empire.

FURTHER READING: Crampton, R.J. *Bulgaria, 1878–1918.* New York: Columbia University Press, 1983; Kohn, Hans. *Pan-Slavism: Its History and Ideology.* New York; Vintage, 1960.

CARL CAVANAGH HODGE

## Bülow, Bernhard Heinrich Martin Carl, Count von (1849–1929)

A German politician and diplomat, Count von Bülow was German Chancellor and Prussian *Ministerpresident* from 1900 to 1909. Born into one of the oldest German aristocratic families on May 3, 1849, he studied law and then had a rapid diplomatic career, including placements in Paris, St Petersburg, Bucharest and Rome. Bülow was Secretary of State for Foreign Affairs from 1897 and the Kaiser **Wilhelm II**'s preferred candidate to replace Hohenlohe as Chancellor in 1900. Under his Chancellorship, he initially tried to further tensions among the other great powers and intended to turn Germany into a world power, although he eventually changed his strategy when his policy arguably resulted in anti-German alliances. He demanded Germany's "place in the sun" and nurtured much of Germany's bellicose foreign policy, such as in during the First Moroccan Crisis. Bülow personifies, like no other politician, Wilhelmine expansive foreign policy aspirations, yet eventually fell out of favor with the monarch after the Daily Telegraph Affair of 1908 and was forced to resign in July 1909, although he continued to harbor hope of reinstatement.

During the World War I, Bülow was critical of his successor's policy, blaming Theobald von **Bethmann-Hollweg** for the escalation of the July Crisis. At the end of 1914 he was called upon to use his influence in Rome as Germany's ambassador, but he had no success in convincing Italy to join its Triple Alliance partners in the hostilities. Bülow hoped he might be recalled to the office of Chancellor following Bethmann-Hollweg's and then Michaelis' dismissals in 1917. After the war, he wrote his memoirs in which he blamed Bethmann-Hollweg for the escalation of the July

Crisis. Bülow died following an earlier stroke in October 1929. *See also*: German Empire; *Weltpolitik*.

FURTHER READING: Bülow, Prince von. *Memoirs*. 2 vols. London, 1931–32; Lerman, Katharine A. *The Chancellor as Courtier: Bernhard von Bülow and the Governance of Germany 1900–1909*. Cambridge: Cambridge University Press, 1990; Winzen, Peter. *Bernhard Fürst von Bülow*. Göttingen: Muster-Schmidt Verlag, 2003.

ANNIKA MOMBAUER

## Bundesrat

One of the two legislative chambers of the German **Reich.** The Bundesrat represented the 20 states, as well as the three free cities and held considerable power when it came to the passage of laws, the formulation of policy, and the dissolving of the Reichstag. The Bundesrat epitomized the federal element of the Reich constitution and was especially designed to guard against parliamentarianism. At its inception in 1871, the Bundesrat was the highest constitutional body of the Empire. Modeled on the constitution of the North German Confederation, the Bundesrat was intended by Bismarck as a hybrid between legislature and executive. In practice, however, its main function was to make, not to implement, laws. All legislative proposals were first introduced in the Bundesrat. Only if the upper house approved of the proposal would the bill be passed on to the popularly elected Reichstag. Apart from making law, the Bundesrat decided on a possible declaration of war as well as over constitutional quarrels among the member states of the Reich.

In the Bundesrat, the otherwise obvious Prussian hegemony was disguised. Although the kingdom made up nearly two-thirds of the Empire's population and territory, it disposed of only 17 of a total of 58 votes (61 after the reform of 1911). Next to Prussia, Bavaria had six, Saxony and Wurttemberg four, and Hesse and Bade three votes each. The other votes were distributed among the smaller states, many of them enclaves surrounded by Prussian territory. Accordingly, Prussia wielded an often overwhelming influence in the chamber.

The position of both the Bundesrat and the smaller federal states was further checked by the fact that the chamber did not consist of independent deputies but of envoys who took their orders from the state governments. Because for a long time most of the legislative proposals were drafted in the Prussian state ministries and the committee chairmanships were monopolized by the Prussian envoys to the Bundesrat, Prussia marginalized the smaller German states. Only on important matters did the chancellor hold preliminary talks with some of the envoys, and this was largely confined to the representatives of Bavaria, Saxony, and of the other kingdoms. Because of ever-growing centralizing tendencies in the Reich, however, the Bundesrat as an institution increasingly lost influence to the Kaiser, to the Reichstag, and to national pressure groups. *See also* German Empire.

FURTHER READING: Boldt, Hans. *Deutsche Verfassungsgeschichte*. vol. 2. München: Deutscher Taschenbuch Verlag, 1993; Craig, Gordon. *Germany, 1866–1945*. New York: Oxford University Press, 1978; Fulbrook, Mary. *A Concise History of Gremany*. New York: Cambridge University

Press, 1990; Mann, Golo. *The History of Germany Since 1789.* London: Chatto & Windus, 1968; Nipperdey, Thomas. *Deutsche Geschichte.* München: Beck, 1985.

ULRICH SCHNAKENBERG

## Burke, Edmund (1729–1797)

A British parliamentarian, statesman, and philosopher, Edmund Burke was born and educated in Dublin. Burke studied law before becoming a political writer and, in later life, a leading parliamentarian. He served as secretary to the Lord Lieutenant of Ireland, during which time he wrote *Tracts on the Popery Laws,* a critique of the laws that restricted the civil and political rights of Catholics. On returning to England, he was elected to Parliament in 1765, a Whig with strong ties to the faction led by Lord Rockingham. When Rockingham left office the next year, Burke declined a position in the new government and opposed it. In his *Thoughts on the Present Discontents* (1770), he argued against the power of the Crown under **George III.** He later fought in Parliament and in print against political corruption and the maladministration of Bengal under the governor-generalship of Warren Hastings. Burke supported the grievances of the American colonists respecting taxation and, in March 1775, made a speech on reconciliation with America that, although eloquently delivered, failed to avert the conflict that broke out later that year.

Although many Whigs supported the French Revolution that broke out in 1789, Burke became an early critic of "Jacobinism," viewing the increasing radicalism of the movement as dangerous to his country's liberal political traditions. He was the anonymous editor of *The Annual Register* from 1759 to 1797, but is best known for his *Reflections on the Revolution in France* (1790), which, although it lost him the support of the leading Whig statesman, Charles James Fox, attracted a large following inside and outside Parliament among those who saw the Revolution as a danger to the social and political stability provided by British constitutionalism. As Anglo-French relations deteriorated with the invasion of strategically important Belgium, Burke redoubled his attacks on the Republic and strongly supported war, which began in February 1793. In 1796, he wrote *Letters on a Regicide Peace* (1796) in which he accused the revolutionaries of threatening the right of property-holding. Burke's stature at home grew in proportion to the violence of the Revolution, particularly during the Terror. He died in 1797, an icon of his political adherents and one of several eighteenth-century statesmen—above all William **Pitt**—whose political philosophy spawned modern conservatism.

FURTHER READING: Burke, Edmund. *Reflections on the Revolution in France.* Edited by Frank M. Turner. New Haven, CT: Yale University Press, 2003; Lambert, Elizabeth. *Edmund Burke of Beaconsfield.* Newark, DE: University of Delaware Press, 2003.

GREGORY FREMONT-BARNES

## Burkersdorf, Battle of (1866)

Also known as the Battle of Soor, Burkersdorf was an engagement of the **Austro-Prussian War.** The Prussian invasion of Bohemia in June 1866 consisted of two prongs. The eastern prong, the Prussian Second Army under Crown Prince Frederick, advanced south and west from Saxony through the mountain passes.

Because the Prussian army had to split up and use several passes, it meant that the Austrian North Army had the opportunity to defeat the Prussians in detail. One Prussian corps was able to establish itself at the Bohemian pass at Skalice, but another was driven back at Trautenau, the northernmost pass, on June 27 by General Ludwig Gablenz's X Corps. Gablenz's initiative left X Corps vulnerable to an attack on its right flank from the other Prussian bridgeheads, so he was ordered to retreat south the next day to Josephstadt and the main Austrian army. On the retreat, X Corps was nearly cut off at Burkersdorf by the Prussian Guard advancing west from Skalice. Austrian artillery helped blunt the Prussian attacks, but X Corps was forced to retire west instead of south. Any chance for the Austrians to stop the Prussians at the passes was lost.

FURTHER READING: Showalter, Dennis. *The Wars of German Unification.* London: Arnold, 2004; Wawro, Geoffrey. *The Austro-Prussian War.* New York: Cambridge University Press, 1996.

DAVID H. OLIVIER

## Burlingame Treaty (1868)

A treaty between the **United States** and China opening the United States to Chinese immigration. It was negotiated by U.S. Secretary of State William H. Seward and a Chinese commission that included Anson Burlingame, signed on July 28, 1868, and proclaimed on February 5, 1870.

China was in the throes of dynastic decline, which European nations eagerly attempted to exploit. Out of altruism and self-interest, the United States followed an "**open door**" policy opposing infringements on Chinese sovereignty. After the Civil War, American interests in China focused on cultivating the "China market," protecting American missionaries, and securing labor for American economic development. The treaty guaranteed most-favored nation treatment for Chinese in the United States and Americans in China and permitted unrestricted immigration of Chinese into the United States while withholding naturalization rights. The United States pledged noninterference in Chinese domestic affairs and granted Chinese consuls in U.S. ports diplomatic equality with European consuls. Finally, Americans in China and Chinese in the United States were guaranteed freedom of religion.

The treaty improved Sino-American relations and the environment for American merchants and missionaries in China. By encouraging Chinese immigration, the treaty helped to meet labor needs in the United States while exacerbating racial tensions.

FURTHER READING: Anderson, David L. "Anson Burlingame: American Architect of the Cooperative Policy in China, 1861–1871." *Diplomatic History* Vol. 1/3 (1977): 239–255; Bevans, Charles I., comp. *Treaties and Other International Agreements of the United States of America 1776–1949.* Vol. 6. Washington, DC: Government Printing Office, 1971.

KENNETH J. BLUME

## Burma

The home of a formidable empire in its own right in the eleventh and twelfth centuries and the site thereafter of chronic civil war until the eighteenth century.

In the nineteenth century, it was increasingly under British control. Britain waged three **Anglo-Burmese Wars,** the last of which was prompted by a concern to secure all of Burma from competition after the French conquest of Tonkin to the East. In 1886, Burma was incorporated into British India, but during the next four years, Burmese resistance to British rule was fierce and British pacification of it brutal. Lowland peasants were jailed, beaten and shot; their villages were burned and livestock killed. Hill tribesmen, along with the help of troops brought in from India, were used by the British to help defeat resistance. The Burmese never accepted British rule and resented incorporation into India until 1937 when Burma was administratively separated from it.

FURTHER READING: Aung, Maung Htin. *A History of Burma.* New York: Columbia University Press, 1967; Farwell, Byron. *Queen Victoria's Little Wars.* New York: W. W. Norton, 1972; Thant Myint-U, *The Making of Modern Burma.* New York: Cambridge University Press, 2001.

CARL CAVANAGH HODGE

## *Burschenschaft*

A German student organization that emerged at the time of the Wars of Liberation against Napoleon between 1813 and 1815. The *Burschenschaft*'s twin goals of the formation of a German nation state and political freedom were disappointed by the Congress of Vienna and the formation of the Holy Alliance, which restored the old order of absolutism and particularism. In spite of being persecuted by Austria and Prussia, former members of the *Burschenschaft* nevertheless played a prominent part in the German Revolution of 1848. It was, however, not until 1871 that their dream of a united Germany was finally realized.

Founded in Jena in 1815, the *Burschenschaft*, with their motto "Freedom, honour, fatherland," quickly spread to other universities in the German-speaking parts of central Europe. Their flag carried the colors black, red, and gold, the colors of the Lützow free corps, of which many students had been members during the Wars of Liberation. Among their main demands figured the abandonment of the confederal system and the creation of a constitutional German central government in place of the German Confederation of 35 independent states and 4 free cities, which they considered as an artificial entity. In October 1817, about 500 members of the Burschenschaft and their academic teachers met at the Wartburg castle near Eisenach to reassert their demands. Yet the fiery speeches given, as well as the burning of reactionary books and military uniforms, by a small number of students intensified the already aroused suspicion of German governments. Prussia was the first to react. She prohibited the fraternities and put the universities under a rigid system of control. The assassination of the author and alleged Russian agent August von Kotzebue one-and-a-half year later by the student Karl Sand, a member of the Burschenschaft, provided count Metternich with an opportunity to curtail civil liberties even more. Metternich, the main defender of the status quo in Europe, secured the approval of the governments of the German Confederation to wipe out what he saw was seditious action. The subsequent Carlsbad Decrees not only outlawed the Burschenschaften but drastically curtailed all efforts for further political reform. The decrees limited freedom of speech and the power of the legislatures, restricted the right of assembly, expanded the authority of the police, and intensified censorship.

Within a short period of time, the opposition had been subdued and throughout Germany the reactionary forces won the day. Most important, the Prussian king revoked his promise to grant his kingdom a constitution, and it was only after the 1830 Paris July Revolution that the German freedom movement began to stir again.

Ultimately, the forces of reaction could not stop the propagation of the modern ideas of nationalism and freedom. During the German Revolution of 1848–1849 former members of the *Burschenschaften,* most prominently Heinrich von Gagern, the speaker of the Frankfurt Parliament, actively participated in the struggle for unity and liberalism. However, the failure of the movement dealt a severe blow to the fraternities. After the foundation of the German Empire, their former espousal of liberal reforms declined. Many *Burschenschaften* now subscribed to a more aggressive nationalism and increasingly anti-Semitism also came to the fore. *See also* German Empire; Nationalism.

FURTHER READING: Elm, Ludwig. *Füxe, Burschen, Alte Herren. Studentische Korporationen vom Wartburgfest bis heute.* Köln: PapyRossa-Verlag, 1993; Randers-Pehrson, Justine. *Germans and the Revolution of 1848–1849.* New York: Peter Lang, 1999; Steiger, Günter. *Aufbruch. Urburschenschaft und Wartburgfest.* Leipzig: Urania-Verlag, 1967; Wentzke, Paul. *Geschichte der deutschen Burschenschaft.* Heidelberg: Winter, 1965.

ULRICH SCHNAKENBURG

## Burton, Captain Sir Richard Francis (1821–1890)

British soldier, explorer, master linguist, and diplomat, Sir Richard Burton was best known for his dispute with John Hanning Speke about the source of the Nile River. While serving in the Indian Army, Burton became an expert in local languages, customs, and political affairs, skills that led to his assignment as an intelligence officer. After his military career ended in a cloud of scandal over his explicit report on the brothels of Karachi, Burton returned to Europe and began writing the first in a series of books and articles about Indian customs, religion, and his own adventures.

Burton's career as an explorer began with an 1853 visit to Mecca and Medina disguised as an Afghan Muslim, a ploy that enabled him to write a highly detailed and accurate description of contemporary Muslim life and culture. Later that same year, he became the first European to visit the east African city of Harar and began planning an expedition to find the source of the Nile river by traveling overland through Somalia. His first Nile expedition, which included John Hanning Speke, ended in disaster when his party was attacked by Somali tribesmen. After recuperating from their wounds and serving in the **Crimean War,** Burton and Speke returned to Africa in 1857 and spent two years marching inland in search of the Nile. Their quarrel over Speke's claims to have discovered the source of the Nile while on a solo side trip began immediately after their return to Britain in 1860 and lasted until Speke's death four years later.

Shortly after his 1860 marriage, Burton began a diplomatic career that was to last for the remainder of his life. His postings, which included Fernando Po, Rio de Janeiro, Damascus, and Trieste, enabled him to continue indulging in his twin passions of travel and publication of translations, erotica, and travelogues. Burton's health began to decline shortly after receipt of his 1886 knighthood for service to the crown. On his death, his devoutly Catholic wife burned the bulk of his papers to protect his reputation. *See also* East India Company; Egypt; India; Somaliland.

FURTHER READING: Brodie, Fawn. *The Devil Drives: A Life of Sir Richard Burton.* New York: W. W. Norton, 1967; Carnochan, W. B. *The Sad Story of Burton, Speke and the Nile, or, Was John Hanning Speke a Cad?* Stanford, CA: Stanford University Press, 2005; Jutzi, Alan H. *In Search of Richard Burton.* Berkeley: University of California Press, 1993; Rice, Edward. *Captain Sir Richard Francis Burton.* New York: Charles Scribner's Sons, 1990.

KENNETH J. OROSZ

# C

## Calcutta

A city of Bengal in Northeast India and, during the nineteenth century, the capital of the British Empire's most valued territorial possession. A principal base of the East India Company as early as the 1690s, Calcutta emerged as the administrative center of British India as the Company consolidated its control of Bengal. It also became a major commercial center and vital port of colonial seaborne trade and enjoyed a position of enormous prestige among colonial cities of the Empire. Also, Calcutta was known for its superb British colonial architecture and its rich cultural and intellectual life, particularly its role in the Bengali Renaissance. In 1885, the formation of the Indian National Congress made Calcutta into a center of nationalist politics, a role that became more important after the partition of Bengal province by Lord Curzon in 1905. In 1912, the Indian capital was moved to Delhi, but Calcutta remained a hotbed of radical nationalism until Indian independence in 1947.

FURTHER READING: Chaudhuri, Sukanta. *Calcutta, The Living City.* 2 vols. New York: Oxford University Press, 1995.

CARL CAVANAGH HODGE

## Caldiero, Second Battle of (1805)

Fought between October 29 and 31, 1805, the Second Battle of Caldiero was an indecisive Austrian victory over Marshal Masséna's 43,000 Franco-Italian troops in northeast Italy during the War of the Third Coalition. Austria's 48,000 men under Archduke Charles were based along the Adige River. Napoleon ordered Masséna to prevent Charles from reinforcing the Austro-Russian armies in Germany. Charles planned a brief action followed by a retreat. The French assault on October 29 reached the entrenched fortifications around Caldiero village, east of Verona. Charles's planned counterattack early the next day was abandoned because of fog, while Massena's renewed assault was unsuccessful. The Austrians advanced around 2 P.M., but failed to break the French center. Charles planned another attack on October 31 to cover his withdrawal, but dawn revealed that Masséna had evacuated the battlefield, so Charles retreated toward Hungary. *See also* Napoleonic Wars.

FURTHER READING: Schneid, F. C. *Napoleon's Italian Campaigns: 1805–1815.* Wesport, CT: Praeger, 2002; Simone, L., et al. *Caldiero 1805* Verona: Regione del Veneto, 2005.

DAVID HOLLINS

## California

A present-day West Coast state of the **United States,** the northern portion of which was initially laid claim to by Russia in the early nineteenth century. Southern California passed from the Spanish Empire to Mexico, but the U.S. Navy took possession of Monterey and claimed California in July 1846. Acquisition of California was an unstated objective of the administration of James A. Polk during the Mexican War, and its cession to the United States by Mexico in the Treaty of Guadalupe Hidalgo in 1848 gave the American republic both superb new ports and a vital interest in the Pacific Ocean. California's admission to the Union as a free soil state in 1849 served to intensify the domestic tensions that ultimately led to the American Civil War. *See also* Manifest Destiny; Russian Empire.

FURTHER READING: Bancroft, Hubert Howe. *History of California.* Santa Barbara, CA: W. Hebberd, 1963.

CARL CAVANAGH HODGE

## Caliph

According to Sunni Islamic tradition, the rightful successor to the Prophet Muhammad and therefore empowered to lead the entire Muslim community. After the death of Muhammad, the first four Caliphs, Abu Bakr (r. 632–634), Umar ibn al-Khattab (r. 634–644), Uthman ibn Affan (r. 644–656), and Ali ibn Abi Talib (r. 656–661), were prominent companions of the prophet who were selected by other companions based on their piety, ability to control the affairs of the Muslims, and membership in the prophet's Quraysh tribe. The issue of succession, however, led to decades of sectarian strife, culminating with the assassination of Ali at the hands of troops loyal to Mu'awiya, the first caliph of the Ummayad Dynasty. This action solidified a rift in Muslim society, causing the formation of the Shi'a branch of Islam and establishing the caliph as an undemocratic dynastic position based purely on heredity.

Over time, various caliphal dynasties came to power, and the resultant changes often included moving the dynastic capital to different cities within the Muslim world such as Damascus, Baghdad, Cairo, and Istanbul. In the mid-thirteenth century, the Mongols razed Baghdad and destroyed the Abbasid caliphal line, effectively ending the traditional power afforded to the caliph. Although the position was quickly restored under the Mamluks of Cairo, it was no longer a strong unifying position, but rather a weak figurehead. The Ottoman conquest of Egypt in the early sixteenth century ended the Abbasid caliphate of Cairo. The Ottoman sultan Selim I (1467–1520) claimed that caliphal authority had been passed to him by the last Abbasid caliph, conferring on him and future sultans the title of caliph. Most early Ottoman sultans, however, did not feel it necessary to call upon caliphal authority to rule their empire, using it mainly as a justification to conquer other Muslim lands.

In the late eighteenth century, the Ottoman sultan's authority became threatened by internal forces for independence and outside pressure from rival European empires. Sultan **Mahmud II** (1785–1839) sought to strengthen the central government's control of his far-flung empire and modernize Ottoman civil society and military forces. The European influence engendered in the modernization process caused friction within the empire, and a growing rivalry developed between the sultan and the universally popular Muhammad Ali of Egypt. Despite all of Mahmud II's efforts to hold the empire together, during his reign he lost Algeria to France and Syria to Muhammad Ali, and saw Greek independence established. By the time Sultan Abdul Hamid II (1842–1918) was firmly in power in the late nineteenth century, the empire was rapidly disintegrating. In response, he asserted his role as caliph in an effort to inspire pan-Islamic unity and support from the disparate ethnic groups within the **Ottoman Empire** and around the Muslim world.

As the Ottoman Empire foundered, its European rivals began to colonize regions previously under the sultan's control, as well as other Muslim lands. Some of the colonized peoples looked to the caliph as the symbol of the broader Muslim world and a last hope to restore their lands to Muslim control; this sentiment was particularly strong in British colonial India. Nonetheless, internal strife, defeat in World War I, and the rise of the secular westernized government of Mustapha **Kemal** in Turkey sealed the fate of the caliphate. The last caliph, Abdul Mejid (1868–1944), was deposed and the position of caliph abolished in 1924. *See also* Caliphate.

FURTHER READING: Crone, Patricia, and Hinds, Martin. *God's Caliph: Religious Authority in the First Centuries of Islam.* Cambridge: Cambridge University Press, 1986; Quataert, Donald. *The Ottoman Empire, 1700–1922.* New York: Cambridge University Press, 2000.

BRENT D. SINGLETON

## Caliphate

A term referring both to the Islamic institution of government led by the unifying office of **Caliph** as well as to the territories and people under his direct control. Until the death of Prophet Muhammad, Islamic lands were limited to the Arabian Peninsula. Under his immediate successors, however, an expansion to nearby territories proceeded quickly. Within a century after Muhammad's death, Muslims controlled a territory stretching from the Indus River in the east through Persia, the Arabian Peninsula, Syria, Palestine, Egypt, North Africa, and across the Strait of Gibraltar, encompassing Spain in the west. The non-Muslim peoples living under the caliph's rule were not forced to convert to Islam; however, the governors and major government figures in the provinces under caliphal control were Muslims, and various taxes and other limits were placed on non-Muslims.

At various times, rival claims to caliphal authority caused separate contemporaneous caliphates to arise. For instance, the Spanish and North African caliphate of Córdoba arose as a continuation of the Umayyad caliphal line after revolutionaries established the Abbasid dynasty in Baghdad. Later, the Shia-controlled Fatimid caliphate, based in Cairo, claimed authority despite the Abbasid caliphate. Time and internecine warfare doomed the rival caliphates until only the Abbasids remained powerful enough to rule. The whole of the Muslim world was not included within the direct purview of the caliph; many far-flung Muslim kingdoms and empires were fully independent of caliphal authority. Nonetheless, most of these states swore at least nominal allegiance to the caliph and often used his name to further their own legitimacy or called on him when in need.

After the demise of the Abbasid caliphs in Baghdad and later Ottoman victory over the Mamluks in Egypt in 1517, the caliphate became synonymous with the sultan and the **Ottoman Empire.** For the first time since the early centuries of the caliphate, authority and governance were completely centralized and encompassed significant areas inhabited predominantly by non-Muslims, such as Greece and Armenia. At the height of Ottoman power, the caliphate controlled Anatolia, large swaths of Eastern Europe, the Caucasus, the Middle East, and most of North Africa.

By the seventeenth century, the caliphate was weakening as a result of expensive wars with its neighbors in Europe and Persia, as well as a fundamental lack of leadership on the part of the sultans. A series of Russo-Turkish wars hampered Ottoman efforts to expand and maintain power just as European technological advances began to overwhelm the increasingly anachronistic Ottoman military, political, and social structures. In the early nineteenth century, these factors resulted in dramatic losses in the caliphate's territory through military defeat, independence movements, and European colonialism. By the end of the nineteenth century, the caliphate was reduced to holding only Anatolia, Syria, Iraq, Palestine, and small portions of Arabia.

The caliphate was effectively impotent but held on for several more decades until it was officially disbanded in 1924 in the aftermath of World War I and the establishment of the secular Turkish state.

FURTHER READING: Crone, Patricia, and Martin Hinds. *God's Caliph: Religious Authority in the First Centuries of Islam.* Cambridge: Cambridge University Press, 1986; Karsh, Efraim, and Inari Karsh. *Empires of the Sand: The Struggle for Mastery in the Middle East 1789–1923.* Cambridge, MA: Harvard University Press, 1999; Yapp, M.E. *The Making of the Modern Near East, 1792–1923.* New York: Longman, 1987.

BRENT D. SINGLETON

## Cambodia

The home of the Khmer Empire from the ninth to the thirteenth centuries and after the seventeenth century the object of rival Siamese and Vietnamese claims until the penetration of Indochina by France in the 1850s. Cambodia became a French protectorate in 1863. The protectorate retained limited Cambodian autonomy along with traditional administrative structures yet privatized land ownership, reformed the tax system, and encouraged commerce. Only in 1897 was the Cambodian king stripped of all power and his authority transferred to ministers who met at the pleasure of the French resident. With French aid Cambodia was able to recover three lost provinces from Siam in 1907. *See also* French Empire.

FURTHER READING: Chandler, David. *A History of Cambodia*. Boulder, CO: Westview, 1983.

CARL CAVANAGH HODGE

## Cameroon

A West African territory and German colony as of 1884. After centuries of intermittent contact with Europeans eager to trade for slaves, ivory, rubber, and palm products, Cameroon was colonized by Germany and quickly became the largest and most important of its West African possessions. The German acquisition of Cameroon came as a shock as Britain initially had stronger claims to the region. Not only had British Baptists established a mission station on the mainland in 1858, but the coastal Duala tribe had repeatedly requested the creation of a protectorate as a means of fending off unscrupulous European merchants. These requests were ignored, thereby opening the door for German merchant firms trading along the West African coast to expand their operations to Cameroon. The resultant competition eventually led the British to raise import duties in the **Gold Coast.** Concerned that this could lead to the exclusion of German merchants from all West African markets, Otto von **Bismarck,** in July 1884, sent a naval expedition under the command of Gustav Nachtigal to establish a German protectorate in Cameroon. The Germans subsequently used uprisings in the 1890s and 1904–1907 as a pretext for launching punitive military expeditions that completed the conquest of the interior and solidified their hold on Cameroon. Germany later obtained an additional 280,000 square kilometers in northeastern Cameroon when France ceded parts of **French Equatorial Africa** as settlement of the 1911 Moroccan crisis.

Bismarck's hope that private merchant firms would run the colony quickly fell apart, necessitating the creation of an official colonial administration . Colonial administrators soon found their efforts to develop the economy hampered by periodic uprisings, extreme linguistic diversity and frequent clashes with Protestant mission societies who championed native rights. Nevertheless, the Germans created a series of rubber, cocoa, and palm tree plantations that soon turned out more exports than any other German colony. Although roads and bridges were built deep into the interior in the hopes of opening up additional plantations, subsequent efforts to expand the agricultural sector were hampered by the need for land and the chronic lack of labor, necessitating the expropriation of African property and the introduction of coercive measures including bribery and the use of forced labor. Ultimately, the combination of continued African resistance to these tactics and the 1906 introduction of the **Dernburg reforms** requiring better treatment of indigenous peoples prevented German Cameroon from reaching its full economic potential. After falling to an allied invasion force in 1916, Cameroon was subsequently divided by Britain and France, a solution confirmed in 1922 with the League of Nation's decision to award them mandates over the former German territory. *See also* Africa, Scramble for; Berlin, Conference of; German Empire, Morocco; Togo.

FURTHER READING: Henderson, W. O. *The German Colonial Empire 1884–1919*. London: Frank Cass, 1993; Mbuagbaw, Tambi Eyongetah, Robert Brain, and Robin Palmer. *A History of the Cameroon.* New York: Longman, 1987; Rudin, Harry R. *Germans in the Cameroons.* London: Jonathan Cape, 1938; Stoecker, Helmuth. "Cameroon 1885–1906." In Helmuth Stoecker, ed. *German Imperialism in Africa.* London: C. Hurst & Company, 1986, pp. 83–92; Wirz, Albert. "The German Colonies in Africa." In Rudolf von Albertini, ed. *European Colonial Rule, 1880–1940. The Impact of the West on India, Southeast Asia, and Africa.* Westport, CT: Greenwood Press, 1982, pp. 388–417.

KENNETH J. OROSZ

### Campbell, Sir Colin, Baron Clyde (1792–1863)

British soldier whose career extended from the Napoleonic Wars to the Indian Mutiny and into almost every corner of the **British Empire.** Born in Glasgow, he entered the British army at age 16 and first saw action in the **Peninsular War** at Ricola in August 1808. As lieutenant Campbell served with distinction at Barossa in 1811 and also fought at Vitoria and San Sebastián in 1813. After surviving the debacle of New Orleans in the **Anglo-American War** of 1812 and participating in suppression of the Demerara rising in British Guiana in 1823, Campbell was promoted to the rank of captain in 1823 and to a lieutenant-colonel in 1832. Real distinction came with service in the First **Opium War,** after which he was made a Commander of the Bath and the First **Sikh War,** which brought him a knighthood.

In the **Crimean War** Campbell was promoted to major general and distinguished himself at Alma and Balaclava. Thus Campbell was already among the most celebrated military heroes of the Empire when in 1857 he was made commander-in-chief of British forces tasked with the suppression of the **Indian Mutiny** and ultimately contributed more than any individual to military victory and the restoration of political order. Campbell was made a peer, Baron Clyde, in 1858.

FURTHER READING: Farwell, Byron. *Queen Victoria's Little Wars.* London: W. W. Norton, 1972; Shadwell, L. S. *Life of Colin Campbell, Lord Clyde.* Edinburgh: W. Blackwood, 1881.

CARL CAVANAGH HODGE

### Campbell-Bannerman, Sir Henry (1836–1908)

British prime minister remembered as a staunch radical and consistent opponent of imperial expansion. His government of 1905–1908 nevertheless began an informal alliance with France that led into World War I.

Campbell-Bannerman was from a Scottish mercantile family. He was educated at the Universities of Glasgow and Cambridge, and entered Parliament as a radical for the Scottish constituency of Stirling Burghs in 1868. He placed himself in the tradition of Richard **Cobden,** and became a lifelong follower of William **Gladstone.** He worked under Edward Cardwell during his reforming tenure at the War Office in the early 1870s, and subsequently served as Chief Secretary for Ireland under Gladstone in 1884–1885. As a Gladstonian, he supported Home Rule in 1886, dismissing Ulster's objections as "Ulsteria." Campbell-Bannerman served at the War Office in the Liberal governments of 1886 and 1892–1895.

During subsequent decade of opposition, Campbell-Bannerman was a leader among the anti-imperialist, the so-called "little Englander" Liberals. In protest against the army's tactics of burning farms and relocating the Boer population in "concentration camps" during the Second Boer War and to counter the government's argument that the army was not bound by the laws of war as the Boer guerilla tactics violated them, Campbell-Bannerman rhetorically demanded "when is a war not a war? When it is carried on by methods of barbarism in South Africa," a remark for which he is often remembered.

Arthur J. **Balfour**'s Conservative government resigned in December 1905, and Campbell-Bannerman became premier. In the subsequent election campaign he called for an international "League of Peace" adumbrating subsequent notions of a League of Nations, but campaigned primarily on the venerable Cobdenite slogan of "Peace, Retrenchment and Reform." He won an imposing victory, and as prime minister he governed as more of a Gladstonian small-government Liberal than a social democratic "new Liberal"—as his old-fashioned electoral cry had implied. As Prime Minister, he agreed reluctantly to the staff conversations with France, initiated by Sir Edward Grey, which prepared the way for British intervention in World War I. He resigned the office due to ill health on April 8, 1908, and died on April 22, with Herbert **Asquith** succeeding him. *See also* Boer Wars; Liberal Party.

FURTHER READING: Spender, J. A. *The Life of Sir Henry Campbell-Bannerman*. London: Hodder and Stoughton, 1923; Wilson, John. *CB: A Life of Sir Henry Campbell-Bannerman*. London: Constable, 1973.

MARK F. PROUDMAN

## Canada

At the beginning of the nineteenth century, Canada comprised the North American territories along the St. Lawrence River and to the north of Lakes Ontario and Erie, not including most of what became in the course of the century the Dominion of Canada. Canada was divided into Upper and Lower Canada by William **Pitt's** Constitution Act of 1791. Lower Canada—subsequently **Québec**—had a French-speaking majority and Upper Canada an English-speaking one. Each colony was granted a representative assembly and an appointive upper house under a British-appointed Governor. Conflicts between the elected assemblies and the Governors led in both colonies to brief rebellions in 1837. The British responded by sending Lord Durham to report on the situation; his report led to the reunion of the two Canadas and the grant of effective local autonomy under the name of **Responsible Government** in 1848. The **Dominion** of Canada was founded on July 1 1867, pursuant to the **British North America Act,** which received its second reading in the British House of Commons on February 28, 1867.

The intention, inspired by the American example, was to create a strong federal government, leaving only local matters to the provinces. Nova Scotia was initially an unwilling province of Canada, but its protests were ignored by the imperial parliament. In 1870, the western territories of the Hudson's Bay Company, known as Rupert's Land, were ceded to Ottawa. This resulted in a brief rebellion under Louis Riel, but rebel forces scattered on the arrival of an Anglo-Canadian force under Colonel Garnet Wolseley. The Province of Manitoba joined Confederation in 1870. **British Columbia** followed in 1871, an agreement having been reached to construct largely at federal expense a transcontinental railway.

In 1905, the remaining territories on the prairies joined the Confederation as the provinces of Saskatchewan and Alberta. The Canadian Pacific railway was completed in 1885, somewhat behind schedule. That same year saw a further rebellion led by Riel in Saskatchewan put down by an expeditionary force from Ontario after the Battle of Batoche; this time Riel was hanged for treason. Initially led by a Conservative government under Sir John A. **Macdonald,** in 1874, the Liberals came to power after a scandal over railway financing. MacDonald came back into power in 1878, remaining prime minister until his death in 1891, and instituting the so-called "National Policy" of tariffs designed to protect Canadian industry. Nevertheless, Canada remained primarily an exporter of primary products, including agricultural products, minerals, and timber, throughout the pre-1914 period.

Canada's connection to the British Empire was controversial: many, likely most, English Canadians were imperialist to some degree, but the imperial connection was less popular with the French-speaking population of Québec. Under the Liberal Sir Wilfrid **Laurier,** Canada made a small contribution to the British war effort in the South African War of 1899–1902, and chose to create its own navy in place of making a contribution to the British. Canada's initial reaction to the outbreak of war in 1914 was summed up by Laurier's cry of "Ready, aye, ready!" but enthusiasm waned, particularly in Québec, as the war went on. *See also* British Empire; United States.

FURTHER READING: Lower, A.R.M. *Colony to Nation.* London: Longmans Green, 1957; Martin, Ged. *Britain and the Origins of Canadian Confederation, 1837–63.* Basingstoke: MacMillan, 1995.

MARK F. PROUDMAN

## Canadian Pacific Railway (CPR)

Canada's first transcontinental railway, built for the most part between 1881 and 1885 to connect the Pacific Coast province of British Columbia with Eastern Canada. British Columbia had made such a rail link the precondition of its membership in the Canadian Confederation, and the Conservative government of Sir John A. Macdonald also saw the railroad as the commercial backbone of British North America, a unified Canadian dominion stretching across North America, invulnerable to economic absorption by the United States, with manufacturing interests in the East fueled by the resources of the West.

The railway's construction had to overcome the engineering difficulties of crossing the Rocky Mountains and the danger of labor in rugged terrain. Immigrants from Europe and imported workers from China made up the manual labor force, the latter group in particular suffering a high rate of fatality in doing the most dangerous work. When complete, the Canadian Pacific Railway was the longest railway ever constructed. Much of the railway's freight consisted of the fundamentals of a developing economy such as coal, timber, and wheat; but after 1890, it also carried raw silk cocoons from the Orient between the Pacific port of Vancouver and silk mills in New York and New Jersey. *See also* British North America Act; Railways.

FURTHER READING: Finley, J. L., and D. N. Sprague. *The Structure of Canadian History.* Scarborough: Prentice-Hall, 1984; McInnis, E. W. *Canada, A Political and Social History.* Toronto: Holt, Rinehart and Winston, 1969.

CARL CAVANAGH HODGE

## Canning, George (1770–1827)

One of the leading British statesmen of the early nineteenth century. Canning forsook his Whig tendencies for more Tory sympathies when he supported William Pitt from 1794. Although a distinguished speaker in Parliament, Canning did not hold a prominent position in government until 1807, when he was appointed Foreign Secretary under the Duke of Portland in which office he served until 1809. In this capacity he sent a punitive expedition against Copenhagen and played a prominent part in Britain's involvement in the Peninsular War against Napoleon in Spain and Portugal. He strongly opposed his country's expedition against Walcheren in 1809, and his disagreements with Castlereagh, the Secretary of State for War, led to an inconclusive duel between them. He served again as Foreign Secretary in 1822–1827 during which time he recognized the newly independent Latin American states, thus securing substantial economic benefits for his country. He served briefly as prime minister in 1827.

FURTHER READING: Dixon, Peter. *Canning: Politician and Statesman.* London: Weidenfeld & Nicolson, 1976; Hinde, Wendy. *George Canning.* London: Collins, 1973; Temperley, Harold. *The Foreign Policy of Canning, 1822–1827.* Hamden, CT: Archon Books, 1966.

GREGORY FREMONT-BARNES

## Cape Colony

One of the original provinces of the Union of South Africa. Originally founded by the Dutch East India Company in 1652 to supply its fleets headed to the East Indies with fresh food, Cape Colony had fallen into British hands by the start of the nineteenth century during the course of the Napoleonic Wars. This sparked European expansion into the interior of southern Africa as the original Boer settlers attempted to flee British control. The arrival of 5,000 British settlers in 1820 not only made it clear that Britain intended to hold on to the Cape, but it also marked the start of declining Anglo-Boer relations. In addition to resenting the introduction of a new language and culture, the Boer settlers, many of whom relied on a combination of cheap African labor and slaves to work their farms, opposed the British policy of granting Africans legal rights and complained about the inadequate compensation for their lost property when Parliament abolished slavery in 1833. Eager to escape further British interference in their daily lives, many Boer families migrated north as part of the **Great Trek** into the **Transvaal** and the **Orange Free State** where they created independent republics.

Despite the loss of population resulting from the Great Trek, Cape Colony prospered throughout the nineteenth century. Immigration continued, and by the mid-1870s, white settlers made up a third of the Cape's population. Although settler demand for land caused periodic clashes with the neighboring Xhosa tribe, these conflicts effectively ended in 1856 when the Xhosa killed off their cattle and destroyed their crops in the belief that doing so would prompt their ancestors to return and drive out the whites. The resultant famine broke the back of Xhosa resistance and ushered in a period of political stability that, combined with the abolition of the British **East India Company**'s monopoly on trade, led to significant economic development. Growing economic prosperity in turn led to increased political autonomy for the Cape. In 1853, a parliament elected on the basis of property ownership and income, rather than race, replaced earlier advisory and legislative councils appointed by the governor. This was followed in 1873 by the creation of responsible government. Thereafter, the newly created prime minister and his cabinet assumed all responsibility for Cape Colony's domestic affairs.

The twin discoveries of diamonds in Griqualand West in 1867 and gold in the Transvaal in 1880 complicated the situation by financing the political career of Cecil **Rhodes.** Although he initially rose to power as prime minister of Cape Colony by championing Boer rights, by the mid-1890s Rhodes began to see an independent Transvaal as a major obstacle to British interests in southern Africa. His backing of the botched **Jameson Raid** not only ended Rhodes's political career, but it also renewed Anglo-Boer tensions and helped trigger the **Boer War** of 1899–1901. Although Britain annexed the former Boer republics in the aftermath of the war, final resolution of the political situation only came in 1910 when Cape Colony changed its name to the Province of Good Hope and joined Natal, Transvaal and the Orange Free State in the newly created Union of South Africa. *See also* Afrikaners; Bonaparte, Napoleon; British Empire; Vereeniging, Treaty of.

FURTHER READING: Davenport, R., and C. Saunders. *South Africa: A Modern History.* London: Macmillan, 2000; Mackinnon, Aran S. *The Making of South Africa.* Upper Saddle River, NJ: Prentice Hall, 2000; McCracken, J. L. *The Cape Parliament, 1854–1910.* Oxford: Clarendon Press, 1967; Ross, Robert. *A Concise History of South Africa.* Cambridge: Cambridge University Press, 1999.

KENNETH J. OROSZ

## Caprivi, Count Leo von (1831–1899)

Otto von **Bismarck**'s successor as German chancellor, serving from 1890 to 1894. Born to a family of Slovenian origin in Berlin-Charlottenburg, Caprivi served as an army officer in the wars of 1866 and 1870–1871 and as Chief of the Admiralty, 1882–1886. His basically sound policies of rapprochement and colonial agreements with **Britain,** replacing **protectionism** with bilateral commercial treaties, and cautious domestic reform earned him severe criticism from contemporaries, especially for his decision not to renew the 1887 Reassurance Treaty with Russia, regarded as one of Bismarck's most important achievements. In the Zanzibar Treaty of 1890, he secured from Britain German control of Heligoland in the North Sea in exchange for British control of Zanzibar off the coast of German East Africa, which prompted howls of protest from colonial pressure groups.

FURTHER READING: Berghahn, Volker Rolf. *Imperial Gremany, 1871–1914: Economy, Society, Culture and Politics.* Providence: Berghahn Books, 1994.

NIELS P. PETERSSON

## Cardwell, Edward, First Viscount Cardwell, (1813–1886)

British colonial secretary who did much to initiate the process of Canadian confederation but best remembered for his army reforms while at the War Office in Gladstone's first government, 1868–1874. Cardwell entered parliament for Liverpool as a Free Trade Conservative in 1842, and was always strongly associated with Sir Robert **Peel,** whose memoirs he edited. He was known for his expertise on financial, mercantile and maritime questions. Losing his Liverpool seat in 1852 because of his support for the repeal of the navigation acts—in effect protection for merchant shipping—he sat as a Liberal for the City of Oxford for the rest of his political career. As colonial secretary under Lord **Palmerston** and John Russell from 1864 to 1866, he prodded Canadian leaders in the direction of confederation and began the process of withdrawing British troops from both Canada and, more controversially, **New Zealand.**

He became secretary for war in 1868, in which office he continued the gradual draw-down of troops in colonial service. Influenced by Prussian successes in the 1870 war with France, he reorganized the War Office and introduced the concept of short service enlistments followed by service in the reserves. Most significantly, however, he abolished the system of army commission purchase, meeting significant opposition in committee and from the Lords. The latter he was able to overcome only with the assistance of a royal warrant, forbidding commission sales. The episode did much to estrange the officer class from the Liberal Party. Cardwell refused to succeed Gladstone as head of the Liberal Party on the latter's, as it turned out, temporary resignation in 1874, and was in poor health for the final dozen years of his life. *See also* Canada; Franco-Prussian War; Gladstone.

FURTHER READING: Biddulph, Sir Robert. *Lord Cardwell at the War Office.* London: John Murray, 1904; Eriskson, Arvel B. "Edward T. Cardwell," *Transactions of the American Philosophical Society* 49/2 (1959).

MARK F. PROUDMAN

## Carlist Wars (1833–1840, 1847–1849, 1872–1876)

Three wars in Spain fought during the period from 1833 to 1876. The Carlists were members of a conservative political movement in Spain with the goal of establishing an alternate branch of the Bourbon dynasty to the throne. Felipe V, grandson of Louis XIV of France and founder of the Spanish Bourbon dynasty, limited the royal succession to male descendants and only to female descendants in the absence of any male heir on any line. In 1830, Fernando VII published the *Pragmatic Sanction,* which was approved by the government in 1832. The decree restored the rights of female descendants to inherit the throne. Fernando VII died in 1833 without a male heir. His wife, Maria Cristina, became regent for their daughter, Isabel II. Ferdinand's brother, Carlos, claimed the Spanish throne under the premise that the *Pragmatic Sanction* was not valid. Carlists supported the ambitions of Carlos, while *Cristinos,* or *Isabelinos,* supported Isabel II and her mother.

Carlos was leader of the staunch royalist and Catholic faction at the Spanish court seeking to counter growing liberal and anticlerical influences after the French

Revolution and Napoleon. Carlism emerged as an umbrella ideology for political Catholics and conservatives, and served as the main group of right-wing opposition to ensuing Spanish governments. Carlists' rallying cry of "God, Country, and King" united them against liberal and later republican forces taking root in Spain. Carlism became a true "mass movement," drawing supporters from all classes, especially peasant and working classes. The areas in Spain where Carlism established a foothold included Navarre, Rioja, Basque Country, Catalonia, and Valencia.

Carlos V (1788–1855) was the first Carlist pretender to the Spanish throne. He abdicated in favor of his son Carlos VI (1818–61), who continued the claim from 1845 to 1860. Carlos's brother, Juan III (1822–1887), carried the Carlist banner from 1860 to 1868. Carlists forced him to abdicate because of his liberal leanings under the idea that the king must be legitimate both in blood and in deeds. Juan became head of the house of Bourbon after the extinction of the elder line of French Bourbons in 1883. Some French legitimists proclaimed him heir to the French throne. Juan's son Carlos VII (1848–1909) represented the Carlists from 1868 to 1909. Carlos was succeeded by his son, Jaime III (1870–1931), and then his brother, Alfonso Carlos (1849–1936). In 1936, the Carlists' male line died out.

The First Carlist War lasted from 1833 to 1840. The cruelties inflicted by both sides forced the European powers to intervene to establish a set of rules for warfare. France, Britain, and Portugal supported Isabel. All three powers gave financial support; Britain and Portugal also lent military support. The Carlists, short on finances, were quickly defeated yet continued to harass the liberal government for several years. The Second Carlist War, also known as the Matiners' War, lasted from 1847 to 1849. Catalonian rebels initiated a guerilla war in the name of the Carlist pretender. Carlist forces came to their aid, but the rebel forces were defeated. In 1868, a revolution forced Isabel II's abdication in favor of her son, Alfonso XII; however, the government elected Amadeo I of the house of Savoy as king of Spain. Shortly thereafter, a republic governed Spain before a Bourbon restoration under Alfonso in 1874. The political upheaval after Isabel II's deposition led to the Third Carlist War, lasting from 1872 to 1876.

FURTHER READING: Aronson, Theo. *Royal Vendetta: The Crown of Spain 1829–1965*. London: Oldbourne, 1966; Gallardo, Alexander. *Britain and the First Carlist War*. Norwood, Yorkshire: Norwood, 1978; Holt, E. *The Carlist Wars in Spain*. London: Putnam, 1967.

ERIC MARTONE

## Carlyle, Thomas (1795–1881)

A prominent biographer, historian, and activist in nineteenth-century Britain. A Scot, Carlyle was educated at the University of Edinburgh before moving to London to pursue a literary career. His knowledge of Germany, its literature, and culture was comprehensive, and he did much to introduce German literature to the British public. His first major work was *The French Revolution*, his last a multivolume biography of Frederick the Great. Carlyle was a friend of the young John Stuart **Mill,** but their relationship cooled somewhat when Mill's maid threw the almost complete manuscript of the *French Revolution* into the fire. Carlyle went on to produce an edition of the letters of Oliver Cromwell and large numbers of shorter essays, polemics, and imaginative histories written in a style at once witty, declamatory, and in places almost poetic. Carlyle gave a series of lectures on heroes in 1840, which became a volume celebrating great men. In imperial affairs, Carlyle played a leading role in defending Governor Eyre of **Jamaica,** accused of committing atrocities in response to an apprehended rising, and he parodied the abolitionist movement with his 1849 suggestion of a "Universal Abolition of Pain Association." He wrote nothing systematic on imperial topics, but his *Past and Present* (1843) enthused that England's epic poem, like that of the ancient Romans, was written on the face of the earth, and called for the misery of urban slums to be relieved by state-organized emigration, a common idea at the time.

Carlyle's main contribution to the Empire, however, was cultural. He celebrated the heroic and the strong, and held that that rule of such men should be unapologetic and not hedged about what he saw as the bad faith of liberal self-justification. Against a background of rationalist, utilitarian liberalism, Carlyle provided a strong defense of authority, tradition, and of the right of conquest, along with, it must be said, a coruscating critique of many individual authorities who failed to live up to his exacting, world-historical standards. *See also* British Empire; Social Darwinism.

FURTHER READING: Carlyle, Thomas. *Carlyle's Works.* 16 vols. New York: Peter Fenelon, 1897; Kaplan, F. *Thomas Carlyle: A Biography.* Ithaca, NY: Cornell University Press, 1983.

MARK F. PROUDMAN

## Carlsbad Decrees (1819)

Measures agreed at an August 1819 conference of ministers from Austria, Prussia, Saxony, Bavaria, Württemberg, Hanover, Baden, Mecklenburg, Saxe-Weimar-Eisenach, and electoral Hesse that took place at Carlsbad (German spelling: Karlsbad; Czech spelling: Karlovy Vary). The meeting at the Bohemian spa was summoned at the behest of Austria's foreign minister Klemens Prince von **Metternich** to discuss measures to be taken by the German Confederation against nationalist and liberal organizations and opinion leaders in Germany. The assassination of the dramatist August Kotzebue by a radical student offered an opportunity to persuade the governments of many German states to approve to harsh methods of repression. Uniform censorship of periodical publications, the dissolution of student clubs, liberal and nationalist *Burschenschaften,* and a central commission to investigate radical activities were agreed in Carlsbad and a few weeks later by the representatives of the German states at Frankfurt. The Carlsbad Decrees became synonymous with the suppression of freedom of speech and an anti-liberal policy of the German states.

FURTHER READING: Blackbourn, David. *A History of Germany, 1780–1918.* Oxford: Blackwell, 2003; Jarausch, Konrad H. *Students, Society and Politics in Imperial Germany.* Princeton, NJ: Princeton University Press, 1982.

GUENTHER KRONENBITTER

## Casement, Sir Roger (1864–1916)

Before his 1916 execution for treason and the British government's subsequent effort to smear his reputation by releasing diaries that graphically detailed his alleged homosexuality, Casement was an Irish-born British diplomat and colonial reformer best known for reporting the horrors of forced labor in the **Belgian Congo** and the Putumayo region of Peru. After several visits to Africa while serving as a ship's purser, in 1884 Casement became an employee of **Leopold II's** International African Association where he worked as a railroad surveyor and construction foreman. Casement left the Congo in 1892 to join the British diplomatic corps. After a brief tour of duty in **Nigeria,** he was promoted rapidly and served as British Consul in Mozambique from 1895 to1898, Angola from 1898 to 1900, and the Congo Free State from 1901 to 1904.

Shortly after his return to the Congo, he began warning the British government about the mistreatment of natives and the damaging effects of forced labor in rubber cultivation. Under pressure from humanitarian groups, in 1903 the British government charged Casement with undertaking an official inquiry. His Congo report, published the next year, provoked an international scandal with its detailed evidence of atrocities and was instrumental in forcing Leopold to relinquish his private colony in the Congo Free State to the Belgian government. Following the appearance of his Congo report, Casement was transferred to **Brazil** where he served in a variety of Consular posts from 1906–1911. In 1910, he was ordered by the Foreign Office to investigate charges of atrocities against the inhabitants of the rubber producing Putumayo region of neighboring Peru. Casement's detailed report substantiated the worst of the allegations, earned him a knighthood in 1911, and eventually led Parliament to dissolve the London-based Peruvian Amazon Company two years later.

In 1913, ill health forced Casement to retire from diplomatic service. On his return to **Ireland** he became actively involved in the campaign for Irish **Home Rule,** helping to organize the paramilitary Irish National Volunteers and traveling to the United States to seek funds for the separatist movement. After the outbreak of World War I, he traveled to Germany in a failed effort to gain diplomatic recognition and possible military assistance for an independent Ireland. Germany's refusal to provide military assistance for the planned Easter rising prompted Casement to return to Ireland in April 1916 in an effort to stop the revolt. He was captured shortly after landing, taken to London for trial, convicted of treason, and executed August 3, 1916. *See also* Portuguese Empire.

FURTHER READING: Campbell, John. "Give a Dog a Bad Name." *History Today* 34 (September 1984): 14–19; Daly, Mary E., ed. *Roger Casement in Irish and World History.* Dublin: Royal Irish Academy, 2005; McCormack, W. J. *Roger Casement in Death, or, Haunting the Free State.* Dublin: University College Dublin Press, 2002; Mitchell, Angus. *Casement.* London: Haus Publishing, 2003; Reid, Benjamin Lawrence. *The Lives of Roger Casement.* New Haven, CT: Yale University Press, 1976; Sawyer, Roger. *Casement, the Flawed Hero.* London: Routledge, 1984.

KENNETH J. OROSZ

## Castlereagh, Robert Stewart, Viscount (1769–1823)

An Anglo-Irish politician and British Foreign Secretary, Castlereagh, a courtesy title he assumed in 1796 owing to his father's Irish marquisate, was initially a Whig, but the events of the French Revolution drove him to the Tories. Elected to the Irish Parliament in 1790, to Westminster in 1794, and sitting for several years in both Parliaments, he was a supporter of William **Pitt** the Younger's Irish Union, and like Pitt he insisted on the need for the redress of Catholic disabilities. This latter cause earned him the displeasure of George III, which complicated his political career. He was at the War Office during the early years of the Peninsular campaign, when it was not popular, and resigned as a result of a series of complicated machinations by Canning coincident with the failure of the 1809 Walcheren expedition. The dispute with Canning led to a duel that both men survived and that did not prevent Castlereagh becoming foreign secretary under Spencer Perceval in 1812.

After the assassination of Perceval, Castlereagh kept his office under the premiership of Lord Liverpool and became known for his deft and moderate diplomacy. In the complicated and many-sided negotiations surrounding the defeat of Napoleonic France, Castlereagh was a consistent opponent of a vindictive peace, and he opposed the counter-revolutionary Holy Alliance. In domestic politics, however, Castlereagh was an equally consistent opponent of parliamentary reform and a supporter of repression, especially in the aftermath of the 1819 "Peterloo massacre," at St. Peter's fields, Manchester. Castlereagh did not believe that the government could or should remedy the commercial depression and widespread suffering that came with the peace. His reputation as a reactionary inspired Shelley's famous lines, "I met death on the way/he had a mask like Castlereagh." Increasingly depressed and unstable, Castlereagh committed suicide in 1823. *See also* Canning, George; Metternich, Clemens von; Napoleonic War; Vienna, Congress of.

FURTHER READING: Hinde, Wendy. *Castlereagh*. London: Collins, 1981; Kissinger, Henry. *A World Restored*. Boston: Houghton Mifflin, 1957.

MARK F. PROUDMAN

## Caucasus

The region between the Black and Caspian Seas and a territorial bone of contention among the Ottoman, Persian, and Russian Empires for centuries. During the nineteenth century, the Caucasus came increasingly under Russian dominance. Georgia was annexed to Russia in 1801; Baku and other parts of Azerbaijan followed in 1813; Persian Armenia and the remainder of Azerbaijan in 1828. Russian expansion into the Western Caucasus thereafter came at direct expense to the **Ottoman Empire,** and after the **Russo-Turkish** War of 1828–1829 the Treaty of **Adrianople** transferred Circassia to the Russian Empire. Between 1830 and 1859, the Muslim peoples of the region waged a *jihad* against Russian rule, known as the Murid Wars. After the deployment of ever larger and better equipped Russian armies brought the local tribes to surrender, the region remained under Russian control until the passing of the Soviet Union in 1991. *See also* Eastern Question; Russian Empire.

FURTHER READING: Hosking, Geoffrey. *Russia, People and Empire*. Cambridge, MA: Harvard University Press, 1997; Rywkin, Michael. *Russian Colonial Expansion to 1917*. London: Mansell, 1988; Seton-Watson, Hugh. *The Russian Empire, 1801–1917*. Oxford: Clarendon Press, 1967.

CARL CAVANAGH HODGE

## Cavour, Count Camillo Benso di (1810–1861)

Italian statesman and prime minister of the Kingdom of Piedmont (1852–60) and the Kingdom of **Italy** in 1861. Cavour was a Piedmontese aristocrat who became the leading statesman of Italian unification. In 1847, he started a respected patriotic journal, *Il Risorgimento,* which brought him to the attention of the government. During the revolutionary outbursts of 1848, it was Cavour who urged King Charles Albert to not only promulgate a constitution but also lead a national struggle for liberation. The war failed, but the new king, **Victor Emmanuel II,** remained steadfast to unification and constitutionalism, and asked Cavour to become Prime Minister in 1852. Despite his idealism, Cavour was a realist prepared to lead his country to a new nation.

Cavour immediately recognized that no amount of reform would prevent Austria from defeating Piedmont unless he had an alliance with another Great Power. He seized the opportunity to do so by aiding the Allies during the Crimean War. Afterward in July 1858, he concluded a secret alliance with Napoleon III and manipulated the Austrians into declaring war in April 1859. By July the Allies had control over most of northern and western Italy, but the cities in central Italy revolted and received protection from the armies of Piedmont. In the south, Cavour permitted Giuseppe Garibaldi to seize Sicily and Naples. When the war concluded, all of these territories except for Rome and the Venetia were annexed to Piedmont and approved by plebiscite. On March 17, 1861, the Kingdom of Italy was proclaimed, with Turin as its capital. Cavour died on June 6 having created modern Italy. *See also* Crimean War; Habsburg Empire.

FURTHER READING: Hearder, Harry. *Italy in the Age of the Risorgimento 1790–1870.* New York: Longman, 1983.

FREDERICK H. DOTOLO

## Central Powers

A term commonly used to refer to the Triple Alliance of Germany, **Austria-Hungary,** and **Italy** pitted against the Triple Entente of Britain, France, and Russia in the period leading to World War I, or alternatively to Germany, Austria-Hungary, the Ottoman Empire, and Bulgaria during World War I. Because Italy declined to fight in 1914, the term was generally applied to the two core allies Germany and Austria-Hungary. The apparent blank check of diplomatic and military support given by Germany to Austria-Hungary in the wake of the assassination of Archduke Franz Ferdinand in July 1914 was critical in prompting Russia to mobilize and therefore in turning the latest Balkan crisis into a general European war.

FURTHER READING: Albertini, Luigi. *The Origins of the War of 1914.* 3 vols. Translated by Isabella M. Massey. New York: Oxford University Press, 1952.

CARL CAVANAGH HODGE

## Ceylon

A large island off the southeast coast of India, present-day Sri Lanka. Ceylon was initially a target of Portuguese and then Dutch colonization, but the conquest of the Netherlands by France during the Napoleonic Wars prompted troops of the East

India Company to seize it against weak Dutch resistance in 1796. British control was then made official by the Treaty of Amiens in 1802. The British abolished slavery, dissolved commercial monopolies in favor of free trade, and established a uniform administrative structure and legal system for the island. Indentured labor was imported from India, and coffee, tea, rubber, and coconut plantations prospered.

FURTHER READING: DeSilva, K. M. *A History of Sri Lanka*. Delhi: Oxford University Press, 1981.

CARL CAVANAGH HODGE

## Chamberlain, Joseph (1836–1914)

A major British politician and from 1895 an imperially ambitious colonial secretary, Joseph Chamberlain made his fortune in the Birmingham manufacturing industry, retired from business, and became one of the ablest public figures of his time. As a city councilor, then mayor of Birmingham, he was a reformer and a driving force behind the Elementary Education Act of 1870. Chamberlain regarded the British aristocracy as a burden on the nation yet cultivated an aristocratic appearance with a monocle and a fresh orchid in his buttonhole—an ambivalence of attitude reflected in his politics. Elected in 1876 as a Liberal member of Parliament, he rose to cabinet rank in **Gladstone**'s government of 1880. Chamberlain's democratic convictions, tinged with republican and socialist views, placed him on the radical wing of the Liberal Party; yet his deepest sentiments were for the ideal of imperial unity. Subscribing to the liberal imperialism of Charles **Dilke,** he favored a degree of Irish autonomy within the Empire yet resigned from Gladstone's cabinet in 1885 over the policy of Irish Home Rule.

Chamberlain emerged the leader of the Liberal Unionists, cooperating with the Conservative Party to bar Gladstone from office. When **Salisbury**'s Conservatives formed a coalition government with the Unionists in 1895, Chamberlain was given his choice of ministries and chose the Colonial Office. "Pushful Joe" involved Britain more intensively in the Scramble for Africa. He favored bringing the Boer republics into the Empire and was accused of colluding in the machinations of Cecil **Rhodes** in the disastrous **Jameson Raid.** Chamberlain negotiated with the government of the Transvaal, but the failure to reach agreement on the rights of British Uitlanders led to the Second Boer War.

Yet Chamberlain was as concerned to consolidate British power as to extend it. He favored the idea of an **imperial federation** of the white peoples of the Empire and broke with the traditional Liberal principle of **free trade,** advocating **imperial preference.** He helped bring about the Anglo-Japanese Alliance of 1902, sought an alliance with Germany, and ultimately favored *entente* with France as an alternative. His tariff policy split the Conservative Party and facilitated a Liberal landslide in the election of 1906. He died in 1914, but his sons, Austen and Neville, carried the family flag into Britain's foreign policy of the 1920s and 1930s. *See also* Africa, Scramble for; Boer Wars.

FURTHER READING: Marsh, Peter T. *Joseph Chamberlain: Entrepreneur in Politics*. New Haven, CT: Yale University Press, 1994; Strauss, William L. *Joseph Chamberlain and the Theory of Imperialism*. Washington, DC: American Council on Public Affairs, 1942.

CARL CAVANAGH HODGE

## Chancellorsville, Battle of (1863)

A pivotal battle of the **American Civil War** fought in Virginia in May 1863. Union General Joseph Hooker assumed command of the Army of the Potomac in January 1863, following the disastrous battle of Fredericksburg. After a period of refitting the army, Hooker hoped to flank Confederate Commander General Robert E. Lee out of his defenses and into a fight on open ground.

Leaving John Sedgwick's corps at Fredericksburg to hold Lee in position, Hooker marched westward along the Rappahannock River. Lee was badly outnumbered, having sent James Longstreet's corps to North Carolina. In an effort to prevent encirclement, Lee boldly split his army and marched west to meet Hooker, leaving a rearguard near Fredericksburg. When Hooker crossed the Rappahannock on April 30, Lee again divided his army, sending Stonewall Jackson's corps to the south and west to flank Hooker in the vicinity of Chancellorsville. Within sight of seizing key terrain, Hooker halted his advancing columns. He lost his nerve completely when Jackson fell on the vulnerable Union right flank late on May 2. Without having used his entire force, Hooker retreated in defeat across the Rappahannock. Lee then turned east and routed Sedgwick's corps, which had successfully pushed the rebel rearguard out of its defenses.

Lee used the victory as a launching pad for his second invasion of the north, which ended in defeat at Gettysburg. Long considered Lee's masterpiece, the Chancellorsville victory proved costly to the Confederacy when Jackson was wounded by his own men while conducting a night reconnaissance, wounds that led to his death.

FURTHER READING: Furgurson, Ernest B. *Chancellorsville, 1863: The Souls of the Brave.* New York: Random House, 1992; Sears, Stephen W. *Chancellorsville.* Boston: Houghton-Mifflin, 1996.

THOMAS D. VEVE

## Charles, Archduke of Austria (1771–1847)

Archduke Charles (Karl) of Austria, Duke of Teschen, was born in September 1771 in Florence, the capital of Tuscany. The third son of the Grand-Duke of Tuscany and Emperor Leopold II made a career in the Austrian army. As General-governor of the Austrian Netherlands in 1793–1794 and as field-commander of Austrian armies operating in southern Germany, northern Italy and Switzerland from 1796 to 1800, he took part in Austria's warfare against revolutionary France.

In 1801, Charles became president of the Aulic War Council, *Hofkriegsrat,* and started to modernize the Austrian forces. In the war against France in 1805, Charles led the Austrian troops in Italy. With the army reform still in its infancy, Charles opposed another war against Napoleon in 1809. But when war had broken out, Charles commanded the Austrian field army and achieved the first victory over Napoleon in the Battle of **Aspern-Essling** in May 1809. Nevertheless, Austria lost the war and Charles his command. He became Austria's most influential military writer and died in Vienna in April 1847. *See also* Habsburg Empire; Napoleonic Wars.

FURTHER READING: Bérenger, Jean. *A History of the Habsburg Empire, 1780–1918*. London: Longman, 1997; Bridge, Francis R. *The Habsburg Monarchy Among the Great Powers, 1815–1918*. New York: St. Martin's, 1990; Kann, Robert A. *A History of the Habsburg Empire, 1526–1918*. Berkeley: University of California Press, 1974.

GUENTHER KRONENBITTER

## Charles X, King of France (1757–1836)

King of France from 1824 to 1830 and the personification of the dissolute life and reactionary politics for which the late Bourbon dynasty was caricatured. Charles fled to Edinburgh with the outbreak of the Revolution in 1789 and returned to France in 1814 as leader of the ultraroyalists. He promptly fell in with clerical forces and authorized a series of penalties for irreligious behavior, which was merely the first of a series of measures that ultimately alienated all shades of political opinion. His Four Ordinances of St. Cloud provoked the July Revolution of 1830, and after three days of street –fighting, Charles was forced to abdicate and take refuge in England. His time on the throne being otherwise a waste of time and space, his most lasting legacy to France was his initiation of the military expedition against **Algeria** in 1830 to distract attention from his manifold failures at home.

FURTHER READING: Cobban, Alfred. *A History of Modern France.* 3 vols. New York: Braziller, 1965.

CARL CAVANAGH HODGE

## Chattanooga, Battle of (1863)

A Union victory in the **American Civil War.** Chattanooga, Tennessee, an important rail center and river port, is situated on the south bank of the Tennessee River Valley at Moccasin Bend where the Ridge and Valley Region of the Appalachian Mountains meets the Appalachian Plateau Region. Missionary Ridge runs southwest to northeast on the eastern side of the city and was occupied by Confederates. They also held the heights of Lookout Mountain, a great plateau on the west.

After the Union defeat at Chickamauga, General Rosecrans was replaced by General Ulysses S. Grant. Opposing him were Confederates under the command of General Braxton Bragg. On November 23, Union forces captured Orchard Knob, a hill centrally located between Chattanooga and Missionary Ridge. The next day Union forces commanded by Major General Joseph Hooker scaled the walls of Lookout Mountain in the "Battle above the Clouds." They then drove its Confederate defenders southward into Georgia. On November 25, assaults on Confederate positions on Missionary Ridge were repulsed until near dusk when Union forces commanded by Major General George H. Thomas attacked Confederate rifle pits at its base. The troops then spontaneously swept up the ridge without orders to attack. The dramatic assault by 23,000 men drove the Confederates off the ridge and back into Georgia. Confederate casualties were 6,600, Union losses at 6,000.

Europe received news of the last of a long series of battles in 1863 with some boredom. It was more news of enormous and deadly conflicts that had not brought an end to the war. Still, the use of railroads for moving troops continued to impress some in Prussian military circles.

FURTHER READING: Cozzens, Peter. *The Shipwreck of Their Hopes: The Battles for Chattanooga.* Urbana: University of Illinois Press, 1994.

ANDREW JACKSON WASKEY

## Chaumont, Treaty of (1814)

A treaty concluded between Austria, Prussia, Russia, and Britain on March 9, 1814, during the campaign in France against Napoleon. By its terms, the Emperor Francis I of Austria, Tsar Alexander I of Russia, King Frederick William III of Prussia, and Lord **Castlereagh,** the British Foreign Secretary, offered Napoleon peace terms that would provide France with her pre-1792 borders in exchange for a general cease fire. If these terms were rejected, the Allies agreed among themselves to pursue the war to a successful conclusion, with each partner supplying at least 100,000 men and promising not to conclude a separate peace with the enemy. Napoleon, who was only weeks away from final defeat, rejected the Chaumont terms, thus discarding the last opportunity to retain his throne through negotiation. *See also* Bonaparte, Napoleon; Napoleonic Wars.

FURTHER READING: Kissinger, Henry. *A World Restored: Metternich, Castlereagh and the Problems of Peace, 1812–1822.* Boston: Houghton Mifflin, 1957; Nicholson, Harold. *The Congress of Vienna: A Study in Allied Unity, 1812–1822.* New York: Viking Press, 1946; Ross, Steven T. *European Diplomatic History, 1789–1815: France against Europe.* Garden City, NY: Anchor Books, 1969; Webster, Sir Charles. *The Foreign Policy of Castlereagh, 1812–1815: Britain and the Reconstruction of Europe.* London: G. Bell and Sons, 1963.

GREGORY FREMONT-BARNES

## Cherniaev, General Mikhail Gregor'evich (1828–1898)

The Russian general whose forces conquered Tashkent in 1865. This was a major turning point in the Russian conquest of Central Asia, as the pace of conquests quickened thereafter. Cherniaev argued that the military conquest of Tashkent was much needed in 1864, despite some opinions to the contrary in the Ministry of Foreign Affairs. Prior to Cherniaev's success, Russian leaders had envisioned Chimkent as the southern point of their empire. Tashkent was surrendered on June 17, 1865 and Cherniaev earned the nickname "The Lion of Tashkent." He served twice as governor-general of **Turkestan,** 1865–1866 and 1882–1884. After his first stint in Turkestan, he strongly criticized the Turkestan regime of his successor, General Konstantin von **Kaufman,** via his job as editor of the *Russkiy Mir* (*The Russian World*) newspaper. Throughout his career he alternated between periods of support and opposition from the tsarist government. *See also* Great Game, Russian Empire.

FURTHER READING: MacKenzie, David. *The Lion of Tashkent, the Career of General M.G. Cherniaev.* Athens: University of Georgia Press, 1974.

SCOTT C. BAILEY

## Chickamauga Creek, Battle of (1863)

One of the bloodiest battles of the **American Civil War,** especially in the western theater. Confederate dead were listed at 2,673 and Union dead at 1,656, with total casualties in killed, wounded, and missing numbering 37,129. Chickamauga (in Cherokee, "river of death") was fought south of Chattanooga, Tennessee, in extreme northwestern Georgia. The Union Army of the Tennessee was commanded by General William S. Rosecrans and the Confederate Army of Tennessee was commanded by General Braxton Bragg. The battle began when Confederate forces tried to move across Chickamauga Creek at the Alexander Bride crossing. During the day, the confused battle raged as small groups fought in the dense woods in thick gun smoke unable to hear officers' commands. At dusk on September 19, the battle line lay along the LaFayette-Chattanooga Road.

On September 20, the renewed battle became a rout after a garbled order caused a gap in the center of the Federal army's line. Confederates commanded by General James Longstreet, who had just arrived by rail from Virginia, poured through the gap. The defense of Snodgrass Hill by General George Thomas, "The Rock of Chickamauga," saved the Union Army, and, as night settled, Union forces slipped away to rejoin Rosecrans in Chattanooga. The battle was a tactical victory for the Confederates, but a strategic nullity because Bragg failed to march to Chattanooga to destroy the Union army or to drive it back to the Ohio River. Sympathizers with the Confederacy in Europe, and especially imperialists in France, were cheered for a short while and others thought it would bring peace. The battlefield is now the Chickamauga National Battlefield.

FURTHER READING: Tucker, Glenn. *Chickamauga: Bloody Battle in the West.* Dayton, OH: Morningside Bookshop, 1984.

ANDREW JACKSON WASKEY

## China

For 2,200 years China was an extraordinarily durable imperial state, yet by 1557, when Portugal took possession of Macao, it became an object of European interest. Ruled since 1644 by the **Qing dynasty** descended from Manchu conquerors, nineteenth-century China was beset by internal convulsions and external challenges until 1912 when a nationalist revolution led by **Sun Yatsen** produced a republic. The first domestic upheaval, the folk-Buddhist White Lotus rebellion of 1796 to 1804, revealed both popular discontent with the Qing government and the flagging competence of its military. The Nian (1851–1868) and the **Taiping** (1850–1864) rebellions further weakened China and left its large territory and extensive coastline increasingly vulnerable to the predations of Britain, Japan, and Russia in particular. Indeed, the Qing's bureaucratic rigidity and China's educational and economic backwardness led to its humiliation as early as the **Opium War** of 1839–1842 with Britain, the Treaty of Nanjing and the loss of Hong Kong. After the **Arrow War** of 1856–1860 against both Britain and France the capital of Beijing was occupied and the Yuan Ming Yuan summer palace burned to the ground by the British. The Forbidden City was spared on the calculation that the disgrace involved might topple the Qing dynasty, which the British in particular preferred to remain in power as a weakened negotiating partner.

The Treaties of **Tientsin** inaugurated the system of harbor treaties similar in many respects with the "capitulations" to which the **Ottoman Empire** had been subjected.

The European powers were thereby given extraterritorial rights in harbor cities such as Shanghai and Canton, where whole districts became enclaves of European culture and legal jurisdiction, and the sovereign authority of China was in effect suspended. Further "unequal treaties" with France, Germany, Russia, and the **United States** further opened up China to trade while displacing Qing authority from the coastal treaty ports. In 1880, France expanded its empire in Indochina with the occupation of Hanoi and Haiphong and also sought concessions from China in **Annam.** When negotiations with France collapsed in 1884, the Chinese navy promptly became the victim of a catastrophic defeat by the French fleet in which virtually every Chinese warship was either sunk or destroyed by fire within scarcely more than an hour of fighting. As a consequence, French control of **Indochina** was consolidated. Meiji Japan (see **Meiji Restoration**) then joined the competition for spheres of influence and commercial privileges and, as trophies of its victory in the **Sino-Japanese War** of 1894, took Taiwan, the Pescadores, and the Liaotung Peninsula. China was forced to recognize the independence of **Korea,** where Japan promptly established a sphere of influence. In wholly accurate anticipation of a future struggle with Japan, Russia protested the Japanese gains recorded in the Treaty of **Shimonoseki.** A revision in which Japan's territorial gains were scaled back was negotiated by Japan, France, Germany, and Russia over the head of the Qing government. Dissatisfied with its lack of a presence on the Chinese coast and under the spell of its naval lobby, Germany struck next by landing troops on the Shantung Peninsula in 1896 and extracting a 99-year lease on the port of Tsingtao. In 1898, Russia gained **Port Arthur**—under Shimonoseki initially given to Japan—on similar terms; the same year France secured its own 99-year lease of Kwang Chou Wan.

Thus China had by the turn of the century been the object of foreign competition every bit as intense as Africa. The fundamental contrast, however, was that the whole of China had at least a nominal government and was never taken over, made into a protectorate, or partitioned. Having behaved like jealous sisters in the scramble for Chinese ports, the Great Powers buried their rivalries in response to the antiforeign **Boxer Insurrection** in 1900 and cooperated in the comprehensive defeat of the revolt. They declined to partition the country, as each sought guaranteed maximum access to the Chinese market, along with the harbor rights entailed, at a minimal cost of administrative responsibility. The **Open Door** policy proposed by the United States, according to which extensive spheres of influence were forbidden to keep China open to all comers, secured the support of the British government as result of a convergence of interest. Whereas the United States as a latecomer did not want to be left out of China altogether, Britain sought to ease the direct cost of maintaining its worldwide empire and commercial interests. The Boxer Rebellion's impact otherwise was to expose the final bankruptcy of the Qing. In 1903, Sun Yatsen praised the Fighting Fists for standing up to foreign bullies in a way that its impotent court had been unable to for the better part of a century. Thereafter China's progress to the Revolution of 1912 gathered unstoppable momentum. *See also* Extraterritoriality; Japanese Empire; Portuguese Empire; Russian Empire.

FURTHER READING: Hsieh, P. C. *The Government of China, 1644–1911.* Baltimore: Johns Hopkins Press, 1925; Preston, Diana. *The Boxer Rebellion: China's War on Foreigners.* London:

Constable and Co. Ltd., 1999; Spence, Jonathan D. *The Search for Modern China*. New York: W. W. Norton, 1990.

CARL CAVANAGH HODGE

## Ch'ing Dynasty

*See* Qing Dynasty

## Chrysanthemum Throne

Based on the flower that is the official seal of the Japanese imperial family, the term *Chrysanthemum Throne* is a common English-language reference to the Japanese emperor. Although obscured by the warrior government that ruled Japan from the twelfth through early nineteenth centuries, the Japanese emperor became the ultimate locus of national authority after the toppling of the feudal regime in 1868. The 1889 Meiji constitution placed full sovereignty in the emperor. And although actual policy-making through the early twentieth century rested in the hands of the samurai founders of the modern nation, the emperor remained the ultimate symbol of nation and empire. That symbol would increasingly be imbued with spiritual and cultural, as well as political, significance and would become, by 1940, the focal point of a colossal new conception of a Greater East Asian world order. *See also* Japanese Empire.

FURTHER READING: Beasley, William G. *The Meiji Restoration*. Stanford, CA: Stanford University Press, 1972; Jansen, Marius, ed. *The Emergence of Meiji Japan*. Cambridge: Cambridge University Press, 1995.

FREDERICK R. DICKINSON

## Churchill, Lord Randolph (1849–1894)

The father of Winston **Churchill** and a prominent Conservative politician and Secretary for India in the Marquess of **Salisbury**'s government of 1885–1886, Lord Randolph Churchill was largely responsible for the British annexation of Upper Burma in 1886. Born at Blenheim Palace on February 13, 1849, Churchill was the third son of the seventh Duke of Marlborough. His political career began with election to Parliament in 1874, after which he emerged as the leader of "Tory Democracy," a progressive group of Conservative Members of Parliament who sought to secure a strong working-class vote for the government of Benjamin **Disraeli** by promoting its policies of social reform.

Churchill quickly made himself useful, and his rise to cabinet responsibility was rapid; after his tenure in the India portfolio he became Chancellor of the Exchequer and Conservative leader in the House Commons, in each case the youngest member to hold the position for more than a century. Churchill was, however, of an impetuous temperament. He resigned after only five months because of quarrels with fellow ministers over budget estimates and never rose to cabinet level again, a lesson in unrealized potential. He was troubled by poor health for the remainder of his life.

FURTHER READING: Foster, R. F. *Lord Randolf Churchill: A Political Life.* New York: Oxford University Press, 1981.

CARL CAVANAGH HODGE

## Churchill, Sir Winston Leonard Spencer Churchill (1874–1965)

Twice prime minister of the United Kingdom, Winston Churchill is remembered for his great achievement during World War II, especially during the period between the fall of France in June 1940 and the entry into the war of the United States in December 1941, when Britain stood alone against Nazi Germany.

In the pre-1914 period, however, Churchill was notable as an author on imperial wars, as a reforming cabinet minister, and as an energetic First Lord of the Admiralty. Educated at Harrow and Sandhurst, he was commissioned in the Queen's Own Hussars in 1895. In that same year, he took up a parallel vocation as a journalist, reporting on the Spanish campaign in Cuba. In 1896, he sailed with his regiment to India. Deploying his mother's extensive contacts in high places, he managed to attach himself to a punitive expedition to the northwest frontier in1897, and to Lord Kitchener's reconquest of the Sudan the next year. During the latter, Churchill famously took part in one of the British army's last cavalry charges. Both experiences resulted in books, Churchill's *River War* on the Sudanese campaign being marked by a guarded sympathy for the defeated enemy, and remaining a valuable account. Resigning his army commission in 1899, Churchill went to South Africa as a journalist on the outbreak of the Second **Boer War,** but after taking command of the unsuccessful defense of armored train, he was captured by the Boers. His subsequent escape from prison in Pretoria and return to Durban via Portuguese East Africa made him a popular hero. He had stood unsuccessfully for Parliament in 1899, but in the "khaki" election of 1900, by now a national hero, he was successful.

Churchill crossed the floor to the Liberals in 1904 on the issue of **free trade**, the Tories having taken up the question of an imperial tariff wall. His crossing of the floor coincided with the rapid decline of Conservative fortunes and earned him a reputation as an opportunist. On the formation of a Liberal government in 1905, Churchill became undersecretary to the Colonial Office; as the Secretary, Lord **Elgin,** was in the Lords, Churchill represented the department in the Commons. When Herbert **Asquith** succeeded Sir Henry **Campbell-Bannerman** in 1908, Churchill became President of the Board of Trade—a cabinet minister at age 33. Under the influence of David **Lloyd George,** Churchill campaigned for the "peoples' budget" of 1909 and for the restriction on the powers of Lords contained in the Parliament Act of 1911. Although originally skeptical of higher naval spending, as First Lord of the Admiralty from 1911, he pushed for new and modern battleships, and for other technical innovations, such as submarines and aircraft. At the approach of war in 1914, Churchill ordered the fleet to move from its channel bases to its war station at Scapa Flow.

An aggressive advocate of the potential of naval power, he pushed the Dardanelles expedition of 1915, which of course went badly wrong, and cost Churchill the Admiralty. After a period in the trenches, he returned to office as minister of munitions, and then after the war at the War Office. Following his service as chancellor of the exchequer in the 1920s, Churchill's career once more seemed over, this time because of his obstinate opposition to Indian self-government and his warnings about Hitler's rearmament. The rest, as they say, is history. *See also* Churchill, Lord Randolph; Fisher, Sir John; Navalism.

FURTHER READING: Churchill, Winston. *The River War.* 2 vols. London: Longmans, 1899; Gilbert, Martin, and Randolph S. Churchill. *Winston S. Churchill.* 8 vols. London: Heinemann, 1966–1988.

MARK F. PROUDMAN

## Civil War

*See* American Civil War

## Clark, William

*See* Lewis and Clark Expedition

## Clausewitz, Carl von (1780–1831)

A Prussian general and military theorist, Clausewitz is best known for his magnum opus, *On War.* Born at Burg, near Magdeburg, Clausewitz joined the Prussian army in 1792 as a cadet and served on the Rhine front against the French from 1793–1794. He later trained at the War Academy in Berlin, where he became a protégé of Gerhard von **Scharnhorst,** a staff officer later to play a prominent part in the army reforms of 1807–1813. On the recommendation of Scharnhorst, Clausewitz was transferred to an appointment on the general staff. He was captured in the wake of the Battle of Auerstädt in October 1806. On his release three years later, Clausewitz assisted Scharnhorst and General Augustus **Gneisenau** in the complete reform and remodeling of the Prussian army. Clausewitz served in the Prussian contingent that formed the northern wing of the French invasion of Russian in 1812, but he defected to the Russians, with whom he served at the siege of Riga. He later persuaded General Yorck to sign the Convention of Tauroggen by which the Prussian contingent declared its neutrality. Clausewitz remained in Russian service until 1814, when he returned to the Prussian army and became chief of staff to Baron von Thielmann, one of the corps commanders at the battles of Ligny and Wavre during the **Waterloo** campaign of 1815.

In 1818, Clausewitz was promoted to major general and served as director of the staff college in Berlin until his retirement in 1830. Among his various books he wrote an account of his experiences on campaign in 1812, published posthumously, although his most highly acclaimed work, *Vom Krieg* (*On War*), also published posthumously, focused on the theoretical problems of war rather than on narrative history. Clausewitz argued that war constituted merely an extension of politics through violence—and therefore a natural tool of national policy. The supreme objective was the decisive encounter between the principal armies of opposing states, wherein the overwhelming success of one side enabled it to impose its political will on its opponent. This cardinal principle was applied with overwhelming success during Prussia's wars of unification (1864, 1866, 1870–1871) and the idea has become axiomatic since. Indeed, by extolling Napoleon's tactics and the principles he had applied to warfare as models of good generalship, Clausewitz ensured that his work would become the standard, orthodox text for army officers and military theorists not only of his own century, but of our own. *See also* Liberation, War of; Napoleonic Wars.

FURTHER READING: Clausewitz, Carl von. *On War.* Princeton, NJ: Princeton University Press, 1984; Paret, Peter. *Clausewitz and the State.* Oxford: Oxford University Press, 1976; Paret, Peter, and Gordon Craig, eds. *Makers of Modern Strategy from Machiavelli to the Nuclear Age.* Princeton, NJ: Princeton University Press, 1986; Parkinson, Roger. *Clausewitz.* London: Wayland, 1970.

GREGORY FREMONT-BARNES

### Clayton-Bulwer Treaty (1850)

Negotiated and signed in Washington, D.C. by American Secretary of State John Clayton and the British Minister to the United States, Sir Henry Lytton Bulwer, the treaty was a compromise between competing Anglo-American imperial ambitions in Central America. Both powers refused exclusive control over any transisthmian interoceanic canal project, but agreed to cooperate in its development and ensure its neutrality, guaranteeing to neither fortify nor exercise dominion over the route.

The project was a popular idea in both countries for years. The conclusion of the **Mexican-American War** (1846–1848) and the emerging Anglo-American rivalry for Oriental markets sharpened interest in a mid-hemispheric isthmus canal. Reacting to American territorial expansion in the Southwest and a treaty with New Granada (Colombia) that reserved canal rights through Panama for the United States, in 1848, the Russell Ministry augmented Britain's presence on the Mosquito Coast (parts of Honduras and Belize) to a protectorate. Domestic and foreign appeals prompted U.S. diplomats to negotiate commercial treaties with Honduras, El Salvador, and Nicaragua, the latter granting the United States perpetual rights to build, operate, and fortify a canal. Although none of the Central American treaties were submitted to the U.S. Senate for ratification, they were enough to spur the British to compromise with the United States.

The Clayton-Bulwer Treaty was not without controversy, but it proved enduring. The Zachary Taylor Administration (1849–1850), which faced significant domestic opposition to the treaty, interpreted the noncolonization clauses to apply retroactively to Britain's existing colonies, but Westminster refused to relinquish Belize or the Bay Islands. From 1856 to 1860, amid heightened American filibustering expeditions, the United States and Britain quietly settled on the status quo, guaranteeing Britain's Central American possessions while allowing Americans to reaffirm their commitment to the Monroe Doctrine. The treaty remained in effect for a half century, but as the United States became increasingly involved in Latin American affairs and the British more attentive to Continental Europe, mutual cooperation required modification. The **Hay-Pauncefote Treaty** of 1901 abrogated the terms of Clayton-Bulwer, granting the United States rights to unilaterally construct, control, and fortify an isthmus canal. The Clayton-Bulwer Treaty was an early expression of American **Open Door** imperialism, which later became the stated policy of the United States, but also helped pave the way for eventual direct U.S. intervention in Latin America affairs. Anglo-American intrusion significantly disrupted local political alignments, altered traditional social relations, and permanently rearranged Central American international relations. *See also* Monroe Doctrine; Panama Canal; Roosevelt, Theodore.

FURTHER READING: Merk, Frederick. *The Monroe Doctrine and American Expansion, 1943–1849.* New York: Knopf, 1966; Perkins, Dexter. *The Monroe Doctrine, 1826–1867.* Baltimore: The Johns Hopkins University Press, 1933.

JONATHAN GANTT

## Clemençeau, Georges (1841–1929)

Twice French premier (1906–1909 and 1917–1920), Georges Clemençeau was a major radical figure of the Third Republic whose combative nature earned him the nickname "The Tiger." He was born in Mouilleron-en-Pared on September 28, 1841. His political career began after becoming mayor of Montmartre in Paris in 1870. Even before the German unification was completed, as a deputy for Paris at the National Assembly at Bordeaux, he had voted against making peace with Prussia. He opposed colonialism on the grounds that it would divert national energies from the imperative of recovering Alsace-Lorraine, and he was a relentless opponent of Jules **Ferry**'s colonial policy.

Clemençeau's career was damaged by the Panama Scandal but recovered when he championed the republican cause during the **Dreyfus Affair.** In his first premiership, his policies led to cementing friendship with Britain. The ***Entente Cordiale*** of April 1904 between France and Britain had led to formal recognition of the French influence in Morocco, and the First Morocco Crisis demonstrated the solidarity of the *Entente.* There was revival of nationalist feeling in France during his premiership nurtured in part by the revanchist spirit of Clemençeau's policy. His government fell in 1909, but he continued to advocate greater readiness in case of a war and returned as a particularly energetic and effective wartime premier from 1917 to 1920. World War I made Clemençeau a legendary figure; indeed, his tough leadership in a struggle that nearly bled France white brought him the new title of "Father Victory." At the Paris Peace Conference of 1919, Clemençeau was the most forceful advocate of punitive peace terms for Germany.

FURTHER READING: Dallas, Gregor. *At the Heart of a Tiger. Clemenceau and His World 1841–1929.* New York: Carroll & Graf, 1993; Jackson, J. Hampden. *Clemenceau and the Third Republic.* New York: Collier Books, 1962; Lecomte, Georges. *Georges Clemenceau: The Tiger of France.* Translated by Donald Clive Stuart. New York: Appleton & Company, 1919; Martet, Jean. *Georges Clemenceau.* London: Longmans, Green & Company, 1930; Watson, David Robin. *Georges Clemenceau; A Political Biography.* London: Eyre Methuen, 1974.

PATIT PABAN MISHRA

## Cleveland, Grover (1837–1908)

Because he served two nonconsecutive terms (1885–1889 and 1893–1897), Grover Cleveland is considered the 22nd and 24th President of the United States. He was born Stephen Grover Cleveland on March 18, 1837, in Caldwell, New Jersey. A Democrat in a Republican age, Cleveland nonetheless had a meteoric rise from mayoralty of Buffalo, New York to the presidency within four years. A courageous and upright man, he believed in the call of conscience in handling the external affairs of the nation. He opposed the rising imperialist sentiment in the country, and in his second term refused the annexation of **Hawaii.** He was against assigning Hawaii the status of a protectorate, doubting that the U.S. Constitution could be made to work for a non-Caucasian society so far away, yet saw islands as an ideal location for a naval base to help defend the Pacific Coast. In the Venezuela-British Guiana boundary dispute of 1895, Cleveland applied the **Monroe Doctrine,** a bellicose turn that annoyed the British government yet ultimately led it to agree to arbitration. Cleveland died in Princeton on June 24, 1908.

FURTHER READING: Ford, Henry Jones. *The Cleveland Era: A Chronicle of the New Order in Politics.* New Haven, CT: Yale University Press, 1919; Welch, Richard E. *The Presidencies of Grover Cleveland.* Lawrence: University Press of Kansas, 1988.

PATIT PABAN MISHRA

## Cobden, Richard (1804–1865)

A British **free trade** and peace campaigner, Richard Cobden was possibly the most effective political activist of his time. Cobden was born to an unsuccessful farmer and shopkeeper in Sussex. After the failure of his father's business, he was sent away to a minor and abusive boarding school where he was extremely unhappy. Taken into an uncle's firm at age 15, he became a successful commercial traveler selling calico and other textiles. He learned French, read widely, and soon set up his own business.

In 1832, he moved from London to Manchester, where he continued to prosper. In 1835, Cobden published his first "pamphlet," a work of some 150 pages entitled "England, Ireland and America," under the pseudonym "a Manchester manufacturer." Cobden argued that Ireland and America were of far greater economic importance to England than any of the European countries with which traditional great power diplomacy concerned itself. Arguing that force could not make markets for bad or expensive goods, Cobden foresaw that the United States would soon be Britain's greatest economic competitor. He urged that wars and colonies be avoided, and taxes and debts reduced. In subsequent writings, he argued that not merely war but international diplomacy itself served only the interests of a parasitic aristocracy: "As little intercourse as possible betwixt the *Governments,* as much connection as possible between the *nations,* of the world," was one of his more compelling slogans. Colonies, for Cobden, were likewise of no commercial value, a doctrine reinforced by his reading of Adam Smith. The **Anti-Corn Law League** was started by a group of Manchester manufacturers in 1839 to oppose tariffs on imported wheat imposed after the Napoleonic wars. By the early 1840s, Cobden and his associate John Bright took the lead in organizing the league. Cobden's rural background and knowledge of Adam Smith enabled him to effectively frame the arguments for free trade as more than mere capitalist self-interest.

Elected to Parliament in 1841, Cobden became the Parliamentary spokesman for a national movement. Sir Robert Peel moved to abolish the Corn Laws in 1846, personally praising Cobden's advocacy. After the Corn Laws' repeal, Cobden toured Europe as the triumphant advocate of free trade and expressed great confidence that Britain's move would be followed by other nations. Free trade, Cobden argued, would lead the nations of the world to appreciate their true inter-dependence, and thus to live in peace with one another. Cobden was offered the possibility of a place in the cabinets of both Lord John Russell and Lord Palmerston, but he refused, wishing to maintain his role as the voice of principle. He was probably the most consistent and effective ideologue in Victorian England. Free trade assumed in England, if not elsewhere, a kind of totemic status, the cause of "protection"—tariffs—becoming in Benjamin **Disraeli**'s words, "not merely dead, but damned." The Cobden Club, founded by leading Liberals after Cobden's death in 1865, adopted the device, "Free Trade, Peace, Goodwill among Nations," a classic statement of mid-Victorian bourgeois optimism. In the later years of the century, at a time when many considered Cobden's "little England" doctrines to be obsolete, his followers were among the most obdurate opponents of imperialism. *See also* Liberal Party.

FURTHER READING: Cobden, Richard. *Political Writings*. 2 vols. Edited by Peter Cain. London: Routledge, 1995; Hinde, Wendy. *Richard Cobden: A Victorian Outsider.* New Haven, CT: Yale University Press, 1987; Hobson, J.A. *Richard Cobden: The International Man.* London: T. Fisher Unwin, 1919.

MARK F. PROUDMAN

## Cochin China

Nam Kỳ, the southernmost region of contemporary Vietnam, was named *Cochinchine* by the French, who in 1858 occupied Da Nang on the coast to the north and from there moved southward. By early 1859, French forces occupied Saigon, and in 1862 the emperor of **Annam** ceded his provinces around the Mekong Delta. In 1867, these new possessions became officially France's new colony of Cochin China. In the wake of the sudden absence of the Annamite officials, French naval officers were forced to improvise an administrative apparatus, so they established a school for training staff from France in the customs of the country. After France's defeat in the **Franco-Prussian War,** however, the Third Republic abolished this system and replaced the naval staff with civil governors who made no attempt to learn the local language. French republican law was also imposed with ideological fervor, and its stress on individual liberty in a society constructed around the family unit was highly, and unnecessarily, disruptive.

In 1881, Cochin China was given the authority to elect a local deputy, but some of the administration and much of the commerce in the province were conducted by subject peoples of other French colonies. Despite the offense given to a local population thus doubly subjugated, Cochin China's fertile soil enabled the colony to generate sufficient revenue to make it financially independent of France. *See also* Indochina; French Empire.

FURTHER READING: Chapius, Oscar. *A History of Vietnam: From Hong Bang to Tu Duc.* Westport, CT: Greenwood, 1995; Power, Thomas F. *Jules Ferry and the Renaissance of French Imperialism.* New York: King's Crown Press, 1944; Wesseling, H.L. *The European Colonial Empires 1815–1919.* New York: Pearson Education, 2004.

CARL CAVANAGH HODGE

## Code Napoléon

*See* Napoleonic Code

## Colenso, Battle of (1899)

The third and most disastrous for British forces of three early engagements in the Second Boer War—the others being at Magersfontein and Stormberg—in which the Boer forces under General Louis **Botha** inflicted heavy losses on British regulars led by General Sir Redvers Buller. Buller subjected the Boers to a preliminary and ineffective bombardment before launching a frontal assault of three brigades against the Boer positions. As the Boers were in well-concealed trenches and firing German-made Mauser rifles loaded with smokeless cartridges, British forces were never sure of the exact location of their enemy. Buller's forces suffered 145 killed, 762 wounded, and 220 missing or captured. Of Botha's forces only 8 were killed and 30 wounded.

FURTHER READING: Pakenham, Thomas. *The Boer War.* New York: Random House, 1979.

CARL CAVANAGH HODGE

## *Colons*

White settlers in France's overseas colonies. The term was usually applied to **Algeria** specifically or French North Africa more generally, as it was here that a particularly large white settler population posed the greatest threat to the indigenous population and in time constituted the greatest nuisance to the French government. *Colons* often came from poor economic backgrounds or were political exiles of the Second Empire, and many were not French but Italian, Spanish, and Maltese. Those with energy and an eye for the main chance quickly realized that in the newly conquered territories, they could secure a level of material comfort impossible for them in Europe. Native Algerians unfamiliar with European property rights could be persuaded to partition land hitherto held in common and sell off small parcels to *colons*, the most enterprising of whom within a generation employed them as landless wage laborers on prosperous estates. The *colons* also had full political representation in France, whereas native Algerians did not. The *colons* were therefore fanatical about maintaining France's overseas empire and, in the case of Algeria, made Algerian independence into a national crisis for France. *See also* Abd-al-Qādir.

FURTHER READING: Ageron, Charles Robert. *Modern Algeria: A History from 1830 to the Present.* Trenton, NJ: Africa World Press, 1991; Bennoune, Mahfoud. *The Making of Contemporary Algeria, 1830–1987: Colonial Upheavals and Post-independence Development.* Cambridge: Cambridge University Press, 2002.

CARL CAVANAGH HODGE

## Colony

The term *colony* is derived from the Latin *colonia,* which named an agricultural settlement created for soldiers who had finished their service. In English, until the late nineteenth century the term *colony* retained its etymological meaning, designating a place to which settlers went, usually to establish themselves in agriculture. The term had connotations of natural, wholesome, and healthy expansion; "colonists" were engaged in bettering themselves, settling unimproved lands, and adding to the wealth of the world and of the nation.

Some mid-Victorian writers insisted that the **United States** was Britain's best colony, because that was where British settlers found the best opportunities. The term had no necessary connotations of political subordination, and Victorians often compared their colonies to those of the Hellenistic world, which had of course not been governed from their home cities. Increasingly, however, influenced by the fact that the largest and most prominent British dependencies, those in **Canada** and Australasia, were also colonies in the etymological sense. It became common to refer to all imperial dependencies as "colonies." The Royal Colonial Society, for instance, later the Royal Colonial Institute, was founded in 1868 and subsumed all imperial topics under the rubric of "colonial." Although critics of imperial expansion often observed that many British possessions, particularly those acquired in Africa in the late nineteenth century, were not really colonies in the original sense, the term came to apply to all dependent territories, and therefore acquired by the twentieth century a connotation of subordination. Since World War II, the term *colonialism* has become a synonym for the term *imperialism* and has come to denote unjust political subjection. The British government at this writing still retains a small number of colonies but finds it necessary to refer to them as "British Overseas Territories."

FURTHER READING: Bodelsen, C. A. *Studies in Mid-Victorian Imperialism*. London: Heinemann, 1960; Lewis, George Cornewall. *An Essay on the Government of Dependencies*. London: John Murray, 1841.

MARK PROUDMAN

## Commonwealth

Like its close cognate Commonweal, the term *commonwealth* implies the idea of a common good. The word came into use in the seventeenth century to name states deriving their legitimacy from a claim to pursue that good, as against legitimacy based on royal or prescriptive right. The term thus had republican connotations. The Commonwealth of England was the formal name of the English republic of Oliver Cromwell, and after the American Revolution former colonies such as Massachusetts named themselves commonwealths. The term was used occasionally in the pre-1914 period as a synonym for the **British Empire,** especially by those who wanted to emphasize its constitutional nature.

The Balfour Declaration of 1926 recognized all the **dominions** as being of equal status within "the British Commonwealth of Nations," and became for a generation something of a synonym for the British Empire, particularly in discussions pertaining to the emigrant dominions. After World War II, the adjective *British* was dropped, and the Commonwealth devolved in the rather ethereal entity it is today. The name, which once clothed absolute authority, in the twentieth century served thinly to camouflage the dissolution of power.

FURTHER READING: Mansergh, Nicholas. *The Commonwealth Experience*. London: Weidenfeld and Nicolson, 1969.

MARK F. PROUDMAN

## Communism

Communism is a theory and system of social and political organization that negates the capitalist profit-based system of private ownership and argues for a communist society in which the means of production are communally owned. Largely shaped by the socialist movement of nineteenth-century Europe, modern communism derives its structural and logical core from the *Communist Manifesto,* written by Karl Marx and Friedrich Engels in 1848. In the last half of the nineteenth century, the terms *socialism* and *communism* were often used interchangeably. Marx and Engels, however, came to see socialism as merely an intermediate stage of society in which most industry and property were owned in common but some class differences remained. They reserved the term *communism* for a final stage of society in which class differences would finally disappear, people would live in harmony, and the state would no longer be needed. Once again the meaning of the word communism shifted after 1917, when Vladimir **Lenin** (1870–1924) and his Bolshevik Party seized power in Czarist Russia. The **Bolsheviks** changed their name to the Communist Party and installed a repressive, single-party regime clearly devoted to the implementation of socialist ideals.

The origin of the communist notion can be traced back to ancient times, such as in Plato's *The Republic;* or in the life of the early Christian Church, as described in the *Acts of the Apostles.* As early as the sixteenth century, Thomas More, in his treatise *Utopia* (1516), envisioned a society based on common ownership of property, whose rulers administered it by applying pure reason. Enlightenment thinkers such as Immanuel Kant (1724–1804) in Germany and Jean Jacques Rousseau (1712–1778) in France criticized the idea of private property. The upheaval generated by the French Revolution brought forth a flurry of communistic ideas. A revolutionary firebrand, Francois-Noel Babeuf (1760–1797) argued for the common ownership of land and total economic and political equality among citizens.

French socialist Louis Blanc (1811–1882) advocated "associations of workers" or "social workshops," funded by the state and controlled by the workers. According to him, these would promote the development of balanced human personalities, instead of cutthroat competition encouraged by capitalism. Louis Blanc is perhaps the best known for developing the social principle, later adopted by Karl Marx that clarifies the distribution of labor and income. Another French revolutionary of the nineteenth century, Louis Auguste Blanqui (1805–1881), made an important contribution to communism, although by promoting the idea that a working-class revolution could not succeed without a small group of disciplined conspirators to lead the way.

In the late nineteenth century, Marxism increased in popularity, particularly in countries whose urban population was impoverished and whose intellectuals were given no voice in government. Marx and Engels flung themselves into national and international political movements dedicated to promoting socialism and their end goal of communism. They were active in the International Workingmen's Association—popularly known as the First International—an alliance of trade-union groups founded in 1864. A less disjointed union of socialist parties, the Socialist International (also known as the Second International), was formed in 1889 in Paris, France. Just before the revolution in Russia, in 1912 its constituent political parties claimed to have 9 million members.

FURTHER READING: Aptheker, Herbert, ed. *Marxism & Democracy*. Monograph Series Number One. New York: American Institute for Marxist Studies/Humanities Press, 1965; Collier, Andrew. *Socialist Reasoning: An Inquiry into the Political Philosophy of Scientific Socialism.* London: Pluto Press, 1990; Furet, Francois, and Deborah F. Furet. *Passing of an Illusion: The Idea of Communism in the Twentieth Century.* Chicago: University of Chicago Press, 1999; Patsouras, Louis, and Thomas, Jack Roy. *Essays on Socialism.* San Francisco: Mellen Research University Press, 1992.

JITENDRA UTTAM

## Communist Manifesto (1848)

A pamphlet originally published in London in 1848 as a declaration of principles and objectives of the Communist League, a clandestine organization of expatriate German artisans and intellectuals. In 1847, the Communist League commissioned two new prominent members of the league, Karl **Marx** (1818–1883) and Friedrich **Engels** (1820–1895), to write a manifesto clearly stating its basic objectives and the underlying philosophy. Friedrich Engels first drafted *Principles of Communism* and handed it over to Karl Marx for revision. Drawing on Engels's *Principles,* Marx produced the theoretical and literary masterpiece that the world now knows as the *Communist Manifesto.* Among all the documents of the socialist movement, it is the most widely read, talked about, and hotly debated document. Manifesto is a carefully written systematic statement of a radical philosophy that was used to change political, social, and economic life of common people and finally come to be known as Marxism.

Although the *Communist Manifesto* was composed against the background of larger, long-term historical developments, it was written just before the outbreak of the 1848 revolution that swept across Europe—from France to Germany, Hungary, Italy, and beyond. In just a few weeks, one government after another fell. Although it cannot be said that the pamphlet played a major part in the events that followed, it is a product of that very specific time and that very specific revolutionary climate. In that historical fact lie both many of its strengths and some unresolved problems. The revolution, or revolutions, of 1848 took place in countries with diverse social, economic, and political conditions: from a relatively "developed" country like France, or parts of Germany such as the Rhineland, to "backward" areas like southern Italy or Transylvania. One thing they had in common, however, was that capitalism was not well advanced in any of them, and in some cases not at all. For all their differences, they all had predominantly rural populations. If the various continental revolutions had a common political program, it was not the overthrow of something like a capitalist system. It was rather the establishment of unified liberal or constitutional states with a degree of civil equality, inspired above all by the French Revolution. In some cases, like Hungary or Italy, the struggle for a more democratic state was closely linked with the fight for national autonomy.

At any rate, when Marx and Engels wrote the *Manifesto,* they did not believe that a socialist revolution, or a proletarian revolution of any kind, was in the offing. They briefly hoped that the events, and the failures, of 1848 might lead to something more, some further longer term development, a "permanent revolution" that would push beyond the bourgeois republic to proletarian rule and finally socialism. Any reader of the Manifesto must be struck by the fact that the revolutionary hero of its eloquent narrative is the bourgeoisie. The revolutionary victories of the bourgeoisie were, of course, deeply contradictory for Marx and Engels, combining benefits and costs in equal measure. They hoped, and confidently expected, that the bourgeoisie's conquests would eventually be overtaken by the triumph of the working class and socialism. But even while the Manifesto calls workers to arms and foresees their emergence as a truly revolutionary force, it tells the triumphal story of the bourgeoisie. The impact of the *Manifesto* was nevertheless remarkable. It has been translated into all the major languages and has remained an inspiration for generations of socialists. *See also* Communism.

FURTHER READING: Ehrenberg, J. *The Dictatorship of the Proletariat: Marxism's Theory of Socialist Democracy*. London: Routledge, 1992; Labriola, Antonio. *Essays on the Materialist Conception of History*. Translated by Charles H. Kerr. Chicago: Charles H. Kerr Co-operative, 1908; Tucker, Robert C., ed. *The Marx-Engels Reader*. New York: W. W. Norton & Company, 1978.

JITENDRA UTTAM

## Comparative Advantage

The idea of "comparative advantage" is a principal component of the doctrine of **free trade;** it was articulated most coherently in *The Principles of Political Economy*, published in 1819 by the economist David **Ricardo.** Developing ideas on national economic specialization also discussed by Adam **Smith** in *The Wealth of Nations*, Ricardo argued that a national economy benefits most from international trade by specializing in the production of goods and services in which it enjoys an advantage in efficiency relative to other national economies.

In an ideally free trading world economy, he maintained, each country would export the goods and services of which it is the most efficient producer, in terms of quality and price, but import those goods and services in which it is at a comparative *dis*advantage. The resulting international division of labor in a free trading world would therefore produce the highest quality goods and competitive prices. In practice, even governments nominally committed to free trade routinely protected industries in which they were less efficient as a result of the political costs imposed by uncompetitive domestic producers: electoral defeat at best, violent unrest at worst. Moreover, the doctrine was at odds with many of the economic motivations—ranging from privileged access to raw materials for industry to monopoly control of strategic materials crucial to survival in war—that prompted the Great Powers to seek overseas colonies.

FURTHER READING: Peach, Terry. *Interpreting Ricardo*. Cambridge: Cambridge University Press, 1993; Sraffa, Piero, and M. H. Dobb. *The Works and Correspondence of David Ricardo*. 11 vols. Cambridge: Cambridge University Press, 1951–1973.

CARL CAVANAGH HODGE

## Concentration Camps

Before their use as the internment and death camps built by Nazi Germany starting in 1933, *concentration camp* was a term coined by Lord Kitchener for internment centers developed as a counter to Boer guerrilla tactics in the final stages of the

Second **Boer War.** Kitchener attacked the very means of the Boers' sustenance by destroying their farms and livestock and herded Boer women and children, along with their black African laborers, into internment facilities. As a consequence of inadequate medical and sanitary standards, the camps were swept by disease and their populations devastated. A report later calculated that more than 27,000 Boers, 22,000 of whom were children, and some 14,000 black Africans perished in the camps. In 1900, Salisbury's government had won reelection in the "khaki election," partly on the back of popular enthusiasm for recent victories in South Africa. Now, Liberal Party and Socialist domestic critics of the war attacked the Conservative government's prosecution of the war as "barbaric," and the government itself felt mounting humiliation at its apparent inability to extract a Boer surrender.

Although Kitchener first used the term, he did not initiate the method. Reconcentration camps, as they were called, were used by Spain in Cuba during the rebellions of the 1860s and 1890s. In the latter instance, General Valeriano Weyler relocated 300,000 Cuba civilians sympathetic to the rebels. Here, too, thousands perished of hunger and disease. Liberals back in Spain denounced the policy, and the American press had additional outrage to justify the belligerent stand that ultimately led to the Spanish-American War.

FURTHER READING: Farwell, Byron. *The Great-Anglo-Boer War.* New York: Norton, 1990; Fremont-Barnes, Gregory. *The Boer War, 1899–1902.* Oxford: Osprey, 2003.

CARL CAVANAGH HODGE

## Concordat of 1801

A form of truce signed by Napoleon **Bonaparte** (1769–1821), as First Consul of France, and the new Roman Catholic Pope, Pius VII (1742–1823). Roman Catholicism was recognized as the religion of the majority of French citizens, which came into full communion with the Vatican. The Concordat accepted supremacy of the state over the Church in the nomination of bishops. The general law of public worship of April 1802 was applied to other religious orders and clergy was placed under state laws. Although the concordat did not satisfy diehard anticlericals and devoted Catholics; it healed the schism between the priests, and Napoleon received the support of the papacy. When he was crowned Emperor in December 1804, the pope was present.

FURTHER READING: Alexander, R. S. *Napoleon.* London: Arnold, 2001; Englund, S. *Napoleon: A Political Life.* New York: Scribner, 2004; Furet, François. *The French Revolution, 1770–1815.* Cambridge: Basil Blackwell, 1996.

PATIT PABAN MISHRA

## Confederation of the Rhine (1806–1813)

A puppet state created by Napoleon I after his abolition of the Holy Roman Empire. It was in effect a new constitutional arrangement for 16 states and territories of western Germany following on Napoleon's military successes at Ulm and Austerlitz in 1805. The Act of Confederation, established by a treaty signed in Paris on July 17, 1806, made some 8 million Germans subjects of the French Empire and bound states such as Baden, Bavaria, Hesse-Darmstadt, and Württemberg to assist in the creation of an army of 63,000 men for their collective defense. The Confederation disintegrated after Napoleon's defeat at Leipzig in 1813 and the withdrawal of French forces. *See also* Bonaparte, Napoleon; Napoleonic Wars.

FURTHER READING: Rose, J. Holland. *The Revolutionary and Napoleonic Era, 1789–1815.* Cambridge: Cambridge University Press, 1935.

CARL CAVANAGH HODGE

## Congo

*See* Belgian Congo

## Congress System

A new form of diplomacy whereby the Great Powers agreed to meet at regularly fixed conferences, established by Article VI of the Quadruple Alliance signed in Paris on November 20, 1815 among Britain, Russia, Austria, and Prussia. The system was not, strictly speaking, meant to mimic the Congress of Vienna, which had met between 1814 and 1815 to discuss the political reconstruction of Europe in the aftermath of the Napoleonic Wars, but rather to serve as an opportunity with which to hammer out their diplomatic differences and seek to maintain peace.

France was returned to the diplomatic fold at the Congress of Aix-la-Chapelle (September–November 1818); at **Aix-la-Chapelle** the powers discussed affairs connected with the occupation and rehabilitation of France; at **Troppau,** in October–December 1820, the revolution in Spain, which had began as an army revolt in January, occupied the chief concerns of the delegates, together with the crisis arising out of the Neapolitan revolt. Significantly, the three autocratic powers of Russia, Austria, and Prussia maintained their right to military intervention in the name of the alliance in the event that revolution threatened the stability of other states. At **Laibach,** January–May 1821, the powers considered the constitution of Naples and the mandate given to Austria to march troops into Italy; and at Verona, October–December 1822, the Russians and Austrians sought to support a French expeditionary force dispatched to Spain to put down a revolt there. Russia also argued for intervention in the Greek revolt against Turkish rule. The British, represented by the Duke of Wellington, opposed this policy and withdrew from the conference before it concluded its business.

For France, the various congresses permitted her to reestablish her reputation as a stable nation dedicated to the balance of power and international cooperation against radicalism. As early as the Congress of Troppau, Britain attended with the status of little more than that of an observer, wishing to distant herself from the other powers' wish to interfere in the internal affairs of states whose autocratic governments stood at risk from revolution. So little did the Congress System appear to benefit her interests that Britain abandoned it after Verona. Austria, Russia, and Prussia met for a final congress at St. Petersburg in 1825, although when major differences arose between the first two, no further congresses were held. International conferences later met at Berlin in 1878 and, of course, in 1919 at Versailles, where the delegates established a permanent system of conferences in the form of the League of Nations, the forerunner of the United Nations created in 1945. *See also* Balance of Power; Quadruple Alliance; Vienna, Congress of.

FURTHER READING: Kissinger, Henry. *A World Restored: Metternich, Castlereagh, and the Problem of Peace 1812–1822.* London: Weidenfeld & Nicolson, 2000; Lowe, John. *The Concert of Europe: International Relations, 1814–70.* London: Hodder & Stoughton, 1991.

GREGORY FREMONT-BARNES

## Conrad, Joseph (1857–1924)

Born Teodor Józef Konrad Korzeniowski, Polish-born British novelist Joseph Conrad used his experiences of more than 16 years in the British merchant marine and as a steamboat captain on the Congo River to give him the material for such novels as *An Outcast of the Islands* (1896), *The Nigger of the Narcissus* (1897), *Heart of Darkness* (1899), and *Lord Jim* (1900). Today widely considered one of the greatest modern writers in the English language, Conrad was one of an increasing number of serious writers who, in the late nineteenth century, made themselves intermediaries of the collision between the European world and the overseas indigenous cultures into which it encroached. In Conrad's work this involved immensely disturbing accounts of the brutalities committed in the pursuit of commerce or in the name of advancing civilization. The Congo Free State he characterized as "the vilest scramble for loot that ever disfigured the history of human conscience." It served equally as the setting for Conrad's *Heart of Darkness* as it did for Roger **Casement**'s report on abuses in the Upper Congo River rubber trade. *See also* Belgian Congo; Stanley, Henry Morton.

FURTHER READING: Sherry, Norman. *Conrad's Western World.* Cambridge: Cambridge University Press, 1971.

CARL CAVANAGH HODGE

## Conrad von Hötzendorf, Franz (1852–1925)

A military leader of the late **Habsburg Empire** bearing significant responsibility for Vienna's policy in the crisis of July 1914. Conrad was born in November 1925 in Penzing in Lower Austria. Like his father, he joined the Austrian officer corps. In 1878–1879 and in 1882, he took part in military operations in Bosnia-Herzegovina and Dalmatia, gaining battlefield experience. A general staff officer and teacher at the War Academy in Vienna, Conrad became known for his publications on battlefield tactics. As commander of an infantry brigade in Trieste and of an infantry division in the Tyrol, he became interested in war preparations against Italy. In 1906, on the behest of Archduke Francis Ferdinand, Conrad was chosen to succeed Friedrich von Beck-Rzikowsky as chief of the general staff of the Austro-Hungarian armed forces.

He launched a rigorous reform of the general staff and the system of maneuvers and training. War planning became more professional and war preparations were taken more seriously than before. With Italy and Romania being unreliable allies, and with Russia, Serbia, and Montenegro as probable enemies in a future war, the strategic situation looked bleak to Conrad. A social Darwinist afraid of the dismemberment of the multiethnic Habsburg Empire in an age of nationalism, Conrad propagated preventive war as the only viable solution to Austria-Hungary's security problems. In 1911, he provoked a clash with the Foreign Office and lost his position by calling for a preventive war against Italy. After the First **Balkan War,** Conrad was reinstalled as Chief of the general staff in 1912, but the heir to the throne, Archduke Francis Ferdinand, was pondering a replacement when the assassination plot in Sarajevo changed the political landscape.

In 1914, Conrad did not have to persuade foreign minister Berchtold or the Emperor to risk a Great Power war. Relying on his agreement with the German general staff, Conrad ordered an offensive against Russia's armies. Russian victories brought the Austro-Hungarian army close to a complete collapse in 1914–1915 and again in 1916, but with German, and partly Bulgarian, support Habsburg armies scored victories over Russian, Serbian, and Romanian armies in 1915–1916. The Italian offensive, on the other hand, could be contained but not beaten. Conrad's leadership was shaped by overambitious operational plans and a striking disregard of the numbers and the morale of his troops. He lost his post again in 1917, served as commander of an army, and was sent into early retirement in 1918. After the war, Conrad started publishing his memoirs. He died in Bad Mergentheim in Germany in August 1925. *See also* July Crisis.

FURTHER READING: Rothenberg, Gunther. *The Army of Franz Joseph.* West Lafayette: Indiana University Press, 1976.

GUENTHER KRONENBITTER

## Conscription

Compulsory military service, in principle for all adult males, was increasingly the practice of all serious Great Powers in the late nineteenth century. With the exception of Britain and the United States, who were both secure against sudden invasion by land, all major powers accepted the notion that the triumph of Prussian armies over Austria in 1866 and France in 1871 pointed to the prudence of universal military training. The maintenance of large numbers of reservists capable of supplementing the strength of the professional army on short notice became the norm. The movement toward larger armies had been inaugurated by the French Revolutionary concept of the *levée en masse* and Napoleon's successful use of large conscript forces, but the prospect of general war in Europe retreated over the next half century to reemerge with united Germany's challenge to the continental balance of power after 1871.

Conscription's appeal to national governments thereafter gathered further strength from the intensification of Great Power competition within Europe. The popular appeal of European nationalist movements, along with the increasing commonness of men in uniform, meanwhile contributed to acceptance of the idea that service to the nation and experience of war was the rite of passage to manhood. Militarization of European society was thereby nurtured. Even socialist movements often used military symbols and values to further youth recruitment. Conscription among the rival powers also ratcheted up the prospective scale and cost of a European war, although after 1914 the reality was far worse than anyone had anticipated. *See also* Railways.

FURTHER READING: Keegan, John. *The First World War.* New York: Alfred A. Knopf, 1999; Strachen, Hew. *The First World War.* New York: Oxford University Press, 2001.

CARL CAVANAGH HODGE

## Conservative Party

A political party of the United Kingdom that introduced the term *conservative* in its current meaning into the English language. The party was not commonly known by that name until the 1830s. It traces its roots through the antirevolutionary politics of William **Pitt** the Younger to the eighteenth-century oppositional or "country" Tory party, and thence to the Anglican and royalist successors to the cavaliers of the English Civil War. By the 1820s, however, egalitarian political reform was gaining wide support, even among some Tories, and those generally opposed to reform and supportive of Anglican and aristocratic privilege came to describe themselves as "conservatives." With the fracturing of Lord Grey's Whig administration after the 1832 Reform Act, the Tories of Sir Robert Peel were able to attract a wider body of supporters by styling themselves Conservatives rather than Tories.

By the late nineteenth century, the Conservative Party, as it came to be known, was associated with imperialism, but it had not always been so. In the middle years of the century, self-assertive foreign policies were more commonly associated with Lord Palmerston, and plans for imperial expansion were often put forward by radicals. The Liberals, however, were also partisans of colonial self-government and were accused by Conservative leader Benjamin **Disraeli** of plotting "the disintegration of the empire of England." Given at times to florid imperial rhetoric, Disraeli's administration of 1874–1880 managed to become embroiled in a series of wars in Afghanistan and South Africa, which opponents linked to what was beginning to be called "**imperialism.**" Disraeli's successor, Lord Salisbury, was able to use imperial feeling—and the parallel and far from unintended implication that the Liberals were lacking in imperial patriotism—to cement a broad-based "Conservative and Unionist" party. Imperialism, in the sense of support for the Empire, remained a key part of Conservative ideology through the 1950s, when the Suez crisis served to emphasize the extent of its costs and the paucity of its rewards.

FURTHER READING: Blake, Robert. *The Conservative Party from Peel to Churchill.* London: Eyre and Spottiswoode, 1970.

MARK F. PROUDMAN

## Continental System

A policy of economic strangulation intended by Napoleon I (see **Bonaparte, Napoleon**) to cause fatal disruption to British commercial activity and concomitant advantage to French trade and agriculture. Unable to defeat Britain by direct invasion, Napoleon set out this grandiose objective through the Berlin Decree of November 21, 1806, which declared the ports of continental Europe closed to British trade. The Continental System was partly a response to British Orders in Council of January 1807 and others thereafter, which applied sanctions on maritime trade with France. In reply, all British goods found in territories under French or French allied control were confiscated. After the Treaty of **Tilsit** with Russia in July 1807, Napoleon applied the system to Russian ports, from which considerable trade was carried on with Britain. In this respect the system began to have its intended effect. Napoleon issued the Fontainebleau Decree on October 13, 1807, followed by the First Milan Decree on November 23 to reinforce the Berlin Decrees. Harsher measures still came into force with a Second Milan Decree of December 1807, which authorized seizure of neutral vessels unless they could produce on demand a certificate indicating place of origin. If evidence showed that at any point in their journey they had docked at a British port, they were to be seized along with their entire cargo. Napoleon's Second Milan Decree stated that any neutral vessel that allowed British warships to stop and search it for contraband articles thereby lost its neutral status and could be confiscated as if it were British. Thus no vessel was free from the restrictions and depredations of either combatant; all nations, including the United States, found its maritime trade severely curtailed.

The system was effective in its early stages, but when it became clear that Spain and Portugal were evading its stipulations, Napoleon invaded the Iberian Peninsula, extending his conquests to an area over which he was never able to establish effective control and opening a theater of operations for the British. From 1810, moreover, Tsar Alexander began to flout the regulations, a course of action that ultimately led Napoleon to invade Russia two years later. The Continental System suffered from numerous flaws, not least that it was impossible for the French to monitor every continental port. The system proved unpopular with those over whom French rule extended, depressing economies and causing great resentment, especially in the Low Countries and the northern port towns along the Baltic. *See also* Napoleonic Wars; Nelson, Horatio; Peninsular War; Russian Empire.

FURTHER READING: Bergeron, Louis. *France under Napoleon*. Princeton, NJ: Princeton University Press, 1981; Broers, Michael. *Europe under Napoleon, 1799–1815*. London: Arnold, 1996; Ellis, Geoffrey J. *Continental Blockade: The Case of Alsace*. Oxford: Oxford University Press, 1989; Ellis, Geoffrey J. *The Napoleonic Empire*. Atlantic Highlands, NJ: Humanities Press International, 1991; Heckscher, E. F. *The Continental System: An Economic Interpretation*. Gloucester, MA: Peter Smith, 1964.

GREGORY FREMONT-BARNES

### Convention for the Amelioration of the Condition of the Wounded and Sick in Armed Forces in the Field

*See* Geneva Convention

### Convention of 1818

*See* Anglo-American Treaty

### Copenhagen, First Battle of (1801)

An early naval engagement of the Napoleonic Wars. Great Britain claimed the right to search neutral ships for what she considered inappropriate goods and even to confiscate them. This led Russian Tsar Paul I to get Denmark, Prussia,

Russia, and Sweden to form the League of **Armed Neutrality** of the North, a unity easier to obtain after the defeat of the Second Coalition. This move was a direct threat to Britain's attempted economic blockade of France and she was determined to act.

Of the League members, Denmark had the only significant naval force. Britain sent a force under Admiral Hyde-Parker of 26 ships-of-the-line, supported by a number of frigates and other smaller ships. Hyde-Parker was not particularly aggressive, but his second in command was Admiral Horatio **Nelson,** who was determined to destroy the Danish fleet. That fleet was anchored in an inner harbor and was well protected by coastal batteries and warships. While Hyde-Parker led an essentially diversionary move against the western front, Nelson took 12 ships-of-the-line and the support vessels against the main part of the Danish fleet. The battle raged all day, as Nelson pounded the center of the Danish line. Several ships ran aground and Hyde-Parker's effort to come in support of the attack was unsuccessful. The Danish flagship, *Dannebroge,* exploded, and one by one the Danish ships were silenced, if not boarded. Nelson's northern attack faltered, however, and to Hyde-Parker, who was watching from afar, it seemed that Nelson was losing. He signaled Nelson to withdraw, but Nelson was having none of it. He famously held his spyglass to his blind eye to "see" any signal, and the fighting continued. By late afternoon the British were winning, but both sides accepted a truce. Each side lost approximately 1,000 men. Denmark left the Armed Neutrality League, which in any event collapsed with the assassination of Tsar Paul on March 24, 1801. *See also* Copenhagen, Second Battle of.

FURTHER READING: Knight, Roger. *The Pursuit of Victory;* New York: Basic Books, 2005; Rodger, N.A.M. *The Command of the Ocean.* New York: W. W. Norton, 2004.

J. DAVID MARKHAM

## Copenhagen, Second Battle of (1807)

A naval engagement of the Napoleonic Wars that followed the defeat of the Fifth Coalition and that lasted from August 16 to September 5, 1807. Great Britain was harassing Danish ships and relations between the two nations were cool. Napoleonic France was courting an alliance with Denmark, and Great Britain, anticipating hostility, chose to strike preemptively against the Danish fleet. On September 2, Britain sent 25 ships-of-the-line and 29,000 soldiers against the Danish capital of Copenhagen. For two nights the city was attacked and bombarded. The largely wooden city was badly damaged and more than 2,000 of its citizens killed. Disheartened, the Danish government surrendered its 17-ship fleet and a large quantity of stores. Britain's military objectives were achieved, but they came at a high diplomatic and political cost. Most of Europe, as well as the United States, condemned her unilateral and illegal action and the opposition party at home was equally outraged. Napoleon took good advantage of this diplomatic disaster and gained both stature and adherents to his **Continental System.** *See also* Copenhagen, First Battle of; Tilsit, Treaty of.

FURTHER READING: Rodger, N.A.M. *The Command of the Ocean.* New York: W. W. Norton, 2004.

J. DAVID MARKHAM

### Corn Laws (1804, 1815)

British statutes that controlled the import and export of grains, the word *corn* being commonly used to denote a variety of basic food grains. The effect of the tariff on imports was to raise the price of food, but the 1804 law did not raise prohibitive opposition because of Britain's struggle against the **Continental System.** The Corn Law of 1815, however, was passed after the final defeat of Napoleon **Bonaparte** and was widely viewed as a duty to restrict the import of grain to protect the economic interests of the large landowners who dominated Parliament. Because it guaranteed enormous profits to agriculture while raising the price of food to the wage laborers of an industrializing economy, agitation against the 1815 Corn Law linked industrial interests and workers in a campaign for free trade and greater democracy. With the creation of the **Anti-Corn Law League** in 1839, Liberal reformers such as Richard **Cobden** tied their attack on protectionism to demands for both economic and constitutional reforms in Britain itself and in Britain's trading relationship with its empire.

FURTHER READING: Barnes, Donald Grove. *A History of the English Corn Laws, 1660–1846.* New York: A. M. Kelly, 1965.

CARL CAVANAGH HODGE

### Corunna, Battle of (1809)

Otherwise known as La Coruña, an early battle of the **Peninsular War.** British troops under the command of Sir John Moore were evacuated from Spain through the port of Corruna on the northwest coast. The evacuation began on January 14, but on January 15, a French army of 24,000 and 36 guns appeared at a point in the operation when Moore had fewer than 15,000 men and 12 guns left on land. Moore was killed in the action to beat off a French attempt at envelopment, and his successor command, Sir John Hope, led a gallant defense that inflicted heavy casualties on the French army under Marshal Nicolas Soult. Although the British expeditionary force was returned to England, it had lost immense quantities of material and had been forced to destroy almost all its horses. At this point the campaign on the Iberian Peninsula seemed a disaster. Anglo-Spanish relations were damaged, and Foreign Secretary George **Canning,** who had led Britain into the Peninsular War, faced a personal and political crisis. *See also* Wellington, Duke of.

FURTHER READING: Esdaile, Charles. *The Peninsular War.* London: Allen Lane, 2002.

CARL CAVANAGH HODGE

### CPR

*See* Canadian Pacific Railway

### Crete

An island on the eastern Mediterranean under the control of the **Ottoman Empire** since 1669 and a major battleground for the expansion of the newly independent

Greek state. The Cretans, Orthodox, and Muslims, the latter numbering 30 percent of the population, had lived relatively harmoniously for centuries, but the introduction of modernity resulted in nationalism coming to determine the response of the Orthodox Cretans to Ottoman rule.

Cretan revolts against Ottoman rule subsequently occurred, notably during the Greek War of Independence (1821–1829), but the Ottomans maintained control of the island until 1830. In that year, by agreement of the European powers, Crete was ceded to Egypt, which in 1840 returned control of the island to the Ottoman Empire. Thereafter, friction between the Orthodox and Muslim Cretans resulted in successive rebellions by the Christians. There was a revolt in 1858, but a more serious uprising occurred in 1866. **Greece** prepared for war and made an alliance with **Serbia,** but British pressure prevented Greek intervention and the revolt collapsed.

In October 1878, the Halepa Pact provided for an assembly with a Christian majority. But in the 1890s, insurrections led the Porte to strengthen Ottoman direct rule and suspend representative institutions. In 1896, a full-scale revolt was led by a Cretan Liberal, Eleutherios Venizelos, and the next year Greek forces intervened on behalf of the insurgents. The ensuing war between Greece and the Ottoman Empire was terminated in 1898 when British, Russian, Italian, and Austro-Hungarian battleships and marines arrived to force the Ottoman army out. Crete was granted autonomy within the Ottoman Empire and, under pressure from the European powers, Prince George of Greece was made high commissioner.

George was popular at first, but he became autocratic, and popular unrest, led by Venizelos, forced him to resign in 1906. Despite insistent Cretan demands for annexation to Greece and support for that from various European powers, namely France and Russia, the island remained an Ottoman possession under international protection until 1912. A Cretan uprising in March 1912 resulted in the establishment of an independent provisional government, with the delegates installed in the Greek parliament the following October. By the terms of the Treaty of London of 1913, which ended the First **Balkan War** between Greece—joined by Serbia, Bulgaria, Montenegro, and Romania—and the Ottoman Empire, the Ottomans formally ceded Crete to Greece. The Muslim minority initially remained on the island but was later relocated to Turkey under the general population exchange agreed to between Greece and Kemalist Turkey in the 1923 Treaty of Lausanne. *See also* Kemal Mustapha.

FURTHER READING: Dakin, D. *The Unification of Greece.* New York: St. Martin's 1972; Schurman, Jacob Gould. *The Balkan Wars, 1912–1913.* New York: Cosimo Classics, 2005.

ANDREKOS VARNAVA

## Crimean War (1853–1856)

A Great Power conflict occurring midway between the Napoleonic Wars and World War I; it pitted the **Ottoman Empire** and its allies Britain, France, and Sardinia against the **Russian Empire.** The war had many causes, among which were Russia's ambitions in the Balkans and its ostensible desire for Constantinople, Anglo-Russian tensions over central Asia and access to India, the British public's distaste for the tsar as a result of his role in repressing the revolutions of 1848, Louis Napoleon's desire to play a leading part in European power politics, and a series of obscure disputes about the status of Christians and their holy places in Palestine, then a part of the Ottoman Empire.

The latter disputes were the official *casus belli,* which led Russia to invade the Ottoman Balkan provinces in 1853. In November 1853, the Russian Black Sea fleet destroyed the Turkish Fleet at Sinope, which provoked a British ultimatum demanding the return to port of the Russian fleet. The British and their French allies declared war on Russia in March 1854. Allied forced landed in the Crimea in September of that year and advanced on Sebastopol. The allied armies shortly ran in troubles with supplies, disease, and the weather, notwithstanding initial victories. The episode of the charge of the Light Brigade at **Balaklava** in response to botched orders, immortalized by Tennyson, came to symbolize the incompetence of the army staff. The new technology of the **telegraph** and the presence of war correspondents brought the sufferings of the army rapidly to popular attention. Motivated by the descriptions of William Russell of the *Times,* Florence Nightingale led a party of nurses who reformed the infamous hospital at Scutari in Turkey, and impressed on the military authorities the importance of sanitation. A motion was made in the House of Commons for an inquiry into the conduct of the war in January 1855, as a result of which the government of Lord Aberdeen fell.

A government of a similar political complexion was formed under Lord **Palmerston,** who became prime minister for the first time with a mandate to prosecute the war with greater energy. Sebastopol was at length taken by a French assault in September 1855, a year after the allied troops had landed. Negotiations among the three major combatants resulted in the Treaty of Paris of March 1856, which in many ways restored the *status quo ante* with the qualification that the Black Sea was closed to warships. The Russians denounced the latter codicil in 1870, which is to say at the first opportunity. The Treaty of Paris was followed by the Declaration of Paris, which outlawed privateering, possibly the only enduring legal result of the Crimean war. The Crimean War had little effect on the expansion of European empires outside Europe. It did, however, mark the increasing importance of public opinion on the methods and conditions under which wars were waged. *See also:* Balkan Wars; Eastern Question.

FURTHER READING: Lambert, Andrew. *The Crimean War.* Manchester: Manchester University Press, 1990; Royle, Trevor. *Crimea: The Great Crimean War, 1854–56.* Basingstoke: Palgrave-Macmillian, 2004; Woodham-Smith, Cecil. *The Reason Why,* London: Readers' Union, 1957.

MARK F. PROUDMAN

## Croatia-Slavonia

A kingdom created in 1868 by merging the kingdoms of Croatia and Slavonia. It was part of the Greater Hungarian kingdom. The **Ausgleich** of 1867 strengthened Hungarian sovereignty, but Croatia-Slavonia retained a privileged position within the framework of the kingdom of Hungary. With a clear South Slav majority, Croatia-Slavonia's ethnic composition differed profoundly from Hungary proper. The strongest group were Catholic Croats, but there was a sizable Serbian community as well. The Nagodba (Compromise) of 1868 provided for cultural and limited political autonomy. Nevertheless, Hungarian efforts to undermine Croatian autonomy and a struggle between rival versions of Croatian and South-Slavic nationalism led to political instability in Croatia-Slavonia in the early twentieth century. *See also* Habsburg Empire; Pan-Slavism.

FURTHER READING: Kann, Robert A. *The Multinational Empire: Nationalism and National Reform in the Habsburg Monarchy, 1848–1918.* 2 vols. New York: Octagon Books, 1964; Mason, John W. *The Dissolution of the Austro-Hungarian Empire, 1867–1918.* London and New York: Longman 1985.

GUENTHER KRONENBITTER

## Cromer, Sir Evelyn Baring, First Earl of (1841–1917)

A British diplomat and longtime proconsul in **Egypt,** Evelyn Baring was a younger son of the Baring banking family. Baring was sent to the Royal Military Academy at Woolwich and then posted to the Mediterranean, where he focused on learning Greek and Italian. After passing out first from the Staff College in 1870, he went to the War Office where he worked for the abolition of commission purchase under his cousin Lord Northbrook, the Liberal peer and junior minister. When Northbrook went to **India** as Viceroy in 1872, Baring followed him as private secretary. Baring acquired a reputation for self-confidence to the point of arrogance—he was known in India as "over," as in over-Baring—and financial skill that led to his appointment as the British member of a commission on the Egyptian debt.

After the British occupation of Egypt in 1882, Baring went to Cairo, formally as British Consul, but in reality as a proconsul with final say over the policies of the Khedive's government. Baring—or Lord Cromer as he became in 1892—reconstructed the Egyptian army and civil service under the leadership of British officers and officials, worked with some success to put the country's finances, ruined by Khedivial excess, in order. Notwithstanding that the temporary occupation intended in 1882, Cromer and British opinion generally came to favor an extended British hold over Egypt, perhaps formalized as a protectorate, and often justified by the same kind of philanthropic rhetoric that had come to characterize the Raj. Following the death of General Gordon in the Sudan, Cromer temporized over future Anglo-Egyptian policy there, on the one hand wanting to preserve the prestige of the Khedive's government and restrain other European powers, while on the other fearing the expense and difficulty of a reconquest. After many hesitations, the British finally sent Horatio **Kitchener** all the way to Khartoum in 1898. Cromer designed the government of the "Anglo-Egyptian **Sudan**" so as to preserve the myth of Egyptian independence. Cromer's 1907 retirement from a long career as the ultimate authority in Egypt was marred by the scandal surrounding the Dinshawai incident of 1906, in which a number of Egyptians were hanged after an altercation with a party of British officers. In 1908, Cromer published *Modern Egypt,* a defense of his conduct there, and in 1910, *Ancient and Modern Imperialism,* a comparative study of imperialism that anticipated the work of modern scholars, especially in its remarks on imperialism and racial prejudice. Cromer presided over the 1916 commission of inquiry into the Dardanelles expedition and died the next year.

FURTHER READING: Cromer, Lord. *Ancient and Modern Imperialism.* London: John Murray, 1910; Owen, Roger. *Lord Cromer.* Oxford: University Press, 2004; Zetland, Marquess of. *Lord Cromer.* London: Hodder and Stoughton, 1932.

MARK F. PROUDMAN

## Cuba

The largest island of the Greater Antilles is located at the entrance to the Gulf of Mexico and the Caribbean Sea. Between 1511 and 1899, Cuba was part of Spain's overseas colonial empire. During the nineteenth century, Cubans repeatedly struggled for independence of their island from the increasingly oppressive imperial center. The resulting Ten Years' War (1868–1878) produced limited political reforms but caused widespread destruction and damage to foreign, in particular American investments. Beginning in the 1820s, the **United States** had become a powerful commercial and cultural presence on the island and replaced Spain by mid-century as Cuba's most important trading partner with powerful investments in sugar, coffee, tobacco, iron ore and copper, railroads, telegraphs, and public utilities. This bilateral relationship, described by President William **McKinley** as "ties of singular intimacy," held special significance for both sides: Americans were attracted to Cuba for geostrategic and commercial reasons. Many regarded the island as a "natural appendage" to the United States and several administrations since the presidency of James Madison made repeated unsuccessful attempts to purchase the island from Spain. Many Cubans were equally attracted to American political freedoms, economic power, and popular culture, whereas others feared domination by the United States. The annexationists hoped to defend their own social and political status through further integration with the United States; the interventionists worked for ultimate independence after a transitional period of U.S. control; the nationalists were repelled by North American contempt for Hispanic culture and wanted complete independence from Spain and the United States.

Cuban rejection of Spanish rule resulted in two wars. Whereas the Ten Year's War prompted tightened Spanish rule, the Cuban War of Independence (1895–1898) culminated with the U.S. intervention of 1898, ended Spanish colonial rule in 1899, and enabled the creation of a semi-sovereign Cuban Republic in 1902. The reasons for American military intervention of 1898 that resulted in the **Spanish-American War,** dubbed "the splendid little war" by Ambassador John Hay, encompassed public outrage over the brutal oppression of the Cuban population, in particular the strategy of forced removals, *reconcentrado,* initiated by General Valeriano Weyler y Nicolau; the fear of geostrategic instability in the Caribbean; the explosion of the *U.S.S. Maine* in Havana harbor, blamed on Spanish sabotage; and the desire to protect American commercial investments.

As the Teller Amendment to the U.S. declaration of war prohibited annexation and limited military occupation to Cuba's pacification, Americans developed alternative strategies for continued effective control over the island. The military occupation ended in 1902 after American troops had disbanded the Cuban revolutionary army, worked on infrastructure improvements, and laid the foundations for health and educational reforms. Through the **Platt Amendment** of 1901, which became part of the Cuban constitution, and the U.S.-Cuban Treaty of 1903, the United States reserved intervention rights, control over Cuban foreign and economic affairs, and base rights at Guantánamo Bay. Between 1906 and 1909, Cuba, which had effectively become a U.S. **protectorate,** was again placed under American military occupation with additional military interventions in 1912 and 1917. *See also* Monroe Doctrine; Roosevelt, Theodore; Spanish-American War.

FURTHER READING: Ferrer, Ada. *Insurgent Cuba: Race, Nation, and Revolution, 1868–1898.* Chapel Hill: University of North Carolina Press, 1999; Hernández, José M. *Cuba and the United States: Intervention and Militarism, 1868–1933.* Austin: University of Texas Press, 1993; Pérez, Louis A., Jr. *The War of 1898: The United States and Cuba in History and Historiography.* Chapel Hill: University of North Carolina Press, 1998; Pérez, Louis A., Jr. *Cuba and the United States: Ties of Singular Intimacy.* Athens: University of Georgia Press, 1997; Pérez, Louis A., Jr. *Cuba under the Platt Amendment, 1902–1934.* Pittsburgh: University of Pittsburgh Press, 1986.

FRANK SCHUMACHER

## Cuban Reciprocity Treaty (1902)

A treaty reducing tariff barriers between the **United States** and the newly independent Republic of Cuba by 20 percent or more and successfully binding the Cuban economy to the United States. Since as early as 1899, representatives of the United States military government in Cuba had called for trade reciprocity as a way to rebuild the agricultural sector of the Cuban economy destroyed by the Cuban Revolution. Initial efforts met with stiff resistance in the U.S. Congress where representatives of the American Beet Sugar Association successfully countered a massive lobbying campaign organized by Military Governor Leonard **Wood,** Cuban sugar interests, and the American Sugar Refining Company. Efforts to pass legislation to lower the tariff and to ratify the treaty failed in 1902. Intense pressure from President Theodore **Roosevelt,** changes in the world economic situation, and the buyout of many in the beet sugar industry by the American Sugar Refining Company, allowed the treaty to pass in 1903. The treaty succeeded in binding the Cuban economy, primarily depended on agricultural products like sugar, to the American manufacturing economy.

FURTHER READING: Healy, David. *The United States in Cuba, 1898–1902: Generals, Politicians, and the Search for Policy.* Madison: University of Wisconsin Press, 1963.

JAMES PRUITT

## Curzon, George Nathaniel, Marquess Curzon of Kedleston (1859–1925)

Viceroy of **India** and British foreign secretary, Curzon was a younger son of an ancient Norman family, and always had a burning desire to add luster to his family's name by conspicuous political achievement. Educated at Eton and Balliol College, Oxford, he had numerous connections to England's political elite. Curzon, however, acquired an early fascination with Asia and used that interest as a basis for his political career. He spent a number of years traveling in central and eastern Asia, explored the sources of the River Oxus, and published a series of respected volumes on Persia, central Asia, and the Far East.

First elected to Parliament as a member of the **Conservative Party** in 1886, he briefly held office as undersecretary for India in 1891–1892, where he supervised the passage through the Commons of the India Councils Bill, a first halting step to representative government in that country. After serving from 1895 to 1898 as undersecretary to the Foreign Office under Lord **Salisbury,** also prime minister, in

1899 he was made viceroy of India. It was as viceroy that Curzon made his name as the epitome of the ostentatious imperial governor, at the same time justifying his position by the improvements, moral and material, conferred on the governed. But through his ham-handed attempt to partition **Bengal,** the power base of the emerging Indian National Congress, Curzon also acquired a reputation as the enemy of Indian self-government. Leaving India under a cloud created by a long-running bureaucratic battle with Lord Horatio **Kitchener,** commander of the Indian Army, Curzon's political career appeared over.

He returned to active politics, however, in the wartime coalition cabinet of 1915, and in 1916 joined David Lloyd George's war cabinet. In 1919, he became foreign secretary, in which post he negotiated the Dawes plan concerning postwar reparations, the withdrawal of the French from the Ruhr, and the 1923 Treaty of Lausanne with Turkey, one of the most enduring of the post-World War I treaties. Curzon expected to be asked to form a government on the 1923 resignation of Andrew Bonar Law, but he was passed over, in part because he sat in the House of Lords, in favor of Stanley Baldwin.

FURTHER READING: Dilks, David. *Curzon in India.* New York; Taplinger, 1970; Gilmour, Ian. *Curzon: Imperial Statesman.* London: John Murray, 1994; Zetland, Lord. *Life of Lord Curzon.* 3 vols. New York: Boni and Liveright, 1928.

MARK F. PROUDMAN

## Custoza, Battles of (1849, 1866)

Two engagements in the Italian Wars of Independence that occurred at Custoza in eastern Lombardy, southwest of Verona and south of the Lake Garda (Lago di Garda). During the Revolution of 1848, Italian nationalists, striving to establish an Italian nation state, tried to get rid of Austrian rule over most of northern **Italy.** The kingdom of **Piedmont-Sardinia** took the lead in those efforts in 1849. In the First Battle of Custoza on July 24, 1849, the troops of Piedmont-Sardinia were defeated by the Austrians under Field Marshall Count Radetzky. As a result of this victory, the **Habsburg Empire** was able to reestablish control over Lombardy and northeastern Italy, but nationalist leanings and resentment against Austrian rule were common in northern Italy throughout the 1850s.

With French support, Sardinia defeated Austria in 1859 and formed an Italian nation-state at Austria's expense. In 1866, an alliance with Prussia was formed to complete the expulsion of Austria from Italy. On June 24, 1866, the Italian army under King **Victor Emmanuel** II was beaten by Austrian forces under Archduke Albrecht of Austria despite Italian superiority in numbers. Like the naval Battle of Lissa, the second Austrian victory at Custoza was of political insignificance because Austria had already agreed to hand over Venetia to Italy and had no choice but to honor this obligation after the crushing defeat against Italy's ally Prussia at the Battle of **Königgrätz.** *See also* Austro-Prussian War.

FURTHER READING: Holmes, George, ed. *The Oxford History of Italy.* New York: Oxford University Press, 1997.

GUENTHER KRONENBITTER

## Cyprus

An island of 3,572 square miles off the coast of Turkey in the eastern Mediterranean. The British Conservative government of Benjamin **Disraeli** occupied Cyprus in 1878 by virtue of the Anglo-Turkish Convention, which aimed to protect the Ottoman Empire from further Russian attack after the 1877–1878 Russo-Turkish War, but protecting the Ottoman Empire was incidental to the aim of safeguarding British financial and strategic interests in the Near East and India. Disraeli's government perceived that Cyprus, with its central location and special place in the imperial imagination as a strategic base for various Crusades and the Venetians, would become a British stronghold. But neither his nor Gladstone's Liberal government made any effort to make Cyprus into a military or naval station. Within months of occupying Cyprus, most of the 10,000 strong army of occupation was withdrawn after the troops contracted fever from the summer heat and insalubrity of the plains. The Liberals and numerous naval experts criticized the selection of Cyprus because the island lacked a harbor. The port of Famagusta on the east coast was clogged, needed a breakwater, and was unhealthy. The Conservative government postponed the work.

When the Liberals came to power in 1880, they set in motion the future course of Cyprus until 1915. The island was run on the cheap to divert the tribute due to the Porte to pay for the defaulted 1855 loan repayments guaranteed by London and Paris. Consequently, expenditure on public works was curbed. There was a change only after Joseph Chamberlain became colonial secretary in 1895 and embarked on an expensive program of improving sericulture, agriculture, and irrigation; constructing a railway; and improving the inner harbor at Famagusta. The success of the works was mixed and had no aim to alter the place of Cyprus in the strategic structure of the Empire. This position was fixed in 1888 when the Colonial Defence Committee established that Cyprus was not worth defending and was indeed a defense liability. It accordingly advocated the removal of the British garrison, which was subsequently reduced, first by a Conservative government in 1892 and then by the Liberal government in 1895. Subsequent efforts to remove all of it failed because the Colonial and Foreign Offices were concerned about the rise of Geek nationalism and the potential clashes that may result from calls within the island to unite Cyprus to **Greece.**

The population of Cyprus, which was 74 percent Orthodox Christian and 24.5 percent Muslim in 1881, was multicultural during Ottoman rule, but by 1912 British policy had allowed for the rise of Greek nationalism to divide the population into a multinational society. The Cypriots were integrated during Ottoman rule: the Cypriot hierarchy and governing councils comprised Orthodox and Muslims. The peasants shared economic hardships; a language based on a mixture of dialects, various Greek, Ottoman, Medieval French and Venetian; a folklore; and interacted socially, even intermarrying. Between 1850 and 1890, mixed villages increased by more than 100. The British, who rejected occupying Crete because of the threat of Greek nationalism there, failed to maintain the structures that had produced this multicultural society. They rejected coopting an Orthodox Church willing to work with them and desirous of preserving Orthodox-Muslim integration, because such a relationship conflicted with modern ideas of civil government. Cyprus, unlike most other possessions where cooption had been practiced, was perceived as being on the European periphery. Hence, the island received a legislative council in 1882 that had a local majority, *Katharevousa*. An artificially created version of Greek adopted by the Greek state was accepted for government business, English was not introduced to schools, and the nationalist curricula of Greece were adopted. Furthermore, because early opposition was minor, the British did nothing to curb the rising agitation of a small but vociferous group of Greek nationals and local Cypriots imbued in the Hellenic ideal, which instilled fear in the Muslim community. In 1912, the Orthodox and Muslim Cypriots clashed in Nicosia and Limassol and the garrison and reinforcements from Egypt were called in.

By 1912, Cyprus had become unviable economically, politically, and strategically to the extent that the Liberal government of Herbert **Asquith** wanted to cede the island to Greece. Winston **Churchill,** then the first lord of the admiralty, along with David Lloyd George, made such a proposal to the prime minister of Greece, Eleutherios Venizelos, in 1912. The context was the protection of British interests in the eastern Mediterranean after much of the British naval presence was withdrawn to the western Mediterranean and the Atlantic to combat the rising German threat. Churchill wanted to give Cyprus to Greece in exchange for being allowed to establish a naval base at Argostoli Harbor on the island of Cephallonia in the Ionian Sea to block the Austro-Hungarian fleet. Talks were postponed because of the instability in the Balkans stemming from the Balkan Wars and the outbreak of World War I. *See also* British Empire; Eastern Question; Royal Navy.

FURTHER READING: Alastros, Doros. *Cyprus in History.* London: Zeno, 1955; Halil, Salih Ibrahim. *Cyprus: The Impact of Diverse Nationalism on a State.* Mobile: University of Alabama Press, 1978.

ANDREKOS VARNAVA

# D

## Dalhousie, George Ramsay, Ninth Earl of Dalhousie (1770–1838)

Governor-general of **Canada** from 1891 to 1828, Dalhousie served extensively in the Napoleonic wars, rising to the rank of lieutenant-general during the Peninsular campaign. In 1816, he was appointed lieutenant-governor of Nova Scotia, where his support for nonsectarian education led to the founding of the university that now bears his name, on the model of the University of Edinburgh. Appointed governor-general of Canada in 1819, he fell into quarrels with French-Canadian politicians about the prerogatives of the executive and control of finances. His aggressive intervention in a local election led Colonial Secretary William Huskisson to transfer Dalhousie to India, where he served as commander-in-chief of the army.

FURTHER READING: McInnis, E. W. *Canada A Political and Social History.* Toronto: Holt, Rinehart and Winston, 1970.

MARK F. PROUDMAN

## Dalhousie, James Andrew Broun Ramsay, First Marquess of Dalhousie (1812–1860)

Son of the ninth Earl of Dalhousie, James, first marquess of Dalhousie, was educated at Harrow and Christ Church, Oxford. He became a convinced Tory. Elected to Parliament in 1837, he joined the cabinet of Sir Robert Peel as president of the Board of Trade in 1845. After the fall of Peel, he refused an offer to join Russell's government. Russell appointed Dalhousie governor-general of **India,** where he served from 1848 to 1856. Dalhousie pursued a policy of internal economic modernization and external expansion within what were called the natural frontiers of India. He energetically pushed **railway** and **telegraph** building, within the limits of the **East India Company**'s finances, and made it a matter of policy that the law should apply equally to all, regardless of religion. Externally, under Dalhousie, the Sikhs were defeated and the Punjab annexed, and the doctrine of "lapse," which stated that Indian states without a clear succession should come under company rule, was enunciated. Dalhousie's annexation of Oudh, along with the rapid modernization he set in motion, has been blamed for the mutiny that followed shortly after his departure from the subcontinent. *See also* Burma; Indian Mutiny.

FURTHER READING: Lee-Warner, William. *The Life of the Marquis of Dalhousie K. T.* Shannon: Irish University Press, 1972.

MARK F. PROUDMAN

## Danish West Indies

Also known as the Danish Virgin Islands, these islands in the northeastern Caribbean's Lesser Antilles accounted for all the Danish New World colonies. They consisted of settlements on the islands of Saint Thomas (28 square miles), Saint John (20 square miles), and Saint Croix (84 square miles). The Ciboney, an Arawak-speaking people, first inhabited the islands. Around 1300, the Caribs migrated to the islands of the Caribbean Sea from northeastern South America. Caribs had conquered the Lesser Antilles when Christopher Columbus and his crew became the first Europeans to visit the Caribbean.

During the seventeenth century, the Virgin Islands were divided between **Denmark** and Britain, although the British occupied the Danish islands from 1801–1802 and 1807–1815. Denmark's first settlement on Saint Thomas in 1655 failed. In 1670, Christian V ascended to the thrown of Denmark and Norway. The next year, the new king chartered the West India Company in Copenhagen to resettle Saint Thomas. In May 1672, Governor Jorgen Iversen arrived with settlers, many of whom were indentured servants and convicts, and established the town of Charlotte Amalie, named in honor of the wife of King Christian V.

Company land grants attracted immigrants and a lucrative plantation economy emerged. Most were not Danes, but other Europeans, including Dutch, English, and French settlers. The planters' labor needs were met by importing African slaves, the first slave ship bringing 103 Africans in 1673. African slaves, who vastly outnumbered Europeans in the Danish West Indies, primarily produced sugar, along with cotton, indigo, and tobacco. In 1674, the company changed its name to the West India and Guinea Company, reflecting merged Danish interests in both West Indian and African colonies. The company claimed Saint John in 1684 but did not settle it with colonists and slaves from Saint Thomas until 1718.

Saint Thomas opened its harbor in 1724 to the flags of all nations and subsequently thrived as a free port trading center. Saint John also became a free port 40 years later. Slave-cultivated agricultural commodities remained the basis of the Danish West Indies' prosperity throughout the eighteenth and early nineteenth centuries. Dependence on slave labor was problematic and authorities brutally suppressed several slave revolts. Newly arrived slaves from the West African kingdom of Akwamu led the most infamous rebellion, which destroyed a quarter of Saint John's plantations in November 1733. That same year, Denmark purchased Saint Croix from France.

Convinced by private investors' arguments that the company monopoly was no longer necessary to colonize the West Indies and was impeding the nation's economic progress, the Danish government bought out the shareholders and liquidated the company in 1754. The following year, the Danish Crown took over administration of the islands. Crown rule increased economic prosperity. Freed of the company's monopoly, planters could now sell their products at higher free-market prices. A Lutheran mission under the national church of Denmark was also created after the establishment of Crown rule.

Slavery in the Danish West Indies accounted for nearly 90 percent of the total population from the 1750s to the 1830s. The slave population peaked at 35,000 in 1802, the year before abolition of the slave trade restricted the slave supply, despite persistent illegal importation. An ordinance in June 1839 provided for free and compulsory education in the islands for both freepersons and slaves. Literacy became a distinctive feature of the Danish West Indies thanks to state support, the Lutheran Church, Moravian missionaries, and black educators.

Only those considered white could vote and hold office before April 1834, when a royal decree granted all "free people of color" the status of citizens, allowing them full legal and economic rights. In 1847, King Christian VIII issued a decree of free birth and declared the emancipation of all slaves in 12 years. Thousands of impatient slaves gathered in Frederiksted, Saint Croix in July 1848 to demand immediate freedom under the leadership of the slave Moses Gottlieb, also known as General Buddhoe. Consequently, the startled Governor-General Peter von Scholten issued an emancipation proclamation on July 3, 1848, which the Crown soon confirmed; however, financial qualifications continued to restrict the franchise to economically privileged men.

The Labor Act of 1849, which regulated and restrained the newly freed workers, established a system of yearly contract labor to replace slave labor. Opposition to the system erupted into violence on contract day in Frederiksted on October 1, 1878. Protesters pillaged and burned homes and shops in town, along with plantations and cane fields in the countryside. Mary Thomas, hailed as Queen Mary by her supporters, was one of the leaders of the rebellion, which led authorities to abolish the act and allow contract negotiation. The first labor union in the islands was organized by D. Hamilton Jackson in 1915.

Profits from plantations, commerce, and shipping dwindled in the Danish West Indies after the mid-nineteenth century. In 1850, Denmark ceded its properties in West Africa to Great Britain. Continuous budget deficits bolstered economic arguments in Denmark for selling the Danish West Indies to the United States, which first became interested in buying them during the American Civil War. Denmark desired to sell the islands for economic reasons, whereas the United States wished to purchase them for strategic purposes. The United States sought the islands as a naval base for controlling the sea lanes between the Panama Canal, which opened in 1914, and southern U.S. ports and Europe. Fearing that Germany would acquire control over the islands during World War I, the United States paid $25 million for the Danish West Indies. Formal transfer of the islands, henceforth known as the United States Virgin Islands, took place in March 1917. The islands have the distinction of being the most expensive land acquisition in the history of the United States.

FURTHER READING: Boyer, William W. *America's Virgin Islands: A History of Human Rights and Wrongs.* Durham, NC: Carolina Academic Press, 1983; Creque, Darwin D. *The U.S. Virgins and the Eastern Caribbean.* Philadelphia: Whitmore Publishing Company, 1968; Dookhan, Isaac. *A History of the Virgin Islands of the United States.* Epping: Caribbean Universities Press, 1974; Hall, Neville A. T. *Slave Society in the Danish West Indies: St. Thomas, St. John, and St. Croix.* Baltimore: Johns Hopkins University Press, 1992; Paquette, Robert L., and Stanley L. Engerman, eds. *The Lesser Antilles in the Age of European Expansion.* Gainesville: University Press of Florida, 1996; Taylor, Charles Edwin. *Leaflets from the Danish West Indies.* Westport, CT: Negro Universities Press, 1970.

DAVID M. CARLETTA

## Danubian Principalities

Moldavia and Wallachia, located astride the mouth of the Danube River where it empties into the Black Sea, were known as the Danubian Principalities. They were provinces of the **Ottoman Empire** from the thirteenth century, were occupied by Russia during the Russo-Turkish War of 1768–1774, but were recovered in the Treaty of Kuchuk-Kainardji in 1774. The Porte nonetheless acknowledged Russia's right to intervene in the principalities on behalf of the Christian peoples living there. This Russian protectorate over Danubian Christians led to occupation from 1829 to 1834 and had the effect of making them autonomous. Russia intervened again in 1848 to put down a nationalist vote in Wallachia and in 1853 reoccupied them to apply pressure on the Ottoman Empire during the diplomatic dispute that ultimately led to the **Crimean War.**

From 1854 to 1857, the Principalities were occupied by Austria to keep peace on the Lower Danube between the Ottoman and **Russian Empire**s. Russia sought to make the provinces formal protectorates, but in 1856 the Treaty of Paris gave a Great Power guarantee to their continuing autonomy. In 1858, they merged into Rumania yet remained within the Ottoman Empire until the Treaty of San Stefano concluding the Russo-Turkish War of 1877–1878 made them fully independent. *See also* Eastern Question.

FURTHER READING: Duggan, Stephen. *The Eastern Question: A Study in Diplomacy.* New York: AMS Press, 1970; Hitchins, Keith. *Rumania, 1866–1947.* Oxford: Clarendon Press, 1994.

CARL CAVANAGH HODGE

## Dardanelles

A waterway connecting the Aegean Sea with the Sea of Marmara and separating Europe from the Asian mainland. In the eighteenth century, Russia emerged as the major antagonist of the Ottoman Empire, in part because of the desire to dominate the Black Sea and have access to the Mediterranean Sea. The question of the Dardanelle Straits thus became important strategically.

Control of passage through the Dardanelles was an Ottoman prerogative so long as the Black Sea remained its lake, but when Russia gained a foothold there in 1774, the rules governing passage became contested. As a consequence of the Ottoman Empire's defeat in the Russo-Turkish War of 1828–1829, St Petersburg forced the Porte to sign the Treaty of **Inkiar Skelessi** in 1833, which closed the straits to warships of countries other than those of Russia.

The treaty alarmed the other European governments, especially the British, who feared the consequences of Russian expansion in the Mediterranean. The British government saw its chance to overturn Russia's advantage and joined the Ottomans to defeat Muhammad Ali, the ruler of Egypt, whose armies threatened the disintegration of the **Ottoman Empire.** The successful military intervention of European powers resulted in the **London Straits Convention** in July 1841, where Russia agreed that only Ottoman warships could traverse the Dardanelles in peacetime. Consequently, the Ottoman government let the British and French fleets through the straits to attack the Crimea during the **Crimean War** in 1853. The Congress of Paris in 1856 reaffirmed the London Straits Convention, and it remained theoretically in force into the twentieth century, although it was broken numerous times, notably by the British in 1878.

During World War I the Entente Powers tried to seize the Dardanelles in an effort to knock the Ottoman Empire out of the conflict, but they failed. Winston **Churchill,** the First Lord of the Admiralty, strongly advocated the attack over the expedition on Alexandretta favored by War Secretary Lord **Kitchener.** The failure damaged Churchill's career. Sir Ian Hamilton's Mediterranean Expeditionary Force failed to capture the Gallipoli peninsula and a withdrawal was ordered in January 1916. *See also* Eastern Question; Russian Empire.

FURTHER READING: Anderson, M. S. *The Eastern Question, 1774–1923: A Study in International Relations.* London: Macmillan, 1966; Macfie, A. L. *The Eastern Question, 1774–1923.* New York; Longman, 1996.

ANDREKOS VARNAVA

## Darwin, Charles (1809–1882)

The immensely influential theorist of evolution, Charles Darwin was the grandson of the biologist Erasmus Darwin and was descended on his mother's side from the Wedgwood pottery family, which made him independently wealthy. After failing to do well in medicine, Darwin was educated in theology at Cambridge, being intended by his family for a clerical career. He had always been fascinated by botany and zoology, however, and was recommended by one of his Cambridge tutors as a naturalist on the proposed expedition of HMS *Beagle.* The *Beagle's* mission was hydrographic, and Darwin went along as a supernumerary, thus giving him considerable time during the five-year voyage from 1831 to 1836 to explore and to collect zoological, botanical, and geological specimens. Darwin published a significant number of scientific articles as a result of the voyage, along with a memoir.

Darwin's numerous writings made him famous in the scientific world, and he became a member of, among others, the Athenaeum, the Royal Society and the Linnean Society. Dating back to his voyage on the *Beagle,* Darwin had suspected that both continents and species changed over time, an idea shared by many contemporary naturalists and geologists. He found in Thomas Malthus's *Essay on Population* the theory of competition for resources that he needed to explain change in species. Darwin also supported his theorization with experiments on the breeding of plants and animals. Friends put him in touch with A. R. Wallace, who had contemporaneously come to similar conclusions about species change, and the two wrote simultaneous papers for the Linnean Society in 1858. The next year, Darwin published his epochal *Origin of Species*. In 1871, Darwin published *The Descent of Man*, which applied his ideas to the evolution of humans, although he was by no means the first to do so.

For much of his life in frail health, Darwin was not a controversialist, and he left public polemics to supporters such as T. H. "Darwin's bulldog" Huxley, himself taking refuge in botanical researches. Darwin was, from his earliest years, opposed to slavery and believed that all humans were essentially biologically the same; indeed he went so far in egalitarianism as to note the similarity of human and animal suffering. In religion he was basically a liberal Anglican, although his faith weakened later in life and his precise religious and political views have been controversial. He would not have recognized some of the more bellicose and dogmatic among the ideas that came to be called "Darwinism," especially in its more extreme social Darwinist variants. *See also* Social Darwinism.

FURTHER READING: Browne, Janet. *Charles Darwin*, 2 vols. London: Jonathan Cape, 1995–2002; Himmelfarb, Gertrude. *Darwin and the Darwinian Revolution*. New York, W. W. Norton, 1968.

MARK F. PROUDMAN

## David, Jacques Louis (1748–1825)

One of the greatest of the French neoclassicist painters. Among his most famous works, the *Oath of the Horatii,* completed in 1784, idealized the classical virtues of stoicism and masculine patriotism and established a severe yet seductive aesthetic David applied to his support for the French Revolution, most effectively in his *Death of Marat* painted in 1793. A supporter of Maximilien Robespierre, who voted for the execution of Louis XVI, David was imprisoned by the Directory but saved by the intervention of his estranged wife. Less a committed revolutionary than an avid propagandist for the heroes of his age, David promptly transferred his loyalty to Napoleon **Bonaparte** after 1799 and produced, in works such as *Napoleon Crossing the Saint Bernard* and the *Sacre de Joséphine,* the opulent and romantic image for which the first military genius and tyrant of modern times is remembered. It is, indeed, no exaggeration to say that the subsequent idealized legacy of **Bonapartism** to French politics was in part the work of David's brush.

FURTHER READING: Brookner, Anita. *Romanticism and Its Discontents*. New York: Viking, 2000; Honour, Hugh. *Neo-Classicism*. Harmondsworth: Penguin, 1975.

CARL CAVANAGH HODGE

## Deák, Ferenc (1803–1876)

A Hungarian statesman, Ferenc Deák was born in Söjtör, **Hungary,** in October 1803. His father belonged to the landowning elite of Hungary. Ferenc Deák studied law, joined the civil service, and became a member of the Hungarian Diet for the first time in 1833. As a leader of the reform movement, Deák grew to political prominence. The Revolution of 1848 led to a new independent Hungarian ministry, and

Deák served in this government as minister of justice and was therefore responsible for drafting the "April Laws" of 1848, the legal basis for Hungarian independence under a Habsburg king. He left government in September 1848 and his political career suffered a severe setback in the aftermath of Hungarian defeat in the war against Austria in 1849.

In the following decade of neoabsolutist rule, Deák was the leader of the opposition in Hungary and played a decisive role in the negotiations with the Viennese authorities that finally led to the **Ausgleich** of 1867. The reestablishment of Hungarian independence within the framework of the Dual monarchy was the major achievement of Deák and his supporters. He died in Budapest in January 1876. *See also* Austria-Hungary; Habsburg Empire.

FURTHER READING: Kann, Robert A. *A History of the Habsburg Empire, 1526–1918.* Berkeley: University of California Press, 1974; Sinor, Denis. *History of Hungary.* Westport, CT: Greenwood, 1976.

GUENTHER KRONENBITTER

## Decembrists (1825)

A group of Russian nobles who staged a failed coup d'état. During the first half of **Alexander I**'s reign, Russia's educated elite, encouraged by the tsar's liberal tendencies, had high hopes for the possibility of reform. These intellectuals, many of them military officers, had been educated in the ideas of the Enlightenment. After Napoleon **Bonaparte**'s invasion of 1812, many had experienced life in the West during Russia's subsequent invasion of France and became aware that Russia's political system and social structure were exceedingly conservative and repressive. When Alexander became more conservative after 1812, they formed secret societies that eventually discussed overthrowing the monarchy. When Alexander died in December 1825, confusion over succession to the throne gave the Decembrists the perfect opportunity to stage their coup. The new tsar, **Nicholas I,** hesitated but finally used force and crushed the rebellion. Many of the participants were exiled and five were hanged. *See also* Russian Empire.

FURTHER READING: Mazour, Anatole G. *The First Russian Revolution, 1825—The Decembrist Movement: Its Origins, Development, and Significance.* Berkeley: University of California Press, 1937; Pomper, Philip. *The Russian Revolutionary Intelligentsia.* Arlington Heights, IL: Harlan Davidson, 1970.

LEE A. FARROW

## Delcassé, Théophile (1852–1923)

A French journalist and statesman, Théophile Delcassé may be regarded as the founder of the Third Republic's strategic diplomacy. Elected to the Chamber of Deputies in 1889, he held various cabinet posts throughout his distinguished career in government. Delcassé was a staunch supporter of France's colonial ambitions, and as minister of colonies authorized Marchand's expedition to Fashoda. He is also known for his diplomatic efforts to cordon off the German Reich through a system of alliances.

As Minister of Foreign Affairs between 1898 and 1905, he labored to tighten the Franco-Russian alliance and was instrumental to the signing of the Anglo-French **Entente Cordiale** in 1904. He was criticized by his opponents for his uncompromising and allegedly bellicose anti-German policy and was forced to resign on June 6, 1905, in the midst of the **Moroccan Crisis** and its attending rumors of war. As naval minister from 1911 to 1913, Delcassé worked to strengthen Anglo-French naval cooperation, particularly in the Mediterranean, in anticipation of war. *See also* Africa, Scramble for; French Empire.

FURTHER READING: Andrew, Christopher M. *Théophile Delcassé and the Making of the Entente Cordiale: A Reappraisal of French Foreign Policy, 1898–1905.* London: Macmillan, 1968; Zorgbibe, Charles. *Delcassé: le grand ministre des Affaires étrangères de la IIIe République.* Paris: Olbia, 2001.

SERGE RICARD

## Delhi, Battle of (1803)

A key battle of the Second **Maratha War** in **India.** When war broke out between the Marathas and the British **East India Company** in August 1803, General Louis Bourquein took command of the French-trained Maratha infantry in north India. Bourquein decided for a battle near Delhi on the bank of the Hindun River, a tributary of the Jamuna. He deployed 100 guns for support of the infantry. To prevent any outflanking move by the company's cavalry, the two flanks of the Maratha line rested on marshes. When, on September 11, 1803, General Gerald Lake, commander of the company's force in north India, discovered the Maratha position on the bank of Hindun, his infantry was still half a mile in the rear. Lake needed to buy some time to allow his infantry to come up. So he ordered his cavalry to charge the Maratha line. When the Maratha artillery opened fire, Lake's cavalry turned back.

The Marathas believed that the company's troops were retiring in confusion and left their entrenchments to come out in pursuit. Lake immediately ordered his cavalry to turn back and charge the Maratha infantry. The Maratha infantry, in their eagerness to attack, had broken ranks. Now they were disordered as a result of the sudden counterattack of Lake's cavalry. At that juncture, the company's infantry arrived. As they advanced, Maratha artillery opened up with grape and chain shot. When the infantry advanced within 100 yards of the Maratha artillery line, they bought their muskets at their shoulder level and fired a volley. After firing, they charged with their bayonets at the Marathas who broke and ran. Lake's army suffered 485 casualties and the Marathas lost more than 1,500 men. The Marathas vacated the fort of Delhi, and on September 15, Lake occupied it without opposition.

FURTHER READING: Cooper, Randolf G. S. *The Anglo Maratha Wars and the Contest for India.* New York: Cambridge University Press, 2003.

KAUSHIK ROY

## Delhi, Siege of (1857)

A grinding and bloody engagement of the **Indian Mutiny.** On May 11, 1857, the Third Cavalry rebelled at Meerut and started for Delhi. The next morning the troopers entered Delhi, cut down the British garrison, and proclaimed Bahadur Shah as Emperor. General Henry William Barnard the commander-in-chief of India cobbled up a force and, on June 5, reached Alipur, 10 miles from Delhi. On June 7, Brigadier Archdale Wilson's Meerut Brigade crossed the Jamuna River and joined Barnard's force. Then they took up position before Delhi.

The commander of the rebel army at Delhi was Bakht Khan, an ex-subedar, a rank equivalent of sergeant in the Indian army, of the British East India Company's artillery. The city of Delhi situated on the right bank of the Jamuna was surrounded on the north, west, and southern sides by a stone wall that was five and half miles long. The wall on the eastern side of Delhi was two miles long and ran parallel to the river. The wall was 24 feet high and around it ran a dry ditch 25 feet wide and 25 feet deep. The rebel guns of Delhi bombarded the British batteries constructed by the Punjabi sappers. The rebels repeatedly launched infantry attacks for capturing the British outposts, but they were turned back by grape shot.

With the arrival of the siege train in front of Delhi on September 7 1857, the company's troops numbered 12,588. On September 14, 1857, after intense bombardment by 18 and 24 pounder guns, the company's soldiers organized in four columns and assaulted Delhi, held by 30,000 rebels. Inside Delhi, the fighting was furious. The narrow streets were barricaded and swept by guns. The rebels took positions behind the windows and on the roofs of the houses and shot at the British soldiers. On the first day of the assault, the company's troops were able to capture only one-sixth of the town and suffered 1,166 casualties. Six days of street fighting finally secured the city for the British forces at the cost of some 4,000 casualties. Rebel losses are unknown. *See also* Dalhousie, James Andrew Broun Ramsay, First Marquess of Dalhousie; Lucknow, Siege of.

FURTHER READING: Harris, John. *The Indian Mutiny.* London: Hart-Davis MacGibbon, 1973; Hibbert, Christopher. *The Great Mutiny: India, 1857.* London: Allen Lane, 1980.

KAUSHIK ROY

## Denmark

In 1800, the Scandinavian country of Denmark was an absolutist monarchy with overseas colonies; by 1914, it was a parliamentary democracy. The possession of the **Danish West Indies** in the Caribbean—St. Thomas, St. Croix, and St. John—made Denmark an imperial power, albeit on a minor scale. Sugar production was quite profitable until the abolition of slavery in 1848. Danes were also heavily engaged in the trans-Atlantic slave trade. The Danish islands were sold for $25 million to the United States in 1917 and became part of the Virgin Islands. From 1620 to 1845, Denmark also held the island of Trankebar (present-day Tarangambadi), southeast of India. From 1750 to 1848, attempts were also made to colonize the nearby Nicobar Islands but failed.

Denmark gained control of the North Atlantic islands of Greenland, Iceland, and the Faeroe Islands by dynastic tradeoffs in 1380. On Iceland, a series of disasters—ranging from volcanic eruptions to epidemics—led to serious considerations of evacuating the whole population to Denmark, but after the mid-eighteenth century the situation improved, and by the nineteenth century cottage industry and fisheries flourished. Political upheaval in Europe and change in Denmark also led to reforms demands in Iceland. The Althing, the medieval Icelandic parliament, was resurrected in 1843 and a constitution promulgated in 1874. From 1854, Iceland also had status of a free trade area. Iceland became autonomous in 1918 and fully independent from 1944. The Faeroe Islands had a parliament of medieval origin until 1816 that was reestablished as a provincial council after the Danish constitution came into force in 1849, but a growing awareness of local cultural identity lead to a forceful movement of national revival that has lasted into the twentieth and twenty-first centuries.

Denmark was initially a member of the League of **Armed Neutrality** and then joined the Napoleonic Wars war on France's side in 1799, a move that heralded disaster. In 1801, the capital of Copenhagen was shelled by the Royal Navy, and in 1807, the British captured or destroyed the entire Danish navy. The 1814 peace treaty of Kiel forced Denmark to cede Norway to Sweden and Helgoland to the British. The West Indies was occupied by Britain but was returned after the war. German unification threatened Schleswig and Holstein, which the Danish king ruled as duchies, and in 1864, Austria and Prussia conquered the two duchies and parts of remaining Jutland. The latter territory was returned to Denmark in 1920 after the German defeat in World War I, in which Denmark remained neutral. The Napoleonic Wars also led to an economic crisis that lasted until the establishment of a central bank in 1818 and also a crisis in the agricultural sector that lingered until 1828 as a result of low grain prices. The already efficient Danish farming sector improved its output, especially in the latter half of the nineteenth century. Falling grain prices again in the 1870s stimulated the emergence of export-oriented dairy farming and a mechanization of production. Agricultural produce such as eggs, bacon, and butter accounted for 85–90 percent of Danish exports, Great Britain being the major market. From the 1880s, cooperatives owned by the farmers themselves did most of the food processing, thus creating a market-oriented rural class.

Economic problems fed growing demands for political reform around the mid-nineteenth century, and a constitutional monarchy was established in 1849, the year after the great upheavals of 1848 all over Europe. Civil liberties were guaranteed and a bicameral legislature, the lower-house Folketinget and the upper-house Landting, was introduced, while the King retained partial legislative powers. As a consequence of the defeat by Prussia and Austria in 1864, Denmark was forced to surrender its claim on Schleswig-Holstein and thereafter was vulnerable to German power. Conservative, wealthy landowners controlled a reformed upper house; but after 1864, modern political parties emerged, the conservative *Høire* and liberal *Venstre* being the dominant factions. The emerging urban working class became politically more active from the 1870s, and the Social Democrat Party was established in 1880. Organized labor followed a confrontational line until 1899, when disputes between employers and employees became institutionalized and subject to negotiations and general agreements. The Social Democratic party was voted into the Folketing in 1884. Toward the end of the nineteenth century, Denmark saw a process of further democratization of the constitution and introduction of parliamentarianism in 1901, giving the Folketing a dominant position over the Landting and the King. *See also* Copenhagen, Battles of; Napoleonic Wars; Schleswig-Holstein Conflict.

FURTHER READING: Jespersen, Knud J. V. *A History of Denmark.* Basingstoke: Palgrave, 2004; Jones, W. Glyn. *Denmark. A Modern History.* London: Croom Helm 1986; Oakley, Stewart. *A Short History of Denmark.* New York: Praeger Publishers, 1972.

FRODE LINDGJERDET

## Derby, Edward George Geoffrey Smith Stanley, Fourteenth Earl of (1799–1869)

Three times Conservative minority prime minister of the United Kingdom, Derby came from an old Whig family and served as a young man in the reforming administrations of **Lord Grey,** in which, in 1833, he oversaw the abolition of slavery throughout the British Empire. In the mid-1830s, disenchanted with Lord Melbourne's government, he moved toward the Conservative Party of Sir Robert **Peel.** His devotion to stability led him to break with Peel over **Corn Law** repeal, and he became a leading member of the Tory rump. Divisions among the Whig, Peelite, and Radical supporters of the governments of Russell and Palmerston allowed Tory minorities to hold office briefly in 1852, again in 1858–1859, and most significantly from 1866–1868.

The latter ministry passed the Second Reform Act, with significant Liberal support, effectively doubling the size of the electorate. In imperial affairs, it oversaw Lord Robert Napier's successful but expensive punitive expedition of 1867–1868 against Emperor Theodore of **Abyssinia,** who had kidnapped British personnel in reaction to an imagined diplomatic slight. Derby resigned the premiership in February 1868 and was succeeded by Benjamin **Disraeli.**

FURTHER READING: Saintsbury, George. *The Earl of Derby.* London; J. M. Dent, 1906.

MARK F. PROUDMAN

## Derby, Edward Henry Stanley, Fifteenth Earl of (1826–1893)

British Foreign Secretary under Benjamin **Disraeli** and Colonial Secretary under William **Gladstone.** The son of the 14th Earl of **Derby,** he served in his father's 1858 cabinet as the first secretary of state for **India** after the abolition of **East India Company** rule. When the Tories came back into office with Disraeli's large majority of 1874, Derby became foreign secretary, as he had been under his father in 1866–1868. He became alarmed at the risks of war that Disraeli was taking in his confrontation with Russia during the eastern crisis of 1876–1878, and resigned from the Cabinet.

Reversing his father's path, he moved back to the Liberals and served as colonial secretary under Gladstone from 1882–1885, in which capacity he must bear some responsibility for negotiating the London Convention of 1884 with the Afrikaner republics, leaving their precise status a topic of later contention and eventually war in 1899. When Liberals split over **Home Rule,** Derby followed the Unionists, and was Liberal Unionist leader in the House of Lords until 1891. *See also* Africa, Scramble for; Boer Wars; Eastern Question; Ireland.

FURTHER READING: Blake, Robert. *Disraeli*. New York: St. Martin's, 1967; Vincent, John, ed. *Disraeli, Derby and the Conservative Party*. Hassocks: Harvester Press, 1978.

MARK F. PROUDMAN

## Dernburg Reforms (1909–1910)

Reforms that overhauled the German colonial system following public outrage over colonial corruption scandals and the bloody suppression of the **Herero** and **Maji Maji** revolts. Under the guidance of former businessman Bernhard von Dernburg (1865–1937), the German government ended the influence of special interest groups by abolishing an advisory body known as the *Kolonialrat* and transferred control over colonial matters from a subdivision of the Foreign Office to a newly created Colonial Ministry. As colonial minister, Dernburg sought to reduce corruption and professionalize colonial service by ensuring that those serving overseas received the same salaries, pensions, and opportunities for promotion as their counterparts at home in Germany. Starting in 1908 with the creation of the Hamburg-based *Koloninstitut*, which provided formal training in colonial administration as well as classes in the languages and culture of colonized peoples, Dernburg made a concerted effort to staff his ministry with experts in the hopes of creating more rational, productive, and humane colonial policies.

As a staunch supporter of economic development, he used his business connections to attract new investment in the colonies, leading to an expansion of mining, agriculture, and railroad construction projects throughout the German colonial empire. At the same time, Dernburg also advocated better treatment of the indigenous peoples, arguing that they were crucial to the long-term development of the colonies both as a labor force and as the primary suppliers of raw materials. Consequently, his reforms also abolished corporal punishment, the use of forced labor, and the expropriation of native lands. Although the outbreak of World War I ended Germany's colonial experiment, the effect of the Dernburg reforms was a significant liberalization of German colonial administration during the final years of the Empire. *See also* Africa, Scramble for; Bülow, Bernhard von; German Empire; Trotha, General Lothar von.

FURTHER READING: Gann, L. H., and Peter Duignan. *The Rulers of German Africa 1884–1914*. Stanford, CA: Stanford University Press, 1977; Henderson, W. O. *The German Colonial Empire 1884–1919*. London: Frank Cass, 1993; Smith, Woodruff D. *The German Colonial Empire*. Chapel Hill, NC: University of North Carolina Press, 1978; Stoecker, Helmuth, ed. *German Imperialism in Africa*. London: C. Hurst & Company, 1986.

KENNETH J. OROSZ

## De Valera, Eamon (1882–1975)

An Irish Nationalist and later prime minister and president of the Irish Republic, De Valera was born in 1882 in New York City of an Irish mother and a Spanish-Cuban father. At the age of two, he and his mother moved to **Ireland.** In the 1900s, he obtained degrees from several Irish universities and was appointed a professor of mathematics at an Irish Teachers' College. During this period, he became enamored of the revival of the Gaelic language of the early 1900s, and this attraction led him to the Irish independence movement.

De Valera became a member of the Irish Volunteers, an Irish Nationalist Army, and by 1913, rose to the rank of captain. He was subsequently initiated into the secret Irish Republican Brotherhood, the shadowy leadership group of the Irish Volunteers. He was one of the leaders of the 1916 Easter Rebellion and avoided execution by the British only because of his American citizenship. He went on to be both the political and symbolic leader of the Irish nation for most of the mid-century.

FURTHER READING: Coogan, Tim Pat. *Eamon de Valera: The Man Who Was Ireland*. New York: Harper Collins, 1995; Coogan, Tim Pat. *Michael Collins: The Man Who Made Ireland*. Boulder: Robert Rhinehart, 1996; Dwyer, T. Ryle. *Eamon de Valera*. Dublin: Gill and Macmillan, 1998; Kee, Robert, *The Green Flag*. Bergenfield: Viking-Penguin, 1972.

JOSEPH ADAMCZYK

## Díaz, Porfirio (1830–1915)

Porfirio Díaz was the Mexican president and dictator from 1877 to 1880 and 1884 to 1911. Educated for the Church, Díaz entered politics in the mid-1850s and in the 1860s served as a military commander in support of the republican leader Benito Juárez against the French and Emperor Maximilian. Díaz later broke with Juárez and in 1876 seized power in a coup, arranged elections, and thereafter established a brutal dictatorship that lasted for 34 years. He governed ruthlessly yet often efficiently, in close cooperation with Mexico's landed oligarchy, and packed both the civil service and the judiciary with his personal supporters.

He cultivated generally positive relations with all the Great Powers, but in particular with the United States, and offered attractive terms for foreign investors. Although the country experienced a significant improvement in its standard of living, its benefits were narrowly distributed among the wealthy. Díaz's liberal land reforms, moreover, alienated Mexico's Indians by breaking up communal property and putting it on the market. Although he put down an Indian rebellion in the 1880s, he was overthrown by the Mexican Revolution of 1911 and died in French exile.

FURTHER READING: Bazant, Jan. *A Concise History of Mexico, From Hidalgo to Cárdenas, 1805–1940*. New York: Cambridge University Press, 1977; Beals, Carleton. *Porfirio Díaz, Dictator of Mexico*. Westport, CT: Greenwood, 1971.

CARL CAVANAGH HODGE

## Dilke, Sir Charles (1843–1911)

A fervent Liberal imperialist, Charles Dilke was born into the bosom of the British Liberal establishment. His father was given a baronetcy for his work with Prince Albert on the Great Exhibition of 1851, which Dilke inherited in 1869. As a boy he was introduced to most of the great figures of the age, from Victoria herself to the Duke of **Wellington** and Lord **Palmerston.** Dilke was educated at Cambridge, and after graduation he embarked on a then unusual grand tour around the world. The result was a two-volume memoir, *Greater Britain: A Record of Travel in English-Speaking*

*Countries during 1866 and 1867.* The work was an instant success, going through many editions, and propelling Dilke into Parliament.

*Greater Britain* tells the tale of an observant but highly opinionated young man traveling westward across the United States, with a brief excursion to Canada, then across the Pacific to New Zealand and Australia, and thence to India, returning to England by the Suez Canal. Although often remembered today as a celebration of imperialism, Dilke's vision was that of a free-trading radical, and his volumes were not uncritical of the British Empire. In India, for instance, he labeled the Anglo-Indian government "a mere imperialism, where one man rules and the rest are slaves," and saw with some prescience that "by means of centralization and railroads, we have created an India which we cannot fight."

For Dilke, the term *Greater Britain* meant the countries that had been influenced by British emigration and culture or by British rule. It was the United States in which he was most interested, and which was for him Britain's exemplary colony. For Dilke, as for many Victorians, the term *colony* had classical associations and did not necessarily imply political subordination. In his preface, Dilke wrote, "In America, the peoples of the world are being fused together, but they are run into an English mould . . . through America, England is speaking to the world . . . If two small islands are by courtesy styled 'Great,' America, Australia, India must form a 'Greater Britain.'"

It was a combination of ethnic and cultural pride in his country that was rather more self-confident, and less inclined to focus purely on political ties, than the avowed imperialism of later decades. Nevertheless, the primary impact of Dilke's volumes, aside from giving an initial boost to his own political career, was to raise the profile of Britain's overseas possessions in the minds of the book-buying public, and to suggest that colonies might be a source not merely of expense and danger, but also of pride and strength to Britain. In that way, he played some role in preparing the ground for the more aggressive imperialism of subsequent decades.

Dilke began his political career as a radical, going so far to the left as to dally with republicanism in the early 1870s. He served as the representative of William **Gladstone**'s 1880–1885 government during the unsuccessful attempt to renew the Cobden-Chevalier Free Trade treaty of 1860, and represented the Admiralty in the House of Commons during the British occupation of **Egypt** in 1882. He was seen as a man of great ability and a potential future Prime Minister, but his political career was destroyed by a divorce scandal in 1886. He became in his later years a respected and cautiously imperialist commentator on imperial and military affairs, publishing *Problems of Greater Britain* in 1890, and in 1899, a volume of essays entitled *The British Empire. See also* Liberal Imperialism; Liberal Party.

FURTHER READING: Jenkins, Roy. *Sir Charles Dilke, A Victorian Tragedy.* London: Collins, 1958; Matthew, H.C.G. *The Liberal Imperialists.* London: Oxford University Press, 1973.

MARK PROUDMAN

## Disraeli, Benjamin, Earl of Beaconsfield (1804–1881)

A politician, statesman, and Conservative prime minister, Benjamin Disraeli was a commanding figure of British imperialism. The term *imperialism* was invented in its modern sense to describe—indeed to condemn—his foreign and imperial policies. Disraeli was born into an assimilated Jewish family and was baptized an Anglican in 1817. His father was a bookseller and antiquarian, and Disraeli grew up in literary circles. He initially attempted a literary career, publishing witty autobiographical novels and historical romances now remembered largely for their biographical significance. Although his novels made some money, Disraeli lived a fast life, dressed extravagantly, traveled extensively, and ran up large debts in financial speculations. He first ran for Parliament in 1832, as a radical. In 1835, he joined the Tory party, arguing that Tories shared with radicals a concern for the people as against the Whig oligarchy. That the Whigs were a self-interested ruling class hiding behind spurious appeals to liberty was an argument he made repeatedly, and most notably in his 1835 *Vindication of the English Constitution.*

Disraeli was finally elected to Parliament in 1837. In 1839, he married the widow of another Tory member of Parliament, whose independent income, along with his own prodigious novel-writing, helped to salvage his parlous finances. In the 1840s, Disraeli became known as a member of the "Young England" group of socially conscious Tory members of Parliament. He continued to write novels in which Whig oligarchs and utilitarian politicians were the villains, and enlightened noblemen the heroes: his most famous, *Sybil* of 1845, proclaimed that England consisted of two nations, the rich and the poor, and offered a kind of enlightened *noblesse oblige* as the solution. Another of Disraeli's so-called "Young England" trilogy, *Tancred, or the New Crusade,* has been famously accused by the theorist of Orientalism, Edward Said, of creating the model for future imperialism in the Middle East, although the novel in fact says little about the empire. The great political crisis of the 1840s was the rupture of the governing Tory party over Sir Robert **Peel's** 1846 repeal of the **Corn Laws,** in the name of free trade. The Whigs and radicals had been clamoring for repeal; in response to Peel's conversion to their cause, Disraeli famously denounced him as "a burglar of others' intellect."

Disraeli took the leadership of the protectionist Tories, whose defection pushed Peel out of office in December 1846. As Peel was able to carry most of his cabinet with him, Disraeli became one of the fewer remaining effective parliamentary speakers on the Tory front bench. As a consequence of the death of the initial protectionist leader Lord George Bentinck, he became almost by default the Tory leader in the House of Commons, notwithstanding the lingering anti-Semitism of some backbenchers. Disraeli became chancellor of the exchequer and leader of the House of Commons in the 1852 minority Tory government of Lord **Derby,** during which time he led the Tories to accept that a return to protection was politically impossible. The Tories were out of power until 1858, when, owing to Lord Palmerston's missteps, they once again formed a minority government with Disraeli as chancellor. The minority government lasted until June 1859, when the Liberals came back into power, and the Tories went once more into opposition for an extended period. The failure of **Russell's** 1866 Reform bill, however, presented an opportunity. Disraeli, once again chancellor and leader in the House of Commons under the minority premiership of Derby, was able to fashion with great tactical skill a working if unstable majority of Tories and radicals, which put through the Second Reform Act of 1867.

On the resignation of Derby, Disraeli became prime minister, for the first time in February 1868. His minority administration, its major achievement the Reform

Bill behind it, lasted only until the end of the year; it was nevertheless a great and improbable achievement for an assimilated middle class Jew, a man-about-town, and a sometime novelist to have, in Disraeli's own words, reached "the top of the greasy pole." In imperial affairs, Disraeli's administration was notable for the successful completion of the **Abyssinian** expedition, which demonstrated the long reach of British power. The election of 1868, held under the new franchise, resulted in a great Liberal victory, the Liberals now being under William **Gladstone.** It did not appear that Disraeli would ever again be prime minister, and it seemed that the Tories' minority status had once again been confirmed. But Gladstone shortly ran into difficulties with his own supporters over ecclesiastical and subsequently educational issues. The perceived indifference to the empire of the Liberals—many of whom, given the orthodoxies of free trade, did in fact regard the empire as an albatross—also offered Disraeli an opportunity. In 1872, he made a speech at the Crystal Palace in which he denounced in stirring tones, "the attempts of Liberalism to effect the disintegration of the Empire of England."

Although Disraeli himself had once likened the colonies to "millstones round our necks," there was enough truth to the charge of Liberal indifference that it stuck, and Disraeli was able to reappropriate to the Tory party the mantle of popular nationalism that had for a generation belonged to the party of Palmerston: Disraeli, like Lord **Palmerston,** saw himself as the inheritor of a tradition of national greatness going back to the two Pitts. The appeal, in combination with Liberal divisions, was successful in producing, with the election of 1874, the first outright Tory majority since the days of Peel. In government, however, Disraeli had little in the way of a clear domestic agenda, his entire career, spent largely in opportunist opposition to a liberal consensus, having spared him the need for such a thing. Like many Tories, he regarded programmatic state activity with suspicion, although at the same time was less bound by the more dogmatic aspects of classical *laisser-faire* political economy than were many Liberals. Disraeli was open to opportunistic and piecemeal social reforms, his government putting through such measures as slum clearance, sanitary legislation, and labor laws. But Disraeli himself was primarily interested in foreign and imperial affairs—"politics worth managing"—which appealed to his sense of national greatness. In 1876, Disraeli, by then feeling his age and not being up to managing the House of Commons, moved to the House of Lords as Earl of Beaconsfield. In the same year, he put through the Royal Titles Act, at Victoria's request, making the Queen Empress of India.

Like much of Disraeli's legacy, the imperial title was symbolic without being purely symbolic: it demonstrated a concerted effort to associate national greatness with England and not coincidentally with conservatism. The outcome of the Franco-Prussian war and the preeminence of Bismarck called into question what had come to appear Britain's almost effortless prominence in earlier years. In 1876, Disraeli masterminded the purchase of the Egyptian Khedive's Suez Canal shares, thus reasserting Britain's imperial status; it was a move that led unintentionally to Gladstone's later occupation of Egypt. The Eastern question and the Bulgarian atrocities of 1876, in which Balkan nationalist risings encouraged by Russia were put down with ferocity by the Turks, gave Disraeli his opportunity to assert British power by opposing Russian expansion and defending Turkey, a traditional British ally. But the Liberals, led by Gladstone, were outraged that Britain should go to the brink of war in support of an Islamic despotism guilty of atrocities against Christian populations. The Liberals became the party of international morality and cooperation, tarring Disraeli and Tories with immoral cynicism.

The 1878 Berlin Conference, in which Disraeli played an equal part with Bismarck, secured Britain's objectives and temporarily settled the Balkan question. Along the way, Britain had taken **Cyprus,** a move denounced as superfluous and arrogant expansionism by many Liberals. It was during these crises that the term *jingoism* ("we don't want to fight/but by Jingo if we do/we've got the ships/we've got the men/we've got the money too") became associated with Tory imperialism. In 1877, Britain annexed the Transvaal, largely as a result of the initiative by the "man on the spot," Sir Theophilus Shepstone. This led rapidly to difficulties with both the Transvaal Boers and the Zulus, the traditional enemies of the Boers. In 1879, war broke out in Zululand. The Zulu War began with the catastrophic defeat of Isandhlwana, but concluded successfully, if bloodily and expensively, with the collapse of Zulu power in the wake of Lord Chelmsford's victory at Ulundi. In 1878, war had also broken out in Afghanistan, prompted by Britain's objections to a Russian ambassador at Kabul. Abandoning the traditional Liberal policy of "masterly inactivity" on the Northwest frontier, Disraeli's Viceroy Lord Lytton issued an ultimatum that led to a declaration of war. Initially successful at marching to Kabul and installing a British candidate on the Afghan throne, Britain shortly found itself embroiled in a guerilla war that dragged on through the election of 1880, until Gladstone ordered a withdrawal in 1881.

The term *imperialism*, initially used to compare Disraeli's Royal Titles Act to the tinsel regime of Napoleon III (see **Bonaparte, Louis Napoleon**), came to be applied to forward imperial policies in general, and in particular with the numerous wars and threats of war associated with Beaconsfield's government. Gladstone, in his Midlothian speeches of 1879, called for Britain to respect the rights of other nations and to avoid unnecessary wars. It was, however, to the partisan uses of imperial jingoism that Gladstone primarily objected. The latter's convincing victory in the election of 1880 was in part a verdict on Beaconsfield's imperialism, although rising taxes and the state of the economy, which in the 1870s had entered what until 1929 was called the "great depression," also played a large part in Disraeli's defeat. Disreali, by then infirm, resigned the premiership on April 21, 1880. He died a year later, on April 19, 1881. Disraeli's legacy has been extensively fought over. He was at once the original "imperialist" and something of a progressive reformer; he spoke in edifying, not to say magniloquent, terms of imperial greatness, but could also be cynical and manipulative; he split the Tory party over the Corn Laws, but then weaned the party away from protection and did much to get it through its long subsequent period of exclusion from more than minority office; an opponent of Liberalism and a defender of an aristocracy to which he did not belong, his Reform Act made Britain effectively a democracy; he was always an English nationalist, although at times indifferent to the colonies; a consistent opponent of Palmerston, he was yet able to appropriate the forces of popular nationalism and to make them seem synonymous with Toryism. The Earl of Beaconsfield was above all an imitable personality—a self-made man. *See also* Afghan Wars; Berlin, Congress of; British Empire; Cape Colony; Eastern Question; Ottoman Empire; San Stefano, Treaty of; Straits Question; Transvaal; Zulu Wars.

FURTHER READING: Blake, Robert. *Disraeli,* London: Eyre and Spottiswoode, 1966; Eldridge, C. C. *Disraeli and the Rise of a New Imperialism.* Cardiff: University of Wales Press, 1996; Monypenny, W. F., and G. E. Buckle. *The Life of Benjamin Disraeli, Earl of Beaconsfield.* 6 vols. London: John Murray, 1910–1929.

MARK F. PROUDMAN

## Dogger Bank Incident (1904)

An Anglo-Russian crisis occurring during the **Russo-Japanese War.** On October 21, 1904, the Russian battle fleet, proceeding from their Baltic Sea ports via the North Sea to the Far East for service in the Russo-Japanese War, mistook a British fishing fleet on the Dogger Bank for Japanese torpedo boats and opened fire, killing two men, wounding half a dozen, and sinking a trawler. The incident briefly brought Britain and Russia to the edge of war, but a rapid apology from the tsar and the appointment of an international investigative commission defused the situation. The commission placed blame on the Russian commander, Admiral Rozhdestventski, who went on to be defeated by the Japanese navy at the battle of the Straits of Tsushima on May 27, 1905. *See also Dreadnought;* Tsushima, Battle of.

FURTHER READING: Hough, Richard Alexander. *The Fleet That Had to Die.* London: Hamish Hamilton, 1958; Warner, Denis Ashston. *The Tide at Sunrise.* London: Frank Cass, 2002; Westwood, J. N. *Russia Against Japan, 1904–05: A New Look at Russo-Japanese War.* Albany: State University of New York Press, 1986.

MARK F. PROUDMAN

## Dominion

From the latin *dominus* ("lord"), the term *dominion* means an area of rule or domination. The word was used in this sense to name the seventeenth-century Dominion of New England and the "Old Dominion" of Virginia, both so named under the Stuarts. In 1867, the term was adopted by the new Canadian Confederation as an attractively vague alternative to "Kingdom," which, it was feared, might offend the republican sensibilities of the United States. In 1901, the perceived importance of the empire was recognized by the addition of the phrase "and of the British dominions beyond the seas" to the royal style, the term *dominion*—in lower case—again being sufficiently imprecise as to encompass all manner of dependent territories along with the self-governing colonies, without offending anyone's sensibilities.

Although the federal **Australia** created by the Australian Colonies Act of 1901 called itself a Commonwealth, the term dominion came to designate the status of a self-governing member of the **British Empire** or **Commonwealth,** thus acquiring in the twentieth century a connotation opposite to its etymological meaning. In the first half of the twentieth century, it was common to refer to the self-governing emigrant members of the commonwealth as British dominions, and indeed the British government maintained a dominions secretary to deal with them. Although the Dominion of Canada, as originally constituted, had in most respects complete autonomy, it assumed control over foreign policy only in the twentieth century and did not enjoy full international sovereignty until the 1931 Statute of Westminster, so even in its later, more attenuated sense, the precise meaning of dominion status was not entirely fixed. In discussions about the future of India, South Africa, and other territories such as Southern Rhodesia, reference to dominion status referred to full local self-government and sovereignty under the British crown, on the Canadian model. *See also* Canada; Durham, John George Lambton, First Earl of; New Zealand.

FURTHER READING: Martin, Ged. *Britain and the Origins of Canadian Confederation.* Vancouver: UBC Press, 1995; Wheare, K. C. *The Constitutional Structure of the Commonwealth.* Westport, CT: Greenwood, 1982.

MARK F. PROUDMAN

## Dost Muhammad Khan (1793–1863)

A nineteenth-century Afghan leader who established the Barakzai Dynasty and attempted to add to his realm or defend it, as circumstance dictated, by making alliances with the **British Empire** and the **Russian Empire.** He fought against British attempts to put Shah Shuja-ul-Mulk on the Afghan throne and managed in 1824 to put himself in power in Kabul. In 1834, Dost Muhammad defeated Ranjit Singh, the Sikh ruler of the Junjab, in battle at Kandahar but was unable to stop Ranjit's annexation of Peshawar. He miscalculated in approaching the Russians for assistance when the installation of a Russian representative in Kabul prompted the British to invade. In July 1839, British forces captured Kabul and promptly placed Shah Shuja on the throne.

After being imprisoned in India for two years, Dost Muhammad was freed and returned to power in Afghanistan to maintain order in the country. In 1846, he turned against the British again, this time in alliance with Sikhs of the Punjab, but in 1849 was again defeated in the Battle of Gujarat. He thereafter worked to consolidate his position back in Afghanistan and by 1854 had established his personal authority over the tribes in the south of the country. In recognition of his position, the British sought and secured an alliance with Dost Muhammad, which paid off. Although he remained neutral during the Indian Mutiny, he aided Britain in its wars with Persia and, in 1863, was responsible for the capture of the city of Herat. *See also* Afghan Wars, Great Game, Sikh Wars.

FURTHER READING: Farwell, Byron. *Queen Victoria's Little Wars.* New York: W. W. Norton, 1972; Heathcote, T. A. *The Afghan Wars, 1839–1919.* Staplehurst: Spellmount, 2003.

CARL CAVANAGH HODGE

## *Dreadnought*

Built in 1905–1906, the British battleship *H.M.S. Dreadnought,* literally "Fear Nothing," revolutionized the world's navies because of its powerful turbine-driven propulsion and heavy armament and thereby gave its name to a whole class of battleships. The launching of *H.M.S. Dreadnought* sparked a new phase in the naval arms race between Britain and the German Reich, which was a major factor in pre-World War I Anglo-German antagonism. The first of a series of dreadnoughts displaced a total of 18,000 tons, was 527 feet long, and carried a crew of about 800 men. Because it was equipped with modern steam turbines instead of traditional steam pistons, the *Dreadnought* was as fast as 21 knots. Its mighty armament of ten 12-inch guns and torpedo tubes was designed to fight enemy ships from considerably long distances. The name "Dreadnought" quickly became synonymous for a new type of battleship, because when it was launched in 1906, it made all preceding warships obsolete.

The launching of the *Dreadnought* can be considered as the British response to the challenge posed by the increasing output of German battleships under what later came to be called the Tirpitz Plan. Germany's apparent strategy to outstrip or at least neutralize the Royal Navy's impressive superiority fueled a costly arms race between the Reich and the United Kingdom. Although the parliaments in both countries repeatedly showed reluctance to finance the escalating costs of navy expenditure, they were unable to stop the arms race. Most important, German efforts to keep up with British dreadnought-style production both in terms of quality and quantity increasingly poisoned Anglo-German relations. By the beginning of World War I, the original *Dreadnought* became obsolete, but it was soon succeeded by faster and still heavier armed "superdreadnoughts." These new battleships continued to dominate the navies of the world until around 1940. *See also* Fisher, Sir John; Mahan, Alfred Thayer; Navalism, Tirpitz Plan.

FURTHER READING: Berghahn, V. R. *Der Tirpitz-Plan: Genesis und Verfall einer innenpolitischen Krisenstrategie unter Wilhelm II.* Düsseldorf: Droste, 1971; Herwig, H. H. *Luxury Fleet.* London: Allen & Unwin, 1980; Kennedy, Paul M. *The Rise of the Anglo-German Antagonism.* London: Allen & Unwin, 1980; Lambert, Nicholas A. *Sir John Fisher's Naval Revolution.* Columbia: University of South Carolina Press, 1999; Massie, Robert K. *Dreadnought: Britain, Germany and the Coming of the Great War.* London: Pimlico, 2004; Roberts, John. *The Battleship Dreadnought.* London: Conway Maritime, 1992.

ULRICH SCHNAKENBERG

## *Dreikaiserbund* (1873–1887)

The *Dreikaiserbund,* or Three Emperors' League, was an informal system of cooperation involving **Austria-Hungary,** Germany, and Russia in regard to their interactions with the **Ottoman Empire** in the Balkans. From the German perspective, the league was also a means of blocking an alliance of France and Russia against the newly formed **German Empire.** German chancellor Otto von **Bismarck** appreciated that the emergence of Germany as a new Great Power in Central Europe as a consequence of the **Franco-Prussian War** could make Russia a natural ally of France in any project to undermine or weaken Germany. Yet he also grasped that tsarist Russia—troubled by anarchist, nihilist, and socialist subversion—had much more in common politically with Germany than with republican France. Tsar **Alexander II** also sought German support for Russian interests in the Balkans against the Ottoman Empire and in Central Asia against the British Empire. Bismarck therefore arranged a meeting of Wilhelm I, Tsar Alexander II, and Emperor Franz Joseph at Berlin in September 1872, and the three thereafter held frequent conferences between 1872 and 1876. The system nonetheless collapsed in the 1880s over Austro-Russian differences in the Balkans. *See also* Central Powers; Entente Cordiale; Holy Alliance; Reinsurance Treaty; Triple Alliance.

FURTHER READING: Langer, William L. *European Alliances and Alignments, 1871–1890.* New York: Alfred A. Knopf, 1939; Taylor, A.J.P. *The Struggle for Master in Europe, 1848–1918.* Oxford: Clarendon, 1954; Wehler, Hans Ulrich. *The German Empire, 1871–1918.* New York: Berg Publishers, 1997.

CARL CAVANAGH HODGE

## Dresden, Battle of (1813)

Fought on August 26–27, 1813, the Battle of Dresden was Napoleon **Bonaparte**'s only major victory over Allied forces in the 1813 War of Liberation. After Austria joined the Allies on August 11, its Army of Bohemia, under Feldmarschall Karl Fürst zu Schwarzenberg and reinforced with Prussian and Russian troops to 80,000 men, marched to the vital city of Dresden in Saxony on August 25, while Napoleon's army was thought to be in Silesia. Marshal Gouvion St-Cyr held the city with 20,000 men, but Allied planning delays allowed Napoleon to arrive with 90,000 troops on August 26. Uninformed of the French reinforcements, Schwarzenberg's orders permitted him to mount only five half-hearted demonstrations against the city. The attack columns had marched to within cannon shot range of the city at midday, but at 5 P.M., as they prepared to assault the city, Napoleon unleashed his reinforcements and by midnight, the Allies were back in their starting positions. In the pouring rain of the next morning, further reinforced to 140,000 men, Napoleon launched a double flank attack, with a reinforced center holding its positions to force the expanded Allied army of 170,000 to withdraw.

Although the French left under Marshal Mortier became bogged down against General Wittgenstein's 35,000 Russians, Marshal Murat had overwhelmed the Allied left flank under Austrian Feldzugmeister Ignaz Gyulai by 3 P.M., just as an additional French corps under Marshal Vandamme seized Pirna 16 miles to the southeast to threaten the Allied rear. An hour later, Schwarzenberg issued orders for a withdrawal of Bohemia, leaving 12,000 prisoners behind. *See also* Napoleonic Wars.

FURTHER READING: Brett-James, A. *Europe Against Napoleon: the Leipzig Campaign 1813.* London: Macmillan, 1970. London; Hofschröer, P. *Leipzig 1813.* Oxford: Osprey Military Publishing, 1993.

DAVID HOLLINS

## Dreyfus Affair (1894–1906)

A pivotal political crisis of turn-of-the century France that broadly pitted the forces of left and right against each other. The episode involved the fate of Alfred Dreyfus, a Jewish French army officer who was wrongly court-martialed for treason, degraded, and sentenced to the Devil's Island penal colony in French Guyana in 1894. George Picquart, a colonel of intelligence, and Dreyfus's brother subsequently revealed evidence showing that the real guilty party was a Catholic, Major

Walsin Esterhazy. Dreyfus had been the victim not only of incompetence but also of the anti-German xenophobia rampant in French society, as well as of widespread anti-Semitism inside the army. When Esterhazy was tried and acquitted, the French Radical and Socialist Parties were aroused to fight for Dreyfus with the argument that the army general staff was a club of royalist and clericalist anti-Semites guilty of prejudiced error, a reactionary threat to the Third Republic, and an institution ripe for purge.

The novelist Emile Zola leveled the same charge at the army in his famous letter *J'accuse,* and prominent politicians such as Georges **Clemençeau** and Jean Jaurès also took up Dreyfus's case. It was revealed that the evidence against Dreyfus had been forged. He was pardoned, but the Dreyfusards demanded nothing less than acquittal and secured it with quashing of the verdict in 1906. At its height "The Affair" utterly dominated French political life; it occasioned impassioned debate and occasionally violence. The test of strength between intellectuals, Radicals, and Socialists on the one hand and the Church and army on the other reawakened hatreds dating back to 1789 and polarized French politics for the remainder of the Third Republic. The Dreyfus Affair exposed ugly sentiments below the surface of the otherwise opulent optimism of the *belle époque.* *See also* Action Française.

FURTHER READING: Derfler, Leslie. *The Dreyfus Affair.* Westport, CT: Greenwood, 2002; Kayser, Jacques. *The Dreyfus Affair.* New York: Civici-Friede, 1931.

CARL CAVANAGH HODGE

## Dual Alliance

A term commonly applied alternatively to the Austro-German alliance dating to 1879, which, with the later addition of Italy, became the **Triple Alliance,** or to the Franco-Russian alliance of 1890. The first was a secret alliance, a centerpiece of Bismarck's system, in which Austria and Germany pledged military aid and cooperation if either were attacked by Russia. The second was its mirror image insofar as it was a Franco-German pact against the very Central European powers of that formed the anti-Russian coalition of 1879. In 1893, France and Russia signed a secret military convention in which Russia promised to commit all its forces against Germany if it should be attacked either by Germany or by Italy with German support. For its part, France committed to attack Germany if Russia were attacked either by Germany or by **Austria-Hungary** backed by Germany.

FURTHER READING: Langer, William L. *The Diplomacy of Imperialism, 1890–1902.* New York: Alfred A. Knopf, 1968; Taylor, A.J.P. *The Struggle for Mastery in Europe, 1848–1918.* Oxford: Clarendon, 1954.

CARL CAVANAGH HODGE

## Durbar

Persian for "prince's court," the durbar in British **India** was a grand court ceremonial used to commemorate special occasions involving the monarchy. Three durbars were held in India by the British. They took the form of receptions, balls, parties, and a grand military parade. The first of the Durbars was held to commemorate the bestowing of the title "Queen Empress of India" on Queen **Victoria** by Parliament at the behest of British Prime Minister Benjamin **Disraeli.** It took place on January 1, 1877, in Delhi and was designed to rally the princes of India to British rule. The second durbar was also held in Delhi when Victoria's son, **Edward VII,** was proclaimed "King-Emperor" on January 1, 1903. The third and last of the durbars took place to commemorate the accession of King **George V** to the throne of the United Kingdom upon the death of his father in 1910. It was marked in India by the durbar held at Delhi in the presence of King George and his wife on December 12, 1911.

To ensure maximum publicity of the occasion, the rulers of states were excused the payment of succession duties; military and lower-ranked civil servants received bonuses; grants were provided for schools; and, for the first time, officers, men, and reservists of the Indian Army became eligible for the Victoria Cross. Most important, the king himself announced the well-kept secret that the capital of India would be transferred from Calcutta to Delhi and the partition of **Bengal** of 1905 would be reversed, a new province of Bihar and Orissa would be created, and Assam would once again be under a chief commissioner. The durbar became controversial because these costly administrative moves were announced without consulting Parliament, but the changes were the most important, as they had far-reaching consequences. *See also* Raj.

FURTHER READING: James, Lawrence. *Raj: The Making and Unmaking of British India.* New York: St. Martin's Griffin, 1997; Wolpert, Stanley. *A New History of India* New York: Oxford University. Press, 2005.

ROGER D. LONG

## Durham, John George Lambton, First Earl of (1792–1840)

A reforming governor-in-chief of British North America, Lord Durham (as Lambton became in 1829) was a wealthy land and coal owner. He entered politics as a fierce and often intemperate radical and proponent of parliamentary reform. He served in the reforming government of his father-in-law, Earl Grey, helping to draft the great reform bill. From 1835 to 1837, he was ambassador to Russia. Although he initially refused the governorship of Canada, he accepted the post after the arrival of news of the rebellion of 1838. Returning to England after only five months in **Canada** because of the cabinet's disallowance of an order sending rebel leaders into exile, Durham and his entourage set about producing his famous report.

Durham's report was probably written in large part by his secretary, Charles Buller, and was inspired in many respects by the colonization theories of Edward Gibbon Wakefield, also on his staff. It was leaked to the *Times* in February 1839, likely by Wakefield. The report recommended the Anglicization and assimilation of the French Canadians through a union of Upper and Lower Canada. It also, more successfully, urged significant grants of self-government to the colony, although tariff and land policy was reserved to the imperial government, the latter in accordance with Wakefield's theories. Durham was long remembered, with some element of exaggeration, as the father of responsible government in the colonies, although his report did not use that term. He died, likely of tuberculosis, in 1840. *See also* British North America Act; Commonwealth; Dominion.

FURTHER READING: Durham, Lord. *Report on the Affairs of British North America.* London, 1839; Ged, Martin. *The Durham Report and British Colonial Policy.* Cambridge: Cambridge University Press, 1972.

MARK F. PROUDMAN

## Dutch East Indies

The name given to the island colonies founded by the Dutch East India Company, mostly in present-day Indonesia, starting in the seventeenth century. As the Netherlands became part of France when Napoleon **Bonaparte** invaded in 1795 and was annexed outright in 1811, British hostility toward France was extended to the Netherlands and all Dutch possessions. Britain therefore assumed colonial authority in the East Indies in 1811, yet in 1814 England was obliged by the Treaty of Vienna to return the territory. This was only imperfectly implemented, and disputes arising from continuing British interest in the Indies produced the Anglo-Dutch Treaty of 1823, which divided the islands between British control in Singapore and Malacca and Dutch control of Sumatra along with the islands between Malacca and Sumatra. Principal Dutch interest focused on the island of Java, but a rebellious population made it difficult to reestablish control. The Java Uprising of 1825–1829—also referred to as the Great Java War and also the Dippa Negara War—cost the Dutch colonial garrison 15,000 soldiers.

FURTHER READING: Spruyt, J., and J. B. Robertson. *History of Indonesia.* New York: St. Martin's, 1967; Vandenbosch, Amry. *The Dutch East Indies.* Berkeley: University of California Press, 1942.

CARL CAVANAGH HODGE

## Dvořák, Antonín (1841–1904)

Czech composer of romantic music whose work is usually categorized as a "national" by virtue of its incorporation of folk material—Slavonic dance and song rhythm—into symphonies, symphonic poems, and even chamber music. Dvořák was born in Nelahozeves, Bohemia, and was an apprentice butcher in his father's shop when his musical gifts diverted him toward formal training in Prague and an early career as a viola player. From 1873 onward, he produced a steady flow of new compositions, won a succession of prizes, and came to the attention of Johannes Brahms, who helped him get his scores published in Berlin. From opera, symphonies, and choral pieces to incidental music and string quartets, Dvořák's output was impressive. It reveals an authentic genius for the use of strings in any format, unexpected and refreshing harmonies, and an unforced capacity to absorb and adapt the themes of Central European folk traditions.

In the mid-1990s, Dvořák taught, performed, and composed in the United States and is possibly best known for his Symphony No.9 "From the New World," which was influenced by his exposure to American spiritual music. A subject of the Habsburg Empire loyal to his Czech nationality and to the notion of national school of music, Dvořák was nonetheless refreshingly comfortable with the local, the national, and the cosmopolitan.

FURTHER READING: Clapham, John. *Dvořák.* New York: W. W. Norton, 1979.

CARL CAVANAGH HODGE

# E

## Eastern Question

A long-term problem in European diplomatic affairs, the Eastern Question involved three sets of interrelated issues having to do with the fate of the **Ottoman Empire.** The first issue was an international one. Could the Ottomans fend off the territorial and strategic desires of the European Great Powers for pieces of Ottoman territory, and if not then how should the competing Great Powers partition the Ottoman Empire? The resolution of the Eastern Question through a solution of partition became tightly bound up with the maintenance of the European **balance of power,** because Ottoman losses might not be equitably divided among the European rivals. As a result of Great Power jealousies, the Turks could usually find at least one European power among France, Britain, Russia, Austria, or Germany (after 1871) that would choose to support the territorial integrity and status quo for fear that the demise of the Ottoman Empire would benefit its rivals more than itself. The second issue concerned the continued viability of the Ottoman Empire. Could the Porte reform the Ottoman system sufficiently to reverse its decline, ensure its internal order, and stave off rebellions? The third issue, closely tied up with the second, grew from the challenges posed by nationalisms of the subject Christian peoples in the **Balkans.** Should these peoples have their own independent national states, or could they be accommodated within the multinational Muslim Ottoman Empire?

The origins of the Eastern Question can be traced to Russian military advances against the Ottomans during the eighteenth century. Seeking a position on the lands around the Black Sea coast, Russia, usually in cooperation with Austria, waged a series of wars against the Turks. Eventually, the Russians advanced to the Pruth River, and the Austrians reached the Danube-Sava River line. As a consequence of their defeat at the hands of the Russians in 1774, the Ottomans signed the Treaty of Kuchuk Kainardji, which ended centuries of Ottoman dominance on the Black Sea and gave Russia the right to speak for the Orthodox Christians under Ottoman rule, including Romanians, Greeks, Serbs, and Montenegrins. The Ottoman government promised to protect Orthodox Christians and their churches and allowed the Russian government to construct its own church in Constantinople that would be under the protection of Russian officials. Russia would subsequently use these treaty provisions as the basis to intervene in Ottoman affairs in the name of protecting the Orthodox Christian subjects of the sultan. In contrast, France served as a supporter of the Ottomans in this period, and Britain did not yet play much of a role.

Austrian attitudes changed after the **Napoleonic Wars.** After gaining the Dalmatian coast in 1815, Austria already had difficulties maintaining its hold over the multinational population in its empire and no longer desired to incorporate any more Balkan peoples. Not wanting to expand any further into the Balkans, the Austrians grew wary of further Russian advances against the Ottomans because such Russian gains would give Russia dominance in the Balkan Peninsula and pose problems for Austrian defenses by creating Russian borders to the south and east. As a result Austria had come to support the status quo in the Eastern Question through the first half of the nineteenth century. Nevertheless, Austria did annex the Ottoman territory of **Bosnia-Herzegovina** in1908, after having exercised administrative authority there since 1878.

At the same time that Austrian interests were weakening, British interests in the region were strengthening. As British holdings in India grew, the British government became increasingly preoccupied with protecting the lines of communication to its most lucrative colonial and trading colony, and those routes ran across Ottoman lands. The expanding British concern for its Indian possessions generated a corresponding heightened fear of Russian encroachment. The British feared that a powerful Russian army could deal a mortal blow to the Ottomans and then seize the Turkish straits at the **Bosporus** and **Dardanelles** as a prelude to Russian expansion beyond the Black Sea into the Eastern Mediterranean. Thus as part of its Indian defenses, the British generally tried to prop up Ottoman power. Britain encouraged Turkish administrative reform as the means to alleviate grounds for discontent and restiveness on the part of the sultan's Christian subjects so that the Russians would have no excuse to intervene in Turkish affairs as a prelude to the final dismemberment of the Ottoman Empire. For this reason, the British actively encouraged the Tanzimat Reforms (1839–1876), which were intended to promote the equality of all Ottoman subjects, regardless of religion, and strengthen the efficiency and administrative power of the central government. On the other hand, Russia worried that a British naval squadron could force the straits, enter the Black Sea, and threaten the entire Russian southern coast or even the Caucasus. This scenario actually came to pass during the **Crimean War** (1853–1856), when British troops landed on the Crimean Peninsula.

As the nineteenth century wore on, it became clear that the Balkan Christian peoples considered national independence preferable to potential equality within a reformed Ottoman system. In their armed struggles, the Balkan peoples received the greatest aid from Russia. The first to rebel against Ottoman rule were the Serbs, from 1804 to 1815, who managed to achieve an autonomous principality within the Ottoman Empire under Russian protection. The Serbian prince still recognized the Ottoman sultan as his sovereign, but the prince exercised control over local affairs. With the help of the Great Powers, the Greek Revolution of 1821–1833 led to the first successful Balkan independence movement. Britain, France, and Russia oversaw the establishment of a Greek kingdom independent of the Ottoman Empire in the wake of the **Russo-Turkish War** (1828–1829). In the aftermath of that war, Russia also gained administrative control over the principalities of Wallachia and

Moldavia, the core of the future Romanian national state. Serbia, Romania, and Montenegro received recognition as national kingdoms after the Russo-Turkish War (1877–1878). Also, at this time Bulgaria was granted autonomous status within the Ottoman Empire. Independence did not bring an end to the nationalist struggles, however, because the borders of these new states did not include all the national lands based on historical or population claims. For example, Serbia desired Bosnia and Greece wanted Crete.

The conflicting irredentist claims of Serbia, Greece, and Bulgaria on remaining Ottoman lands in Macedonia brought intense competition among the Balkan governments for control over that region. In response to the potentially destabilizing set of rivalries among the Balkan states, Russia and Austria found common interest in preserving the status quo in the peninsula. The two Great Powers signed the Austro-Russian Balkan Agreement of 1897 and reiterated their cooperation in the Murzsteg Agreement of 1903. Under these agreements, Austria and Russia agreed to put the Balkans "on ice," meaning that they would not countenance any territorial changes in the region and they would impose Ottoman administrative reforms in Macedonia to quell the revolutionary potential.

In 1908, a revolution did break out in Macedonia, but it was a Turkish one. The Ottoman Third Army Corps, stationed in Macedonia, spearheaded the **Young Turk** Revolution by marching on Constantinople and forcing Sultan Abdul Hamid II to restore the constitution in June–July 1908. The Young Turks held out the prospect that the Ottoman Empire would at last be thoroughly reformed, and they promised that all Ottoman citizens would receive equal constitutional rights and participation in a parliamentary democracy. Therefore, the Young Turk government wanted to reclaim administrative control over Bosnia from Austria on the grounds that Turkish constitutional reforms obviated the need for Austrian administration. The promise of reform meant also that the autonomous Bulgarian principality would find its road to independence blocked. Austria therefore coordinated with Bulgaria to secure their territories against Turkish control. In 1908, Austria declared its annexation of Bosnia while simultaneously Bulgaria declared its national independence from the Ottoman Empire. Serbian officials expressed outrage that Austria had taken Bosnia, and Belgrade appealed to the Russians to force Austria to renounce its annexation. Stymied in their expansion to the east, the Serbs refocused their attention on expansion southward towards the Kosovo region of Macedonia.

Meanwhile, the Russians encouraged all the Christian Balkan states to come together in an alliance to serve as a check on any further Austrian expansion into southeastern Europe, and these efforts resulted in the formation of the Balkan League in 1912. Having facilitated the military coordination of Bulgaria, Serbia, Greece, and Montenegro as a defensive bloc against Austria, the Russians watched helplessly as the countries of the **Balkan League** redirected their energies into an offensive alliance against the Turks. In concert, the Balkan League attacked the Ottoman Empire in the First **Balkan War** (October 1912–May 1913) with the goal of driving the Turks from Europe once and for all. Although the Balkan allies were spectacularly successful in pushing the Turks back, the conflicting claims on Macedonia soon divided them against one another. These divisions led to the Second Balkan War (June–August 1913), in which Bulgaria launched an attack against its former allies Serbia and Greece to gain most of the territory of north-central Macedonia. The Romanians and the Ottomans quickly entered the war against Bulgaria too. Beaten back on all sides, the Bulgarians were forced to capitulate. After World War I, the emergence of the Turkish Republic in 1923 brought the Eastern Question to a close. *See also* Berlin, Congress of; British Empire; Habsburg Empire; Russian Empire; Pan-Slavism; Paris, Treaty of; San Stefano, Treaty of.

FURTHER READING: Anderson, Matthew S. *The Eastern Question, 1774–1923.* New York: St. Martin's, 1966; Clayton, Gerald. *Britain and the Eastern Question.* London: University of London Press, 1971; Duggan, Stephen. *The Eastern Question, A Study in Diplomacy.* New York: AMS Press, 1970.

JONATHAN GRANT

## East India Companies

English, French, and Dutch chartered trading companies, in each case dating to the seventeenth century. In the case of the Netherlands, the Vereenigde Oostindische Compaagnie (VOC) was chartered in 1602 to govern and extend Dutch colonial holdings in **India,** Java, and Sumatra, and by 1650 its wealth and naval reach made the Netherlands a world power and the world's foremost trading nation. The French Revolutionary and Napoleonic Wars, however, were devastating to the Netherlands as well as to Dutch overseas possessions, so that by 1815 many of the VOC's holdings had been lost and the company was nationalized and reemerged as the Dutch Colonial Office.

The French Compagnie des Indes Orientales was established in 1664. It was active in India, as well as in Mauritius and Bourbon in the Indian Ocean until French defeats in the War of Austrian Succession, 1740–1748, and the Seven Years' War, 1756–1763.

The English East India Company, by far the most durable and successful of the three, was chartered by Elizabeth I in 1600. Initially in competition with Portuguese, Dutch, and French ventures, the company nonetheless secured a foothold on the Indian subcontinent in 1619 and never let go. In 1657, it was reconstituted as a joint stock company and developed a capacity for surviving intact the violent changes of English politics in the eighteenth century. Between 1740 and 1793, it also vied with its French rival for advantage in India until the wars of the late eighteenth century shunted circumstance decidedly in its favor. The company then profited again during the **Napoleonic Wars** by the virtual elimination of its Dutch rival and the acquisition of formerly Dutch possessions.

Nicknamed the John Company, the British East India company often operated as a state unto itself—raising troops, fighting wars, and bribing local officials—until by mid-nineteenth century, the company controlled roughly two-thirds of India. Its considerable independence made it a routine item of political controversy in Britain, so that successive acts of Parliament and charter renewals were used to limit its financial and administrative autonomy until the Indian Mutiny of 1857 prompted the British government to terminate the company. The passage of the India Act in 1858 brought India under the direct control of the British Crown. *See also* British Empire; Hudson's Bay Company; Free Trade.

FURTHER READING: Furber, Holden. *John Company at Work.* New York: Octagon Books, 1948; Glamann, Kristof. *Dutch-Asiatic Trade.* Copenhagen: Danish Science Press, 1958; Lawson,

Philip. *The East India Company: A History.* New York: Longman, 1993; Philips, C. H. *The East India Company.* Manchester: Manchester University Press, 1961; Wesseling, H. L. *The European Colonial Empires, 1815–1919.* London: Longman, 2004.

CARL CAVANAGH HODGE

## Eckmühl, Battle of (1809)

Napoleon **Bonaparte**'s victory in Bavaria over the Austrian army under Archduke **Charles.** After the battle of **Abensberg,** Marshal Davout's French Third Corps engaged a reinforced 17,000 strong Austrian IV Korps around the Laiching villages, just west of Eckmühl, eight miles south of Regensburg, on April 21. Napoleon had taken the main French army 18 miles south to Landshut, but turned his troops north. As Davout's 20,000 men renewed their attack from the west around 2 P.M. on April 22, Napoleon arrived with another 60,000 Franco-German troops. While Davout pinned the Austrian right wing, Napoleon's troops seized Eckmühl village, crossed the Grosse Laaber River and shattered the Austrian center on the Bettelberg hill. Left unsupported, Rosenberg retreated northwards up the Regensburg road at about 4 P.M.

FURTHER READING: Castle, I. *Eckmühl 1809.* Oxford: Osprey Military Publishing, 1998.

DAVID HOLLINS

## Edward VII, King of Great Britain (1841–1910)

King of Great Britain and Ireland and Emperor of India from 1901 to 1910, Edward VII was the eldest son of Queen **Victoria.** Owing to his mother's longevity he did not ascend the throne until late middle age. He had in the meantime acquired a justified reputation as a *bon vivant,* although he always took his royal duties seriously, becoming as Prince of Wales something of a model for the future role of royals as roving public ambassadors. As king, he played an active and at times independent role in foreign affairs, being perhaps the last monarch to do so. In pre-1914 Europe, with most of the continent still under monarchical rule, he had close personal connections to most countries, including Germany, although there was no love lost between Edward and his nephew Kaiser **Wilhelm II,** whose naval building program was in some measure motivated by imagined slights from his uncle. Edward was a Francophile, and his visit to Paris in 1903 foreshadowed the Anglo-French *Entente Cordiale* of the following year.

Edward also played a role in reconciling Britain and Russia, long divided over the Balkans, Central Asia, and Persia, with his 1908 visit. He was opposed to the overuse of the Lords' veto against the reforming measures of Herbert **Asquith**'s Liberals, but he was also hostile to a threatened mass creation of peers to overcome the problem, going so far as to contemplate abdication. Edward died on May 6, 1910 before he had to confront the issue. He is remembered for his post-Victorian geniality, his large lifestyle, and his diplomatic skills. He was the last monarch to give his name to an era; the Edwardian era, in fact bedeviled by international crises and social tensions, is often seen through spectacles given an anachronistic rose tint by the disasters of the next decade.

FURTHER READING: Lee, Sidney. *King Edward the Seventh.* 2 vols. London: MacMillan, 1925–1927; Magnus, Philip. *King Edward the Seventh.* London: John Murray, 1964.

MARK F. PROUDMAN

## Egypt

Although in fact largely independent from much of the period, Egypt was formally a tributary province of the **Ottoman Empire** from 1800 to 1914. Napoleon **Bonaparte,** hoping to enhance his own prestige and to threaten India, invaded in 1898, but his forces were shortly evicted by the British. Power in Egypt fell to **Mehmet Ali,** an Albanian janissary in the Turkish service, who rapidly established himself as Viceroy in Egypt, killing many of the former Mameluke upper classes in the process and defeating British troops in 1807. Mehmet Ali became the forebear of the Egyptian dynasty that reigned until it was overthrown by Gamal Abdel Nasser's "Free Officers" movement in 1952. In theory subject to the Sultan, Mehmet Ali supported his ostensible master during the Greek civil war, losing his fleet at the battle of Navarino (1827) in consequence. In 1838, Mehmet Ali declared his intention of becoming independent of Turkey, which provoked a war that went badly for the Turks, the Egyptians invading Anatolia and threatening Constantinople. Lord **Palmerston,** as foreign secretary, saw Mehmet Ali as a French client and in 1840, he sent forces to Egypt to force his withdrawal. Mehmet Ali died in 1849.

By the 1850s, the introduction of steamships having made the Red Sea navigable all year round, an increasing quantity of British trade to India went through Egypt. Napoleon III proposed to Palmerston that England should occupy Egypt and France Morocco; the latter demurred on the grounds—justified by later events—that such an occupation would lead to innumerable diplomatic complications. The introduction of cotton cultivation further attracted Europeans and European capital, and the cotton famine caused by the U.S. Civil War resulted in a windfall for Egypt's rulers. Borrowing for investment and for vice, Egypt descended into debt as regal spending boomed and the American war ended. Various schemes for the construction of a canal through the Isthmus of Suez had been proposed over the decades. In 1859, against Palmerston's objections, construction started on a canal, the effort being led by Ferdinand de Lesseps; the Egyptian viceroy held a minority stake. The **Suez Canal** was complete in 1869, vastly increasing the strategic value of Egypt.

In the 1870s, Egypt's finances fell into complete disarray, and the Khedive was forced to both sell his shares in the canal—snapped up by Benjamin **Disraeli**'s government to keep them out of French hands—and to accept foreign financial oversight in the form of a "dual control" staffed by French and British representatives. In 1879, Khedive Ismail attempted to free himself from foreign control and for his pains was replaced by his son Tewfik on the orders of the Porte, the latter acting at Anglo-French prompting. A nationalist movement under Colonel Ahmed Arabi began to gather force in Egypt, objecting to both Turkish overlordship and European control and also to the military cuts insisted on by European comptrollers. An Anglo-French note of January 1882 offered support to Tewfik, but it had only the effect of making him appear a foreign puppet. The growing power of Arabi, and anti-European riots in Alexandria in June 1882, prompted the arrival of an Anglo-French fleet. But the French government then fell, and the French fleet was ordered to sail. The British admiral on the spot considered that the arming of

Alexandria's forts by Arabi constituted a danger to his force, and on July 11, 1882, he bombarded the city. An expeditionary force under Sir Garnet Wolseley defeated Arabi's army at Tel el-Kebir in the Canal Zone on September 13, 1882.

While out of power, William **Gladstone** had urged strongly against intervention in Egypt, famously arguing that a British foothold there would become "the certain egg of a North African empire"; he found, in 1882, that, driven by force of circumstance, he had acquired just such an egg. Britain was soon drawn into the **Sudan,** and thence into Uganda and East Africa. As Gladstone had feared, dreamers like Cecil Rhodes spoke of a "Cape to Cairo" empire. From 1882 until Nasser's coup, Egypt was effectively a British client, although it remained through 1914 formally an Ottoman province. In 1883, the British installed Sir Evelyn Baring, later Lord **Cromer,** as consul-general and effective mayor of the palace to the Khedive. Cromer later proclaimed that "we do not govern Egypt; we only govern the governors of Egypt." He set about rationalizing Egypt's finances, and he did a creditable job of paying creditors, reigning in corruption, increasing exports, restoring a healthy balance of payments, and incurring the enduring hostility of Egyptian nationalists. Cromer was skeptical of the Sudanese interventions of 1884–1885and 1896–1898 as too expensive, although others saw them as essential to Egypt or Britain's prestige. In 1914, Britain, on going to war with Turkey, proclaimed a protectorate over Egypt, although that had in practice been the case since 1882. *See also* Aboukir Bay, Battle of; Africa, Scramble for; Napoleonic Wars.

FURTHER READING: Cromer, Lord. *Modern Egypt.* London: MacMillan, 1908; Karabell, Zachary. *Parting the Waters: The Creation of the Suez Canal.* New York: Random House, 2003; Marlowe, John. *Spoiling the Egyptians.* London: André Deutsch, 1974; Robinson, Ronald, John Gallagher, and Alice Denny. *Africa and the Victorians: The Official Mind of Imperialism.* London: MacMillan, 1961.

MARK F. PROUDMAN

## Elgar, Edward (1857–1934)

A significant contributor to late romantic European music and possibly the greatest English composer of his generation, Edward Elgar is best known for his major works, which include *The Dream of Gerontius* and *Variations on an Original Theme "Enigma."* His less substantial *Pomp & Circumstance Marches,* however, became standards of popular national sentiment. Most notably, A. C. Benson's *Land of Hope & Glory,* set to Elgar's *Pomp & Circumstance March No.1,* is to this day sung at the last night of the Prom Concerts, its words evoking the patriotism of power.

FURTHER READING: Kennedy, Michael. *Portrait of Elgar.* London: Oxford University Press, 1968.

CARL CAVANAGH HODGE

## Elgin, James Bruce, Eighth Earl of (1811–1863)

Governor-in-chief of British North America, Elgin inherited his earldom and a heavily encumbered estate in 1841. In 1842, he accepted appointment as governor of Jamaica and spent the rest of his career in imperial employment. In Jamaica, he was unable to resolve conflicts between planters and former slaves—now "apprentices"—caused by the abolition of slavery in the previous decade.

In 1846, he went to **Canada,** where he oversaw the adoption of **responsible government.** In Canada, he outraged Tory opinion by speaking French in the legislature and by assenting to the Rebellion Losses bill, which in the Tory view rewarded disloyalty. He also oversaw the negotiation of the 1854 reciprocity treaty with the United States. Refusing a cabinet post in Lord **Palmerston**'s government, in 1857, Elgin was made plenipotentiary to **China** and **Japan,** responsible for opening up trade with those nations with the aid of a large expeditionary force that sailed with him. He was successful in both countries.

In 1859, however, Chinese forts fired on a British emissary—who happened to be Elgin's brother—and Palmerston sent Elgin back to China with a combined Anglo-French force which in 1860 sacked the Chinese emperor's summer palace and entered Peking in triumph. In 1862, he was made Viceroy of **India,** where he died the following year.

FURTHER READING: Checkland, S. G. *The Elgins: A Tale of Aristocrats, Pronconsuls and Their Wives.* Aberdeeen: Aberdeen University Press, 1988.

MARK F. PROUDMAN

### Elgin, Victor Alexander Bruce, Ninth Earl of (1849–1917)

Victor Bruce, ninth earl of Elgin was viceroy of **India.** The son of the eighth earl of **Elgin,** Victor was born in **Canada** but educated at Eton and Balliol, Oxford. Appointed Viceroy of India by the Liberal Prime Minister Lord Rosebery in 1894, he served through 1899. In India, he was a moderate reformer, overseeing the operation of the Tories' Indian Councils Act of 1892, which introduced a small degree of representative government in India, and he also worked energetically on famine relief. His viceroyalty, however, has tended to be overshadowed by the more programmatic tenure of his successor, Lord **Curzon.**

Elgin served as colonial secretary in the ministry of Henry **Campbell-Bannerman,** where he oversaw the grant of self-government to the conquered Boer republics. He is best remembered, however, for controlling his bumptious young parliamentary secretary, Winston **Churchill.** Churchill began his tenure of office by sending Elgin a long memorandum describing the Empire's problems and ending with the words "these are my views." Elgin returned the paper with the annotation, "but not mine."

FURTHER READING: Checkland, S. G. *The Elgins: A Tale of Aristocrats, Pronconsuls and Their Wives.* Aberdeeen: Aberdeen University Press, 1988.

MARK F. PROUDMAN

### Ems Telegram (1870)

Document that instigated the **Franco-Prussian War.** The Ems Telegram was a message from the Prussian King, **Wilhelm I,** to Prime Minister **Otto von Bismarck.** On July 13, 1870, the telegram was sent from Bad Ems where Wilhelm spent his holidays. It reported an encounter between Wilhelm and the French ambassador, in which the king politely refused to promise that no member of his family would seek the Spanish throne. Bismarck changed the wording of the telegram. By abridgement, Bismarck made it look like outright provocation on the part of France, and he had it published in the newspapers. Bismarck's intention was to start a war with France. The French considered the doctored telegram a provocation. On July 19, France declared war on the North German Confederation. *See also* Bonaparte, Louis Napoleon; German Empire.

FURTHER READING: Howard, Michael. *The Franco-Prussian War.* New York: Collier, 1969; Wawro, Geoffrey. *The Franco-Prussian War: The German Conquest of France in 1870–1871.* Cambridge: Cambridge University Press, 2003; Wetzel, David. *A Duel of Giants: Bismarck, Napoleon III and the Origins of the Franco-Prussian War.* Madison: University of Wisconsin Press, 2001.

MARTIN MOLL

## Engels, Friedrich (1820–1895)

A philosopher and political economist, Friedrich Engels is best known as Karl **Marx**'s lifetime friend and ally. Engels was born in Barmen, present-day Wuppertal, Germany on November 28, 1820, the eldest son of a successful textile manufacturer. The works of the radical German poet Heinrich Heine (1797–1856) and the German philosopher Georg Wilhelm Friedrich Hegel (1770–1831) greatly influenced Engels. The German Socialist Moses Hess (1812–1875) converted Engels to Communist beliefs. While passing through Paris in 1844, Engels met Marx, and their lifelong association began.

In Manchester, England, Engels came into contact with chartism, the movement for extension of suffrage to workers. He contributed to the *Northern Star* and other publications and made a study of political economy. His experience and studies convinced him that politics and history could be explained only in terms of the economic development of society. He firmly believed that the social evils of the time were the inevitable result of the age-old institution of private property. These conclusions were embodied in a historical study, *Condition of the Working Class in England* (1844), a creditable piece of factual research that was highly praised by Karl Marx and established Engels's reputation as a revolutionary political economist.

In 1844, Engels visited Marx in Paris. Marx had published works sympathetic to **communism.** The two men found that they had arrived independently at identical views on capitalism. Engels wrote that there was virtually "complete agreement in all theoretical fields." Their many-sided collaboration, which continued until the death of Marx in 1883, had two principal aspects: systematic development of the principles of communism, later known as Marxism; and the organization of an international Communist movement. Lesser aspects of their collaboration included journalistic writing for the *New York Tribune* and other publications.

In elaborating Communist ideas and principles, the two men delved into the field of philosophy but subsequently turned to other fields. Marx dealt particularly with political thought, political economy, and economic history; Engels's interests included the physical sciences, mathematics, anthropology, military science, and languages. *The Communist Manifesto* (1848), written by Marx, partly on the basis of a draft prepared by Engels, influenced all subsequent Communist literature and is regarded as a classic articulation of modern Communist views.

After the death of Marx in 1883, Engels, in his own words, had to play the first fiddle for the first time. He did it through his writings that suggested the "orthodox" ways of interpreting Marx and through advising numerous newly emerging Marxist groups in various countries. Sometimes Engels tried to serve as a moderating influence, raising his voice against extreme emphasis on "revolutionary violence." He could not, however, prevent Leninist-Stalinist orthodoxy from shaping some of the most oppressive totalitarian regimes of the time. Engels died in London on August 5, 1895, long before it all happened; but his name, just as the name of Marx, cannot be dissociated from the most traumatic experiment of the twentieth century. Engels was also a military critic, and he held out the hope that the universal conscription common in his time might become the vehicle of social revolution—a hope not wholly unfounded. *See also* Lenin, Vladimir.

FURTHER READING: Henderson, W. O. *Marx and Engels and the English Workers and Other Essays.* London: Taylor & Francis, 1989; Marcus, S. *Engels, Manchester, and the Working Class.* New York: Random House, 1974; Riazanov, David. *Karl Marx and Friedrich Engels.* New York: International Publishers, 1927; Schumpeter, Joseph A. *Capitalism, Socialism, and Democracy.* New York: Harper, New York, 1950; Tucker, R. C. *The Marx-Engels Reader.* New York: Norton, 1972.

JITENDRA UTTAM

## Entente Cordiale (1904)

A "friendly understanding," the Entente Cordiale was an agreement signed on April 8, 1904, between France and Britain resolving longstanding colonial grievances. The agreement initiated a policy of Anglo-French cooperation and served as the embryo for the Triple Entente between Britain, France, and Russia during World War I.

Before the entente, Britain focused on maintaining a policy of "splendid isolation" from continental European affairs, and France became increasingly preoccupied with the preservation of its security after its 1871 defeat by Prussia, which subsequently unified a German state. A temporary shift in German policy, emphasizing relations with Britain, prompted Russia to fear isolation. France, seeking an ally against Germany, sought an 1891 Russian entente and eventually signed a military pact in 1894 that became a cornerstone of foreign policy for both countries.

Recent developments in Egypt had strained France's relations with Britain. The khedive declared bankruptcy in 1876, and a system of Anglo-French control, using an international financial commission, worked to eliminate Egypt's debt. But in 1882, an uprising prompted Britain to secure the Suez Canal. When France refused to assist, Britain occupied Egypt unilaterally and dissolved dual control. A humiliated France used its creditor position to complicate British attempts to reform international financial control. French foreign minister Théophile Declassé believed that Britain would negotiate over Egypt if pressured at a vital location. He chose Fashoda on the upper Nile River, but the venture led to another humiliation in the **Fashoda Incident** of 1898. After Fashoda, France altered its Egyptian policy from confrontation to compensation and focused on Morocco to complete its North African empire and to improve its Mediterranean position.

Fear of German naval expansion and tension with Russia, meanwhile, made France attractive to Britain. In 1903, King **Edward VII** of Britain and French President Émile Loubet made reciprocal state visits to mend Anglo-French relations. Negotiations between Paul Cambon, French ambassador, and Lord Lansdowne, British foreign secretary, then ran from July 1903 to April 1904. The talks involved Madagascar, the New Hebrides, Newfoundland fishing rights, Siam, and West Africa. At the center of negotiations, however, was the future of Egypt and Morocco. Britain jettisoned its Moroccan ambitions in return for promises of free trade lasting 30 years. France agreed to give Britain a free hand in Egypt and to refrain from Mediterranean coastal fortifications that could menace Gibraltar. To prevent a German alliance, Britain also argued Spain's Moroccan interests needed consideration. Subsequent German behavior in the Moroccan Crisis of 1905 served to deepen Anglo-French collaboration and led to the military conversations of 1906–1914.

An Anglo-Russian entente followed in 1907, establishing a spheres-of-influence understanding in Afghanistan, Persia, and Tibet, but also paving the path toward formation of the Triple Entente and ultimately an alliance that confronted Germany with a two-front war in August 1914. *See also:* Anglo-Japanese Alliance; Balance of Power; Triple Alliance.

FURTHER READING: Andrew, Christopher. *Théophile Declassé and the Making of the Entente Cordiale.* New York: St. Martin's Press, 1968; Dunlop, Ian. *Edward VII and the Entente Cordiale.* London: Constable, 2004; Rolo, P.J.V. *Entente Cordiale: The Origins of the Anglo-French Agreements of April 8, 1904.* New York: St. Martin's Press, 1969.

ERIC MARTONE

## Eritrea

Eritrea was an Italian colony on the Red Sea coast of east Africa. In 1869, the Rubattino Steamship Company had purchased the port of Assab to use as a trading station on the Red Sea. When the port proved less than successful, Italian investors acquired Massawa in 1885 with the connivance of the British. This angered **Ethiopia,** which believed that Italy had infringed on its rights to the city. To avoid a conflict, the Italians agreed to halt further expansion. The Ethiopian Emperor Yohannes IV, however, believed that the Italians violated this promise and attacked an Italian military column at Dogali in 1887, before advancing toward Massawa. There were only a small number of Italian forces in East Africa, and Italy was unwilling to send metropolitan troops. So colonial officials reached an understanding with Menelik, king of Shoa, against Johannes, thereby embroiling Italy in Ethiopian politics.

Menelik gave Asmara and Keren to the Italians, who also gained further territory from warring Moslem tribes. The informal colonial administration, which until 1882 was a mixed private-public company, proved inadequate. Rome appointed military governors, but imperial enthusiasts went further and argued that a single colony in East Africa would better aid the spread of Italian influence. In 1890, the Italian government therefore merged the scattered holdings along the Red Sea into Eritrea. Yet the hopes to use Eritrea as a base for colonial expansion ended with Italy's defeat at the Battle of **Adowa** in 1896. With its territorial ambitions shattered, Italy transferred control of Eritrea to civilian authority and moved the capital to Asmara. Otherwise, Italy neglected the colony, hoping it would absorb the nation's excess population and become self-sufficient. Eritrea exported a limited variety of agricultural products—coffee, gum, and hides—but lacked other natural resources and was ill-suited for large-scale farming. It required constant subsidization. The only benefit the colony provided was in the large number of Eritreans who fought during the Italo-Ottoman War of 1911–1912. *See also* Africa, Scramble for.

FURTHER READING: Berkeley, G.F.H. *The Campaign of Adowa and the Rise of Menelik.* London: Constable, 1902; Tekeste, Negash. *Italian Colonialism in Eritrea, 1882–1941: Policies, Praxis, and Impact.* Stockholm: Uppsala University Press, 1987.

FREDERICK H. DOTOLO

## Ethiopia

The reunification of Ethiopia, an ancient east African kingdom also known as **Abyssinia,** was begun in the nineteenth century by Lij Kasa, who conquered Amhara, Gojjam, Tigray, and Shoa, and in 1855 had himself crowned emperor as Tewodros II. He began to modernize and centralize the legal and administrative systems, despite the opposition of local governors. Tensions developed with Great Britain, and Tewodros imprisoned several Britons in 1867, including the British consul. A British military expedition under Robert Napier, later Lord Napier, was sent out and easily defeated the emperor's forces near Magdala in 1868. To avoid capture, Tewodros committed suicide.

A brief civil war followed, and in 1872, a chieftain of Tigray became emperor as Yohannes IV. Yohannes's attempts to further centralize the government led to revolts by local leaders. In addition, his regime was threatened during the years 1875–1876 by Egyptian incursions and, after 1881, by raids of followers of the **Mahdi** in **Sudan.** The opening of the **Suez Canal** in 1869 increased the strategic importance of Ethiopia, and several European powers—particularly Italy, France, and Great Britain—vied for influence in the area. **Italy** focused its attention on Ethiopia, seizing Aseb in 1872 and Massawa in 1885. In 1889, Yohannes was killed fighting the Mahdists. After a brief succession crisis, the king of Shoa, who had Italian support, was crowned Emperor **Menelik II.**

Menelik signed a treaty of friendship and cooperation with Italy at Wuchale in 1889. In response to a dispute over the meaning of the treaty—Rome claimed it had been given a protectorate over Ethiopia, which Menelik denied—Italy invaded Ethiopia in 1895 but was decisively defeated by Menelik's forces at **Adowa** on March 1, 1896. By the subsequent Treaty of Addis Ababa, signed in October 1896, the Treaty of Wuchale was annulled, and Italy recognized the independence of Ethiopia while retaining its Eritrean colonial base. During his reign, Menelik greatly expanded the size of Ethiopia, adding the provinces of Harar, Sidamo, and Kaffa. In addition, he further modernized both the military and government and made Addis Ababa the capital of the country in 1889, developed the economy, and promoted the building of the country's first railroad.

Thus Ethiopia was the only independent sub-Saharan African state at the end of the nineteenth century. In October 1935, Italy invaded the country. Addis Ababa fell to the invaders, and in May 1936, Mussolini proclaimed Italy's King Victor Emmanuel III Emperor of Ethiopia. *See also* Africa, Scramble for; Egypt; Eritrea.

FURTHER READING: Marcus, Harold G. *A History of Ethiopia*. Berkeley: University of California Press, 1994; Zewde, Bahru. *A History of Modern Ethiopia, 1855–1974*. London: J. Currey, 1991.

MOSHE TERDMAN

## Extraterritoriality

Extraterritoriality refers to immunity from the jurisdiction of one's territory of residence, arising in large part from the demands of Europeans resident in non-Christian states. It is usually reserved for the official representatives of states and international organizations, but European powers obtained extraterritorial privileges for their citizens in all the independent states of the "East" in the middle of the nineteenth century. The origins of this form of extraterritoriality can be traced back to the southern Mediterranean, where rulers since the Middle Ages dealt with communities of Western traders by allowing them to govern themselves in the so-called "capitulations." Rulers in the Far East may likewise have perceived extraterritoriality as a means of dealing with isolated communities of alien coastal traders. But where it formed part of "unequal treaties," such as those extracted from China in 1842, Japan in 1854, and Siam in 1855, it became a tool in the arsenal of informal imperialism and a humiliating sign that the states forced to grant extraterritorial privileges to foreigners were regarded as inferior and incapable of "civilized" government.

Extraterritorial jurisdiction was exercised by foreign consuls and therefore entailed the establishment of consular outposts wherever foreigners were allowed to reside. It was claimed to imply freedom from taxation for Western nationals and businesses and was not always exercised without partiality toward Western defendants. As it applied also to subjects of the European powers' colonies, groups like citizens of Hong Kong in mainland China or Burmese and Laotians in Siam were effectively beyond the reach of the local administration.

One of the main political aims of Asia's modernizing nations was to free themselves of the infringement on sovereignty that extraterritoriality implied. The only way to do so was to establish a Western-style legal system with an independent judiciary and published laws. Japan obtained the renunciation of extraterritoriality in this manner in 1899, and Britain renounced extraterritoriality in Siam in 1909, tough on condition that justice be administered by a Western judge when the defendant was British. Therefore extraterritoriality and the struggle to remove it were a powerful agent of institutional westernization.

Germany lost all of her extraterritorial privileges in the Versailles peace settlement of 1919. In China, Britain and the United States held on to extraterritoriality until 1943, when China became their military ally. *See also* Ottoman Empire; Qing Dynasty.

FURTHER READING: Gong, Gerrit W. *The Standard of "Civilization" in International Society*. Oxford: Clarendon, 1984; Scully, Eileen P. *Bargaining with the State from Afar: American Citizenship in Treaty Port China, 1844–1942*. New York: Columbia University Press, 2001.

NIELS P. PETERSSON

## Eylau, Battle of (1807)

A bloody yet indecisive battle of the **Napoleonic Wars** between Russian Field Marshal Levin Bennigsen's 67,000 men and Napoleon **Bonaparte**'s 45,000. On

February 7, in bitter cold, the French took possession of the town of Eylau, southeast of Königsberg in East Prussia. The next day, Bennigsen attacked in the midst of a sudden blizzard. Napoleon's flanks were under heavy pressure and Marshal Pierre Augereau's moves against the Russian center were ineffective, as in the confusion of the blizzard they swerved off course into the fire of the Russian guns. The Russians even threatened Napoleon's headquarters, but the Imperial Guard prevented disaster. Seeking the initiative, Marshal Joachim Murat led more than 10,000 cavalry in a dramatic attack, overrunning the Russian guns and center before returning to safety. With reinforcements arriving on both sides, the battle continued under awful conditions until 11 P.M. that evening, after which Bennigsen withdrew. Tired and numbed by the weather and slaughter, both sides withdrew to their winter quarters to await a spring campaign. The battle is commemorated by the painting *Napoleon at Eylau* by Antoine-Jean Gros in the Musée du Louvre. *See also* Tilsit, Treaty of.

FURTHER READING: Goltz, Colmar, Freiherr von der. *Jena to Eylau: The Disgrace and Redemption of the Old Russian Army*. Translated by C. F. Atkinson. New York: E. P. Dutton, 1913; Summerville, C. J. *Napoleon's Polish Gamble: Eylau and Friedland, 1807*. Barnsley, England: Pen & Sword Military, 2005.

J. DAVID MARKHAM

# F

## Falkenhayn, Erich von (1861–1922)

A Prussian general and chief of the German general staff from 1914 to 1916, Erich von Falkenhayn was born into a Prussian **Junker** family. His military career began at the age of 10 with his entry in a military school. He interrupted his successful military career and became a military adviser in China in 1896. Falkenhayn came to the attention of the kaiser while working as a general staff officer in the East Asian Expeditionary Corps. The peak of his prewar career was the appointment to Prussian minister of war in July 1913. Following Helmuth von Moltke's dismissal after the Battle of the Marne in September 1914, Falkenhayn replaced him as the chief of the general staff. He initially attempted to achieve a victory by continuing the campaign on the Western Front but failed in the Battle of Ypres.

He aimed at a negotiated peace, but was unable to convince the chancellor or other influential military leaders, above all Paul von Hindenburg and Erich von Ludendorff, of his strategy. Their attempts to achieve his dismissal in early 1915 failed, and Falkenhayn continued in his post until August 1916, when Rumania declared war on Germany and he lost the kaiser's support, which had thus far protected him from his critics. He was replaced by Hindenburg and Ludendorff. His name is closely linked with the disastrous Verdun campaign and with a **strategy** of attrition aimed at a negotiated peace. After his dismissal he commanded the Ninth Army in Rumania, followed by stints in Turkey and Russia. In 1920, Falkenhayn published his memoirs; he died in 1922 from kidney failure. *See also* German Empire; Schlieffen Plan.

FURTHER READING: Afflerbach, Holger. *Falkenhayn. Politisches Denken und Handeln im Kaiserreich.* Munich: Oldenbourg, 1996; Falkenhayn, Erich von. *Die Oberste Heeresleitung 1914–1916 in ihren wichtigsten Entschliessungen,* Berlin: E. S. Mitter, 1919; Foley, Robert T. *German Strategy and the Path to Verdun: Erich von Falkenhayn and the Development of Attrition, 1870–1916.* New York: Cambridge University Press, 2005.

ANNIKA MOMBAUER

**Far East**

Usually referred to today as East and Southeast Asia, the Far East encompasses the region of Asia that reaches geographically from the Malay Peninsula in the southwest to **Korea** and **Japan** in the northeast. Politically, a large part of the region belonged to the old Chinese world at the beginning of the Age of Imperialism, bound to the Manchu court in Peking by cultural ties and tributary relationships. Europeans had only a tenuous foothold there at that time: the Philippines were part of the Spanish Empire, and the Portuguese held **Macao** and, in present-day Indonesia, had accepted various forms of subservience to the Dutch. Western traders were allowed limited intercourse with Chinese merchants in the southern port city of Canton, but China had twice, in 1793–95 and 1816, rejected Britain's demand for more regular diplomatic and commercial relations. Japan finally refused commercial or political intercourse with the outside world.

Imperialism, understood in a cultural sense, includes the development of a system of meanings in which the Far East was "far away" from a West that began to perceive itself as the sole and undisputed center of civilization. Notions like the Chinese view according to which China was the center of the world and countries beyond East Asia did not count for much were swept away by the superior force of Western industry, arms, and organization. And although eighteenth-century Europeans were ready to admire China and Japan as ancient civilizations with important cultural achievements to their credit, this attitude gave way, around 1830, to the picture of a stagnant, decadent East to be uplifted and civilized by the more advanced West. Confidence in the superiority of the West remained predominant for the rest of the Age of Imperialism and was rattled only by the experience of Europe's near self-destruction in World War I. Imperialism was not primarily a cultural process, however, and it was power in its various forms that determined that the Far East was "far away," China was no longer "central," not even for the Chinese, and Japan was no longer able to maintain her self-imposed isolation.

The geopolitical situation after the defeat of France in 1815 was marked by the predominant position of the **British Empire.** In the Far East, British policy was shaped by her rule over India and by her trading interests, especially in the highly profitable exchange of Chinese tea and silver against Indian opium. By mid-century, the increasing superiority of British—and later, more generally Western—industry, technology, arms, and organization had markedly increased the cost-benefit ratio of overseas expansion; and additional incentives for expansion were provided by the search for new markets, whether demanded by industrialists and traders or preemptively pursued by politicians, the desire for national greatness, competition between the imperialist powers, and the revival of the Christian missionary enterprise.

Britain took **Singapore,** controlling the Malacca Straits, which link the Indian Ocean with the South China Sea, in 1819. In three wars in 1824–26, 1852–53 and 1885, India's neighbor **Burma,** which was unwilling to accept commercial relations and a subservient position vis-à-vis **India,** was also conquered. But otherwise the British were reluctant to expand territorially and kept in check Indian officials and local adventurers who sought to extend British possessions. In 1816, they returned the Dutch colonies seized during the Napoleonic Wars, and they continued to respect the domains of Spain and the Netherlands because these smaller powers kept out stronger rivals and ensured a minimum of order and commercial openness.

Therefore throughout Southeast Asia, Western direct administration remained limited to the pre-1815 colonies for much of the century, and expansion took the form of private adventurism or of contractual relationships with local rulers.

Indeed, in the most important instances, imperialism in the Far East led to "informal empire" rather than to outright colonial rule. **China, Siam,** and Japan all escaped colonialism—the latter even acquiring colonies of her own—but they did not escape other forms of institutionalized Western privilege and predominance. The First **Opium War,** 1839–1842, was the starting point of this form of expansionism: China, concerned about the economic and social dislocation caused by the opium trade, outlawed the importation of the drug and ordered the destruction of stocks accumulated in Canton. Britain retaliated and quickly defeated China. The policy of Britain's foreign minister, Lord **Palmerston,** is a perfect illustration of the "imperialism of free trade." Palmerston did not want to conquer China, but to make her accept **free trade**—notably, but not exclusively, in opium—and diplomatic relations following the forms developed among Western nations. Consequently, the peace settlement, the Treaty of Nanking of 1842, did not mention opium except in connection with compensation for unlawfully destroyed property. Instead, it forced China to open five **treaty ports** to foreign trade and residence, to limit her import duties to 5 percent, to grant foreigners **extraterritoriality,** and to accept official relations with foreign consuls. Further provisions included the cession of **Hong Kong** and a war indemnity. In 1856–1860, Britain, joined by France, again went to war against China, imposing a revised treaty, the Treaty of **Tientsin,** that provided for diplomatic representation at Peking, the creation of a Chinese foreign ministry, the Tsungli yamen, the opening of ports on the Yangtze River, freedom of movement for Christian missionaries, and an end to the Chinese practice of referring to Westerners as "barbarians" in official communication.

Elsewhere, the fate of China did not go unnoticed. Japan signed treaties modeled on the Treaty of Nanking in 1854 and 1858 under the threat of naval action from the **United States,** while Siam's leadership correctly figured a slightly less onerous settlement might be possible when entered into voluntarily, which happened in 1855. Korea accepted treaty relations with Japan and with Western powers in 1876. Informal empire thus rested on a series of "unequal treaties" between Western and Asian powers—"unequal," because the privileges conferred on the Western side were not reciprocal. Asian states retained their independent statehood, but lost part of their sovereignty and were constantly exposed to political or military interference. An important element of the treaty regime was the most-favored-nation clause, which automatically granted each "treaty power" all the privileges acquired by any one of them. This clause guaranteed the cosmopolitan character of Western dominance in the Far East, embodying the spirit of "a fair field and no favours" in which Britain, confident in her industrial, financial, and commercial superiority, led the opening up of the world for free trade and civil international relations—voluntarily if possible and by force if necessary.

Informal empire presupposed a measure of stability and efficiency on the part of Asian states, and restraint on the part of the West. However, the new character and urgency of Asian-Western relations was an important factor of destabilization throughout the Far East, although often in conjunction with internal factors such as ethnic and religious tensions and economic difficulties. In many parts of the Far East, the mid-nineteenth century therefore was a time of turbulence and rapid change. In China, the decline of the state's institutions and limits to economic growth—even as the population increased from 150 million to 430 million between 1700 and 1850—became apparent at the end of the eighteenth century. Conditions were aggravated by opium imports, corruption, and the political and military pressure of the West. Rebellions occurred with increasing frequency, the largest of which, the **Taiping Rebellion** cost 20 million lives between 1850 and 1864 and severely weakened the power and finances of the Chinese state.

Still following the lead of Britain, the powers pursued the "co-operative policy" of seeking to keep in power the Qing Dynasty during the years from 1860 to1895. Having accepted the Treaties of Tientsin, the Qing upheld the treaty regime, as the Western powers gently prodded them in the direction of reforms. Western soldiers under Charles **Gordon** fought against the Taiping, and the Imperial Maritime Customs was created, an administrative branch of the Chinese state organized on Western lines and staffed by Westerners, mostly Britons, under the leadership of Sir Robert Hart (1835–1911), which collected China's maritime duties and thereby provided the central government with its most important and most reliable source of income. The leading role in defeating the Taiping and introducing economic and military reforms, however, was played neither by Westerners nor by the imperial administration, but by local elites and provincial governors such as Tseng Kuo-fan (1811–1872) and Li Hung-chang (1823–1901). While the central government remained skeptical of modern technology and refused to authorize the construction of railways, provincial governors established China's first modern shipyards, arsenals, iron, and textile plants. The principles on which these enterprises were organized, "official supervision and merchant management" and "Chinese essence-Western application", however, implied that reforms stopped short of institutional change and in the end failed.

Meanwhile, Western penetration of the Chinese interior remained limited. Commerce did not develop in the proportions expected by those who had enthused about the "market with 400 million customers," and the activity of Western trading houses, although profitable, mostly remained confined to the treaty ports. As a result of quickly expanding Chinese emigration, there quickly were more East Asians in America than Westerners in East Asia. The only Westerners to penetrate deeply into the Chinese interior were Christian **missionaries.** The success they encountered in their endeavors was, like that of traders, disappointing. Nevertheless, missionary activity was the cause of severe and permanent conflict with local elites and populations and of frequent disturbances, sometimes involving the loss of life and always leading to demands for compensation supported by foreign consuls and, occasionally, gunboats.

A stark contrast to developments in China is presented by Japan. Like China, Japan experienced economic and social problems in the early nineteenth century and was pushed into internal conflict over how to deal with the threat from the West and the enforced opening to foreign commerce. There was violent opposition against the **Tokugawa shōgunate** that for many Japanese seemed too accommodating toward the Western powers, and in response to antiforeign rebellions, Western gunboats shelled Japanese cities in 1863–64. The Shogunate lost support and was abolished in 1868, power passing back into the hands of the *tenno,* the emperor. The **Meiji Restoration** was restorative only insofar as it reestablished the power of the *tenno;* otherwise, it started one of the most remarkable, comprehensive, and swift social transformations in human history. Guidance for the changes was provided by the slogan "rich country-strong army." The old class system of samurai, farmers, artisans and merchants was abolished and a Western-style administration replaced the old feudal system. A new centralized tax system provided the state with the means to put itself at the forefront of change. Compulsory education and military service were introduced. Modern industrial enterprises were set up by the state, some of them becoming competitive exporters after their privatization in the 1880s. High-ranking statesmen were sent on study missions abroad and foreign experts brought to Japan.

Japan passed through a phase of enthusiasm for things Western in the 1870s and experienced a conservative backlash in the 1880s, all the while developing her own version of modernity. Under the influence of conservative statesmen with first-hand experience of the West like Iwakura Tomomi (1825–83) and Hirobumi **Ito** (1841–1909), a concept for Japan's future political institutions took shape. Partly to fend off demands for parliamentary democracy, the *tenno* in 1881 promised a constitution and a national assembly. In 1889, Japan adopted a constitution influenced by that of imperial Germany, with an elected legislature and a government responsible only to the emperor. Legal and constitutional reform allowed Japan to negotiate an end to the "unequal treaties" by 1899. Thus within two decades after the Meiji restoration, Japan was a constitutional centralized state with a modern army and modern industry, Western-style legal institutions, and a modern education system. Within two more decades, she would become a great power with colonies of her own, and a cultural hub from which Western knowledge and methods were diffused, in adapted form, throughout the Far East.

On the fringes of the Far East, European territorial expansion accelerated when France and, later, Germany, the United States, and Japan became more active, and also because the opening of the **Suez Canal** in 1869 greatly improved communication with Europe. The nature of colonial rule, however, did not change much until the turn of the century. In 1859, France occupied Saigon in response to the murder of Christian missionaries, and in 1862, she acquired the surrounding territory of Cochinchina from Annam. **Cambodia,** feeling threatened by her neighbor Siam, accepted a French protectorate in 1863. France then concentrated on the search for an access to the China market via the Mekong and the Red River in **Tonkin.** These advances, not always authorized from Paris, provoked the British move against Burma in 1885, and a war with China that defended France's traditional hegemony over Annam, 1883–85. The war cost Premier Jules **Ferry** his job, but nevertheless resulted in the acquisition of Annam and Tonkin. The French possessions in Indochina were unified in the "Union Indochinoise" in 1887, and rounded off in 1893, after France had sent gunboats to Bangkok and forced Siam to surrender the Western part of **Laos.**

The Dutch were confronted with armed uprisings in their empire, especially the Java war, of 1825–30, and with the need to cover the costs of colonial administration. For the latter purpose the exploitative "cultivation system" was created, under which peasants were required to produce crops for export instead of being taxed. From the 1870s, state influence and monopolies were reduced and a free trade regime set up, and trade greatly expanded. In the Spanish Philippines, restrictions on foreign trade were lifted already in 1834, and British and American merchants quickly acquired a dominant position in the commercial life of the colony, which developed a strong export agriculture. Spanish rule, however, was increasingly resented as nationalist and liberal sentiment strengthened. When conflict over Cuba led to the **Spanish-American War** in 1898, the government of the United States was negotiating with the Philippine rebels, but the rebels quickly changed their attitude when they saw that the Spanish were prepared to surrender and hand the colony over to the Americans. Thus the United States, long an unlikely colonial power, acquired an empire of its own. To the north, finally, Russia occupied Siberia in 1858, and by the end of the century, the rivalry between Russia and Britain stretched all along Asia, from the **Bosporus** to **Manchuria.**

The intensified imperialist competition resulting from new challenges to Britain's geopolitical hegemony apparent from the late 1870s reached China after the **Sino-Japanese War** of 1894–95 and the "Triple Intervention" of Russia, France and Germany against Japan's territorial demands. Military defeat exposed China's weakness, and she became the focus of great power rivalry. The Far East took center stage in world politics for the next decade, drawing Japan and the United States into a regional balance of power that was no longer purely European. An intense rivalry developed under the close scrutiny of millions of jingoistic armchair strategists in living rooms, universities, parliaments, and editorial offices. When Germany, disappointed in her demands for "compensation" for the 1895 intervention, seized the port of **Kiaochow** in 1897, the "scramble for concessions" was on: China was forced by the other powers to grant them advantages comparable to those extracted by Germany, such as the 99-year lease of Kiaochow plus mining and railway concessions in the surrounding province of Shantung. Thus Russia acquired **Port Arthur** and the right to build a railway across Manchuria, France obtained **Kwang-chow Wan** and permission to build a railway from Tonkin into Yunnan, Britain got **Weihaiwei,** the enlargement of **Hong Kong,** and contracts to build several large railway lines for the Chinese government. Governments and public opinion in Europe began to debate the future of China—Could she remain independent? Should she be divided into semi-independent "spheres of influence" allotted to the great powers? Or would she collapse and have to be partitioned? In the end, the United States, fearing exclusion from China, proposed a joint declaration to guarantee an "open door," to the trade and investment of third powers and preclude any exclusive spheres of influence, which was unenthusiastically accepted by all the powers except Russia.

The surge of imperialist aggression triggered varied responses in China. A movement demanding much more radical change than the "self-strengtheners" appeared and their leaders, K'ang Yu-wei (1858–1927) and Liang Ch'i-ch'ao (1873–1929) gained the ear of emperor Kuang-hsü (1875–1908) during the "Hundred days" of reforms in 1898, but the reformers were removed from power—and some of them executed—when ex-regent **Ts'u Hsi** placed the emperor under house arrest and reasserted her leadership. At the same time, the Boxer movement opposed to anything Western was gaining ground in Northern China, strengthened by indignation at expansionism in the region, especially by Germany, ecological and economic problems, as well as constant conflict with Christian missionaries. When the movement became too strong to control, Ts'u Hsi decided to give it official sanction and to allow the siege of the diplomatic quarter in Peking by the Boxers in summer

1900. In the face of this situation, the unity underlying the rivalry between the powers quickly asserted itself, and all powers with interests in China jointly intervened. China was defeated and had to accept yet another indemnity, as well as the stationing of foreign troops in Peking.

The **Boxer Insurrection** and the expensive occupation of parts of North China convinced most of the powers that colonizing China was too costly to contemplate. Most of them also sought to avoid a major international crisis in the Far East. The only clash between imperialist powers involved Russia and Japan, for whom the Far East was geographically *not* far away. Russia had systematically strengthened her position in the Far East through the construction of the **Trans-Siberian Railway** between 1891and 1905 and by stationing troops in Northern China during the Boxer Insurrection. Japan, concerned about her position in Manchuria and in neighboring Korea, demanded Russia's withdrawal, and attacked Port Arthur when Russia refused. The **Russo-Japanese War** of 1904/05 was won decisively by Japan, after resource-intensive combat foreshadowing World War I. It was the last major international crisis concerning the Far East before the Great War, and it is seen as a major turning point in diplomatic, military, and indeed world history.

In international relations generally, the decade witnessed significant realignments. Britain, feeling threatened by Germany and Russia, concluded the **Anglo-Japanese Alliance** in 1902 and resolved her difficulties with France in the Entente Cordiale of 1904. Japan's victory permitted the completion of this diplomatic realignment with the "Far Eastern Agreements," a series of separate bilateral treaties that removed the remaining tensions between defeated Russia, financially exhausted Japan, Britain, and France. Germany was left out and started complaining about being "encircled," forgetting that the rash methods of German *Weltpolitik* had provided the spur for the others to liquidate their differences in the first place. For some, the year 1905 marked the beginning of a global challenge against the West. Fears of a "Yellow Peril," initially drummed up in Europe to help justify the Triple Intervention, now gripped the United States, where Japan was seen as a new rival in the Pacific. The challenge, however, was an ambivalent one. As contemporary observers noted, Japan's victory was not only that of an Asian over a European power, but also of a constitutional, rapidly industrializing state over an autocratic peasant empire. It gave an important boost and a new direction to anti-imperialist sentiment throughout the Far East and beyond, and it convinced Asian nationalists that the way to emancipation was to follow the model of Japan by concentrating on the creation of an industrial economy, a constitutional political system and a modern army. Chinese students went to Japan in ever greater numbers, some joining revolutionary Kuomintang, and returned to staff the modern army and government departments that were being created after the Boxer fiasco.

In China, Britain and the United States, now supported by France and Germany, sought to defend informal empire by pitting Western financial power against the weakened military-backed expansionism of Russia and Japan. Most of China's railways were constructed with Western capital in the short period between 1903 and 1914. Large investments in China's railways and government loans made the powers interested in propping up the Qing and the conservative reformers around Chang Chi-tung (1837–1909) and Yuan Shih-k'ai (1859–1916) who wished to centralize power in Peking with the help of Western money and technology. But China's increasingly nationalist reform movement demanded railway construction under Chinese control. Nationalists turned against both the powers and a dynasty that nationalists accused of being both alien, "Manchu," and weak in foreign policy. Both grievances combined in the revolution of October 1911, which led to the downfall of the Qing and the establishment of a republic. Revolutionary troubles further weakened China politically and financially and left her without defenses against Japan when the European powers started fighting each other in 1914.

Japanese nationalism remained intense after the war against Russia, and Japan committed strongly to colonization in Korea—a Japanese protectorate since 1905 and a colony since 1910—and to the exploitation of the Japanese sphere of influence in Manchuria. Economic growth continued after 1900, in part fuelled by government subsidies paid out of the Chinese war indemnity of 1895. In politics, government based on parties and parliamentary majorities slowly became the rule; however, military and colonial expenditure and domestic investments caused financial strains and political crises.

The process of carving up the region was completed by 1910. Korea was absorbed by Japan, Siam's existence had been guaranteed in Anglo-French agreements in 1896 and 1904, and her borders with the neighboring colonial territories were finally settled in 1907–09. In the Philippines, the United States had to impose direct rule in a costly war against the liberation movement it had initially supported when the islands were Spanish, but then succeeded in coopting the nationalist elites by setting up an elected legislature and promising eventual independence. The Dutch fought a long war from the 1870s to the early 1900s to impose rule on Sumatra. In all colonial territories, the creation of an administrative and economic infrastructure accelerated after the turn of the century. Direct administration through Western-style institutions now replaced earlier forms of rule by local vassals of a dominant—either colonial or domestic—government. Railway construction was the most important aspect of infrastructure improvement in most territories, and the development of natural resources—plantation crops, tin, rice—for export on the world markets was the focus of economic policies.

By 1914, the process of imperial expansion in the Far East seemed to have brought about a new equilibrium. Colonial frontiers were now neatly drawn and largely undisputed; China and Siam were seeking to play the role of independent nation states; Japan was already integrated into the great power system. Yet there were strains, such as Japanese expansionism, China's fragility, and the beginnings of modern anticolonial resistance everywhere. Events in the Far East since the turn of the century began to foreshadow those of the post-1914 world: the end of European hegemony, the rise of the United States and of Japan, economic nationalism, and the destructive character of industrialized mass warfare. *See also* Balance of Power; Japanese Empire; *Mission Civilisatrice;* Russian Empire.

FURTHER READING: Bayly, C. A. *The Birth of the Modern World, 1780–1914: Global Connections and Comparisons.* Oxford: Blackwell, 2004; Beasley, William G. *The Rise of Modern Japan: Political, Economic and Social Change since 1850.* London: Weidenfeld & Nicholson, 2000; Cain, Peter J., and A. G. Hopkins. *British Imperialism, 1688–2000.* Harlow: Longman, 2001; Girault, René. *Diplomatie européenne: Nations et impérialismes, 1871–1914.* Paris: Armand Colin, 1997; Hsü, Immanuel C. *The Rise of Modern China.* New York: Oxford University Press, 2000; Osterhammel, Jürgen. *Colonialism: A Theoretical Overview.* Princeton, NJ: Markus Wiener, 2002; Spence, Jonathan D. *The Search for Modern China.* London: Hutchinson, 1990; Tarling,

Nicholas, ed. *The Cambridge History of Southeast Asia.* Vol. 2/1: From c. 1800 to the 1930s. Cambridge: Cambridge University Press, 1999.

NIELS P. PETERSSON

## Fashoda Incident (1898)

An Anglo-French confrontation that determined the spheres of influence of the French and the British in sub-Saharan Africa and averted the French spread into Sudan and East Africa. Fashoda was a village in the southern **Sudan** on the White Nile. Its modern name is Kodok. In 1898, a French expedition led by Major Jean-Baptiste Marchand occupied Fashoda, laying claim to the upper Nile for France. An international crisis followed when Anglo-Egyptian forces under H. H. **Kitchener** reached Fashoda, where he met Marchand and had long discussions with him to settle the matter peacefully. The outcome of the discussions was that the French and Egyptian flags would be flown, and the decision over the Upper Nile would be settled in discussions conducted by the French and British governments. Ultimately, French claims were withdrawn and the area became part of the Anglo-Egyptian **Sudan.** The incident left a legacy of anti-British bitterness in France that was not overcome until the **Entente Cordiale** of 1904. *See also* Africa, Scramble for.

FURTHER READING: Lewis, David Levering. *The Race to Fashoda: European Colonialism and African Resistance in The Scramble for Africa.* New York: Weidenfeld & Nicholson, 1987; Neillands, Robin. *The Dervish Wars: Gordon and Kitchener in the Sudan 1880–1898.* London: John Murray Ltd., 1996.

MOSHE TERDMAN

## Fenian Brotherhood

The modern derivation of the ancient *Feonin Erin*, pre-Christian Irish militants, the Fenian Brotherhood was a secret, oath-bound Irish nationalist society dedicated to ending English imperial rule in **Ireland** through physical force, political agitation, or economic pressure. Formally known as the Irish Revolutionary Brotherhood, in 1858 radical nationalists organized into small units, known as circles, with branches throughout the United Kingdom, Continental Europe, North America, and **Australia** to provide funding, material resources, and logistical support for a nationalist revolution.

In an effort to exacerbate Anglo-American tensions, American Fenians attempted several unsuccessful invasions of **Canada.** Fenian violence peaked in 1867, with an insurrection on March 5–6, followed in December by a terrorist bombing of Clerkenwell Prison in London. Although nominally existent through the early 1880s, ultraviolent factions supplanted the Fenian organization, but the name continued in usage among Anglophiles for decades as a pejorative label for Irish nationalists.

FURTHER READING: Brown, T. N. *Irish-American Nationalism.* Philadelphia: Lippincott, 1966; Morton, W. L. *The Critical Years: The Union of British North America, 1857–1873.* New York: Oxford University Press, 1964.

JONATHAN GANTT

## Ferozeshah, Battle of (1845)

A sequel engagement to **Mudki** in the First **Sikh War.** Less than two days after the battle at Mudki, the British army and the Sikh army met again, at Ferozeshah on December 21, 1845. About 13,000 Sikh troops under the command of Lal Singh were entrenched there, and General Sir Hugh Gough began the march toward the enemy at 4 A.M. Seven hours later, at 11 A.M., Gough wanted to attack but was overruled by his second-in-command, Lieutenant General Sir Henry Hardinge, in his capacity as governor-general of India. Gough did not have all available troops with him, and Lord Hardinge made the decision to wait for the rest to arrive. Once they arrived, the attack commenced late in the afternoon. With the addition of Sir John Littler's men, the British had about 18,000 troops. The attack began with an artillery duel. Then Littler's infantry charged, but was repulsed.

As at Mudki, nighttime came and confusion reigned. The British forces had taken the field, though, and camped in the former Sikh position. On the second day of the battle, December 22, a new Sikh army, led by Tej Singh, arrived. Gough ordered a cavalry charge, which was successful, but then the cavalry rode off, as ordered by their commander. This surprised many on both sides, and, fearing a trick, Singh withdrew and led his army back across the Sutlej into Sikh territory. It was a costly victory for the British: 700 killed out of a total of 2,415 casualties. The Sikhs had an estimated 3,000 casualties. *See also* Afghan Wars; India.

FURTHER READING: Bruce, George. *Six Battles for India: The Anglo-Sikh Wars, 1845–6, 1848–9.* London: Arthur Barker, 1969; Cook, Hugh. *The Sikh Wars: The British Army in the Punjab, 1845–1849.* London: Leo Cooper, 1975; Crawford, E. R. "The Sikh Wars, 1845–9." In Brian Bond, ed. *Victorian Military Campaigns.* New York: Frederick A. Praeger Publishers, 1967; Farwell, Byron. *Queen Victoria's Little Wars.* New York: W. W. Norton, 1972.

DAVID TURPIE

## Ferry, Jules François Camille (1832–1893)

French politician and colonial theorist who, during his two terms as prime minister, initiated major educational reforms and oversaw a significant expansion of the French overseas empire. After brief stints as a lawyer and a liberal Republican journalist known for his critiques of the Second Empire, Ferry entered politics and was elected to the French National Assembly in 1869. Following the French defeat in the **Franco-Prussian War,** he became head of the Republican Left and from 1879–85 held a variety of ministerial posts in the new Third Republic. Although initially more interested in domestic policy, in the wake of the Battle of **Sedan** Ferry became convinced that France needed to obtain colonies to maintain her status as a great power and compete effectively in the growing international economy. In exchange for new markets and guaranteed sources of raw materials, Ferry argued that France in turn had a moral obligation, dubbed the *mission civilisatrice,* to uplift the indigenous peoples of colonized areas by exposing them to French culture, education, industry, and a Western work ethic. These principles became the cornerstone of French colonial policy until the end of World War II.

During his first term as prime minister from September 1880 to November 1881, Ferry supported Pierre Savorgnan de **Brazza**'s efforts to establish a protectorate in the French Congo and authorized the French acquisition of **Tunisia** as a preemptive measure to forestall its annexation by Italy. This measure and its associated expenses proved unpopular and led to the downfall of his first government. In his second term as prime minister, running from February 1883 to March 1885, Ferry served simultaneously as foreign minister and became increasingly involved in colonial policymaking. In 1884, increasing international tensions provoked by German, Belgian and French colonial expansion in Africa led Ferry to join forces with Otto von **Bismarck** in arranging the Conference of **Berlin,** which set ground rules for the acquisition of additional colonies, thereby unleashing the Scramble for Africa. Early the next year, Ferry expanded the existing French protectorate in **Madagascar** at the behest of colonial interest groups. In addition to authorizing colonial expansion in Africa, Ferry also oversaw the growth of French holdings in **Indochina.** Eager to undo the damage caused to French prestige by two earlier failed ventures in the region, in 1883 Ferry dispatched a military expedition to create protectorates over **Annam** and **Tonkin.** Confused reports over temporary military setbacks in Tonkin became a lightning rod for anticolonial sentiment and toppled his second government in 1885. Despite this political setback, Ferry was elected to the Senate in 1891 and became its president less than a month before his 1893 assassination by a religious fanatic. *See also* Africa, Scramble for; Belgian Congo; French Empire; French Equatorial Africa; German Empire.

FURTHER READING: Cooke, James J. *The New French Imperialism, 1880–1910: The Third Republic and Colonial Expansion.* Hamden, CT: Archon Books, 1973; Gaillard, Jean-Michel. *Jules Ferry.* Paris: Fayard, 1989; Power, Thomas F. *Jules Ferry and the Renaissance of French Imperialism.* New York: King's Crown Press, 1944; Wesseling, H. L. *The European Colonial Empires 1815–1919.* New York: Pearson Education, 2004.

KENNETH J. OROSZ

## Fichte, Johann Gottieb (1762–1814)

Johann Fichte, a German nationalist philosopher, was born in the duchy of Saxony on May 19, 1762. In 1780, Fichte entered the University of Jena as a theology student. In 1791 he traveled to Königsberg to Immanuel Kant's lectures. While there, Fichte's *Critique of All Revelation* was published; however, the printer accidentally identified it as Kant's work. As a consequence it gained a wide readership and made Fichte's reputation when the mistake was corrected. It also led to a professorship at the University of Jena in 1793.

While at Jena, Fichte began to discuss the French Revolution with private student groups who favored French political ideas. Fichte's admiration for the French Revolution led him to defend it in "Contributions to the Rectification of Public Opinion Concerning the French Revolution," despite its excesses. Between 1796 and 1798, Fichte published his legal and ethical ideas in *Basis of Natural Right* and *System of Ethics.* He claimed that monarchy would soon disappear and be replaced by democratic government. His "Jacobinism" and his atheistic reputation led to his dismissal from his teaching position in 1799. In the spring of that year, Fichte moved to Berlin where he began to change from an enthusiast of French revolutionary ideas into a German patriot. That same year he published the *Vocation of Man;* the next year he published *The Closed Commercial State,* which engages the idea of an economic autarchy.

Fichte left Berlin for Königsberg after Prussia was defeated by Napoleon in the 1806–07 campaign; however, he returned to a French-occupied Berlin to deliver his "Addresses to the German Nation." They mark the beginning of German nationalism. In them he urged the creation of a national educational system that would teach patriotism. From 1810 until 1814, he taught at the University of Berlin as a professor of philosophy. He died on January 27, 1814, from typhus contracted while serving as a volunteer in a hospital during a local epidemic.

FURTHER READING: Breazeale, Daniel, and Tom Rockmore, eds. *Fichte: Historical Contexts/ Contemporary Controversies.* New York: Prometheus Books, 1994; Fichte, Johann Gottlieb. *Addresses to the German Nation.* Edited by George A. Kelly. New York: Harper Torch Books, 1968.

ANDREW JACKSON WASKEY

## Filibuster

A term derived from Dutch (*vrijbuiter*) and Spanish (*filibustero*) expressions for "free booty." It was commonly applied during the nineteenth century to the activities of American entrepreneur-adventurers who undertook small-scale military operations and insurrectionist activities against the governments of Latin American countries, often with the goal of drawing the United States into the conflict to thereby secure their own personal political or commercial interests.

Among the more notorious filibusterers was William Walker (1824–1860), who, after leading a failed filibustering expedition to California in 1853, in 1855 exploited the outbreak of a civil war in Nicaragua to divide the country and establish himself as dictator. Walker, a Southerner, promptly issued a decree opening Nicaragua to slavery. A coalition of neighboring republics ousted him in 1857, but he immediately organized a new expedition. By this time he had become an embarrassment to U.S. foreign policy, specifically regarding the sensitive and strategically important question of the construction and control of a future interoceanic canal across the Central American isthmus. His expedition was therefore apprehended by the U.S. Navy. An expedition to Honduras in the 1860s finally saw him captured, convicted, and executed. Despite the common usage of the term in the United States, filibustering was hardly a uniquely American activity. In terms of its ambition and consequences, the **Jameson Raid** against the government of the Transvaal in 1896 is among the more spectacular examples. *See also* Manifest Destiny, Monroe Doctrine, Panama Canal.

FURTHER READING: Danziger, Christopher. *The Jameson Raid.* Cape Town: Macdonald South Africa, 1978; Stephanson, Anders. *Manifest Destiny: American Expansionism and the Empire of Right.* New York: Hill & Wang, 1995.

CARL CAVANAGH HODGE

## Finland

Finland was part of the Kingdom of Sweden from the twelfth century until Tsar **Alexander I** launched the **Russo-Swedish War** of 1808–09, after which it became a grand duchy of the **Russian Empire.** Finland was guaranteed constitutional government, and its autonomy was generally respected until 1898, when a Pan-Slavist policy of Russification decreed by Tsar **Nicholas II** made Russian the state language of Finland and prompted native Finns and Swedes to make common cause in resistance. This climaxed in 1904 with the assassination of Nikolai Bobrikov, the Russian governer-general.

During the Russo-Japanese War, Japan sought to support a Finnish uprising with a shipment of rifles, but the plan was abandoned when the supply ship was wrecked off the Finnish coast. Russification was suspended in any event with the onset of the 1905 revolution in Russia. In 1906, Finland regained its autonomy and was also permitted to elect a diet by universal suffrage. A period of repression returned in 1910, but the Bolshevik Revolution of 1917 afforded Finns an opportunity to declare their independence. The next year Finnish "Whites" led by Carl Mannerheim and supported by Germany fought off the Red Army, and Finland's independence was recognized by Russia in December 1918. *See also* Napoleonic Wars; Pan-Slavism.

FURTHER READING: Singleton, Frederick Bernard. *A Short History of Finland.* New York: Cambridge University Press, 1989.

CARL CAVANAGH HODGE

## Fisher, John Arbuthnot, Lord Fisher (1841–1920)

An influential British naval officer, and first sea lord before and again during World War I. Fisher was nominated a cadet in the **Royal Navy** at the age of 13 and served without seeing action in the **Crimean War.** He then served as a midshipman in the China War of 1857. Academically excellent and extremely ambitious, he rose rapidly through the officer ranks. Promoted captain in 1874, he held numerous sea-going commands and also increasing senior posts with the fleet gunnery school, HMS *Excellent.* In 1882, he commanded HMS *Inflexible,* the most powerful ship in the navy, during the bombardment of Alexandria, and went on to command the naval brigade that held the city until the arrival of the army's expeditionary force. Fisher caught dysentery in **Egypt,** but nevertheless went back to England to take command of *Excellent,* going on to become director of ordnance at the Admiralty.

In 1899, Fisher became commander-in-chief in the Mediterranean, at the time the most important command in the navy. He became second sea lord, responsible for naval personnel, in 1902. In 1904, he succeeded, as had been expected, to the post of first sea lord, the senior officer of the navy—not to be confused with first lord of the admiralty, the cabinet minister for the navy. In an era dominated by a growing German threat on the one hand and financial pressures on the other, Fisher introduced reforms to the reserve system, recalled from far-flung stations and retired numerous obsolete ships to save money for first-class ones, consolidated the Channel and Home fleets, and introduced torpedo-firing destroyers. His most important innovation, however, was the turbine-powered, all-big-gun ***Dreadnought*** class of battleships, which all made all previous ships obsolete. Fisher, however, really wished to move to a class of battle cruisers fast and powerful enough to replace battleships entirely, an ambition never realized.

In retirement after 1910, Fisher pined for recall. He advised the admiralty on the use of oil in place of coal, and correctly foresaw the importance of the submarine.

Shortly after the outbreak of war in 1914, Winston **Churchill,** then first lord of the admiralty, and an admirer of Fisher's dynamism, recalled him as first sea lord. After the abortive attacks on the Dardanelles in April and May 1915, however, Fisher resigned in protest against what he took to be Churchill's obsession with that campaign. For the remainder of the war, Fisher advised on technical innovations, playing a part in the development of ASDIC, an early form of sonar named after the Anti-Submarine Detection Investigation Committee, the antisubmarine technology that was essential to victory in World War II. Fisher is remembered for his focus on technology and gunnery over brass-polishing and painting, but most of all for his immense if sometimes controversial reforming energy. *See also* Mahan, Alfred Thayer; Navalism; Tirpitz Plan.

FURTHER READING: Lambert, Nicholas A. *Sir John Fisher's Naval Revolution.* Columbia: University of South Carolina Press, 1999; Marder, A. J. *From the Dreadnought to Scapa Flow: The Royal Navy in the Fisher Era.* 5 vols. London: Oxford University Press, 1961–70; Massie, Alex. *Dreadnought: Britain, Germany and the Coming of the Great War.* London: Cape, 1992.

MARK F. PROUDMAN

## Florida Purchase Treaty

*See* Adams-Onís Treaty

## Foch, Ferdinand (1851–1929)

Marshal of France and commander of Entente forces in 1918, Ferdinand Foch joined the French army in 1871. With the onset of World War I, Foch commanded the Ninth Army. During the Battle of the Marne he launched the counterattack. He subsequently led the Northern Army since October 1914 until the Battle of the Somme in the summer of 1916 for which he was sacrificed as a scapegoat. In 1917, Foch was recalled as chief of the general staff. He was given overall command of the Entente forces in March 1918. Foch managed to stop the German advance during spring 1918, mounting the counterattack that turned the tide of the war. Foch accepted the German surrender in November 1918 and played a major advisory role at the Paris Peace Conference.

FURTHER READING: Neiberg, Michael S. *Foch: Supreme Allied Commander in the Great War.* Washington, DC: Brassey's, 2003.

MARTIN MOLL

## Fontane, Theodor (1819–1898)

A German novelist and poet, Theodor Fontane is usually noted for his comparatively gentle criticisms of the Prussian class system, its social conventions, and of the spirit of German politics after the 1871 establishment of the Second Reich. Fontane worked for the conservative *Kreuzzeitung,* but in 1870, he became the drama critic of the comparatively liberal *Vossische Zeitung.* He wrote about Prussia's War with Denmark in 1864 and with Austria in 1866, before tackling the **Franco-Prussian War** and being held in French captivity for three months. For all three wars he published his personal observations. Not until the age of 57 did Fontane begin to work on the novels for which he is best remembered. The most noteworthy are *Vor dem Sturm* (1878), *Irrungen, Wirrungen* (1888), *Frau Jenny Treibel* (1892), *Effi Briest* (1896), and *Der Stechlin* (1899).

FURTHER READING: Craig, Gordon A. *Theodore Fontane: Literature and History in the Bismarck Reich.* New York: Oxford University Press, 1999.

CARL CAVANAGH HODGE

## Foraker Amendment (1899)

An amendment to an army appropriations bill adopted by the U.S. Congress prohibiting the granting of "property franchises, or concessions of any kind whatsoever" in **Cuba** during the American occupation following the **Spanish-American War.** Senator Joseph Foraker of Ohio, an opponent of President William McKinley's policies in Cuba, introduced the measure in response to efforts by the War Department to grant public franchises during the American military governance of Cuba. Foraker feared that American economic penetration of Cuba would commit the United States to remain in the island indefinitely. Despite opposition from supporters of the McKinley administration, the Senate passed the amendment by a vote of 47 to 11. Although the measure hindered large-scale economic penetration of the island, it had the unintended consequence of hindering efforts by the military government to harness foreign investments to rebuild the Cuban infrastructure. *See also* Monroe Doctrine; Teller Amendment.

FURTHER READING: Healy, David. *The United States in Cuba, 1898–1902: Generals, Politicians, and the Search for Policy.* Madison: University of Wisconsin Press, 1963.

JAMES PRUITT

## Fox, Charles James (1749–1806)

One of the most prominent British statesmen of the era of the American and French Revolutions. Fox led the Whigs in arguing against Britain's attempt at maintaining the American colonies within the **British Empire** through force of arms, and later opposed British military intervention on the Continent against revolutionary France. He was an expert on economic and constitutional issues and spoke eloquently in Parliament from 1768 until his death in 1806. He served as foreign secretary under Lord Rockingham's government in 1782 and later became a close personal friend and political ally of the prince regent, later King George IV.

A staunch political opponent of William **Pitt,** Fox opposed the prime minister's determined prosecution of the war against revolutionary and Napoleonic France that had begun in 1793. Greatly disliked by King George III, who for many years refused to contemplate him holding a prominent government position, Fox did not become a cabinet minister again until 1806, when, on the death of Pitt, he became foreign secretary in Lord Grenville's government. Only months before his death, Fox sought an abortive peace with France and moved a bill for the abolition of the slave trade. *See also* Napoleonic Wars.

FURTHER READING: Ayling, Stanley. *Fox: The Life of Charles James Fox.* London: J. Murray, 1991; Mitchell, Leslie. *Charles James Fox.* Oxford: Oxford University Press, 1992; Powell, David. *Charles James Fox: Man of the People.* London: Hutchinson, 1989.

GREGORY FREMONT-BARNES

## Francia, José Gaspar Rodríguez de (1766–1840)

Dictator of Paraguay and key figure in Paraguay's struggle for independence from Spain in 1810. Born in Asunción, Francia received training in theology and law before serving on the town council between 1807 and 1809. When Paraguay declared its independence from Spain, he took command of the ruling junta. He pushed Paraguay to break from Spain and to resist any effort by the independence forces in Buenos Aires to assert authority over his new country. His supporters granted him the title of "perpetual dictator" in 1816. He ruled in an idiosyncratic fashion until his death. He closed Paraguay's borders and used his army and river patrols to prevent foreigners from entering the country. He stripped Spanish residents of most political and economic rights. He also promoted state-owned rural industries to generate revenue from a rigidly controlled export trading system.

FURTHER READING: Williams, John Hoyt *The Rise and Fall of the Paraguayan Republic, 1800–1870.* Austin: University of Texas Press, 1979.

DANIEL K. LEWIS

## Francis Ferdinand, Archduke of Austria (1863–1914)

Heir to the Austrian throne, whose assassination in Sarajevo in July 1914 triggered the diplomatic crisis leading to World War I. Archduke Francis (Franz) Ferdinand of Austria-Este was born in December 1863 in Graz, the capital of the Austrian crownland Styria. After the suicide of Archduke Rudolph, Emperor Francis Joseph's only son in 1889, and the death of his father, Archduke Charles Louis in 1896, Francis Ferdinand became the heir apparent and served as the Emperor's deputy in military affairs since 1898. In 1913, he was appointed inspector-general of all Austro-Hungarian forces. After 1906, Francis Ferdinand used his military chancellery as the institutional basis for his efforts to reinvigorate the position of the crown in Austro-Hungarian politics.

The focus of his political maneuvers was on the role of Hungary within the framework of the Habsburg monarchy. Francis Ferdinand resented nationalist groups and politicians in general because he perceived nationalism as a deadly challenge to the multiethnic realm of his dynasty. The Magyar political elite, who had revolted against Habsburg rule in 1848–49 and had taken control of Hungary since the **Ausgleich** of 1867, looked like the most dangerous of those groups to him. He sabotaged his uncle's policy of accommodating the Magyars and toppled several ministers and high-ranking officials because they seemed to be too lenient in dealing with Magyar politicians. His chancellery in the Belvedere palace in Vienna became the rallying point of conservatives who wanted to strengthen the authority of the crown and the Catholic Church in the Habsburg monarchy. Some of them called for a strong political role for **Austria-Hungary**'s south Slav population or a higher degree of autonomy for the Habsburg crownlands. Francis Ferdinand's interest in these projects was limited to their tactical value as tools to undermine Hungary's privileged position. Embittered by the emperor's resistance against his marriage with Sophie Chotek in 1900, he felt a strong dislike for his uncle's advisors and the court.

In the final years before World War I, Francis Ferdinand played the role of leader of the opposition to the governments installed by the emperor. While he destabilized domestic politics, he usually was an advocate of a cautious foreign policy. He warned against a military confrontation with Russia and acted as the leading "dove" within the decision-making circles in Vienna in 1913. His assassination by a Bosnian terrorist group supported by Serbian ultranationalists in Sarajevo July 28, 1914 gave the war party in Austria-Hungary the upper hand and opened the way to wage war on **Serbia.** *See also* Bosnia-Herzegovina; Habsburg Empire; Pan-Slavism.

FURTHER READING: Bérenger, Jean. *A History of the Habsburg Empire.* London, New York: Longman, 1994; Fichtner, Paula Sutter. *The Habsburg Empire: From Dynasticism to Multinationalism.* Malabar: Krieger, 1997; Macartney, Carlile A. *The Habsburg Empire, 1790–1918.* London: Weidenfeld & Nicolson, 1971.

GUENTHER KRONENBITTER

## Francis Joseph, Emperor of Austria (1830–1916)

Last of the major Habsburg rulers, Archduke Francis Joseph of Austria was born in Schloss Schönbrunn near Vienna in August 1830. In the revolution of 1848, he replaced his uncle, Ferdinand I, as emperor of Austria. Ferdinand was persuaded to resign by the dynasty and the political advisors of the crown because a more energetic monarch seemed to be necessary for the Habsburg monarchy's survival. The victory of counter-revolution the next year marked the beginning of neoabsolutist rule, characterized by a rigorous suppression of nationalist and liberal groups.

As a result of Austria's diplomacy during the **Crimean War,** the Habsburg monarchy was rather isolated when it had to face the alliance of Napoleon III (see **Bonapart, Louis Napoleon**) and Piemont-Sardinia in the late 1850s. Francis Joseph commanded his troops in the Battle of **Solferino** in 1859, and the disastrous defeat forced him to accept the loss of Lombardy. In the following years, the Habsburg monarchy not only lost other territories to the newly created kingdom of Italy but after the Austrian defeat in the Battle of **Königgrätz** in 1866, Prussia could build a German nation state and diminish decisively Austria's position in central Europe. Ultimate responsibility for these setbacks rested with Francis Joseph who had the final say in all matters of diplomacy and warfare and who had chosen the top officials and commanders.

The series of defeats forced the Emperor to offer constitutional reforms in all Habsburg territories and to offer a high degree of Hungarian autonomy. The **Ausgleich** of 1867 with the Magyar elite restricted Francis Joseph's power, but he accepted Austria-Hungary's new constitutional framework and used a divide-and-rule strategy, playing the antagonistic nationalist groups against each other. By picking the prime ministers in Vienna and Budapest, the common ministers and all the highest ranking officers and civil servants, Francis Joseph could still shape domestic politics and foreign affairs. Austria-Hungary's position as a Great Power was secured by the occupation of **Bosnia-Herzegovina** in 1878–79 and an alliance system based on the cooperation with Germany. The annexation of Bosnia-Herzegovina in 1908 led to an international crisis and the growing isolation of Austria-Hungary. In 1914, Francis Joseph gave his approval to a war against **Serbia,** knowing that this would probably lead to a Great Power war. During World War I, the octogenarian monarch lost more and more control to military leaders and politicians. He died in Schloss Schönbrunn in November 1916, two years before the Habsburg monarchy's collapse. *See also* Austro-Prussian War; Habsburg Empire.

FURTHER READING: Beller, Steven. *Francis Joseph.* London: Longman, 1996; Cassels, Lavender. *Clash of Generations: A Habsburg Family Drama in the Nineteenth Century.* London: J. Murray, 1973; Okey, Robin. *The Habsburg Monarchy. c. 1765–1918 from Enlightenment to Eclipse.* Basingstoke: MacMillan Press, 2001.

GUENTHER KRONENBITTER

## Franco-Italian Convention (1902)

The completion of an entente began in 1900. Since the period of "Risorgimento" in the 1830s, Giuseppe Mazzini, the Italian nationalist politician, had claimed North Africa for the nation of Italy. At the Congress of Berlin in 1878, the fate of Tripoli was discussed. Britain encouraged Italy to consider acquiring Tripoli as a colony and France ideally to occupy Tunis. This arrangement was considered favorable to ensure that the status quo in the Mediterranean be maintained. But Italian imperial ambitions grew after Britain and France expanded their respective empires in North Africa. France began to rule Tunis as a protectorate in 1881, and Britain occupied Egypt in 1882. Italy became increasingly worried about French expansion in North Africa and saw the acquisition of Tripoli as a necessity to provide safety and defense. Suspicions of French colonial ambitions persisted. An entente was agreed on with France in 1900, although the terms were ratified only in 1902. France was allowed to gain predominance in Morocco without Italy's intervention, and Italy was granted a similar guarantee by France in Tripoli and Cyrenaica. Italy began a series of "peaceful penetrations" soon after. In 1902, France and Italy then agreed that each would maintain neutrality, not only in the event of direct of indirect aggression by a third party but also if one or the other of them "as a result of direct provocation, should find itself compelled, in defense of its honor or security, to take the initiative of a declaration of war."

In Africa, Italy faced strong opposition from Turkey with regard to Tripoli, yet invaded it in 1911, and finally possessed it by virtue of the Treaty of Lausanne in 1912. In Europe the 1902 agreement, which remained officially secret until 1918, made Italy's membership in the Triple Alliance with Germany and Austria-Hungary altogether worthless. *See also* Dual Alliance; Entente Cordiale.

FURTHER READING: Hayes, Carlton J. H. *A Political and Social History of Modern Europe.* New York: Macmillan, 1926; Langer, William H. *The Diplomacy of Imperialism, 1890–1902.* New

York: Afred A. Knopf, 1968; Taylor, A.J.P. *The Struggle for Master in Europe, 1848–1918.* Oxford: Clarendon, 1954.

NURFADZILAH YAHAYA

## Franco-Prussian War (1870–1871)

The final and most significant of the wars of German unification, the Franco-Prussian War lasted from July 19, 1870, to May 10, 1871. It pitted France against Prussia and its allies, which included the states of the North German Confederation, as well as the south German states of Baden, Württemberg, and Bavaria. Presented to the peoples of all belligerent lands as a test of national honor, its deeper causes were Prussia's ambition to bring about the national unification of the German states of Central Europe under its aegis and France's attempt to buttress its flagging geopolitical position, especially against the surging power of Prussia. The war was a decisive victory for the Prussian monarchy. The French Second Empire collapsed in military debacle and Prussia unified Central Europe largely on its own terms. The war was therefore a diplomatic revolution in Europe and a grave portent of the violent national conflicts to come in the twentieth century.

The war resulted from such pan-European developments as the technological creativity of industrial economies, the growth of bureaucratic states, and the explosive power of popular nationalism; but its immediate causes were the deliberate actions of Count Otto von **Bismarck,** the chief minister of the Kingdom of Prussia, and Louis-Napoleon **Bonaparte** (Napoleon III), emperor of France. Bismarck's primary strategic objective was the unification of the quasi-independent territories of Central Europe into a national polity. To reach this objective, in the 1860s he provoked a series of international crises, including wars with Denmark in 1864 and the Austrian Empire in 1866, to marginalize Austria in Central European affairs and to encourage the smaller German lands in the north and south to accept national unification under Prussian control. The confessional affinities of a common Protestantism coaxed the northern lands into the Prussia-dominated **North German Confederation** in 1867, but the southern Catholic lands of Baden, Württemberg, and Bavaria resisted Prussian claims to national leadership. Bismarck hoped that by goading France to attack Prussia, these lands would fly to the flag of a victimized Germany and accede to Prussian supremacy in a unified Second **Reich.**

Louis-Napoleon Bonaparte, the nephew of Napoleon I (see **Bonaparte, Napoleon**) and ruler of the French Second Empire, played into Bismarck's scheme. By the 1860s, his empire suffered from chronic political rancor and widespread institutional corruption, as well as from a series of foreign policy fiascoes, whose fallout put the lie to his boast that he would restore the greatness of France in the international arena. Living off the legend of his uncle, and alarmed at Prussia's audacity and military competence, he was determined to check Prussian ambitions for the control of Central Europe. Victory in war against a hated national enemy promised to restore public confidence in his unstable regime and achieve political integration by appeals to patriotic unity.

Bismarck exploited Louis-Napoleon's saber rattling to provoke a conflict in which France would be seen as the aggressor. The *casus belli* concerned the succession to the Spanish throne. Spain offered its throne to Prince Leopold von Hohenzollern-Sigmaringen, the nephew of Wilhelm I, the Prussian king. France opposed the move and in a needless provocation, insisted that Wilhelm renounce for all time any Prussian designs on the Spanish crown. Wilhelm registered his resistance to this demand in a telegram he dispatched from the spa at Ems to his foreign ministry in Berlin. When the **Ems Telegram** arrived, Bismarck edited it to make it look like Wilhelm and the French ambassador, Count Vincent Benedetti, had insulted one another. Then he released the doctored version to the diplomatic corps and the press. Feeling rebuffed, and keen to capitalize on the anger of a humiliated French public, Louis-Napoleon ordered mobilization against Prussia and declared war on July 19, 1870.

France expected to enjoy the early advantage in the conflict, but this optimism rested on serious miscalculations. The French took courage in the Chassepot rifle, whose long range and stopping power would reverse any Prussian invasion, and the *mitrailleuse,* a precursor to the machine gun, whose shock effect would deter infantry assault. They also banked on their smaller force of long-term service professionals, whose experience and veteran resolve would break the attacks of less formidably armed German conscripts. The Prussian army, however, led by Helmuth von **Moltke,** the hero of the 1866 Battle of **Königgrätz** against Austria, was matchless in Europe. When the army was arrayed to inflict concentrated and cross fire, the poundage, accuracy, and range of its artillery could shatter any defensive position. Its soldiery, although conscripted, were fit, disciplined, and skilled in small-unit tactics that promoted initiative and aggressive maneuver. These tactics ensured high casualties when applied to well-secured defenses, but Prussian expertise in mobilizing reserves by use of the civilian **railway** system furnished a constant supply of reinforcements. The French generals expected the Prussians to take seven weeks to arrive at the front. Within 18 days, Moltke had more than 300,000 of his best troops deployed on the forward edge of the battle area with tens of thousands of replacements filing into line behind them. Huddled into defensive positions and suffering from insufficient logistical supply and flaccid morale, the French army was vulnerable to Moltke's ferocious strategy of encirclement and pocket annihilation.

The war between these unbalanced forces began on August 2 with a French probing action into the German border town of Saarbrücken. Over the next four days, massive counterstrokes at Wissembourg, Spicheren, and Froeschwiller by Prussian forces and the armies of their allies overwhelmed this half-hearted assault. The Prussians exploited these victories by attacking French supply lines, cutting communications, and pursuing retreating French formations. The French command at the front, led by the vacillating Marshal François Achille Bazaine, gathered 200,000 French troops at Metz, where Moltke trapped them. On August 16–18, Moltke attacked outlying French positions northwest of Metz at Mars-la-Tour and Gravelotte, severing the besieged French garrison from the hinterland and blocking any escape attempts to the West. Hoping to relieve the pressure on Metz, Louis-Napoleon and Marshal Patrice MacMahon led a new French army northwest of Metz to the old fortress town of **Sedan,** intending from there to attack Moltke and rescue Bazaine. Moltke took advantage of this clumsy move and, on August 30, encircled the French in and around the fortress. On September 1, he opened a withering assault of massed artillery barrage and converging infantry attack from all sides, which decimated French initiatives to break out. By the end of the day, Louis-Napoleon canceled resistance as futile, and on September 2, he surrendered his army to Moltke and Bismarck, who had arrived to witness the capitulation of his adversary.

Louis-Napoleon's fatigued regime was altogether too fragile to withstand the shock of national disaster on the battlefield. The Paris crowd, astonished by the precipitous collapse of the French army, proclaimed the end of the empire on September 4 and established a Government of National Defense to continue the struggle against Prussia. Although Bismarck hoped for a quick peace, the revolution evolved a regime, led by the radical republican Léon **Gambetta,** hardened against surrender to an enemy with annexationist aims, so the war continued inconclusively. On October 29, however, Marshal Bazaine, his troops starving and succumbing to epidemic dysentery, surrendered the garrison at Metz. Paris had been encircled as well, despite the harassment fire of irregular *franc-tireurs* against Prussian targets, and famine and disease loomed as winter approached. On January 28, 1871 the city capitulated and French leaders sought an armistice. The new French National Assembly, led by its provisional executive Adolphe **Thiers,** then accepted Bismarck's humiliating terms in the Treaty of **Frankfurt,** which was signed on May 10: cession of the fortresses of Metz and Strasbourg, as well as the province of Alsace, loss of one-third of the province of Lorraine, including its rich coal and iron-ore deposits, the payment of a five-billion franc indemnity for starting the war, and payment of all German occupation costs.

The arresting outcomes of the war were evident to all observers. The war was a devastating blow to French patriotic culture. Disputes over the assignment of blame for the catastrophe poisoned French politics for decades and stoked a furious *revanchism,* which insisted that the confiscated territories of **Alsace-Lorraine** be restored to a rehabilitated France. More alarming still was the emergence of a unified German Empire led by militaristic Prussia, a development long feared by European strategists. Industrially strong and culturally provocative yet lacking in domestic concord owing to inherent constitutional inequalities, imperial Germany represented a new and potentially disruptive force in world affairs. These developments encouraged national chauvinists on both sides, whose shrill discourses of friend and foe threatened European stability in an era of growing international competition.

The human costs of the war were evident as well. In just six months of combat, France suffered 150,000 killed and wounded. Prussia and her allies lost 117,000. The unprecedented lethality of modern weapons, especially concentrated large-bore artillery and overlapping machine gun fire, wiped out whole formations of men, inflicting massive wounds, mutilating the human body, and leaving hundreds dead in infantry assaults to be shoveled into mass graves. The brutalizing effects of this experience, which left long-lasting psychological damage on many of its veterans, led to frightful wartime atrocities. These included the summary execution of *franc-tireurs,* retaliation burnings of entire villages, the murder and neglect of prisoners of war, and the subjection of cities to starvation and disease to break civilian resistance. Such incidents as these suggested the "total wars" of the twentieth century, which would engulf soldiers and civilians alike. *See also* Austro-Prussian War; Balance of Power; German Empire.

FURTHER READING: Howard, Michael. *The Franco-Prussian War: The German Invasion of France, 1870–71.* Oxford: Taylor & Francis, 2001; Wawro, Geoffrey. *The Franco-Prussian War: The German Conquest of France in 1870–1871.* Cambridge: Cambridge University Press, 2003; Wetzel, David. *A Duel of Giants: Bismarck, Napoleon III, and the Origins of the Franco-Prussian War.* Madison: University of Wisconsin Press, 2001.

JEFFREY T. ZALAR

## Franco-Russian Alliance (1891)

*See* Dual Alliance

## Franco-Spanish Agreement (1904)

Signed on October 3, 1904, between the French and Spanish governments, the Franco-Spanish Agreement supplemented the **Entente Cordiale** established between Britain and France only six months earlier. It clarified the respective spheres of influence of the two countries in Morocco by publicly reaffirming the independence and integrity of Morocco yet secretly providing for the partition of the North African territory. Spain was to have the Mediterranean coast of Morocco and a portion of its hinterland. Spain pledged to erect no fortifications and to take no actions without the consent of France. Considering the 1904 agreement together with the Anglo-French Entente and **Franco-Italian Convention** of 1902, Germany felt threatened by provisions governing access to North Africa in which Berlin was no so much as consulted. Rightly guessing that such provisions were in part crafted to contain German ambition, Berlin resolved to test their durability, starting with the First Morocco Crisis in 1905. *See also* Algerciras Congress.

FURTHER READING: Hayes, Carlton J. H. *A Political and Social History of Modern Europe.* New York: Macmillan, 1926; Langer, William H. *The Diplomacy of Imperialism, 1890–1902.* New York: Afred A. Knopf, 1968; Taylor, A.J.P. *The Struggle for Mastery in Europe, 1848–1918.* Oxford: Clarendon, 1954.

CARL CAVANAGH HODGE

## Frankfurt Parliament (1848–1849)

A *Vorparlament,* or provisional parliament, established as the German National Assembly during the revolutionary upheavals of 1848, the Frankfurt Parliament convened in the rotunda of Paulskirche in Frankfurt am Main and authorized the organization of elections by direct male suffrage throughout Germany and Austria. The parliament was a hastily improvised response of liberal reformers to the decision by Prussian King Friedrich Wilhelm IV to consent to a combined Prussian diet to discuss German unification.

The parliament was chiefly concerned with preparation of a constitution for all the German lands. The parliament was briefly the heartbeat of German national aspirations, but it came to grief because of a lack of unanimity specifically over the construction of a national government. It offended **Austria-Hungary** with a resolution to exclude from the German Empire all non-German lands. The parliament then offered the title of hereditary emperor to Friedrich Wilhelm, who was both loath to accept a throne offered by social inferiors and fearful of provoking Austria or Russia. Having stood partly on the principle of divine right, he weakly put it aside and asked for the consent of the various German states. When Bavaria, Hanover, Saxony, and Württemberg objected and Austria disapproved, he refused the crown. Its plan defeated, the assembly melted away, and the day of German unity was postponed until 1870. Meaningful liberal reform was postponed much longer. *See also* Bismarck, Otto von; German Empire; North German Confederation.

FURTHER READING: Eyck, Frank. *Frankfurt Parliament, 1848–1849*. New York: St. Martin's, 1968.

CARL CAVANAGH HODGE

## Frankfurt, Treaty of (1871)

The diplomatic settlement concluding the **Franco-Prussian War.** The war was effectively over after the German victory at Sedan in September 1870. With the fall of the empire, however, Napoleon III (see **Bonaparte, Louis Napoleon**) left the Germans with no recognized government with which to negotiate terms of surrender. It took the protracted siege of Paris to convince the provisional government that the cause was lost and to agree to an armistice in late January 1871. Elections held across France in early February led to a victory of the pro-peace factions. Louis Adolfe **Thiers** was chosen to head the new government and to serve as chief negotiator. The preliminary negotiations were held in Versailles, February 21–26, with the final treaty signed at Frankfurt on May 10.

The chief goal of the German Chancellor, Otto von **Bismarck,** was to leave France too weakened to wage a war of revenge in the foreseeable future. He pursued two means to achieve this: territory from France to be annexed to the newly created German Empire and a financial indemnity of 5 billion francs to keep the French treasury from financing rearmament. Bismarck demanded all of the province of Alsace and most of Lorraine, including the fortress of Metz. Much of this territory contained a mixture of French and German peoples, but the area around Metz was French. For that reason Bismarck wanted to exclude it from the German Empire, but both the kaiser and general staff insisted that Metz and its fortress become German territory in order to secure the frontier and to deprive France's border of a key component of its defenses. Furthermore, the German public believed that the peace should punish France. Faced with the combined determination of king, military, and public, Bismarck gave way and made Metz a condition of the settlement.

Thiers had little leverage. With significant portions of France already occupied, it would have required little effort from the Germans to take compensation from the occupied territory. As well, Bismarck could threaten to let the armistice lapse and permit the resumption of hostilities against a French government, army, and people no longer capable or willing to fight. As a result, Thiers accepted Bismarck's demands and the provisional government ratified them.

The treaty has been blamed as a source of the heightening tensions in Europe ultimately leading to World War I. In particular, the desire to restore the "lost provinces" of Alsace and Lorraine served as a rallying point for French nationalists keen on another war with Germany. The indemnity was paid in full in three years and thus failed to scupper French rearmament. In 1919, finally, the punitive nature of the treaty served as model for diplomats who sought to impose a similar peace of Germany after World War I, featuring both territorial losses and reparations. *See also* Alsace-Lorraine; Clemençeau, Georges; German Empire.

FURTHER READING: Giesberg, Robert I. *The Treaty of Frankfort: A Study of Diplomatic History, September, 1870-September 1873*. Philadelphia: University of Philadelphia Press, 1966; Pflanze,

Otto. *Bismarck and the Development of Germany*. Princeton, NJ: Princeton University Press, 1963.

DAVID H. OLIVIER

## Fredericksburg, Battle of (1862)

A disastrous defeat of Union forces in the American Civil War. Although the Army of the Potomac had checked Robert E. Lee's advance into the North at **Antietam** in Maryland in September, President Abraham Lincoln cashiered George McClellan for having allowed the Confederate army to reach the safety of Virginia. Ambrose Burnside assumed command of Union forces and marched to outflank Lee at Fredericksburg, hoping to force Lee out into the open for a battle that would favor the superior numbers in the Union Army. Burnside was delayed crossing the Rappahannock River awaiting pontoon bridges. The delay allowed Lee the time to set up a powerful defense on high ground south and west of Fredericksburg. On the morning of December 13, 1862, Burnside launched a series of fruitless frontal assaults against well-defended Confederate positions under James Longstreet and Stonewall Jackson. Only the early darkness halted the massacre of Union troops.

Burnside planned to renew the frontal attacks the next day, but was talked out of it by his subordinates. After Burnside ordered new movements against Lee in January, mockingly called the "mud marches" by the Union troops, Lincoln removed him from army command in favor of Joseph Hooker.

FURTHER READING: O'Reilly, Francis Augustin. *The Fredericksburg Campaign: Winter War of the Rappahannock*. Baton Rouge: Louisiana State University Press, 2006.

THOMAS D. VEVE

## Freemasonry

Initially a secret fraternity that developed a system of allegory and symbolism based on the temple of King Solomon and medieval stonemasonry, Freemasonry experienced its most tumultuous episodes in the eighteenth and nineteenth centuries, and its lodges and their most prominent members were directly involved in the social-political transformations of those times.

The speculations on the origins of Freemasonry are numerous, but the most circulated hypothesis is that it started in 1356, with the formation of the London Masons Company, a guild of stonemasons and builders, *cementarii* in Latin. The earliest known mention of the term *Freemason* dates from 1376, and it is considered to be derived from "freestone," a soft limestone commonly used then by builders in the South of England. In 1425, King Henry VI of England banned the yearly congregation of the Masons. The first Masonic Grand Lodge of England was publicly formed in London in 1717. Thereafter, Freemasonry spread rapidly throughout Europe and beyond. The first lodge on the American continent, in what was to become the United States, was opened in 1733.

The theories on the purpose and objectives of Freemasonry are also multiple. In general it is believed that it was created as a haven for medieval religious dissidence. In time the need for secrecy has gradually subsided; however, its practices and rituals, as well as its spiritual content have expanded. Freemasonry is known to have experienced two schisms. The first one took place in 1753, when a newer faction, of a lower class standing and more religious, known as the Antients, broke away from the Grand Lodge of England and their acolytes, a more aristocratic and unorthodox—mostly Deist or Pantheist—group, which would come to be known as the Moderns. The second schism started in 1877, when the French branch, the *Grand Orient de France,* started accepting atheists and women and also tolerating religious and political discussions in the Lodge. Atheism and revolution had increasingly become popular with the continental European and Latin American lodges, so that governments often regarded them as fronts for subversive activity. Despite all the metaphysical and ethereal constitutional claims of Free Masonry, its ultimately concrete social objectives and interests have become apparent through its recruiting choices and strategies, generally directed towards the upper echelons of the social and religious hierarchy.

Some of the most well-known members of the nineteenth-century lodges included British Kings George IV (1762–1830), William IV (1765–1837), and Edward VII (1841–1910); Giuseppe Garibaldi (1807–1882) of the Italian Orient, a leader in the Risorgimento that led to the unification of Italy; Giacomo Casanova (1725–98); American Presidents George Washington (1732–99), James Monroe (1758–1831), Andrew Jackson (1767–1845), James Knox Polk (1795–1849), James Buchanan (1791–1868), Andrew Johnson (1808–75), William McKinley (1843–1901), and Theodore Roosevelt (1858–1919); American abolitionist John Brown (1800–59); French sculptor Frédéric Bartholdi (1834–1904), the creator of the *Statue of Liberty;* the Portuguese "Dom Pedro" (1798–1834), briefly King Pedro IV of Portugal and then Pedro I, first Emperor of Brazil when Brazil declared its independence in 1822; Mexican Presidents Benito Juárez (1806–72), the first and only Native American Mexican president, and Porfirio **Díaz** (1830–1915), the dictator; Argentinean general José de San Martín (1778–1850), a leader in South America's fight for independence from the Spanish Empire; Venezuelan general and statesman Antonio José de Sucre (1795–1830), one of Simón **Bolívar**'s closest friends; Bernardo O'Higgins (1778–1842), the first head of state of independent Chile; and the Cuban poet José Martí (1853–95), a leader of Cuba's fight for independence.

FURTHER READING: Naudon, Paul. *The Secret History of Freemasonry: Its Origins and Connection to the Knights Templar.* Rochester, VT: Inner Traditions, 2005; Ridley, Jasper. *The Freemasons: A History of the World's Most Powerful Secret Society.* New York: Arcade, 2002.

GEORGIA TRES

## Free Trade

The doctrine that international trade should be neither discouraged nor distorted by government policy. It normally refers to the idea that tariff barriers to the entry of foreign products into a domestic market should be abjured; in more sophisticated forms, it also holds that government policy should avoid bounties and other policies designed to enhance exports. The canonical authority to which free traders looked throughout the nineteenth century for intellectual and moral support was Adam **Smith,** although the vast majority of classical political economists were hostile to protection except in select circumstances. Arguments for free trade generally rested on the theory of **comparative advantage,** which held that each nation should focus on those products that it could make most cheaply and efficiently, a system of free trade ensuring that the benefits were distributed. Some, such as the free trade campaigner Richard **Cobden,** hoped that peaceful trade would bind nations together by ties of common interest, thereby leading to international peace.

Free trade was one of the most emotive causes in nineteenth-century British politics. The abandonment of agricultural protection—the so-called **Corn Laws**—in 1846 caused the Tory or **Conservative Party** of Sir Robert **Peel** to split, many of the free traders going at length into the Liberal Party. Free trade exerted a powerful hold on the Liberal Party until the 1940s. Britain abandoned free trade for revenue reasons during World War I. Between the mid-nineteenth century and that war, opposition to free trade was limited to the **Tariff Reform** wing of the Conservative or **Unionist** Party, and even there it was a minority position. Supporters of free trade urged a "free breakfast table"—in other words they opposed tariffs on sugar and tea. Although free trade had its supporters in other countries, Britain's policy of unilateral free trade, not emulated by other powers, was unique.

From an imperial point of view, arguments for free trade cut both ways: in a free trading world, empires would be irrelevant to the economics of trade, but in a world in which many major colonial powers—France and Germany chief among them—practiced protection, there was an argument for other powers to expand their empires so as to retain access to colonial markets. The cause of free trade could serve as a motive for war, often by interimperial forces, in the name of opening markets, as it did in China and Japan. In practice, in British politics dogmatic free traders were often radicals and anti-imperialists, whereas protectionist policies were associated with such enthusiastic imperialists as Joseph **Chamberlain.** *See also* Anti-Corn Law League; British Empire; Continental System; Open Door.

FURTHER READING: Forster, Jakob. *Business, Politics, and Tariffs, 1825–1879.* Toronto: University of Toronto Press, 1986; Hinde, Wendy. *Richard Cobden: A Victorian Outsider.* New Haven, CT: Yale University Press, 1987; McCord, Norman. *The Anti-Corn Law League, 1838–1846.* London: Allen & Unwin, 1968; Muller, Jerry. *Adam Smith in His Time and Ours.* Princeton, NJ: Princeton University Press, 1993.

MARK F. PROUDMAN

## French Empire

During the Age of Imperialism France had, after Britain, the second largest and most diverse colonial empire, with a wide mix of settler colonies, penal settlements, plantations, trading bases, and **protectorates** that literally spanned the globe. The bulk of French colonial possessions date from the nineteenth century, but the origins of the empire actually go back 300 years earlier when men like Jacques Cartier and Samuel de Champlain were sent by the monarchy to explore and colonize parts of the New World. Although the French subsequently expanded their possessions in **Canada** and the **Caribbean** to include slaving bases in West Africa, several Indian Ocean island colonies, and five trading bases in **India,** nearly all were lost in a series of eighteenth-century wars against Britain and Spain. In the early nineteenth century, during the reign of Napoleon **Bonaparte,** whose conquests came mostly at the expense of other great powers in Europe itself, France lost still more overseas colonies. The Haitian Revolution, led by **Toussaint l'Ouverture,** not only cost France her most prosperous plantation colony, it also led to the sale of recently restored French holdings in the Mississippi basin to the United States in what has become known as the **Louisiana Purchase** (1803). Consequently, at the start of the nineteenth century, the French overseas empire was limited to a handful of trading bases in India and **Senegal,** Caribbean plantation colonies in Guadeloupe and Martinique, the islands of St. Pierre and Miquelon off the coast of Canada, and Guiana on the South American mainland. Subsequent French colonial expansion overseas was haphazard and devoid of any grand master plan. Instead, colonies were taken either to satisfy the vagaries of domestic French politics or in response to the activities of individual colonial officials and special interest groups. The result was continuous, if somewhat chaotic, expansion that reached a fever pitch in the 1880s as part of the **Scramble for Africa.**

### Colonial Expansion

The first bout of French colonial expansion in the nineteenth century came in **Algeria,** which at the time was a semi-autonomous province of the **Ottoman Empire** ruled by a local viceroy. After the final restoration of the Bourbon Dynasty in 1815, Franco-Algerian relations suffered a sharp decline when the French objected to the high interest rates charged for grain borrowed by Napoleon's armies and refused to take responsibility for debts incurred by the Revolutionary government. The situation came to a head in April 1827, when an argument over unpaid debts escalated and led the Algerian viceroy to destroy French trading posts and expel the French consul after swatting him with a ceremonial whisk. **Charles X,** the increasingly unpopular king, later seized on this incident as justification for launching a March 1830 invasion in a vain effort to divert the attention of the French masses from his attempts to restore autocratic royal power. Despite the success of the French invasion, Charles was toppled from power and replaced by the **July Monarchy** of his distant cousin Louis Philippe. The new king opted to keep Algeria in the hopes of placating competing economic pressure groups by granting contracts and concessions in Algeria. Shortly thereafter the eruption of a long and bloody revolt by the Algerian masses led the French to expand their initial holdings by pushing deeply and permanently into the Algerian interior.

The July Monarchy also oversaw the expansion of French interests in sub-Saharan Africa, the Indian Ocean, and Polynesia. In an effort to compete with the British for trade along the **Guinea** coast of West Africa during the late 1830s and 1840s, French merchants and naval officers began signing a series of treaties granting French protection to coastal tribes in Guinea, the Ivory Coast, and the river estuary of Gabon, thereby turning an old string of trading posts dating to the seventeenth century into a larger informal sphere of influence. This sphere later served as the nucleus for additional French incursions into West and Equatorial Africa during the "new imperialism" of the 1880s. In the Indian Ocean, the desire for sugar plantations and the need for resupply bases for naval vessels led the French governor of Reunion to annex the islands of Nosy Bé in1840 and Mayotte in 1841, giving France a toehold in the Comoros Islands and a base from which to intervene in the affairs of neighboring **Madagascar.** Similarly, longstanding demands from missionaries and colonial enthusiasts for annexation of various Polynesian islands in the hopes that they would yield plantations and resupply bases for the French navy finally bore fruit in the early 1840s when Admiral Abel Aubert Dupetit-Thouars acted on his own authority by annexing the Marquesas and declaring a protectorate over Tahiti.

Additional expansion in Africa, the Pacific, and Indochina in Southeast Asia took place during the Second Empire of Louis Napoleon **Bonaparte** (Napoleon III), who opted to pursue an active and aggressive foreign policy to live up to his namesake, increase popularity at home, and divert attention from his failed foreign policy ventures in Italy and Mexico. During his time in power (1852–1870), Napoleon III continued the conquest and pacification of the Algerian interior and dispatched French troops to Guinea and Dahomey on the pretext of protecting French merchants and securing access to the increasingly important peanut and palm oil trade. A combination of military power, diplomacy, and bribery was then used to get local chiefs to accept protectorates over additional West African coastal regions. In the South Pacific, the existence of good pasture land, a strategic location near Australia, and the need for a healthier penal settlement than Guiana led France to annex New Caledonia in 1853. Over the next several decades, New Caledonia was turned into a small settlement colony composed of a handful of free settlers and thousands of convicts and political prisoners exiled from metropolitan France. In nearby China and **Indochina,** France was goaded into action by the persecution of missionaries and their converts, culminating in French participation in the Second **Opium War** in 1860. Similarly, the French government intervened in nearby Indochina by sending in the navy in 1847 and again in 1858 to bombard the port of Da Nang in an effort to force Tu-Duc, the emperor of Annam, to grant freedom of worship to Christians. Tu-Duc was eventually forced to sign a treaty in 1862 that granted religious toleration throughout his realm and ceded the southern province of Cochin-China, including Saigon, to France.

Not all colonial activities during the reign of Napoleon III were orchestrated or even officially sanctioned by his government. In eastern Africa, a French merchant and occasional diplomat, Henri Lambert, visited the Somali coast in 1855 and convinced the local chief to cede the port of Obock to him on behalf of France. Although the ministry of foreign affairs convinced Napoleon III to turn down the cession owing to suspicions about Lambert's motives, the French negotiated a new treaty in 1862 after Lambert's death purchasing Obock outright so as to counter the British presence in Aden and guarantee access to the Red Sea. French expansion in Senegal was similarly driven by a single individual who forced the government's hand. Starting in the mid 1850s, Louis Faidherbe, the newly appointed governor of Senegal, embarked on an unofficial and unsanctioned program of colonial expansion by invading the interior after provoking border disputes with neighboring Muslim communities in an effort to gain land for plantations.

In 1870, the Second Empire's defeat in the **Franco-Prussian War** swept Napoleon III from power, triggered the **Paris Commune** uprising, and ushered in the Third Republic. Given its bloody beginnings and the French public's loss of confidence in the new regime over a series of scandals, including the Boulanger Affair, the Panama scandal, the **Dreyfus Affair,** and the turn of the century anticlerical campaign, the new regime was forced to compensate with an aggressive foreign policy in the hopes of preserving France's geopolitical position and, above all, reinvigorating French patriotism via the acquisition of allies and new colonies overseas. In the process, the Third Republic hoped to use the new territories, their resources, and peoples to restore French military and economic power on a global scale. Indeed, by the turn of the century, French politicians were openly talking about using their empire as a base for creating a nation of 100 million Frenchmen that would ensure France's status as major world power.

The renewed French interest in colonies was not just motivated by geopolitics. As in other European powers, by the 1870s, national attitudes toward empire were also changing because of industrialization, persistent action by special interest groups, and belief in the twin ideologies of **social Darwinism** and the **white man's burden.** Industrialization caused domestic misery and unrest in metropolitan France as the masses adjusted to urbanization and factory-based means of production. Like Charles X before them, Third Republic politicians often saw the acquisition of colonies as a means of diverting public attention from domestic crises. Given the intensified competition among industrial powers, colonies were also seen as a major arena of investment and an attractive safety net providing guaranteed markets and raw materials; interest groups, which now included leading industrialists, continued to push European governments to acquire colonies. France was no exception. In addition to bankers and overseas investors, French merchants and **missionaries** also made strident demands for annexation to protect their activities. The military and their suppliers soon joined in, reasoning that the pursuit of empire would both demonstrate French power and legitimate their own claims on national fiscal resources. Lastly, the belief in social Darwinism convinced the French that they were in a struggle for survival in which the strong were entitled to seize resources from weak. In the process, they incurred a moral obligation to elevate and "civilize" their racial inferiors by providing peace, stability, education, good government, and exposure to capitalism.

For all these reasons, the French entered the 1870s increasingly interested in taking on additional colonies. That interest peaked in the late 1870s and early 1880s as a result of events in **Tunisia, Egypt,** and the Congo River basin. Shortly after the turn of the century, the rulers of Tunisia and Egypt, two outlying provinces of the declining Ottoman Empire, began modernization campaigns financed by European capital in an effort to strengthen their lands and secure their independence from the Ottoman Sultan. By mid-century, the size of these debts led to the creation of finance commissions that enabled the Europeans to supervise and reform Tunisian and Egyptian finances. France, as the largest creditor, naturally dominated these finance commissions and regarded both provinces as French spheres of influence. This position of French dominance was threatened at the end of the 1870s when a newly unified **Italy** indicated its intention to annex Tunisia as part of an effort to rally the masses at home behind the new nation. France responded by sending the Algerian army into Tunisia in 1881 in a bid to secure a treaty creating a formal French protectorate. The invasion, although intended to be temporary, provoked a nationalist revolt fueled by Islam that ultimately forced the French to stay permanently in Tunisia.

As in Tunisia, the size of its loans and active involvement in the construction of the **Suez Canal** led the French to regard Egypt as a sphere of influence. They were therefore not pleased when Egypt's debt burden forced the Khedive to sell his 43 percent stake in the Suez Canal to Britain in 1875. This move and the subsequent implementation of Anglo-French control over Egyptian finances proved to be deeply unpopular and helped trigger a nationalist uprising in 1881 that deposed the Khedive and threatened to nationalize the canal. Because Paris was preoccupied with domestic problems and the growing revolt in Tunisia, France refused Britain's offer to send in a joint invasion force to restore order. Britain, after invading alone, subsequently declined to allow France to resume its old role in jointly administering Egyptian finances. Feeling cheated out of its sphere of influence, the French government became increasingly determined both to regain lost influence in Egypt and to contain British influence elsewhere on the continent.

The chance to act on these sentiments was afforded by the actions of **Leopold II** of Belgium. Eager to overcome the limits of his status as a constitutional monarch, Leopold created a private trading company to explore and exploit the Congo River basin in central Africa. These efforts, which peaked in the late 1870s, put him in direct competition with French merchants operating out of Gabon. As French and Belgian company officials raced each other to sign treaties securing monopolies on trade with local African rulers, Leopold tried to preempt further French claims by declaring that he controlled the entire Congo region on the southern side of the river. Concerned that additional paper partitions could lead to conflict between European nations, German Chancellor Otto von **Bismarck** and the French Prime Minister Jules **Ferry** convened the **Berlin Conference** in 1884 to set ground rules for future colonial annexations. Immediately thereafter, France joined other European powers in a race to acquire African territories that was subsequently dubbed the Scramble for Africa.

During the scramble, France engaged in a combination of diplomatic ventures and military expeditions in an attempt to hem in British possessions and regain influence in Egypt by securing access to the upper Nile. Starting in 1884, French expeditions began pushing inland from all the existing African colonies in an effort to drive across the center of the continent in a French equivalent of Cecil **Rhodes**'s Cape to Cairo dream. These efforts culminated in 1896 with an expedition led by Jean-Baptiste Marchand, which marched overland from Equatorial Africa to southern Sudan, claiming everything it encountered along the way for France. Although the Marchand expedition successfully reached the Nile River ahead of advancing British forces, the **Fashoda Incident** effectively put an end to the dream of regaining control over Egypt. Nevertheless, French gains in Africa were enormous, in part because the areas in question were often sparsely populated desert or were divided into large African states that periodically cooperated with French forces in actions against their neighbors. Consequently, by the turn of the twentieth century, French possessions covered more than one-third of the African continent and stretched from Algeria, Senegal, and Equatorial Africa to the Oubangui River. Further adjustments, including the acquisition of **Morocco,** continued right up until the outbreak of World War I and were the result of inter-European negotiations to resolve border disputes.

The Third Republic's colonial efforts were not limited to the African continent. The French also acquired additional Pacific island possessions, but their greatest area of expansion occurred in Indochina. Eager to protect existing holdings in the region, colonial lobbyists in France demanded active military intervention in **Tonkin** in 1884 in a bid to restore order and end endemic piracy. By the end of the decade, the success of these operations enabled France to establish protectorates over Annam, Tonkin, Cochin-China, and Cambodia and to turn the Vietnamese emperor into a puppet ruler. Not satisfied with these conquests, the French invaded neighboring **Laos** in 1893 in an effort to solidify their hold on the Mekong River and gain additional land for plantations. These actions completed the establishment of a French colonial empire that by1914 boasted 63 million colonial subjects and 12 million square kilometers of territory.

### Administrative Policy and Structure

Unlike other colonial powers that thought of their empires as possessions, France regarded its colonial empire as noncontiguous extensions of France itself. They were considered literally part of France, not because they had been annexed, or even because they contained French settlers, but because the French were committed to the idea of assimilation and expected colonial peoples to one day take on the status, rights, and responsibilities of citizenship. Belief in assimilation, which had its roots in the French Revolution, not only led to efforts to "civilize" native peoples through exposure to French language, culture, industry, and education, it also had a profound impact on colonial administration.

Because the colonies were considered part of France, they were afforded no special treatment whatsoever. Metropolitan laws, tariffs, and forms of government were simply extended to newly acquired possessions. Hence, as in France itself, power was concentrated in the hands of the National Assembly in Paris and was transmitted through a series of lower level officials down to towns and villages. As only Frenchmen could fully understand and appreciate this system, France adopted a concept known as direct rule in which all officials in the colonies were French. Africans and Asians were employed by colonial administrations as clerks and aides, but they served in subordinate roles that left all decision-making authority in the hands of white officials. Although bypassing local rulers ensured French political control at all levels, it had the disadvantage of making French colonial policy ponderous and slow to adapt to local conditions. These factors were partly offset by the ability of French citizens in some full colonies such as Algeria, Senegal, and Cochin China to elect deputies to serve in the National Assembly. Since few nonwhites acquired citizenship, however, most indigenous peoples remained unrepresented.

Although the National Assembly could not deal with everyday colonial matters, the French did not develop a colonial minister or colonial office for most of the nineteenth century. Before the Scramble for Africa, France never had a sufficient number of colonies to warrant creating a high-level government position to coordinate colonial policy. Moreover, creating such a position flew in the face of assimilation by implying that, rather than being subject to the jurisdiction of regular government bodies, the colonies instead had some sort of special status. In the absence of a single colonial ministry, France therefore developed a tradition whereby any ministry with sufficient reason could dabble in colonial affairs. This situation, which made the drafting and implementation of colonial policy chaotic and difficult, changed slightly during the 1890s, as France began to acquire newer and larger colonial holdings. France finally created a colonial minister in 1894, but his position remained ambiguous. Not only was the colonial ministry the smallest and least prestigious agency within the government, but, in a nod to tradition, it never took over full responsibility for colonial affairs. Instead, it remained subject to constant budget scrutiny from the National Assembly and continued to face periodic intervention from other ministries, government agencies, and committees representing special interest groups.

Below the colonial minister were governors and governor-generals who administered individual colonies or the three federations of **French West Africa, French Equatorial Africa,** and **French Indochina.** Like the colonial minister, the governors and governor-generals were in an ambiguous position. On the surface they were quite autocratic and could issue decrees; control their own administration, police, military, and legal systems; and run native affairs. At the same time, however, their power was restricted in several ways. In addition to requiring colonies to generate tax revenues to pay for their own administration and share of common expenses like defense, the National Assembly also reviewed all other expenditures by local administrations. Governors who raised additional monies to pay for pet projects inside their own colonies risked signaling Paris that they could possibly afford to contribute more in the future toward joint expenses. As a result, Paris exercised tight fiscal control over the governors. French colonial governors also had to obey orders from the colonial ministry, were watched by inspectors, and were subject to influence from pressure groups and the press. Moreover, they also had to contend with advisory councils made up of local colonial officials who could influence policy by threatening to appeal to metropolitan officials.

Individual colonies were subdivided into districts—Subdivisions and *cercles* or *circonscriptions*—in the hands of white bureaucrats who gathered reports, carried out the governor's policies, administered justice, and collected taxes. Despite having sole authority for huge geographic areas, colonial administrators were usually young men with little training. Furthermore, tropical diseases, long separation from friends and family, lack of amenities, and distance from the metropole combined to make colonial posts less desirable than other branches of government. As a result, in addition to suffering high turnover rates, those who served in the colonies often had little interest in the lives of indigenous peoples, few ideas about how to promote commerce or education, and little incentive to act without specific instructions from Paris. Paris tried to deal with this problem by setting up the *École Coloniale* in the late 1880s to train colonial officials. Still, its curriculum was largely irrelevant and, and, even at its peak, less than 20 percent of colonial administrators were alumnae. Rather than concentrating on practical matters or languages, the *École Coloniale* emphasized French law, history, and obedience to existing government policies. Consequently, French administrators were less well trained, less efficient, less capable, and ultimately less effective than their British counterparts.

By 1900, the French began rethinking the premises behind colonial rule. In particular, they concluded that the policy of assimilation was a failure, as few Africans had renounced local custom and become French citizens. The pull of religion and indigenous social and cultural institutions proved to be too strong. At the same time, the rise of social Darwinism and racism made the French increasingly uncomfortable with the very idea of African assimilation. Consequently, at the turn of the century, France abandoned assimilation in favor of *association*, defined as a cooperative policy of colonial administration in which colonized peoples were recognized as junior partners and native institutions were to be allowed to continue developing according to local needs. In effect, the shift was in principle toward a more indirect form of rule whereby native authorities would retrieve and exercise some power. In practice, however, little changed, as most French colonial officials had been schooled in the old policy of assimilation and either fell back on it out of confusion or in resistance to the prospect of sharing political authority on any level.

## The Colonial Lobby

Often lumped together under the general descriptor of *Parti Colonial*—a loose collection of interest groups rather than a political organization—the French colonial lobby was composed of a wide variety of private organizations eager to highlight the supposed benefits of colonies and acknowledge the achievements of missionaries, explorers, and settlers. In addition to missionary societies, urban chambers of commerce, and academic associations, the colonial lobby also contained large numbers of independent entities like the *Comité de l'Afrique Française,* which were organized around specific colonies or groups of colonies. These committees, most of which were formed between 1890 and 1905, held lectures, supported research, held exhibitions, and published journals to draw attention to colonial affairs or influence government policy. Similarly, in 1893, business interests created their own lobby in the form of the *Union Coloniale Française* to pressure the government regarding trade and colonial development policy. Collectively, these groups found a willing audience in the *Groupe Coloniale,* a caucus of pro-colonial deputies in the lower house of the National Assembly.

The military and settlers also represented important interests. The army continued to lobby on behalf of colonial issues not only because its honor was at stake, but also because the maintenance of empire ensured its budgets from year to year. As for the settlers, they naturally petitioned Paris for protection, land, subsidies, labor, and the development of colonial infrastructure. Paris often distrusted their motives, leading to frequent disputes between settlers and administrators who resented settler demands and the difficulties they created. Colonial authorities were also suspicious of settlers because not all were of French origin. Because the country was relatively stable and prosperous after 1850, finding settlers to send to colonies was often challenging, so that France had to turn to immigrants from Italy and Spain, as well as imported laborers from India and Syria. The result was a heterogeneous colonial population, which, aside from Algeria, was never very large and only a limited success as a lobby.

## Economic Policy

Although colonial propaganda claimed that the colonies were economically valuable, the reality is that they were of limited use to France in part because Paris had no coherent or coordinated economic plan until after World War I. Throughout the nineteenth century, the government paid lip service to the demands of the colonial lobby for public investment in infrastructure but remained wary of the expense and preferred instead to concentrate on the tasks of conquest and administration. Economic development was therefore left in private hands between 1880 and 1914. Private firms in the colonies and in the metropole underwrote and promoted many colonial ventures, but their efforts were insufficient. Consequently, the French colonial empire not only lacked adequate roads, railroads, and port facilities to exploit effectively the mineral and other resources of the interior, French merchants and manufacturers also blocked efforts to develop local manufacturing lest it interfere with their own exports. As a result, most colonies remained underdeveloped and their people too poor to be a real market for French goods. They were confined to supplying tropical raw materials such as coffee, spices, sugar, rice, bananas, coconut, citrus, margarine, peanut oil, cotton, rubber, minerals, and hardwoods.

Although colonial exports were useful for propping up uncompetitive and declining French industries through the provision of cheap raw materials that could be sold internationally or shipped to France to be made into finished goods, by 1914, the colonies accounted for only 10 percent of French foreign trade. The bulk of colonial trade was concentrated in Indochina and parts of West Africa where France had established rubber, peanut, and palm plantations. Much of the remainder of the African empire, however, was desert and economically worthless. Efforts to change this were limited by the combination of direct rule, with its insistence on sending out expensive white administrators and soldiers to the colonies, and the requirement after 1900 that colonies be self-sufficient. Limited spending on health and education also took their toll in the form of higher absenteeism and poorly trained workers, all of which worked to slow economic development. It was not until the 1920s and the effort to rebuild from the destruction of World War I that France began making serious attempts to develop its colonies by expanding plantations, increasing road and railroad construction, and masking improvements in harbor facilities.

### Education Policy

Throughout the nineteenth century, French colonial policy was committed to the *mission civilisatrice*, which held that it was an imperial duty to civilize or uplift backward natives by exposing them to the benefits of French culture, language, education, industry, and justice. For most of the century the intent was to actually assimilate colonized peoples to the point where they would acquire citizenship by renouncing native law and customs in favor of French language and culture. Although education was considered the key to this transition, successive governments continually struggled with the format, content, and direction it should take in the colonies. The result was significant variation in terms of the size and quality of school systems from one colony to the next. Generally speaking, colonial officials refused to spend much time or money on schools, preferring instead to leave them in the hands of missionaries. Government schools were therefore few in number and were geared toward schooling low-level clerks or providing vocational training. Trainees were drawn from native elites and the best students of mission schools and were presented with curricula and textbooks imported from France. Yet the education they received was not equivalent to one received in France. Instead pupils in the colonies were taught basic literacy, acceptance of their secondary status, and obedience to the colonial order. Moreover, because diplomas earned in the colonies were not recognized in France, pupils of government schools found their prospects for future advancement outside the colonial environment highly restricted.

Mission schools were similarly limited. Although missionaries maintained extensive school systems that extended deep into the interior and down to the village level, their curriculum was a mixture of Christianity, manual labor, and limited academics. Because Protestant mission theology held that conversion was best achieved through exposure to Scripture in one's own language, mission schools often taught in local vernaculars. Moreover, as the missions felt that the bulk of their pupils were destined to lead lives as farmers and laborers, mission schools eschewed academic preparation beyond primary school in favor of vocational training, often employing pupils on school farms, plantations, and other money-making ventures in lieu of charging tuition. Although the pupils of mission schools often pushed for more academic instruction, particularly French-language literacy, as a means of obtaining better paid clerical jobs with local business or administration, their requests met with limited success before 1914. The failure of mission schools to be more responsive to these requests led to discontent among pupils and exposed mission schools to criticism from administrators who complained that they were not doing enough to spread French language and culture or even train sufficient numbers of clerks to fill the needs of local government and business firms. The combination of these charges, combined with growing anticlerical sentiment in France, stripped mission schools of government subsidies after 1900, and led to repeated clashes with administrators over the content of curriculum right up until the outbreak of World War I.

### The Status of Native Peoples

France established two forms of political status within the empire. Citizens included nationals from France, whites born in the colonies, and the handful of natives who naturalized. Although citizens enjoyed full civil liberties, voting rights, and preferential treatment under the law, few Africans or Asians were willing or able to meet the conditions for naturalization that varied from place to place yet always included complete linguistic and cultural assimilation. Most colonized peoples were ignorant of the requirements or even the possibility of acquiring full citizenship. They were also discouraged from naturalizing, as it cut them off from their own communities and meant giving up inheritance rights established under native law. Instead, the majority of colonized peoples were classified as colonial subjects and were denied voting rights. They were also subjected to forced labor known as *prestation* and were legally answerable to native courts run by administrators who applied their own interpretation of local customary law in civil cases. Colonial subjects were also subject to the *indigénat*, an extra-judicial code that began in Algeria in the 1870s and was soon extended to all of French Africa. Under the *indigénat*, French administrators could impose punishments in the form of short jail sentences and fines for a series of offenses ranging from failure to pay taxes to disrespect of colonial officials. The arbitrary nature of the *indigénat* was deeply offensive to Africans and continually underscored the inequality of French colonial administration.

With the outbreak of World War I in 1914, France relied heavily on its colonies to provide men and resources for the war effort in Europe. After the armistice of 1918, France clung to its colonies and used their resources to facilitate reconstruction of the metropole. In light of the many sacrifices of colonized peoples during and immediately after the war, the French failure to address the inequities in treatment of colonized peoples—including retention of the hated *indigénat*, the use of forced labor, poor education, and limited economic opportunities—led to a gradual rise in colonial nationalism during the interwar period and eventually triggered decolonization in the 1960s. *See also Belle Époque;* Boulanger, General Georges-Ernest; Entente Cordiale; Brazza, Pierre; Haiti; Somaliland; Triple Entente.

FURTHER READING: Aldrich, Robert. *Greater France: A History of French Overseas Expansion.* New York: St. Martin's, 1996; Canale, Jean-Suret. *French Colonialism in Tropical Africa 1900–1945.* New York: Pica Press, 1971; Cohen, William B. *The French Encounter with Africans: White Response to Blacks, 1530–1880.* Reprint ed. Bloomington: Indiana University Press, 2003;

Cooke, James J. *New French Imperialism 1880–1910: The Third Republic and Colonial Expansion.* Hamden, CT: Archon Books, 1973; Fieldhouse, D. K. *The Colonial Empires: A Comparative Study from the Eighteenth Century.* 2nd ed. London: Macmillan, 1982; Hoisington, William A., Jr. "Colonial Mission: France Overseas in the Nineteenth and Twentieth Centuries." In William B. Cohen, ed. *The Transformation of Modern France.* Boston: Houghton Mifflin, 1997, pp. 97–108; Johnson, G. Wesley. *Double Impact: France and Africa in the Age of Imperialism.* Westport, CT: Greenwood Press, 1985; Manning, Patrick. *Francophone Sub-Saharan Africa 1880–1995.* 2nd ed. Cambridge: Cambridge University Press, 1998; Quinn, Frederick. *The French Overseas Empire.* Westport, CT: Praeger, 2002; Wesseling, H. L. *The European Colonial Empires 1815–1919.* New York: Longman, 2004.

KENNETH J. OROSZ

## French Equatorial Africa

French Equatorial Africa *(Afrique équatoriale française)* was a federation of French colonies, stretching northward from the Congo River into the Sahara Desert. From 1880 to 1910, the French expanded their colonial empire into West and Central Africa. The federation was formed in 1910, as an administrative grouping modeled after the *Afrique Occidentale Francaise,* French West Africa, which was formed in 1895. Savorgna de **Brazza,** the French Commissioner for the French Congo, was largely responsible for its creation. The new federation consisted of Middle Congo, Gabon, and Ubangi-Shari-Chad. In 1920, however, Chad left the federation and was ruled as a separate colony. After the **Agadir Crisis** in 1911, part of French Equatorial Africa was ceded to German Cameroon. This part was later returned to France according to the terms in the Treaty of Versailles signed in 1919. The federation's capital and seat of the governor-general was Brazzaville. With only 3 million inhabitants spread over 965,000 square miles, the federation was sparsely populated and not an attractive target for investment. *See also* Africa, Scramble for; Entente Cordiale, French Empire.

FURTHER READING: Aldrich, Robert. *Greater France: A History of French Overseas Expansion.* New York: St. Martin's Press, 1996; Manning, Patrick. *Francophone Sub-Saharan Africa 1880–1995.* New York: Cambridge University Press, 1998; Wesseling, H. L. *The European Colonial Empires 1815–1919.* New York: Longman, 2004.

NURFADZILAH YAHAYA

## French Foreign Legion

Officially named the *Régiment Étranger,* the French Foreign Legion was the most storied and durable mercenary force attached to a regular army. France had a long history of employing foreign mercenaries before the creation of the legion; of 102 line regiments in the French army before the revolution, 23 were made up of foreign nationals. The French Foreign Legion was established in 1831 by Louis Philippe to mop up refugees coming into France after the Revolution of July 1830 made it illegal for foreigners to enlist in the French army. The Legion quickly became a home for foreign adventurers, social misfits, and every kind of criminal.

The Legion also became a military workhorse of French colonialism, seeing action for the first time in **Algeria** in 1832. In 1835–1836 the Legion served in the

Carlist Wars in Spain, where it fought well yet was so decimated that it had to be rebuilt. Adopting the motto *Legio patria nostra,* "the Legion is our fatherland," in the 1840s, it made its headquarters in Sidi-bel-Abbès in Algeria and played a major role in the French conquest of that country. Legion units also served in the Crimean War, the Austro-Piedmontese War, the Franco-Prussian War, and in French **Indochina.** Captain Jean Danjou, a highly decorated legionnaire who lost a hand in combat in Algeria in 1853, and had a wooden prosthetic made, died with most of his men in a last-ditch stand in the Battle of Camarón in Mexico in 1863. His wooden hand was recovered, is displayed at the legion headquarters in Aubagne in southern France, and is paraded annually on the anniversary of the battle.

FURTHER READING: Porch, Douglas. *The French Foreign Legion.* New York: Harper Collins, 1991; Turnbull, Patrick. *The Foreign Legion.* London: Heinemann, 1964.

CARL CAVANAGH HODGE

## French Indochina

*See* Indochina

## French Restoration (1814)

The return of the Bourbon dynasty to the throne of France in 1814 in the wake of the collapse of the empire of Napoleon I. Despite a brief interruption in their control of government after Napoleon's escape from exile on Elba in 1815, the Bourbons regained control of France until the Revolution of 1830. The period of 1814 to 1830 was characterized by a sharp conservative reaction to the ideas of the French Revolution, which had overthrown the Bourbon monarchy. Louis XVIII, whose brother Louis XVI had been executed during the French Revolution, assumed the French throne in 1814 and ruled until 1824. Louis XVIII was forced to grant a written constitution, known as the Charter of 1814, guaranteeing a bicameral legislature with an appointive Chamber of Peers and an elected Chamber of Deputies. Only men of exceptional wealth, property, and education were eligible to vote. The king argued over the constitution's preamble, steadfastly arguing that his right to rule derived from providence rather than the people.

Although the monarch's return was initially popular, the nostalgia surrounding it dissipated as Louis XVIII's efforts to reverse the changes of the French Revolution mounted. In 1815, Napoleon escaped from his exile on Elba and landed in France, beginning the adventure of the Hundred Days. The king fled to Ghent as Napoleon regained control of the government. After Napoleon's defeat at **Waterloo,** the Bourbon dynasty was restored a second time. What followed was the White Terror, a bloody purge of Bonapartists, who supported Napoleon, and antimonarchists in France conducted by reactionary supporters of the monarchy.

Louis XVIII was a cautious king who relied primarily on moderate ministers to run the government. As a result of the elections of 1815, the Chamber of Deputies became dominated by ultraroyalists, or ultras, staunch conservatives who supported the monarchy and the Catholic Church. The Chamber proved difficult for the king's ministers. Liberals gained control of the Chamber from 1816 to 1820. In 1820, the assassination of the duc de Berry, son of the king's brother, the comte d'Artois, who was leader of the Ultras, prompted the fall of the Liberals and the return of the Chamber to the Ultras, who would dominate government throughout the next decade.

Louis XVIII died in September 1824 and was interred at Saint Denis. His brother, d'Artois, inherited the throne as **Charles X.** A devout Catholic and defender of the absolutist principles of monarchy, Charles X held an elaborate coronation ceremony at Reims Cathedral in the style of medieval French kings. In 1829, Jules de Polignac became chief minister. From 1827 to 1830, a series of economic downturns led to a growing number of liberal deputies in the Chamber. Although Polignac retained support from much of the aristocracy, the Catholic Church, and the peasantry, he was opposed by workers and upper members of the bourgeoisie. Charles X became frustrated with the Chamber as it filled increasingly with liberal deputies who blocked his legislation and threatened his existing policies. The Charter of 1814 established a constitutional monarchy, granting the king extensive power over policymaking, but the Chamber had to pass his legislation. The charter also granted the Chamber the right to determine the election method for its deputies and their rights within the Chamber. The liberal deputies issued a final no-confidence vote in March 1830, prompting Charles X to overstep his constitutional restrictions by attempting to alter the charter by a series of royal decrees known as the Four Ordinances. The decrees called for the dissolution of the Chamber, new elections based on a new electorate, strict censorship of the press, and restriction of voting rights to only the wealthiest in France. Polignac conceived of the 1830 invasion of **Algeria,** partly to shore up Charles' popularity with a foreign triumph reminiscent of Napoleon. In this it failed, but the invasion succeeded, and Algeria became the regime's most lasting legacy.

The decrees led to outcries in the press and urban mobs in Paris mobilized against the king, assembling barricades in the streets. The uprising quickly mounted until it went beyond the means of the monarchy to control. The revolution occurred over three days in 1830, resulting in the abdication of Charles X and his son, the duc d'Angoulême, on July 30, thereby ending the Bourbon monarchy. The liberal, bourgeois Chamber of Deputies refused to recognize Charles X's grandson, the comte de Chambord, as Henry V. Instead, they declared the throne vacant and elected Louis Philippe, duc d'Orleans, a member of a junior branch of the Bourbon family, king of the French. Louis Philippe ruled the "July Monarchy" from 1830 until 1848, when he too was overthrown in revolution. *See also* Bonaparte, Napoleon; Bonapartism; French Empire.

FURTHER READING: Bertier de Sauvigny, Guillaume de. *The Bourbon Restoration.* Translated by Lynn M. Case. Philadelphia: University of Pennsylvania Press, 1966; Mansel, Philip. *Paris between Empires: Monarchy and Revolution, 1814–1852.* New York: St. Martin's Press, 2003; Plibeam, Pamela. *The Constitutional Monarchy in France, 1814–1848.* New York: Longman, 2000; Tudesq, Andre-Jean, and Andre Jardin. *Restoration and Reaction, 1815–1848.* Translated by Elborg Forster. Cambridge: Cambridge University Press, 1983.

ERIC MARTONE

## French West Africa

French West Africa (*Afrique occidentale française*) was by 1913 a federation of eight French colonial possessions in Africa that extended, on an East-West axis, from

Senegal on the Atlantic coast to the border of Chad and, on a North-South axis, from the northern border of **Senegal** and **Algeria** to the Ivory Coast. The explosive growth of the French Empire after the mid-1880s necessitated the consolidation of political authority in an effort to coordinate policy and eliminate intercolonial rivalry, ultimately resulting in the creation of three colonial federations: **French Equatorial Africa,** French West Africa, and French **Indochina.** French West Africa, created in 1895, was the largest and most geographically diverse of the three, combining the colonies of Senegal, Ivory Coast, French Sudan (present-day Mali, Niger, and Burkina Faso) and French **Guinea** into a single administrative unit. Later additions included Dahomey in 1899 (present-day Benin) and Mauritania in 1904.

As in the other federations, political authority in French West Africa was highly centralized. Each colony retained its own governor and local colonial administration, but they were all subject to oversight by a governor-general headquartered in the Senegalese port town of St Louis, moved to Dakar in 1904. The position of governor-general was immensely powerful. The decision to forbid individual governors from having direct contact with Paris meant that the governor-general, who answered directly to the colonial minister and French parliament, served as a clearinghouse for all colonial policies, decisions, and reports. Moreover, in addition to setting federation-wide health, education, and agricultural policies, the governor-general also controlled the purse strings of individual colonial governments, as all revenues from customs duties gathered throughout the federation were sent to Dakar and then reallocated in the form of "subsidies." As such, the governor-general was not only in a position to pressure the colonial governors under his command to follow a common set of policies but was also able to coordinate economic development by directing investment in infrastructure. The result was a growing emphasis throughout the early twentieth century on the cultivation of cash crops such as peanuts, cotton, coffee, and cocoa, as well as intensive railroad construction to open the interior to trade.

During World War II, French West Africa served as a crucial base of operations for Charles de Gaulle and the Free French. As a reward for this service, the French colonies in West Africa were granted increased local autonomy and, once the war ended, were transformed into overseas territories, complete with citizenship and full political rights for their inhabitants. By 1956, however, the rising tide of African nationalism led to demands for independence and the final dissolution of French West Africa as a political entity. *See also* Africa, Scramble for; French Empire.

FURTHER READING: Aldrich, Robert. *Greater France: A History of French Overseas Expansion.* New York: St. Martin's Press, 1996; Chafer, Tony. *The End of Empire in French West Africa: France's Successful Decolonization?* Oxford: Berg, 2002; Johnson, G. Wesley. *Double Impact: France and Africa in the Age of Imperialism.* Westport, CT: Greenwood Press, 1985; Manning, Patrick. *Francophone Sub-Saharan Africa 1880–1995.* 2nd ed. Cambridge: Cambridge University Press, 1998; von Albertini, Rudolf. *European Colonial Rule, 1880–1940: The Impact of the West on India, Southeast Asia, and Africa.* Westport, CT: Greenwood Press, 1982; Wesseling, H. L. *The European Colonial Empires 1815–1919.* New York: Longman, 2004.

KENNETH J. OROSZ

## Gambetta, Léon (1838–1882)

A leading politician of the French Third Republic. Gambetta was called to the Bar in 1859 and as a lawyer exhibited strong political views, above all hostility to Napoleon III (see **Bonaparte, Louis Napoleon**). He was elected as a Republican to the National Assembly in 1869, and in 1870, he voted against going to war against Prussia. On September 4, 1870, Gambetta proclaimed the Third Republic and, as a member of the Committee of National Defense, displayed immense energy and political skill to supplying the French Army. Gambetta opposed both the peace of 1871 and its terms, fighting with patriotic zeal against the cession of **Alsace-Lorraine** in particular. He was suspicious of Adolfe **Thiers** but contemptuous of the Paris Commune that Thiers destroyed. In these attitudes he was typical of the militant moderation of many Radicals, Georges **Clemençeau** among them: middle class republicans who hated the monarchy and the Church equally, who were dedicated to the prosperity of business, and who were absolutely devoted to France.

Gambetta was among the most important republicans of his generation, playing a key role in the defeat of President MacMahon and the triumph in the elections of 1879 of a republican majority under Jules Grévy. In 1881, he supported the policy of Jules **Ferry** in sending a French expeditionary force across the Algerian border to seize the ailing Ottoman province of Tunis before Italy could do so and thereby reclaim France's status as Great Power. Gambetta then served briefly as prime minister and died suddenly of an accident at age 42. He was mourned as a hero of the Third Republic. At his funeral Victor Hugo took his grandchildren to see the coffin and said "there lies a great citizen."

FURTHER READING: Brogan, Denis. *The Development of Modern France, 1870–1939*. London: Hamish Hamilton, 1940; Deschanel, Paul. *Gambetta*. New York: Dodd, Mead, 1920; Zeldin, Theodore. *France, 1848–1945*. Oxford: Clarendon, 1977.

CARL CAVANAGH HODGE

### Garibaldi, Giuseppe (1807–1882)

An Italian patriot, soldier, adventurer, revolutionary, and politician instrumental in the unification of **Italy,** Giuseppe Garibaldi was born in Nice in 1807 in what was then the kingdom of Sardinia. Garibaldi joined **Young Italy,** a patriotic society, in 1833, and became a follower of nationalist Giuseppe **Mazzini.** The French Revolutionary Wars had brought the Italian peninsula reforms, giving Italians a taste of republicanism. The return of absolutist governments after the **French Empire**'s 1814 demise prompted the Risorgimento, a revolutionary movement. Secret nationalist societies formed and unsuccessful revolts flared throughout the peninsula.

Garibaldi participated in a failed nationalist insurrection in 1834. He barely escaped arrest and execution, fleeing to Marseilles and then Brazil. During his 12 years in South America (1836–1848), Garibaldi met his first wife, Anita, who became his comrade-in-arms, and won fame fighting for the province of Rio Grande do Sul, then in revolt against the Brazilian government. He became a member of its navy, operating as a pirate. Garibaldi gained military leadership experience as a **guerrilla** in Uruguay, which was fighting Argentina for independence. The Revolutions of 1848, a liberal nationalist movement in Europe, saw mostly unsuccessful uprisings throughout the Italian peninsula against its foreign rulers. Sicily rebelled against its Bourbon king, and anti-Austrian riots ensued in the north. Garibaldi offered his services to the Sardinian king, leader of the Italian independence movement. Mazzini established a Roman Republic against Franco-Austrian troops sent to restore the pope. He summoned Garibaldi to help defend the Republic. Garibaldi's forces were driven from Rome in 1849; during the retreat, Anita died.

Several revolutionaries went into exile, including Garibaldi. He worked in New York making candles, leaving to become the skipper of cargo ships. In 1854, Garibaldi returned to the Italian peninsula after Count **Cavour,** Sardinia's prime minister, granted his consent. Garibaldi retired to Caprera, living as a farmer before accepting a commission in the Sardinian army. Sardinia joined the Crimean War in 1855 to gain French support to expel the Austrians for Italian independence. By 1859, victories at **Magenta** and **Solferino** had forced Austria to cede Lombardy, but Venice and Rome remained under foreign control. Napoleon III of France sought peace with Austria without consulting Sardinia and annexed Savoy and Nice as payment for assistance. Tuscany, Romagna, Modena, and Parma opted for annexation to Sardinia.

Garibaldi mounted an invasion of the Italian peninsula via Sicily. He resigned his commission and called for "a million rifles and men." About 1,089 volunteers, known as "Red Shirts," rallied to Garibaldi's call. Most of them were young professionals, journalists, lawyers, artists, and intellectuals. With his army, Garibaldi invaded Sicily and Naples, driving out the Bourbon dynasty. Garibaldi became temporary dictator and continued marching north until halted by Sardinian troops. Garibaldi resigned his command to Victor Emmanuel II of Sardinia, which annexed Sicily and Naples to create Italy. In 1861, Italy became a nation-state under **Victor Emmanuel II.** Rome remained protected by France while under papal rule. Garibaldi led two unsuccessful attacks against Rome in the 1860s and later accepted a position in the French army during the Franco-Prussian war to "aid the cause of International Republicanism." In 1870, French troops withdrew from Rome for war with Prussia. After France lost, Italian forces entered the Papal States, annexing them into Italy. In 1874, Garibaldi became deputy for Rome in parliament. He retired with a government pension to Caprera, where he died in 1882. *See also* Vienna, Congress of.

FURTHER READING: Garibaldi, Giuseppe. *My Life.* Translated by Stephen Parkin. London: Hesperus Press, 2004; Ridley, Jasper. *Garibaldi.* London: Constable, 1974; Smith, Denis Mack. *Garibaldi: A Great Life in Brief.* New York: Alfred A. Knopf, 1956.

ERIC MARTONE

## Gaspirali, Ismail Bey (1851–1914)

Also known as Gasprinskii, Gaspirali, a Crimean Tatar intellectual, and an advocate of educational progress for Turkic peoples. He was especially interested in increasing literacy rates of Turks, seeing that as a key avenue toward future economic and political success. He published many articles and books, including many in his newspaper, *Tercüman* or *Terjüman* (*Interpreter*).

Gaspirali saw education as a means to ultimately challenge Russian political authority, but he never called for more radical measures. He thought gradual measures were the most effective way to create pan-Turkic unity. Gaspirali's ideas paved the way for the late-nineteenth-century movement known as Jadidism, whose supporters advocated new school curricula that combined modern Western subjects, Turkic literature, and traditional Islamic teachings. Gaspirali urged the creation of a common Turkic literary language, which he used in *Tercüman*. He believed that a common language was necessary to advance Pan-Turkism. *See also* Ottoman Empire; Russian Empire.

FURTHER READING: Ekinci, Yusuf. *Gaspirali Ismail.* Ankara: Ocak Yalınları, 1997.

SCOTT C. BAILEY

## Geneva Convention (1864)

The Convention for the Amelioration of the Condition of the Wounded and Sick in Armed Forces in the Field, known as the Geneva Convention, had as its goals the protection of the vulnerable in wartime and the prevention of unnecessary suffering. Its key provision was that once soldiers were wounded, they were no longer legal combatants and should not be targeted as such. Signatories to the convention pledged to protect the wounded and allow representatives of the Red Cross to administer aid. The Geneva Convention also called for those killed in war to be properly identified and given a proper burial, as well as for a prohibition of weapons of war that cause "undue" suffering, notably "dum-dum" bullets. The Geneva Convention was extended in 1906 to cover war at sea, in 1929 to provide protection for prisoners-of-war, and in 1949 to protect civilians during war.

The First Geneva Convention was inspired by the Swiss doctor Jean Henri Dunant, the founder of the International Red Cross. Dunant was in the Italian town of Solferino in 1859 during a battle between Franco-Sardinian and Austrian troops. He was horrified by the suffering of battle casualties, who were left to die on the field because neither side would agree to a truce to retrieve them. He helped some of the injured himself and subsequently wrote *A Memory of Solferino*, published in 1862, proposing the creation of a civilian relief organization to aid the wounded in war. Dunant's work led to the formation of a private Red Cross organization in Geneva and to the international conference in Geneva in 1864, which drafted the Geneva Convention. The convention recognized the work of the International Red Cross, the new international organization comprised of the private Red Cross organizations that had begun to form in other European nations. Its headquarters was also in Geneva. Although the International Red Cross was technically an independent body, its member organizations often worked in close collaboration with national military and medical staffs, illustrating the connections between national and international ideals in the nineteenth century.

The Geneva Convention was an early step in the establishment of international humanitarian law. It provided a moral standard against which foreign policies and military affairs could be judged and gave legitimacy to later humanitarian campaigns against some of the more egregious examples of imperial rule. The desire to attenuate the violence of war also inspired the 1899 **Hague Peace Conference** and the 1907 Hague Convention on Land Warfare, both of which put forth rules of warfare in the spirit of the First Geneva Convention.

FURTHER READING: Hutchinson, John F. *Champions of Charity: War and the Rise of the Red Cross.* Boulder, CO: Westview Press, 1996; Hutchinson, John F. "Rethinking the Origins of the Red Cross." *Bulletin of the History of Medicine* 63, 4 (1989): 557–578; Moorehead, Caroline. *Dunant's Dream: War, Switzerland and the History of the Red Cross.* London: Harper Collins, 1998; Reisman, Michael W., and Chras T. Antoniou. *The Laws of War.* New York: Vintage, 1994.

DANIEL GORMAN

## George III, King of Great Britain (1738–1820)

George III was the king of the United Kingdom of Great Britain and Ireland from 1760 to 1820. George III began his rein in the midst of the Seven Years' War from which he swiftly brought his country after he removed from office the elder William Pitt, Earl of Chatham. During the rebellion of the American colonies, 1775–1783, he gave full support to Lord North's ministry and staunchly refused to come to any terms with the colonists short of their remaining part of the British Empire. He later supported William **Pitt** the Younger during his long period as prime minister (1783–1801, 1804–1806), not least the government's vigorous prosecution of the war against revolutionary France after the execution of Louis XVI in 1793.

He suffered bouts of illness, probably prophyria, which led to periodic political crises, most significantly in 1788–1789, when talks of a regency and the rise of the Whigs would almost certainly have led to Pitt's fall and peace with France. The king, however, recovered, and continued to support the war, although disagreement with Pitt over Catholic Emancipation led to the former's resignation in 1801. From 1811, as a result of a return of insanity, George III withdrew from politics, succeeded by his son, the future **George IV,** as Prince Regent until 1820. *See also* British Empire; Napoleonic Wars.

FURTHER READING: Brooke, John. *King George III.* New York: McGraw-Hill, 1972; Ditchfield, G. M. *George III: An Essay in Monarchy.* New York: Palgrave Macmillan, 2002; Hibbert, Christopher. *George III: A Personal History.* London: Viking, 1998.

GREGORY FREMONT-BARNES

## George IV, King of Great Britain (1762–1830)

Prince Regent, and later King of the United Kingdom of Great Britain and Ireland. He served in the capacity of regent from 1811 when the madness of his father, **George III,** rendered him unfit to continue as sovereign. Politically, George was a close ally of the Whigs, particularly Charles James **Fox**—his father's political nemesis—and this association, together with his inveterate gambling, strained relations with his father. He consistently ran up enormous debts, much to the embarrassment of the royal family, which regularly appealed to Parliament for relief. Despite his Whig loyalties, George worked with the Tory government under Lord Liverpool from 1812, supporting the nation's war against Napoleon **Bonaparte,** which ended three years later. George's divorce from Queen Caroline led to a scandalous public trial, and his later years as regent and king were characterized by domestic unrest and a gradual weakening of royal power. *See also* Napoleonic Wars.

FURTHER READING: David, Saul. *The Prince of Pleasure: the Prince of Wales and the Making of the Regency.* London: Little, Brown, 1998; Parissien, Steven. *George IV: The Grand Entertainment.* London: John Murray, 2001; Smith, E. A., *George IV.* New Haven, CT: Yale University Press, 1999.

GREGORY FREMONT-BARNES

## George V, King of Great Britain and Emperor of India (1865–1936)

The second son of **Edward VII** and among the most conscientious and popular of British monarchs. He served in the **Royal Navy** from 1877 to 1892, a career path suddenly closed to him by the sudden death of his older brother and his consequent emergence as heir to the throne. With the death of Edward VII in May 1910, George V followed his coronation with a trip to **Ireland** and Wales and fives months later made the first visit to **India** of a reigning monarch, although he had visited the country in 1905 as the Prince of Wales. On the advice of his constitutional advisors, he intervened in the political crisis over the Parliament Act of 1910–1911 and urged compromise during the Irish Home Rule crisis in 1912–1914. During World War I, he insisted that the royal household abide by national rationing guidelines and personally donated £100,000 to the war effort. He made seven visits to the front in Belgium and France and hundreds of visits to hospitals and factories, and he personally awarded 58,000 military decorations. To top it all off he changed the family name from the German Saxe-Coburg-Gotha to the English Windsor.

FURTHER READING: Judd, Denis. *The Life and Times of George V.* London: Weidenfeld and Nicolson, 1973.

CARL CAVANAGH HODGE

## German Confederation

The German Confederation (*Deutscher Bund*), a loose association of Central European states, mostly but not exclusively German, was created in 1815 by the Congress of **Vienna.** The *Bund* was a reorganization of the surviving states of the Holy Roman Empire, abolished by Napoleon Bonaparte in 1806 and replaced by the **Confederation of the Rhine.** It consisted of 39 states in all and covered a territory stretching from Westphalia in the west to Moravia in the east, from Prussia in the north to Tyrol in the south. The member states were formally committed to mutual defense yet were fully sovereign and had no overarching authority. Hanover was a German state yet also a co-sovereignty under the crown of England; Luxemburg was governed by the Netherlands. Whereas the Rhine confederation had been a creature of Napoleonic hegemony in Central Europe, the *Bund* became the object of the post-Napoleonic rivalry of Prussia and Austria until the **Austro-Prussian War** of 1866 decided the matter in Prussia's favor. Most of the *Bund*'s members were integrated in to the new **German Empire** established in 1871.

FURTHER READING: Fulbrook, Mary. *A Concise History of Germany.* New York: Cambridge University Press, 2004; Mann, Golo. *The History of Germany since 1789.* Translated by Marian Jackson. New York: Praeger, 1968.

CARL CAVANAGH HODGE

## German East Africa

Although dwarfed as a settlement colony by **German Southwest Africa,** German East Africa was the largest and most populous German colony. During the early nineteenth century Arab slavers expanded their activities deeper into the interior of East Africa, thereby attracting the interest of European abolitionists, merchants, explorers, and missionaries. By the 1840s, early European contacts with East Africa had evolved into an informal British protectorate over **Zanzibar** and its coastal possessions. Formal colonization of the region began in late 1884 as part of the Scramble for Africa when the German explorer and adventurer Carl **Peters** induced interior chiefs to sign treaties of protection that placed their lands under his control. Although Otto von **Bismarck** had initially opposed Peters' activities lest they provoke an unnecessary confrontation with Britain, the German government established a formal protectorate over East Africa in February 1885. Germany's creation of a protectorate caught Britain by surprise and triggered a race for territory in which British and German agents competed with each other to expand their respective colonial holdings by signing additional treaties with tribes located much further inland. Anglo-German rivalry in East Africa finally ended 1890 with the **Heligoland-Zanzibar** treaty, which formalized the borders of German East Africa.

Although Bismarck had initially hoped to leave the task of administering the new protectorate to Peters and his *Deutsch-Ostafrikanische Gesellschaft* (German East Africa Company [DOAG]), the combination of DOAG mismanagement, arrogant treatment of the local Muslim population, and increased competition for trade triggered a revolt in 1888 that forced the German government to intervene militarily and eventually assume control of colonial administration three years later. Although the outbreak of additional revolts over the next several years required ongoing military campaigns to pacify the interior, the new administration's primary task was fostering economic development. To that end, the Germans began an ambitious program of railroad construction, created coffee and rubber tree plantations, and introduced a variety of new crops including cotton, sisal, and sesame.

Despite German East Africa's economic growth, by the turn of the century German relations with the indigenous peoples were again in decline, as a result of a combination of taxes, forced labor, and the arrival of white settlers and Indian im-migrants. The situation finally came to a head with the outbreak of the 1905–1907 **Maji-Maji** revolt, which the Germans suppressed with extreme brutality. Neverthe-less, after the outbreak of World War I, German forces composed predominantly of African recruits under the command of Paul von Lettow-Vorbeck retreated into the interior and launched a highly successful guerilla campaign, only surrender-ing after the war had officially ended. After the war, Germany was stripped of all her colonies and in 1922 the newly created League of Nations split German East Africa into mandates, assigning Tanganyika to Britain and the smaller territories of Rwanda and Burundi to **Belgium.** *See also* Burton, Captain Sir Richard Francis; Berlin, Conference of; Dernburg Reforms; German Empire; Livingstone, David; Lugard, Lord Frederick; Uganda.

FURTHER READING: Henderson, W. O. *The German Colonial Empire 1884–1919.* London: Frank Cass, 1993; Iliffe, John. *Tanganyika under German Rule, 1905–1912.* Cambridge: Cambridge University Press, 1969; Rudolf von Albertini, ed. *European Colonial Rule, 1880–1940. The Impact of the West on India, Southeast Asia, and Africa.* Westport, CT: Greenwood, 1982; Stoecker, Helmuth, ed. *German Imperialism in Africa.* London: C. Hurst & Company, 1986.

KENNETH J. OROSZ

## German Empire

The German Empire was proclaimed on January 18, 1871, in the Hall of Mirrors at Versailles, not far from where the Prussian army besieged Paris in the final days of the **Franco-Prussian War.** The German Empire, occasionally referred to as the Second **Reich,** also died in battle, on November 9, 1918, when **Wilhelm II** abdicated his throne in the final days of World War I. Strife-ridden at home because of unre-solved institutional contradictions and provocative abroad as the result of an eco-nomically powerful and culturally volatile nation on the make, Imperial Germany was for the 50 years of its existence a source of instability in Europe and throughout the world. The regime's tenuous compromise between monarchical privilege and constitutional provision, combined political authoritarianism with an industrialized social order that made Germany both the most admired and feared nation on the European Continent. Its history illustrates the critical dilemmas of political, social, and cultural upheaval in modern times and the folly of chauvinistic nationalism in the era of "total" war.

### The Foundation of the Reich

The architect of the German Empire was Prussian Prime Minister Otto von **Bismarck.** In the 1860s, Bismarck orchestrated a series of international crises, in-cluding wars with **Denmark** in 1864, the **Austrian Empire** in 1866, and France in 1870–1871. With these conflicts, Bismarck sought to marginalize Austria in Central European affairs and then to unite the many small states of Germany under Prussian leadership. With the leaders of these states, Bismarck established a federalist system of government capped by the Prussian hereditary monarchy. The constitution of the German Empire reflected the priorities of the **Junkers,** Prussia's land-owning aristocracy, from whom Bismarck himself descended. The emperor alone directed foreign affairs and had the authority to declare war. He called and dissolved parliament and appointed imperial officials, who served at his sufferance independent of parliamentary oversight. His chancellor, almost always a Junker as well, had broad executive and legislative powers. The lower house or Reichstag was elected by universal manhood suffrage, but it had no ministerial responsibility and its decisions had to be approved by the upper house or *Bundesrat,* which was dominated by the delegation from Prussia. This arrangement gave Prussia and in particular its Junker elites *de facto* veto power over Reich legislation, guaranteeing a political authoritarianism that was out of step with a rapidly industrializing and modernizing German society.

At the core of the German imperial government, then, was a fundamental contradiction. The system provided for mass political action in a parliamentary body, but such action, above all when it advocated socialism, was unwelcome. When parliament addressed foreign or military affairs, it was constitutionally enfeebled. The system possessed little flexibility for adapting to the complicated politics of an increasingly mobilized electorate and hampered the creation of a national political consensus. The basic institutions of the state—the emperor, the constitution, the Reich ministry, and the voting system—bore enormous stress as recurring topics of acrimonious debate. The country's numerous divisions between workers and the middle class, urbanites and farmers, Catholics and Protestants, and Germans and ethnic "others," such as Danes, Poles, Alsace-Lorrainers, and East European Jews, were neither resolved nor mitigated by democratic compromise. More dangerously imperial authorities attempted to generate popular support for the regime less by mollifying disagreement through meaningful political reform than by foreign policy adventurism and emotional appeals to aggressive nationalism that imperiled Germany's strategic position. The temptation to overcome domestic squabbling through grand foreign undertakings assumed increasing importance in the planning of Reich officials in the military, ministry, and imperial court.

### Problems of National Integration

In the early years of the empire, Bismarck attempted to solve the problems of national unity by marginalizing the two groups that seemed to menace the interests of his chief allies in the Protestant middle class and Junker aristocracy, socialists and Roman Catholics. From 1871 to 1890, German society experienced the tumults of rapid industrialization and urbanization. The agricultural base of the country, strong in rye, potato, and sugar beet production in the east, and dairy farming and winemaking in the west, was solid. But the increasing intensity of cultivation, resulting primarily from the growing use of artificial fertilizers and the mechanization of seed and processing work, expanded yields while reducing labor requirements, releasing rural inhabitants from the demands of the soil to seek employment elsewhere. These populations found work in heavy industry, above all in the teeming cities of central Germany, the Ruhr Valley, and along the Rhine River, such as Cologne, Düsseldorf, and Duisburg.

As elsewhere in Europe, life for industrial workers was hard. In massive numbers, German workers joined the Social Democratic Party (SPD), founded in 1875, and the labor unions affiliated with it to address concerns such as job safety and security, reduced working hours, protections for women and children, and the right to strike. To Bismarck, socialist criticism of the highly stratified industrial social order and aristocratic claims to political authority, combined with sympathy for laborers abroad, posed intolerable risks to the nation's unity and long-term stability. Socialism threatened perpetual social unrest and undermined the national loyalty of industrial workers, the fastest growing segment of the population. In the late 1870s, he therefore disbanded the SPD and its unions, outlawed socialist propaganda, and criminalized associations that promoted socialist ideas. These Antisocialist Laws only drove more workers into the socialist camp and honed the parliamentary skills of SPD delegates, who, in the 1880s, pushed a government motivated both by fear of a radicalized working class and real humanistic concern to enact sweeping social welfare legislation, including national health and accident insurance. This legislation also established a social security system for the aged. In an 1890 political crisis that cost Bismarck his chancellorship, the Antisocialist Laws were officially retired, and the SPD emerged stronger and more politically astute than ever.

Roman Catholics, the other major category of *Reichsfeinde* or "enemies of the Reich" in Bismarckian Germany, accounted for roughly one-third of the country's 1871 population of 41 million inhabitants. They lived in regions such as Bavaria, Württemberg, and the Rhineland, which had either been annexed to Prussia early in the nineteenth century or had to be cajoled into joining the Prussian-dominated empire at the expense of cherished political and cultural traditions. Bismarck always mistrusted them. Their adherence to the "infallible" pronouncements of a foreign pope, their clericalism and dogmatic traditionalism, and their low social status clashed with the national consensus he was attempting to construct on the basis of liberal-Protestant anticlericalism, modern scholarly endeavor, and middle class social advancement. The participation of the clergy in mobilizing Catholic voters in the nation's first elections emboldened Bismarck to strike against German Catholicism in the classic church-state confrontation of the nineteenth century, the *Kulturkampf.* Prussia led the way in this "struggle for culture" with legislation that expelled foreign Jesuits, imposed lay inspectors on Catholic-run schools, established civil marriage as compulsory in law, and dispatched state supervisors to seminaries and the houses of monastic orders. Priests in Prussia were even compelled to sit for "cultural" exams to test their knowledge of—and support for—the prevailing liberal-Protestant ethos. These measures galvanized Catholic support behind the Center Party, established in 1870 to defend Catholic interests against a hostile government. Led by the irrepressible Hanovarian Ludwig Windthorst, the Center became a thorn in Bismarck's side and forced the Prussian government to rescind nearly all anti-Catholic legislation by the end of the decade.

The *Kulturkampf,* however, was more than a Church-State struggle. It was also a conflict over the very definition of what it meant to be German in the infant national community. One reason nationalism had such powerful resonance in modern Germany was that Germans found defining a durable collective identity so difficult. Catholics and Protestants lived in different sociocultural "publics." Better educated and more upwardly mobile, Protestants supported Imperial Germany's official culture as articulated by the monarchy, the army, liberal business and academic elites, and their churches. This culture celebrated the ancient Germans and their revolt against the Roman Empire, as well as Martin Luther and his revolt against the Roman popes. It also respected modern knowledge and honored the philosophical contributions of Protestant titans like Immanuel Kant and Georg Wilhelm Friedrich **Hegel.** Lastly, it promoted a middle class domestic experience of cultural attainment that shaped the personality through regular consumption of art, the Bible, the glorious histories of Protestant Prussia in arms, and the fiction of such giants of German literature and letters as Johann Wolfgang von Goethe and Friedrich Schiller. Roman Catholics, especially when antagonized by the Prussian state, reveled in an idealized medieval and pastoral past, when Church and State existed in harmony and society rested untroubled in organic integration. More modestly educated and provincial than urbanized Protestants, they welcomed the achievements of scientific learning but resisted the fragmentation of knowledge promoted by German universities and rejected any intellectual extremism that did not recognize the limits on science suggested by religion. Their philosophical champion remained the medieval Spanish saint Thomas Aquinas; their literary heroes still included venerable figures like the fourteenth-century Italian Dante Alighieri and the seventeenth-century Spaniard Miguel de Cervantes. They viewed the Protestant Reformation of the sixteenth century as a diabolical tragedy.

So, whereas the social divide in Bismarck's Germany had to do with disputes over economic structure and access to power, the confessional divide touched on core historical narratives and bedrock cultural commitments that originated from and reinforced competing identities. The polemics generated by this cleavage poisoned every aspect of public life. Middle class Protestants saw in the mass of lower-class rural, small-town, and working class Catholics a hostile population, whose alleged intellectual backwardness and cultural impoverishment thwarted the upward drive of the nation. Consequently, they discriminated against Catholics in all areas of civil society, from university and military appointments to job promotions and access to positions of cultural leadership, such as the boards of provincial museums and libraries. As late as 1914, only 18 percent of all civil servants were Catholics—half their percentage of the total population. This inequality and the ugly confessional rancor it generated, not least among Catholics who deeply resented their lack of parity with Protestant Germans, was a perpetual irritant to social relationships at the national and local levels and testifies that, despite national political unification, the German Empire was still building a German nation well into its history. The problems of national identity only intensified under the reign of the young Emperor Wilhelm II (r. 1888–1918), who proved inept at reforming a political system headed toward institutional paralysis and unable to establish a popular consensus behind the regime any more durable than the visceral fears and impulsiveness of patriotic nationalism.

### Society and Culture in Wilhelmine Germany

Many historians have argued that the German Empire's uneasy commingle of authoritarianism and democracy, as well as its forestalled national integration resulting from the persistence of premodern social relations and strident religious argument, explains Germany's political catastrophe in the twentieth century. Germany followed a *Sonderweg*, or "special path," to modernity, the thesis holds, which led from the Bismarckian constitution to world war and to Adolf Hitler's Third Reich in the 1930s. This picture of Germany under Wilhelm II as a stagnant and stifled, "misdeveloped" nation can be drawn too tightly. If imperial authorities felt constrained in their rule, it was because civil society in Wilhelmine Germany was so dynamic, the cultural voices within it so diverse and divergent, that it impinged on the monarchy's maneuverability and undermined the government's efforts in moving legislation to sustain the system and thereby to reassert its legitimacy. The élan of this civil society derived principally from the German middle class.

The expansion of the German economy in the years 1888–1914 was striking. Annual growth ran at a brisk 4.5 percent. The heavy industries of mining and steel production increased in size and scope of enterprise, and metalworking took off owing to the rapidly expanding need for specialized parts, precision tools, and finely calibrated measuring instruments. German industrial research and applied science created new industrial sectors as well. Germany led the way in the lucrative electrical and heavy chemical industries. In 1891, the production of electricity contributed about 45 million marks to the economy. By 1913, this figure had risen to 1.3 billion. Thanks to innovations in pharmaceuticals and electrochemical production, Germany had become the world's leading exporter of synthetic dyes by 1900. Germany was also a major European exporter of capital through an impressive network of banks centered in Berlin. The country's enormous fleet of merchant ships, operating out of the ports of Hamburg, Kiel, and other maritime sites, helped increase Reich exports of manufactured goods and textiles 81 percent from 1889 to 1910. "Made in Germany" became a prestigious and highly coveted label in European and world markets, broadcasting Imperial Germany's arrival as a major economic powerhouse.

The occupational profile of German workers changed just as dramatically as the economy that shaped it. The percentage of workers employed in industry and craft production, as well as in trade, commerce, and transportation, rose to 55 percent by 1907; those involved in agriculture fell to less than 30 percent. As the economy diversified and as labor became more specialized, many new types of jobs appeared. These included legal and health aides, government service work in building code inspection, postal and railroad administration, and fishery management, as well as positions in the booming "white collar" sector of the economy, which offered employment—to women as well as men—as clerks and typists, small business assistants, and teachers and officials in Germany's large public school system. Most German workers saw their real wages increase between 1885 and 1913, sometimes as high as 30 percent. National unemployment rarely exceeded 3 percent, and the average workweek fell from more than 70 hours in the late 1870s to 60 hours or less in the years before the war.

Germany's highly integrated and robust industrial economy also created yawning social inequalities. Industrial workers, for example, experienced rising real wages, greater job security, and shorter hours but also suffered from squalid living conditions, high food prices, and, unlike their comrades in other industrialized nations such as Britain and France, strained social and political segregation that limited their ability to improve their circumstances. There was very little social mobility between the classes in Germany and great gulfs of wealth and income distribution. Doomed to perennial penury, German industrial laborers grew increasingly frustrated with a social order that offered greater opportunities to slide down than move up.

The winners in this economy were male members of the middle class—propertied and educated men who occupied positions of social and cultural influence. They were doctors, lawyers, professors, and other credentialed experts; writers, journalists, and cultural producers; and industrial captains and other business elite. Although a highly differentiated and ideologically fragmented stratum, they were united socially by their distance from the Junker aristocracy above and the impecunious wage laboring classes below, and culturally by the values of hard work, thrift, competition, and enterprise. Intensely nationalistic and concerned for the diffusion of German literary *Kultur* as an integrating force in a fractious polity, they valued public education and popular literacy; manners in a well-regulated everyday life; conspicuous consumption of approved art, books, and music; and the celebration of the nuclear and patriarchal middle class family. They presided over a vigorous civil society, which demonstrated their dynamic capacity for self-mobilization and social leadership.

Wilhelmine Germany produced an extraordinarily rich artistic culture. New styles developed in painting, drama, poetry, opera, literature, and architecture. Publishing elites took advantage of mass literacy to create, by 1912, some 4,000 journals and newspapers addressing all audiences and interests, as well as an explosive pulp fiction market that filled leisure time with romance novellas, serialized crime stories, escapist travel accounts, tabloid spectacle, and an alarming volume of nationalist tracts that proclaimed Germany's national and ethnic superiority over other European and world populations. Creative energy channeled into other pastimes as well, including cinemas, dance halls and cabarets, theaters, **zoological gardens**, convivial societies of every kind, such as hiking, choral, and gymnastics groups, and spectator sports, which drew massive weekend crowds. Complemented by aristocratic and court ceremonial; thousands of faith-based social, cultural, and charitable voluntary associations; and proletarian institutions that shaped the everyday experience of the working class, the sociability of Wilhelmine Germany supported a wide and colorful spectrum of cultural voices that lent essential substance to public opinion. When this opinion mobilized in Germany's numerous elections, the flux, incoherence, and instability of German society became only more evident.

### Politics, Foreign Policy, and War

Before 1890, elections in Imperial Germany could still appeal to a shared purpose of national community building. After 1890, elections turned primarily on concrete issues concerning, above all, reform of the Prussian electoral system and the achievement of social justice. The emergence of interest-based politics fragmented the electorate more than ever. It also sharpened a political rhetoric that was already drenched in **militarism.** This rhetoric, along with more sophisticated techniques of voter mobilization, placed added pressure on a Prusso-German authoritarian system, already under stress, by introducing new tensions and energies into the political arena. Voter mobilization in the countryside, for instance, engaged new strata of the rural population in agitation for such controversial measures as tariff protection, progressive taxation, and the abolition of the Reich's restricted suffrage provision. Mobilization in the cities produced a number of anti-Semitic parties, which, although irrelevant by 1900, nonetheless testified to a society at odds with itself and a politics deeply tinged with the irrational. The introduction of other new voices into Germany's political culture, including those of feminists, who demanded, however fruitlessly, access to the franchise, undermined even solid blocs of support, such as the Center Party had enjoyed, and made coalition politics difficult due to constantly shifting parliamentary majorities.

The greatest threat to the system and the most dramatic development in German politics after 1890 was the rise of the SPD as a dominant party with enormous support among unhappy urban voters. While the Conservative Party receded and both the National Liberals and Progressives stagnated, the SPD skyrocketed in electoral

power. With the retirement of the Antisocialist Laws in 1890, the SPD sent 35 delegates to the Reichstag, a new high. By 1912, this number had grown to 110, as
the SPD drew almost 35 percent of all ballots cast. The red tide of the SPD was
dangerous because it mobilized public opinion hostile to the core institutions of political authoritarianism, even as its broader critique of the social order destabilized
the status quo. The party's insistence on the urgency of political and social reform
would not go away. The Center Party and the left-of-center Progressives occasionally worked with the SPD in a parliamentary coalition on some reformist policies,
but the right-of-center National Liberals and Conservatives, which represented the
entrenched interests of the state, would not. This intransigence in the face of the
SPD's advance threatened, as early as 1909 but certainly after the elections of 1912,
political stalemate, in which the government could not obtain parliamentary backing for its policies.

The gathering specter of political paralysis encouraged imperial elites to relieve
domestic pressure by diverting public attention to foreign involvements. No one
embraced the idea with greater ardor than Wilhelm II himself. Incapable of reforming the system he inherited from Bismarck, whom he unceremoniously dismissed
from public service in 1890, he sought a way out of the crisis by demanding that
Germany be recognized as a World Power. In this policy of *Weltpolitik*, he enjoyed
broad-based popular support, voters for SPD candidates excluded, although patriotism was also lively enough among workers. Indeed, pride in the nation's many economic and cultural achievements; regard for the army, which had an exceptional
influence in determining national culture; and jingoist enthusiasm for an assertive
foreign policy were the few matters on which there was parliamentary consensus.
Naturally, national chauvinism was strongest in the military and naval leadership,
in the Reich Foreign Office, and among Wilhelm's court advisors. Transmitting nationalistic ideas to the population and often shaping elite opinion were a number of
powerful extra-parliamentary pressure groups that whipped up the middle class for
militarism, imperialism, and the notion of building a blue water navy as a platform
for projecting German power abroad. These groups included the Colonial League,
the Naval League, the Central Association of German Industrialists, and the Pan-
German League, which was led by the vitriolic anti-Semite Heinrich Class.

Germany's foreign policy under Wilhelm II left the country wreathed with enemies. Bismarck's preoccupation had been to solve the strategic conundrum of a
country located in Central Europe with few natural borders and faced on multiple
fronts with the prospect of war against a coalition of forces. Accordingly, he sought
alliances with the conservative empires of **Austria-Hungary** and Russia to the south
and east and the isolation of Germany's traditional enemy, France, in the west, in
part by an understanding with Great Britain. These arrangements, already in disarray when Wilhelm assumed the throne, were abandoned by the kaiser's foreign ministry. In 1890, Wilhelm refused to extend the **Reinsurance Treaty** that Bismarck had
signed with Russia. This prompted a precipitous decline in relations with Russia,
whose government now approached France, thus leaving Germany with only the weak
Austro-Hungarian monarchy to the south as a principal ally. Wilhelm then alienated
Britain in two grave respects. Bismarck had resisted colonialism as an unnecessary
impediment to good relations with the **British Empire** but, in 1884, nevertheless
gave in to gathering domestic pressure to establish colonies in sub-Saharan Africa
and East Asia. These possessions brought negligible economic benefit to the Reich

yet alarmed the British, whom Bismarck had reassured repeatedly that Germany was satisfied territorially. Under Wilhelm, however, German colonialism expanded to include such possessions as Togoland, the **Cameroons, German East Africa** (Tanzania), **German Southwest Africa** (Namibia), a handful of islands in the Pacific, a strip of land on the Southeastern coast of **New Guinea,** and **Kiaochow** off the coast of China. Further irritating to the British was Wilhelm's obsession with building a "deterrent fleet" to dissuade any power from attacking Germany or challenging the Reich's colonial interests. Germany's 1897 decision to build a large surface fleet, and the provocative Naval Bills subsequently passed through the Reichstag, drove Great Britain and France, themselves colonial rivals, closer together. In 1904, they concluded a series of friendly agreements known as the **Entente Cordiale;** Russia, in fear of rising German militarism, joined them in 1907 in the **Triple Entente.** With the exception of its alliance with Austria-Hungary, Germany was now isolated. Yet its foreign policy only became more erratic, as it attempted to exploit diplomatic crises in such places as **Morocco** and the Balkans to weaken the ties of the powers now arrayed against it.

Stalemated politically at home and all but encircled on its borders, Germany faced a nightmare scenario. Imperial elites in the military and foreign ministry talked openly of resolving the desperate domestic and geostrategic situation through war. Other Germans, including leading intellectuals and religious authorities, believed that a war might put an end to materialism, decadence, and the malaise of cultural despair by elevating the atoning values of righteous suffering and heroic self-sacrifice. Although it cannot be said that these Germans intrigued to provoke a war—and they certainly did not get the war they wanted—it is true that when an unexpected event set the march toward military conflict in motion they chose escalation and defiance over moderation and restraint.

World War I (1914–1918) was a catastrophe for Imperial Germany and the German people. The general staff of the German army, led by Helmuth von **Moltke,** the nephew of the hero of the Seven Weeks' War against Austria and the Franco-Prussian War, responded to the assassination of Archduke **Francis Ferdinand,** the heir to the throne of the Austro-Hungarian Empire, by running the calculated risk of a localized, short war that Germany could win by implementing the **Schlieffen Plan.** Drawn up by General Alfred von Schlieffen, the plan called for rapid mobilization to the west against France, which would be defeated in six weeks, followed by a rapid redeployment of forces to the east, by way of Germany's dense **railway** network, to face Russia. Inflexible in its minute design, fantastical in its ignorance of the manpower and logistical requirements of moving massive armies burdened with tremendous strategic and tactical expectations and, above all, dismissive of the dreadful new realities of industrialized combat, the Schlieffen Plan broke down just miles outside of Paris. Its violation of Belgian neutrality triggered the Allied alliance system, bringing the full weight of the British Empire against Germany. The great trench and attrition battles on the Western Front against France, Britain, and eventually the United States—the Marne and Ypres in 1914, the Somme and Verdun in 1916, Passchendaele and Cambrai in 1917, and the Ludendorff Offensives of the spring of 1918—in addition to its bloody engagements with Russia and its allies and Italy, cost the German Army an astonishing 6 million casualties, including 2,043,000 war dead.

The *Burgfrieden,* or "civil peace," that Wilhelm declared at the outbreak of the war—which was supposed to subordinate party politics to the exigencies of the national enterprise—could not hold up against these terrible losses. The war did not resolve the manifold tensions that had long afflicted Germany, and whatever enthusiasm there may have been in August 1914 dissipated rapidly. Morale at home sagged as casualties mounted, consumer goods disappeared, crime rose, strikes broke out, censorship was imposed, people starved as a consequence of Britain's naval blockade, and children came down with typhoid fever, tuberculosis, and rickets. Unable to relieve the misery and unwilling to open up the political structure until October 1918, when the German Army had already lost the war and was streaming back dejected across the nation's frontiers, the Reich collapsed in utter exhaustion and comprehensive defeat. The army, led by Generals Paul von **Hindenburg** and Erich Ludendorff, both of whom would figure prominently in the later rise to power of the war veteran and political crusader Adolf Hitler, blamed this defeat on civilian elites in the Reichstag, whose interminable squabbling had "stabbed the army in the back." Wilhelm II abdicated his throne on November 9 and fled to Holland, there to spend the rest of his life splitting wood, dreaming of what might have been, and uttering vile anti-Semitic diatribes. The German people, meanwhile, staggered forward into revolution, massive debt, international opprobrium, and a future no less divisive—politically, socially, or culturally—than that of the ill-fated Empire. *See also* Austro-Prussian War; Balkan Crises; Bülow, Bernhard von; Russian Empire; Tirpitz Plan.

FURTHER READING: Anderson, Margaret Lavinia. *Practicing Democracy: Elections and Political Culture in Imperial Germany.* Princeton, NJ: Princeton University Press, 2000; Berghahn, Volker R. *Imperial Germany, 1871–1914: Economy, Society, Culture and Politics.* Providence, RI, and Oxford: Berghahn Books, 1994; Chickering, Roger. *Imperial Germany and the Great War, 1914–1918.* Rev. ed. Cambridge: Cambridge University Press, 2004; Hull, Isabel V. *Absolute Destruction: Military Culture and the Practices of War in Imperial Germany.* Ithaca, NY: Cornell University Press, 2004; Röhl, John C. G. *The Kaiser and His Court: Wilhelm II and the Government of Germany.* Cambridge: Cambridge University Press, 1996; Smith, Helmut Walser. *German Nationalism and Religious Conflict: Culture, Ideology, Politics, 1870–1914.* Princeton, NJ: Princeton University Press, 1995; Smith, Woodruff D. *The German Colonial Empire.* Chapel Hill: University of North Carolina Press, 1978.

JEFFREY T. ZALAR

## German Southwest Africa

The largest of the German colonial possessions in Africa, approximately three times the size of Germany itself. The initial German acquisition of the territory was almost solely the result of the efforts of Frans **Lüderitz** and Heinrich Vogelsang who together purchased land from the local Khoikhoi people in 1883. In 1884, Berlin announced that Lüderitzland was to become a German protectorate, and, after some diplomatic difficulties with London, the claim was recognized by Britain. Berlin then promptly annexed adjacent territory until the western coast of Africa north of the British Cape Colony and south of Portuguese Angola was a German protectorate. This policy represented a reversal for the German government under the leadership of Otto von **Bismarck,** who had hitherto been skeptical of the benefit of overseas possessions to the Second Reich. It marked Germany's belated participation in the intensified competition among European powers for African territory. Although it was not financially solvent until 1912, German Southwest Africa was the object of such vigorous promotion by the *Kolonialverein,* especially for cattle breeding, that a significant immigration of European farmers resulted. Territorial pressure on the indigenous Herero—a semi-nomadic, cattle-herding people of the interior threatened by the enclosure of grazing land on which they assumed usufruct rights—exploded into violent revolt when disease then diminished the Herero herds. A number of colonists were murdered, but the German reaction quickly transformed the **Herero Revolt** of 1904–1907 into one of the most brutal of the colonial wars prosecuted by Europeans in Africa. In Germany the revolt occasioned the "Hottentot Elections" of 1907 in which pro-colonial parties inflicted a defeat on the anti-colonial Social Democrats. *See also* Africa, Scramble for; Bülow, Bernhard von; German Empire.

FURTHER READING: Hull, Isabel V. *Absolute Destruction: Military Culture and the Practices of War in Imperial Germany.* Ithaca, NY: Cornell University Press, 2005; Pakenham, Thomas. *The Scramble for Africa.* New York: Random House, 1991.

CARL CAVANAGH HODGE

## Gettysburg, Battle of (1863)

A pivotal battle of the American Civil War. It was fought in Gettysburg, Pennsylvania, between the Confederate Army of Northern Virginia, numbering 75,000 men and commanded by General Robert E. Lee, and Union forces, eventually numbering 90,000. Arriving piecemeal, they were commanded by General George G. Meade.

On July 1, Confederate troops looking for shoes at a Gettysburg factory encountered Union cavalry commanded by Brigadier General John Buford. Lee's cavalry, command by Major General J.E.B. Stuart, was off raiding for supplies. This left Lee militarily blind. On July 2, he nevertheless attacked the Union flanks. His generals failed to effectively execute his orders, so that intense fighting all day for the high ground left many dead with two key hills, Big Round Top and Little Round Top to the south of Gettysburg, still in the hands of the Union. At the same time, fierce fighting took place in a wheat field and peach orchard below as the tide of battle swayed back and forth. On July 3, 15,000 Confederates charged the Union lines on the high ground on Cemetery Ridge led by Major General George Pickett after the greatest artillery duel in American history. They were cut to pieces and too few gained the high ground to achieve a victory.

Gettysburg was thus one of the most decisive battles in the American Civil War and was the high watermark of the Confederacy. The news of Gettysburg—combined with the simultaneous surrender of Vicksburg, Mississippi, to the Union army of General Ulysses Grant—ended the diplomatic efforts of the Confederacy to gain diplomatic recognition from Britain or the Continental powers.

FURTHER READING: Coddington, Edwin B. *The Gettysburg Campaign: A Study in Command.* New York: Charles Scribner's Sons, 1984; Foote, Shelby. *The Stars in Their Courses: The Gettysburg Campaign.* New York: Modern Library, 1994.

ANDREW JACKSON WASKEY

## Gibraltar

A tiny peninsula on the eastern coast of the Bay of Algeciras at the exit of the Mediterranean Sea into the Atlantic Ocean and a British crown colony after 1830. A British fleet first seized Gibraltar in 1704 during the War of the Spanish Succession, and it was formally ceded to Britain by Spain in the Treaty of Utrecht ending the war in 1713. Although Spain laid siege to Gibraltar during the American Revolution, British sovereignty was confirmed by the Treaty of Versailles in 1783. Owing to its position at the gateway between the Mediterranean and the Atlantic, Gibraltar acquired enormous strategic value to the **Royal Navy** during the Napoleonic Wars and thereafter in policing the oceanic waterways of the **British Empire.** John **Fisher,** First Sea Lord from 1904 to 1910, referred to Gibraltar as one of the "five strategic keys" of British world dominion, the others being Alexandria and Suez, Singapore, the Cape of Good Hope, and the Straits of Dover. *See also* Navalism.

FURTHER READING: Herman, Arthur. *To Rule the Waves.* New York: Harper Collins, 2004; Morriss, Roger. *The Royal Dockyards during the Revolutionary and Napoleonic Wars.* Leicester: University of Leicester Press, 1983.

CARL CAVANAGH HODGE

## Giolitti, Giovanni (1842–1928)

Italian Premier in 1892–1893 and for most of the period from 1903 to 1915. At the beginning of the twentieth century, two factions dominated Italian politics. The first represented nondemocratic and authoritarian political and economic elites. The second was a parliamentary alliance of Mazzinians, Radicals, and independent Socialists who advocated more democratic government. In 1900, this "extreme left" defeated an attempt by the right to restrict constitutional law, and thereby ushered in a democratic government under Giuseppe Zanardelli, a longtime reformer. When health issues forced Zanardelli to retire, Giuseppe Giolitti returned to power.

Giolitti was from Piedmont and entered public life shortly after national unification, holding various civil service positions. He believed that southern peasants and northern industrial workers could be entrusted with political choice but realized that both authoritarian conservatives and nondemocratic radicals threatened democratic government. In 1899, Giolitti announced a sweeping program of reforms, including respect for civil rights, administrative reorganization, a progressive tax, and free trade. To ensure that his reforms were passed, Giolitti practiced *transforismo,* that is, bringing men into government regardless of political ideology and ensuring their loyalty through political patronage. He played the various parliamentary factions against each other to divide opposition, undermining the Socialists, for example, by supporting Catholic and Nationalist parliamentarians. Giolotti was responsible for the annexation of Tripoli and led a successful imperialist war against Turkey in 1911–1912 in which Italy gained **Libya,** Rhodes, and Dodecanese, but his government was rampant with corruption and the costs of war high. When he pushed through universal male suffrage and social welfare programs, moreover, he alienated industrialists and Catholics, split the Socialist Party, thereby crippling it as a political force, and had few political allies left. Giolotti supported the **Triple**

**Alliance** with Germany and Austria-Hungary but sought to keep Italy neutral at the outbreak of World War I. *See also* Italo-Turkish War.

FURTHER READINGS: Coppa, Frank J. "Economic and Ethical Liberalism in Conflict: The Extraordinary Liberalism of Giovanni Giolotti." *Journal of Modern History, 42*, 2, 1970: 191–215; Sprigge, Cecil. *The Development of Modern Italy.* New York: Fertig, 1969.

FREDERICK H. DOTOLO

## Gladstone, William Ewart (1809–1898)

William Gladstone was four times British prime minister, and leader of the **Liberal Party** at the height of its power in the late nineteenth century. Gladstone's name became synonymous with a central kind of Victorian liberalism, combining prudent and skillful public finance, earnest moralism, cautious reform, a broadly pacific foreign policy, and retrenchment on the defense expenditure. Known for his profound religious belief, prodigious industry, and argumentative skill, Gladstone's relation to British imperialism is ambiguous. Although he presided over periods of rapid imperial expansion, he resisted many acquisitions and professed a stern belief in the importance of consensual relations with foreign powers.

Gladstone came from a family of prosperous Liverpool merchants and was educated at Eton and Christ Church, Oxford. Influenced by his family's evangelicalism in his youth, he was all his life a devout Anglican. Although he was as a young man primarily interested in theological questions, Gladstone first entered the cabinet in 1843 as president of the Board of Trade under Sir Robert **Peel** and shortly distinguished himself as a master of complex fiscal detail. In 1845, however, Gladstone resigned from Peel's cabinet in protest against a public subvention in support of a Catholic seminary in Ireland. He shortly rejoined Peel's cabinet as secretary for war and colonies, and served in the administration that, in 1846, split the Tory Party by repealing the protectionist **Corn Laws** in the name of free trade. Gladstone thus became associated with the Peelite group that formed much of the core of the early Liberal Party.

In opposition, Gladstone opposed on legal grounds **Palmerston's** use of the British fleet to compel Greece to compensate a British subject for losses in an anti-Semitic riot, the famous Don Pacifico affair of 1850. Shortly thereafter, Gladstone traveled to Italy and published a pamphlet on Neapolitan prisons, describing the government of that country as "the negation of God erected into a system of government." These were his first ventures into foreign policy and gave voice to the moralistic liberalism for which he became famous.

Gladstone became Chancellor of the Exchequer under his fellow Peelite Lord Aberdeen in 1852. In his four terms as Chancellor over the following 30 years, he did much to turn that office into the chief controller of public funds that it has been ever since, as opposed to a mere accounting office recording decisions made elsewhere: the well-known battered briefcase in which chancellors carry their budgets to the House was originally Gladstone's. His first budget envisioned continuing tariff simplification and the abolition of the income tax by 1860, a hope not realized because of the outbreak of the **Crimean War** with Russia in 1853. With the fall of Aberdeen, he was out of office from 1855 to 1859. Gladstone returned to the Exchequer under Palmerston in 1859, a government generally held to have marked the birth of the British Liberal Party. Gladstone served as Chancellor under Palmerston until 1865, and in the subsequent short-lived administration of Earl (formerly Lord John) **Russell.** As Chancellor, he cut tariffs further, and was leader in the Commons during Russell's failed attempt at franchise reform in 1866.

Gladstone first became prime minister on the strength of the Liberal election victory of 1868, famously proclaiming on receiving his summons to the Queen that, "my mission is to pacify Ireland." His government disestablished the Anglican Church of Ireland and also reformed Irish land laws, introduced in the 1870 primary education bill, abolished commission purchase in the army, and introduced the secret ballot. In foreign policy, Gladstone's first government remained neutral in the Franco-Prussian war while successfully persuading the belligerents to respect the neutrality of Belgium, and also negotiated the 1872 Anglo-American arbitration treaty under which American claims for compensation for the depredations of the British-built confederate cruiser *Alabama* in the American Civil War were settled. This government saw the withdrawal of most British troops from the New Zealand Maori Wars and from Canada, which led to charges that, in Disraeli's words of 1872, the Liberals were intent on "the disintegration of the empire of England." This was untrue—Gladstone's government in fact in its final years annexed the Diamond Fields of South Africa, a move pregnant with future consequences, and also made war on the King of Ashanti—but the charge that Liberals were indifferent to imperial concerns did reflect much Liberal opinion, and so had some traction.

Gladstone lost the election of 1874 by a large margin, bringing the Tories under Benjamin **Disraeli** into office with a majority for the first time since that party's split over protection in 1846. There was widespread feeling that the Liberals had run out of ideas, and Gladstone surprised the party by resigning the leadership. In 1876, the Tory government supported Muslim Turkey in its campaign against Christian Bulgarian nationalists, a consequence of Britain's traditional policy of supporting Turkey to contain Russia. With his famous pamphlet, *Bulgarian Horrors and the Question of the East,* Gladstone became the voice of popular anger, particularly but not exclusively among Liberals and nonconformists, at Turkish outrages.

A number of foreign and imperial incidents followed on the heels of the Bulgarian crisis: Disraeli's acquisition of Suez Canal shares in 1876, the Royal Titles Act making Queen Victoria Empress of **India,** and the 1878 acquisition of Cyprus, among them. They combined with Disraeli's own pro-imperial rhetoric and the jingoism of his supporters to associate the Tories with a kind of bombastic and expansionist imperialism, which Gladstone found morally offensive. Gladstone was among those who first used the term *imperialism* to describe not support for the empire but rather its aggressive expansion, and for Gladstone there was always a suspicion that imperialism was as much as anything a set of what he called "theatrical displays and tricks" designed to divert the voters from more serious issues.

Disraeli's government blundered into the Second Anglo-Afghan War in 1878. In the previous year it had faced a war in the eastern Cape Colony and in 1878 another with the Basuto. By early 1879, Britain also found itself at war with the Zulus in Natal, an indirect consequence of the annexation of the Transvaal in 1877. The Zulu War was marked by the catastrophic defeat of Isandhlwana, although it was won by the end of the year. Gladstone was adopted as Liberal candidate for the

Scottish constituency of Midlothian, and there, in the fall of 1879, he made an epochal series of speeches laying out a detailed critique of Disraeli's imperialism.

On being returned to office as prime minister in 1880, Gladstone shortly found himself confronted with the difficulties of these not-always-consistent principles. He ordered withdrawals from Afghanistan and the Transvaal. Lord Roberts' victory at Kandahar allowed the former to be accompanied by a satisfactory agreement with Afghanistan, and relative peace prevailed on the Northwest frontier of India until 1919. But a Boer Victory at Majuba in 1881 made the Transvaal withdrawal appear, to both the Boers and the Tories, an ignominious defeat.

In opposition, Gladstone had protested against Disraeli's purchase of Suez Canal shares and against other encroachments on **Egypt.** In office, however, disorder in Alexandria and the threat of an Egyptian default on its international debts led to British intervention. The Royal Navy bombarded Alexandria on July 11, 1882. A force under Sir Garnet Wolseley then landed in the canal zone and defeated the Egyptian Army at Tel el-Kebir on September 13, 1882, leading to an effective British protectorate—although Egypt remained nominally subject to the Ottoman Empire.

Britain's intervention in Egypt led to strains with France, which was pursuing its own ambitions in Tunisia and in West Africa. The so-called Scramble for Africa was to some extent provoked by the British occupation of Egypt and led to the 1884 Berlin conference on the partition of West Africa. Gladstone resisted large annexations in tropical Africa and saw some merit in German claims in East Africa. He only permitted the 1884 Warren expedition into Bechuanaland because the rest of his cabinet insisted. Gladstone saw a large empire as a source of "needless and entangling engagements," rather than strength, and viewed imperial problems through the lens of European relations. That fear of entanglements and a parallel desire to avoid expense led Gladstone's government to countenance the reinvention of the semi-sovereign chartered company with the chartering of the British North Borneo Company in 1881. Little noticed at the time, the revival of the chartered company nonetheless prepared the way for subsequent and more prominent exercises in private imperialism, most notably of course that of Cecil Rhodes and the British South Africa Company.

The Egyptian occupation also led to British involvement in the Sudan, a territory in which the Egyptian Khedive had claims. General Charles "Chinese" **Gordon** was sent out to arrange an Anglo-Egyptian withdrawal from the Sudan in the face of an Islamic rising. But Gordon did not withdraw, and soon found himself besieged in Khartoum. Gladstone hesitated in sending Wolseley down the Nile to relieve Gordon, with the result that the latter was killed as the Mahdi's forces took the city. By this point the septuagenarian Gladstone was known in his party as "The Grand Old Man," or GOM: the Tories turned this around, calling him MOG, or "Murderer of Gordon."

After a brief interval of Tory minority government, Gladstone returned to power in 1886, determined, as in 1868, to bring peace to **Ireland.** His solution was **Home Rule,** an Irish legislature that was to have strikingly limited powers well short of the Dominion status extended to the settlement colonies. The question was not adroitly handled, and many of the more Whiggish or right-wing Liberals bolted the party, leading to the fall of Gladstone's third government. But they were accompanied by radicals like Joseph Chamberlain and John Bright, who saw in Home Rule a set of special privileges for Ireland, and who also saw the end of the Union of 1801 as a possible prelude to the breakup of the Empire. The 1886 split of the Liberal Party ushered in a period of largely Tory rule that lasted until 1906, as the Liberal Unionists found places within an increasing middle class and imperialist Tory Party.

Gladstone returned to office for the fourth time as prime minister in 1892 at the age of 82, but he was increasingly out of sympathy with the imperialist temper of the times, and also less than equal to the strains of office. He resigned in 1894 over a dispute in which the rest of his cabinet insisted on the need for an increase in the naval estimates. Gladstone died on May 19, 1898, and was given a state funeral and buried in Westminster Abbey. Gladstone was in favor of the British Empire as an association of self-governing states and considered the empire and British power more generally a liberal force. But he was opposed to what he called "**imperialism**"—the expansion of the empire for its own sake or simply to obstruct the expansion of others. Although he occupied Egypt, he was also willing to pay a political price for retrocession in the Sudan and South Africa. He saw the empire as a consequence rather than a source of power. With the exception of Ireland, his primary interests were elsewhere. *See also* Boer Wars; Liberalism; Ottoman Empire.

FURTHER READING: Gladstone, W. E. *Midlothian Speeches*. Edited by M.R.D. Foot. New York: Humanities Press, 1971; Jenkins, Roy. *Gladstone*. London: Macmillan, 1995; Matthew, H.C.G. *Gladstone, 1809–1898*. Oxford: Oxford: University Press, 1998. Morley, John. *The Life of William Ewart Gladstone*. 3 vols. London: MacMillan, 1903.

MARK F. PROUDMAN

## Globalization

Globalization is best defined as increasing interconnectedness between human beings on a global scale, plus increasing awareness of such interconnectedness. On both accounts, the Age of **Imperialism** was an age of rapid globalization in all dimensions of life, experienced firsthand by many people who increasingly conceived of the world as a single sphere of action where faraway events affected their daily lives.

Nineteenth-century globalization was based on the development of ever more efficient technologies of transport and communication—chiefly the **railway,** the **steamship** and the **telegraph.** The first steamship traveled from London to Bombay in 1850, and the opening of the **Suez Canal** in 1869 cut the travel time from Europe to India in half. Perhaps more important, steam navigation significantly reduced transportation costs and risks for both passengers and freight. Transatlantic freight rates fell by roughly half between the mid-nineteenth century and 1910. Railways opened up vast inland spaces to settlement and intensive agriculture and connected them to world markets. The telegraph for the first time in history allowed information to travel faster than goods and people, creating new possibilities for centralized decision making in business, diplomacy, and war. The first transatlantic cable laid in 1866 increased the velocity of communication between Europe and the United States by a factor of 10,000.

For economic historians, the mid-nineteenth century marks the beginnings of globalization. World trade grew 25-fold between 1800 and 1913, but globally integrated markets for labor, capital, and goods emerged in the century's third quarter. For the first time in human history, basic commodities such as grain and meat were traded between continents. Europe was henceforth supplied with food produced on America's temperate plains, and farmers in Prussia and the United States and in Argentina and India were put in direct competition with each other. South African gold and diamonds, Indian textiles, Malayan rubber, and American manufactured goods likewise found markets halfway around the world, while developing economies soaked up European investment. Centers of production, trade, and consumption in different continents were now closely connected. The availability of telegraphic information on prices, supply, and demand completely transformed long-distance trade, as well as the stock exchanges and financial markets. Thus multilateral networks of exchange and global interdependence linking the great importers and exporters of people, goods, and capital emerged after mid-century; and soon there were economic cycles affecting the world economy as a whole, such as the first "Great Depression" beginning in 1873, and a first worldwide economic boom starting in 1896. By the end of the nineteenth century, nearly everyone in Europe, North America, and the settler societies was integrated into global markets as a consumer and producer.

Likewise at mid-century, a great wave of global migration set in, helped by cheaper travel, but also by a steady stream of information passing between migrants and those who had stayed behind. Nearly 70 million people permanently left their homes between 1850 and 1914. Migration from Europe to the temperate zones of the American continent was especially important, but millions also went from China to Southeast Asia, tens of thousands from China to South Africa, from Japan to California, and from India to East and South Africa. Immigration and emigration transformed entire societies, drawing large regions into the movement of global exchanges, pushing aside indigenous populations, and giving those staying behind room to breathe. Temporary migration was scarcely less consequential in its impact on China, for example, students returning from Japan with the foundations of Western learning and migrant workers taking back several years' savings from plantations and mines in Southeast Asia.

Increasingly, people became aware that they were part of globally interconnected markets and social relationships. This is evident in the outlook of seasonal laborers working in Sicily in summer and in Argentina in winter, or in that of Chinese emigrants worldwide contributing money to **Sun Yatsen**'s revolutionary endeavors, but also in the global business strategies of trading houses, banks, and large manufacturing firms and in the global dimensions of military and naval strategic thinking. Widely read newspapers and telegraphic news agencies such as Reuter's made people react to important information from other continents as quickly as to local news.

Global consciousness was expressed in various forms: in visions of peace and unity, in humanitarian aid given to distant victims of flood or famine, notions of a Western *mission civilisatrice,* and of global economic competition and of global Great Power rivalry. Only against the background of a widespread sentiment that economic and political globalization had set in is it possible to understand the racial fear of the "Yellow Peril" that gripped Europe in the 1890s and the United States a decade later. Other evidence of an emerging global consciousness is the agreement by 25 states in 1884 to divide the world into a system of time zones and establish a global time based on the Greenwich meridian. The success of Jules Verne's *Around the World in 80 Days*, published in 1873, rested on the striking novelty of the feat performed by Phileas Fogg and his companions; yet only 30 years later it was theoretically possible to make this voyage in half the time. Europe's return to protectionism and interventionism starting in the 1880s must been seen as a reaction to economic globalization. Finally, *Weltpolitik*—the idea that Great Power competition had become global—must count as evidence of a global consciousness that, just as today, focused with particular intensity on the dangers and conflicts of globalization.

Political globalization developed more slowly and with more ambiguous consequences. Western forms of political organization—administration, justice, government by law—were exported into the entire world. But the example of the new Latin American republics demonstrated that global institutional homogenization—the establishment of new nation-states—could imply political fragmentation in the form of the destruction of the Spanish colonial empire. By mid-century, the powerful and industrialized nation state seemed the only model available to societies that wished to retain independence and control over their destiny, and Westernizing reform and modernization were attempted from Egypt to Japan, from Siam to Madagascar. The world's empty or loosely organized spaces were relentlessly filled by the structures of clearly demarcated, competing nation states and empires. Still, nationalism and internationalism remained compatible. Globalization was furthered by nation states that remained reasonably open even when turning to protectionism after the mid-century interlude of **free trade.**

Political globalization was evident also in intensified global competition between states, but especially between the major imperial powers. In the mid-century era of "free-trade imperialism," competition was left to private traders and producers; military force was used to make non-European societies accept free trade and diplomatic relations rather to conquer territory. Gradually, however, as economic competition and popular belief in the political and economic importance of overseas possessions increased, states began to play a more important role overseas. Africa was partitioned between the powers at the Conference of **Berlin** in 1884. The playing field of the **Great Game,** the struggle for mastery in Asia between Russia and Britain, was extended ever farther eastward, up to Northern China after the **Sino-Japanese War** of 1894–1895. Soon, the United States, the first non-European Great Power, and Japan, the first non-Western Great Power, were drawn into a balance of power that, by the end of the nineteenth century, was a global rather than European. Confrontation between rival Great Powers now meant fragmentation on a global scale. The Age of Imperialism ended with a world war.

World War I quickly became a global conflict as colonial peoples and overseas resources were marshaled for the war effort, yet its causes lay in local conflicts between powers that were among the least globally connected. Neither the Age of Imperialism nor, for that matter, the present era should be analyzed as a "global age" where everything and everyone is affected instantly, primarily, and homogeneously by the same, global structures and processes. There were, and are, many different ways in which people participate in globalization—as agents or victims, voluntarily or involuntarily, economically, politically, culturally or socially. Although half of **Ireland**'s population emigrated in the mid-nineteenth century, France experienced hardly any emigration. Many territories were integrated into the world economy only partly, or hardly at all. Institutional homogenization and integration within the great colonial empires often meant the disruption of older, continental, and transcontinental trading links, as in Africa. Where Westernizing reform really took hold, such as in Japan, the result was a new and rival variant of modernity, not merely an imitation of the Western civilization. Global consciousness and especially fear and envy of supposed enemies and competitors on other continents were often much more acute than warranted by substantive global interdependence. *See also* Navalism; Strategy.

FURTHER READING: Bayly, C. A. *The Birth of the Modern World, 1780–1914: Global Connections and Comparisons.* Oxford: Blackwell, 2004; Bordo, Michael D., Alan M. Taylor, and Jeffrey G. Williamson, eds. *Globalization in Historical Perspective.* Chicago: University of Chicago Press, 2003; Osterhammel, Jürgen, and Niels P. Petersson. *Globalization: A Short History.* Princeton, NJ: Princeton University Press, 2005.

NIELS P. PETERSSON

## Gneisenau, August Wilhelm von (1760–1831)

A Prussian field marshal and German nationalist hero, August Wilhelm von Gneisenau gained early experience serving in a mercenary regiment of the Margrave of Bayreuth Ansbach in the pay of Britain during the American Revolution. In 1786, Frederick the Great commissioned him as a first-lieutenant in the Prussian Army. Gneisenau fought against Napoleon at **Jena** in 1806 and as a major was awarded the coveted *pour le mérite* for his defense of Colberg in 1807. He then worked with **Scharnhorst** in reorganizing the Prussian Army to meet the Napoleonic challenge, introducing among other reforms the revolutionary concept of the general staff. As an aide to **Blücher,** Gneisenau distinguished himself at **Leipzig** and **Waterloo.** After retirement to his Silesian estate in 1816, he became governor of Berlin and a member of the Council State. During the Polish Revolution of 1831, Gneisenau came briefly out of retirement as a field marshal and commanded an army of observation on the Polish border with Carl von **Clausewitz** as his chief of staff. After his death, his name entered the pantheon of **Junker** resistance to Napoleon, the promotion Prussian professional militarism, and German nationalism.

FURTHER READING: Citino, Robert M. *The German Way of War.* Lawrence: University of Kansas Press, 2005; Craig, Gordon A. *The Politics of the Prussian Army, 1640–1945.* Oxford: Oxford University Press, 1955; Rothenberg, Gunther E. *The Art of Warfare in the Age of Napoleon.* Bloomington: Indiana University Press, 1978.

CARL CAVANAGH HODGE

## Gold Coast

A territory on the coast of West Africa and the hub of British involvement in the **slave trade** during the seventeenth and eighteenth centuries. Britain gradually extended its authority over the Gold Coast during the nineteenth century as it sought to enforce the abolition of the slave trade. During the twentieth century the Gold Coast rapidly developed its economy and in 1957, it attained independence, as the state of Ghana.

During the nineteenth century the major obstacle to the extension of British control over the Gold Coast was not the Fanti coastal traders, with whom the British had a well-established commercial relationship, but the Ashanti confederacy that dominated the interior. In 1824, the British fought an unsuccessful war against the Ashanti and it took until the 1840s for Britain to establish permanent control over the coastal trading forts. The Coast of Africa and Falklands Act of 1843 proclaimed British jurisdiction over the territories adjacent to the coastal forts and settlements, but it took another two decades to extend the writ of the British Empire further inland. The British fought an inconclusive war against the Ashanti in 1863–1864, which was sufficiently expensive to persuade Parliament to bring British expansion to a temporary halt. In 1873, however, Sir Garnet Wolseley led a punitive expedition against the Ashanti in which his forces, equipped with breech-loading rifles and protected against malaria by the use of quinine, were much more successful than in earlier campaigns. In 1874, the Aborigines' Protection Society and the British and Foreign Anti-Slavery Society persuaded the British government to commit itself to the abolition of domestic slavery on the Gold Coast. British missionary activity increased during the late nineteenth century and the Fanti, who were very willing to accommodate Christianity, developed into a reliable urban elite of imperial collaborators. The Asanti, however, refused to cooperate, and in 1895 the British government established a protectorate to exercise jurisdiction over the entire indigenous population.

The imposition of formal British control coincided with the articulation of a radical economic vision by Joseph Chamberlain at the Colonial Office, who argued forcefully that Britain must develop the empire with investment capital. Yet during the twentieth century, the economy of the Gold Coast developed almost entirely independently of British investment capital. African farmers responded to increasing demand for chocolate by cultivating cocoa, which turned the Gold Coast into one of the richest countries in Africa. This economic development was accompanied by political aspirations and Africans were brought into the higher civil service of the colony. The process of political integration accelerated after the World War II as a consequence of a new constitution and the growth of African nationalism, and in 1957 Kwame Nkrumah became president of the newly independent state of Ghana. *See also* Ashanti Wars; British Empire; Chamberlain, Joseph; Gold Coast, Exchange of Forts on; Slavery.

FURTHER READING: Havinden, Michael, and Meredith, David. *Colonialism and Development: Britain and Its Tropical Colonies, 1850–1960.* London: Routledge, 1993; Kimble, David. *A Political History of Ghana: The Rise of Gold Coast Nationalism, 1850–1928.* Oxford: Clarendon Press, 1963; Newbury, Colin, ed. *British Policy Towards West Africa. Select Documents, 1875–1914.* Oxford: Clarendon Press, 1971.

CARL PETER WATTS

## Gold Coast, Exchanges of Forts on (1850, 1868)

A series of agreements among Britain, Denmark, and the Netherlands to effectively bring the African **Gold Coast** under British control. Centuries of European rivalry on the Gold Coast led to the construction of a series of coastal forts built by the European powers to defend their commercial interests. Two dozen of these forts were still in use by British, Dutch, and Danish merchants in the nineteenth century.

As the century progressed, Britain negotiated agreements with Denmark in 1850 and the Netherlands in 1868 and 1872 to take possession of these forts. These agreements acknowledged British ascendancy in the region and helped clear the way for the assumption of colonial rule over the Gold Coast in 1874, despite the sometimes violent responses they aroused among the indigenous population. Formally, the forts themselves were the only European possessions on the Gold Coast. Nonetheless, in practice European officials exercised considerable political, economic, and military influence over the districts surrounding their forts. By the middle of the nineteenth century, Britain, Denmark, and the Netherlands all claimed substantial protectorates or spheres of influence, although the nature and extent of their authority varied.

The British maintained an extensive judicial presence and were more actively engaged in the administration of their protectorate. This was especially true in the 1850s, when they attempted unsuccessfully to impose a poll tax on the protectorate to fund the extension of the judicial system, the construction of schools, and the improvement of roads. Pressure to reduce administrative costs also led to the institution of customs duties in the British forts. In contrast, the Dutch and the Danish preferred a more limited scale of administration. They avoided the imposition of taxes and had little interest in humanitarian measures, although the Danes provided a small annual grant to the Basel Mission Society. The primary interest of the Dutch on the Gold Coast was the recruitment of young men, primarily Ashanti slaves, to serve in their East Indian colonies. In any case, the existence of these limited territorial claims proved a source of conflict as the exchanges of forts were carried out.

The first of these transactions was prompted by the Danish decision to withdraw completely from the coast. All the European powers had suffered from a prolonged commercial slump in the first decades of the century caused by an **Ashanti** invasion and occupation of the coastal districts between 1807 and 1826 and the abolition of the slave trade. Faced with mounting commercial losses, Danish officials began looking to sell the five forts they controlled in the mid-1840s. Alarmed by Danish negotiations with France and eager to stamp out the illicit slave trade that persisted in the area, Britain agreed to purchase the forts for £10,000 in 1850. Difficulties with the transaction arose, however, when the British attempted to impose their legal jurisdiction over the local Ga polities, enforce strict rules against slave trading, and collect the poll tax. Neither Britain nor Denmark had sought their consent to the transfer of authority, and the Ga soon chafed under the transition from laissez-faire Danish rule to the more invasive British administration. The inhabitants of several former Danish towns rebelled against British rule in 1854 with "Danish flags flying." The riots were ended by British naval bombardment of the towns of Osu, Labadi, and Teshie.

The second set of transactions arose out of British and Dutch efforts to ease the difficulty of administering their protectorates by exchanging territory and consolidating their spheres of influence. Both faced recurrent problems related to the poorly defined boundaries of their respective protectorates. British and Dutch forts were intermingled along the entire length of the coast, and in the complete absence of reliable maps, the inland boundaries of their protectorates were even more problematic. Attempts to collect taxes and issues summons in certain areas were continually obstructed by disputes over jurisdiction. After a decade of negotiations, the exchange was carried out in early 1868. The Dutch took possession of four British forts in the western Gold Coast; the British took over five Dutch forts in the east. The new border between the reconstituted protectorates was the Sweet River, between Elmina and Cape Coast.

The exchange effectively shifted a number of independent polities from one protectorate to the other, again without their consent. Although the British took possession of the Dutch forts without incident, several of the states transferred into the Dutch protectorate refused to acknowledge Dutch authority. The inland states of Wassaw, Denkira, and Twifu were neighbors and longstanding enemies of the Ashanti empire. As the Dutch were close allies of Ashanti, they regarded Dutch rule as tantamount to an Ashanti occupation. Dutch authorities also faced resistance when they attempted to take control of British Commenda, which had a long history of conflict with nearby Dutch Commenda. Unable to occupy the British fort, the Dutch eventually destroyed it and the town with a naval bombardment. Within months the former British dependencies had placed Elmina under siege; the Ashanti army responded by invading the belligerent states; and the Dutch were plunged into a costly and unanticipated war. The Dutch eventually abandoned their forts in 1872, selling them to the British for the nominal fee of £4000. Two years later a British proclamation placed the Gold Coast under direct colonial rule. *See also* Africa, Scramble for; Ashanti Wars.

FURTHER READING: Claridge, William Walton. *A History of the Gold Coast and the Ashanti.* New York: Barnes & Noble, 1964; Fage, J. D. *Ghana, A Historical Interpretation.* Westport, CT: Greenwood, 1983; Ward, W.E.F. *A History of Ghana.* New York: Praeger, 1963.

SCOTT ANDERSON

## Gold Standard

A standard defining a national currency in terms of a fixed weight of gold, and allowing a free exchange and trade of gold. Until the nineteenth century, most of the countries maintained a bimetallic monetary system, in which national monetary units were valued against a certain weight of either gold or silver. The widespread adoption of the gold standard during the second half of the nineteenth century was largely due to the Industrial Revolution that brought a tremendous increase in the production of goods and widened the basis of world trade. During its existence, the classical gold standard is widely seen to have contributed to equilibrium of balances of payments worldwide. The same institutions that lent support to a period of remarkable globalization and economic modernization later contributed to interwar instability and the depth and length of the Great Depression of the 1930s. By the late 1930s, the gold standard as a species of monetary policy was mostly extinct.

The countries that accepted the gold standard had three principal objectives: to facilitate the settlement of international commercial and financial transactions, to establish stability in foreign exchange rates, and to maintain domestic monetary stability. Monetary authorities in different countries believed these aims could best be accomplished by having a single standard of universal validity and relative stability.

In the early part of the nineteenth century, virtually no country had a gold-based currency. The gold standard was introduced by Great Britain in 1821 and adopted by Australia and Canada in 1852 and 1853, respectively. Between 1870 and 1910, however, most nations came to adopt it. The far-reaching changes of 1871 led Germany, Scandinavia, Holland, Belgium, Switzerland, France, Finland, and the United States to adopt gold standards by 1879. In the 1880s, Argentina, Chile, Greece, and Italy chose gold-based regimes, but these experiments did not last. Many of the countries soon reverted to fiat currency regimes where it became impossible to trade a fixed number of domestic notes for gold specie at the legally mandated quantity. By the first decade of the twentieth century, most of these nations nonetheless adopted the gold standard again. In the 20 years after 1890, Asian nations also linked up to the gold standard. With some exceptions, the prevalence of the gold standard lasted until the economic crisis of 1929 and the ensuing depression. *See also* British Empire; Free Trade; Globalization.

FURTHER READING: Eichengreen, Barry J. *Golden Fetters: The Gold Standard and the Great Depression, 1919–1939.* Oxford: Oxford University Press, 1992; Flandreau, Marc. "The French Crime of 1873: An Essay on the Emergence of the International Gold Standard." *Journal of Economic History* 56, 4 (1996): 862–897; Gallarotti, Giulio, M. *The Anatomy of an International Monetary Regime: The Classical Gold Standard, 1880–1914.* Oxford: Oxford University Press, 1995.

JITENDRA UTTAM

## Gołuchowski, Agenor (1849–1921)

Austro-Hungarian minister for foreign affairs from 1895 to 1906. Count Agenor Gołuchowski was born in March 1849 in Lemberg (Lviv) in the Austrian crown land of Galicia. The son of a governor of Galicia and a member of the Polish aristocracy dominating the crown land, he entered the diplomatic service. His diplomatic career in Berlin, Paris, and Bucharest culminated in 1895 when he succeeded Count Kalnóky at the head of the Austro-Hungarian foreign ministry. Traditionally, relations with Germany, Austria-Hungary's closest ally, and Great Britain were quite good, and Gołuchowski used them as a basis for his foreign policy, but his Polish background did not hinder him from trying to ease tensions between the Habsburg monarchy and Russia.

In the Cretan insurrection against Ottoman rule (1895–1897), Gołuchowski achieved a consensus of the Great Powers, and in the Macedonian revolt of 1902, he cooperated with Russia. He managed to improve relations with Italy's foreign minister, Tommaso Tittoni. Gołuchowski was less successful in coping with in his opponents back home. Hungarian politicians and the heir to the throne, Archduke Franz Ferdinand, disliked him for opposite reasons but pushed for his resignation in October 1906. He died in Lemberg in March 1921. *See also* Balkan Crises; Habsburg Empire.

FURTHER READING: Albertini, Luigi. *The Origins of the War of 1914.* 3 vols. Translated by Isabella M. Massey. New York: Oxford University Press, 1952; Bridge, F. R. *From Sadowa to Sarajevo: The Foreign Policy of Austria-Hungary, 1866–1914.* Boston: Routledge and Kegan Paul, 1972.

GUENTHER KRONENBITTER

## Gorchakov, Alexander (1798–1883)

Russian foreign minister from 1856 to 1882 under Tsar **Alexander II.** Gorchakov's main diplomatic mission was to revise Russia's weakened position resulting from defeat in the **Crimean War.** To that end Gorchakov threw Russian support behind **Prussia** in its drive for German unification in competition with Austria. In return for Russian support, Germany endorsed Russia's remilitarization of the Black Sea in 1871. In Asia, Gorchakov opposed further Russian expansion, and he issued the famous "Gorchakov Circular" to European capitals in December 1864. The circular asserted that Russian expansion was simply a civilizing mission to secure a stable frontier against barbaric nomads and that Russia did not covet a single inch of Central Asian territories from the settled areas of the Uzbek khanates. His assertions proved hollow when Russian armies advanced against the khanates and ultimately conquered them all by 1873. *See also* Great Game; Russian Empire.

FURTHER READING: Geyer, Dietrich. *Russian Imperialism: The Interaction of Domestic and Foreign Policy, 1860–1914.* New York: Berg, 1987; Kazemzedeh, Firuz. *Russia and Britain in Persia, 1864–1914.* New Haven, CT: Yale University Press, 1968; Lieven, Dominic. *Empire, The Russian Empire and Its Rivals.* New Haven, CT: Yale University Press, 2002; Ragsdale, Hugh. *Imperial Russian Foreign Policy.* Cambridge: Cambridge University Press, 1993; Rywkin, Michael. *Russian Colonial Expansion to 1917.* London: Mansell, 1988.

JONATHAN GRANT

## Gordon, Charles George (1833–1885)

A British army officer famous for his leadership of native troops, killed at Khartoum by the forces of the self-proclaimed Mahdi, or messiah. As a young officer of Engineers, Gordon was converted to evangelical Christianity, which he practiced in earnest but unconventional ways throughout his life, housing paupers and at times going so far as to demand that his own salary be reduced. He fought with conspicuous courage at **Balaklava** during the **Crimean War.** In 1860, he volunteered to go to China as part of the Anglo-French expedition of that year. Two years later, he took command of what was audaciously called "the ever-victorious army," a disorganized force of mercenaries hired to protect the merchants of Shanghai. Gordon in fact did make it victorious against the **Taiping** insurgents. "Chinese Gordon" became a popular hero.

In 1873, Gordon was offered the governor-generalship of the southern **Sudan** by the Khedive of **Egypt,** a territory claimed by Egypt but not in fact under the Khedive's control. Traveling with only a small escort, Gordon made the abolition of slavery a personal priority, on one occasion riding almost alone into an enemy camp in Darfur to order the rebels' disbandment. Gordon left the Egyptian service in 1879 and undertook brief missions in Africa and **India.** When Britain occupied Egypt in 1882, it inherited Egypt's dubious claims to the Sudan. In response to the defeat of an Anglo-Egyptian force there, a popular clamor arose in London, assisted by the press, to send Gordon to fight the Mahdi. William **Gladstone**'s cabinet decided instead to send Gordon not to fight the Mahdi but to extract the remaining Anglo-Egyptian troops from the country. Gordon reached Khartoum, but instead of evacuating he prepared to defend the city, which he managed to do for almost a year. In the face of a further popular outcry, Gladstone was at length forced to send an expedition to relieve him. In the event, Khartoum fell and Gordon was killed on January 26, 1885, two days before the relief expedition's boats sighted the city. Gordon's courage and charisma combined with his ascetic Christianity to make him an imperial martyr in the sight of much of the public—the martyr's blood being on Gladstone's hands. Many who knew him closely thought him close to mad, and more recent critics have followed the lead of Lytton Strachey's infamous caricature, portraying Gordon as egocentric, given to drinking bouts, possibly homosexual, and obsessed by death. Not even his critics have denied his courage.

FURTHER READING: Elton, Godfrey. *Gordon of Khartoum: The Life of General Charles Gordon.* New York: Knopf, 1955; Pollock, John. *Gordon: The Man behind the Legend,* London: Constable, 1993; Strachey, Lytton. *Eminent Victorians,* London: G. P. Putnam's Sons, 1918.

MARK F. PROUDMAN

## Grant, Ulysses S. (1822–1885)

Ulysses S. Grant was an **American Civil War** hero and eighteenth President of the United States (1869–1877). In 1822, Grant was born in Point Pleasant, Ohio, to Jesse and Hannah Grant. His father was a farmer and a tanner. Grant was the oldest of six children and he had many different occupations throughout his younger years, but he was best known as a talented horse trainer. In 1839, he enlisted in the military, where he excelled in horsemanship, but was otherwise not an outstanding student. After graduation, Grant married Julia Dent and was assigned to General Zachary Taylor's army in Texas around the same time as the outbreak of the Mexican War in 1846. He was involved in major battles and was promoted to first lieutenant.

In 1854, he was promoted to captain and moved to California but became very depressed. He resigned from the military and wasted the next few years separated from his family and in many different and insignificant jobs. When Grant rejoined his family, the Civil War was looming. This national tragedy became Grant's finest hour. He returned to the army and, in June 1861, was made a colonel at the head of the 21st Illinois Volunteers of the Union forces. His career then proceeded from minor victories at Fort Henry and Fort Donelson to a pivotal near-defeat at Shiloh and a major victory at **Vicksburg,** the capture of which on July 4, 1863, did more to doom the Confederate cause than the more storied Union victory at **Gettysburg** the same day. Late the same year Grant's victory at Chattanooga opened the state of Georgia to a Union invasion. In March 1864, President Lincoln placed Grant in command of the entire Union Army. Grant's aggressiveness and superior grasp of strategy thereafter relentlessly pursued the destruction the Confederate army led by Robert E. Lee, from whom he accepted the Confederate surrender on April 9, 1865. Grant is credited by many with having invented the American way of war.

Grant served as secretary of war under President Andrew Johnson, but it was his military background and popularity that led to his own election to the presidency in 1868. As president he governed during the bitter era of Reconstruction yet presided over the historic amendments to the constitution that ended **slavery** and gave the electoral franchise to the freed slaves. In foreign policy Grant settled the *Alabama* claims with Britain and avoided war with Spain over the future of **Cuba.** His attempt to annex Santo Domingo as a naval base was thwarted by Congress. Grant nonetheless announced that henceforth no territory on the American continent was to be transferable to any European power, a reiteration of the **Monroe Doctrine.** Grant secured a treaty with Hawaii in 1875 providing for freer trade—a down payment on an eventual American protectorate there. He sought but failed to secure a treaty with Samoa in the southern Pacific and also failed to secure congressional approval for a treaty with Colombia for the rights to a Panamanian canal—in both cases revealing a personal awareness that the United States could not long delay a presence in strategically important waters.

Grant's presidency lasted two terms but was marred by charges of corruption, many of them valid, on the part of members of his administration. He died in 1885 in Mount McGregor, New York only four days after finishing his memoirs, widely considered one of the masterpieces of the English language. *See also* Strategy.

FURTHER READING: Fuller J.F.C. *Grant and Lee: A Study in Personality and Generalship.* Bloomington: Indiana University Press, 1957; Grant, Ulysses. *Personal Memoirs of U.S. Grant.* New York: Penguin Classics, 1999; Korda Michael, *Ulysses S. Grant: The Unlikely Hero.* New York: Harper Collins, 2004; Smith, Jean Edward. *Grant.* New York: Simon and Schuster, 2001; Weigley, Russell F. *The American Way of War.* Bloomington: Indiana University Press, 1973.

ARTHUR HOLST

## Gravelotte-St. Privat, Battle of (1870)

One of the largest and most important engagements of the **Franco-Prussian War.** By mid-August of 1870, the invading German armies faced east; and the French army faced west, its back to the German frontier and to the key French fortress of Metz. The French commander, Marshal François Achille Bazaine, chose to fall back on Metz and spaced out his forces along a strong defensive ridge from Gravelotte in the south to St. Privat in the north. General Helmuth von **Moltke** intended to use his artillery to weaken the French, then outflank the French position around St. Privat and roll up the French lines from north to south, but subordinates launched frontal assaults on prepared French positions. German artillery took a toll on the French, but French rifle fire tore up the German attacks.

By the evening, it appeared that the Germans were at the end of their tether, and a counterattack by the French would have carried the day. Instead, Bazaine ordered the troops to hold their positions. This gave the Germans time to conduct their flanking move around St. Privat, and the French were forced to retreat to the false security of **Metz,** where they were besieged. French losses were nearly 13,000; the Germans lost more than 20,000 men.

FURTHER READING: Howard, Michael. *The Franco-Prussian War.* New York: Collier, 1969.

DAVID H. OLIVIER

## Great Exhibition (1851)

A celebration of British achievements in science and technology. Organized by the Society of Arts, Manufactures and Commerce under the chairmanship of Prince Albert, consort of Queen Victoria, it featured 14,000 exhibitors and attracted more than 6 million visitors. The Exhibition took place in Hyde Park in the so-called "Crystal Palace"—as it was dubbed by *Punch* magazine—a prefabricated building of iron and glass, later dismantled and moved to its permanent location at Sydenham, Kent. The Great Exhibition became the model for future world's fairs and similar exhibitions. Although 1851 by no means marked the height of the territorial expansion of the British Empire, the Great Exhibition has been held to mark the height of Victorian power and self-confidence; it certainly marked one of the last decades in which England's global technological and economic primacy was uncontested.

FURTHER READING: Hobhouse, Hermione. *The Crystal Palace and the Great Exhibition.* New York: Athlone Press, 2001.

MARK F. PROUDMAN

## Great Game

The name attributed to the nineteenth- and early twentieth-century competition for colonial territory in Central Eurasia. Tsarist Russia and Great Britain were the primary actors in this ongoing diplomatic, political, and military rivalry. The term Great Game was first widely popularized in Rudyard **Kipling**'s novel *Kim,* first published in 1901. British Captain Arthur Connolly, however, was believed to have coined the phrase in his *Narrative of an Overland Journey to the North of India* in 1835. Since then, it has been the subject of countless historical studies. It should be noted that Russian speakers did not refer to this period of colonial rivalry as the Great Game, but certainly acknowledged this important period of its own historical record. Among Russian speakers, the Great Game competition is referred to as the "Tournament of Shadows."

The Great Game is generally accepted to date from the early nineteenth century until the 1907 **Anglo-Russian Convention,** although some scholars date its conclusion to later in the twentieth century. The Anglo-Russian Convention is also referred to as the Convention of Mutual Cordiality or the Anglo-Russian Agreement and was signed on August 31, 1907. The convention gave formal unity to the Triple Entente powers, consisting of France, Great Britain, and Russia, who would soon engage in future diplomatic and military struggles against the earlier-formed **Triple Alliance,** consisting of Austria-Hungary, Germany, and Italy. The agreement also confirmed existing colonial borders. Great Britain and Russia agreed not to invade Afghanistan, Persia, or Tibet, but were allowed certain areas of economic or political influence within those regions.

In contemporary history, popular media often speak of many new "Great Games." This term has become customary for discussing any sort of diplomatic or state-organized conflicts or competitions in the Central Eurasian region. These new Great Games are often mentioned in disputes over oil or natural resources, diplomatic influence or alliances, economic competition, the opening or closing of military bases, the outcomes and maneuvering for political elections and offices, or any number of other contemporary issues in Central Eurasia. Russia, the United States, China, Turkey, the European Union countries, East Asian states, and various Islamic-influenced countries are often portrayed as the major competitors of these contemporary Great Games.

The historical roots of the Great Game are planted in a period of sustained mutual fear and mistrust on the part of Britain and Russia throughout most of the nineteenth and early twentieth centuries. Both British and Russian leaders feared that the other side would encroach on their territorial holdings and would establish preeminent colonial control in the Central Eurasian region. It was widely believed that this would escalate into a war between the two powers at some point, but this never happened. Russia and Britain, however, did engage in a considerable amount of military ventures against various peoples of Central Eurasia. The conflicts ranged from diplomatic squabbles to shows of military force to full-blown wars.

During the early nineteenth century, Russia became increasingly interested in solidifying its southern borders. The Russians gained allegiance from various Kazakh hordes during the late eighteenth and early nineteenth centuries. They still faced opposition from many Kazakhs, however, including Kenesary **Kasimov,** who led a sustained rebellion of Kazakhs against Russia from 1837–1846. Much of the early nineteenth-century Russian attention in Central Eurasia was directed toward quelling Kazakh resistance and ensuring secure southern borders for the empire. By 1847, the Russians finally succeeded in bringing the Greater, Middle, and Lesser Kazakh hordes under Russian control. In response to its defeat in the Crimean War (1854–1856), Russia turned its military attention away from the Ottoman Empire and the Caucasus and instead toward eastward and southward expansion in Central Eurasia. The terms of the 1856 Treaty of **Paris** effectively forced Russia to relinquish its interests in Southwest Asia, spurring a new round of imperial interest in Central Eurasia. Russian advances in Central Eurasia were both offensive and defensive moves, as they conquered the only areas left to them and hoped to position themselves against future British encroachment in the region.

The British government became increasingly alarmed over the southward movement of the Russian armies throughout the nineteenth century. Russian conquest of the Kazakh steppe was followed by mid-century attacks on the Central Eurasian oasis empires of Khokand, Khiva, and **Bukhara.** The Russians began a new wave of conquest in 1864 by conquering the cities of Chimkent and Aulie Ata. Khokand was defeated in 1865 and with the unexpected Russian attack and conquest of Tashkent in 1865 by General Mikhail **Cherniaev,** tsarist Russia was in a position to launch a string of attacks in the latter 1860s and throughout the 1870s that struck fear in the hearts of the British. The Russians then conquered the Bukhara state in 1868 and the **Khiva khanate** in 1873. Both Bukhara and Khiva were granted the status of Russian protectorates in 1873. The Turkmen of Central Eurasia put up particularly strong resistance to Russian conquest during a long period of fighting between 1869 and 1885. As with most of the other areas, the Russians considered controlling the Turkmen and their territory as essential for resisting possible British incursions. The Russian victory over the Turkmen at the Battle of Göktepe in 1881 was crucial. The final Russian territorial acquisition in Central Eurasia was at the oasis of Merv in 1884. The Russians considered this conquest especially important because of its proximity to **Afghanistan.** As the Russian southward advance continued, British colonial officials became increasingly concerned that Russia may attempt to continue southward and attempt to take the jewel in the British colonial crown, **India.** The British had maintained economic and political influence over South Asia since the early seventeenth century, initially through the British East India Company's economic ventures. Although India was not a formal British colony until 1858, with the suppression of the Sepoy rebellion, Britain enjoyed strong commercial and political influence over the area throughout the nineteenth century. Russians feared British interest in areas they considered to be in their own colonial backyard—especially Afghanistan, Persia, and Tibet.

The Great Game included two major wars between the British and the leaders of Afghanistan, with disastrous results for the British. The British hoped that Afghanistan could serve as a buffer state in defense of Russian advances toward India. The First Anglo-Afghan war lasted from 1839 until 1842. In this war, the British attempted to replace current Afghan leader Dost Muhammad Khan with a leader more amenable to British control, Shuja Shah. The Second Anglo-Afghan War was fought from 1878–1880, again over issues of British political and diplomatic influence in Afghanistan. In both conflicts the British faced harsh opposition in Afghanistan; however, after the second conflict, they were able to establish considerable control over Afghan politics by placing Abdur Rahman Khan in power. Abdur Rahman Khan ruled Afghanistan until 1901, largely in service of British interests in the region. He was able to quell opposition to the idea of a unified Afghanistan during this period. Perhaps his biggest test of political leadership came in 1885 in Panjdeh, in northern Afghanistan. Panjdeh was an oasis area, which the Russians wished to claim. After much diplomatic wrangling, the dispute was resolved and the Russians and Afghanis agreed to a border at the Amu Darya River, ceding Panjdeh to the Russian Empire. During the early 1890s, the Russians attempted to continue a southward push through the Pamir Mountains to India's frontier of Kashmir. At this point mutual fears had reached a crisis situation, but they were temporarily resolved through the work of the Pamir Boundary Commission in 1895. This agreement paved the way for the formal acknowledgment of Russian and British colonial possessions in Central Eurasia through the 1907 Anglo-Russian Convention. The Pamir Boundary Commission of 1895 set the definitive boundaries for the Russian Empire in Central Eurasia.

The Russians faced two major setbacks in the early twentieth century, the Russo-Japanese War of 1904–1905, and the Revolution of 1905. As a result of these two reversals and amidst the backdrop of an emerging alliance system among the major European powers, the Russians became interested in resolving their disputes with Great Britain. In 1907, both sides agreed to a cessation of the Great Game competition by agreeing to the **Anglo-Russian Convention** on August 31. Under the terms of this agreement, both sides settled their disputes over territories in Central Eurasia—including Afghanistan, Persia, and Tibet—and forged a military and diplomatic alliance that they would carry into World War I. *See also* Afghan Wars; British Empire; Russian Empire; Russo-Japanese War; Triple Entente.

FURTHER READING: Hopkirk, Peter. *The Great Game: The Struggle for Empire in Central Asia.* New York: Kodansha International, 1994; Morgan, Gerald. *Anglo-Russian Rivalry in Central Asia: 1810–1895.* London: Frank Cass, 1981; Siegel, Jennifer. *Endgame: Britain, Russia, and the Final Struggle for Central Asia.* London: I. B. Tauris Publishers, 2002; Soucek, Svat. *A History of Inner Asia.* Cambridge: Cambridge University Press, 2000.

SCOTT C. BAILEY

## Great Powers

States whose economic resources, military power, and diplomatic prestige make their policies and actions an inescapable concern of all states in an international system. The term was first adopted as an orthodox diplomatic concept in 1817, with the signing of the Treaty of Chaumont and was elevated to common usage by the Prussian historian Leopold von Ranke in 1833. In the period between the Napoleonic Wars and World War I, the Great Power club included Austria, Britain, France, Italy after 1861, the Ottoman Empire, Prussia—succeeded by the **German Empire** after 1871—Russia, Japan after 1895, and the **United States** after 1865. *See also* Balance of Power; Strategy; Navalism.

FURTHER READING: Kennedy, Paul. *The Rise and Fall of the Great Powers.* New York: Random House, 1987; Taylor, A.J.P. *The Struggle for Mastery in Europe, 1848–1918.* Oxford: Clarendon Press, 1954.

CARL CAVANAGH HODGE

## Great Trek (1863–1867)

Often dated to 1837, the Great Trek was an overland migration over a number of years of Dutch-speaking **Afrikaners,** or Boers as they were then called, away from the British-controlled Cape Colony and into the interior of what is now South Africa. Boers traveled through the Eastern Cape north and east toward what became the **Orange Free State,** into the **Transvaal,** and some south again into Natal. Although some areas were relatively depopulated as a result of the African intertribal warfare known as the Mfecane, the Boers clashed with several black African tribes, most notably the Zulu at the battle of Blood River in 1838.

The Great Trek was motivated by a desire for land and pasture, but also by opposition to the anglicizing influences brought to the Cape by the British, and specifically to the abolition of slavery and tentative moves toward racial equality in the British Empire. The Great Trek led to the founding of militantly independent Boer republics in the interior, the predecessors of those—the Transvaal and the Orange Free State—that went to war with Britain in 1879 and again in 1899. The Great Trek and its myths of survival in the face of great odds and native hostility became a foundational event in the historical consciousness of the Afrikaners, the eventual capital of South Africa being named Pretoria in honor of Andries Pretorius, their leader at **Blood River.** *See also* Africa, Scramble for; Boer Wars; British Empire.

FURTHER READING: Davenport, T.R.H. *South Africa: A Modern History,* Basingstoke: MacMillan, 1987; Etherington, Norman. *The Great Treks: The Transformation of South Africa, 1815–1854.* New York: Longman, 2001; Ransford, Oliver. *The Great Trek.* London: Murray, 1972.

MARK F. PROUDMAN

## Great White Fleet

A popular name for the newly established Atlantic Fleet of the United States Navy, which was sent on a round-the-world-cruise between December 16, 1907, and February 22, 1909, to demonstrate the ascendancy of American sea power. The ships set out from Hampton Roads, Virginia under the command of Civil War veteran Rear Admiral Robley D. Evans to arrive back there after completing a 43,000-mile voyage. The fleet first circumnavigated South America, reaching San Francisco, California.

At that point Rear Admiral Charles S. Sperry assumed command and his fleet traversed the Pacific with calls in Hawaii, New Zealand, Australia, China, the Philippines, and Japan, then steaming west into the Mediterranean by way of Ceylon and the Suez Canal. His units participated in relief efforts after the Sicily earthquake while other ships reached Constantinople, capital of the Ottoman Empire before returning home via the Strait of **Gibraltar.**

The 16 battleships, all painted white for the occasion, comprised the single largest concentration of capital ships in the world. This underscored the United States' recently acquired great power status, signaled its entry to the global naval building race, and also dealt a warning to potential challengers of the **Monroe Doctrine,** such as Germany or Japan. At the same time the fleet was not merely formed for display, but reflected organizational reform in the U.S. Navy: doctrinal reform proposed by Captain Alfred Thayer Mahan, and the assertive policies of President Theodore Roosevelt called for the concentration of formerly scattered capital ships in a single battle fleet able to deliver decisive victory in the theater it was deployed. *See also* Great Powers; Navalism; Mahan, Alfred Thayer; Roosevelt; Theodore; Strategy.

FURTHER READING: Baer, George W. *One Hundred Years of Sea Power: The U.S. Navy, 1890–1990.* Stanford, CA: Stanford University Press, 1993; Hart, Robert A. *The Great White Fleet: Its Voyage Around the World, 1907–1909.* Boston: Little, Brown, 1965; The Great White Fleet. Naval Historical Center. See www.history.navy.mil/faqs/faq42–1.htm

GÁBOR BERCZELI

## Greece

The **Ottoman Empire** ruled Greece from the fifteenth to the early nineteenth century. Ottoman rule preserved the religious traditions of the Orthodox Church and ruled along with the cooperation of the Church and the Orthodox elite. During the enlightenment Europe created a unitary ideal of ancient Greece and appropriated its perceived righteousness and made it its intellectual and political ancestor. Soon a unitary ideal of a modern Greece emerged and many Orthodox Christians, who had a religious identity and lived in peace and in many cases integration with Muslims, began to consider themselves Greeks.

In 1821, the "Greeks" rebelled and declared their independence yet did not succeed in winning it until 1829. The Patriarch, Gregory V, was hanged, not for supporting the revolt, but after advising the Sultan that it would be shortly suppressed. Indeed, the Ottomans often seemed on the verge of suppressing the Greek revolt, but the intervention of the Russian, British, and French governments brought a different result. The intellectuals and elites of France and Britain saw the war as a chance to "liberate" their spiritual ancestors. Many French and English men volunteered to fight for the cause, including, most famously, Lord Byron, who died fighting for Greece. The Russians saw the Greeks as their coreligionists and wanted to gain an influence over them. The military intervention of Russia, France, and Britain resulted in the Porte ultimately agreeing to Greek independence. The former Russian minister of foreign affairs, Ioannis Capodistrias, a Greek noble from the Ionian Islands, became president of the new republic, but the **Great Powers** had ideas of controlling the Greek state. They instituted a monarchy, the Greek Kingdom, under the Convention of London in 1832 and, in the person of the 17-year-old Otto of Bavaria of the German House of Wittelsbach, the second son of King Ludwig I of Bavaria and Therese of Saxe-Altenburg, and Greece's first king.

Otto's reign lasted for 30 years. In the beginning a group of Bavarian regents ruled in his name and made themselves unpopular by trying to impose German ideas of orderly government. Nevertheless they laid the foundations of a Greek administration, army, justice system, and education system. Otto sought to give Greece a good government, but refused to renounce his Roman Catholic faith in favor of Orthodox Christianity. His marriage to Queen Amalia remained childless and he was autocratic. The Bavarian regents ruled until 1837, at which point the governments of Britain and France, which considered Greece a part of their informal empire, forced Otto to appoint Greek ministers, although Bavarians still ran most of the administration and the army. Greek discontent grew until a revolt broke out in Athens in September 1843, and Otto agreed to grant a constitution. A National Assembly created a bicameral parliament, consisting of an Assembly and a Senate. Power passed into the hands of a group of politicians, many of whom had been commanders in the revolt against the Ottoman rule.

Nationalism and nation-building dominated Greek politics throughout the nineteenth century. When Greece was created in 1832, its people, who called themselves *Romiee*, were not homogenous—language, culture, and social norms were entangled with other linguistic and religious groups: Turkish, Slavic, Latin, Frankish, and even the Romaic. With the majority of Orthodox Christians living under Ottoman rule, Otto and many Greek politicians dreamt of liberating them to form a Greater Greece, with Constantinople as its capital. This was called the Great Idea (*Megali Idea*), and it was sustained by almost continuous rebellions against Ottoman rule in many Christian Orthodox territories. But Greece was too poor and too weak to wage war on the Ottoman Empire, and London, to whom Greece was heavily in debt, opposed expansion. During the **Crimean War** the British occupied Piraeus to prevent Athens from declaring war on the Ottomans as a Russian ally.

Meanwhile, Otto's interference in government was beginning to upset Greek politicians wanting to rule their own back yard. In 1862, Otto dismissed the prime minister, the former admiral Constantine Canaris, provoking a military rebellion that forced Otto to leave. The Greeks then asked Whitehall to send Queen Victoria's son, Prince Alfred, as their new king, but the other Great Powers rejected this idea. Instead, a young Danish Prince of the Gluckburg house became King George I. George was a popular choice. At London's urging, Greece adopted a more democratic constitution in 1864. The powers of the king were reduced, the Senate was abolished, and the franchise was extended to all adult males. Yet politics remained dynastic. Two parties soon started to alternate in office: the Liberals, led first by Charilaos Trikoupis and later by Eleftherios Venizelos, and the Conservatives, led initially by Theodoros Deligiannis and later by Thrasivoulos Zaimis. His son, Alexandros. Trikoupis, who favored social and economic reform, dominated Greek politics in the later nineteenth century. Deligiannis, on the other hand, promoted Greek nationalism and the *Megali Idea*, especially in Crete and Macedonia, but also in Cyprus. By the 1890s, Greece was virtually bankrupt, and poverty in the rural areas was eased only by emigration to the United States. Despite its poverty, Greece managed to host the first Olympic games of the modern age in 1896.

The issue of nation-formation continued to dominate the political landscape and gave rise to the language question. The Orthodox Christian or Romiee spoke a language that had evolved during the centuries of integration with other linguistic traditions into many unique variations of Greek. Many of the educated elite saw this as a peasant dialect and wanted to restore the glories of ancient Greek. Government documents and newspapers were published in *Katharevousa,* an artificial purified language, which few people could understand. Liberals favored recognizing the spoken tongues, but Conservatives, the University, and the Orthodox Church resisted. When the New Testament was translated into the popular Demotic in 1901, riots in Athens brought down the government. Hellenization had succeeded in transforming Orthodox Christian Romiee into Hellenized Orthodox Christians.

The result was that many Greeks increasingly became active in "liberating" Orthodox Christian territories that they perceived were part of Greece *irredenta,* namely Crete, Macedonia, Epirus, and to a lesser extent Cyprus. The Treaty of Berlin of 1881 gave Greece Thessaly and parts of Epirus, while frustrating hopes of securing Crete. Greeks in Crete continued to stage regular revolts, and in 1897 the government of the firebrand nationalist Deligiannis declared war on the Ottomans. Ottoman forces defeated the Greek army. Disturbances in Macedonia also increased. Here the Greeks were in conflict not only with the Ottoman rule but also with the Slavs and Bulgarians. The Cretan Greeks, led by Eleftherios **Venizelos,** rebelled again in 1908. When the Greek government refused to rescue them, the army and navy rebelled. Venizelos was soon asked to take control and instituted sweeping reforms.

Venizelos successfully steered Greece through the two Balkan Wars, dramatically increasing the borders of the country, but his support of the Entente was rejected by the new king, Constantine I. Despite parliament approving Venizelos' policy to enter the war on the Entente's side after Bulgaria joined the Central Powers, Constantine forced Venizelos to resign. Venizelos established a rival government at Salonica and with allied backing managed to bring Greece into the war in 1917. *See also* Balkan Crises; Balkan Wars.

FURTHER READING: Clogg, R. *A Short History of Modern Greece.* New York: Cambridge University Press, 1988; Dakin, D. *The Unification of Greece, 1770–1923.* London: Benn, 1972.

ANDREKOS VARNAVA

## Grey, Charles, Second Earl Grey (1764–1845)

Prime minister of the United Kingdom from 1830–1834, Earl Grey oversaw the passage of the Great Reform Act of 1832. Although from a Tory family, he became from his election to Parliament in 1786 a Foxite Whig, and, unlike many others, he remained true to his Foxite principles throughout the 1790s. As foreign secretary in the Ministry of All the Talents, however, he came to see Napoleonic France as a threat to Britain, and he supported the war effort through 1815. Grey was out of office during the years of Tory rule up to 1830. He became prime minister on November 16, 1830, and immediately set about satisfying the widespread demand for electoral and franchise reform, although his aims in that effort were essentially conservative. With great determination and some assistance from public agitation and a threat to create a mass of new peers, Grey overcame the resistance of the Lords, and the great Reform Bill received royal assent in June 1832. Grey's government also oversaw the abolition of **slavery** in the British Empire in 1833. His ministry fell over Irish questions in 1834.

FURTHER READING: Smith, E. A. *Lord Grey, 1764–1845*. Oxford: Clarendon Press, 1990; Trevelyan, G. M. *Lord Grey of the Reform Bill*. London: Longmans, Green, 1920.

MARK F. PROUDMAN

## Grey, Henry, Third Earl Grey (1802–1894)

Colonial secretary under Lord John Russell, Grey oversaw the introduction of **responsible government** in the British settlement colonies. Grey became parliamentary undersecretary at the Colonial Office under the ministry of his father, Charles **Grey,** Second Earl Grey, in 1830. His ideas about colonial governance were influenced by the contemporary writings of Edward Gibbon Wakefield, who urged the sale of colonial lands, with the proceeds used to subsidize emigration. In the 1830s, he argued for a conciliatory reaction to the Canadian rebellions, and also became interested in reforming the conditions of life for enlisted soldiers in the army.

Becoming colonial secretary under Lord John Russell in 1846, Grey oversaw the introduction of responsible government in **Canada** and the effective grant of similar local self-government in the major Australian colonies. He also oversaw the introduction of limited forms of representative government in South Africa and **New Zealand,** two colonies beset by chronic native wars, for which neither Grey nor anyone else had an adequate solution. He left office when Russell's ministry fell in 1852, and produced *The Colonial Policy of Lord John Russell's Administration,* a defense of his conduct in office, which remains a useful source on early Victorian colonial policy.

FURTHER READING: Grey, Earl. *The Colonial Policy of Lord John Russell's Administration*. London: R. Bentley, 1853; Morrell, William Parker. *British Colonial Policy in the Age of Peel and Russell*. New York: Barnes & Noble, 1966.

MARK F. PROUDMAN

## Grey, Sir Edward, First Viscount Grey of Fallodon (1862–1933)

British foreign secretary from 1905 to 1916, Sir Edward Grey had much to do with taking the country in World War I. Descended from an old Whig family with a tradition of military and political service, and distantly related to the Earl Grey of the great reform bill, Grey had an undistinguished academic career at Balliol, Oxford. In 1884, he became private secretary to Sir Evelyn Baring, later Lord **Cromer,** effectively the British proconsul in **Egypt.** Elected to parliament as a Liberal in 1885, Grey remained loyal to William **Gladstone** during the split of the **Liberal Party** over **home rule** the next year. When Lord Rosebery went to the Foreign Office in Gladstone's 1892 government, Grey became his parliamentary undersecretary , and thus the department's voice in the Commons.

In opposition after the Liberal defeat of 1895, Grey aligned himself with the Liberal imperialists in supporting British actions at **Fashoda** and in South Africa. When the Liberals returned to power under Henry **Campbell-Bannerman** in 1905, Grey went to the foreign office. Although ruling out a firm commitment to defend France against Germany, Grey permitted the Anglo-French military staff talks begun under the Tories to continue. The Anglo-Russian Convention of 1907 drew Britain yet closer to the Entente powers. In 1914, Grey strongly insisted to the House of Commons that Britain must intervene against Germany; however, he also remarked, famously and prophetically, that "the lamps are going out all over Europe; we shall not see them lit again in our lifetime." Grey was left out of Lloyd George's 1916 cabinet, thus ending his official life after more than a decade at the foreign office. *See also* Entente Cordiale; July Crisis (1914); Liberal Imperialists; Military Conversations.

FURTHER READING: Albertini, Luigi. *The Origins of the War of 1914.* 3 vols. Translated by Isabella Mellis Massey. New York: Oxford University Press, 1952; Robbins, Keith. *Sir Edward Grey: A Biography of Lord Grey of Fallodon,* London: Cassell, 1971; Trevelyan, G. M. *Grey of Fallodon,* London: Longmans, Green, 1937.

MARK F. PROUDMAN

## Grey, Sir George (1812–1898)

Governor of **New Zealand** and the **Cape Colony,** Sir George Grey was an enthusiastic follower of Thomas Carlyle and protagonist of British power who believed fervently in Britain's civilizing mission. Grey was born into a military family and educated at Sandhurst. Temporarily posted to Western Australia as a captain in 1839, he shortly sold his army commission and returned as governor. Appointed governor of New Zealand in 1845, shortly after the outbreak of war with Maoris, Grey waged war with enthusiasm while denying full self-government to the New Zealanders.

In 1854, he went to South Africa as high commissioner and governor of the Cape Colony, where he waged war against the Xhosa and tried to incorporate the Boer republics into the British Empire, contrary to London's policy. He went back to New Zealand in 1861, where he again made war, with some success, against the Maori nationalist "King movement." He was replaced by the British government, tired of the expense of his New Zealand campaigns, in 1868. His campaigns against the Maori had made him popular with some settlers, and he was elected premier of New Zealand from 1877–1879. This eccentric but ruthless man died in 1898. *See also* Maori Wars.

FURTHER READING: Milne, James. *The Romance of a Pro-Consul.* London: Chatto & Windus, 1899.

MARK F. PROUDMAN

## Guadeloupe

*See* French Empire

## Guadalupe Hidalgo, Treaty of (1848)

The treaty ending the **Mexican War** of 1845–1848 and transferring over half of the Mexican territory to the **United States.** Negotiated by Nicholas P. Trist for the United States and Luis Gonzaga Cuevas, Bernardo Couto, and Miguel Aristrain for

Mexico, the treaty was signed on February 2, ratified by the U.S. Senate on March 10 and the Mexican government on May 30, and proclaimed July 4, 1848.

American interest in territory south of the Louisiana Purchase had been long-standing. In 1836, **Texas** declared itself independent of Mexico, and in 1845 the United States annexed Texas. After a clash between American and Mexican troops on Mexican territory, Congress declared war on May 13, 1846. American troops captured Mexico City on September 17, 1847, and Trist, without official authorization, opened negotiations later that year.

By the treaty, Mexico ceded what later became Arizona, **California,** New Mexico, Texas, and parts of Colorado, Nevada, and Utah, to the United States, in all some 55 percent of Mexican territory. Washington compensated Mexico with $15 million for war-related damages to Mexican property and assumed up to $3.5 million of claims by American citizens against Mexico. The border was set at the Rio Grande and the two nations agreed to cooperate on any future road, canal, or railway project along the Gila River, later the basis of the 1853 Gadsden Purchase.

The treaty benefited mainly the United States, which completed, except for the Gadsden Purchase of 1853, its contiguous continental expansion by increasing its national territory by approximately one-quarter. Many Americans viewed the treaty as a validation of the nation's **Manifest Destiny** to expand across the continent, but the terms soured Mexican-American relations for decades and the territorial acquisition exacerbated sectional divisions in the United States. The treaty and the circumstances surrounding it exemplify America's antebellum expansionist thrust.

FURTHER READING: Hunter Miller, ed. *Treaties and other International Acts of the United States of America.* Vol. V. Washington: U.S. Government Printing Office, 1937, pp. 207–428; Pletcher, David M. *The Diplomacy of Annexation: Texas, Oregon, and the Mexican War.* Columbia: University of Missouri Press, 1973.

KENNETH J. BLUME

## Guam

*See* Spanish-American War

## Guatemala

Guatemala is the Central American home of the Mayan civilization (c. 301–900) and a Spanish colony after 1524. Guatemala was the core of the Captaincy-General of Guatemala—comprising present-day Belize, Costa Rica, El Salvador, Guatemala, Honduras, Nicaragua, and Panama—until it achieved independence from Spain with Mexico in 1821. Guatemala ceded from Mexico to join the Central American Union, 1824–1838, and finally to become a wholly separate republic in 1839. It lost the territory of present-day Belize to Britain in 1859. Guatemala frequently intervened in the affairs of its neighbors, but after 1880 it came progressively under the domination of the United States. *See also* Monroe Doctrine.

FURTHER READING: Handy, J. *The Gift of the Devil: A History of Guatemala.* Boston: South End Press, 1984.

CARL CAVANAGH HODGE

## Guerrilla

The word commonly used to refer to an irregular fighter, the term *guerrilla* is widely acknowledged to have entered usage in the English language during the **Peninsular War,** when *la guerrilla* referred to the struggle of irregulars practicing harassment and sabotage of the Napoleonic army in Spain. Insofar as one in every four French casualties suffered in Spain is thought to have been inflicted by them, *guerrilleros*—the more appropriate Spanish term for the fighters themselves—were obviously effective fighting allies for Wellington but were also a source of valuable intelligence.

Romanticized as the champions of a "people's war" against Bonapartist tyranny, they were also famed for extraordinary cruelty to the French soldiers they captured and were blamed by the victims of the harsh French reprisals they provoked. Carl von **Clausewitz** dealt with the conditions facilitating guerrilla tactics, and C. E. Callwell devoted a chapter to guerrilla war in his classic *Small Wars,* first published in 1896, citing among others the followers of **Abd-al-Qādir,** the **Khalsa,** and the **Boers** as especially effective practitioners. *See also* Afghan Wars; Boer Wars; Peninsular War.

FURTHER READING: Callwell, C. E. *Small Wars: Their Principles and Practice.* London: HMSO, 1906; Esdaile, Charles. *The Peninsular War.* London: Allen Lane, 2002.

CARL CAVANAGH HODGE

## Guinea

Guinea, or Guinea Coast, is a geographical term of Berber origins used by Europeans from the fourteenth to the nineteenth centuries to designate varying sections of the western coast of Africa, a region that formed one apex of the Atlantic Triangle trade, and lay along the route to the Asian lands formerly known as the East Indies. Taken in the broadest sense, that is, stretching from the southern edge of the Sahara Desert to Angola, it was divided into Upper and Lower Guinea at the Equator. Further subdivisions indicated the most lucrative export commodities, hence the Pepper or Grain Coast, the Ivory Coast, the Mina or **Gold Coast,** and the Slave Coast. Given that these items originated in the hinterland, and their procurers were known to have supplied the Trans-Saharan and internal Sudan trade beforehand, such labels point to the existence of an extensive and efficient distribution system.

It is well documented in Arabic written sources that the region's resources prompted the rise of indigenous empires especially from the tenth century onward and occasionally lasting into the twentieth century, including those of the Mande, Soninke, Yoruba, Edo, Akan, and Fulbe people. Enabled by a technological revolution, and pressed by a shortage of bullion, the Portuguese Prince Henry the Navigator (1394–1460) initiated the European exploration of the Atlantic seaboard, primarily to gain direct access to the goldfields of the western Sudan. A further advantage of establishing trading posts on the Guinea Coast lay in their utility as a stepping stone to the spice trade of Asia, until then monopolized by the Levant traders of Genoa and Venice, and also disrupted by the expansion of the Ottoman Empire.

Even though the Treaty of Tordesillas of 1494 made the region a formal Portuguese sphere of interest, Portugal's emerging seaborne empire was soon challenged by Dutch, English, French, Danish, Swedish, Brandenburger, and even Courland competitors from the 1520s on. Having organized chartered companies with commercial monopolies, Europeans constructed a network of factories and forts along the seaboard and built up a profitable trade first in gold then slaves to satisfy the need of an emerging plantation complex in the Americas. The capital thus accumulated and access to lubricants derived from palm or peanut oil contributed to the rise of industrial Europe. Imports included European metal ware, textiles, and firearms; American silver and tobacco; and Asian and African cowries and cloth. Such early commercial links to the Guinea helped establish the modern interdependent world economy. Partaking in the Columbian exchange, the transfer of disease, plant and animal species, as well as technology, ideas and religious currents across continents formed part of the transactions at the same time. The hinterland, however, was less affected until the so-called Scramble for Africa, the period of direct territorial annexation that is commonly dated from the 1870s. Obstacles included resistance by the powerful indigenous states of the interior, efficient competition from other trading systems, the limited length of navigable rivers, few suitable natural harbors, a disease environment that earned the coast the epithet "White Man's Grave," and finally the lack of sufficient funds or official support. By the 1870s, France and Britain remained the two dominant European powers that also carried the lead in colonization and territorial annexations. *See also* Africa, Scramble for; British Empire; Globalization.

FURTHER READING: Birmingham, David. *Trade and Empire in the Atlantic, 1400–1600.* New York: Routledge, 2000; Hopkins, Anthony G. *An Economic History of West Africa.* New York: Longman, 1973.

GÁBOR BERCZELI

## Guizot, François (1787–1874)

French statesman and historian whose father was executed during the Reign of Terror in 1794. Guizot started a legal career in Paris in 1805, but from 1812 to 1830 he was a professor of modern history at the Sorbonne, where his intellectually formative publications included *Sur l'histoire de France* and *Histoire de la revolution d'Angleterre.* Guizot's sympathy with moderate royalists drew him into politics after the **July Revolution** of 1830 as an advocate of a constitutional monarchy with limited suffrage and supporter of the **July Monarchy** of Louis Philippe. As minister of education, 1832–1837, he introduced a new system of primary instruction.

Guizot served briefly as French ambassador to London, before becoming foreign minister and finally prime minister in 1847. Guizot was fond of British gradualism in political reform, but his conservatism led to the fall of his government and the abdication of Louis Philippe in the February Revolution of 1848. He devoted the rest of his life to writing.

FURTHER READING: Brush, Elizabeth Parnham. *Guizot in the Early Years of the Orleanist Monarchy.* Urbana: University of Illinois Press, 1929.

CARL CAVANAGH HODGE

## Gujarat, Battle of (1849)

The final and decisive engagement of the Second **Sikh War.** After the Battle of Chillianwala, the Sikh commander, Sher Singh, received reinforcements from his father Chattar Singh and also from the Amir of Kabul. On January 26, 1849, the Sikh fort of Multan in West Punjab surrendered to British forces and reinforcement was on its way to meet Baron Hugh Gough, commander-in-chief of British forces in **India.** Sher Singh decided to outflank Gough's army at Gujarat by crossing the Chenab River but was thwarted in the venture by British irregular cavalry and forced instead to face a British attack in open country south of Gujarat. The Sikh defensive position was in the form of a crescent. A dry sandy *nullah* named Dwarah protected the Sikh right; their left was on a rivulet named Katela. The Sikh center rested on the two villages named Bara Kalra and Chota Kalra, respectively. Gough brought 24,000 soldiers to the field to engage a Sikh army 50,000 to 60,000 in number.

The battle started on February 21 at 7.30 A.M. with a furious cannonade that continued for three hours. The distance between the Sikh forces and the British lines was 800 yards. Gough enjoyed qualitative and quantitative superiority in artillery over the Sikhs, and the 59 Sikh guns were silenced by 96 British guns. Gough then launched the First and Second divisions against the Sikh center and, at a cost of 600 casualties, captured the two villages. The Sikhs then retreated to their second defensive line. Meanwhile, the Third Division and the Bombay Brigade supported by field artillery advanced towards the Sikh left. About 1,500 Afghan cavalry charged from the Sikh left but were routed by Sindh Horse and the Ninth Lancers. The Sikh left then launched another attack of combined infantry and cavalry but were again driven back by the field battery and horse artillery of the Third Division. By one o'clock, the Sikhs were in full retreat. Gough won at the cost of 96 killed and 710 wounded. Sikh losses are unknown. Aside from ending the Second Sikh War in Britain's favor, Gujarat witnessed the first ever use of anesthetics on British soldiers. *See also* Khalsa; Punjab.

FURTHER READING: Cook, Hugh C. B. *The Sikh Wars: The British Army in the Punjab, 1845–1849.* London: L. Cooper, 1975.

KAUSHIK ROY

## Gurkha War

*See* Anglo-Nepal War

# H

## Haakon VII, King of Norway (1872–1957)

Born Christian Fredrick Charles George Valdemar Axel, Prince Charles for short, the future Haakon VII of Norway was the son of King Fredrick VIII of Denmark (1843–1912). In 1896, he married Princess Maud (1869–1938), daughter of King **Edward VII** of Great Britain (1841–1910). When Norway declared independence from Sweden in 1905, the Norwegian parliament offered Prince Charles the throne, which he accepted after a plebiscite held November 13–14 of that year. He took the name Haakon after several of his old Norse predecessors.

Many of the founding fathers of the new Norwegian state were republicans, but they realized that the public was largely monarchist. The choice of Haakon affirmed the ties to Denmark, which Norway was a dependency of from 1380 to 1814, and through his wife, the ties with Britain. The latter was paramount, as the British Empire was Norway's largest trading partner and also commanded the high seas on which Norway's important merchant fleet was navigating. Good relations with Britain also lessened the prospects of Swedish intervention aimed at quashing Norwegian independence, and that other great power would support Sweden in doing that.

In a constitutional monarchy based on parliamentarism, King Haakon's role as head of state made him more a ceremonial symbol than a real political force. At certain pivotal points in Norwegian history, however, he rose to the occasion. He became an important advisor on foreign policy to the government during World War I, in which Norway stayed neutral. In a 1927 political crisis, Haakon turned to the Labor Party and asked them to form a new government, as they were the largest party in the parliament. The task was formally assigned to the king by the Constitution, but reduced to a formality under normal circumstances after the introduction of parliamentarism in 1884.

FURTHER READING: Barton, H. Arnold. *Sweden and Visions of Norway Politics and Culture, 1814–1905.* Carbondale: Southern Illinois University Press, 2003; Stenersen, Øivind, and Ivar Libey. *A History of Norway from the Ice Age to the Age of Petroleum.* Lysaker: Dinamo Forlag, 2003.

FRODE LINDGJERDET

## Habsburg Dynasty

One of Europe's great dynasties, the Habsburgs were a royal and imperial Austro-German family that ruled Austria from 1282 until 1918. The Habsburgs also controlled **Hungary** and **Bohemia** from 1526 to1918 and ruled Spain and its empire from 1504 to 1506 and again from 1516 to 1700. The family name is derived from the Habichtsburg, or "Hawk's Castle," erected around 1000 in the Aargau region of Switzerland. From southwest Germany the family extended its holdings to the eastern reaches of the Holy Roman Empire, roughly today's Austria.

After 1521, the family split into the Austrian and the Spanish Habsburgs. The Austrian line held the title of Roman Emperor, as well as their hereditary lands and the kingdoms of Bohemia and Hungary; the Spanish Habsburgs ruled over Spain, the Netherlands, the Habsburgs' Italian possessions, and Portugal. With this enormous empire, the Habsburgs inherited a bulk of problems. Cooperation between Spanish and Imperial Habsburgs in the seventeenth century failed to maintain the hegemony that the dynasty had enjoyed in the sixteenth century. During these two centuries, the Habsburgs were preoccupied with halting the Ottoman advance into Europe. The Spanish Habsburgs died out in 1700.

In 1806, the Holy Roman Empire was ended by **Napoleon** Bonaparte's reorganization of the German states into the Confederation of the Rhine. Because of the possibility that Napoleon could be elected Roman Emperor, Franz II took steps to protect Habsburg interests. To guarantee his family's continued imperial status, he adopted a new hereditary title, Emperor of Austria, in 1804, thus becoming Franz I of Austria. To preclude the possibility of Napoleon's election, he officially dissolved the Holy Roman Empire in 1806. The Congress of **Vienna,** 1814–1815, then redrew the map of Europe. The Holy Roman Empire was replaced with a **German Confederation,** and Austria's Emperor held the permanent presidency of the confederation. Franz I's conservative outlook set the parameters especially for domestic policy, which Franz personally controlled until his death in 1835. The state council that Franz selected to rule in the name of his mentally incompetent son Ferdinand I ensured the continuance of his policies until revolution shocked Habsburg rule in 1848. Ferdinand abdicated on December 2, 1848, and his 18-year-old nephew was crowned Emperor Franz Joseph I. He would rule Austria for no less than 68 years.

In 1854, Franz Joseph married Duchess Elisabeth of the Bavarian House of Wittelsbach. She bore him four children: three daughters and the crown prince, Rudolf, who, in contrast with his conservative, if not reactionary, father, held liberal views. In 1881, he married Princess Stephanie of Belgium, daughter of King **Leopold II.** By the time their only child was born in 1883, the couple had drifted apart, and Rudolf found solace in drink and female companionship.

Rudolf's death, apparently through suicide, along with that of his mistress, Baroness Mary Vetsera, in 1889 at the estate of Mayerling near Vienna, made international headlines and fueled conspiracy rumors. According to official reports, their deaths were a result of Franz Joseph's demand that the couple end the relationship. Rudolf was declared to have been in a state of mental imbalance. Many people, however, doubted the veracity of the reports and claimed that Rudolf had been murdered as part of a conspiracy. Rudolf's death was an extremely grim chapter in the long line of outbreaks of mental instability in the Habsburg Dynasty caused by inbreeding. One younger brother to Franz Joseph, Archduke Viktor Ludwig, spent most of his life exiled, following scandals involving dressing up in women's clothes. Franz Joseph's brother, Archduke Maximilian, was crowned Emperor of **Mexico,** but his regime was overcome by insurgents after the French Emperor **Napoleon III** had withdrawn military aid for Maximilian. He was captured and executed on June 19, 1867.

In 1867, autonomy was given to Hungary under the terms of the **Ausgleich** or "compromise," turning the empire into the Dual Monarchy of **Austria-Hungary.** The December Constitution of 1867 placed no significant restrictions on the Emperor with regard to foreign and military affairs. Franz Joseph thus remained the ultimate arbiter of all important decisions. After the death of Crown Prince Rudolf, Franz Joseph's nephew, Archduke **Franz Ferdinand,** became heir to the throne. His marriage to the low-ranking Countess Sophie Chotek was permitted only after the couple had agreed that their children would have no access to the throne. Franz Ferdinand, an impatient and cynical character, had a strained relationship with the aged emperor and established a shadow government at his place of residence, the Belvedere Palace in Vienna. He alienated many sections of Austro-Hungarian political opinion with vague plans to be carried out after his accession to the throne. Both supporters and opponents of Austria-Hungary's dualist structure were suspicious of his ideas for a reform of the monarchy. When Franz Ferdinand and his wife were assassinated in Sarajevo on June 28, 1914, the attack on Habsburg imperial continuity led to a Great Power diplomatic crisis and ultimately a war of unprecedented scale.

The death of Franz Joseph on November 21, 1916 then deprived Austria-Hungary of his symbolic unifying presence. His grand-nephew Charles I, age 29, became his successor but was unprepared for the role. Although Charles was a pious Catholic of conciliatory nature, his good intentions were not reinforced by gifts beyond the ordinary. He was unable to put forward a meaningful program of reform and could not resist the centrifugal forces pulling the monarchy apart. On November 11, 1918, he renounced his state duties but did not abdicate his throne. He fled to Switzerland after Austria-Hungary had collapsed. Encouraged by Hungarian nationalists, Charles sought twice to reclaim the throne of Hungary, but failed. He died in exile in 1922. In Austria and Hungary, the monarchies were abolished and republics established. The Austrian parliament expelled the Habsburgs and confiscated all the official property in 1919. *See also* Habsburg Empire; Napoleonic Wars; Ottoman Empire; July Crisis.

FURTHER READING: Beller, Steven. *Francis Joseph.* London, New York: Longman, 1996; Bérenger, Jean. *A History of the Habsburg Empire.* London, New York: Longman, 1994; Cassels, Lavender. *Clash of Generations: A Habsburg Family Drama in the Nineteenth Century.* London: J. Murray, 1973; Fichtner, Paula Sutter. *The Habsburg Empire. From Dynasticism to Multinationalism.* Malabar, FL: Krieger, 1997; Macartney, Carlile A. *The Habsburg Empire, 1790–1918.* London: Weidenfeld & Nicolson, 1971; Okey, Robin. *The Habsburg Monarchy. c. 1765–1918 from Enlightenment to Eclipse.* Basingstoke: MacMillan Press, 2001.

MARTIN MOLL

## Habsburg Empire

The Habsburg Empire comprised the territories ruled by the Habsburg family, one of the most prominent royal dynasties in European history. The Habsburgs originated in the southwestern regions of the Holy Roman Empire, a conglomeration of territories in central Europe that lasted from the early Middle Ages to the start of the nineteenth century. The name of the dynasty derived in the eleventh century from a castle, the *Habichtsburg,* or Hawk's Castle, in what is today the Swiss canton of Aargau. In the following centuries, the Habsburgs lost control over their Swiss holdings but acquired smaller territories in southwestern Germany. The election of Rudolph I as German king and Holy Roman Emperor in 1271 marked the Habsburgs' rise to political prominence. In 1278, Rudolph seized control of Austria from King Ottokar of Bohemia who was killed by Habsburg forces at the Battle of Marchfeld. In the following centuries, the Habsburgs acquired the Tyrol and Carinthia, elevated themselves to the rank of Archdukes by using a forged document, and formed dynastic relations with the ruling houses of Poland, Bohemia, and **Hungary,** becoming, as a result, kings of the latter two realms. Effective control over Bohemia was limited by the power of the Bohemian estates, and the situation in Hungary was even more complex, with most of the territory inherited from King Louis (Lajos), who had been killed at the Battle of Mohács in 1526, controlled by the Ottomans or their vassals until the late seventeenth century. From the fifteenth century until the collapse of the Habsburg Empire in 1918, the Austrian, Bohemian, and Hungarian duchies and kingdoms formed the core of Habsburg territory in central Europe.

### The Ascent of the Habsburg Dynasty

The position of the Habsburgs as one of the most powerful dynasties in Europe rested on their ability to secure election as German kings and Holy Roman emperors from 1438 to 1806 with only a brief interlude in the eighteenth century. Holding the imperial crown enhanced the dynasty's prestige and allowed the Habsburgs to profit from the loyalty of imperial cities and estates. Another decisive factor in the Habsburgs' rise as a political force was their success in making politically advantageous marriages. In 1477, Maximilian, the son of Emperor Frederick III, married Mary, the daughter of Charles the Bold, duke of Burgundy, and in 1496, their son, Philip the Handsome, married Juana, the daughter of the Catholic monarchs of Spain, Ferdinand of Aragon and Isabella of Castile. Through these two matches, Philip and Juana's son, Charles of Ghent, succeeded his maternal grandfather, Ferdinand, as Charles I, king of **Spain,** in 1516, and his paternal grandfather, Maximilian, as Charles V, Holy Roman emperor, in 1519. By the end of the sixteenth century, the Habsburgs ruled not only Spain and the empire, but the **Netherlands** (part of the old Burgundian state), the vast Spanish empire in the Americas, southern Italy, and Portugal. For a time in the 1550s, Charles's son Philip, as husband to Queen Mary, the daughter of Henry VIII, was also king of England. After Charles's death in 1558, the Habsburg domains, which had nearly encircled France, the dynasty's main rival, split into two parts. Descending from Charles's brother Ferdinand, the Austrian branch, the *Casa d'Austria,* or House of Austria, ruled over the family's central European possessions and maintained the succession to the throne of the Holy Roman Empire from 1548–56 to 1740. After the Ottoman defeat at the Battle of Vienna in 1683, the Austrian Habsburgs also controlled the Kingdom of Hungary. Descended from Charles's son Philip, the Spanish branch of the family ruled Spain and much of the Netherlands until 1700. The two branches of the dynasty intermarried frequently to consolidate their possessions and to cooperate in international politics.

From the point of view of France, with Habsburg domains on its eastern, southern, and northern borders, the dynasty's dominance was a serious threat to European peace. After the death of Charles II, the last Spanish Habsburg, a bitter fight over succession to his throne led to the War of Spanish Succession (1700–1713), which pitted Austria, in alliance with other states, against France. Although they lost the Spanish Crown to the French House of Bourbon, the Austrian Habsburgs successfully seized the Spanish Netherlands (modern Belgium) and parts of northern and central **Italy.** After 1713, the center of the Habsburg Empire was Vienna, not Madrid. Because he lacked a male successor, Emperor Charles VI issued the Pragmatic Sanction (1713), which confirmed provisions for a female succession and insisted on the monarchy's indivisibility. Through concessions, Charles tried to win the approval of the Pragmatic Sanction from the estates in the various Habsburg territories and from other European monarchs. Nevertheless, after his death in 1740, his heir and daughter Maria Theresa had to fight for eight years to secure her rights and titles and to place her husband on the throne of the Holy Roman Empire. Even then, the strategically important and economically valuable province of Silesia was lost to Fredrick II of **Prussia;** however, Maria Theresa launched a number of important reforms of the bureaucracy, the military, and education. Her son Joseph II tried to modernize and militarize his realm in a more radical fashion but provoked violent opposition in Hungary and the Austrian Netherlands. Joseph's failure to centralize governmental structures by following the examples set by France and Prussia demonstrated the limits of the dynasty's grip on power.

### Nationalist and Napoleonic Challenges

Without the cooperation of the traditional elites in the various kingdoms and lands, the multiethnic Habsburg Empire could not be held together. At the same time, it was the dynasty that provided the indispensable unifying bond. Therefore nationalism and the sovereignty of the people were not only anathema to the dynasty, but a deadly threat to the political survival of the union of lands and crowns ruled by the Habsburgs. Since the late eighteenth century, the Austrians sought to contain or destroy revolutionary and nationalist movements. This policy proved costly. In the wars against revolutionary France and **Napoleon** from 1789 to 1815, Austria not only lost the Netherlands, southwestern Germany, and northern Italy but, after the defeat at **Wagram** in 1809, was forced to cooperate with Napoleon to avoid another armed clash with the French emperor. The new Austrian foreign minister, Count Klemens von **Metternich,** nevertheless decided to break with Napoleon and rejoin the anti-Napoleonic coalition in 1813. Together with his British counterpart, Lord **Castlereagh,** Metternich worked for a lasting European settlement in 1814–1815, in the wake of Napoleon's final defeat. The **Congress of Vienna** in 1815 and the working of the Congress system until the 1820s gave Austria more than its due share of political influence in Europe. In terms of territory, Austria gave up its former possessions in southwestern Germany and the Netherlands. Instead, Salzburg became Austrian and the Habsburgs kept most of the Polish territory acquired in 1774 and 1795. In Italy, Lombardy and Venetia formed a kingdom united with Austria.

In 1804, in response to the self-coronation of Napoleon as Emperor of the French, Holy Roman Emperor Francis II claimed the title of hereditary Austrian emperor. Under French pressure, Francis in effect dissolved the Holy Roman Empire in 1806. At the Congress of Vienna in 1815, Metternich refrained from any attempt to resurrect the Holy Roman Empire, and in the newly created German Confederation Austria chaired the deliberations of the diet but could not achieve much without Prussian consent. Still, through Metternich's skilful diplomacy, the Habsburg Empire was able to win the support of Prussia and other German states to use the confederation as a tool to suppress liberal and nationalistic groups in Germany. In Italy there was no equivalent of the German Confederation, so Austria intervened militarily when revolutionary movements threatened to destabilize the Italian states. Austrian antirevolutionary zeal undermined the solidarity among the Great Powers and damaged Austro-British cooperation in the 1820s; Metternich found himself isolated when Britain, France, and Russia fought for the independence of **Greece** from Turkey in 1827. Austria refrained from a policy of territorial expansion on the Balkan Peninsula and considered the preservation of the **Ottoman Empire** as indispensable to its own survival. The Habsburg Empire thus acted as the most clear cut case of a status quo power and annexed Kraków only to contain the spread of Polish nationalism. Unable to establish an efficient tax-system, however, the empire suffered from inadequate financial means to play the role of Great Power. Overcommitted and underfinanced, Austria depended on a favorable climate of antirevolutionary consensus and a preference for peaceful crisis settlement among the other Great Powers. Austria's policy of repression, directed against liberals and nationalists at home and abroad, collapsed in 1848.

The revolution of 1848–1849 challenged Habsburg rule in several ways. In Vienna, a liberal government replaced Metternich, and an assembly was summoned to deliberate and decide on a new constitution. In Hungary, nationalists took control and were fighting for independence. In Italy, nationalist uprisings and an attack on Piedmont-Sardinia aimed at the expulsion of Austria from the region. With young Emperor **Francis Joseph** and a conservative government under Prince Felix Schwarzenberg in charge, the Habsburgs were able to fend off the danger. By 1850, the Habsburg rule had been restored, as was the German Confederation. Francis Joseph's neo-absolutist regime was based on tradition, repression, economic progress, and prestige. During the **Crimean War** (1853–56), Austria's policy offended a **Russia Empire** that had supported the Habsburgs against the Hungarian insurgency in 1849 yet did not lead to an alliance with France and Great Britain. In 1858, the French Emperor **Napoleon III** formed an alliance with Piedmont-Sardinia to expel Austria from northern Italy. In response to Sardinian provocations, the Habsburg monarchy went to war. Defeated by the French-Sardinian alliance in the Battles of **Magenta** and **Solferino,** Austria was forced to cede Lombardy in 1859. The Habsburg Empire had no choice but to watch helplessly from the sidelines as the Italian kingdoms and principalities were swept aside by a combination of nationalism and Sardinian power politics. The next blow to Habsburg prestige came in the 1860s when Prussia under Prime Minister Otto von **Bismarck** outmaneuvered Austrian foreign policy in the debate about a reformed German Confederation and the future of the former Danish duchies of Schleswig and Holstein, both occupied by Austrian and Prussian forces after the German-Danish War of 1864. The Prussian secession from the German Confederation led in 1866 to war between Prussia and Austria and most of the other German states. The Battle of **Königgrätz** ended with a clear Prussian victory and forced Francis Joseph to accept Austria's exclusion from Germany. Victories over Prussia's ally Italy in the Battles of Custoza and Lissa were of little political significance and could not prevent the loss of Venetia. The creation of two new nation-states, Germany and Italy, had come at the expense of the Habsburg Empire, which could survive as a Great Power only as long as the opposition within it could be mollified.

### Constitutional Reform

From 1860 to 1867, constitutional reform therefore ranked high on the political agenda. Neo-absolutist rule gave way to broader political participation, lively public debate, and the protection of individual rights. The most difficult aspect was the position of Hungary within the framework of the empire. The Hungarian opposition under leaders like Ferenc **Deák** and Count Gyula **Andrássy** negotiated the **Ausgleich,** or Compromise, of 1867, which transformed the Habsburg possessions into **Austria-Hungary.** From 1867 to 1918, the so-called Dual Monarchy symbolized a union of the Kingdom of Hungary and Austria over the other kingdoms and lands of the Habsburgs; both parts shared the person of the monarch, the King of Hungary and Emperor of Austria, and the settlement of succession laid down in the Pragmatic Sanction of 1713–1723 was the constitutional foundation of Austria-Hungary. According to Law XII of 1867, approved by the Hungarian diet, Hungary also accepted a common foreign policy and a common defense. Currency and foreign trade issues were also to be resolved in common. After 1868, a common Austro-Hungarian army and navy formed the Habsburg monarchy's fighting forces, but there would also be defense forces for Hungary and Austria. The common ministers of foreign affairs, war, and finances and the prime ministers of Austria and Hungary would deliberate on questions of common interest. Delegations from the parliaments in Vienna and Budapest would discuss regularly the common ministers' policy. The contributions of Hungary and Austria to the budget of the common ministries had to be negotiated every 10 years. Among the common ministers, the minister of foreign affairs stood out as minister of the Imperial and Royal House. He presided over the session of the common ministerial council if the monarch were not present in the council. High politics were traditionally the most prestigious aspect of government policy, and the decision to wage war or to make peace was considered to be the monarch's prerogative. In the Dual Monarchy, where there was no common prime minister or chancellor, the foreign minister served as the monarch's most important political advisor.

In domestic affairs, the emperor and king had to rely on the heads of governments in Vienna and Budapest. The prime ministers of both Austria and Hungary were appointed and dismissed by the monarch, who had to approve any legislation, but the prime ministers nonetheless needed the backing of a parliamentary majority to get their budgets and bills through the legislative assemblies. Emergency legislation offered an opportunity to circumvent unruly parliaments, especially in Austria, but only for brief periods. In Hungary, support for the prime minister in the diet was almost indispensable. The composition of the parliaments in Vienna and Budapest differed significantly. Austria's ethnic diversity was adequately reflected in parliament, at least by comparison with the ethnically homogenous Hungarian diet. Magyars, the Hungarian-speaking segment of the population, were overrepresented as a consequence of restrictive electoral laws excluding the less affluent and mostly non-Magyar Hungarian citizens. In Austria, the electorate was gradually expanded and universal male suffrage introduced in 1907. The crown supported this democratization in the hope that nationalistic parties with their middle-class supporters would lose clout. The Austrian crown lands had their own parliaments and electoral rules; the administration of the crown lands was headed by a governor, chosen by the emperor and usually drawn from the high nobility. Within the framework of the Kingdom of Hungary, the Kingdom of Croatia-Slavonia enjoyed a high degree of autonomy, whereas the rest of the Hungarian realm had a more centralized structure than Austria.

On the domestic agenda, dualism and the nationality question stood out. Whether the settlement of 1867 was sufficient to secure Hungarian independence was hotly debated among Hungarian politicians. With the diet in Budapest dominated by the small Hungarian-speaking elite of landowners and bourgeoisie, social or national divisions in the parliament were less significant than the divide between the supporters of the Ausgleich and the followers of almost complete independence. The Liberals under the leadership of Kálmán Tisza accepted the Compromise of 1867 as the legal basis of Hungary's place in the Habsburg monarchy and controlled Hungarian politics until 1890. Over the following decade, the economic success and growing self-confidence of the Magyar middle class fueled a significant rise in Magyar nationalism. The Independence Party followed the tradition of the revolutionaries of 1848–1849 and put pressure on the Hungarian government to aim for Hungary's independence. In 1903, the conflict between Hungary and the crown escalated, when Francis Joseph upheld the status quo of the common army in the face of attempts to establish Hungarian as the language of command. A coalition formed around the Independence Party was forced to give in to Francis Joseph when the king threatened to have a general franchise bill introduced in parliament in 1905. In the last years before World War I, István **Tisza,** the leader of the Hungarian moderates, managed to rein in the opposition within the diet and became the most influential politician in Austro-Hungarian politics. In the late 1880s, Tisza became the first Hungarian prime minister willing to co-finance a massive military buildup. Stability in Hungary and better cooperation between Vienna and Budapest, however, could be achieved only by accepting Magyar dominance in Hungary and Hungarian assertiveness in Austro-Hungarian negotiations. To **Francis Ferdinand,** Francis Joseph's nephew and heir apparent, this was anathema. He believed that Hungary's strong position within the Dual Monarchy would block any sensible solution to nationality problems and would eventually bring down the Habsburg Empire. Yet he and his supporters tried in vain to roll back the political influence of Hungary's elite, so when war broke out in 1914, dualism was still one of the decisive features of the Habsburg Empire's political system.

### The Balkan Tinderbox

The nationality question was no less persistent than the quarreling about dualism. With 11 officially recognized nationalities, none of them constituting a majority, Austria-Hungary certainly was a multiethnic empire. By 1910, the Austrian population broke down into the following percentages: 35.6 percent Germans, 23 percent Czechs, 17.8 percent Poles, and 12.6 percent Ruthenians (Ukrainians). In the same year, the population of the lands of the Hungarian crown was 48.1 percent Magyar, 9.8 percent German, 9.4 percent Slovak, 14.1 percent Rumanian, 8.8 percent Croatian, and 5.3 percent Serb. On the eve of World War I, the Magyars were almost a majority language group in Hungary yet only one-fifth of the Habsburg Empire's population. Even the Germans could claim no more than 23.9

percent of Austria-Hungary's total population. Unlike the Magyars, the Germans watched their share of the population dwindling, albeit rather slowly; the traditional dominance of Germans in most of the crown lands looked threatened by a Slav population, growing stronger in relative terms. In Bohemia, with its Czech majority, German and Czech nationalists were at loggerheads over language policy issues. When the Austrian government under Prime Minister Count Badeni proposed a settlement that strengthened the role of Czech in official use in 1897, Germans in Bohemia and in other parts of Austria protested in the streets, and German politicians obstructed the parliament in Vienna. Badeni's decrees were revoked and the Bohemian nationality problem was still waiting for a viable solution when Austria-Hungary finally collapsed in 1918.

Other nationality conflicts, in Moravia and Bukovina for example, could be solved by compromise. In Galicia, the Poles made some concessions to the Ruthenians. In Hungary, the government's policy of Magyarization worked well in the Hungarian heartland but alienated the Slovak, Rumanian, Croatian, and Serb minorities. The Croats in Croatia-Slavonia were able to defend their cultural autonomy. Among Croatians and Serbs in the lands of the Hungarian crown and in Austria, different strands of nationalism evolved, one of them aiming at the unification of the Habsburg monarchy's South Slavs. This challenged the structure of the Dual Monarchy and called for the incorporation of Bosnia and Herzegovina.

**Bosnia-Herzegovina**, part of the Ottoman Empire and home to Catholic Croats, Orthodox Serbs, and South Slav Muslims, was occupied by Austria-Hungary after the **Congress of Berlin** in 1878. Administered by a special department of the common ministry of finance, Bosnia-Herzegovina belonged to neither Austria nor Hungary. The unilateral annexation of the territory in 1908 at the behest of foreign minister Aloys Lexa von **Aehrenthal** caused an international crisis but failed to stabilize the internal situation in Bosnia-Herzegovina. Radical Serb and South Slav nationalistic groups, encouraged and supported by factions of the elite in the kingdom of Serbia, agitated against Habsburg rule. One such organization, the Black Hand, assassinated Francis Ferdinand and his wife in Sarajevo on July 28, 1914. Austria-Hungary's political leaders, first and foremost the new foreign minister Count Leopold Berchtold, decided to use the murder of the Habsburg Empire's heir apparent as an opportunity to wage punitive war on Serbia for its provocations going back several years. Bosnia-Herzegovina was the only example of Austro-Hungarian territorial expansion in the age of imperialism, and the western half of the Balkan Peninsula was considered to be the Habsburg Empire's "natural" sphere of influence. The **Balkan Wars** of 1912–1913 made a mockery of this miniature version of imperialism. In addition, Serbia's policy in the South Slav question was perceived as a deadly threat to Austria-Hungary's survival as a Great Power. To quell the South Slav opposition within the Habsburg Empire and to defend its Great Power status, Austria-Hungary posted an ultimatum to Serbia that ultimately triggered war against its neighbor in July 1914. The political and military leaders of the Habsburg Empire and Francis Joseph were well aware that an attack on Serbia could lead to Russian military intervention and to a wider Great Power conflict but were not deterred.

There was hope that Russia, because of its domestic instability, might not enter the fray, and, in the event of a European war, Austria-Hungary could rely on German assistance. In 1879, the Habsburg monarchy had formed the Dual Alliance with Germany, which was a defensive alliance against Russia and was supplemented in

1881 by the Triple Alliance with Germany and Italy and in 1882 by a secret alliance treaty with Rumania. As a result of the domestic quarreling about dualism, however, the Habsburg monarchy had neglected the buildup of its reserve armed forces since the late 1880s. Austria-Hungary took part in the European armaments race after 1912 but could not make up for decades of a self-imposed blockade. In addition, Germany would have to face the possibility of a two-front-war against Russia and France, which had been united in a military alliance since the 1890s.

Greatly exaggerated hopes in Italy's and Rumania's support or at least neutrality and extreme optimism with regard to the German and Austro-Hungarian offensives at the beginning of the war proved to be illusory. The Austro-Hungarian army under the leadership of Franz Conrad von Hötzendorf suffered defeat in 1914–1915. With German help, Habsburg troops were able to achieve victories against Russia and Serbia in 1915, against Rumania in 1916, and against Italy in 1917, but coalition warfare led to an ever-increasing dependence on Germany and made it more or less impossible to negotiate a separate peace treaty with the Entente powers. After Francis Joseph's death in November 1916, the new Emperor, Charles I, tried to win more freedom of maneuver, but his policy of secret negotiations with the Entente backfired when the talks were made public by the French in 1918. In the face of growing unrest caused by the hardship of war and calls for independence among the Habsburg Empire's Slavs, Charles offered a root-and-branch reform of Austria-Hungary's political structure in October 1918. It was too late. The Austro-Hungarian front in Italy was already collapsing and nationalists seized effective control in many parts of the empire.

Austria-Hungary broke apart in November 1918, and Charles was helpless to prevent the Habsburg Empire's dismemberment. He went into exile in Switzerland in March 1919. Two attempts to restore Habsburg rule in Hungary failed in 1921, and Charles was forced to leave Europe for the Portuguese island of Madeira, where he died on April 1, 1922. His empire had given way to several newly created states. From beginning to end, the Habsburg Empire had been a union of territories kept together by the ruling house, the court, the crown's advisors, and the military and civilian servants of the Habsburg dynasty. Tradition and convenience had provided for widespread loyalty as long as middle class nationalism was confined to inter-ethnic bickering, but in the face of a long and unsuccessful war, "divide and rule" tactics could not save an empire that had endured for centuries. *See also* Appendix *Words and Deeds,* Doc. 24; Balkan Wars; Black Hand; Congress of Vienna; Eastern Question; Napoleonic Wars.

FURTHER READING: Bérenger, Jean. *A History of the Habsburg Empire, 1780–1918.* London: Longman, 1997; Bridge, Francis R. *The Habsburg Monarchy Among the Great Powers, 1815–1918.* New York: St. Martin's, 1990; Cornwall, Mark, ed. *The Last Years of Austria-Hungary: A Multi-National Experiment in Early Twentieth Century Europe.* Exeter: University of Exeter Press, 2002; Evans, Richard J. W. *The Making of the Habsburg Monarchy 1550–1700: An Interpretation.* Oxford: Clarendon Press, 1984; Ingrao, Charles. *The Habsburg Monarchy, 1618–1815.* Cambridge: Cambridge University Press, 1994; Kann, Robert A. *A History of the Habsburg Empire, 1526–1918.* Berkeley: University of California Press, 1974; Kann, Robert A. *The Multinational Empire: Nationalism and National Reform in the Habsburg Monarchy, 1848–1918.* 2 vols. New York: Octagon Books, 1964; Macartney, C. A. *The Habsburg Empire, 1790–1918.* London: Weidenfeld & Nicolson, 1968; Mason, John W. *The Dissolution of the Austro-Hungarian Empire, 1867–1918.* London and New York: Longman 1985; May, Arthur J. *The Hapsburg Monarchy, 1867–1914.* Cambridge, MA: Harvard University Press, 1951; Sked, Alan. *The Decline and Fall of the Habsburg Empire, 1815–1918.*

London: Longman, 1989; Taylor, A.J.P. *The Habsburg Monarchy, 1809–1918.* Chicago: University of Chicago Press, 1976.

GUENTHER KRONENBITTER

## Hague Conferences (1899, 1907)

International conferences formalizing the laws of war. Many contemporaries imagined that they would show the way to the abolition of war and its replacement by a system of arbitration. The Hague Conference of 1899 was called in response to an 1898 diplomatic note known as the Tsar's Rescript, circulated by Tsar Nicolas II, who wanted to abolish war on Christian grounds. The idea was greeted enthusiastically by pacifists and liberals, with respectful circumspection by most governments, and with some derision in conservative and military circles. The 1899 conference produced some quickly obsolete provisions against dropping bombs from balloons, and some rapidly ignored prohibitions against chemical warfare, but it also led to the formation of the Permanent Court of Arbitration, still in existence, to which consenting states may submit disputes for arbitration.

The 1899 conference led to the Second Hague Conference of 1907, which had more success in formalizing the customary laws of war, in particular those pertaining to the rights of neutrals, the conventions of land warfare, and the opening of conflicts. The 1907 convention also produced statutes pertaining to the long-controversial topic of the status of prizes taken in naval warfare, a topic that submarines, torpedoes, and long-range gunnery shortly made anachronistic. A third Hague conference, planned for 1914, never took place. Initiated by the most autocratic monarch in Europe, the Hague conferences nevertheless attracted high hopes from many on the reformist left. They became the models for many future attempts at multilateral international diplomacy, their statutes on the laws of land warfare are generally accepted today, and the internationalist spirit of the Hague conferences was a precursor to the League of Nations and later the United Nations.

FURTHER READING: Ceadel, Martin. *Semi-Detached Idealists: The British Peace Movement and International Relations, 1854–1945.* Oxford, 2000; Perris, G. H. *A Short History of War and Peace.* London: Williams and Norgate, 1911.

MARK F. PROUDMAN

## Haig, Douglas (1861–1928)

British military leader who became commander-in-chief of all British forces on the Western Front in 1915 and collaborated closely with Marshal Ferdinand **Foch,** the Generalissimo of Allied Armies in France, until the Allied victory of 1918. Haig joined the army in 1885 and served with distinction as a cavalry officer in the Sudan in 1898 and in the Second Boer War, 1899–1902. Thereafter, he served in India but between 1906 and 1909 implemented reforms in the War Office under Richard **Haldane.** With the outbreak of war in 1914, Haig initially commanded a corps of the British Expeditionary Force before succeeding General John French at the head the British army in 1915. Haig was a determined yet unimaginative commander considered by Prime Minister David Lloyd George to be responsible for heavy British losses at the Battle of the Somme and the Third Battle of Ypres.

FURTHER READING: Sixsmith, E.K.G. *Douglas Haig.* London: Weidenfled and Nicolson, 1976; Winter, Denis. *Haig's Command: A Reassessment.* Barnsley: Pen & Sword Military Classics, 2004.

CARL CAVANAGH HODGE

## Haiti

Haiti was the second colony in the Americas, after the United States, to win its independence from European control. Initially a Spanish possession peopled in large part by slaves imported from Africa, Haiti was ceded to France in 1697. A slave revolt led by Toussaint L'Ouverture first erupted in 1791 and defeated the French colonial forces but then united with them to defeat invading British and Spanish forces in response to a decree from the French revolutionary government abolishing slavery. In 1802, a new invasion force was dispatched to Haiti by Napoleon. Toussaint was persuaded to agree to a truce, but was betrayed and shipped to prison in France where he died. The cause was immediately taken up by a former slave, Jacques Dessalines, whose army, aided somewhat by the ravages of yellow fever among the French, won the Battle of Vertières in November 1803. On January 1, Haiti declared its independence. *See also:* French Empire, Slavery.

FURTHER READING: Heinl, Robert Debs, and Nanct Gordon Heinl. *Written in Blood: The Story of the Haitian People.* Lanham, MD: University Press of America, 1996.

CARL CAVANAGH HODGE

## Haldane, Richard Burdon (1856–1928)

Richard Haldane was a British Liberal imperialist in the 1890s and a supporter of the Boer War. He is remembered for his army reforms of 1907, which created the British Territorial Army reserve system still in use, a system that served Britain well in the World Wars. Haldane was born into a Scottish Calvinist family, although like many young men of his generation he developed religious doubts. Educated at the Universities of Edinburgh and Göttingen, he was called to the bar in 1879. Haldane was known throughout his life for his philosophic temperament. Henry **Campbell-Bannerman,** with whom he periodically crossed swords politically, referred to Haldane as "Schopenhauer." Haldane was involved in the founding of the London School of Economics in 1895 and in higher education reform.

He was first elected to Parliament as a Gladstonian Liberal in 1886, along with his friend H. H. **Asquith.** Haldane had friends across the political spectrum, ranging from the Webbs to A. J. **Balfour,** but as a Liberal imperialist he supported, along with Asquith and Lord **Rosebery,** a strong stance against France in the **Fashoda Incident** of 1898. With other Liberal imperialists, he also broke rank with the **Liberal Party** leader Campbell-Bannerman, supporting the Conservative government's policy at the outbreak of the Second Boer War in 1899.

Haldane initially opposed Campbell-Bannerman's accession to the premiership in 1905, thinking the latter too anti-imperial, but he went to the War Office in his government. He became an active reformer and succeeded in gaining the wholehearted cooperation of the army staff. He was responsible for founding the Officers'

Training Corps, which drew many educated young men into the army; the Territorial Army, effectively the army reserves; and the Imperial General Staff. He took relatively little part, owing to ill health, in the passing of the Parliament Act of 1911, but went to the Lords in that year and in 1912 became Lord Chancellor. He briefly returned to the War Office during the crisis of August 1914, and left office for the last time in May 1915. Although attacked for his philo-Germanic leanings by the Tory press, in fact his work at the War Office was a solid contribution to the British cause in the World Wars. *See also* Boer Wars; Liberal Imperialists.

FURTHER READING: Koss, S. E. *Lord Haldane: Scapegoat for Liberalism.* New York: Columbia University Press, 1969; Matthew, H.C.G. *The Liberal Imperialists.* Oxford: University Press, 1973; Maurice, F. B. *Haldane: The Life of Viscount Haldane of Cloan.* 2 vols. London: Faber, 1937–1939.

MARK F. PROUDMAN

## Hamilton, Alexander (1755–1804)

American soldier, politician, statesman, and constitutional theorist of the Federalist Papers, as well as first Secretary of the Treasury of the **United States** (1789–1795). Hamilton was born in the Caribbean on the tiny island of Nevis. When he was 10 years old, his father moved the family to the nearby island of St. Croix and subsequently abandoned them. His mother opened a shop while Hamilton found a job as a clerk at a trading post where he was first immersed in bookkeeping and economics. The main trade in the Caribbean at this time was sugar and slaves formed the majority of workforce. Witnessing the brutal reality of slavery firsthand, Hamilton developed an aversion to the practice that prevented him from ever owning slaves or endorsing the practice. At 17, Hamilton left for the colony of New York in 1772 and enrolled at King's College, now Columbia University. He joined the New York Militia in 1775 and became a captain of an artillery unit. After two years of service, he gained the respect of General George Washington, who appointed him his aide-de-camp with the rank of lieutenant colonel. His intelligence and his proximity to Washington ensured his position as an important political figure after the Revolutionary War was won.

In 1780, Hamilton married Elizabeth Schuyler, began a successful Manhattan law practice, and represented New York at the Continental Congress in Philadelphia. Hamilton led the Federalist side in the constitutional debates, accounting for two-thirds of *The Federalist,* a series of 85 newspaper essays written together with James Madison and John Jay on the fundamental principles and constituent institutions of government that represent both the first major work of political theory produced in America and the blueprint for *The Constitution of the United States of America.* The coherence of Hamilton's ideas and the force with which he articulated them did much to secure ratification of the Constitution. As Secretary of the Treasury to President Washington, Hamilton was able to encourage manufacturing, allow the national government to assume responsibility for the country's debt, create a national bank that standardized and controlled the currency, and was able to maintain friendly ties with the British government. Hamilton found himself in a constant struggle with anti-Federalists, Thomas **Jefferson** and James **Madison** most prominent among them, who wished to keep the federal government's power to a minimum. Federalists and Anti-Federalists disagreed on almost every issue—save that of territorial expansion.

Expansion was deemed not only desirable but also a necessity in ensuring the security of the republic. Hamilton personally went as far as trying to form a permanent standing army to accomplish this task, but he was impeded when then President John **Adams** disagreed. The little republic was, Hamilton maintained, "the embryo of a great empire" and the powers of Europe would happily crush the American experiment. In the meantime he deemed it imperative that the United States avoid any overseas commitments beyond "occasional alliances," a sentiment evident in the Farewell Address of Washington's presidency, which Hamilton co-authored. The speech is often cited as the first article of American isolationism in the first half of the twentieth century. Hamilton used his influence to help his rival Jefferson to the presidency in 1801 over Vice President Aaron Burr, whom he distrusted personally and politically. He also supported Jefferson in the Louisiana Purchase, deeming it important to American security that European power be eliminated from the North American continent and the hemisphere. In this attitude he anticipated the Monroe Doctrine. Hamilton died young and suddenly at the age of 49 in a pistol duel with Burr. *See also* Louisiana Purchase; Monroe Doctrine.

FURTHER READING: Chernow, Rob. *Alexander Hamilton*. New York: Penguin Books, 2004; Ellis, Joseph J. *His Excellency: George Washington*. New York: Knopf Publishing, 2004; Hamilton, Alexander. *Hamilton: Writings*. Washington, DC: Library of America, 2001.

ARTHUR HOLST

## Haussmann, Baron George Eugène (1809–1891)

A civic planner responsible for the radical rebuilding of the city of Paris. Born in Paris to a Protestant family from Alsace, Hausmann had a successful civil service career and was prefect for the department of the Seine from 1853 to 1870. He was appointed in 1853 by **Napoleon III** to modernize the French capital. The city was comprehensively transformed in a massive public works project under Hausmann's direction. Broad and long tree-lines avenues and boulevards were cut through the tangled mass of narrow streets and old urban neighborhoods. The goals of the project were both functional and aesthetic. The city was to be more sanitary with vastly improved traffic flow and commercial accessibility. The broad avenues, meanwhile, made it impossible for insurrectionists to erect barricades as they had in 1848, while the system of converging avenues at *étoiles* and the proximity of both to the main railway stations made it possible for Adolfe Thiers to transport large numbers of troops from the provinces to any point in the capital and thus crush the Paris Commune in 1870. At the same time, the classicism of grand avenues such as the *Avenue de la Grande Armée* radiating out from the *Arc de la Triomphe* evoked Napoleonic might and gave Paris the look and feel of an imperial capital.

FURTHER READING: Saalman, Howard. *Haussmann: Paris Transformed*. New York: G. Braziller, 1971.

CARL CAVANAGH HODGE

# Hawaii

A group of eight major islands located in the Pacific Ocean 2,500 miles off the California coast, Hawaii became the first overseas territory of the **United States** in 1898. Throughout the nineteenth century, Hawaii served as central crossroads of the North Pacific for whaling and the Asia trade. The islands' strategic location in the central Pacific made Hawaii of major importance to all great powers, especially the United States.

Since the 1820s, American protestant **missionaries** turned planters and businessmen helped to maneuver the kingdom of Hawaii, which had been politically unified in 1810 under Kamehameha the Great, into a position of a culturally and commercially dependent **protectorate** of the United States. The new residents on the islands accelerated the "Americanization" of Hawaiian society. Hawaii's first constitution of 1840 reflected the dual influence of American political thought and missionary work, as it was based on the Declaration of Independence and the Bible. Americans shaped the educational system, advised Hawaiian monarchs, achieved government positions, and increased the Hawaiian aristocracy's economic dependency through debt stimulation.

From 1842 up to the 1890s, successive U.S. administrations supported the Tyler Doctrine, which extended the **Monroe Doctrine** to Hawaii and warned Britain and France against any attempts at annexation. In 1881, Secretary of State James G. Blaine even described Hawaii as an essential part of the American system of states and key to the North Pacific trade. The 1875 reciprocity treaty gave the islands' most important product, Hawaiian sugar, duty-free entry into the United States provided Hawaiians would not allow territorial concessions to other powers. The relationship further intensified when the Hawaiian government granted Washington naval rights in Pearl Harbor.

Expansionist pressure for annexation during mid-century failed to convince the U.S. government, as Americans virtually dominated most aspects of Hawaiian life without the responsibility of formal rule. In 1893, however, an American-supported rebellion deposed Queen Lilioukalana in response to a deepening social and economic crisis in the islands and the queen's efforts to contain American influence. The new government was immediately recognized in Washington, but annexation was heavily debated and ultimately postponed. The prospect of inclusion of a substantial body of "racially diverse" Chinese, Japanese, and native Hawaiians remained a main argument against annexation. Only a few years later, however, changing strategic considerations of control over the Pacific, the fear of Japanese domination of the islands, and the lure of the Asian mainland resulted in the annexation of Hawaii in 1898. The Organic Act of 1900 incorporated the Territory of Hawaii into the United States and granted Hawaiians U.S. citizenship. By the outbreak of World War I, Hawaii had been transformed into a major army and navy base for the protection of America's colonial Pacific empire. *See also* Japanese Empire; Navalism; United States.

FURTHER READING: Kuykendall, Ralph Simpson. *The Hawaiian Kingdom.* 3 vols. Honolulu: University of Hawaii Press, 1965; Merry, Sally E. *Colonizing Hawai'i: The Cultural Power of Law.* Princeton, NJ: Princeton University Press, 1999; Osborne, Thomas J. *"Empire Can Wait": American Opposition to Hawaiian Expansion, 1893–1898.* Kent, OH: Kent State University Press, 1981.

FRANK SCHUMACHER

## Hay-Bunau-Varilla Treaty (1903)

A treaty between the **United States** and **Panama** granting the United States the right to build an Isthmian canal connecting the Atlantic and Pacific Oceans. Signed on November 18, 1903 by U.S. Secretary of State John Hay and Panama's Philippe Bunau-Varilla, the treaty was ratified by the U.S. Senate on February 23, 1904, and it was proclaimed February 26, 1904.

After Colombia rejected the **Hay-Herrán Treaty,** Bunau-Varilla, a canal engineer and organizer of the French New Panama Canal Company, organized a Panamanian uprising. American warships prevented Colombian forces from suppressing the revolt, the United States extended recognition three days later, and Bunau-Varilla and Hay quickly signed the new treaty. The treaty gave the United States effective sovereignty over Panama, which granted "in perpetuity" a 10-mile strip across the Isthmus. The United States also secured the right to construct and operate a canal across the Isthmus and use or control Panama's inland waterways and other Panamanian territory. Panama could not tax the canal, equipment, or workers. The United States was to pay $10 million plus $250,000 annual rent, beginning nine years after ratification, and pledged to maintain Panama's independence and the canal's neutrality. Finally, Washington agreed to purchase the assets of the canal company for $40 million.

The revolution and treaty highlighted American hemispheric power. The United States effectively ran Panama until a 1936 agreement cancelled the most interventionist features of the 1903 treaty. *See also* Monroe Doctrine; Navalism; Roosevelt Corollary.

FURTHER READING: Bevans, Charles I. *Treaties and Other International Agreements of the United States of America 1776–1949.* Vol. 10. Washington: Government Printing Office, 1972, pp. 663–672; Collin, Richard H. *Theodore Roosevelt's Caribbean: The Panama Canal, the Monroe Doctrine, and the Latin American Context.* Baton Rouge: Louisiana State University Press, 1990; Mellander, G. A. *The United States in Panamanian Politics: The Intriguing Formative Years.* Danville: Interstate Publishing, 1967.

KENNETH J. BLUME

## Hay-Herrán Treaty (1903)

A treaty granting the **United States** the right to build a canal across **Panama.** Signed by U.S. Secretary of State John Hay and Colombia Foreign Minister Tomás Herrán on January 22, 1903, and ratified by the U.S. Senate on March 17, 1903, the treaty was rejected by Colombia's congress on August 12, 1903.

By the late nineteenth century, the geopolitical necessities of international trade and a two-ocean navy combined to convince American policymakers of the need for a U.S.-controlled Isthmian canal. Through intense lobbying, agents of the bankrupt French New Panama Canal Company convinced Congress to select the Panama route. Negotiations with the Colombian government commenced shortly thereafter. The treaty provided that the canal company could sell its property to the United States, which received a 90-year lease on a six-mile strip across the Isthmus. The United States would pay $10 million and, after nine years, an annual rental of $250,000, with an option to renew the lease.

Colombia rejected the treaty, saying that it infringed on Colombian sovereignty and set an unacceptably low price for canal rights. Refusing to renegotiate, the United States allowed or assisted a revolution resulting in Panamanian independence and then quickly negotiated the Hay-Bunau-Varilla treaty.

FURTHER READING: Ameringer, Charles D. "The Panama Canal Lobby of Philippe Bunau-Varilla and William Nelson Cromwell." *American Historical Review* 68/2 (1963): 346–363; Christian L. Wiktor, ed. *Unperfected Treaties of the United States of America, 1776–1976.* Vol. 3. Dobbs Ferry, NY: Oceana Publications, 1977, pp. 449–463; Collin, Richard H. *Theodore Roosevelt's Caribbean: The Panama Canal, the Monroe Doctrine, and the Latin American Context.* Baton Rouge: Louisiana State University Press, 1990.

KENNETH J. BLUME

## Hay-Pauncefote Treaty (1901)

Named for U.S. Secretary of State John Hay and the British Ambassador at Washington, Lord Pauncefote, the Hay-Pauncefote Treaty guaranteed free passage for the ships of all nations through the Panama Canal. The treaty superseded the Clayton-Bulwer Treaty of 1850, which had effectively committed both powers not to construct an isthmian canal.

The first Hay-Pauncefote Treaty was signed in 1900. It stipulated that equal tolls would be charged to ships of all nations using the new canal, and that it should not be fortified. The Senate then amended the treaty so as to exclude the second restriction; Britain rejected the amendment. A Second Hay-Pauncefote Treaty was therefore negotiated and signed on November 18, 1901, which was worded so as to permit an interpretation allowing the fortification of the canal. Following, as it did, the resolution of the Venezuela crisis of 1895 and being succeeded immediately by the 1903 treaty providing for arbitration of the Canada-Alaska border, the Hay-Pauncefote Treaty was an important step in ending the Anglo-American tensions that had marked the nineteenth century, and in bringing the two powers closer to the alliances of the twentieth century. *See also* Panama; United States.

FURTHER READING: Tilchin, William N. *Theodore Roosevelt and the British Empire: A Study in Presidential Statecraft.* New York: St. Martin's, 1997.

MARK F. PROUDMAN

## Hegel, Georg Wilhelm Friedrich (1770–1831)

A German idealist philosopher, Georg Hegel was born in Stuttgart, Germany, on August 27, 1770. Through his schooling years Hegel mastered English, Greek, French, and Hebrew; obtained a master's degree in philosophy in 1790; and spent the years 1788–1793 as a theology student in nearby Tübingen. There he formed lasting friendships with Friedrich Hölderlin (1770–1843) and Friedrich von Schelling (1775–1854), both of whom became major figures of the German philosophical scene in the first half of the nineteenth century. All three witnessed the unfolding of the French Revolution and immersed themselves in the emerging criticism of the idealist philosophy of Immanuel Kant.

Hegel belongs to the period of German idealism in the decades after Kant. He was fascinated by the works of Benedictus de Spinoza, Jean-Jacques Rousseau, and by the French Revolution. As the most systematic of the post-Kantian idealists, Hegel effectively elaborated a comprehensive and systematic ontology from a "logical" starting point throughout his published writings as well as in his lectures. He is best known for his teleological account of history, an account that was later taken over by Marx and inverted into a materialist theory of an historical development culminating in communism. Hegel's famous philosophy is his theory of the dialectic. According to this logic, thesis inevitably generates antithesis, its dialectical opposite, and in the next stage the interaction between thesis and antithesis creates a new condition, defined by Hegel as the synthesis. In time, this resultant synthesis transforms into another negative element leading to a more comprehensive synthesis. The final result in this process is the Hegelian "absolute" or the perfect whole. As an absolute idealist, Hegel used this theory to read nature and events through history.

Hegel's conception of history stressed the concept of monarchy as the highest and most permanent situation in society. He distinguished world history into four categories: the Oriental Empire based on absolute monarchy, the Greek Empire where the monarchy was replaced by the republic, the Roman Empire in which the individual is reduced to obedience, and the Germanic Empire in which individual and state are effectively harmonized. Correspondingly, in his studies on aesthetics, Hegel distinguished three periods: the Oriental, the Greek, and the Romantic. In extension he describes architecture's difference from related arts in terms of the externality of function in the architectural work. Further, his three stages of art and architecture are organized around their relation to function: symbolic architecture appearing before any posited separation of function and means, classical architecture achieving a perfect balance of the two, and romantic architecture going beyond the dominance of function.

Hegel's views were widely taught in Germany and elsewhere. His followers were divided into two groups, right wing and left-wing Hegelians. Right-wing followers had a conservative interpretation, and the other group offered a free, frequently controversial, understanding of Hegel. This group included Feuerbach, Bauer, Friedrich **Engels,** and Karl **Marx.** Hegel's philosophies also influenced other philosophies that developed in Europe in the nineteenth century such as post-Hegelian idealism, the existentialism of Kierkegaard and Sartre, the socialism of Marx and Lasalle, and the instrumentalism of Dewey.

FURTHER READING: Avineri, Shlomo. *Hegel's Theory of the Modern State,* Cambridge: Cambridge University Press, 1972; Crites, Stephen. *Dialectic and Gospel in the Development of Hegel's Thinking.* University Park: Pennsylvania State University Press, 1998; Forster, Michael N. *Hegel and Skepticism.* Cambridge: Harvard University Press, 1989; Forster, Michael N. *Hegel's Idea of a Phenomenology of Spirit.* Chicago: University of Chicago Press, 1998; Gadamer, Hans-Georg. *Hegel's Dialectic: Five Hermeneutical Studies.* Translated by P. Christopher Smith. New Haven, CT: Yale University Press, 1976.

MANU P SOBTI AND MOHAMMAD GHARIPOUR

## Heligoland, Battle of (1864)

A naval engagement of the Schleswig-Holstein War. When war broke out between **Denmark** and Austria and Prussia in early 1864, the Danish navy blockaded German ports in the North and Baltic Seas. The only German naval power of note was Austria. A small fleet of two Austrian frigates under the command of Captain Wilhelm von Tegetthoff arrived in the North Sea at Cuxhaven at the end of April. Accompanied by three small Prussian warships, Tegetthoff's makeshift fleet sailed to challenge the Danish fleet of two frigates and a corvette. Although the Austro-Prussian fleet had more ships, the Danes possessed superior firepower. On May 9, the two sides met off the island of Heligoland and exchanged fire for several hours, neither side losing a ship. Tegetthoff withdrew his battered fleet to Cuxhaven. Although the Danes had inflicted heavier damage, they withdrew their forces from the North Sea and did not reestablish the blockade. *See also* German Empire.

FURTHER READING: Dicey, Edward. *The Schleswig-Holstein War.* 2 vols. London: Tinsley Brothers, 1864.

DAVID H. OLIVIER

## Heligoland-Zanzibar Treaty (1890)

Also known as the Anglo-German Heligoland Treaty, the agreement was an attempt to solve territorial disputes in Africa. Heligoland, an island in the North Sea north of the German port of Bremerhaven, was seized by the British in 1807, and kept during the post-1815 peace. In 1890, under the Heligoland-Zanzibar Treaty, Britain ceded Heligoland to Germany in exchange for German recognition of its protectorate of Zanzibar. Some lands in East Africa also changed hands, largely to Britain's advantage. Lord Salisbury's government calculated that Heligoland was in wartime indefensible and so of little practical use. Zanzibar was valued as a base for antislavery operations in Africa, as a naval base, and as an entrepôt for British trade in the region. German recognition reduced conflict over the German claims on the continent behind it, which became Tanganyika.

On the other hand, Germany sought control over Heligoland as a guard for the western end of the Kiel Canal. The agreement represented an instance of cooperation between two increasingly adversarial powers, but the calculations behind it reinforced the perception that Britain and Germany were natural antagonists. The treaty has gone down in history as a small but initial step toward the collision of 1914. *See also* Africa, Scramble for; Anglo-German Treaty.

FURTHER READING: Austen, Ralph A. *Northwest Tanzania under German and British Rule: Colonial and Tribal Politics, 1889–1939.* New Haven, CT: Yale University Press, 1968; Pakenham, Thomas. *The Scramble for Africa.* New York: Random House, 1991.

MARK F. PROUDMAN

## Herero Revolt (1904–1907)

The bloodiest and most protracted colonial war in **German Southwest Africa,** the Herero Revolt resulted in the death of two-thirds of the Herero and half the Nama peoples. The origins of the Herero Revolt date to the mid-1890s when pastoralist tribes in Southwest Africa, now Namibia, came under pressure from business interests and growing numbers of German settlers who wanted their cattle, land, and labor either for railroad construction or the creation of white-owned ranches and farms. This pressure intensified in 1897 as a result of the outbreak of a Rinderpest epidemic that decimated the region's cattle population and led the German colonial administration to seize tribal lands and relocate the inhabitants onto reservations. Although billed as a means of containing the Rinderpest epidemic, the administration's sale of seized property made it clear that in reality the creation of the reservation system was little more than an effort to provide cheap land and cattle to settlers. The resultant African hostility over the loss of their property was soon compounded by rapidly increasing debt incurred in an effort to rebuild their lost herds, perpetually low wages on white owned farms, and a growing awareness of racial inequalities within the legal system.

This long-simmering resentment finally erupted into violence in January 1904, when the Herero, under the command of Chief Samuel Maherero, rose up and attacked and killed more than 100 German settlers near the town of Okahandja. Thereafter, superior numbers and the inexperience of their opponents enabled the Herero to roam at will until the June 1904 arrival of 15,000 German reinforcements under the command of General Lothar von **Trotha,** an experienced officer who had seen service in German East Africa and China's Boxer Rebellion. Shortly after his arrival in the colony, von Trotha engaged and defeated the main Herero force at the Waterberg River in August 1904, driving the survivors into the desert where many died of starvation. Two months later a new uprising by the Nama broke out in the southern portion of the colony. Although their traditional rivalry prevented the Nama and the surviving Herero from joining forces, during the next several years both tribes fought a running guerilla war against the German colonial forces. Determined to suppress both rebellions, von Trotha unleashed a genocidal reprisal campaign that quickly decimated both the Herero and Nama peoples, eventually provoking a public outcry that led to both his recall to Berlin in 1906 and the **Dernburg reforms** that unfolded the next year. *See also* German Empire, Maji-Maji Rebellion.

FURTHER READING: Bley, Helmut. *South-West Africa Under German Rule, 1894–1914.* Evanston, IL: Northwestern University Press, 1971; Bridgman, Jon. *The Revolt of the Hereros.* Berkeley: University of California Press, 1981; Drechsler, Horst. *"Let us Die Fighting:" The Struggle of the Herero and the Nama against German Imperialism (1884–1915).* London: Zed Press, 1982; Hull, Isabel V. "The Military Campaign in Southwest Africa, 1904–1907." *Bulletin of the German Historical Institute* 37 (2005): 39–45.

KENNETH J. OROSZ

## Herzl, Theodor (1860–1904)

The founder of political **Zionism,** Theodor Herzl was born in Budapest, Hungary. Herzl grew up in the spirit of the German-Jewish Enlightenment. In 1878, the family moved to Vienna and Herzl studied law, graduating in 1884. Rather than pursuing a career in law, Herzl became a playwright and a journalist. His early work was of the feuilleton order and in no way related to Jewish matters.

In 1891, he became Paris correspondent for the *New Free Press*, an influential liberal Viennese newspaper. He still regarded the Jewish problem as a social issue and wrote a drama, *The Ghetto* (1894), in which assimilation is rejected. In Paris, Herzl witnessed anti-Semitism, which resulted from the trial of Alfred **Dreyfus**, a Jewish army officer, who was falsely convicted of treason in a humiliating ceremony in 1895. The trial triggered a wave of anti-Semitism in the cradle of European liberal democracy. Herzl resolved that the only solution to the Jewish problem was the exodus of Jews from their places of residence. He eventually realized that a national home in Palestine was the answer.

In 1896, Herzl published a pamphlet, *The Jewish State*. Herzl declared that the Jews could gain acceptance only if they ceased being a national anomaly. The Jews are one people, he argued, and their plight could be transformed into a positive force by the establishment of a Jewish state. He saw the Jewish problem as an international question to be dealt with in the arena of international politics. Reaction to his plan was mixed. Many Jews rejected it as too extreme; others responded with enthusiasm and asked Herzl to head what was to become the Zionist movement. He convened the First Zionist Congress in Basel, Switzerland, on August 29–31, 1897. This first interterritorial gathering of Jews on a national and secular basis adopted the Basel Program and established the World Zionist Organization to help create the economic foundations for a Jewish state as a socialist utopia. Herzl was elected president of the organization. He met with world leaders trying to enlist financial and political support and collected funds from Jews around the world. He died in 1904 before his ideas could become reality.

FURTHER READING: Falk, Avner. *Herzl, King of the Jews: A Psychoanalytic Biography of Theodor Herzl.* Lanham, MD: University Press of America, 1993; Friedman, Isaiah, ed. *The Rise of Israel. Herzl's Political Activity, 1897–1904.* New York: Garland, 1987. See also http://www.zionism-israel.com/bio/biography_herzl.htm

MARTIN MOLL

## Hesse-Cassel

A German principality and, since 1803, an electoral state, Hesse-Cassel was one of the more powerful middle-ranking powers in central Germany. Between 1850 and its dissolution in 1866, Hesse-Cassel found itself at the center of Austro Prussian antagonism. Although the **Holy Roman Empire** already lay in agony and disappeared only three years later, the landgrave of Hesse-Cassel was at last awarded the status of elector in 1803. Soon after, he fled from invading French forces and went into exile. In 1807, Napoleon occupied Hesse-Cassel, made it the capital of the newly founded Kingdom of Westphalia, and installed his brother Jérôme as king in the capital Cassel.

After **Napoleon**'s downfall, the *ancien régime*, which was reinstated at the Congress of Vienna, frustrated hopes for a more liberal future. In November 1831, Hesse-Cassel decided to participate in the **Zollverein,** thus ending widespread smuggling of goods along the Prussian border, which had damaged relations between the two states. Two years later, the Landtag granted Jewish emancipation. In the meantime the elector and his conservative ministers tried largely in vain to slacken the pace of democratic and economic reform. The apex of the struggle between the two camps, however, was reached with the German Revolution of 1848–1849. Initial success of the progressive forces compelled the new elector Frederick William I to reassert and extend the constitution of 1831. However, when the Paulskirche parliament disintegrated in 1849, in Hesse-Cassel, as everywhere else, reactionary forces tried to turn back time.

By now the kingdom was following a policy of its own with the aim of a German union under Prussian leadership. These ambitions predictably aroused the suspicion of Austria, and armies from the two states met near Fulda in the south of Hesse-Cassel. A clash was averted, but on November 29, 1850, Prussia was forced by Russia and Austria to sign the humiliating Punctuation of Olmütz and had to renounce her plans of German political unity for the time being. Prussia also reacknowledged the Frankfurt Diet, the legislative organ of the **German Confederation.** When war between Austria and Prussia finally erupted in 1866, Hesse-Cassel had occupied a central position between the two Great Powers. Against the advice of his ministers and contrary to the opinion of the overwhelming majority in the Landtag, Frederick William faithfully stood by Austria and her south German allies. Prussian troops invaded and occupied the electorate during the Seven Weeks' War. Shortly thereafter, the Hessian army took their orders from the Prussian military command. When Prussia annexed Hesse-Cassel, there was little resistance from the people, and its history as an independent state came quietly to an end. *See also* Austro-Prussian War; German Empire.

FURTHER READING: Ingrao, Charles W. *The Hessian Mercenary State: Ideas, Institutions, and Reform under Frederick II, 1760–1785.* Cambridge: Cambridge University Press, 2002; Showalter, Dennis. *The Wars of German Unification.* London: Arnold, 2004; Taylor, Peter K. *Indentured to Liberty: Peasant Life and the Hessian Military State, 1688–1815.* Ithaca, NY: Cornell University Press, 1994.

ULRICH SCHNAKENBERG

## Hesse-Darmstadt

A central German state that formed a customs union with Prussia in 1828 but sided with Austria in the Seven Weeks' War and became a constituent member of the **German Empire** in 1871.

In response to **Napoleon**'s successful military campaigns, Hesse-Darmstadt sought to come to terms with Europe's new hegemonic power and consequently entered the Confederation of the Rhine in 1806. As a reward, the state was raised to the status of a grand duchy. When the tide turned against Napoleon in 1813, Hesse-Darmstadt joined the triumphant allied forces. After the territorial readjustments made between 1806 and 1815, membership in the Prussian customs union as the first of the south German states in 1828 further increased the prospects for economic growth. Moreover, Hesse-Darmstadt's accession as one of the larger central German states paved the way for the formation and future enlargement of the *Zollverein.*

The grand duchy nonetheless signed an anti-Prussian convention with her traditional ally Austria in 1866. After the end of the Seven Weeks' War, victorious Prussia treated most of the defeated southern states with general benevolence, and Hesse-Darmstadt was the only southern state that had to cede considerable parts of her territory north of the Main River. Although she did not form part of the emerging North German Confederation, the grand duchy later signed a military pact with Prussia and joined the war against France on Prussia's side. In 1871, Hesse-Darmstadt became one of the constituent states of the German Empire. *See also* Austro-Prussian War; Confederation of the Rhine.

FURTHER READING: Lange, Thomas. *Hessen-Darmstadts Beitrag für das heutige Hessen.* Wiesbaden: Hessische Landeszentral für politische Bildung, 1998; Schüßler, Wilhelm. *Hessen-Darmstadt und die deutschen Großmächte.* Darmstadt: Großherzoglich Hessischer Staatsverlag, 1919.

ULRICH SCHNAKENBERG

## Hindenburg, Paul von Beneckendorff und von (1847–1934)

Prussian General Field-Marshall and Chief of the General Staff Paul von Hindenburg began his career with entry into a military school at the age of 12. Hindenburg participated in the German Wars of Unification and served in the German General Staff and the Prussian Ministry of War. His active military service ended in 1911 at the age of 63.

His later military career began in World War I, when he was recalled on August 22, 1914 to command the Eighth Army after its disastrous performance on the Eastern Front. Together with his Chief of Staff Erich Ludendorff, he achieved fame and admiration as the victor of the Battle of Tannenberg, and was subsequently one of Germany's most popular military leaders, rivaling the kaiser in popularity. His military successes included the occupation of large parts of Russian Poland and the Baltic states. Hindenburg and Ludendorff's intrigues against Chief of the General Staff Erich von **Falkenhayn** finally paid off in August 1916 when Hindenburg replaced Falkenhayn and formed, with Ludendorff, the Third Army High Command, which increasingly resembled a military dictatorship. The Hindenburg-Programme aimed at expansion of armament production and the economy for the war effort. The "Hindenburg Line" was the name given to the area of the Western Front where Ludendorff had effected a strategic retreat, and the far-ranging demands he planned for a victor's peace were known as the "Hindenburg-Peace." Hindenburg supported the declaration of the Kingdom of Poland, the unrestricted submarine warfare that brought the United States into the war, and the intrigues against Chancellor Bethmann-Hollweg and other politicians. As the kaiser's popularity waned, Hindenburg's only increased. After Germany's defeat, Hindenburg's popularity continued, but Ludendorff was blamed for the Third Army High Command's shortcomings. Although his military career was finally over upon his second retirement at the age of 71, Hindenburg was to be recalled once more, in April 1925, this time to head the Weimar Republic as its president. It was in that role that he proclaimed Adolf Hitler German Chancellor in January 1933. *See also* Schlieffen Plan; Strategy.

FURTHER READING: Asprey, Robert B. *The German High Command at War. Hindenburg and Ludendorff Conduct World War I.* New York: W. Morrow, 1991; Showalter, Dennis E., and William J. Astore. *Hindenburg: Icon of German Militarism.* Washington, DC: Potomac Books, 2005.

ANNIKA MOMBAUER

## Hindustan

Hindustan, meaning "Land of the Hindus," derives from the word "Hindu," which is the Persian form of "Sindhu," the Indus River. Hindustan is considered one of the earliest historical names for the nation of Bharat or **India**. Although occasionally used to mean all India, historically it refers to northern India, in contrast to the Deccan, or South.

The British East India Company, formed in 1600, made great advances at the expense of the Mughal Empire, seething with corruption, oppression, and revolt and crumbling under the despotic rule of Aurangzeb between 1658 and 1707. Although still in direct competition with French and Dutch interests until 1763, the British East India Company was able to extend its control over almost the whole of the subcontinent in the century after the subjugation of Bengal at the Battle of Plassey in 1757. English and French trading companies had been competing to protect commercial interests against one another for more than a century. By the middle of the eighteenth century, however, the content of battle changed from "commerce" to "empire." During the Seven Years' War, 1756–1763, Robert Clive, the leader of the Company in India, defeated a key Indian ruler of Bengal at the decisive Battle of Plassey in 1757, a victory that ushered an informal British rule in India. Still nominally the sovereign, India's Mughal Emperor increasingly became a puppet ruler, unable to contain the spread of anarchy. Waiting for an appropriate opportunity, the company stepped into political battle field as a policeman of India.

The transition to formal imperialism, characterized by Queen Victoria being crowned "Empress of India" in the 1870s, was a gradual process. The first step dated to the late eighteenth century. The British parliament, disturbed by the idea that a great business concern, interested primarily in profit, was controlling the destinies of millions of people, passed acts in 1773 and 1784 that gave itself the power to control company policies and to appoint the highest company official in India, the governor-general. This system of dual control lasted until 1858. By 1818, the East India Company had become the master of India. Some local rulers were forced to accept its authority; others were deprived of their territories. Some portions of the subcontinent were administered by the British directly; in others native dynasties were retained under British supervision.

Until 1858, however, much of the subcontinent was still officially the dominion of the Mughal emperor. Anger among some social groups, however, seethed under the governor-generalship of James **Dalhousie,** who annexed the Punjab in 1849 after victory in the Second Sikh War; annexed seven princely states on the basis of lapse; annexed the key state of Oudh on the basis of misgovernment, and upset cultural sensibilities by banning Hindu practices such as *sati.* The 1857 Indian Mutiny, or Sepoy Rebellion, was the key turning point. After fierce fighting the revolt was crushed. One important consequence of the mutiny was the final collapse of the Mughal dynasty. The mutiny also ended the system of dual control under which the British government and the British East India Company shared authority. The government relieved the company of its political responsibilities, and in 1858 the company relinquished its role. Trained civil servants were recruited from graduates of British universities, and these men set out to rule India. Lord **Canning** was appointed governor-general of India in 1856. When the government of India was transferred from the company to the Crown, Canning became the first viceroy of India.

The core logic of British colonialism—the extraction of natural resources and creation of captive market place—resulted in the modernization of certain sectors of Indian economy. The spread of railroads from 1853 contributed to the expansion of business, and cotton, tea and indigo plantations drew new areas into the commercial economy. The removal of import duties in 1883, however, exposed India's emerging industries to unfettered British competition, provoking another quite modern development, the rise of a nationalist movement. The denial of equal status to Indians was the immediate stimulus for the formation of Indian National Congress in 1885. Congress was initially loyal to the empire, but after 1905 showed an increased commitment to self-government and by 1930 supported outright independence. The "Home charges," payments transferred from India for administrative costs, were a lasting source of nationalist grievance, although the flow declined in relative importance over the decades to independence in 1947. Although majority Hindu and minority Muslim political leaders were able to collaborate closely in their criticism of British policy into the 1920s, British support for a distinct Muslim political organization from 1906 and insistence from the 1920s on separate electorates for religious minorities, is seen by many in India as having contributed to Hindu-Muslim discord and the country's eventual partition. *See also* East India Company; Indian Mutiny; Sikh Wars.

FURTHER READING: Basham, A. L., ed. *A Cultural History of India*. Oxford: Clarendon, 1975; Chandra, Bipan. *Essays on Contemporary India*. New Delhi: Har-Anand, 1993; Featherstone, Donald. *India from the Conquest of Sind to the Indian Mutiny*. London: Blandell, 1992; Henderson, C. E. *Culture and Customs of India*. Westport, CT: Greenwood Press, 2002; Lewis, Martin D. *The British in India: Imperialism or Trusteeship*. Lexington, MA: Heath, 1962.

JITENDRA UTTAM

## Hobson, John Atkinson (1858–1940)

John Hobson, an economist, political commentator, and activist, formulated what has been probably the single most influential theory of **imperialism** in his volume *Imperialism: A Study* (1902).

Hobson was the son of a Derbyshire businessman and newspaper owner. He was educated in Derby and at Lincoln College, Oxford, before becoming a schoolteacher and contributor to his father's newspaper in the 1880s. In his youth, he was a Liberal Unionist, which is to say an opponent of Gladstone's Home Rule Bill and a supporter of the generally more conservative side of the post-1886 **Liberal Party.** After the death of his prosperous father, Hobson had a modest private income, which allowed him the freedom to travel and write on social, economic, and political topics. Motivated by a work ethic and perhaps a sense of guilt derived from his northern, middle class but privileged beginnings, Hobson's lifetime output was prodigious. Peter Cain, one of the foremost Hobson scholars, has gone so far as to say that he wrote too much. From these relatively conservative, middle class beginnings, Hobson, an inveterate questioner of established verities, moved rapidly leftwards.

By the late 1880s, Hobson had become one of a number of so-called new Liberals, questioning the earlier dogmas of classical *laissez-faire* political economy. Motivated by continuing lower class poverty and endemic unemployment, Hobson began to question the idea that the minimally taxed and relatively unregulated free market economy of Gladstonian England would or could provide full employment or economic well-being to the mass of the population. Hobson's first book, *The Physiology of Industry,* co-written with his friend the businessman A. F. Mummery and published in 1889, was an attack on the classical economic dogma that production could not outstrip consumption. Contending that the economy as then structured created unusable surpluses of capital in the hands of the rich, Hobson and Mummery argued for taxes on savings and an increase in consumption through a higher minimum wage. They also questioned the fiercely defended dogmas of **free trade** and called for reductions in working hours and controls on immigration to help raise wages. Hobson did not hold to all these ideas throughout his life, but his lack of faith in the automatic economic balance mechanism of Adam **Smith**'s famous "invisible hand," and his perception that problems of consumption rather than production could be the key to persistent economic imbalances anticipated the insights of John Maynard Keynes a generation later, as Keynes himself recognized.

Hobson continued his attack on traditional economics in two subsequent books, *Problems of Poverty* in 1891 and *The Problem of the Unemployed* in 1896. Hobson also produced a more conventional, relentlessly empirical, much reprinted, and still quite useful economic history, *The Evolution of Modern Capitalism: A Study of Machine Production,* in 1894. As the titles of his books indicated, Hobson was centrally concerned with problems of poverty and unemployment. Throughout his life, he evinced a very liberal concern for personal autonomy and for the development of the full potential of each human being. Hobson shared fully the sensibility that had led John Stuart Mill, the central figure in British liberalism, to call for a maximum diversity of "experiments in living." But Hobson, unlike many liberals, observed that industrial conditions in his society minimized the life choices of many, and arguably most, people, and set about asking why this was. Hobson insisted throughout his career on the social character of human beings and always insisted, with some element of paradox, that the realization of individual potential required an intelligent understanding of the "organic" (one of his favorite words) character of society.

Hobson's attack on classical political economy ran strongly counter to the ingrained ideas of the period, and he never secured fulltime academic employment. As Hobson and Mummery noted, it was at the time considered "positively impious" to question the moral and economic benefits of saving, two categories that ran together in the minds of many Victorians. But despite his attack on these economic dogmas, Hobson always remained a very Victorian man: a deep moral sensibility, and a Gladstonian talent for moral outrage, runs through all his writings. He believed that reason could guide man to a better and more just future. He also believed implicitly that progress toward such a future was the natural direction of history, and so any reversion to earlier, less rational and more coercive social conditions attracted the full weight of his very Victorian moral outrage.

These moral concerns were evident in his first writing on imperialism, an 1897 article entitled "The Ethics of Imperialism" in the short-lived *Progressive Review,* a journal he participated in founding. In that article, he compared the ethics of imperialists to those of thieves grabbing as much land and wealth as possible. In 1898, Hobson published an article in the Liberal *Contemporary Review* linking capital export to imperial expansion. In 1899, Hobson was sent to South Africa, the scene of crises that culminated in the Second **Boer War** of 1899–1902, as a correspondent for the *Manchester Guardian.* A book of essays resulting from that journey, *The War* *in South Africa* (1900) developed that moral theme. In 1901, Hobson published a small volume, *The Psychology of Jingoism,* which analyzed the ideology of imperialism. Hobson synthesized his earlier analyses of the economic distempers of the time, the politics of imperialism in South Africa and elsewhere, and the ideology of imperialism in his volume of 1902.

*Imperialism: A Study* was a systematic examination of what Hobson called "the new Imperialism," by which he meant the rapid expansion of European empires in the previous two or three decades, with particular emphasis on the British Empire. Hobson began by dealing with what were then prominent pro-imperial arguments. He argued that, contrary to the popular late Victorian slogan that "trade follows the flag," recent imperial acquisitions, largely in Africa, were of little commercial significance. He also argued that such territories were unlikely to support large numbers of British emigrants. The Empire, however, did serve the interests of powerful classes, among them the aristocracy, the related military and diplomatic services, arms makers, and traders with colonial connections, who in alliance with conservative domestic interests had been able to persuade the nation that imperialism served the national interest. In making these charges, Hobson echoed a long tradition of radical complaint that British foreign policy was, in the famous words of John Bright, "neither more nor less than a gigantic program of outdoor relief (Victorian term for welfare) for the aristocracy of Great Britain."

But Hobson did not stop there. The decisive factor, "the economic taproot of Imperialism," as he called it, was the role of investors and speculators in pushing overseas expansion. Here, he came to his particular *bête noire,* the role of the diamond magnate Cecil **Rhodes** and his **British South Africa Company** in pushing the expansion of the British Empire in southern Africa and in provoking the Anglo-Boer War. Building on ideas that he had first developed in his books of the previous decade, Hobson argued that the lightly taxed capitalism of his time accumulated surpluses of capital in the hands of the wealthy that could not profitably be invested in the domestic economy. These surpluses were therefore exported, thus creating pressure for imperial expansion to safeguard foreign investments in unstable regions of the globe. There were numerous forces driving the rapid imperial expansion of the time, but Hobson held that financial capital was "the governor of the imperial engine."

Rhodes's South Africa Company, with its vast sovereign holdings in Africa, its control of much of South Africa's "Rhodesian" press, its prominent aristocratic and Tory government connections, and its dubious stock exchange manipulations, appeared to Hobson and many others to be the epitome of capitalist imperialism. Hobson also pointed to the alleged role of J. P. Morgan and other capitalists in provoking the advent of overseas U.S. imperialism at the time of the **Spanish-American War** of 1898. Hobson's solution to the problem of imperialism and its wars abroad was intelligent redistribution of the nation's wealth at home, raising working class living standards and thereby diffusing the surpluses of investment capital that were understood to drive imperialism.

Hobson's *Imperialism* did not meet with an immediate success—it was praised in the Liberal and radical press, and ignored in the Tory and imperialist press—but it was reprinted in a slightly revised edition in 1905 and became one of the standard textbooks of anti-imperialism in subsequent years. Lenin drew heavily on Hobson's *Imperialism* in his *Imperialism: The Highest Stage of Capitalism* of 1916, thereby significantly distorting the memory of Hobson's essential liberalism, and the reformist, social democratic character of his prescriptions, and leaving many to think of Hobson as a proto-Marxist and an economic determinist.

Hobson's later works included *Towards International Government* of 1915, which advocated a variety of liberal internationalism that led to the League of Nations, and he played a role in the antiwar internationalist group the Union of Democratic Control, although he was rapidly disappointed by the reality of the League of Nations. In 1938, Hobson published a brief autobiography, *Confessions of an Economic Heretic*, which remains among the best sources on his life, and in which he reproved his earlier self for having been too economically deterministic in his *Imperialism* of 1902.

A.J.P. Taylor said of Hobson that, "it was no mean achievement for Hobson to anticipate Keynesian economics with one flick of the wrist and to lay the foundations for Soviet foreign policy with another. No wonder that he never received academic acknowledgment or held a university chair." Taylor might have added that Hobson also played a large role in framing the liberal internationalism championed by President Woodrow Wilson after 1918. Hobson's thought was central to both the crusading internationalisms of the twentieth century, the Leninist, and the Wilsonian, and anticipated in many respects that century's most significant economic innovations. *See also* Africa, Scramble for; Jingoism; Lenin, Vladimir; Liberalism.

FURTHER READING: Cain, P. J. *Hobson and Imperialism: Radicalism, New Liberalism, and Finance, 1887–1938*. New York: Oxford University Press, 2002; Kemp, Tom. *Theories of Imperialism*. London: Dobson, 1967; Mommsen, Wolfgang J. *Theories of Imperialism*. Translated by P. S. Falla. Chicago: University of Chicago Press, 1982; Nemmers, Erwin Esser. *Hobson and Underconsumption*. Clifton, NJ: A. M. Kelly, 1972.

MARK PROUDMAN

## Hohenlinden, Battle of (1800)

The last victory of Republican French armies over the Austrians in Germany. Fought in the forests 16 miles east of Munich, Bavaria, on December 3 between General Moreau with 56,000 men and 61,000 Austro-Bavarian troops led by 18-year-old Archduke John. The armistice was terminated by the French on November 28, but John won the opening action at Ampfing on December 1. On December 3, the Allied army advanced in four columns from Haag through the forest toward Hohenlinden, where Moreau was concentrating his army to counterattack as the allied columns emerged from the woodland. At dawn as snow fell, the central Allied column opened fire on French positions, but the side columns were three hours behind, marching along woodland tracks. The fighting raged along the main road, but it was stalemated around the entrance to the Haag Forest until about 11 A.M., when Feldmarschalleutnant Kollowrat's center column had to give ground as it ran out of reserves. The two Allied northern columns had arrived, however, and they engaged the French left wing under General Grenier, but they were forced to withdraw as the advance of the French center threatened their line of retreat.

In the south, Feldmarschalleutnant Riesch's column was even more delayed and was halted around St. Christoph by two French divisions under General Decaen. The French center, led by Generals Ney and Grouchy, steadily advanced down the forest road as Generals Grenier and Richepanse advanced along the northern tracks, throwing the retreating allied army into increasing disorder. With losses of 12,000 troops, John hastily withdrew at 6 P.M. and an armistice was concluded at Steyr on December 25. *See also* Napoleonic Wars.

FURTHER READING: Arnold, J. *Marengo and Hohenlinden*. Lexington, VA: Napoleon Books, 1999; Schneider, G. *Hohenlinden: Die vergessene Schlacht*. Munich: Kurt Vowinckel, 2000.

DAVID HOLLINS

## Hohenzollern Dynasty

The ruling house of Brandenburg-**Prussia** from 1415 to 1918 and of imperial **Germany** from 1871 to 1918. Originating in southwestern of Germany and traceable back to the eleventh century, the family took its name from the German word *Zöller*, meaning watchtower or castle, and in particular from the Castle of Hohenzollern, the ancestral seat, today in the German state of Baden-Württemberg. Around 1200, the family split into the Swabian and the Franconian line. From the latter all the branches surviving into modern times derived.

In 1415, Holy Roman Emperor Sigismund made Frederick VI of Hohenzollern elector of Brandenburg. He and his successors had the right to participate in the elections of the German kings. Brandenburg, becoming the center of Hohenzollern power, was one of the most important principalities in the **Holy Roman Empire.** In 1525, Grand Master of the Teutonic Knights Albert of Brandenburg secularized the order's domains as the Duchy of Prussia. Joachim II, who reigned from 1535 to 1571, converted to Lutheranism. In 1614, the acquisition of Cleve, Mark, Ravensburg, and the Duchy of Prussia marked the Hohenzollern rise as a leading German power. With the help of France and England, the dynasty rose further after the Peace of Westphalia in 1648. Frederick William, the Great Elector obtained Pomerania, the secularized bishoprics of Cammin, Minden, and Halberstadt. His reign brought centralization and absolutism to the still scattered Hohenzollern lands. In 1701, Frederick III of Brandenburg secured from the Roman Emperor the title "King in Prussia." The change to "King of Prussia" was not formally recognized until 1772. The Prussian royal title was a new symbol of the unity of the family holdings. The Prussian kings retained their title of electors until the dissolution of the **Holy Roman Empire** in 1806.

Frederick William I, on the Prussian throne from 1713 to 1740, was the real architect of Hohenzollern greatness through his administrative, fiscal, and military reforms. His son Frederick II, called "The Great," seized Silesia and acquired West Prussia in 1772. By 1800, Germany included nearly 2,000 separate entitles, among which were several dozen territories ruled by the Hohenzollerns. They were subject to the Roman emperor in the western part of their domains and had been subject to the Kingdom of Poland in the east. The Revolutionary and Napoleonic Wars resulted in the end of the old empire and the creation of a **German Confederation.** The **Congress of Vienna** settlement of 1814–1815 resulted in a substantial extension of Hohenzollern territory in the west, and the period between 1815 and 1866 was marked by the struggle of Hohenzollern-Prussia against Habsburg-Austria for domination of Germany. The question of whether there should be a unified Germany was one of the most contentious issues over this entire half century.

Frederick William IV, whose reign began in 1840, was a draftsman interested in both architecture and landscape gardening and a patron of several great German artists. Frederick William was a staunch Romanticist, and his devotion to this movement was largely responsible for his developing into a conservative at an early age. Upon his accession, he toned down the reactionary policies enacted by his father, promising to enact a constitution. In March 1848, Frederick William was overwhelmed by the revolutionary movement that shook Germany and much of the rest of Europe. He offered concessions, promising to promulgate a constitution and agreed that Prussia and other German states should merge into a single nation. When the revolution collapsed, conservative forces regrouped and gained the support of the king. The king nonetheless remained dedicated to German unification, leading the Frankfurt Parliament to offer him the crown of Germany on April 3, 1849, which he refused, saying that he would not accept a crown from the gutter.

In 1857, Frederick William suffered a stroke that left him mentally disabled. His brother William took over as regent and became King **William I** upon his brother's death on January 2, 1861. The new monarch was often in conflict with the liberal Prussian Diet. A crisis arose in 1862, when the Diet refused to authorize funding for a reorganization of the army. The king's government was unable to convince legislators to sanction the budget, and the king was unwilling to give in, so the deadlock continued. William resolved that Otto von **Bismarck** was the only politician capable of handling the crisis, and in September 1862 appointed Bismarck minister-president of Prussia. It was thereafter Bismarck who effectively directed politics, interior as well as foreign. On several occasions he gained William's assent by threatening to resign. Under Bismarck's direction, Prussia's army triumphed over its rivals Austria and France in 1866 and 1870–1871, respectively. On January 18, 1871, William was proclaimed emperor of a unified Germany. He accepted the title "German Emperor" grudgingly; he would have preferred "Emperor of Germany," which, however, was unacceptable to the federated monarchs. In his memoirs, Bismarck describes William as an old-fashioned, courteous, polite gentleman, whose common sense was occasionally undermined by female influences.

In 1829, William had married Augusta of Saxony-Weimar and had two children, Frederick and Princess Louise of Prussia. Upon his death on March 9, 1888, William I was succeeded by Frederick III. In 1858, Frederick had married Princess Victoria of Great Britain and Ireland, the eldest daughter of Queen Victoria and Prince Albert. By the time he became Emperor in 1888, Frederick had incurable cancer of the larynx, which had been misdiagnosed. He ruled for only 99 days before his death on June 15, 1888 and was succeeded by his eldest son **William II.**

A traumatic breech birth left William with a withered left arm, which he tried with some success to conceal. Additionally, he may have experienced some brain trauma. Historians are divided on whether such a mental incapacity may have contributed to his frequently aggressive, tactless, and bullying approach to problems and people, which was evident in both his personal and political life. On several occasions, he publicly offended foreign statesmen and countries. His personality certainly damaged German policy, most notably in his dismissal of Bismarck in 1890. The emperor was accused of megalomania as early as 1894 by German pacifist Ludwig Quidde, and his reign was noted for his push to increase German military power. He also sought to expand German colonial holdings, and under the **Tirpitz Plan** the German navy was built up to challenge that of Great Britain. Despite these policies it is misleading to say that he was eager to unleash World War I, although he did little to prevent it. During the war, he was commander-in-chief but soon lost all control of German policy.

After Germany's defeat, William could not make up his mind to abdicate. He was still confident that even if he were forced to renounce the German throne, he would still retain the Prussian kingship. Thus his abdication both as emperor and king of Prussia was announced for him by Chancellor Prince Max von Baden on November 9, 1918. The next day William fled into exile in the Netherlands where he died on June 4, 1941.

The Hohenzollern Swabian line remained Catholic at the Reformation. Charles of Hohenzollern-Sigmaringen became prince of Romania in 1866 and king as Carol I in 1881. Ferdinand succeeded his uncle in Romania in 1914, where his descendants ruled until 1947. There are currently no reigning Hohenzollerns left. *See also* German Empire; *Weltpolitik.*

FURTHER READING: Eulenberg, Herbert. *The Hohenzollerns.* London: G. Allen & Unwin, 1929; Koch, Hannsjoachim Wolfgang. *A History of Prussia.* London, New York: Longman, 1978; Röhl, John C. G. *Young Wilhelm: The Kaiser's Early Life, 1859–1888.* Cambridge and New York: Cambridge University Press, 1998; Röhl, John C. G. *Wilhelm II: The Kaiser's Personal Monarchy, 1888–1900.* New York: Cambridge University Press, 2004.

MARTIN MOLL

## Holland

*See* Netherlands, Kingdom of the

## Holy Alliance

A compact signed by Austria, Prussia, and Russian in the wake of the **Napoleonic Wars.** Tsar **Alexander I** of Russia, acting under the influence of the religious mystic, Baroness von Krüdener, drew up a document declaring that the actions of European sovereigns ought to be guided by the principles of justice, peace, and Christian charity. Specifically, that it was "their fixed resolution, both in the administration of their respective States and in their political relations with every other Government, to take for their sole guide the precepts of that Holy Religion, namely, the precepts of Justice, Christian Charity and Peace, which . . . must have an immediate influence on the councils of Princes, and guide all their steps, as being the only means of consolidating human institutions and remedying the imperfections." To this lofty goal, on September 26, 1815 the tsar put his name, together with King Frederick William III of Prussia and Emperor Francis I of Austria. Practically every other Christian ruler—significant and insignificant—later followed suit, although there were three notable exceptions to the list of adherents: the British prince regent refused on constitutional grounds, although he recognized the solemnity and importance of its sentiments; the sultan of Turkey, not being Christian, was not invited to sign; and Pope Pius VII refused to sign it on grounds that it would associate him with Protestants. The Holy Alliance was innocuous at best and meaningless at worst—indeed, both Viscount **Castlereagh** and Prince Klemens **Metternich** dismissed it as verbal nonsense—and it became synonymous with reactionary autocracy for the subsequent generation, although it exercised little if any effect on the policies of those who had promised to govern according to its principles.

FURTHER READING: Hurst, Michael, ed. *Key Treaties of the Great Powers, 1814–1914.* 2 vols. *Vol. I: 1814–1870.* Newton Abbot, UK: David & Charles, 1972; Lowe, John. *The Concert of Europe: International Relations, 1814–70.* London: Hodder & Stoughton, 1991.

GREGORY FREMONT-BARNES

## Home Rule

In British history, home rule signified the idea that the separate countries of the United Kingdom should have separate parliaments. Home rule in the Victorian era normally referred to Irish Home Rule, which is to say to the restoration of a separate but subordinate parliament at Dublin. In 1873, the Protestant lawyer, Isaac Butt, formed the Home Rule League, the first Irish party fully independent of the British parties In the 1890s, there were relatively minor movements for Scottish and Welsh Home Rule, but they had little immediate consequence. The Liberal governments of William **Gladstone** attempted to pass Home Rule Bills for **Ireland** in 1886 and 1893 but failed in both instances. The issue was rejoined in 1912, after the Parliament Act of 1911 had trimmed the power of the House of Lords. In 1914, the third Home Rule Bill was in its third reading, and Ireland on the cusp of civil war over it, when the **July Crisis** eclipsed all other events. Irish Home Rule waited until 1921. *See also* Act of Union.

FURTHER READING: Jalland, Patricia. *The Liberals and Ireland.* New York: St. Martin's, 1980.

MARK F. PROUDMAN

## Hong Kong

A village at the mouth of the Pearl River on the southern coast of China until 1841, when it was seized by Britain during the First **Opium War** as a resettlement site for British merchants expelled from Guangzhou and Macao. In 1842, the British forced the Chinese to sign the Treaty of Nanking, which stipulated that Hong Kong would remain a British possession in perpetuity. The next year, Hong Kong was proclaimed a British crown colony. In 1860, the colony was expanded by the Convention of Peking and in 1898 reconfigured again to take in an area named the New Territories enclosing more than 360 square miles. It was then leased to Britain for 99 years.

FURTHER READING: Endacott, G. B. *Government and People in Hong Kong, 1841–1962.* Hong Kong: Hong Kong University Press, 1964.

CARL CAVANAGH HODGE

## Hudson's Bay Company

A British trading company established by Royal Charter in 1670 to explore and develop northern **Canada.** Henry Hudson first entered the bay that was later named after him in 1610 in search of the Northwest Passage. This led to a realization of the wealth to be attained through the fur trade, which the French, based in Montreal, then held the monopoly. Two French fur traders, Médard Chouart, sieur de Groseilliers (1618–1696) and his brother-in-law Pierre Esprit Radisson (1632–1710), who felt they had been cheated in Montreal, turned to the British and argued that Hudson Bay would be a good place to establish a trading center. This argument appealed to traders and "The Governor and Company of Adventurers trading into Hudson's Bay" (the Company) was given its charter to trade on May 2 by King Charles II. It established a monopoly of the Indian trade, especially the fur trade, in the area fed by all the rivers and streams that drained into Hudson's Bay, 1.5 million square miles encompassing more than one-third of Canada and parts of the **United States**. This territory was named Rupert's Land after Charles's cousin, Prince Rupert of the Rhine, who became the first governor of the company. The company controlled the fur trade throughout much of North America from its headquarters at York Factory on Hudson's Bay.

After the Treaty of Paris of 1763, when the British acquired New France, Scottish, English and American traders arrived in Montreal to take advantage of the new opportunities. In 1784, they established the North West Company and, operating through the Great Lakes and bypassing Hudson's Bay, the Nor'Westers became a serious rival to the company, which had established 97 trading posts in the west by 1870. The company and the Nor'Westers both built forts along the Saskatchewan River and competed for furs. Nor'Westers were the first to reach the Pacific. In 1816, Lord Selkirk of the company established the Red River colony at Winnipeg, Manitoba to compete with the North West Company. The colony was attacked by Métis on June 19, 1816, in the "Seven Oaks Massacre" when 21 people were killed. The result was that the two companies were merged by the British government in 1821 but retained the company's name. This extended the company's territory to the Pacific.

George Simpson (1786–1860), who was knighted in 1841, had become the governor of the company in 1820, and he was to direct and dominate the affairs of the merged company until his death. A ruthless and efficient governor who acquired the nickname "The Little Emperor," he reduced the number of employees from 2,000 to 800 but awarded traders a share of the profits to ensure their loyalty and productivity. He substituted Indian canoes with sturdier York boats based on an Orkney design 30 feet long. The greatest threat to the company came from the American Mountain men coming from the Oregon Country along the Platte and Snake Rivers from Saint Paul. Simpson decided on a scorched earth policy by trapping out the entire area from northern California to Nevada. In 1846, the United States and Great Britain set the boundary between the United States and Rupert's Land at the 49th parallel, and Simpson relocated the company's West Coast headquarters to Vancouver Island where it became the *de facto* government in the west.

In 1867, the Dominion of Canada was formed and three years later the company was forced to give up Rupert's Land to the Dominion in exchange for land, cash, and property around its trading posts. By the 1870s, the company had lost its monopoly of trade, the beaver hat went out of fashion, and furs from other areas of the world had taken over the market. The company turned increasingly to retail merchandising, especially through its department stores. York Factory finally closed its doors in 1957.

FURTHER READING: Galbraith, John S. *The Little Emperor: Governor Simpson of the Hudson's Bay Company.* Toronto: Macmillan, 1976; Newman, Peter Charles. *Empire of the Bay: The Company of Adventurers that Seized a Continent.* New York: Penguin Books, 2000.

ROGER D. LONG

## Huerta, José Victoriano (1854–1916)

President of Mexico (1913–1914), Victoriano Huerta rose to the rank of general and fought against both the Mayan people of the Yucatán and the rebel Emiliano Zapata. After the revolution of 1910, Huerta was officially loyal to the new government of Francisco Madero yet plotted simultaneously, with the knowledge and cooperation of the **United States,** to overthrow Madero. The ensuing power struggle saw Huerta emerge triumphant as the provisional president of Mexico in February 1913. He established a dictatorship, which provoked from U.S. President Woodrow **Wilson** a demand for democratic elections. When Huerta refused, Wilson sent American forces to seize the Mexican port of Veracruz. This united Huerta's enemies against him, and, after a series of military defeats, he resigned the presidency and went into exile. *See also* Monroe Doctrine.

FURTHER READING: Kirkwood, Burton. *The History of Mexico.* Westport, CT: Greenwood, 2000.

CARL CAVANAGH HODGE

## Hugo, Victor (1802–1885)

Among the greatest French writers of the nineteenth century and a major contributor to French national mythology, Hugo was born on February 26, the son of Léopold Hugo, a general in **Napoleon**'s army and Sophie Trébuchet. Hugo's mother ensured that he received an excellent education in the classics and languages. To a significant extent, Hugo determined the directions of French literature during the nineteenth century and contributed to the intellectual milieu of his time, with his wide-ranging ideas on politics, religion, poverty, capital punishment, and social injustice. He is largely regarded as the leader of the romantic movement, whose essence is mostly captured in his poetry. Apart from poetry, Hugo also wrote novels, as well as plays, including the famous masterpiece, *The Hunchback of Notre Dame.* Hugo lived in exile in the Channel Islands for his anti-Bonapartist political beliefs. While there he wrote *Les Miserables,* later made into a musical play. Hugo died in May 1885. His funeral procession was extremely long, leading to the Panthéon as the French mourned the death of the respected French literary artist.

FURTHER READING: Robb, Graham. *Victor Hugo, A Biography.* New York: W. W. Norton, 1997.

NURFADZILAH YAHAYA

## Human Zoo

A public exhibit of human beings, as ethnological displays, that became increasingly popular after the 1870s. Facilitated by the possession of overseas colonies, human zoos were common, either in their own right or as an integral feature of international exhibitions, in major cities of most of the Great Powers. The German zoo entrepreneur Karl Hagenbeck organized a traveling exhibit of wild animals and

Nubians from the Sudan, which was a hit in Berlin, London, and Paris. The 1889 Parisian World's Fair featured 400 colonial peoples. The format varied from the simple display of human beings in cages to elaborate dioramas of entire villages with primitive peoples in their "natural" setting. *See also* Racism; Social Darwinism.

FURTHER READING: Osborne, Michael A. *Nature, the Exotic, and the Science of French Colonialism.* Bloomington: Indiana University Press, 1994.

CARL CAVANAGH HODGE

## Hungary

Hungary is a country of Eastern Europe that, following the Battle of Mohács in 1526, became part of the **Ottoman Empire** until its conquest by Austria in 1687, when the crown of Hungary fell to the Habsburgs. The Hungarian nobility strived to defend its political privileges, while modern nationalism resulted in a movement of cultural self-assertion and political reform that culminated in the revolution of 1848–1849 and Hungary's unsuccessful attempt to break away from Habsburg rule. The Hungarian opposition finally negotiated the **Ausgleich** of 1867 with the Austrian Emperor Francis Joseph, which stipulated the restoration Hungary's political autonomy within the framework of Austria-Hungary until 1918, when the Habsburg Empire collapsed. The Kingdom of Croatia-Slavonia was a semi-autonomous part of the Kingdom of Hungary. Among Hungary's leading politician in the nineteenth and early twentieth centuries were Count Gyula **Andrássy,** Ferenc **Deák,** Kálmán **Tisza,** and István **Tisza.** *See also* Austria-Hungary; Habsburg Empire.

FURTHER READING: Sugar, P. F. *A History of Hungary.* Bloomington: Indiana University Press, 1990.

GUENTHER KRONENBITTER

## Huskisson, William (1770–1830)

William Huskisson was a British Tory politician, president of the Board of Trade, and probably the first man in history to die in a motor vehicle accident. Raised in enlightenment circles in Britain and France, he became in 1790 secretary to the British ambassador at Paris and witnessed many of the events of the revolution. Huskisson entered Parliament as a Pittite in 1796. Appointed to posts at the War Office and the Treasury, Huskisson developed a reputation as a financial expert. After the death of Pitt, he became a follower of Canning, who brought him into Lord Liverpool's government in 1814. Huskisson had much to do with framing the **Corn Law** of 1815, and was also an energetic supporter of a return to a bullion-based currency after the Napoleonic wars. Influenced by the teachings of Smith and Ricardo, Huskisson saw that Britain's future was as a manufacturing country and worked for the rationalization and reduction of tariff barriers and the reform of the navigation laws during his tenure of the Board of Trade from 1823 to 1827. He nevertheless supported preferences for imperial goods.

Huskisson, a so-called liberal Tory, did not get along with the Duke of **Wellington,** and did not last long in the latter's 1828 government. Huskisson sat in the Commons for Liverpool, and in 1830 traveled there for the opening of the first public railway, the Liverpool and Manchester. Getting off his train, he was struck by an oncoming engine and died as a result of his injuries. Huskisson became a model for future financial reformers such as Peel and Gladstone, whose roots were also in liberal Toryism.

FURTHER READING: Cookson, J. E. *Lord Liverpool's Administration: The Crucial Years, 1815–1822.* London: Chatto & Windus, 1975.

MARK F. PROUDMAN

## Hyderabad

Among the largest of the Princely States of **India,** Hyderabad was a virtually independent state under the Nizam dynasty of Asaf Jah between 1724 and 1748. Thereafter, Britain and France were rivals for influence with his successor, with the British finally prevailing in the person of Nizam Ali. In 1798, it became the first Indian princely state formally to ask for British protection and proved to be useful British ally during the **Maratha Wars.**

Hyderabad was also the proximate site of a battle fought in March 1843 between an Anglo-Indian force of 5,000 led by General Charles Napier against 26,000 Baluchis led by Amir Shir Muhammad on the east bank of Indus River in present-day Pakistan. The battle was a spectacular victory for Napier, producing 270 casualties among Napier's men against 6,000 of the Baluchis.

FURTHER READING: Lambrick, H. T. *Sir Charles Napier and Sind.* Oxford: Caltendon Press. 1952.

CARL CAVANAGH HODGE

## Ibn Saud (1880–1953)

Abd al-Aziz ibn Saud, commonly known as Ibn Saud, united most of the Arabian Peninsula through decades of astute political maneuvers and military campaigns, resulting in the foundation of the modern Kingdom of Saudi Arabia. The Al-Saud family had long been leaders in the north-central Najd region of Arabia. In the late nineteenth century, the Al-Sauds were exiled to Kuwait as a result of a power struggle with the rival Al-Rashid clan. In 1902, however, a young Ibn Saud led 40 loyalists of the puritanical Wahhabi sect of Islam in wresting control of Riyadh away from the Al-Rashids, a first step in the eventual reestablishment of Al-Saud control of the Najd.

Throughout the hostilities the Al-Rashids had nominal Ottoman support, but the Turks did not trust their ambitions and never sufficiently supported them militarily against Ibn Saud. Ibn Saud staved off Ottoman intervention through a constant stream of correspondence to Istanbul feigning loyalty to the sultan. He also conducted a guerilla campaign against Turkish interests to discourage aid to Al-Rashid and sought assistance from the British in the event the Turks did intercede more forcefully.

By 1916, Ibn Saud had gained British recognition of his control of the Najd and Al-Hasa as well as a promise of protection if attacked. Within a decade, he had taken the southern portions of modern Saudi Arabia and expanded throughout the remaining Al-Rashid controlled northern regions. In 1925, he made a move on the religiously important Hijaz province, decisively beating Hashemite King Hussein ibn Ali and taking control of Mecca and Medina. In doing so, he had completed his consolidation of nearly all of Arabia and became the king of the Najd and king of the Hijaz.

In 1932, the formation of the Kingdom of Saudi Arabia was officially declared and recognized internationally. Soon after, Ibn Saud began to tap Arabia's petroleum wealth, inviting American oil companies to the country to develop the industry. Much of the country's future oil wealth went to the Al-Saud family; however, Ibn Saud lived a relatively austere life and used some funds to improve the infrastructure and public institutions of his country. *See also* British Empire; Ottoman Empire; Wahhabis.

FURTHER READING: Al-Rasheed, Madawi. *A History of Saudi Arabia.* New York: Cambridge University Press, 2002; Anscombe, Frederick F. *The Ottoman Gulf: The Creation of Kuwait, Saudi Arabia, and Qatar.* New York: Columbia University Press, 1997.

BRENT D. SINGLETON

## Ibrahim Pasha (1789–1848)

The eldest son of **Mehmet Ali** Pasha of **Egypt** and an Egyptian general, Ibrahim Pasha conducted largely successful campaigns against the **Wahhabis** in Arabia between 1816 and 1819. He fought against the Greeks, but the European coalition defeated him in **Navarino,** and he was forced to withdraw from the country. Ibrahim conquered Palestine and Syria in 1832–1833. His attempts to apply to Syria and Palestine the reforms that his father had introduced in Egypt caused a series of disorders. In 1839, Ibrahim fought again against the Ottomans, but European intervention on behalf of the **Ottoman Empire** compelled Ibrahim to evacuate back to Egypt. In 1848, he was regent of Egypt during his father's insanity.

FURTHER READING: Goldschmidt, Arthur, Jr. *Modern Egypt: The Formation of A Nation-State,* Boulder, CO: Westview Press, 1988; Karsh, Efraim, and Inari Karsh. *Empires of the Sand: The Struggle for Mastery in the Middle East 1789–1923,* Cambridge, MA: Harvard University Press, 2001.

MOSHE TERDMAN

## Iceland

Iceland is a large volcanic island in the North Atlantic Ocean that was thought by many scholars to have been reached first by monks from **Ireland** in the eighth century. It was certainly reached and taken by Vikings in the ninth century under whom Iceland established the *Althing,* the oldest continuous parliament in the world. Along with Greenland and the Faeroe Islands, Iceland became a Danish possession after **Denmark**'s conquest of Norway in 1380. As a consequence of volcanic eruptions, disease, and neglect, Iceland atrophied as a colony until the eighteenth century, when cottage industries and fishing began to flourish. As of 1854, Iceland became a **free trade** area. Nineteenth-century change in Denmark also brought reform to Iceland. The *Althing* was reestablished in 1843, and a constitution provided for limited Home Rule in 1874. Iceland became autonomous in 1918 but did not sever its ties to the Danish crown until 1944.

FURTHER READING: Gjerset, Knut. *History of Iceland.* New York: Macmillan, 1924; Hjálmarsson, Jón R. *History of Iceland, From the Settlement to the Present Day.* Reykjavik: Iceland Review, 1993.

CARL CAVANAGH HODGE

## Immigration Restrictions

Laws passed during the second half of the nineteenth and early twentieth centuries by most self-governing colonies in the British Empire to restrict the immigration of Asians, mainly from **China, India,** and **Japan.** The European settlers in these colonies, having taken the land from the indigenous inhabitants, sought to avoid the arrival of non-Europeans, whom they perceived as racial inferiors and economic competitors.

The first immigration restriction laws were passed during the Australian gold rush. A small but steady flow of Chinese, mostly from Guangdong and Fujian provinces, had been arriving in eastern **Australia** during the 1840s, but this number increased with the discovery in 1854 of rich gold fields in the colony of Victoria. In 1855, the Victorian parliament limited the number of Chinese migrants a ship could carry to one person per 10 tons of ship's weight and levied a poll or head tax of £10 on each arrival. The neighboring colonies of South Australia and New South Wales passed similar laws to prevent Chinese landing in their territory and then traveling overland to Victoria. When the gold rush declined in the 1860s, all three colonies repealed their legislation.

Chinese immigration to the west coast of North America led the U.S. Congress to pass the *Chinese Exclusion Act* of 1881. **British Columbia** likewise enacted a series of racist laws from 1878. Some of these laws were struck down by the government of **Canada,** but then in 1885 Ottawa passed an act to restrict Chinese immigration and introduced a head tax. By 1903, this tax had been increased to $300 per person, and in 1906 Newfoundland established a similar levy. The American legislation led the Australian colonies to fear that the American ban on Chinese arrivals would lead to an influx to Australia. During the 1880s, the Australian colonies reintroduced poll taxes and limits on the number allowed to be landed per ship's tonnage. Western Australia enacted immigration restrictions for the first time, but still allowed Chinese to land in the underpopulated north of the colony.

European settlers in the southern African colony of Natal targeted their immigration restriction laws against Indians. In 1896, the government stripped Indians of voting rights on the grounds that the country they came from did not have a parliament (there is no record that this argument was used to similarly prevent Russian migrants from voting). In 1897, Natal introduced a law requiring migrants to be able to pass a dictation test in a European language. The dictation test soon became the accepted method to restrict non-European migration throughout the British Empire. In 1902, neighboring **Cape Colony** copied the Natal legislation. British Columbia had done the same in 1900, although again the Canadian government disallowed the law. **New Zealand** adopted the dictation test in 1907.

The creation of the Commonwealth of Australia in 1901 enabled the passing of national laws to enforce the "White Australia" policy. The Immigration Restriction Act was passed in 1901, although it was not, as has sometimes been suggested, the first law created by the federal parliament. Once introduced, the dictation test rarely had to be enforced, as it deterred most Asian migrants from even attempting to sail to a country where it was in place.

The Republic of **Transvaal** and **Orange Free State** had introduced immigration restrictions toward Indians while they were independent states, and these remained in place after British annexation. After the establishment of the Union of South Africa in 1910, more anti-Indian laws were passed. Mohandas Karamchand (Mahatma) Gandhi began his career of civil disobedience by leading the protests against this legislation, and eventually forced the government of **South Africa** to compromise.

FURTHER READING: Hexham, Irving. *The Irony of Apartheid*. New York: Edwin Mellen Press, 1918; Macdonald, Norman. *Canada: Immigration and Colonization, 1841–1903*. Toronto; Macmillan, 1966; Markuc, Andrew. *Australian Race Relations, 1788–1993*. St. Leondards: Allen & Unwin, 1994; Rich, Paul B. *Race and Empire in British Politics*. New York: Cambridge University Press, 1990; Saxon, Alexander. *The Indispensable Enemy: Labor and the Anti-Chinese Movement in California*. Berkeley: University of California, 1971; Windschuttle, Keith. *The White Australia Policy*. Sydney: Macleay Press, 2004.

JOHN CONNOR

## Imperial Conferences

Initially known as colonial conferences, imperial conferences were meetings of representatives of the British government and the governments of the self-governing colonies of the **British Empire.** The first was held in London in 1887 during Queen Victoria's Golden Jubilee celebrations. The conference took place as advocates of the Imperial Federation called for formal political structures linking the United Kingdom and the self-governing colonies, but these sentiments would never gain widespread support. Defense, trade, and communications were discussed and some decisions were made. The British government agreed to fortify Simon's Town naval base in **Cape Colony,** and the Australian colonies and **New Zealand** agreed to contribute 5 percent of the cost of maintaining a squadron of Royal Navy warships on the **Australia** Station. The next conference in 1894 was unique in that it was held in Ottawa, **Canada,** and was the only meeting that did not deal with defense issues. A resolution was passed supporting Imperial tariff preference, although this would not become a reality until a later economic conference was held in Ottawa at the height of the Great Depression in 1932.

Queen Victoria's Diamond Jubilee provided the backdrop for the 1897 Colonial Conference in London. Colonial Secretary Joseph Chamberlain proposed the creation of an Imperial Council, but this was firmly rejected. The issue of anti-Asian **immigration restriction** laws was discussed, as was the laying of a **telegraph** cable across the Pacific from Vancouver to Sydney, which was completed in 1902.

The 1902 Colonial Conference was held to coincide with King **Edward VII**'s coronation. During the recently concluded South African War, colonial forces had been hastily created to serve alongside the British army. New Zealand Prime Minister Richard Seddon proposed that this *ad hoc* response should be regularized with the creation of an "Imperial and Colonial Reserve Force," but this met with Canadian and Australian opposition. The conference agreed to meetings on a regular basis.

During the 1907 conference, hostility to the term *colonial* led to the self-governing colonies being renamed *dominions*, and the creation within the Colonial Office of a Dominions Department. Henceforth the meetings would be known as the Imperial Conference. Defense issues dominated the conference with a British proposal for an Imperial General Staff, which was established in 1909, and Canadian and Australian calls for the creation of dominion navies. The *Dreadnought* Crisis led to a conference in 1909 to discuss naval issues. This was the first meeting to hold closed sessions and laid the basis for the establishment of dominion navies, although the Royal Australian Navy was the only one to be created before World War I.

The 1911 Imperial Conference, which was held alongside King **George V**'s coronation, was the first to circulate an agenda before the meeting. New Zealand Prime

Minister Sir Joseph Ward proposed the creation of an Imperial Parliament, but attracted no support from the other dominions. The conference discussed whether the British and dominion governments should communicate through British-appointed governors or through dominion-appointed high commissioners. The most significant part of the conference were the closed sessions on defense and foreign affairs. In the Committee of Imperial Defense, Foreign Secretary Sir Edward **Grey** briefed the dominions on the decline in Anglo-German relations. Imperial military cooperation in the event of war was discussed in meetings at the Admiralty and the War Office. The dominion representatives refused to make definite commitments, saying this was a decision to be made by the government of the day; but Australia, Canada, and New Zealand all began making plans for expeditionary forces. These plans became the basis for the Australia and New Zealand expeditionary forces on the outbreak of World War I, although Sam Hughes, the quixotic Canadian defense minister, threw out the Canadian scheme for an improvised scheme of his own creation.

Imperial conferences continued to meet. During World War I, an Imperial War Conference convened during 1917 and 1918. After the war, Imperial conferences were held in 1921, 1923, 1926, 1930, and 1937, coinciding with the coronation of King George VI. The changed relationship between the British government and the dominions was evident when the next meeting in 1944 was renamed the Commonwealth Prime Minister's Meeting. Since 1961, the conferences have been known as Commonwealth Heads of Government Meetings (CHOGM).

These conferences never became the vehicle for the **Imperial Federation** that some had hoped for, but by creating an atmosphere of loose cooperation among states developing their own independence, they established the means by which the British Empire would evolve through decolonization to become the Commonwealth of Nations. *See also* Commonwealth; Dominion; Navalism; South Africa.

FURTHER READING: Kendle, John Edward. *The Colonial and Imperial Conferences, 1887–1911: A Study in Imperial Organization.* London: Longman, 1967.

JOHN CONNOR

## Imperial Federation

*Imperial Federation,* a term used to define a multitude of political schemes that promoted closer union between the **British Empire**'s various constituencies, was an idea that gained support in Great Britain in the late nineteenth century. Its most vocal proponent was The Imperial Federation League, a pressure group that drew support mainly from conservatives and **liberal imperialists.** Lionel Curtis, a co-founder of the imperial pressure group, the Round Table, proposed an actual imperial federation, with a central imperial parliament in London with representatives from the white settlement colonies. Other schemes were less formal, envisioning an imperial federation working through informal imperial conferences—the first such conference was held in 1887—common economic policies, a customs union similar to the German *Zollverein,* or simply the strengthening of social and cultural ties among what some historians have retroactively termed *the British world.* The motivations for imperial federation were varied. Some advocates of imperial federation wanted to improve imperial defense, some to relieve legislative congestion at Westminster, others still to prevent the secession of colonies after they received responsible government. All, however, shared a desire to strengthen the British Empire as a single geopolitical unit.

Imperial federation had been discussed periodically from the 1820s, and attracted the attention of writers such as E. A. Freeman and J. A. Froude from the 1850s to the early 1870s. The idea began to attract broader attention in the last quarter of the nineteenth century, reflecting imperial concerns about the rise of new imperial rivals such as the **United States** and Germany. Both challenged, and sometimes surpassed, Great Britain's economic supremacy in various sectors, calling into question the British Empire's position of international hegemony. Supporters of imperial federation argued that Britain could best resist its rivals by more fully mobilizing the resources of empire through closer political union. They also worried about Britain's increasing isolation from continental affairs and the potential for imperial rivalries to cause war. The latter fear only increased as the "Scramble for Africa" began in earnest in the 1880s. The Imperial Federation League was formed in 1884, with branch associations in the dominions.

Despite the lobbying efforts of supporters, however, imperial federation never achieved significant political support. While the settlement colonies continued to be loyal to the Empire, they were also developing a separate sense of what the writer Richard Jebb termed "colonial nationalism," a separate sense of independent identity that precluded membership in a formal political union. In Britain itself, critics were leery of the potentially onerous financial and military responsibilities imperial federation might entail. The Imperial Federation League itself broke up in 1894 over the question of an imperial tariff. The idea of imperial federation continued to have its advocates, notably those members of Alfred, Lord Milner's "kindergarten," his group of his young assistants in **South Africa,** which included Curtis. Imperial federation, however, never received popular support and was never adopted by any major political party. Ultimately, imperial federation was not feasible because the empire was too multifaceted, too diverse, and too widespread to be encompassed in any single, coherent political structure. Imperial federation received no serious discussion in the twentieth century; still, weaker notions of imperial unity did exist, as reflected in large-scale migration within the empire and a shared loyalty to the crown. *See also* Africa, Scramble for; Commonweath; Dominion.

FURTHER READING: Jebb, Richard. *Studies in Colonial Nationalism.* London: E. Arnold, 1905; Kendle, John. *Federal Britain: A History.* London: Routledge, 1997; Martin, Ged. "The Idea of 'Imperial Federation.'" In Ronald Hyam and Ged Martin, Eds. *Reappraisals in British Imperial History.* London: Macmillan, 1975.

DANIEL GORMAN

## Imperialism

A word of polemical power, analytical imprecision, and historically variant meaning, the term *imperialism* is used in this volume to describe the period of rapid European expansion in the nineteenth and early twentieth centuries. Imperialism is thus not merely a policy but also a tendency, a period, and even a civilization. The shifting meanings and connotations of the term have themselves been influenced by, and been influential on, the history of imperialism. The word *imperialism* is a noun derived from the word *imperial*, itself the adjectival cognate of *empire*. Imperialism might, and often does, denote the policy or the belief in the desirability of the policy of conquering territories and constructing empires. Indeed, the terms *empire* and *imperial* are both derived from the Latin *imperator*, and that term was for the Romans purely military in significance and was adopted by the Emperor Augustus precisely because its meaning was limited. To insist, however, on the directly etymological use of imperialism to denote military conquest alone would neglect the fact that over a century of invective has indelibly tainted the term with various competing meanings. A purely nominalist understanding of language might assert the possibility of defining any sign in any way; with political language this is obviously not possible, because however one may insist on some precise and limited meaning, the affective and polemical residues of other, earlier meanings and associations linger. *Imperialism* has become a particularly encrusted term.

Before the late 1870s, the term referred in English specifically to the politics of Napoleonic France, or alternatively to despotic government in general. Imperialism first entered the English language in something like its present sense in the late 1870s, when it was used to describe the ostentatious and allegedly aggressive imperial policies of the British Prime Minister Benjamin **Disraeli.** It became a synonym for Beaconsfieldism—a reference to Disraeli's title from 1876, the Earl of Beaconsfield—which the Earl of Derby described as a policy of "occupy, fortify, grab and brag." The term thus named a policy of aggressive expansion, but also had clear connotations of the celebration of empire for partisan purposes. **Jingoism,** from a bellicose music hall song that boasted "we don't want to fight, but, by Jingo, if we do/we got the ships, we've got the men, we've got the money too"—was a contemporary term for the bombastic and vainglorious spirit which critics associated with imperialism. The Liberal leader and four-time Prime Minister W. E. **Gladstone** in particular attacked the "theatrical displays and tricks" of Beaconsfield's foreign and imperial policies as much as their aggressive character. The term *imperialism* thus denoted a policy orientation, but also had connotations of vainglory and specious or unsound partisanship. The historian of empire Sir John Seeley used the term in this sense when he referred in 1883 to Cromwell's West Indian expedition as an attempt to establish an empire "prematurely and on the unsound basis of imperialism."

The term was shortly taken over by advocates of imperialism, be they those who wanted to expand the empire or merely to consolidate and strengthen it. In the 1890s, theorists of imperialism began to find social Darwinist and philanthropic reasons for the programmatic expansion of European, British or Anglo-Saxon empires. The acquisition by the United States of overseas colonies as a consequence of the Spanish American War of 1898 provoked a particular flood of advocacy, including most famously Rudyard **Kipling**'s poetic injunction to "take up the white man's burden . . . to seek another's profit, to work another's gain." The idea that imperialism was good for humanity rather than merely for a particular nation was a relative innovation, as was the air of moral sanctimony that surrounded imperialism in many minds. But that air of morality ensured that imperialism as a policy commanded wide support in this period, as was indicated by the fact that mainstream Liberal leaders such as H. H. **Asquith** and the Earl of Rosebery—both prime ministers at different points and leaders of the so-called **Liberal Imperialists**—felt it necessary to distance themselves from their anti-imperialist "little Englander" cohorts.

The positive moral valence of imperialism was not uncontested. Many of those "little Englanders" argued that it was little more than theft on a grand scale, and the revival in the 1880s of the institution of the Chartered Company—a private company given sovereign or legal powers over a territory—increased suspicion of the philanthropic claims made for imperialism. The most (in)famous such company, Cecil Rhodes' British South Africa Company, known for its stock-exchange manipulations and its African wars, fed the charges of those like J. A. **Hobson** who denounced, "the moneylending classes dressed as Imperialists and patriots."

Hobson made that charge in the context of the South African War of 1899–1902, which saw the deployment of a quarter of a million British troops against two small agricultural republics, and which, after some initial victories, degenerated into an ugly and expensive counterinsurgent campaign. This took the shine off the policy of imperialism, and by the 1905 edition of his *Imperialism: A Study,* Hobson—the canonical radical theorist of economic imperialism—was speaking of imperialism in the past tense. The **British Empire** of course still existed, covering its famous quarter of the globe, but the policy and the period of programmatic and bombastically celebrated expansion initially designated by the term was thought, not inaccurately, to be over. Simultaneously, by insisting on the economic dynamics of capital export that he argued motivated imperialism, Hobson and his followers gave the term a specifically economic significance: imperialism came to connote not merely conquest but conquest in the interests of finance capital, or in more vulgar accounts, in those of the propertied classes.

V. I. **Lenin** redefined imperialism as the "highest stage of capitalism." Borrowing many of his figures and much of his argument from the liberal Hobson, Lenin argued that the final stage of capitalism was so inherently expansionist that it could be renamed "imperialism." The argument had been widely anticipated by other Marxists such as the American H. G. Wilshire, the Austrian Rudolph Hilferding and—Lenin's particular bête noir—the German Karl Kautsky. But Lenin had done something important to the meaning of the term: he applied it not to a policy but to a stage of history, and of course for a Marxist, a stage of history is a part of an inevitable process largely immune to individual agency. Imperialism definitely retained, in Leninist hands, its pejorative connotations, but it simultaneously acquired a systemic or structural denotation and came to be used as the name for a period of history and a stage of the historical process rather than for a given policy. Lenin's polemical redefinition of the term has been both influential and confusing: those who accept Leninist theory and those who merely assimilate its ways of speaking can now show with the air of deductive rigor that Marxists once liked that any capitalist power, no matter what its foreign policy, is by definition imperialist. Simultaneously Leninist powers cannot, again as a matter of dogmatic necessity, be imperialist, even if they are expansionist by policy. They are instead described by terms such as *hegemonist,* a dogmatic nicety that was scrupulously observed even when Communist China and Communist Russia were at nuclear daggers drawn.

If, by insisting that imperialism and the highest or last stage of capitalism were synonymous, Lenin made specific speech difficult, he also made an ideological move of great eristic power: he associated the increasingly discredited practice of colonial conquest with the Marxists' class enemies and the associated Western democratic powers, and did so in a way that made it difficult to speak of the two separately. Polemical power can flow from analytical conflation. After Lenin, and influenced by the immense quantity of invective produced by Marxist parties and their camp followers, imperialism and its cognates became almost entirely pejorative terms and were often used as insults without much positive content.

Scholars of imperialism still use the term, however, and it is of course possible to speak intelligibly of Roman, Ottoman, or eighteenth-century imperialism, using the term in its etymological or late Victorian sense. But simultaneously, other scholars have followed Lenin in applying the term to either a global economic structure or a historical period. World systems theorists see it as a structure evolving over centuries. Analysts of third world poverty can speak of "imperialism without colonies." Leftist scholars define imperialism as any world system producing a rich north and a poor global south. The term *imperialism* has become completely divorced from its military and even political implications; its essence is considered to be purely economic and structural, and no demonstration of policy intent is needed to show the existence of imperialism.

The term is not always used in a purely economic sense. It has become common to hear of "cultural imperialism," which can describe phenomena from the use of the English language to the sale of a hamburger. Any kind of international power or influence, however indirect or even apparently consensual, can be defined as imperialist. It is also possible to speak of "ecological imperialism," meaning the spread of one species at the expense of others. In such usages, the term retains it systemic or structural connotations, while abandoning much of the specific economic arguments used by more orthodox Marxists.

As imperialism has acquired a structural meaning, it has simultaneously expanded temporally. Lenin, like Hobson and like the advocates of imperialism, used the term to describe a relatively brief period of post-free-trading capitalism, running from approximately 1870 forward. Recent scholars, including the editor of this volume, use the term to describe the entire period of European global preeminence, dated back to about 1800. Edward Said, possibly the most influential recent academic analyst of imperialism, defines it as the "unprecedented power" on a global scale of European civilization, which he dates to about 1800, implying that the imperialist period is not yet over. Other recent scholars have backdated imperialism to Christopher Columbus, and in some accounts to the crusades. As imperialism has shed its specific policy denotation and acquired systemic and civilizational connotations, it has also expanded in time.

Imperialism therefore began as a largely pejorative term, but acquired and then rapidly lost positive moral and philanthropic connotations. It was initially primarily military and political in significance, but acquired economic overtones as its philanthropic and patriotic claims were questioned. It was initially used to describe a policy, but in the hands of Lenin and many since has come to denote an economic structure largely independent of the volition of any one actor. Where the term once had an air of specious braggadocio, it now more often names a deep structure, and for many scholars it is a structure inclined to hide rather than to advertise the reality of its power. Imperialism has in recent scholarship been expanded from the brief period of decades analyzed by Hobson and Lenin, and now for many denotes the entire period of Western global exploration and expansion.

As the Euro-American civilization created by imperialism—in the long-term structural sense—has lost confidence in itself, writers within that civilization's chief ideological establishments have decided that imperialism, by which they mean their own culture's power, is almost wholly a bad thing; in the process they have in a period of a little more than a century changed its meaning along moral, economic, structural, intentional, and temporal axes. The historian of British imperialism, W. K. Hancock, is said to have complained that "imperialism is not a word for scholars," but it is not going to go away. It should be used with care. *See also* Bismarck, Otto von; Bonaparte, Napoleon; Colony; Great Power; *Weltpolitik*.

FURTHER READING: Hobson, John A. *Imperialism: A Study.* London: Nisbet, 1902; Kipling, Rudyard. "The White Man's Burden." In Martin Seymour Smith, ed. *Rudyard Kipling.* New York: St. Martin's Press, 1990; Koebner, Richard, and Helmut Dan Schmidt. *Imperialism: The Story and Significance of a Political Word, 1840–1960,* Cambridge: Cambridge University Press, 1964; Lenin, V. I. "Imperialism: the Highest Stage of Capitalism." *Collected Works,* v. 22, *December 1915-July 1916.* Moscow: Progress Publishers, 1964; Magdoff, Harry. *Imperialism without Colonies.* New York: Monthly Review, 2003; Robert, Andrew. *Salisbury: Victorian Titan.* London: Phoenix, 1999; Said, Edward. *Culture and Imperialism.* London: Chatto and Windus, 1993; Seeley, J. R. *The Expansion of England.* London: Macmillan, 1911; Thornton, A. P. *The Imperial Idea and Its Enemies.* New York: St. Martin's, 1959.

MARK F. PROUDMAN

## Imperial Preference

Ideas for a British imperial tariff that became popular in the late nineteenth and early twentieth centuries. Ideas for Imperial Preference took many specific forms, but in general imports from outside the Empire would be taxed at a higher rate than those from within the imperial tariff wall. Most famously advocated by the then-colonial secretary and enthusiastic imperialist Joseph **Chamberlain** in a speech of May 1903, the idea had support primarily in Tory circles. For many supporters, an Imperial *Zollverein* on the German model would serve as a precursor to closer imperial integration, possibly including imperial political and representative institutions. The doctrine of free trade, however, had an almost iconic status in British politics, and proposals to set up a British tariff wall excited great opposition, particularly but not solely among Liberals and Laborites. It caused deep fissures even within the Tory party, and contributed to the marginalization of Chamberlain in his later years. The idea of Imperial Preference had some impact on politics in the **Dominions,** although colonial statesmen were jealous of local control of trade policy for both revenue and protective purposes. Imperial Preference became something of a standby at interwar **Commonwealth** conferences, but the practical difficulties in the way of reconciling local autonomy with a centrally administered tariff policy were insuperable.

FURTHER READING: Pigou, A. C. *Protective and Preferential Import Duties.* London: Macmillan, 1906.

MARK F. PROUDMAN

## Impressionism

Impressionism was an artistic movement that developed among French painters between 1870 and 1885. Leading practitioners include Claude Monet, Edgar Degas, and Pierre-Auguste Renoir. The new movement consciously rejected the rigid rules of the French Art Academy concerning canvas size, subject matter, composition, and technique. Rather than paint historical scenes or moral allegories, the impressionists preferred landscapes, intimate portraits, and middle class entertainments made possible by the Industrial Revolution. Above all, the impressionists sought to capture a fleeting moment in time. As a result, they worked quickly and abandoned the fine details prized in academic circles in favor of loose, broken brushwork and a brighter palette of unmixed paints. Inspired by the influx of Japanese prints made possible by the 1853 American expedition to open Japan to Western trade, impressionist paintings also adopted a revolutionary new compositional style that employed unexpected angles of vision and cut off portions of their subjects. By the mid-1880s, impressionism was gradually replaced by a younger generation of postimpressionist artists like Paul Gauguin and Georges Seurat who used strong, unnatural colors and distorted perspective to convey an emotional response to the industrial changes of late nineteenth-century Europe. *See also Belle Époque;* French Empire; Japanese Empire.

FURTHER READING: Pool, Phoebe. *Impressionism.* London: Thames and Hudson, 1994; Thompson, Belinda. *Impressionism: Origins, Practice, Reception.* London: Thames and Hudson, 2000.

KENNETH J. OROSZ

## India

The most valued colonial possession of the **British Empire.** The Mughal Empire (1526–1857) had been broken, as a unified political entity to be reckoned with, for competing British and French commercial interests in India by the early eighteenth century. By 1761, moreover, the British had managed to reduce France's role in India to that of tertiary commercial presence alone, and over the next century the subcontinent came slowly but relentlessly under British commercial and political dominance. Between the 1760s and 1858, nonetheless, the principal vehicle of British power was the **East India Company,** established in 1600. As the company established a monopoly over the opium trade and salt production, it simultaneously brought more Indian territory under its control by persuading or forcing the small successor states to the Mughal Empire to accept its protection and authority. In the effort, the company fought four wars against the Muslim rulers of Mysore and the Hindu rulers of Maratha. Although the company had pacified most of India by 1818, its appetite for territory had not been sated, so it expanded into Sind between 1838 and 1842 and waged two campaigns against the Sikhs of the Punjab in 1845 and 1849 before it was able to annex the region to its other Indian possessions. Under the direction of James **Dalhousie,** it built **railroads** and **telegraph** networks. As the company slackened its control over missionary activity, however, Hindu traditions such as *sati* and *thugee* came under criticism from English custom and legal attack by officials such as Lord William **Bentinck** and Thomas Babington **Macaulay.** The company's hold on India snapped entirely, when indigenous resentment of foreign rule and the destruction of India's textile industry by the cheaper imports produced by industrializing Britain evolved into the **Indian Mutiny** of 1857.

The ultimate defeat of the rebellion also brought with it the overthrow of the last Mughal emperor who had sided with the rebels. In the **India Act** of 1858, the British

Parliament then transferred authority in India from the company to the Crown, thus beginning the ear of the British *Rāj,* which lasted until India's independence in 1947. Between the passage of the India Act and the onset of the European crisis in 1914, India became a unified political and administrative entity again, this time endowed with the rudiments of a modern infrastructure. While trade boomed and an Indian posting became one of the most prestigious to which a British civil servant could aspire, a period of rapid progress was accompanied by a succession of famines, claiming tens of millions of lives, as the priority of commercial agriculture for export depleted local food supplies. Thus, the middle class of educated administrators from among the Indian population who ran the day-to-day affairs of British India found themselves in the service, although not in possession, of a fledgling Indian state even as the mass discontentment caused by human catastrophe nurtured a political base for the nationalist cause of independence. The Indian National Congress was founded in 1885 by liberal nationalists who sought progress toward independence within the framework of British rule. In 1907, the Congress split between moderates who sought **dominion** status and radicals who demanded immediate independence. In the meantime, a separate Muslim League was founded under the leadership of Dr. Muhammad Ali Jinnah. In 1905, violent protests against the partition of **Bengal** by the Marquis of **Curzon** created a tentative unity of Hindu and Muslim nationalists, in large part because the partition was itself viewed as a divide-and-rule response to the independence cause. The extremists overplayed their hand and were imprisoned or driven into exile, which left Congress forces under the control of moderates. They created the All-India Congress Committee as a centralized executive body of elected delegates. The passage of a series of Indian Councils Acts in 1861, 1892, and 1909 introduced and then increased the indirect election of Indians to recommending bodies that provided a generation of nationalists with training in government.

During World War I, India supplied more than a million men to the British cause and was transformed by the conflict. The war also increased pressure for reform and independence, to which the India Acts of 1919 and 1935 responded but not to the satisfaction of the nationalists. It was remarkable not that Indian independence waited until the conclusion of another world war but rather that the British hold on the country endured, remarkably, until 1947. *See also* Afghan Wars; Anglo-Burmese Wars; Dalhousie, James; Great Game; Hyderabad; Maratha Wars; Sikh Wars.

FURTHER READING: Embree, A. T. *1857 in India: Mutiny or War of Independence.* Boston: Heath, 1963; Gautam, O. P. *The Indian National Congress.* Delhi: D. K. Publishers, 1984; James, Lawrence. *Raj: The Making and Unmaking of British India.* New York: St. Martin's, 1997; Metcalf, T. R. *The Aftermath of Revolt.* Oxford: Oxford University Press, 1964; Wolpert, Stanley. *A New History of India.* Princeton, NJ: Princeton University Press, 1979.

CARL CAVANAGH HODGE

## India Act (1858)

An act of the British parliament abolishing the **East India Company,** which had conquered a large Indian empire, and replaced its rule with that of a viceroy directly responsible to the British government. The East India Company, originally formed in 1600, had acquired, often through force of circumstance rather than policy, a large territorial empire, an empire that had the not unintended effect of enriching many of its owners and employees. Indian government became controversial in the eighteenth century more because of the feared influence of its wealth upon Parliament than because of concerns about the government of **India** itself. William **Pitt**'s India Bills of 1784 and 1793 established a board of control, whose name made it clear that the object was to control the company rather than to govern India.

Throughout the early nineteenth century, successive India bills renewed the company's charter on a 20-year basis, the final one being in 1853. Each bill reduced the company's powers and patronage under the vague idea that it ought eventually to be abolished entirely and under the influence of those like Thomas Babington **Macaulay** who held to the then relatively novel doctrine that English government in India could be justified only if it served the good of India. The systematizing and progressive Victorian mind felt it increasingly anomalous that a commercial organization should simultaneously exercise sovereign powers.

The Indian **sepoy** mutiny of 1857–1858, perceived to have been the result of company misgovernment, crystallized support for this view. An India bill introduced by Lord **Palmerston** commanded such bipartisan support that when his government fell on an unrelated matter, it was reintroduced in much the same form by Benjamin **Disraeli,** acting for the new administration of Lord **Derby.** The Government of India Act established the post of secretary of state for India, who sat in the cabinet, advised by an Indian council, and communicated with a viceroy at Calcutta. It brought the company's armies under crown control and paid off its owners and creditors. Lord Stanley, later the fifteenth Earl of **Derby,** became the first Indian secretary of state, and Lord Canning the first viceroy. *See also* Indian Mutiny.

FURTHER READING: Dodwell, H. H., ed. *The Cambridge History of the British Empire,* Vol. 5, *India, 1858–1918.* Cambridge: Cambridge University Press, 1932; Metcalf, T. R. *The Aftermath of Revolt.* Oxford: Oxford University Press, 1964.

MARK F. PROUDMAN

## Indian Mutiny (1857–1858)

A serious attempt by rebellious Indian elements in the army of the British **East India Company,** supported in some areas by civilians, intended to expel the British from the subcontinent. There were a number of underlying causes, but the mutiny was sparked off by the issuing to **sepoy** troops the Minié rifle cartridge, greased with pork and beef fat, and offensive to Muslims and Hindus, respectively. The mutiny began at Meerut in May 1857 and quickly spread across northern and central India, leading to the general massacre of British troops and civilians. After the initial shock, the British marched to besiege Delhi, taken by the rebels, and to relieve **Lucknow,** which contained a small British military and civilian garrison. Sir Henry Havelock, with 2,500 troops, reached Lucknow on September 25, but was unable to relieve the city until Sir Colin Campbell arrived with reinforcements in November. The small British force before Delhi, despite constant rebel sorties and intense heat, managed to maintain a loose siege of the capital before successfully storming it in mid-September. All but sporadic fighting ended with General Rose's victory at Gwalior in central India in June 1858. Harsh British repression and reprisal followed. *See also* Bentinck, Lord William; Macaulay, Thomas; Missionaries.

FURTHER READING: David, Saul. Th*e Indian Mutiny, 1857.* London, Viking, 2002; Harris, John. *The Indian Mutiny.* London: Wordsworth Editions, 2000; Ward, Andrew. *Our Bones Are Scattered: The Cawnpore Massacre and the Indian Mutiny of 1857.* New York: Henry Holt & Co., 1996; Watson, Bruce. *The Great Indian Mutiny.* New York: Praeger, 1991.

GREGORY FREMONT-BARNES

## Indian Wars

The name commonly given to conflict between indigenous North American peoples, referred to almost uniformly as "Indians," and European settlers encroaching on their territory, starting in the sixteenth century and lasting into the late nineteenth century. In the United States clashes of either settlers or soldiers with various Indian peoples over enormous tracts of territory in the American interior were almost continuous between the 1840s and 1890s, but most accounts of American history set the period of the Indian Wars between the conclusion of the **American Civil War** in 1865 and the Battle of Wounded Knee in December 1890, the last major engagement between the United States Army and indigenous American peoples.

The most storied campaigns were those waged against the Apache, Comanche, Cheyenne, Modoc, Navajo, Nez Percé, and Sioux tribes, many of them organized by General Philip H. Sheridan, a veteran commander in the Union army during the Civil War and commander of the entire U.S. Army between 1883 and 1888. There was immense savagery on both sides and, as most of the campaigns were badly reported or ignored altogether by the press, an equally immense popular mythology constructed about the nature and nobility of the relentless campaign to bring ever more territory under white settlement.

A parallel campaign took place in Canada to the north. Although the scale of westward settlement was smaller and the reaction less violent, where resistance to settlement became an inconvenience, force was routinely used to effect the "resettlement" of tribes such as the Cree, Crow, and Blackfoot by frontier constabularies such as the Northwest Mounted Police and the Royal Canadian Mounted Police. The most famous of these was the Red River Rebellion of 1869–1870, actually a rising of Métis people of mixed French-Canadian and Indian ancestry led by Louis Riel, to this day a hero of French-Canadian and Métis history.

FURTHER READING: Morris, R. B. *The Indian Wars.* Minneapolis: Lerner Publications, 1985; Ostler, Jeffrey. *The Plains Sioux and U.S. Colonialism from Lewis and Clarke to Wounded Knee.* New York: Cambridge University Press, 2004; Steele, Ian. *Warpaths: The Invasion of North America.* New York: Oxford University Press, 1995.

CARL CAVANAGH HODGE

## Indirect Rule

The administration of a colony through a local intermediary. The use of an indigenous leader with a traditional base of authority and legitimacy among the colonial population was usually far less costly than the assumption of direct authority, the posting of troops, and the adjudication of local quarrels. Equally, indirect rule could be defended as a liberal form of colonial administration, because it permitted Africans to retain their traditional authority figures while Africa customs could be codified and used as a basis for settling disputes. Indirect rule was difficult to maintain, as competition among European imperial power intensified, especially during the Scramble for **Africa,** but colonial governors such as Frederick **Lugard** nonetheless developed indirect rule in theory and practice, particularly in Nigeria.

FURTHER READING: Lugard, Frederick Dealtry. *The Dual Mandate in British Tropical Africa.* London: W. Blackwood and Sons, 1922; Perham, Margery. *Lugard.* 2 vols. Hamden: Archon, 1968.

CARL CAVANAGH HODGE

## Indochina

Derived from *Indochine française,* a common label for French territories in Southeast Asia, Indochina included present-day Vietnam, Cambodia, and Laos. French interest in the region dated to the establishment of the *Compagnie de Chine* in 1660. In 1787 the Annamite ruler Nguyen Anh gave France a monopoly of trade in return for military security. In the mid-nineteenth century, French interest in the region intensified, partly as a result of the rise of the silk industry in France and partly in response to competition from Britain to the south, in Hong Kong and Singapore, and from the **United States** in the form of Commodore Perry's visit to Japan in 1853. The French were also keen to gain access to the Chinese market without being hindered by the British, so they concentrated their energies on colonizing Indochina during the 1860s and 1870s primarily for economic reasons and a desire to reclaim national glory wounded by defeat in the **Franco-Prussian War.**

Indochina was nonetheless to be a problematic area in the French colonial project. French Indochina was a federation comprised of **Annam,** Tonkin, and Cochin China. Only Cochin China became a full colony; the remainder became the protectorate of Annam-Tonkin. After the Sino-French War of 1883–1885, Tonkin, Annam and Cochin China came under French control. But the war with China involved some embarrassing setbacks that brought down the government of Jules **Ferry** before secret talks with the Chinese produced an acceptable outcome in the Second Treaty of **Tientsin.**

In October 1887, Cambodia was added, and in 1893 Laos, too, became part of the federation. Its capital was Hanoi. While Annam, Tonkin, Laos, and Cambodia functioned as a protectorate, the kings of Luang Prabang and Cambodia and the Emperor of Vietnam were allowed to retain their positions This was only a façade, as a substantive authority was in the hands of the French governor-general. The control of military and naval forces was his alone. To boost national morale and prestige in the metropole, the government presented French presence in Indochina as benign and admirable through active propaganda. Artifacts from Indochina were exhibited in the grand expositions in Paris, popular during the *belle époque* to illustrate the grandeur of French *mission civilisatrice. See also* French Empire.

FURTHER READING: Chapius, Oscar. *The Last Emperors of Vietnam: From Tu Duc to Bao Dai.* Westport, CT: Greenwood Press, 2000; Power, Thomas F. *Jules Ferry and the Renaissance of*

*French Imperialism.* New York: King's Crown Press, 1944; Wesseling, H. L. *The European Colonial Empires 1815–1919.* New York: Pearson Education, 2004.

NURFADZILAH YAHAYA

## Inkerman, Battle of (1854)

An engagement of the **Crimean War** fought on November 5, 1854. Inkerman became known as the "soldier's battle," for, with a heavy mist shrouding the field, officers were unable to direct their troops and the fighting was left to the ordinary ranks armed with muskets and bayonets. Inkerman was the last of three attempts by the Russians under Prince Menshikov to raise the Allied siege of the Black Sea port of Sevastopol by British and French forces. The brunt of the fighting fell to the British infantry, which, in a confused and bloody action, held the Russians at bay until French reinforcements arrived to shift the balance in the Allies' favor. The Russians withdrew with losses of 12,000 to the Allies losses of 3,300, mostly British. *See also* Balaklava, Battle of; Ottoman Empire; Russian Empire.

FURTHER READING: Barthorp, Michael. *Heroes of the Crimea: Balaclava and Inkerman.* London: Blandford, 1991; Mercer, Patrick. *Give Them a Volley and Charge!: The Battle of Inkerman, 1854.* Staplehurst: Spellmount, 1998; Mercer, Patrick. *Inkerman 1854: The Soldier's Battle.* Oxford: Osprey Publishing, 1998.

GREGORY FREMONT-BARNES

## Inkiar Skelessi, Treaty of (1833)

Also spelled Hunkar-Iskelesi and Unkiar-Skelessi, this defensive alliance between the **Ottoman Empire** and the **Russian Empire** was signed on July 8, 1833. The Ottomans had been forced to turn to the Russians for aid when earlier appeals to the French and British for assistance against the Sultan's own overly ambitious vassal, Mehmet Ali, the governor of **Egypt,** were rebuffed. Egyptian troops led by Mehmet Ali's son, Ibrahim, had conducted an extraordinarily successful campaign against Ottoman forces in the province of Syria during 1832, inflicted a defeat on a numerically superior Ottoman army in Konia in Anatolia, and were on the verge of occupying Constantinople itself by late January 1833. The Ottoman sultan, Mahmud II, turned to his traditional foe, Tsar **Nicholas I** of Russia for aid.

The Russians, on the premise that a weak and beholden Ottoman Empire as a neighbor was preferable to a newly invigorated Egyptian Empire under Mehmet Ali or a great power scramble for territory should the Ottoman Empire dissolve, sent naval forces through the Bosporus in February 1833 to shield the city. The forces were soon reinforced by troops sent ashore in Constantinople itself. Faced with Russian intervention, Mehmet Ali accepted the Peace of Kutahia, which gave him the governorship of an additional four Ottoman provinces in Syria in addition to Egypt, and in return he regained the status of nominally loyal vassal, and Ibrahim withdrew the Egyptian forces south of the Taurus Mountains. To cement their newfound position with the Ottoman Empire, the Russians negotiated the Treaty of Inkiar Skelessi. Officially both the Ottomans and Russians agreed to guarantee the territorial integrity of one another's domains, but in an attached secret clause, the Russians relieved the Ottomans of any obligation to render them military aid in return for an agreement to close the Dardanelles to the warships of any other nations. The treaty had a term of eight years, at which time it was subject to renegotiation.

The secret clause of the treaty was interpreted by the British and French, who soon got wind of it, as granting the Russians a virtual protectorate of the Ottoman Empire. The Russians, on the other hand, claimed that the treaty violated no existing agreements with regard to the straits and simply reaffirmed the "ancient custom" that the straits were to be closed to the warships of all foreign powers in time of peace. During the eight years it was in force, the Treaty of Inkiar Skelessi was a point of major concern within the context of the Eastern Question, and ultimately it was another crisis involving **Mehmet Ali** and the Ottoman Empire that began in 1839, which brought about the treaty's replacement. That occurred when the treaty was superseded by the terms of the London Straits Convention of 1840. *See also* Eastern Question; London Straits Convention.

FURTHER READING: Anderson, M. S. *The Eastern Question 1774–1923*. London: Macmillan, 1966; Hale, William. *Turkish Foreign Policy 1774–2000*. London: Frank Cass, 2000; Hurewitz, C., ed. *The Diplomacy of the Near and Middle East, A Documentary Record: 1535–1914*. Vol. 1. Princeton, NJ: D. Van Nostrand and Co., 1956; Jelavich, Barbara. *A Century of Russian Foreign Policy 1814–1914*. Philadelphia: J. B. Lippincott, 1964; Karsh, Efraim, and Inari Karsh. *Empires of the Sand: The Struggle for Mastery in the Middle East 1789–1923*. Cambridge, MA: Harvard University Press, 1999; MacKenzie, David. *Imperial Dreams, Harsh Realities: Tsarist Russian Foreign Policy, 1815–1917*. Fort Worth, TX: Harcourt Brace College Publishers, 1994.

ROBERT DAVIS

## Intelligence

Intelligence, in the military sense, is knowledge about actual or potential enemies in peace and war that is possibly of decisive advantage when coherently and imaginatively interpreted and acted upon. Carl von **Clausewitz** noted that information obtained in war was often contradictory and more often than not mostly false. He added to this that "the timidity of men acts as a multiplier of lies and untruths." Yet when combined with "firm reliance in self," he conceded, accurate intelligence could make a critical difference. Horatio **Nelson** is generally regarded as a first-class intelligence analyst. His ability to filter through facts in search of probabilities enabled him to calculate in August 1798 that he would find the French fleet in **Aboukir Bay** at the mouth of the Nile and, with the element of surprise, he was able to destroy it. Based in large part on the experience of British colonial conflicts, C. E. Callwell cited the absence of trustworthy information to be an inherent characteristic of small wars in remote areas.

Another British hero of the Napoleonic Wars, the Duke of **Wellington,** was able to overcome this problem during his command of armies in **India,** 1799–1804, simply by adopting the *harkara* system invented by the Mughal Empire of writers and runners who carried news reports over long distances and difficult terrain. Kipling's *Kim* is a creature of the **Great Game,** itself in large part an intelligence contest between the British and Russian Empires. The arts of intelligence were romanticized in the *Kim* tradition by writers such as John Buchan in thrillers such as *Greenmantle*. The attempt to transform intelligence work into science over the course of the nineteenth century—an era of **telegraph** and **railroad**—meant that by far the greatest labors were committed to the gathering of masses of information to improve the quality of intelligence in the service of the calculation behind peacetime diplomacy. Still, conflict stimulated innovation. The **United States** created a Bureau of Military Information in 1862 during the **American Civil War,** a conflict in which rail transportation and telegraph brought significant advantage to the Union cause.

In the final decades of the nineteenth century, cable and wireless communication increased the speed and range in the transmission of information even as global imperial competition and a gathering naval arms race increased the demand for actionable intelligence exponentially. When the British government created the Secret Service Bureau in a joint venture of the Admiralty and the War Office in 1909, it was merely answering a deeply felt need of its national security—a need felt strongest perhaps in the status quo power but nonetheless shared by enemies and allies alike. In 1917, the British effort paid off, when the admiralty intercepted and deciphered German diplomatic efforts to prompt Mexico to attack the United States, an intelligence coup now famous as the Zimmerman Telegram that helped to draft American arms to the Allied cause.

FURTHER READING: Bayley, A. *Empire and Information: Intelligence Gathering and Social Communication in India, 1780–1870.* New York: Cambridge University Press, 1996; Callwell, C. E. *Small Wars, Their Principles and Practice.* London: HMSO, 1906; Clauswitz, Carl von. *On War.* Translated by J. J. Graham. London: Routledge & Kegan Paul, 1908; Keegan, John. *Intelligence in War: Knowledge of the Enemy from Napoleon to Al Qaeda.* Toronto: Key Porter Books, 1903; Tuchman, Barbara. *The Zimmerman Telegram.* New York: Viking, 1958.

CARL CAVANAGH HODGE

## Internationalism

Internationalism is the idea that nations should cooperate to solve common problems and prevent national disputes, rather than pursue primarily their national interests. Internationalism became an increasingly strong ideology as the nineteenth century progressed and has become a dominant ideology of the twentieth century. Modern internationalism can trace its roots to the eighteenth-century Enlightenment, when thinkers such as Immanuel Kant, Voltaire, and Rousseau argued for the universalism of human values and interests. Kant even envisioned a form of world government. Romantic nationalism, which emerged in the early nineteenth century as a reaction to the materialism of many Enlightenment thinkers, also played a role in advancing internationalism. Following the example of the French Revolution, many Europeans sought to form their own nation-states, where a single ethnic population would have its own political state. German and Italian nationalism were notable examples. The widespread revolutions of 1848, however, also reflected a broad, or international, desire for nationalism. These movements, many of which eventually succeeded as the nineteenth century wore on, helped create a larger community of nations, which eventually became the basis for an international community. Conflicts between nations were common, but so, too, was a desire to cooperate and preserve peace. These were the goals of the Concert of Europe, the agreement struck amongst the victorious powers after the Napoleonic Wars to regularly consult each other on issues of perceived common interest. They were also the goals of the new international organizations that began to form in the 1860s and 1870s, including the Universal Postal Union and the International Telegraph Union.

Internationalism also gained strength below the state level. International organizations such as the International Olympic Committee and The International Red Cross, the latter formed in 1864 through the inspiration of the Swiss doctor Jean Henri Dunant, were private organizations that, although they worked with national governments, reflected a spirit of individual amity. Working people also embraced internationalism as a new and potentially revolutionary ideology. The First International, also known as the International Working Men's Association, was founded in London in 1864 under the leadership of Karl **Marx.** Its aim was an international socialist revolution, and it worked to generate cooperation between socialist groups in different nations. The First International attracted both communist and noncommunist socialist organizations, but it eventually split up over the question of whether revolution was a short- or long-term goal, a division mirrored in the personal animosity between Marx and Mikael Bakunin, the Russian anarchist and fellow leading international socialist. The Second International was formed in Paris in 1889, and pursued more reformist goals. It broke up in 1914 over the war, with members choosing nationalism over internationalist goals. The Bolshevist leader V. I. **Lenin** formed the Third International in 1919, representing the international goals of communism. International socialism represented a major ideological challenge to imperialism during the half-century before World War I.

Internationalism also entailed the unprecedented relations of trade and social interaction that marked especially the period from 1870 to 1914. This period, sometimes termed "the first era of globalization," witnessed a marked rise in international cooperation and investment. The British writer Norman Angell, reflecting the temper of the age, declared that any future war, regardless of who won, would in fact harm all participants through the mutual damage it would cause to international trade. In the same spirit, European nations pledged support for international cooperation at The **Hague Conferences** of 1899 and 1907, inspired by the Russian Czar Nicholas II. Internationalism, however, remained stronger as an ideal than a reality. National rivalries remained and were particularly intense regarding imperial competition in Africa and Asia, economic protectionism, and arms production. Internationalism also remained largely a European idea. The United States remained a largely isolationist nation, while much of the rest of the world was excluded because of unequal economic development and colonial paternalism. Nonetheless, although World War I proved a serious setback for internationalism, the idea reemerged after the war in the form of the League of Nations. *See also* Commonwealth; Communism; Globalization; Imperial Federation; Railroad; Telegraph.

FURTHER READING: Cooper, Sandi. *Internationalism in Nineteenth Century Europe: The Crisis of Ideas and Purpose.* New York: Garland Publishing, 1976; Haupt, Georges. *Aspects of International*

*Socialism, 1871–1914: Essays.* Cambridge: Cambridge University Press, 1986; Woolf, Leonard. *International Government.* London, 1916.

DANIEL GORMAN

## International Law

International law, or public international law, is the body of customs, norms, principles, procedures, rules, and standards among sovereign states for the purpose of enhancing peaceful coexistence and cooperation among them. It is generally accepted that the evolution of international law can be broken into two periods: the first between the Peace of Westphalia and World War I (1649–1914), and the second after World War I. During the Age of Imperialism the development of international law was primarily a project of the Great Powers. It addressed matters of war and peace as exemplified in the **Congress System**'s determination to put European diplomacy, "public peace," on a calculable footing following the Napoleonic Wars—in its more confident moments an innovation referred to as the "Concert of Europe."

Despite four limited conflicts involving the **Great Powers** in the mid-nineteenth century, tentative progress was made in the articulation of international norms, for example, in the 1856 Declaration of Paris on matters of commerce and conflict. The Paris declaration's attention to the protection of neutral trade in war, in fact, itself both captured the preoccupations of the Great Powers and expressed the division of modern international law into law of the sea and laws of war. With the progress of industrialization and the rapid increase in international trade, most new norms developed in the second half of the nineteenth century had a wholly practical basis: the International Telegraph Union of 1865, International Postal Union of 1875, and International Conference for Promoting Technical Uniformity in Railways in 1882, all underpinned by treaty or statute in the member states. But issues of moral import were not entirely neglected. The 1864 **Geneva Convention** determined that not only wounded soldiers in the field but also ambulance staff were to be considered neutral and not liable to be taken prisoners of war. It also invented the International Red Cross and gave it a flag, the Swiss flag with colors reversed, to uphold the convention.

In its General Act, the 1884 Conference of **Berlin** not only authorized the colonial partition of Africa but also obliged the signatories to suppress slavery and the **slave trade**. The **Hague** Peace Conference of 1899 was attended by 26 states, that of 1907 by 44; the first sought a systematic codification of the customs of war, and the second furthered this work. It is symptomatic of the intensifying Great Power competition of the time, however, that neither achieved an agreement on arms limitations. The idea of internationalism was much more robust than the substance of international cooperation. The popular nationalism aroused by the July Crisis of 1914 promptly disabused internationalists and pacifists of their roseate outlook. A new day for international law awaited the military outcome of 1918. *See also* Globalization; Internationalism.

FURTHER READING: Glahn, Gerhard von. *Law Among Nations.* New York: Pearson-Longman, 1954; Nussbaum, A. *A Concise History of the Law of Nations.* New York: Macmillan, 1954.

CARL CAVANAGH HODGE

## Iran

*See* Persia

## Ireland

Since the Middle Ages, and especially since the late sixteenth century, Ireland was an object of English rule, colonial plantation, and settlement by English and Scottish Protestants against the resistance of an Irish population that had been Catholic since the fifth century. With the **Act of Union** passed by the government of William **Pitt** the Younger in 1801, Ireland was incorporated into the United Kingdom of Great Britain and Northern Ireland and subsequently required to bear part of the burden of Britain's serial wars against Napoleon **Bonaparte.**

Until 1829, Catholics were barred from serving in parliament. This constitutional exclusion laid a political foundation for Irish nationalism, and despite Catholic Emancipation, the continuing ill treatment of the rural population by Protestant landlords gave it deep social and cultural roots. The **Irish Famine** of the 1840s further deepened Irish resentment, so that the **Home Rule** movement led by Charles Parnell starting in the 1860s enjoyed broad support, and more violent manifestations of Irish nationalism eventually prompted the Coercion Act from the British Parliament in 1881.

In 1902, the owner of the weekly newspaper, *United Irishman,* founded a political organization dedicated to Ireland's complete independence, *Sinn Fein,* "Ourselves Alone." Protestants in the northern province of Ulster began to campaign to defend the Union, fearing that in a sovereign Ireland they would be a small and hated minority. William **Gladstone**'s successive attempts at Home Rule failed, and Irish nationalist stepped up agitation during World War I, climaxing in the Easter Rebellion of 1916 by the Irish Republican Brotherhood. *See also* De Valera, Eamon.

FURTHER READING: Foster, R. F. *Modern Ireland, 1600–1972.* New York: Penguin, 1989; Norman, E. R. *A History of Modern Ireland.* Coral Gables, FL: University of Miami Press, 1971.

CARL CAVANAGH HODGE

## Irish Famine (1845–1850)

A disaster for **Ireland** when disease destroyed the potato crop in 1845–1849. A fungus rotted potatoes in other parts of Europe, too, but the blight affected Ireland most severely because potatoes were the staple food for agricultural laborers and small tenant farmers. Almost a million men, women, and children died of starvation or related diseases. Hundreds of thousands emigrated, either to nearby England and Scotland or to distant North America in so-called coffin ships, aboard which many steerage passengers died.

In the worst year, 1846, the British Prime Minister Sir Robert Peel responded by repealing the **Corn Laws** to encourage the importation of cheap foreign wheat. In practice this did the starving Irish little good, as they lacked the means to buy any kind of food. Lord John Russell's Whig government, succeeding Peel's Conservative ministry, was ideologically rigid. Out of local Irish taxes, Russell provided some ill-paid employment at public works for a minority of starving peasants, but in accord with the principle of laissez-faire, the Whigs believed that only private charities should provide food relief. During the famine the civil servant Charles Edward Trevelyan defended the export of grain and livestock from Ireland to Britain. In the crisis years, the small Quaker denomination showed the greatest generosity. There also was a British Relief Association, helped by Queen **Victoria**'s appeal for contributions.

The potato famine had long-term consequences. Ireland may be unique among European countries to have a smaller population in the twenty-first century than in the mid-1840s. Estimated at 8 million on the eve of the famine, it had fallen to about 5 million at the 1850 census. With less competition for land, small farmers were better off after the famine than before. The population continued to fall during decades of relative prosperity. The age of marriage rose, and the habit of emigration strengthened, particularly among young women. For instance, in the **United States** during the mid and late nineteenth century, Irish Catholic immigrants became numerous. Bridey (for Bridget) became the stereotypical housemaid, while Paddy (for Patrick) the stereotypical unskilled laborer. The overseas Irish helped fund **Fenian** violence and, after World War I, IRA violence. The famine both intensified bitterness toward Britain in the Irish Catholic diaspora and greatly enlarged its numbers. *See also* Act of Union.

FURTHER READING: Woodham-Smith, Cecil. *The Great Hunger: Ireland 1845–1849* New York: Harper & Row, 1962.

DAVID M. FAHEY

## Irish Land Acts (1870–1909)

British legislation passed between 1870 and 1909 to benefit Irish tenant farmers. As a result of wars, confiscations, and anti-Catholic laws, **Ireland**'s wealthy landlords almost always were Protestants of English descent. Fewer than 800 families owned half of Ireland. Except in the northeast, tenant farmers were mostly Roman Catholic. Tenants argued that their insecure status discouraged them from making improvements on their land such as draining marshes. Landlords might respond by imposing higher rents and evicting tenants unwilling to pay them. Economic historians have questioned that many landlords extracted the maximum or rack rent.

In 1870, William **Gladstone,** Britain's Liberal prime minister, persuaded Parliament to pass the first of his Irish land acts. It safeguarded the tenant from arbitrary eviction and compensated the tenant who made improvements. Unfortunately, cheap imports from North America depressed agricultural prices in the 1870s. Frustrated tenants flocked to the National Land League, organized by Michael Davitt. In a context of agrarian violence and intimidation, Gladstone passed a second land act in 1881. It put on the statute book the so-called three Fs that already were customary practice for tenants in Ulster: fair rent, fixity of tenure, and freedom of sale (of the tenant's lease to a new tenant). A land commission established what qualified as fair rents. The 1881 legislation created what was virtually dual ownership by landlord and tenant, but the agenda of Irish land reform quickly moved on to a new demand: land purchase. Conservative ministries played the decisive role. First, in 1885 Parliament passed the Ashbourne Act that provided a loan fund to help tenants buy the land that they leased. The Congested Districts Board, established in 1891, also helped smallholders acquire land. Most important, in 1903 Parliament adopted the Wyndham Act. It reduced the interest rate that tenants paid loans and offered bonuses to landlords who agreed to sell. After the Liberals returned to power, they made sale compulsory in 1907 and reduced the landlord bonuses in 1909.

By 1921, when Ireland was partitioned and an Irish Free State created, two-thirds of land belonged to working farmers and big landlords were rare. Political motives explain this rapid transfer of ownership. Both Liberal and Conservative politicians hoped to restrain Irish nationalism by appeasing small farmers in a mostly agricultural country. *See also* Irish Famine.

FURTHER READING: Solow, Barbara Lewis. *The Land Question and the Irish Economy, 1870–1903*. Cambridge, MA: Harvard University Press, 1971.

DAVID M. FAHEY

## Irredentism

The policy of a state to "liberate" or "redeem" an ethnic minority belonging to its own nation and the territory in which it lives from the domination of another state. In its moderate form irredentism aggressively defends that minority's rights and interests.

The term is derived from the Italian *terra irredenta,* unredeemed land, and was first used to refer to the Italian-speaking areas under Austrian rule after 1866. **Italy,** after achieving unification, fought Austria repeatedly in order to annex Trentino, Trieste, Istria, Fiume, and parts of Dalmatia. Agitation took place both inside Austria-Hungary and in Italy itself. The liberation of *Italia irredenta* was perhaps the strongest motive for the entry of Italy into World War I. By this time, however, the term had lost much of its initial meaning because many Italian acquisitions were not "unredeemed lands" but rather strategic acquisitions, like the Orthodox Christian- and Muslim-inhabited Dodecanese Islands. Nevertheless, in 1919 the Treaty of Versailles satisfied most of the Italian irredentist claims.

The term irredentism has, by extension, been applied to nationalist agitation in other countries, based on historical, ethnic, and geographical reasons, for the incorporation of territories under foreign rule. The best examples of these nationalist irredentist movements before World War I were in the Balkans. Greece sought to resurrect the "Greece of the Five Seas"—a new Byzantine Empire on the ruins of the Ottoman. Bulgaria and Serbia also sought "greater" empires at the expense of the **Ottoman Empire** and its neighbors. *See also* Balkan Wars.

FURTHER READING: Di Scala, Spencer M. *Italy: From Revolution to Republic, 1700 to the Present.* Boulder, CO: Westview Press, 1998.

ANDREKOS VARNAVA

## Isandhlwana, Battle of (1879)

A major Zulu victory over British forces led by Frederic Thesiger, Viscount Chelmsford, in the Zulu War of 1879 in South Africa. In January 1879, Chelmsford led an army of 5,000 British troops and 8,000 Africans in an invasion of Zululand, where Zulu strength was estimated to be 40,000. Chelmsford had requested and been denied additional troops but was nonetheless confident enough to divide his army into three invasion columns that were ultimately to converge on the Zulu capital at Ulundi. Commanding the center column himself, Chelmsford was camped near a hill called Isandhlwana when he received word that a scouting party had made contact with the Zulu. He then compounded imprudence with recklessness by dividing his force and taking half of it in support, leaving 1,800 men behind at Isandhlwana under an inexperienced command. A disciplined force of 20,000 Zulu was able to approach the British camp at Isandhlwana by stealth and overrun its poorly deployed defenses. Only 55 Europeans and 300 Africans survived. The defeat registered shock all over Britain and temporarily brought the invasion of Zululand to a halt. It was partially redeemed at **Rorke's Drift** before Chelmsford won a decisive victory over the Zulu at Ulundi. *See also* Zulu Wars.

FURTHER READING: Duminey, Andrew, and Charles Ballard. *The Anglo-Zulu War: New Prespectives.* Pietermartizburg: University of Natal Press 1981; Morris, Donald. *The Washing of the Spears.* London: Cape, 1965.

CARL CAVANAGH HODGE

## Italo-Abyssinian War (1887–1896)

An imperial African misadventure of the newly unified Italian state. Having secured a foothold on the coast of **Abyssinia** during the 1870s, **Italy** in the 1880s sought to add to its territory either by purchase or conquest. In 1887, the Abyssinian chieftain of the Shoa defeated a small Italian force at Dongali, and by the spring of 1888 more than 20,000 reinforcements had arrived from Italy. There was only scattered fighting, but after the Italians redeemed themselves at Gallabat in March 1889, **Menelik II** signed a treaty with them giving Italy the coastal colony of **Eritrea.** A dispute over the wording of the treaty led to a new round of conflict in which Italian forces under Oreste Baratiera were initially successful but then overplayed their hand and were beaten at Amba Alagai in late 1895.

The stage was thus set for a showdown when in February, 1896 Baratiera's army was reinforced and set out to attack Menelik's much larger force established in a strong defensive position in mountainous terrain near **Adowa.** The engagement was a disaster for Italy and led ultimately to the Treaty of Addis Ababa in which Abyssinian independence was acknowledged and Italian efforts for territory beyond Eritrea abandoned. *See also* Ethiopia; Italo-Turkish War.

FURTHER READING: Berkeley, G.F.H. *The Campaign of Adowa and the Rise of Menelik.* London: Archibald Constable, 1902.

CARL CAVANAGH HODGE

### Italo-Turkish War (1911–1912)

A conflict between **Italy** and the **Ottoman Empire** over the Ottoman North African province of **Libya.** Italian imperialists had long wanted to acquire Tunis, already home to a substantial number of Italian émigrés. Surprising the Italians, however, the French occupied the city in 1881, humiliating Italy and forcing it to seek compensation in **Abyssinia.** The defeat at the Battle of **Adowa** dashed these hopes as well and marred Italian prestige until growing economic prosperity inspired a new generation of imperialists. In parliament these Nationalist deputies urged Prime Minister Giovanni Giolitti to seize the Ottoman provinces of Tripolitania and Cyrenaica to restore Italy's lost military honor. Other politicians wanted the government to address the emigration problem by turning Libya into Italy's "Fourth Shore," an agricultural colony where its excess population would not be lost to the economic benefit of foreign states.

The Ottomans maintained a system of **indirect rule** over their two provinces, which encouraged political instability and independence among the Arab tribes. According to Rome this endangered the region, hurt Italian interests in Tripoli, specifically the Bank of Rome, and might entice France to occupy the two provinces being so close to Tunisia. On September 28, 1911, Italy demanded the surrender of Tripolitania and Cyrenaica on the grounds that the Ottomans were incapable of governing. The Turks naturally refused, so Italy declared war the next day expecting to quickly defeat the Turks and liberate the Arabs. In the first week of October, Italian naval forces attacked and seized the provinces' ports. The Italian army then began a limited advance toward the highlands and desert, as the Turks retreated and drew support from the Arab tribes, which dragged the fighting out well into the next year.

The Italians expanded the war with naval attacks against Turkish ports in the eastern Mediterranean, Aegean, and Red Seas, the occupation of the Dodecanese Islands, and a quick raid into the Turkish Straits. Peace negotiations lingered on into 1912, with continued Arab and Turkish attacks inside Libya, and were concluded only after the Balkan states attacked the Ottomans during the First **Balkan War.** The Treaty of Ouchy in 1912 ended the Italo-Turkish conflict and awarded sovereignty over Libya to Italy. The Arabs, however, continued to resist until 1932, which hindered the exploitation of the colony and forced Italy to maintain a garrison of 50,000 troops. *See also* Africa, Scramble for; Tripoli.

FURTHER READING: Beehler, W. H. *The History of the Italian-Turkish War.* Annapolis: Advertiser-Republican, 1913.

FREDERICK H. DOTOLO

### Italy

Italy became a fully unified state only after 1870. To this point Italy had been divided into numerous medieval states that lost their independence in the early modern period. When Napoleon crossed the Alps seeking military glory, he brought with him the Enlightenment principles of the French Revolution, which inspired generations of Italians in their long struggle for national unity. Napoleon

**Bonaparte** annexed portions of the peninsula to the French Empire, ending the pope's temporal power, but also consolidated the rest into the Kingdom of Italy and the Kingdom of Naples. He extended constitutions, centralized administration, and introduced a modern legal code based on equality before the law. Napoleon's **Continental System** integrated the Italian economy with the rest of Empire's, and, although often exploitive, provided Italian workers with the technical expertise to sustain a modest industrial expansion. The reforms created a meritocracy that supported the Napoleonic regime for a time but, more important, provided invaluable experience and inspiration to those who later completed Italian unification after the fall of Napoleon.

Napoleonic rule with its onerous conscription, taxation, repression, and economic exploitation alienated many Italians who formed secret societies and started insurrections across the peninsula. One group, the *Carbonari*, the coal-burners, consisted primarily of bourgeois democrats who wanted true constitutional government and pressured Joachim Murat, the king of Naples and one of Napoleon's marshals, into granting them one. Murat refused, but domestic opposition weakened him and his eventual defection to the Allies was one factor in Napoleon's loss of Italy. Interestingly, the former rulers were then returned to power, but Murat kept his throne. Murat hated the Austrians, and when Napoleon returned for the Hundred Days, Murat declared war on Austria asking the Italians to join him in a war of national liberation. They did not. Murat failed miserably, was captured and executed. With him, however, died the hope for unification for the time being.

The Congress of **Vienna** restored the absolutist rulers and extended to them the protection of the **Holy Alliance,** a military agreement between Austria, Prussia, and Russia. Prince Metternich of Austria announced that the Alliance would intervene in Italy to stop revolutionary violence and thus suppress liberalism and nationalism. The *Carbonari* returned, joined by other patriots in the movement for national freedom known as the Risorgimento, or resurrection. Insurrections again erupted throughout the 1820s, but these were localized and easily crushed. In the midst of the Italian-wide revolutions in 1848, King Charles Albert of Piedmont granted his people a constitution in defiance of Austria. Reminiscent of Murat, he then went to war against Austria on their behalf but also failed.

In 1831, the *Carbonari* had given way to a more ideological group, **Young Italy,** led by Giuseppe **Mazzini.** Mazzini believed the Risorgimento should first concentrate on deposing the Italian monarchs, including the pope, to encourage the growth of republics, and Young Italy was involved in several plots against Charles Albert. The violence alienated moderate supporters who hoped the pope and the king would both cooperate in freeing Italy. Pope Pius IX was sympathetic to liberalism but rejected its adherence to secularism and anticlericalism, and the violent methods of Young Italy distressed him. The reasonable leadership remaining for the Risorgimento was with Piedmont.

Prime Minister Count Benso di **Cavour** of Piedmont believed only a unified state could make the necessary political, military, and diplomat preparations to defeat Austria. He reformed the finances and trade policies, built railways, enlarged the army, and concluded a military alliance with France. In June–July of 1860, the allies drove the Austrians from northwestern and central Italy, which were then annexed to Piedmont by plebiscites. Southern Italy, except for Rome, was similarly disposed of after Giuseppe **Garibaldi** wrestled Sicily and Naples from the Kingdom of the Two

Sicilies. Once the plebiscites were finished, the Kingdom of Italy was proclaimed in March 1861, although Venice, Rome, and Trieste were not incorporated until 1866, 1870, and 1919, respectively.

The consequences of the Risorgimento emerged over the next several decades and lingered well after 1914. State and Church relations were marked by mistrust and hostility. The Papal *Non Expedit* forbade Catholics from participating in politics, thus denying the new state a natural constituency. In return, Italy passed the Law of Guarantees in 1870 that allowed the pope to occupy the Vatican and granted him diplomatic rights but withheld compensation for the loss of the papal states. Second, the unification alienated reactionaries, republicans, and socialists many of whom remained outside of politics with a minority embracing violence. In 1900, an anarchist killed King Umberto I, an event the political right tried to use to end constitutionalism. The new King **Victor Emmanuel III** came out strongly in favor of democratic reforms.

During this period aristocratic, monarchial, northern, and agricultural interests dominated parliament under the rubric of the right. Its members had fought in the Risorgimento, not out of nationalist sentiments but out of loyalty to the king. The right supported limited constitutional government, but feared social revolution and favored those policies that enforced stability. Although most members of the right were believers, they wanted the State to control secular life, not the Church. Finally, the right supported free trade, balanced budgets, and fiscal stability. Unification had rendered the political left divided between radicals who advocated violence and rejected parliamentarianism, and constitutional liberals and moderate republicans, socialists, and Catholics who were committed to the democratic process but who were excluded from it. The left agreed with the right on secularism and was hostile to ecclesiastical interests. It supported the expansion of civil rights, universal male suffrage, and opposed militarism. Finally, the left believed in state intervention in economics and social welfare. The *Statuto* that Charles Albert had issued for Piedmont and which **Victor Emmanuel II** had extended to the rest of country formed Italy's basic law. It established a constitutional monarchy with an elected parliament chosen by a limited male franchise, and had certain civil rights protections. Integration, however, was accomplished by weakening the traditional local governments that undermined any balance to central authority. The constitution also failed to establish an independent judiciary, civil marriage, and divorce, which were the prerogatives of the Church, or a common penal code.

Giovanni Giolitti, prime minister from 1903 to 1915, was exactly what Italy needed to address these frustrations. He pushed through universal male suffrage, an extensive welfare system, and pledged state neutrality in labor disputes. Giolitti, however, manipulated parliamentarians through the practice of *trasformismo,* which relied on political patronage to buy the loyalty of deputies regardless of ideology. Corruption was rampant, people distrusted the democratic process, and the government's politics had angered major population groups—Catholic, Socialist, and Libera—leaving Giolitti unable to stop a vocal minority who then convinced parliament to enter World War I in 1915.

Italian foreign and colonial policies were conservative in scope. Under Prime Minister Francesco Crispi, who served from 1887 to 1891 and again 1893 to 1896, Italy began to construct an overseas empire, by acquiring Eritria but then overreaching in Abyssinia and suffering humiliation at Adowa in 1896. Italy was also a member of the **Triple Alliance** with Austria and Germany, which brought stability with the Austrians following the wars of the Risorgimento. Irredentist desires to acquire Italian-populated areas of Austria, remained a dead issue for the government. Anglo-Italian relations were cooperative because Italian colonialism was limited. Changes began to occur after 1910 when segments of the population demanded a more activist foreign policy in line with Italy's growing prosperity. At that time Giolitti was trying to court Catholic and Nationalist deputies against the Socialists, and agreed to their demands to implement imperialism, which led to war against the Turks for Libya.

Industrial expansion, which was slow before 1903, became more evident by 1910. Steel, railroads, ships, and automobile production became major segments of the industrial economy. The country had enough workers, its population was approximately 30 million, to sustain further growth. But Italy lacked necessary raw materials, such as coal, and a modern infrastructure: roads and railroads. Millions of Italians also emigrated to work outside the country. Education was problematic because technical subjects were not taught and mandatory education ended at grammar school. Social and cultural unity proved even more difficult. Italians shared a common religious tradition but little else. Each region had its own traditions, dialects, and practices that it sought to maintain after unification. Before 1914, Italians thought of themselves as Florentines, Neapolitans, or Romans, with the government doing little, except increase conscription, to build a common identity. Certainly the acquisition of Rome, which became the capital of Italy after 1870, provided a common historical reference, but the state did little to develop it. In the south, banditry was rampant and in the north irredentism led a minority of intellectuals to criticize Rome for ignoring the plight of Italians still living under Austrian occupation.

The great struggle for unification was completed, but its legacy took time to solve. Modern Italy entered World War I as a unified state but not a united nation. Although it was independent, it was also underdeveloped and torn by deep social and economic fissures.

FURTHER READING: Berkeley, G.F.-H. *Italy in the Making.* Cambridge: Cambridge University Press, 1932; Clark, Martin. *Modern Italy, 1871–1995.* New York: Longman, 1996; Di Scala, Spencer M. *Italy: From Revolution to Republic, 1700 to the Present.* Boulder, CO: Westview Press, 1998; Hearder, Harry. *Italy in the Age of the Risorgimento, 1790–1870.* New York: Longman, 1983.

FREDERICK H. DOTOLO

## Itō, Hirobumi (1841–1909)

The preeminent Japanese statesman of the Meiji period, Hirobumi Itō served as prime minister on four occasions (1885–1888, 1892–1896, 1898, 1900–1901). While studying in Europe as a young man, Itō became convinced of the need for Japan to abandon its insularity and modernize. Returning to Japan, Itō was instrumental in establishing the political institutions of the **Meiji Restoration.** From 1883 to 1889, he supervised the drafting of Japan's first constitution. In 1885, he created a modern civil service, established a cabinet and became the first prime minister of the Japanese empire. Itō supported the **Sino-Japanese War** and negotiated the Treaty of **Shimono-seki,** but subsequently failed to negotiate a peaceful settlement with Russia.

In 1906, he was appointed resident-general in **Korea.** In 1909, Itō was assassinated by a Korean nationalist while visiting Manchuria, and the military used the pretext of his death to annex Korea to the empire. *See also* Japanese Empire; Russian Empire.

FURTHER READING: Beasley, W. G. *The Meiji Restoration.* Stanford, CA: Stanford University Press, 1972; Nish, Ian. *Japanese Foreign Policy, 1869–1942: Kasumigaseki to Miyakezaka.* London: Routledge, 1977.

ADRIAN U-JIN ANG

## Izvolsky, Alexander (1856–1919)

A Russian diplomat and foreign minister from 1906 to 1910 under **Nicholas II.** Izvolsky's nationalist tendencies led to his involvement in a potentially disastrous episode of foreign diplomacy in 1908. In a meeting between Izvolsky and the Austrian foreign minister, Count von **Aehrenthal,** the two agreed to support each other in the following way: Austria would annex Bosnia, and Russia would declare the Straights of the Bosphorus and Dardenelles as open to Russian ships.

Izvolsky did not, however, inform his superiors of this agreement. When the arrangement was made public, it nearly brought Europe to war. The Serbs, who had long considered **Bosnia-Herzegovina** their own, started to prepare for action, and Austria moved troops to the Serb border. Britain came to the support of Russia; Germany supported Austria. In the end, both sides backed down, but Austria retained its new territory and Russia got nothing. Following this embarrassment, Izvolsky began to actively support Serbian nationalism. *See also* July Crisis; Russian Empire; Serbia.

FURTHER READING: Izvolski, Alexander. *The Memoirs of Alexander Izvolsky, Formerly Russian Minister of Foreign Affairs and Ambassador to France.* Edited and translated by Charles Seeger. Gulf Breeze, FL: Academic International Press, 1974; Lieven, D.C.B. *Russian and the Origins of the First World War.* New York: St. Martin's Press, 1983.

LEE A. FARROW

# J

## Jackson, Andrew (1767–1845)

An American nationalist and military leader, Andrew Jackson was the seventh president of the United States (1829–1837). Jackson was the last president to have fought in the American Revolution—he was captured by the British at age 13—and the first to be a product of the frontier. He was born in western South Carolina, but in 1787 moved west of the Appalachian Mountains, becoming a prosperous attorney and political leader. When Tennessee was admitted to the Union in 1796, Jackson became the state's first congressional representative; he became a senator the next year.

By 1801, he was a judge of the state's supreme court and the leader of the state's militia. At the outbreak of the War of 1812, Jackson was appointed a general in the U.S. Army, and given command in the southwest, in present-day Alabama and Mississippi. In this role, he led the war against the Creek Indians in 1813. After winning a decisive victory over the hostile Creeks, he imposed a harsh treaty on both the hostile Creeks and the "friendly" Creeks who actually worked with him during the campaign. In 1815, as commander of the American garrison at New Orleans, he won a smashing victory over a British invasion force made up of veterans from the Napoleonic Wars. This victory made Jackson a national hero.

Two years later, he again commanded a military expedition, this time against the Seminole Indians who had been attacking settlers in southern Alabama and Georgia. In the process of fighting the Seminoles, he also invaded Florida, then a Spanish possession, occupied Pensacola, and executed two English nationals he accused of helping the Indians. The extent to which his actions exceeded his orders from President Monroe is unclear, but he was certainly supported by the president after the fact. Spain was coerced into ceding Florida to the United States. As military leader and governor of Florida, Jackson continued to impose harsh treaties on the Indians in the region, coercing agreements turning over as much as three quarters of what is now Alabama and Florida, as well as parts of neighboring states.

Jackson ran unsuccessfully for president in 1824. He accused the winner, John Quincy Adams, of stealing the election through a "corrupt bargain" with a third candidate, Henry Clay, whom Adams appointed secretary of state. In 1828, Jackson overwhelmingly defeated Adams to become president. His presidency saw much the same spirit of confrontation, bullying, authoritarianism, and occasional extra-legality as his years as a military commander. During the course of his eight years, he repeatedly ignored congressional legislation and Supreme Court rulings. He threatened to invade South Carolina to enforce an unpopular tariff law.

One of the most enduring legacies of his presidency was his policy toward the Indians. Put simply, he did everything in his power to expel them west of the Mississippi. By the late 1820s, the major tribes in the south, the Chickasaw, Creek, Choctaw, Seminole, and, especially, the Cherokee, had largely assimilated the ways of the white Europeans. They controlled distinct territories stretching from the southern Appalachians into what is now Mississippi. They had established farms, towns, organized governments with written constitutions, and, in the case of the Cherokee, a written language.

Nevertheless, the whites wanted their land. In 1830, the U.S. Congress passed the Indian Removal Act, which authorized Jackson to negotiate land-exchange treaties with tribes living within the boundaries of existing U.S. states. Later that year, the State of Georgia attempted to enforce its laws in Cherokee territory. The Cherokee fought back in court, eventually winning a U.S. Supreme Court determination that Georgia had no jurisdiction. Jackson and the Georgians ignored the decision and continued to pressure the Indians to leave. By 1836, a small faction of Cherokees, selected by the U.S. government, had signed a treaty ceding the eastern land for land in what is now Oklahoma. In 1838, Jackson's successor, Martin Van Buren, ordered the army to begin an involuntary removal. Anywhere from 2,000 to 8,000 people died among the approximately 17,000 Cherokees—along with their approximately 2,000 black slaves—during the forced march, known as the "Trail of Tears." Each of the other civilized tribes were forced into similar exoduses, starting with the Choctaw in 1831. The Seminoles resisted fiercely, fighting against the army from 1835 to 1837, when Osceola was tricked into being captured while negotiating a truce. Most of the Seminoles accepted exile, but some withdrew into the Everglades, where they continued to resist until the 1840s. Approximately 17,000 Creeks in 1835, and the Chickasaw in 1837, were also expelled. Each of the tribes suffered their own "Trail of Tears" during the relocations.

Jackson's attitude toward the Indians was paternalistic and patronizing. He probably genuinely believed they were "children" in need of guidance and believed the removal policy was actually beneficial to the Indians. In the 1820s and 1830s, most Americans assumed the nation would never expand much beyond the Mississippi River, so removal to "Indian Territory" would save the Indians from the depredations of whites, allowing them to govern themselves in peace. *See also* Anglo-American War; Indian Wars; Manifest Destiny.

FURTHER READING: Heidler, David S., and Jeanne T. Heidler. *Old Hickory's War: Andrew Jackson and the Quest for Empire.* Baton Rouge: Louisiana State University Press, 2003; Remini, Robert V. *Andrew Jackson.* 3 vols. Baltimore: The Johns Hopkins University Press, 1998.

JOSEPH ADAMCZYK

## Jadidism

A Muslim educational reform movement of the late-nineteenth and early-twentieth centuries. The term derives from the word for the new method of teaching the Arabic alphabet. This movement was started by Ismail Bey **Gaspirali** (or Gasprin-skii) during the 1880s in the Crimea. Gaspirali first articulated the reform ideas of Jadidism in his newpaper *Tercüman.* Jadidism drew a particularly large following among the populations of the Crimea and the Volga-Urals, as well as the intellectual populations of Turkestan.

Jadidism took on many forms among Muslim peoples of Central Eurasia, but the general contours of the movement were similar: reformed education that combined Islamic principles with modern techniques and curricula; creation of a pan-Turkic unity both culturally and politically; and the creation of a common Turkic literary language. Jadidism can be seen historically as a reaction to Russian imperialism and modernization. The movement strived to reconcile elements of the past while adapting to the present and future of Muslim peoples living under Russian imperial rule. *See also* Russian Empire; Tatars.

FURTHER READING: Khalid, Adeeb. *The Politics of Muslim Cultural Reform: Jadidism in Central Asia.* Berkeley: University of California Press, 1998.

SCOTT C. BAILEY

## Jamaica

Jamaica, a large island in the Caribbean Sea, was originally colonized by the Spanish, but conquered by the British in 1660. Along with many smaller islands, it was often referred to simply as the "sugar islands," sugar, along with its by-products rum and molasses, being a great source of wealth. From the period of the Napoleonic Wars, coffee was also grown. By the late eighteenth century, it was estimated that the capital invested in the West Indies amounted to four times that invested in India. All of Jamaica's exports were grown on slave-worked plantations. Its nonwhite population included "maroons," descended from escaped slaves, who lived in the mountainous interior; although the Maroons often cooperated with the British, encouraged by the example of Haiti, they rose unsuccessfully against the crown in 1797.

Jamaica's representative institutions were dominated by the white planter class, and that class and its London representatives energetically opposed the abolition of slavery and of the slave trade in the **British Empire,** the Jamaican assembly going so far as to contest the right of Parliament to enact abolition. The abolition of the slave trade in 1807 marked the beginning of a decline in West Indian influence in London. Growing pressure from abolitionists and their evangelical supporters made it clear that slavery could not long survive. A slave rebellion in 1831, occasioned by confused rumors about the emancipation policy of the new reforming government in London, probably had little effect on the eventual abolition of slavery throughout the empire in 1833. The introduction of a system of "apprenticeship"—in effect indentured labor—in 1835 was intended to address the fact that former slaves often refused to work on plantations, but it occasioned many problems, and was abolished in 1838. The movement for free trade in England led to an end to preferential treatment for West Indian sugar, and compounded the island's economic difficulties. An attempt to overcome labor problems by importing indentured workers from India failed. The domination of Jamaican politics by a tiny white planter electorate did not prevent the conflicts between the local legislature and the colonial executive familiar throughout the empire in this period; if anything they were more vituperative than usual, and Jamaica's economic problems in the wake of abolition led some planters to muse about joining the **United States.**

At the same time American slaveholders held up Jamaica as an example of the problems consequent on abolition. At Morant Bay in 1865, riots among the black population killed about 30 people; official reprisals ordered by Governor Edward Eyre killed several hundred, and a colored member of the legislature was hanged after a dubious trial. This led to the recall of Eyre and a long controversy in Britain between his supporters led by Thomas **Carlyle** and emancipationists led by J. S. **Mill;** this issue displayed in sharp relief both sides of Victorian attitudes to race. In the wake of the massacres, the Jamaican assembly was disbanded. The Jamaican constitution of 1885 created a semi-representative government, but it did not work well. By 1899, the island was close to bankrupt and the Colonial Office imposed direct rule. Some improvement in Jamaica's fortunes followed in the Edwardian period. The age of high imperialism thus saw one of the original and most profitable of colonies fall into a state of relative unimportance.

FURTHER READING: Brown, Aggery. *Color, Class, and Politics of Jamaica.* New Brunswick, NJ: Transaction Books, 1979.

MARK F. PROUDMAN

## Jameson Raid (1895)

Occurring in December 1895, the Jameson Raid was an armed incursion into the territory of the South African Republic, also known as the Transvaal, by a battalion-size force of British South Africa Company Police under the command of Dr. Leander Starr Jameson, a close associate of Cecil Rhodes. Jameson and others in South African imperialist circles imagined that the large number of discontented British subjects, most of whom were attached to the gold mining industry, living in the Afrikaner-ruled Transvaal would rise in rebellion against the government of Paul Kruger, if offered support from an outside force.

No rising occurred, however, and Jameson's force ignominiously surrendered to Transvaal forces. The raid was important from four points of view, in roughly declining order of importance: it hardened Afrikaner attitudes to the British in the run-up to the South African War of 1899; it provoked the Kaiser's congratulatory telegram to Kruger of January 1896, thereby increasing Anglo-German antagonism; it called into question the close links between Cecil **Rhodes,** chairman of the British South Africa Company and at that point also prime minister of the Cape Colony, and Tory ministers, among them Joseph **Chamberlain,** in London, leading to the resignation of Rhodes; finally, the absence of the company's police from Rhodesia helped to provoke rebellions on the part of the African tribes in that colony, thereby leading to the Second Matabele War of 1896. Without the ill-advised and impetuous Jameson Raid, undertaken on the initiative of Jameson and with the connivance although without the immediate permission of Rhodes and Chamberlain, the South African War of 1899 might well have been avoided. *See also* Boer Wars; British South Africa Company; Matabele Wars.

FURTHER READING: Danziger, Christopher. *The Jameson Raid.* Cape Town: Macdonald South Africa, 1978; Longford, Elizabeth. *Jameson's Raid.* London: Weidenfeld and Nicolson,

1960; Rotberg, Robert I. *The Founder: Cecil Rhodes and the Pursuit of Power.* New York: Oxford University Press, 1988.

MARK F. PROUDMAN

## Jammu and Kashmir, State of

*See* Kashmir

## Janissaries

Created in the fourteenth century as a personal bodyguard by Sultan Orkhan (1326–1360) and named in Turkish *jeniçeri,* meaning "new militia," Janissaries were the elite soldiers of the **Ottoman Empire.** The Janissaries became the first regular infantry unit maintained in constant employment by any European ruler. Composed of recruits from the European parts of the empire, Christian prisoners of war, and even slaves, the Janissaries were also the first Ottoman troops to be trained in the use of firearms. They became politically as well as militarily powerful, demonstrating on many occasions a capacity to depose sultans and dictate Ottoman policy. By the nineteenth century the Janissaries became a law unto themselves. In 1825, Sultan Mahmud II created the *eshkenjisa,* a new military unit based on European standards, and attempted to reform the Janissaries along similar lines. They revolted, were defeated by the *eshkenjisa* on June 15, 1826, and then hunted down and slaughtered by the civilian population of Constantinople. Between 6,000 and 20,000 were massacred, their bodies tossed in to the Bosphorus.

FURTHER READING: Goodwin, Godfrey. *The Janissaries.* London: Saqi, 1997.

MOSHE TERDMAN

## Japanese Empire

Japan was the only non-Western nation to construct an empire in the Age of Imperialism. Modeled in large part upon European empires, the Japanese Empire by 1914 included Taiwan, the adjacent Pescadore Islands, Korea, southern Sakhalin Island, and nearly 1,400 islands in the Marshal, Mariana, and Caroline Island chains in the South Pacific. In China, Japan occupied 1,300 square miles of territory in South Manchuria (Guandong) and 200 square miles of land in Kiaochow Bay, Shandong. The Guandong leasehold included the South Manchuria Railway, a first-class naval base at Port Arthur, and Dairen, one of the best ice-free ports on the coast of Northeast Asia. The Kiaochow lease included another first-class naval base and commercial port, Qingdao, and rights to the Shandong Railway.

Japan acquired the Guandong lease and Kiaochow Bay from Russia and Germany, respectively. But Japanese empire-builders themselves were responsible for constructing much of the modern infrastructure of Taiwan, Korea, southern Sakhalin, and the South Pacific Islands. A renewed spurt of empire building from 1931 added enormously to the geographic scope of the Japanese empire. But military defeat in 1945 stripped Japan completely of her overseas territories.

## A Timeline of Japanese Expansion

The modern expansion of Japanese borders began during the **Tokugawa Shōgunate** between 1600 and 1868. The nominal authority of the Japanese archipelago was the *shōgun*—the strongest warrior in the land—whose government was headquartered in Edo, present-day Tokyo. In 1807, the *shōgun* assumed administrative control of the northern-most of the four main Japanese islands, Ezo, present-day Hokkaido. The Treaty of **Shimoda,** concluded in 1855 with Russia, added the southern half of the Kuril Island chain up to Iturup to Japan's northern border and recognized joint Russo-Japanese occupation of **Sakhalin** Island in the Sea of Okhotsk. To the south-east, the *shōgun* dispatched immigrants and established administrative control over the Bonin Islands in 1861.

The geographic scope of Japanese rule expanded apace with the emergence of modern Japan after the **Meiji Restoration** of 1868. In 1875, another treaty with Russia traded Japanese interests in Sakhalin Island for ownership of the entire Kuril island chain. To the west, Tsushima Island became part of Nagasaki Prefecture. To the south, the Ryukyus, present-day Okinawa, were incorporated into the new state in 1879. In 1880, the Bonin Islands became part of the Tokyo metropolitan prefecture. Japan acquired her first formal colonies after her successful participation in three modern wars. After the **Sino-Japanese War** (1894–95), Tokyo received title to Taiwan and the Pescadore Islands; as a result of the **Russo-Japanese War** (1904–1905), Japan acquired its first foothold in **China** in the former Russian leasehold in southern **Manchuria.** By 1913, almost 90,000 Japanese lived in the leasehold, including a division-strength garrison of the Japanese Army at **Port Arthur**—named in 1919 the Guandong Army— and six battalions of special guard troops in the Railway zone. In 1905, Japan also received full title to the southern Sakhalin Island of Karafuto and preponderant polit-ical and economic influence in **Korea.** More than 42,000 Japanese resided in Korea in 1905, when Japan established a protectorate there, and she annexed the peninsula formally in 1910. In the first month of World War I in 1914, the Japanese navy chased the German East India Squadron out of the Marshal, Mariana, and Caroline Islands, establishing Japan for the first time as a Pacific empire. In November of the same year, Japanese troops ejected German forces from Qingdao, China.

## The Japanese Empire and Western Imperialism

Although commercial activity between the Matsumae fiefdom in southern Ezo and the Ainu peoples who inhabited the rest of the island steadily expanded Japa-nese political and economic reach in the eighteenth century, the modern expan-sion of Japanese borders came overwhelmingly in response to the growing imperial activity of the Western powers in Asia. The *shōgun* authorized a geographic survey of Ezo and explorations of the Kuril Islands and Sakhalin Island in response to sev-eral intrusions by Russian ships in the eighteenth and early nineteenth centuries. Administrative control of the Bonin Islands in 1861 followed earlier claims to the islands by Britain in 1827 and the United States in 1853.

The immediate context for the founding of modern Japan was the renewed Western imperial thrust to the east after the conclusion of the **Napoleonic Wars** in 1815. Seeking an expansion of the highly lucrative tea trade, London abolished the British **East India Company** monopoly of trade with China in 1813 and in 1834 dispatched an official representative of the British crown, a superintendent of trade at Canton, to oversee a liberalization of commerce. When Beijing attempted to eradicate opium, Britain's principal currency of exchange for tea, a fleet of 16 British warships set sail for China. China's crushing defeat in the **Opium War** transformed the balance of power in East Asia. The Chinese had for more than 80 years confined trade with the Western maritime powers to Canton and maintained a tight control on foreign commerce. After 1842, Beijing was forced to conclude a series of " unequal treaties" with the Western powers that opened several Chinese ports to foreign commerce and residence and deprived China of its ability to set its own tariffs or to try foreign nationals in domestic courts.

Just 11 years after China capitulated to British firepower, U.S. Commodore Matthew Perry steamed into Uraga Bay outside of present-day Tokyo to make similar demands of Japan. Like China, Japanese leaders were compelled to conclude a series of treaties, beginning with the Treaty of **Kanagawa** with the United States in 1854, which opened Japanese ports to foreign commerce and residence on disadvantageous terms. Yet unlike China, the capitulation incited a civil war that brought down the shōgunate and spurred the founding of modern Japan.

Modern Japan's founders understood the projection of power as an integral symbol and prerogative of a modern nation. Just one year after the **Meiji Restoration,** influential statesmen urged an invasion of Korea in response to Seoul's refusal to normalize relations. By 1873, a "Conquer Korea" debate among the Japanese ruling circle had rejected invasion in favor of industrial development at home, but in 1874, Japan nonetheless sent 3,600 samurai warriors to Taiwan in retaliation for the massacre of 54 shipwrecked Ryukyuans by Taiwanese aborigines. Originally aimed at colonizing eastern Taiwan, Tokyo soon abandoned the scheme for fear of war with China and possible intervention by the Western powers. In the Peking Treaty of 1874, China instead agreed to pay an indemnity to the Ryukyuans, thereby weakening Chinese claim to suzerainty over the Ryukyus and paving the way for incorporation of the islands into the Japanese empire.

Although the Korea debate of 1873 had rejected an immediate invasion, Japanese policymakers continued to seek Korean recognition of Japan's newfound status as a modern nation, and Japanese warships made periodic forays to the Korean coast after 1873. In 1875, Japanese troops seized a Korean fort on Kanghwa Island, south of Seoul, after being fired on by Korean shore batteries. The next year, Tokyo sent an emissary with military support to demand a normalization of relations. On the model of Commodore Perry's 1854 "opening" of Japan, Kuroda Kiyotaka forced Korea to conclude the Treaty of Kanghwa in 1876, which, like earlier treaties forced on China and Japan by the Western powers, compelled Korea to open its ports to international commerce on disadvantageous terms.

The Kanghwa treaty marked the beginning of a long-term Japanese interest in Korea that would bring Japan to successive blows against two other regional rivals, China and Russia. First, having upset Korea's traditional deference to Chinese regional hegemony, the treaty marked the beginning of almost two decades of Sino-Japanese jockeying for position on the peninsula. Although Tokyo had negotiated the Kanghwa treaty directly with Seoul, a new Chinese Imperial Commissioner for Northern Ports concluded the remainder of Korea's treaties with the Western powers in the early 1880s. From the late 1870s through the early 1890s, Japan and

China allied with rival Korean political factions to vie for political, economic, and diplomatic influence in Seoul. By 1882, Japan had 700 and China 1,500 troops stationed permanently in the Korean capital to safeguard their burgeoning interests.

Japan's military defeat of China in 1895 marked the end of Chinese regional hegemony. It also spelled the beginning of a new round of Great Power competition that would noticeably expand the influence of a formidable new Western presence in Asia, that of Russia. After the initial conquest of Siberia in the seventeenth century, Russian pressure in Northeast Asia eased until after the Second **Opium War,** when St. Petersburg joined the powers in the unequal treaty regime imposed on Beijing. Most conspicuously, the Supplemental Treaty of Peking in 1860 granted the tsar almost 400,000 square miles of territory in the Maritime Provinces northeast of Manchuria and Korea. The start of construction on a **Trans-Siberian Railway** in 1891 confirmed St. Petersburg's commitment to colonization of the Russian Far East. By 1895, Vladivostok, the proposed terminus of the railway, had become a substantial port city. Having amassed a fleet of 29 warships there, Russia confidently initiated the Triple Intervention in that year, allying with France and Germany to force Japan to relinquish claims to the Liaodong Peninsula in south Manchuria at the peace conference with China. By the Treaty of Li-Lobanov in1896, China permitted Russian construction of a railway through north Manchuria, the Chinese Eastern Railway, shortening the route of the Trans-Siberian Railway to Vladivostok.

One year later, using the murder of two German missionaries in Shandong province as a pretext, imperial Germany began a scramble for "spheres of influence" in China, whereby the powers vied for exclusive rights to build railways, mines, and fortified ports in strategic areas throughout the continent. By 1898, Germany had acquired a leasehold in Kiaochow Bay, the British in **Weihaiwei** and Kowloon near Hong Kong, the French in Kwangchow near the border of French Indochina, and Russia in the Liaodong Peninsula. Japan obtained only a simple pledge from Beijing not to grant special rights to any other power in Fujian province, across the straits from Taiwan.

The growing Russian presence in Northeast Asia also placed new pressure on Korea. Forever in search of a warm-water port in the Pacific, St. Petersburg had sent a warship to Tsushima Island in 1861 and proceeded to build permanent shore facilities. Although two British men-of-war foiled the mission, Russia began making demands for trade at the Korean border after the 1860 acquisition of the Maritime Provinces. The tsar joined the unequal treaty regime in Seoul with the 1884 Russo-Korean Treaty. Japan therefore moved aggressively after the Sino-Japanese War to consolidate its position in Korea. But in 1895, when the new Japanese minister in Seoul supported a plot to assassinate the Korean queen, the crown prince sought asylum in the Russian legation. During the year that the prince remained with the Russians, he looked to St. Petersburg for substantial political, economic, and military advice. In 1896, Russia received mining and timber rights near the Russo-Korean border, in North Hamgyong province and the Yalu Basin and Ullung Island, respectively. The Li-Lobanov Treaty between Russia and China also outlined mutual military assistance in the event of a Japanese attack on either signatory or Korea.

American, French, German, and British concessionaires joined the Russians after the Sino-Japanese War in the rush to construct and finance railway, mining, electricity, and waterworks projects in Korea, just as they proceeded in China. Initially, Russian pressure excluded Japanese interests from this competition. In 1898, however, Russian demands for a coaling station at Deer Island in Pusan Harbor in southern Korea provoked a backlash from the Western powers that spelled opportunity for Tokyo. In the same year, Japanese interests received rights to finance and construct two rail lines in Korea, from the capital to Pusan on the south coast and to Inchon on the west coast. The Nishi-Rosen Agreement concluded with Russia in the same year barred both signatories from direct interference in Korean internal affairs yet recognized Japan's preferential economic and commercial position in Korea.

Like the Sino-Japanese War, the **Boxer Insurrection** (1899–1901) transformed the balance of power in East Asia. Responding to the penetration of Western missionaries into rural China after the 1858 Treaty of Tianjin, the Boxers United in Righteousness arose in northwest Shandong province in 1898 and in 1900 laid siege to the foreign legation quarters in Beijing. The Great Powers dispatched a combined a force of 20,000, 8,000 of whom came from Japan, to liberate their respective countrymen. But like the Sino-Japanese War, the Boxer disturbance sparked a renewed scramble for position among the intervening powers. In the south, the Japanese civilian administrator in Taiwan plotted an expedition to seize the principal port of Fujian province, Amoy, across the straits from the Japanese colony. Tokyo eventually vetoed the scheme for fear of upsetting Great Britain, a potential ally in the accelerating rivalry with Russia. In the north, Russia had used the outbreak of the Boxer uprising to flood Manchuria with 200,000 troops. This dramatic new military presence became the immediate catalyst for the **Russo-Japanese War,** in which Japan's spectacular victories on land at **Mukden** and at sea in the Straits of **Tsushima** marked its coming-out as a power of the first rank.

Japan again followed military victory in 1905 with swift efforts to consolidate control in Korea. With no remaining regional rivals after Russia's defeat, the door now stood open to Japanese hegemony on the peninsula. Even before the Treaty of **Portsmouth** ended the war, the United States concluded an executive agreement with Tokyo recognizing Japanese "suzerainty over Korea," the Taft-Katsura Agreement of July 1905. Four months later, Japan compelled Korean officials to sign a Protectorate Treaty, calling for a Japanese resident-general in Seoul. The new executive head possessed sweeping powers to supervise Japanese officials and advisers in Korea, intervene directly in Korean decision making, issue regulations enforceable by imprisonment or fines, and use Japanese troops to maintain law and order. Seoul continued to resist Japanese encroachments, but the assassination of Resident General Hirobumi **Itō** in 1909 led to formal incorporation of the peninsula via the 1910 Treaty of Annexation.

One month after the Protectorate Treaty with Korea, China confirmed a new position for Japan in South Manchuria. Japan had been shut out of the scramble for spheres of influence in China after the Sino-Japanese War, but the Sino-Japanese Treaty of December 1905 now recognized the transfer to Japan of Russian rights and leases in Liaodong Peninsula. The **South Manchuria Railway,** Dairen, Port Arthur, and the Guandong Army would become the backbone of Japanese power and influence in China until the end of World War II.

In light of the country's steady expansion through successive wars, Japan's leadership looked to the outbreak of war in Europe in 1914 as another opportunity. By November 1914, Japan had made two notable additions to her burgeoning empire: the Japanese navy occupied German Micronesia—the Marshal, Mariana, and Caroline Islands—while Japanese troops ejected German forces from Kiaochow Bay. Although Tokyo formally returned its Shandong possessions to China in 1922, the islands of German Micronesia remained in Japanese hands as Class C mandates under the League of Nations covenant through 1945.

### Japanese Empire through Western Inspiration and Aid

If the Japanese Empire grew largely within the context of Western imperialism in Asia, it was also inspired by the same principals that underlay the rapid expansion of Western power in the late nineteenth century. The first full Japanese-language translation of Henry Wheaton's 1836 classic, *Elements of International Law: With a Sketch of the History of the Science,* appeared in 1869 and became a critical guide for Japan's crusade to behave and be treated like a "civilized" nation. Herbert Spencer's evolutionary theories came to Japan through the University of Tokyo, where Toyama Masakazu, who had become devoted to Spencer after several years of study at the University of Michigan, began lecturing in 1876 on Spencer's ideas on biology, psychology, and sociology. At the same time, American Ernest Fenellosa taught philosophy at Tokyo University through a distinctly Spencerian lens. Spencer's *Principles of Sociology* and Charles **Darwin**'s *Origin of Species* were both translated into Japanese in the early 1880s.

Although Japan did not enjoy the racial disparity with its subject peoples typical of Western colonialism, Japanese empire-builders shared with their Western counterparts a faith in human progress and the universality of the principles defined by international law, a belief in the "survival of the fittest" and a conviction that they, as members of a "civilized" race, possessed both the right and responsibility to uplift their less enlightened neighbors. In 1875, Fukuzawa Yukichi, a Japanese man of letters, published the wildly popular *Outline of Civilization,* which defined civilization as intellectual and moral progress. Just one year earlier, Japanese policymakers had contemplated the colonization of eastern Taiwan to bring civilization to an area where China exercised no legal jurisdiction. Kuroda Kiyotaka was dispatched to Korea in 1876 to negotiate a treaty based on the "law of nations." And on the eve of the Sino-Japanese War, Japan demanded of Seoul the removal of "old, deep-rooted abuses," which "endangered peace and order."

Taiwan, South Manchuria, southern Sakhalin, Korea, and German Micronesia were eventually incorporated into the Japanese empire in the name of civilizing the "lesser peoples" of Asia. Japanese statesmen meticulously established legal title to all territories through internationally recognized treaties, and they exported to their colonies those institutions that had, by their introduction into Japan in the late nineteenth century, come to define a modern nation: a modern bureaucracy, national education, taxation, policing, and a new industrial infrastructure of railroads, telegraphs, and factories. Even the physical layout of Western capitals and colonial territories that had made their way to Japan in the nineteenth century were reexported to Japanese colonies in the form of large, Western-style stone buildings with imposing columns and arches and wide, tree-lined boulevards.

In its initial forays into colonial governance, Japanese imperialism clearly looked West for much of its inspiration. Early efforts to raise Japanese influence in Korea through railway construction and loans identified British Egypt as a suitable model. The first Japanese civilian administrator of Taiwan and later head of the South

Manchuria Railway, Goto Shinpei, encouraged his subordinates to read widely about British colonialism and commissioned a Japanese translation of Sir Charles Lucas' *Historical Geography of the British Colonies.* Having spent several years of study in Germany in the 1880s, Goto also avidly subscribed to German ideas of "scientific colonialism."

If Japanese empire-builders referenced the same literature on international relations and colonial governance as their Western counterparts, they equally received critical direct guidance from leading Western practitioners of empire building. The Japanese policymakers who had advised against the invasion of Korea in 1873 did so after close observation of the West. During a 22-month sojourn to the United States and Europe, these men had surveyed every trapping of modern national power: parliaments, factories, foundries, and shipyards. And they listened intently as the leader of a powerful newcomer to the international stage, German chancellor Otto von **Bismarck,** advised them to build up and rely on Japan's own strength. When conversely Japan's young leaders decided in 1874 to send a military expedition to colonize eastern Taiwan, they did so on the advice of former U.S. consul to Amoy Charles LeGendre. A French legal adviser to the Japanese government, Gustave Boissanade, aided the 1874 negotiations with China that recognized *de facto* Japanese suzerainty over the Ryukyus. And the conversion of Japan's modern army from small-scale garrisons to a large, mobile force capable of projecting Japanese military strength was facilitated by the Prussian officer, Major Klemens Meckel, who in 1885 began teaching at Japan's new army staff college that Korea was a "dagger pointed at the heart of Japan." In 1895, Japanese negotiators at the peace conference with China followed the guidance of veteran American legal adviser to the Japanese Foreign Ministry, Henry W. Denison. Four years later, Denison helped arrange the transfer from American to Japanese interests of a concession to build the Seoul-Inchon rail link in Korea.

Japanese imperialism also received inspiration and direct guidance from abroad, often relying on Western technical and material support. Through advice and help from the Netherlands, the only Western power with which the Tokugawa regime engaged in active trade, Japan had already constructed Western-style ironworks, steam engines, and dockyards by 1868. In the waning years of the Tokugawa era, Russian interests advised the construction of a series of Western-style sailing vessels, and French technicians helped build the Yokosuka Foundry and Shipyards.

Western technical support swelled with the advent of modern Japan and the arrival of more than 6,000 foreign technical experts in the late nineteenth century. In 1876, the Japanese government employed more than 100 British engineers and technicians to advise the construction of a modern rail system. Until 1912, all steam locomotives running on Japanese rails came from foreign factories, and two of the six ships that comprised Kuroda Kiyotaka's show of strength to Korea in 1876 were piloted by foreign captains. British engineers helped construct the first Japanese integrated ironworks in the late 1870s and, in 1901, German know-how produced Japan's first modern steelworks. Japanese technicians regularly received training in major Western armaments firms, such as Vickers and **Krupp.** By the turn of the century, Japanese arsenals and dockyards used sophisticated imported techniques. Nonetheless, all four Japanese battleships in the Japanese armada that decimated the Russian Baltic fleet in the Battle of Tsushima Straits in 1905 came from British shipyards. British diplomatic and financial support, facilitated by the **Anglo-Japanese Alliance** of 1902, also played a critical role in Japan's victory over tsarist Russia.

### The Japanese Empire as an Anomaly

Although the Japanese empire fit comfortably within the late nineteenth-century scramble for colonies and strategic position initiated in the West, certain factors distinguish Japan from its Western counterparts. Most fundamentally, as a former victim of Great Power imperialism, Japan's rise in international status lagged behind that of the other industrial nations, and Japanese empire-building through 1914 remained an exercise in catch-up. Heavy reliance on Western models, and technical and material support was an important consequence of the particular timing of Japan's emergence on the world stage, as was the intensely political and top-down quality of Japanese expansion. Japan remained primarily an agricultural economy until the eve of the Sino-Japanese War in 1894, whereas emigration to subject territories did not lead but rather followed the Japanese flag.

Another fundamental contrast with Western colonialism, geographic proximity to new territory, facilitated Japanese expansion. Whereas most European powers vied for influence in the far reaches of the globe, Japanese policymakers had the luxury of expanding into contiguous territory. Although Japan lagged behind the other powers in the level of industrial maturity, military capacity, and capitalization, it greatly benefited from lower transportation costs, rapid communications, and familiarity with the climate and cultures of its subject territories. Cultural affinity would become the foundation of an entirely new Japanese imperial enterprise from 1931 to 1945. The architects of empire in 1930s, Japan built on earlier territorial acquisitions. The Manchurian Incident, which inaugurated the new era, sprang from an explosion on the South Manchuria Railway, and during the 14 years of war that followed, Tokyo tightened its control of its original territories in Taiwan, South Manchuria, Korea, Karafuto, and German Micronesia.

The new Imperial Japan at its farthest reach dwarfed the scope of the original empire. By 1942, in addition to the original territories, Tokyo controlled all of Manchuria, Inner Mongolia, the entire Chinese coast and industrial centers, most of Southeast Asia, and the South Pacific to the Solomon Islands. More important, the new Japanese Empire grew not as an expression of compliance with international legal norms but as an explicit rejection of Western imperialism in Asia. Rather than seek open association with the Western powers and distinct detachment from "lesser" Asian neighbors, Japanese expansion in the 1930s unambiguously played on the historical and cultural affinities enjoyed with many of its subject peoples to call for "Greater East Asian Co-prosperity." *See also* Chrysanthemum Throne; Mutsuhito, Emperor; Restoration War; Satsuma Rebellion; Taisho Democracy; *Zaibatsu; Z*-flag.

FURTHER READING: Beasley, W. G. *Japanese Imperialism, 1894–1945.* New York: Oxford University Press, 1987; Berger, Gordon, ed. and trans. *Kenkenroku: A Diplomatic Record of the Sino-Japanese War, 1894–1895.* Princeton, NJ: Princeton University Press, 1982; Duus, Peter. *The Abacus and the Sword: The Japanese Penetration of Korea, 1895–1910.* Berkeley: University of California Press, 1995; Eskildsen, Robert. "Of Civilization and Savages: The Mimetic Imperialism of Japan's 1874 Expedition to Taiwan." *The American Historical Review* 107, 2 (Apr. 2002): 388–418; Kim, Key-Hiuk. *The Last Phase of the East Asian World Order: Korea, Japan and the Chinese Empire, 1860–1882.* Berkeley: University of California Press, 1980; Matsusaka, Yoshihisa

Tak. *The Making of Japanese Manchuria, 1904–1932.* Cambridge, MA: Harvard University Asia Center, 2001; Myers, Ramon H., and Mark R. Peattie, eds. *The Japanese Colonial Empire, 1895–1945.* Princeton, NJ: Princeton University Press, 1984.

FREDERICK R. DICKINSON

## Java

The most populous inland of present-day Indonesia, Java was of interest to sixteenth-century Portuguese traders, who were promptly followed by the Dutch **East India Company** and the establishment of the port of Batavia in 1619 as an entrepôt for inter-Asian trade. When the Dutch Republic was invaded by Napoleonic armies in 1795, the company dissolved and a governor-general appointed, Herman Willem Daendels, who established an administrative system on the French model and constructed a postal road in large part with forced labor. In 1810, Napoleonic France then annexed the Netherlands outright, thereby making all Dutch colonies of strategic interest to Britain in its war with Napoleon. In 1811, a British invasion fleet arrived in Java, and Batavia surrendered shortly thereafter. The British controlled Java until 1816, when it was returned to the Netherlands. During the British occupation, the lieutenant-governor of Java, Thomas Stamford **Raffles,** applied a "forward policy" in Java, claiming Borneo, the Celebes, the Moluccas, Java, and Sumatra, much to the annoyance of the British East India Company whose directors were skeptical of Java's profitability. Raffles also conducted the first population census of Java and attempted economic, fiscal, and land tenure reforms—along with the abolition of **slavery**—but with little success before Java was returned to the Dutch.

Through the introduction of the infamous "cultivation system," whereby the Dutch government produced agricultural goods in Java for sale at auction back in Amsterdam, hundreds of millions of guilders flowed into the coffers of the Dutch treasury. Some reforms were introduced in response to violent rebellions between 1825 and 1830, but the population of Java suffered enormously under a system geared to the demands of Dutch consumers and negligent of the most elementary needs of Javanese producers. Central Java was struck by famine in 1849–1850. Incremental reforms were introduced starting in 1848, but it was not until the 1860s that most forced cultivation was phased out. *See also* East India Companies; Napoleonic Wars; Netherlands.

FURTHER READING: Bayly, C. A., and D.H.A. Kolff, eds. *Two Colonial Empires: Comparative Essays on the History of India and Indonesia in the Nineteenth Century.* Dortrecht: M. Nijhoff, 1986; Carey, Peter. *The British in Java, 1811–1816: A Javanese Account.* New York: Oxford University Press, 1992; Wesseling, H. L. *The European Colonial Empires, 1815–1919.* Harlow: Pearson-Longman, 2004.

CARL CAVANAGH HODGE

## Jefferson, Thomas (1743–1826)

Thomas Jefferson was an American founding father, author of the Declaration of Independence, minister to Paris, secretary of state, and third president of the **United States** (1801–1809). Jefferson was born on April 13, 1743, to wealthy landowners,

Peter Jefferson and Jane Randolph. He attended the College of William and Mary where he also participated in the secret Flat Hat Club. He studied law and philosophy and headed the American Philosophical Society.

As president, Jefferson accomplished many things that benefited the United States. He authorized the Lewis and Clarke expedition to the Pacific and negotiated the **Louisiana Purchase** in which Washington purchased in 1803 from Napoleonic France 529,911,680 acres of land for $15 million, doubling the size of the country and thereby expanding, in his own words, "the empire of liberty." The purchase was in part facilitated by the conflict in Europe. Spain's transfer of territory in North America to France closed the Mississippi and prompted a call for war from Congress. Jefferson's decision to send James Monroe to both France and Spain to negotiate a peaceful settlement was more astute than he could have guessed, as Napoleon's decision to make war against England encouraged him to part with overseas territory of no use to him in the impending struggle. Monroe came home with much more than he had sought and, due to circumstance, at a bargain price. He also responded to the slave revolt in **Haiti** by sending rebellious American slaves to Haiti, thereby in effect aiding the rebellion there while forestalling it at home. He also engaged in a prolonged but worthwhile struggle with the **Barbary States,** 1801–1807, over their commerce raiding in the Mediterranean. By neglecting the maintenance of the navy constructed by his predecessor, John Adams, he made the American effort more difficult, but he nonetheless thought it imperative that a trading nation reach out to chastise the insolence of piracy.

Yet in 1807, Jefferson also unnecessarily harmed relations with Britain by transforming his insistence of rights of neutral states into a policy of embargo against both Britain and France, now properly at war. Anglo-American relations were equally damaged by the British policy of seizing American crews for service in the Royal Navy, but the embargo damaged the maritime economy of the New England states, benefited the **Continental System** of Napoleon, and set American affairs on a course that led ultimately to the **Anglo-American War** of 1812. *See also* Manifest Destiny; Napoleonic Wars.

FURTHER READING: Bernstein, R. B. *Thomas Jefferson.* Oxford: Oxford University Press, 2003; Ellis, Joseph J. *American Sphinx: The Character of Thomas Jefferson.* New York: Knopf, 1997; Onuf, Peter S. *Jefferson's Empire: The Language of American Nationhood.* Charlottesville: University Press of Virginia, 2000.

ARTHUR HOLST

## Jellicoe, John Rushworth (1859–1935)

British naval officer and commander of the Grand Fleet at the Battle of Jutland in 1916. Small in stature but academically brilliant, Jellicoe joined the Royal Navy as a cadet in 1872 and rapidly climbed the officer ranks. He served in the Egyptian expedition of 1882 and subsequently became chief of staff to John **Fisher** at the naval gunnery school, HMS *Excellent.* He remained close to Fisher throughout his career. He served with distinction in the **Boxer Insurrection** in 1900, being severely wounded in action. He played, under Fisher as First Sea Lord, a part in the development of the *Dreadnought.* Jellicoe was placed in command of the Grand Fleet in 1914, thanks to Fisher's influence. The long-expected battle with the Germans arrived on May 31, 1916. After an initial clash of battle-cruiser squadrons in which

British losses were significant, Jellicoe succeeded in engaging the main body of the German High Seas fleet in favorable circumstances, and inflicting significant damage. But when the Germans retreated, Jellicoe did not aggressively pursue, in part because of his fear of torpedoes, and therefore did not win the second Trafalgar that many had hoped for.

The **Royal Navy** in the pre-World War I period has been accused of becoming a rigidly hierarchical and conservative organization far removed in spirit from the initiative and risk-taking of the age of Nelson. Jellicoe's critics accuse him of exemplifying these faults, pointing to both his love of detail and his caution at Jutland. Characterized by Churchill as the only man who could lose the war in an afternoon, his caution was not unjustified. It is the case that the German fleet remained in harbor for the rest of the war, making Jutland a strategic victory even if it was not a tactical one. *See also* Mahan, Alfred Thayer; Navalism; Tirpitz Plan.

FURTHER READING: Marder, A. J. *From the Dreadnought to Scapa Flow: The Royal Navy in the Fisher Era.* 5 vols. London: Oxford University Press, 1961–1970; Massie, Robert K. *Castles of Steel.* New York: Random House, 2003; Patterson, A. T. *Jellicoe: A Biography.* London: Macmillan, 1969.

MARK F. PROUDMAN

## Jena, Battle of (1806)

Often referred to as Jena-Auerstädt, one of two battles fought on the same day, October 14, 1806, in which the French decisively defeated the Prussians. Napoleon, initially with 46,000 men but later rising to 54,000, plus 70 guns, engaged Prince Friedrich von Hohenlohe, with 55,000 men and 120 guns. Advancing at a rapid pace, Napoleon maneuvered his army around the Prussian left flank, putting himself between Berlin and Hohenlohe's forces. Moving toward the west, Marshals Davout and Bernadotte sought to sever the Prussian lines of communication, while the remainder of the French under Napoleon proceeded in the direction of Jena. The Prussians turned around to face their opponents and divided their forces in two, with 63,000 men under the duke of Brunswick marching to Auerstädt, 15 miles to the north. Napoleon opened an assault at dawn. The Prussians counterattacked, but when their offensive began to waver under heavy French musket and artillery fire, Napoleon ordered forward three corps, forcing their opponents back. The French lost only 4,000 killed and wounded, as compared to the Prussians' 25,000 killed, wounded, and captured.

The significance of Jena cannot be understood without reference to its counterpart fought at Auerstädt, where Davout found himself assailed by the bulk of the Prussian army. The French commander, with 26,000 men and 44 guns, held his position against more than twice his strength—50,000 Prussians and 230 guns under Brunswick—who was mortally wounded in the course of the fighting. The Prussians launched a series of small-scale attacks over the course of six hours, but when news of the defeat at Jena began to circulate in the ranks, Prussian morale began to wane and caused troops to retire on both flanks, thereby exposing the center to enfilading fire from the French artillery. Prussian cohesion soon faltered, and after 20,000 fresh French troops arrived and pounced on the Prussian rear, the whole of Brunswick's force dissolved into a rout. The French lost 7,000 killed and wounded, and the Prussians suffered more than 10,000 casualties. Between the two engagements, the French captured more than 200 pieces of artillery. **Prussia**'s twin defeats ended all speculation as to the superiority of the army bequeathed by Frederick the Great and ended all further organized resistance. The French quickly occupied Berlin and mopped up the remainder of Prussian forces in a brilliantly conducted campaign of pursuit and blockade. *See also* Clausewitz, Carl von; Napoleonic Wars.

FURTHER READING: Chandler, David. *Jena 1806: Napoleon Destroys Prussia.* London: Osprey Publishing, 1993; Petre, F. Loraine. *Napoleon's Conquest of Prussia, 1806.* London: Greenhill Books, 1993.

GREGORY FREMONT-BARNES

## Jhansi, Siege of (1858)

A battle of the **Indian Mutiny** of 1857–1858. The strongest position of the rebels in Central India was the city of Jhansi, 130 miles south of Agra, dominated by a fort. Inside the fort there was a foundry capable of manufacturing cast iron mortars. On March 22, 1858, British General Sir Hugh Rose, commanding the Central India Force, laid siege to Jhansi. When Tantia Tope with 20,000 men attempted to relieve Jhansi, on April 1, Rose defeated him on the bank of River Betwa. On April 3, Rose's troops opened the assault on Jhansi. Once the breaching batteries had blasted the walls of the city, the British troops entered the town. A grim hand to hand struggle broke out in the narrow streets and houses within the city. Jhansi was defended by 1,500 **sepoys** and 9,500 rebels armed with matchlocks, but they failed before the siege guns and professional infantry of Rose. On April 4, the *Rani* Lakshmi Bai, a charismatic woman who led the mutineers of Jhansi—*rani* is Hindi for "queen"— fled and on April 6 all resistance ended.

FURTHER READING: David, Saul. *The Indian Mutiny, 1857.* London: Viking, 2002; Harris, John. *The Indian Mutiny.* London: Wordsworth Editions, 2000; Watson, Bruce. *The Great Indian Mutiny.* New York: Praeger, 1991.

KAUSHIK ROY

## Jihad

Meaning "On the path of God," *jihad* is a Muslim doctrine of struggle against unbelievers for the protection or expansion of the realm of Islam. For a believer engaged in *jihad* sins are remitted, whereas death encountered on God's path secures immediate admittance to paradise. The first *jihad* was led by the Prophet Muhammad in the seventh century and was integral to the unification of the Beduin tribes of the Arabian Peninsula into an Arab nation. In the nineteenth century, *jihad*-*ist* activity was usually defensive or insurgent in nature, such as in that of Janangir against the Qing Dynasty in Turkmenistan in 1821; the serial *jihads* of **Abd-al-Qādir** against French control of **Algeria** starting in the 1830s; and the Sudanese Mahdi of Dongola's campaign against the British Empire climaxing in the capture of Khartoum and the collapse of William **Gladstone**'s government in 1885.

FURTHER READING: Johnson, James T., and John Kelsey. *Cross, Crescent and Sword.* New York: Greenwood, 1990; Peters, Rudolph. *Islam and Colonialism: The Doctrine of Jihad in Modern History.* The Hague: Mouton, 1979.

CARL CAVANAGH HODGE

## Jingoism

Clamorous and pugnacious patriotism commonly used to describe popular bellicosity leading up to or during foreign wars. "Jingo" is a corruption of the name of Jingū Kōgō, a legendary Japanese goddess credited with subduing the kingdoms of **Korea.** Its popular use in Britain dates to 1877–1878 when public opinion mobilized in support of Benjamin **Disraeli**'s dispatch of naval forces and Indian colonial troops to oppose Russia's invasion of the Balkans and possible seizure of the **Dardanelles.** Music hall audiences sang that "We don't want to fight, but, by Jingo if we do, we've got the men, we've got the ships, we've got the money too."

One of the more noteworthy episodes of jingoism came during the Boer War on May 18, 1900, when news reached Britain of the relief of a British garrison at Mafeking after a seven-month siege. Mobs celebrated the victory by taking to the streets and in some instances attacking the houses of anti-imperialists or reputed "pro-Boers." The event, in turn, coined a new term: *mafficking. See also* Boer Wars; John Bull; Russo-Turkish War.

FURTHER READING: Hobson, J. A. *The Psychology of Jingoism.* London: G. Richards, 1901.

CARL CAVANAGH HODGE

## John Bull

The name used to personify the English people and British imperialism. Although first used in the seventeenth century, it was John Arbuthnot, a Scottish writer and Queen Anne's physician, who popularized it in his 1712 *The History of John Bull,* a political allegory advocating the end of the War of the Spanish Succession. John Bull was an honest, jolly, hot-tempered cloth merchant, embroiled in a lawsuit with his European neighbors.

From the 1760s, John Bull began a long history in the visual media. The *John Bull* newspaper, a Tory organ, was established. By the mid-nineteenth century he was defined as a rotund, usually rural, shabby farmer or squire. John Tenniel's drawings for *Punch* are the most recognizable version: a portly, ruddy-cheeked and side-whiskered but dignified gentleman, with boots and a shabby hat, usually with a Union Jack waistcoat and a bulldog at heel.

John Bull was in partisan terms neutral, as the Liberal *Punch* and the Tory *Judy* enlisted him with equal credibility. By 1900, John Bull had lost most of his every-man and apolitical character. In 1906, a journalist, swindler, and politician, Horatio Bottomley founded *John Bull* as a weekly journal. Bottomley's John Bull dressed in a short top hat, riding gear, and crop, and savaged Herbert **Asquith**'s Liberal government's fiscal policies. Hereafter John Bull featured mostly on the Conservative side of politics. *See also* Jingoism.

FURTHER READING: Engel, Matthew. *Tickle the Public: One Hundred Years of the Popular Press.* London: V. Gollancz, 1996; Koss, Stephen E. *The Rise and Fall of the Political Press in Britain.* London: Hamish Hamilton, 1984.

ANDREKOS VARNAVA

## July Crisis (1914)

The precipitant diplomatic crisis of World War I, the July Crisis is also referred to as the Mobilization Crisis. The crisis began on Sunday June, 28, 1914 with the assassination of Archduke **Francis Ferdinand,** heir to the Habsburg throne, by Gavrilo Princip, a Bosnian Serb fanatic, during a visit to Sarajevo in **Bosnia-Herzogovina** to view the summer maneuvers of the Austro-Hungarian army. During the month of July it proceeded to an Austrian declaration of war on Serbia on July 28, a general mobilization by Russia the next day, French and German mobilization on August 1 and German declaration of war against Russia later the same day, a German declaration of war on France on August 3 countered by a British declaration against Germany on August 4, and, finally an Austrian declaration against Russia on August 6. Between the assassination and Vienna's war note to Belgrade a series of diplomatic and military measures—not one of which made war inevitable, but equally none of which were unequivocally dedicated to its prevention—ushered the situation among the Great Powers from the possibility to the probability to the near certainty of Armageddon.

These began with Vienna seeking German support for an Austrian war to eliminate Serbia as factor in the Balkans. Because the Austrian government had wanted to destroy Serbia in 1912–1913 and had been thwarted, the assassination was viewed in Vienna as an opportunity to revisit the issue. Until now the German government had seen Austria's fear of Serbian nationalism as hysterical, which it was, but the sensation of the assassination moved Berlin to take the Balkan situation more seriously. Under these circumstances in July 1914 it was possible for the Austro-Hungarian foreign minister, Count Leopold von Berchtold, to obtain what amounted to a "blank check" of support from Germany to undertake against Serbia whatever measures the Austro-Hungarian government deemed imperative. Indeed, Kaiser **Wilhelm II** himself assured Vienna's ambassador, Ladislaus Szögyéni-Marich, of German backing even if Russia intervened on behalf of Serbia. This assurance opened a door between the small regional war Austro-Hungary was preparing to launch against Serbia and a full-out European conflict, unless Russia responded to Serbia's punishment exactly as Berlin and Vienna hoped.

The next step was the Austro-Hungarian 48-hour ultimatum delivered to the Serbian government on July 23. Among other things, it demanded the suppression of publications and organizations engaged in anti-Austrian activities and the dismissal of Serbian officials thought to be involved, directly or otherwise, in such activities; cooperation of Serbian officials with those of Austria in the investigation of the assassination along with legal proceedings against individuals accessory to it; the arrest of Serbian officials found to be involved; and an explanation for the continuing "unjustifiable utterances" of high Serbian officials. The Serbian reply was mostly positive yet rejected outright the demand for proceedings against accessories. Serbia mobilized its forces before even filing the reply; Austria also mobilized and made hostilities official on July 28. On July 26 the British foreign minister, Edward **Grey**—a veteran of successful arbitration during the **Balkan Wars**—had proposed an international conference, but only France and Russia had agreed. Vienna rebuffed outright any submission of an issue of "national honor" to the opinion of other governments, an outrageous articulation given that its position was dependent on German steel.

Thus Austria had the war it sought. It was only from this point forward that the mobilization of their armies became an integral factor in the failure of national governments to prevent its rapid evolution to a general conflagration. Tsar Nicholas II initially ordered Russian mobilization against Austria but came under pressure to mobilize against Germany, too, because Russia's enormous territory made mobilization slow and could put the country at a decisive disadvantage if Germany were to mobilize first. On July 29, this order was temporarily cancelled following a telegram from Wilhelm II with the welcome news that Germany was attempting to restrain Austria. But timely mobilization was actually more critical to Germany, faced with the prospect of war in the east and west against two of the **Entente** powers, Russia and France.

The potential cost of the German blank check was now becoming apparent. A short, sharp Austrian triumph in the Balkans could have altered the European balance of power in favor of the **Triple Alliance** without Germany having to fight. With this calculation now in serious peril, army chief of staff General Helmuth von **Moltke** urged full Austrian and German mobilization. When Russian mobilization resumed on July 30, Germany delivered a 12-hour ultimatum on July 31 that it stop. In addition, Berlin sought clarification from Paris on France's attitude to a Russo-German war, while looking to Britain for assurances of neutrality. France's response was cryptic, and Britain's was a demand that the neutrality of Belgium be respected—a demand Germany rejected. French and German mobilization orders were then almost simultaneous late on the afternoon of August 1, with the difference that Germany now sought British influence to keep France neutral in return for a promise not to attack. At 7:00 P.M., Germany declared war on Russia. The next day Belgium defied Germany's demand for a right of passage for its troops through Belgian territory, and the British cabinet decided that its position would be decided over precisely that issue: if Germany violated Belgium neutrality, guaranteed by the Treaty of London in 1839, Britain would be bound to come to Belgium's aid. When Germany declared war on France on August 3 and promptly launched its invasion of Belguim, therefore, British policy was decided, and the Triple Entente was at war with the Triple Alliance. War was made official on August 4, at which point Austro-Hungary's Serbian war had, in little more than month, become a continental and finally a global conflict that ultimately was to consume a generation of European manhood and draw in Italy, Turkey, and the United States. The Age of Imperialism was over. *See also* Balkan Crises; Black Hand; Eastern Question; Habsburg Empire; London, Treaty of; Military Conversations; Ottoman Empire; Russian Empire; Schlieffen Plan.

FURTHER READING: Albertini, Luigi. *The Origins of the War of 1914*. 3 vols. Translated by Isabella M. Massey. New York: Oxford University Press, 1952; Fromkin, David. *Europe's Last Summer*. New York: Alfred A. Knopf, 2004; Keegan, John. *The First World War*. London: Random House, 1998; Strachen, Hew. *The First World War*. New York: Oxford University Press, 2001.

CARL CAVANAGH HODGE

## July Monarchy (1830–1848)

The reign of the "bourgeois king," Louis Philippe, on the restored throne of France is known as the July Monarchy. After the **July Revolution** of 1830, Louis Philippe (1773–1850) became the French monarch by invitation from the Chamber of Deputies. His rule was hated by conservatives, liberals, and socialists alike. The overwhelmingly bourgeois regime presided over national prosperity until an economic depression in 1846–1847, but it was bereft of any governing principle. It did not look into the grievances of the working class and violently suppressed their revolts in 1831 and 1834.

The regime's foreign policy was uninspiring. Differences with Britain arose over the question of Egypt, and military successes in Algeria were derided as pathetic attempts at reviving Napoleonic glory. The growing upsurge of socialism in the 1840s took the July monarchy to its inevitable end; during its final months, Prime Minister François Pierre **Guizot** failed in his endeavor at reconciling contradictory ideologies—the revolution with the *ancien régime* and authoritarianism with democracy. Discontent against the regime mounted when demands for extension of electoral suffrage were rejected and rioting broke out on February 23, 1848. The next day Louis Philippe abdicated and the Second Republic was established. *See also* Bonapartism.

FURTHER READING: Beik, Paul H. *Louis Philippe and the July Monarchy.* Princeton, NJ: Van Nostrand, 1965; Howarth, T.E.B. *Citizen-King. The Life of Louis-Philippe King of the French.* London: Eyre and Spottiswoode, 1961; Lucas-Dubreton, J. *The Restoration and the July Monarchy.* Putnam, New York, 1929; Rudé, George. *Debate on Europe 1815–1850.* New York: Harper and Row, 1972.

PATIT PABAN MISHRA

## July Revolution (1830)

A revolutionary wave of the 1830s that swept over Europe beginning in France, ending the reign of **Charles X,** the successor of Bourbon ruler Louis XVIII. Charles, unlike his predecessor, believed in an absolute monarchy and tried to revive many features of the *ancien régime*. His measures, like giving compensation to émigrés and the removal of many liberal provisions of the constitution, angered the bourgeoisie. In July 1830, he suspended the liberty of press, dissolved the Chamber of Deputies, and restricted the electoral franchise. An insurrection broke out. Its leaders were from the parliamentary opposition and backed by lower bourgeoisie. After three days of fighting, Charles abdicated in favor of his 10-year-old grandson, the count of Chambord, and then fled to Britain, but he was succeeded by Louis Philippe after the invitation from the Chamber of Deputies. Louis Philippe agreed to rule as a constitutional monarch. Although the July Revolution did not bring lasting political change, its effects were felt in other parts of Europe, including **Belgium, Italy,** the German states, Poland, and Switzerland, where conservatives trembled and liberals took heart. *See also* Bourbon Dynasty.

SUGGESTED READING: Lucas-Dubreton, J. *The Restoration and the July Monarchy.* New York: Putnam, 1929; Merriman, John M. *1830 in France.* New York: Viewpoints, 1975; Pinkney, David H. *The French Revolution of 1830.* Princeton, NJ: Princeton University Press, 1972.

PATIT PABAN MISHRA

## Junker

Derived from *junger Herr*, "young nobleman," a *junker* was a member of the landed aristocracy of Prussia and other regions of northeastern Germany east of the Elbe River. Descended from feudal nobility, in some cases dating as far back as the eleventh century, nineteenth-century Junker families represented a primary buttress of support for the **Hohenzollern** dynasty and held leading positions in the civil service, the army and the navy of the Second Reich. As a social class, Junkers were affiliated with the German Conservative Party and increasingly associated with reactionary politics and Prussian militarism. In 1808, the Scharnhorst-Gneisenau reforms officially ended a Junker monopoly in the Prussian officer corps by opening it up to talent from other social classes, but Junker influence in the army in particular remained strong right up to 1914, and jealousy concerning Kaiser **Wilhelm II**'s enthusiasm for naval power influenced the Junker attitude concerning what might be risked or salvaged by a European war in that fateful year. *See also* Schlieffen Plan; Tirpitz Plan.

FURTHER READING: Craig, Gordon A. *The Politics of the Prussian Army, 1640–1945*. Oxford: Oxford University Press, 1955.

CARL CAVANAGH HODGE

# K

## Kaffir Wars (1781–1879)

Also referred to as the Xhosa Wars, the Kaffir Wars were a series of conflicts, the precise number of which is uncertain, fought along the eastern border of the **Cape Colony** between settlers of Dutch and British origin and local African peoples, mostly Xhoxa and Basuto. The term *kaffir* was initially used by Arab slave traders to refer to non-Muslims, but during the nineteenth century it was increasingly applied by the white population to all Bantu-speaking peoples of southeast Africa. By the end of the century the word *kaffir* was a common racist epithet hurled against black Africans. The wars were fired over competition for grazing land and involved the wanton slaughter of livestock and people. In the 1830s, Boer resentment over how British justice dealt with the conflicts was one of the factors leading to the **Great Trek.** *See also* Boer Wars; British Empire.

FURTHER READING: Smithers, A. J. *The Kaffir Wars, 1779–1877.* London: Leo Cooper, 1973.

CARL CAVANAGH HODGE

## Kaiser-Wilhelm-Kanal

A strategically important waterway in northern Germany. The first plans to link the Baltic and the North Seas by a canal date from the Middle Ages. After the war with Denmark in 1864, Prussia secured herself the right to build a canal through the duchy of Schleswig. It took another 22 years, however, before the Reichstag eventually adopted the project on March 16, 1886. Although the facilitation of trade played a part in the decision, the canal was primarily built for military purposes. The building of the waterway also gave new strategic importance to the North Sea island of **Heligoland,** which had belonged to Great Britain since 1814. Guarding against a British bridgehead off the German shore and close to the new canal, Chancellor Leo von **Caprivi** succeeded in securing the island for the Reich in the **Heligoland-Zanzibar** Treaty on July 1, 1890 in exchange for Zanzibar and other African territories.

After Wilhelm I had launched the construction works of the waterway on June 3, 1887, **Wilhelm II** inaugurated the Kaiser-Wilhelm-Kanal in dedication to his grandfather on June 26, 1895. As the canal was navigable for ships of the size of up to 135 meters of length, 20 meters of breadth and 8 meters of gauge, big warships could now easily and securely be moved from the Baltic into the North Sea and vice versa: a potentially decisive room for maneuver in naval tactics. Because the post-*Dreadnought* ships were considerably larger, however, the canal required an upgrading only 10 years after its opening. The extension works started in 1907 and were duly completed on July 23, 1914, only weeks before the outbreak of World War I. In 1948, after World War II, the Kaiser Wilhelm-Kanal was renamed Nord-Ostsee-Kanal or Kiel Canal. *See also* German Empire; Navalism; Tirpitz Plan; *Weltpolitik.*

FURTHER READING: Behling, Frank. *Kiel-Canal: 100 Jahre Nord-Ostsee-Kanal.* Kiel: Alte-Schiffe-Verlag, 1995.

ULRICH SCHNAKENBERG

## Kálnoky, Gustav (1832–1898)

Count Gustav Kálnoky, Austro-Hungarian foreign minister from 1881 to 1895, was born in December 1832 in Letovice in the Austrian crown land of Moravia. An officer in the Austrian army, he entered the diplomatic service in 1854. He made his diplomatic career in London, Rome, Copenhagen, and St. Petersburg, where he became ambassador in 1880. Kálnoky was appointed minister of foreign affairs in 1881.

The **Triple Alliance** with Germany and Austria's traditional foe, **Italy,** was one of the first of his major achievements. In addition, Romania and Serbia became alliance partners of the Habsburg monarchy. During the 1880s, European Great Power politics was shaped by a series of dangerous crises. Austria-Hungary cooperated closely with Germany and Great Britain and was able to defend her interests on the Balkan Peninsula. But in the early 1890s, relations with Italy deteriorated and there were tensions with Russia. Kálnoky resigned in 1895 and died in February 1898 in Brodek. *See also* German Empire; Habsburg Empire.

FURTHER READING: Pribram, A. F. *The Secret Treaties of Austria-Hungary, 1879–1914.* 2 vols. Cambridge, MA: Harvard University Press, 1921; Taylor, A.J.P. *The Struggle for Mastery in Europe, 1848–1918.* Oxford: Clarendon Press, 1954.

GUENTHER KRONENBITTER

## Kanagawa, Treaty of (1854)

The treaty of amity and friendship between the **United States** and Japan, signed at Kanagawa, now Yokohama, Japan, on March 31, 1854, shortly after the arrival of the American Commodore Mathew C. Perry. The treaty stipulated which Japanese ports were to be opened to American trading vessels and set forth policies regarding the provisioning of American ships and the treatment of shipwrecked sailors. Finally, the treaty established an American consulate in Shikoda.

The Treaty of Kanagawa symbolized the end to Japan's two-century policy of national isolation, or *sakoku*, "closed country," and the opening of the country to foreign intercourse. It was soon followed by similar agreements between Japan and other foreign powers. The rapid and radical changes soon fostered in Japan as a result of its opening resulted in the overthrow of the country's **Tokugawa Shōgunate** in 1868 and Japan's embarkation on a path of modernizing reforms. *See also* Japanese Empire; Meiji Restoration.

FURTHER READING: Beasley, William G. *The Meiji Restoration.* Stanford, CA: Stanford University Press, 1972; Jansen, Marius, ed. *The Emergence of Meiji Japan.* Cambridge: Cambridge University Press, 1995.

DANIEL C. KANE

## Kandahar, Battle of (1880)

The decisive engagement of the Second **Afghan War.** After the defeat of British forces at Maiwand, an Afghan army under Ayub Khan laid siege to the British garrison at Kandahar. A relief force under the command of General Frederick Roberts covered the 313 miles between Kabul and Kandahar in 22 days in one of the most storied marches of British imperial history. Roberts had a force of Gordon and Seaforth Highlanders, Rifles, and Lancers, supplemented by Gurkhas, Sikhs, and Indian cavalry, for a total of just under 10,000 men. He defeated Ayub Khan's army of 11,000 men, inflicting Afghan casualties of 1,200 against 40 British killed and 228 wounded. As the siege and relief of Kandahar had been followed closely in Britain, Roberts was instantly a national hero. Already a recipient of the Victoria Cross, he was showered with further honors. A special Kabul-to-Kandahar medal, subsequently nicknamed the "Roberts Star," was struck and awarded to all who had taken part in the march. *See also* Great Game; India.

FURTHER READING: Heathcote, T. A. *The Afghan Wars, 1839–1919.* Staplehurst: Spellmount, 2003; Tanner, Stephen. *Afghanistan: A Military History from Alexander to the Fall of the Taliban.* Karachi: Oxford University Press, 2003.

CARL CAVANAGH HODGE

## Károlyi, Mihály Count (1875–1955)

Hungarian liberal statesman and landed aristocrat, Count Károlyi was best known for presiding over aspects of the liquidation of the Austro-Hungarian Empire with the end of World War I. Descending from a noble family and owning more than 70,000 acres himself, he seemed an unlikely candidate to challenge the feudal vestiges of the old Austro-Hungarian social and political order. Although lacking reliable political allies, Károlyi's pre-World War I career was by no means obscure. He led the agricultural association of the nobility, then the Hungarian Independence Party, pressed the abandonment of foreign policy in Germany's orbit in favor a of a French and Russian orientation, and also came to advocate the enfranchisement of women, land reform, and limited concessions to ethnic minorities.

A combination of a leftward drifting reform program, Hungarian nationalism, marriage ties with the influential **Andrássy** family, and open support for an early

Wilsonian peace propelled him to leadership in **Hungary** after a decade-long activity in opposition. A short-lived Hungarian People's Republic emerged under his premiership and presidency, prepared by the nearly bloodless revolution of October 28, 1918, formally proclaimed after the abdication of Charles IV on November 16, and ending with his controversial transfer of power to a coalition of communists and social democrats on March 21, 1919. In addressing the legacy of Magyar subimperialism and belated modernization in the eastern half of the dual monarchy, Károlyi's policies and their ineffective execution satisfied neither left nor right, and his significant armistice concessions at Belgrade met a cold Allied reception. Fallen from favor at home and abandoned by the Great Powers in Paris, he eventually lost his fortune, was branded a traitor, and lived most of the remainder of his life in exile. Having become the scapegoat for the harsh terms of the peace treaty of Trianon that detached two-thirds of the Hungarian Crown's former lands, Károlyi only managed to return to Hungarian public life briefly with the end of World War II as a socialist representative in Parliament and then ambassador to France. *See also* Entente; Foch, Ferdinand; Habsburg Empire; Rumania.

FURTHER READING: Glatz, Ferenc, ed. *Hungarians and Their Neighbors in Modern Times, 1867–1950.* New York: Columbia University Press, 1995; Károlyi, Mihály. *Faith without Illusion: Memoirs of Mihály Károlyi.* London: Jonathan Cape, 1956.

GÁBOR BERCZELI

## Kashmir

A creation of the Hindi Dogra dynasty and of the British government of **India,** Kashmir comprises three separate regions of the Valley of Kashmir, predominantly Muslim and Kashmiri-speaking, Jammu; predominantly Hindu-speaking Dogri; and Ladakh, populated mostly by Ladakhi-speaking Buddhists. They existed as separate states, although Kashmir became part of the empire of Ranjit Singh (1780–1839) of the Punjab. After the death of Ranjit Singh, the Sikhs became weakened and after a series of wars, the British took over the Punjab. On March 16, 1846, with the signing of the Treaty of Amritsar, Kashmir was sold by the British to the Dogra chief, Gulab Sigh of Jammu (1792–1857), and he entered Srinagar on November 9, 1846.

Kashmir became a state with an overwhelming majority of Muslim citizens governed by a Hindu maharaja who ruled it as an independent state with regard to internal affairs because the British did not appoint a resident to exercise greater political control until 1884. With the Sikh population in the Punjab still hostile and with strained relations with **Afghanistan,** Kashmir was seen as a frontline state and a valuable ally. With a border shared with Tibet, Chinese Turkistan, Russian Turkistan, and Afghanistan, it was a strategic territory. In addition, the British hoped to share in the trade with Central Asia. When Russia captured Tashkent in 1865, and Samarkand and Bukhara in 1868, there was a recrudescence of the **Great Game** in which the British once again become obsessed for the safety of India and the fear of a Russian invasion of India through Afghanistan. During the viceroyalty of Lord Lytton (1876–1880), Britain adopted a "forward policy," which determined to establish the defensive line for India on the northern heights of the Hindu Kush. Kashmir again became a frontline state. It was not until 1895 that the British and the Russians agreed to the international border between Russia and Afghanistan.

Gulab Singh was survived by his only surviving son Ranbir Sigh (1856–1885) who offered military and financial support to the British during the **Indian Mutiny** of 1857 and the state of Kashmir as a refuge, especially to British women. Pratap Singh (1885–1925) and Hari Singh (1925–1947) succeeded Ranbir. Hari Singh acceded to India rather than Pakistan in spite of the fact that Kashmir was more than 75 percent Muslim and in some areas, more than 90 percent. *See also* British Empire; Russian Empire; Sikh Wars.

FURTHER READING: Huttenback, Robert A. *Kashmir and the British Raj, 1847–1947.* Oxford: Oxford University Press, 2004; Lawrence, James. *Raj: The Making and Unmaking of British India.* New York: St. Martin's, 1997.

ROGER D. LONG

## Kasimov, Kenesary (1802–1847)

Also known as Qasim-uli, Kenesary Kasimov was a Kazakh khan who led one of the most sustained rebellions against Russian colonialism on the Kazakh steppe. Using *guerrilla* tactics of warfare in the northwestern steppe, Kasimov consistently caused problems for the Russian administration, which had enjoyed relatively peaceful relations with the Kazakhs since the late eighteenth century. Kasimov's rebellion lasted from 1837–1846. He also lodged complaints to the imperial administration about the treatment Kazakhs received.

Kasimov garnered widespread support for his rebellion among the Middle Horde Kazakhs. He was the grandson of the famous Kazakh khan Ablai and was born in the Kokchetau area. After leaving the Russian-controlled area of the steppe upon defeat in 1846, Kasimov went south to help the Kyrgyz fight Kokand. He was killed in battle in 1847. Historians have portrayed him as everything from a defender of feudalism and traditional nomadism to a revolutionary and Kazakh nationalist. *See also* Russian Empire.

FURTHER READING: Olcott, Martha Brill. *The Kazakhs.* Stanford, CA: Stanford University Press, 1987, 1995.

SCOTT C. BAILEY

## Kaufman, Konstantin Petrovich von (1818–1882)

Konstantin Kaufman was the first governor-general of the Russian colony of **Turkestan** (1867–1881). During his long tenure as governor-general, he oversaw the conquest or defeat of the Central Eurasian states in **Bukhara, Khiva,** and Kokand. The Russian government generally viewed his administration as successful because it established a certain continuity of Russian rule in Central Eurasia.

Kaufman took a hands-off approach to dealing with the Islamic practices of Turkestan's peoples. He was not reluctant, however, to interfere in such institutions as Islamic law when he found it necessary for the benefit of the state administration.

Kaufman's overall political style can be viewed as a mix of libertarian and authoritarian systems of rule. Although there was considerable autonomy at the local level for traditional rulers and for Islamic courts, their decisions could be ultimately overruled by his decree.

Throughout his tenure, Kaufman argued that Turkestan was a unique colony with unique circumstances that required unique administrative measures. This colonial uniqueness justified the intervention on the part of regional leaders into provincial political or juridical affairs. It also allowed him to often stray from the proscribed statute of Turkestan rule, first promulgated in 1867. At the end of his career, a new statute was to be drafted. The commission found that Kaufman's earlier assertion of certain native rights was faulty. Particularly controversial was Kaufman's claim that Turkestan's people should be free from military conscription. Among the other unique rights of individuals that Kaufman claimed were freedom of religion; preservation of marriage, property, and family traditions; and freedom from physical punishment. The Russian government found the military exemption particularly troubling.

Kaufman's Turkestan administration was progressive by the standards of the time. His administration carried out ethnographic surveys of the region, looked into educational reforms, and commissioned aides to identify social problems. He also instituted plans to improve cotton production and agriculture. He even created a forestry section of his administration to plant trees in the oasis cities of Turkestan. Like many other Western colonial administrators, Kaufman was a firm believer that European or Western civilization was far superior to Eastern or Oriental cultures and societies. He firmly hoped that Turkestan's peoples would adopt Russian and European cultural ways. This would ultimately lead to their conversions to Christianity and their spirited support of the Russian imperial state. *See also* Great Game; Russian Empire.

FURTHER READING: Brower, Daniel. *Turkestan and the Fate of the Russian Empire.* London: Routledge Courzon, 2003; Meyer, Karl E., and Shareen Blair Brysac. *Tournament of Shadows: The Great Game and the Race for Empire in Central Asia.* Washington, DC: Counterpoint, 1999; Schuyler, Eugene. *Notes of a Journey in Russian Turkistan.* New York: C. Scribner's Sons, 1885.

SCOTT C. BAILEY

## Kautsky, Karl (1854–1938)

A noted German-Austrian socialist, Karl Kautsky was born in Prague of middle class Jewish parents. He studied history and philosophy at Vienna University and became a member of the Austrian Social Democratic Party in 1875. In 1880, Kautsky moved to Switzerland, where he was influenced by the Marxist writer, Eduard Bernstein. While living in London between 1885 and 1890, he maintained a close relationship with Friedrich **Engels.** Kautsky founded the journal *Neue Zeit* in 1883. The journal became immensely influential in socialist circles both in Germany and internationally. He joined the German Social Democratic Party (SPD) and, in 1891, drafted the Erfurt Program, which committed the SDP to an evolutionary form of Marxism. Kautsky also wrote the official commentary on the program, called *The Class Struggle.* In 1898, he took up the question of colonialism and the nationalities question in **Austria-Hungary.** He did not believe that **imperialism** would lead to war;

rather, he saw it as a reactionary social phenomenon. He broke with Bernstein after the latter published *Evolutionary Socialism* in 1899. In the book Bernstein argued that the predictions made by Karl **Marx** about the development of capitalism had not transpired. He pointed out that the wages of workers had risen, and the polarization of classes between an oppressed proletariat and capitalist had not materialized. Kautsky strongly criticized these views.

After initial hesitation, Kautsky opposed the SPD's support of the German effort in World War I. He sided with the left-wing socialists and denounced the government's annexationist aims. In April 1917, left-wing members of the SPD formed the Independent Socialist Party. Kautsky reluctantly became a member; however, he continued to oppose the idea of a violent revolution. In September 1917, the SPD dismissed him as editor of *Die Neue Zeit* for his opposition to the war. *See also* Imperialism.

FURTHER READING: Salvadori, Massimo L. *Karl Kautsky and the Socialist Revolution, 1880–1938.* New York: Verso, 1990.

MARTIN MOLL

## Kemal, Mustapha (1880–1938)

More commonly known as Atatürk, soldier and father of modern Turkey, Mustapha Kemal was born in Salonica in 1880, where a museum at the current Turkish Consulate commemorates his birthplace. His father died when Mustapha was seven, and his mother brought him up. Mustapha studied at the military secondary school in Selânik, where his mathematics teacher gave him the additional name Kemal ("perfection") because of his academic excellence. He entered the military academy at Manastır in 1895, graduated as a lieutenant decade later and was posted to Damascus.

Mustapha joined a small secret revolutionary society of reformist officers in Damascus called "Motherland and Liberty" and became an active opponent of the Porte. In 1907, when he was posted to Selânik, he joined the Committee of Union and Progress commonly known as the **Young Turks.** In 1908, the Young Turks seized power from Abdul Hamid II and Mustapha became a senior military figure. In 1911, he was send to defend **Libya** against the Italian invasion, and he was stranded there when the first of the Balkan Wars started and was unable to take part. In July 1913, he was appointed commander of the Ottoman defenses of the Gallipoli Peninsula and in 1914 as military attaché in Sofia.

After a brief period of constitutional rule, power became vested in the triumvirate of Mehmet Talat Pasha, Ahmet Cemal Pasha, and Enver Pasha, who, through secretive negotiations, courted a German alliance. When they joined the **Ottoman Empire** to the side of the Central Powers during World War I, Mustapha was posted to Tekirdağ, on the Sea of Marmara. He was then promoted to colonel and assigned the command of a division in Gallipoli. He played a vital role in the battle against the allied forces in April 1915, holding them off at Conkbayırı and on the Anafarta hills. He was promptly promoted to a brigadier general, thus acquiring the title of pasha.

During 1917 and 1918, Kemal Pasha was sent to the Caucasus to fight against the Russians and then the Hejaz, to suppress the Arab revolt. After resigning his commission, he returned to serve in the unsuccessful defense of Palestine. In October

1918, the Ottomans capitulated to the Allies and he became one of the leaders that favored defending Anatolia and withdrawing from territory not dominated by Turks.

Kemal Pasha, seeing that the disintegration and partition of the Ottoman Empire, even in Anatolia, was a serious possibility, arranged to be sent to Samsun, in Anatolia, with extraordinary powers, as an inspector of the Nineteenth Army and started ordering provincial governors and military commanders to resist occupation. In June 1919, he declared that the government at Constantinople held no legitimate authority and a government-in-exile should be established in Anatolia. In April 1920, a parliament, the Grand National Assembly, was formed in Ankara, and Kemal became the president. This body repudiated the Constantinople government and rejected the Treaty of Sèvres. This was a direct threat to **Greece,** which stood to gain the most, an empire in Anatolia, from that treaty and that country invaded Anatolia. After a series of Greek successes, in January and again in April 1921, Ismet Pasha defeated the Greek army at İnönü. In July, after a third Greek offensive, Kemal took command and routed the Greeks in the 20-day Battle of Sakarya. Victory over the Greeks came in the Battle of Dumlupinar in August 1922 and this assured Turkey's sovereignty and the Treaty of Lausanne delineated the borders. *See also* Balkan Crises; Italy.

FURTHER READING: Lewis, Bernard. *The Emergence of Modern Turkey.* New York: Oxford University Press, 1961; Macfie, A. L. *Atatürk.* London: Longman, 1994; Mango, Andre. *Atatürk.* Woodstock, NY: Overlook, 2000.

ANDREKOS VARNAVA

## Kenya

*See* British East African Protectorate

## Kerensky, Alexander (1881–1970)

Head of the Russian Provisional Government at the time of the Bolshevik revolution in October 1917, Alexander Kerensky was born in Simbirsk in 1881, 11 years after the birth in the same town of Vladimir **Lenin,** the future Bolshevik leader. He attended law school in St. Petersburg and participated in student demonstrations and other protests, activities that eventually resulted in his suspension from the bar. In 1914, Kerensky was elected to the Fourth Duma and was the leader of the Trudoviks, a socialist peasant party. When war broke out in August, he led the radical faction that refused to support a war budget, and throughout the war he continued to push for more responsible government. When the February Revolution overthrew **Nicholas II** in 1917, Kerensky was involved in the formation of both the Provisional Government and the Petrograd Soviet.

During the next months, Kerensky's friendly relationship with both the socialist and the liberal camps strengthened his reputation as the only man who could hold the fragile Provisional Government together; consequently, he was chosen as Prime Minister in the summer of 1917. Once appointed, however, Kerensky assumed many of the trappings of the old regime, moving into the Winter Palace and taking over the luxurious quarters of the tsars. These actions exacerbated the growing unpopularity of the Provisional Government as it faced insurmountable challenges and threats from both the left and the right. The fragility of the Provisional Government became even more evident when recently appointed army commander-in-chief, General Lavr Kornilov, staged an apparent attempted coup d'état. Kerensky was forced to appeal to the Bolsheviks for help, releasing leaders like Lev Trotsky from prison and arming the workers militia, the Red Guard. Kornilov was stopped and captured, but the position of the Provisional Government was greatly weakened by this event. Lenin took advantage of this weakness to press his fellow Marxists for immediate revolution. During the fateful coup d'état, Kerensky escaped the Winter Palace and attempted to amass loyal troops from the northern front to fight the Bolsheviks. He remained in hiding in Russia and Finland until May 1918, when he left for London and Paris in an effort to garner Western support for the creation of a democratic Russia. He spent the next two decades in Paris, working against communism and moved to the **United States** during World War II. *See also* Russian Empire.

FURTHER READING: Abraham, Richard. *Alexander Kerensky: The First Love of the Revolution.* New York: Columbia University Press, 1987; Figes, Orlando. *A People's Tragedy: The Russian Revolution, 1891–1924.* New York: Penguin, 1996; Kerensky, Alexander. *The Catastrophe.* New York: Appleton, 1927.

LEE A. FARROW

## Khalsa

Meaning the "Guru's Own," "Khalsa" was the name given by Guru Gobind Singh to all Sikhs who took the initiation of the double-edged sword. In British **India,** it was the word commonly used to refer to the Sikh army in the Punjab, organized primarily by Ranjit **Singh** who united the loosely federated Sikh clans of the Punjab and created a European-style force using European officers, usually French veterans of Napoleon **Bonaparte**'s *Grande Armée* but also British, Americans, Germans, and Italians. The Khalsa was a military fraternity, a superb fighting force, and after Singh's death almost a government within the Sikh state. After the Khalsa's defeat at the Battle of **Gujarat** in the Second Sikh War, the British army began to raise Sikh battalions.

FURTHER READING: Singh, Amandeep, and Parmot Singh. *Warrior Saints: Three Centuries of Sikh Military Tradition.* New York: I. B. Tauris, 1988.

CARL CAVANAGH HODGE

## Khan, Emir Muhammad Alim (1880–1944)

Emir Muhammad Alim Khan was the last ruler of the Bukharan state in Central Eurasia. Khan ruled as Emir of **Bukhara** from 1911 until Bolshevik conquest in 1920. The Bukharans had pledged allegiance to the Russian state and an economic accord in 1868, in the wake of military defeats at Khojand, Samarkand, and other places. Bukhara became an official protectorate of the **Russian Empire** in 1873. Alim Khan took over rule of the Bukharan state after the death of his father, Emir Abdulahad Khan.

Alim Khan's rule was initially reform-based, but evolved into a more traditionally Islamic administration. Alim Khan's Bukharan state was destroyed during the Basmachi revolt and the ensuing Russian conquest of Bukhara in 1920. The emir saw his regime crumble amid growing support for both Enver Pasha's Basmachis and the opposing Russian Bolsheviks. Alim Khan fled his crumbling regime to Afghanistan in 1920, where he lived until his death in Kabul in 1944.

FURTHER READING: Holdsworth, Mary. *Turkestan in the Nineteenth Century: A Brief History of the Khanates of Bukhara, Kokand and Khiva.* Oxford: St. Anthony's College (Oxford) Soviet Affairs Study Group, 1959.

SCOTT C. BAILEY

## Khiva Khanate

Also known historically as Khorezm or Khwarezm, an Islamic state in Central Eurasia, the Khiva Khanate was centered at the city of Khiva, in modern-day Uzbekistan. The khanate established its capital at Khiva as early as 1619 and was under Chinggisid rule for most of that time. In the early nineteenth century, the Inakids took power, removing the Chinggisid element. The new rulers delegated more power to city-dwellers, called Sarts. In 1717–1718, Peter the Great sent a delegation of approximately 300 men to Khiva, who were killed at the hands of the Khivan Khan Shirghazi. Russian imperial interest in the khanate increased during the middle of the nineteenth century. The Russians attacked Khiva following their earlier conquest of **Bukhara** (1868) and annexed the state as a protectorate in 1873. The khanate faced difficult struggles during the war of 1917–1920. In 1920, the Khivan khanate was ended and replaced by the People's Soviet Republic of Khorezm. *See also* India; Russian Empire.

FURTHER READING: Soucek, Svat. *A History of Inner Asia.* Cambridge: Cambridge University Press, 2000.

SCOTT C. BAILEY

## Khmer Empire

*See* Cambodia

## Kiaochow

Kiaochow includes the bay and the port of Tsingtao, present-day Qindao, in northeastern China. The port was seized by the German navy, ostensibly in response to attacks on missionaries and then to claim mining and railway rights in the adjoining territory, and was subsequently leased for 99 years by Germany in 1897–1888. It then became the core of Germany's sphere of influence in Shandong. The occupation set off the "scramble" for other territorial, mining, and railway concessions and contributed to public outrage culminating in the **Boxer Insurrection.** Kiaochow never became the important naval base and "model colony" surrounded by profitable railway and mining ventures it had been planned to be. Seized by Japanese troops in 1914, Kiaochow was returned to China in 1922. *See also* German Empire; Japanese Empire.

FURTHER READING: Schrecker, John. *Imperialism and Chinese Nationalism: Germany in Shantung.* Cambridge, MA: Harvard University Press, 1971.

NIELS P. PETERSSON

## Kiel

Kiel is a city of northern Germany located on the eastern exit of the **Kaiser-Wilhelm-Kanal**; it was a principal naval base of the **German Empire.** Formerly part of the duchy of Holstein, Kiel became part of Prussia as a result of the Seven Weeks' War in 1866. Provided by nature with an excellent harbor, the small town on the Baltic was the ideal site for a maritime base. Already in 1865, the Prussian navy was moved from Danzig to Kiel and before long, shipbuilding developed into Kiel's major industry. Later the city also became the base for the empire's submarines, together with Wilhelmshaven. As a consequence, the city's population increased 10-fold from 16,000 to 160,000 between 1855 and 1905. It rose by another 50 percent between 1905 and 1914, the high tide of the naval arms race.

During the last days of World War I, Kiel witnessed a major mutiny by navy crews. The mutiny started after a number of stokers had been detained because of their refusal to put to sea. In a reaction to this, marines and sailors held meetings and demanded the release of the prisoners. On November 3, 1918, 3,000 demonstrators clashed violently with loyal troops and one day later a soldier's council was formed and the Communist flag hoisted from the Kiel town hall. After Kaiser Wilhelm II's abdication, however, the uprising soon collapsed. *See also* Navalism; Tirpitz Plan.

FURTHER READING: Dähnhardt, Dirk. *Revolution in Kiel: Der Übergang vom Kaiserreich zur Weimarer Republik 1918/19.* Neumünster: Wachholtz, 1978; Wenzel, Rüdiger. *Bevölkerung, Wirtschaft und Politik im kaiserlichen Kiel zwischen 1870 und 1914.* Kiel: Gesellschaft für Kieler Stadtgeschichte, 1978.

ULRICH SCHNAKENBERG

## Kipling, Joseph Rudyard (1865–1936)

A note British poet and author, Rudyard Kipling is now somewhat inaccurately remembered as an uncritical propagandist of **imperialism.** Kipling was born in India to English parents. He was left alone in England from the age of six, his parents returning to India, and attended minor public schools where his literary talents began to show themselves. He began his career as a journalist with a newspaper in Lahore, the capital of the Punjab. In 1886, he published *Departmental Ditties,* and two years later *Plain Tales from the Hills,* books of stories based on the lives of Anglo-Indian officials and soldiers. *Kim,* published in 1901, is probably his most famous novel. Kipling moved to London in 1889, and although as yet a man in his twenties, enjoyed enhanced fame lubricated by brisk sales. Kipling traveled extensively, particularly in the United States, staying for a time in Vermont, the home of his wife's family. After a serious illness, he moved to South Africa, getting there in time for the South African War, in which he served as a military journalist.

The South African War turned Kipling into an ardent supporter of conscription and national preparedness. In the early years of the twentieth century, his attacks on liberalism were ferocious to the point of alienating many of his readers, and he became an ardent Unionist. During World War I, Kipling, considering it the duty of a writer to support his country, turned out a massive volume of patriotic prose. Unusual for a man of first-rate literary talent, he got along well with the great and the good, becoming a friend even of King **George V.** For the last two decades of his life, he was increasingly ill with an ulcer only belatedly diagnosed; it killed him in 1936. Too often reduced to his well-known 1898 injunction to "take up the **white man's burden,**" Kipling portrayed empire, in that poem as well as elsewhere, as a necessary but unrewarding duty. The year before "White Man's Burden," on the occasion of Queen **Victoria**'s diamond jubilee, he had written the prophetic warning against imperial triumphalism, "lo, all our pomp of yesterday/is one with Nineveh and Tyre." *See also* Boer Wars; British Empire; Intelligence.

FURTHER READING: Kipling, Rudyard. *Something of Myself.* Edited by T. Pinney. Cambridge: Cambridge University Press, 1990; Smith, Martin Seymour. *Rudyard Kipling,* New York: St. Martin's Press, 1990.

MARK F. PROUDMAN

## Kitchener, Horatio Herbert, Lord (1850–1916)

A British soldier best known as minister of war during World War I, Horatio Kitchener began his career as a colonial soldier. He led the Anglo-Egyptian expedition into the Sudan and retook Khartoum and defeated the Dervishes at **Omdurman** in 1898. He served as chief of staff during the Boer War before succeeding to overall command, fighting a harsh campaign punctuated by farm-burning and internment, which eventually brought British victory. He then became commander-in-chief of British forces in **India.**

During World War I, Kitchener raised massive new volunteer armies, although he failed adequately to support the Gallipoli campaign in 1915. The extremely long hours he kept and his refusal to delegate responsibilities endeared him neither to other war planners nor to the politicians with whom he had to deal. By the standards of the Victorian era, he was a competent army administrator; the scale of a world war, however, stretched his abilities beyond their capacity. *See also* Boer Wars; Concentration Camps.

FURTHER READING: Pollock, John. *Kitchener.* London: Constable, 2001; Royle, Trevor. *The Kitchener Enigma.* London: M. Joseph, 1985; Simkins, Peter. *Kitchener's Army: The Raising of the New Armies, 1914–16.* Manchester: Manchester University Press, 1988; Warner, Philip. *Kitchener: The Man behind the Legend.* London: Hamish Hamilton, 1985.

GREGORY FREMONT-BARNES

## Kittery Peace (1905)

The settlement that brought to an end the **Russo-Japanese War** that had begun in the spring of 1904. President Theodore **Roosevelt** offered his and the good offices of the **United States** to the two warring parties at the beginning of June

1905. Japanese Emperor **Mutsuhito** accepted Roosevelt's invitation on June 10, with Russian Tsar **Nicholas II** following suit two days later. Delegations from Moscow and Tokyo conducted their talks at the Portsmouth Naval Shipyard on an island in Kittery, Maine, across from Portsmouth, New Hampshire. After a month of negotiations, a peace treaty, know as the **Treaty of Portsmouth,** was signed on September 5, 1905.

The Japanese arrived in New England following their military successes on land and at sea over the Russians and were led by their foreign minister, Jutaro Komura. The Russian plenipotentiary was Count Sergius Witte, and he was assisted by the Russian minister to the United States, Baron Roman Rosen, as Komura was by Kogoro Takahira, the Japanese minister to the United States. In addition to Roosevelt these four individuals were vital to the eventual conclusion of the treaty. As well as the formal talks that took place at the naval shipyard, informal discussions took place in the relaxed atmosphere of the nearby Wentworth Hotel in New Castle, New Hampshire, where the delegates resided.

After agreement on Japanese preponderance in **Korea,** an evacuation of **Manchuria,** and a commitment to open trading, the key issues that came closest to causing deadlock were those of a Russian indemnity to Japan and the future of the disputed island of **Sakhalin.** They proved sufficiently contentious for Roosevelt to have to intervene to break the impasse in mid-August, with Komura eventually accepting that there would be no reparations and that Sakhalin would be divided in half. This compromise was unpopular in Japan and, the United States was blamed. A feature of the negotiations was unprecedented international media coverage. This had an important conciliatory effect because neither party wanted to be portrayed to the world as being the cause of a failed conference.

Roosevelt earned the 1906 Nobel Peace Prize for his success in bringing the two sides to a negotiated settlement despite not attending any of the discussions in New England. Instead, he exerted influence in preliminary meetings with each delegation at his summer residence, Sagamore Hill in Oyster Bay, New York, by bringing the parties together for an introductory lunch, and once the negotiations had begun through back channels coordinated by Herbert H. D. Pierce, the third under secretary of state. Roosevelt also acted as hub for communications with the delegates and their leaders in the various capitals.

Roosevelt's purpose in the whole enterprise was to prevent the war escalating and upsetting a balance of power in the Pacific with Britain and France taking the sides of Japan and Russia, respectively, and Germany and **Italy** also seeking to expand their influence in the region. Roosevelt was well aware that the scope of American interests in the Pacific had recently increased as a consequence of the acquisition of the Philippines after the **Spanish-American War** of 1898 and that this tended to augment those in Alaska and Hawaii. The successful conclusion of the treaty inaugurated by Roosevelt marked a new era of presidential leadership and of American presence in the international diplomatic arena. For the Japanese the settlement saw their emergence as Great Power, and many consider the treaty the beginning of the end for the tsarist regime in Russia. *See also* Anglo-Japanese Alliance; Japanese Empire; Philippines; Russian Empire.

FURTHER READING: Saul, Norman E. "The Kittery Peace." In John W. Steinberg et al., eds. *The Russo-Japanese War in Global Perspective: World War Zero.* Boston: Brill, 2005; Tilchin,

William N. *Theodore Roosevelt and the British Empire: A Study in Presidential Statecraft.* New York: St. Martin's, 1997.

J. SIMON ROFE

## Königgrätz, Battle of (1866)

Also known as the Battle of Sadowa, Königgrätz was the main battle of the Austro-Prussian War. The three-pronged Prussian advance into Bohemia in late June exposed a number of weaknesses in the Austrian North Army and the competence of its senior officers. First, the Prussian army's needle gun had proven vastly superior to Austrian muskets, producing a casualty rate of four Austrians for each Prussian. Second, the Austrian army was not making use of field telegraphs to coordinate army movements. Most important, the Austrian commander, General Ludwig Benedek, never communicated to his subordinates what his plan of campaign was. On July 1, Benedek inexplicably halted the army north of the Austrian fortress system along the Elbe River, northwest of the town of Königgrätz, far enough away that the fortresses offered no protection. Worse still, the Austrian lines were placed poorly, forming a V-shape that made both left and right wings vulnerable, and the Austrians had their backs to the Elbe, limiting opportunities for retreat or reinforcement.

Meanwhile, two Prussian armies were advancing cautiously toward the Austrian fortress system. The First Army, commanded by Prince Frederick Charles, marched roughly east along the Elbe; the Second Army, under the Crown Prince Frederick, was coming south on the other bank of the Elbe. The Prussians learned of the Austrian halt thanks to a single cavalry patrol on the evening of July 2. Frederick Charles received the news and drafted a plan of attack for the First Army alone for the next morning. When Chief of the Prussian General Staff Helmuth von **Moltke** was advised of the impending battle, he amended Frederick Charles's plan by ordering the Second Army to make all due haste to meet outside Königgrätz, and thus have both armies attack the Austrians at the same time. No one was quite sure where the Second Army was, however, and whether it would arrive in time to engage the enemy. The initial stages of the battle did not go well for the Prussians; superior Austrian artillery fire kept the Prussian attackers at bay. The battle soon began to revolve around possession of the Swiepwald, a dense forest on the Prussian left. The Austrians eventually drove the Prussians out of the forest, but at the cost of thousands of casualties from deadly Prussian rifle fire. This and other assaults kept Benedek's attention focused on the center of his lines, ignoring the increasing peril he faced on the right and left.

Meanwhile, the Crown Prince drove his army toward the sound of the guns, hoping to arrive in time to make a difference. Although the Austrian artillery again proved its superiority over the Prussian artillery, Prussian infantry continued to make steady gains. Eventually, the Austrians had to pull their guns back or abandon them. The entire Austrian North Army was in danger of being enveloped on both sides, by Frederick Charles on their left and by the Crown Prince on the right. It took determined resistance by rearguard elements to buy time for the Austrians to retreat over the Elbe, but the Austrian North Army was in no condition to resume hostilities.

The battle of Königgrätz is considered a classic example of Napoleonic strategy: have several forces march separately but concentrate at the field of battle. Even though Moltke was not certain that the Crown Prince's army would arrive in time, he made sure the day's battle plans took the availability of both armies into account. Without Austrian determination, the double-envelopment would have succeeded and the entire Austrian North Army would have been lost. Nevertheless, the Austrians were incapable of opposing the Prussians, and the road to Vienna lay open to Prussian advance. *See also* Bismarck, Otto von; Clausewitz, Carl von; German Empire; Napoleonic Wars.

FURTHER READING: Craig, Gordon A. *The Battle of Königgrätz: Prussia's Victory over Austria.* Philadelphia: University of Pennsylvania Press, 1997; Showalter, Dennis. *The Wars of German Unification.* London: Arnold, 2004; Wawro, Geoffrey. *The Austro-Prussian War.* New York: Cambridge University Press, 1996.

DAVID H. OLIVIER

## Korea

A peninsula protruding southward from the northeastern corner of the Asian continent, Korea was long a victim of imperial aspirations and colonial subjugation. China was considered in Korea as not only the supplier for culture and civilization but also a military conqueror. The history of Sino-Korea relations can be traced back to the early Han Dynasty (206 B.C.–219 A.D.), when China destroyed Weiman Joseon and built four Chinese prefectures in the northern part of Korea in 108 B.C. In 1392, a Korean general, Yi Seonggye, was sent to China to campaign against the Ming Dynasty, but instead he allied himself with the Chinese and returned to overthrow the Goryeo king and establish a new dynasty. The Joseon Dynasty moved the capital to Hanseong, the present-day capital city of Seoul in 1394 and adopted Confucianism as the state religion, resulting in much loss of power and wealth by the Buddhists. During this period, King Sejong invented the *Hangul* alphabet in 1443. The Joseon Dynasty dealt with invasions by Japan from 1592 to 1598. Korea's most famous military figure, Admiral Yi Sun-sin was instrumental in defeating the Japanese. After the invasions from Manchuria in 1627 and 1636, the dynasty submitted herself to the Qing Empire. On the other hand, Korea permitted the Japanese to trade at Pusan and sent missions to the capital of Edo in Japan. Europeans were never permitted to trade at Korean ports until the 1880s. In spite of some efforts to introduce Western technology through the Jesuit missions at Beijing, the Korean economy remained backward as a result of weak currency circulation. Peasants suffering from famine and exploitation often fled to Manchuria.

The Chinese world order in which Sino-Korean tributary relations were built met the fundamental challenge from Japan and Western powers. They demanded the "independence" and "reform" of Korea. Faced with such pressures and threats from competing powers, some reform-minded Korean leaders attempted in the 1880s to implement the Chinese suggestions on Korea's foreign relations called the "Korean Strategy." The idea in the Korean Strategy was the suggestion from China that Korean leaders should open up diplomatic relations not only with Russia but also with Japan and the **United States** on the condition that traditional Sino-Korean tributary relations be maintained. Russian influence could be balanced by Japan, and Japan could be constrained by the United States. The strategy turned out to be a grand failure, because both China and Korea were too weak to defend themselves against rising imperialist pressures. The Chinese defeat in the **Sino-Japanese War** (1894–1895) meant the collapse of the Chinese world order, as well as Chinese loss of suzerain status in Korea. Indeed, China was forced to agree that Korea be "an independent state," which led progressively to Korean dependence on Japan. After Japanese victories in the **Russo-Japanese War** of 1905, Japan's hegemonic influence over Korea increased, as the Treaty of Portsmouth recognized is a Japanese **protectorate.** Hiroboumi **Itō** was appointed the first resident governor in 1905. In 1907, the Hague Conference recognized Japan's takeover, and in 1908 the Root-Takahira Agreement confirmed American acceptance of Japan's position on the peninsula in return for Japanese recognition of the position of the United States in the **Philippines.** Korea was redefined under Japanese colonial rule. Even before the country was formally annexed, the Japanese forced the last ruling monarch, King Kojong, to abdicate the throne in 1907 in favor of his feeble son, who was soon married to a Japanese woman and given a Japanese peerage. Itō attempted in vain to promote liberal reforms and was in 1909 rewarded for his efforts by assassination at the hands of Korean nationalist. In 1910, Japan annexed Korea outright. In theory the Koreans, as subjects of the Japanese emperor, enjoyed the same status as the Japanese, but in fact the Japanese government tried to assimilate Korea into the so-called Greater Japan. Threat to the Korean identity gave rise to nationalist sentiments and Korean students demonstrated in Japan. On March 1, 1919, street demonstrations erupted throughout the country to protest Japanese rule. *See also* Japanese Empire; Roosevelt, Theodore; Russian Empire.

FURTHER READING: Cumings, Bruce. *Korea's Place in the Sun.* New York: W. W. Norton, 1998; Fairbank, J. K., ed. *The Chinese World Order.* Cambridge, MA: Harvard University Press, 1968; Hsu, Immanuel C. Y., ed. *Readings in Modern Chinese History.* New York: Oxford University Press, 1971; Nahm, Andrew C. *Korea: Tradition and Transformation: A History of the Korean People.* Seoul: Hollym International Corporation, 1996; Wells, Kenneth M. *New God, New Nation: Protestants and Self-Reconstruction Nationalism in Korea, 1896–1937.* Honolulu: University of Hawaii Press, 1991.

JITENDRA UTTAM

## Krasnoi, Battles of (1812)

A series of running skirmishes fought around Krasnoye Selo, southwest of St. Petersburg, during Napoleon **Bonaparte**'s retreat from **Moscow.** As Napoleon closed in on Smolensk in August, he sent Murat's cavalry against Neveroski's division of Barclay's Russian army. Murat's attacks were foiled by the Russian formation of a large square, and the lack of infantry or artillery support doomed his efforts. The Russians withdrew to Smolensk, and Napoleon's delay in pursuit allowed the Russians to strengthen their defensive positions.

Toward the end of the French army's withdrawal from Moscow, Kutuzov's Russian forces were pressing Napoleon and threatening to block the road between Smolensk and Krasnoi, thus dividing Napoleon's strung-out army. Napoleon had one good fighting unit left—the Imperial Guard—and he sent its 18,000 men against Kutuzov's 35,000 on November 17. The Russians were completely surprised and quickly retreated. This cleared the road and allowed the French army to consolidate by late in the day, and they moved on, leaving behind only Ney's missing rearguard. *See also* Napoleonic Wars; Russian Empire.

FURTHER READING: Palmer, Alan. *Napoleon in Russia.* London: Andre Deutsch, 1967.

J. DAVID MARKHAM

## Kruger, Stephanus Johannes Paulus (1825–1904)

Paul Kruger was a Boer politician and statesman, president of the **Transvaal,** and leader in both **Boer Wars** against British rule in South Africa. Born in the **Cape Colony** to a family of strict Puritans, Kruger, at the age of 11, migrated with them in the **Great Trek** of 1834 to the territory beyond the Orange River. A man of high intelligence, Kruger was also an adherent of Old Testament principles and a skilled military commander. He was commandant-general of the Transvaal between 1863 and 1877 and thereafter became vice-president. Kruger bitterly opposed the British annexation of the Transvaal and traveled to London twice in an attempt to reverse it, armed in the second instance with a petition testifying to Boer opposition to British rule. Having failed to secure Boer independence by diplomatic means, Kruger then led the rebellion of 1880 that developed into the First Boer War. Boer forces inflicted a series of small yet shocking defeats on British forces, the most notable at Majuba Hill in February 1881, after which the British agreed to the **Pretoria** Convention restoring self-government to the Boer population.

Kruger became president of the Transvaal in 1883, a position in which he negotiated an improved Pretoria Convention in 1884. In 1886, however, the Transvaal again came under pressure after gold was discovered in Witwatersrand and mining entrepreneurs, known to the Boer population at *Uitlanders,* began to pour into the republic. Rightly apprehensive that the mining boom and the influx of non-Boers threatened the republic's way of life, Kruger's government enacted a 14-year residency requirement for voting rights on the *Uitlanders,* imposed high taxes on mining operations, and controlled the sale of dynamite and spirits. Cecil **Rhodes,** premier of the Cape Colony, saw in *Uitlander* resentment of Kruger's government an opportunity to again attempt British control of Transvaal. After the failure of the **Jameson Raid,** Kaiser **Wilhelm II** of Germany inflamed the situation by sending a congratulatory telegram to Kruger for having preserved the Transvaal's freedom. For his part, Kruger simultaneously built up the Transvaal's fighting capacity—not least of all with the import of 37,000 Mauser rifles and **Krupp** howitzers from Germany—and enticed the **Orange Free State** into an alliance against the British. He also offered concessions to the *Uitlanders* and negotiated with Alfred **Milner,** governor of the Cape Colony and, after 1897, British high commissioner to South Africa. Realizing that Milner intended no compromise acceptable to the Boers, Kruger delivered an ultimatum to the British government and on October 12, 1899, launched an invasion of Natal. After initial Boer successes, it became apparent that Britain intended to prevail. As the tide turned against the Boer forces, Kruger was smuggled out of Pretoria to the frontier of Portuguese Mozambique in May 1900 to travel to Europe in pursuit of aid. He received tea and sympathy, but no more. Kruger was never able to return to the Transvaal. He settled in the **Netherlands** and died in Switzerland in July 1904.

FURTHER READING: Fisher, John. *Paul Kruger: His Life and Times.* London: Secker & Warburg, 1974; Pakenham, Thomas. *The Boer War.* New York: Random House, 1979.

CARL CAVANAGH HODGE

### Krupp, Alfred (1812–1887)

Known as the "cannon king," Alfred Krupp turned the factory inherited from his father, Friedrich **Krupp,** into the biggest steel conglomerate in the world. Krupp started his early career by selling cutlery-producing machines, copying the English cast iron technique. As his works in the town of Essen were part of Prussia, Krupp profited from the formation of the **Zollverein.** In 1848, his experiments with cast iron cannons yielded fruit and his business slowly but inevitably grew. Nevertheless, when revolution broke out in Germany he hardly employed a hundred workers. Only a few years later, he had more than a thousand laborers under contract. This first expansion was made possible by the transport revolution. As Krupp started to produce seamless **railroad** wheels, patented in 1852, his business grew in proportion to the extent of the German railway system. When the patent expired after seven years, the company had outperformed its main competitors and faced a glorious future.

Krupp was now eager to take on other fields of production. He was an able technician but an even better businessman. More than once on the brink of bankruptcy, Krupp reinvested nearly all his earnings in new machinery, huts, and mines. His economic success was largely based on his embrace of innovation, quick adaptation of new technology and outstanding managerial skills. But most of all, Krupp was a marketing genius. Being present at the first world exhibition in London in 1851, his products attracted huge crowds and earned him an excellent international reputation. Although for some time he vainly tried to sell his cast iron cannons, in 1854 his long-term marketing efforts proved successful. On June 15, Prince Wilhelm, later emperor of the Reich, visited the Krupp factory in Essen on a tour through the province of Westphalia. The prince showed great interest in the modern artillery and after Wilhelm had become regent, the Prussian army finally ordered the first 300 cannons in 1859. This was the beginning of a mutually beneficial bargain: the Prussian army was equipped with state-of-the art weaponry and the monarchy bailed Krupp out whenever he was in financial trouble; however, Krupp also sold his artillery to other European powers. During the Schleswig-Holstein War in 1864, Krupp's cannons stood on both sides. Napoleon III also took a keen interest in Krupp's products. To appease angry French weapon manufacturers, however, he had to refrain from buying in Germany.

From 1859 onward, the Prussian army became Krupp's single most important customer, and his provision of cutting-edge steel cannons played a major role in the explanation of the resounding German victory in the **Franco-Prussian War** of 1870. The Krupp guns proved to be decisively superior to the traditional bronze cannons fielded by the French. With the war ending, Krupp was at the height of his powers. Employing more than 10,000 workmen, he owned the biggest ironworks in the German Empire. Moreover, Krupp was on excellent terms with many members of the Reich's political and military elite. Especially generals of the German army were regular guests at his private palace, the Villa Hügel in Essen. Germany had been lagging behind in economic modernization until the middle of the nineteenth century, and Krupp increasingly epitomized German ascent in the age of industry. After Krupp's death, his heirs continued to equip the empire's army until its demise in 1918. *See also* Moltke, Helmuth von; German Empire.

FURTHER READING: Gall, Lothar. *Krupp: Der Aufstieg eines Industrieimperiums.* Berlin: Siedler, 2000; Manchester, William. *The Arms of Krupp, 1587–1968.* Boston: Little, Brown and Company, 1968; Mühlen, Norbert. *The Incredible Krupps.* New York: Holt, 1959.

ULRICH SCHNAKENBERG

## Krupp, Friedrich (1787–1826)

Founder of the Krupp cast iron factory, Friedrich Krupp descended from an old family of merchants. Endowed with a vision and a considerable heritage from his grandmother, he founded a cast iron works outside Essen in the Ruhr area in 1811. The prospects of success seemed excellent: outside England, heavy steel products were not to be found in Europe. Krupp's potential position in the market was further enhanced by Napoleon **Bonaparte**'s **Continental System,** which blockaded European ports and more or less successfully kept out British exports. Despite these advantages, Krupp lacked essential entrepreneurial skills. His business fortunes resembled a roller coaster ride. In addition, Krupp ruined his health in his shop. When he died, at age 39, the factory was heavily in debt and Krupp employed no more than seven workmen. *See also* Krupp, Alfred; Napoleonic Wars.

FURTHER READING: Saur, Karl-Otto. *Friedrich Krupp.* Berlin: Ullstein, 1999; Schröder, Ernst. *Krupp. Geschichte einer Unternehmerfamilie.* Göttingen: Muster-Schmidt, 1991.

ULRICH SCHNAKENBERG

## *Kulturkampf*

The *Kulturkampf* (1871–78), meaning "cultural conflict," was a political struggle that raged between Otto von **Bismarck** and the Catholic Church over the place and power of the church in German society. Given the recent unification of Germany, Bismarck was highly suspicious of any institution that threatened the stability of the Reich or rivaled the new imperial state for the loyalty of the German masses. Although the new **German Empire** largely consisted of the old Protestant-dominated **North German Confederation,** Bismarck worried that the admission of Catholic south German states and the existence of large Catholic minorities in **Alsace-Lorraine** and Prussian Poland might upset the religious balance of power and lead to sectarian conflict, which would rip apart the empire. These fears deepened in 1870 with the creation of the Center Party, formed to represent Catholic political interests, and the Vatican Council's decree that the pope was infallible when speaking on matters of faith and morals. Both measures implied that Catholics owed their primary loyalty to the pope and would use the Center Party to do his bidding.

Bismarck responded to this implied threat by unleashing a series of laws designed to slash the power of the Church and eliminate its ability to indoctrinate German citizens by putting schools under state supervision. In 1871, the imperial government passed laws forbidding priests from using their pulpits to discuss politics, expelling the Jesuit order from Germany, putting religious schools under state supervision, and purging religious teachers from state-run educational institutions. In May 1873, the so-called Falk Laws, named after Prussian Minister of Culture Adalbert

Falk, extended state control over the clergy by regulating the ordination of priests, mandating civil marriage, and granting state agencies disciplinary power over the Church. Priests and bishops who refused to comply faced arrest or expulsion from Germany.

A combination of fierce Catholic resistance to these measures, most visibly expressed by the Center party's doubling of its seats in the 1874 **Reichstag** elections, and pragmatism forced Bismarck to reconsider his anti-Catholic stance. Eager to secure the support of the Center Party for his anti-Socialist campaign and an increase in import tariffs designed to protect his political base, Bismarck began gradually rescinding the more repressive anti-Catholic laws. This process was greatly facilitated by the death of Pius IX and the ascension of the more conciliatory Leo XIII as pope in 1878.

Despite its domestic resolution, the *Kulturkampf* had long-lasting colonial implications. Concerned that hostility from German colonial officials could negatively affect their evangelical efforts, Catholic missionaries attempted to prove their loyalty by becoming staunch supporters of official colonial policies. In particular, German Catholic missionaries tended to accept and implement official directives regarding the shape and content of education in the German colonies. *See also* Missionaries.

FURTHER READING: Clark, Christopher, and Wolfram Kaiser. *Culture Wars: Secular-Catholic Conflict in Nineteenth Century Europe*. Cambridge: Cambridge University Press, 2003; Gross, Michael B. *The War against Catholicism: Liberalism and the Anti-Catholic Imagination in Nineteenth Century Germany*. Ann Arbor: University of Michigan Press, 2000; Ross, Ronald J. *The Failure of Bismarck's Kulturkampf: Catholicism and State Power in Imperial Germany, 1871–1887*. Washington, DC: Catholic University of America Press, 1998; Smith, Helmut Walser. *German Nationalism and Religious Conflict: Culture, Ideology, Politics 1870–1914*. Princeton, NJ: Princeton University Press, 1995.

KENNETH J. OROSZ

## Kunanbaev, Abai (1845–1904)

Also known as Abai Qunan-bai, Abai Kunanbaev was a Kazakh intellectual, poet, writer, and composer whose writings and ideas have been portrayed as both supportive of Kazakh nationalism and critical of Kazakh national shortcomings. Some have seen him, such as the twentieth-century Kazakh writer Mukhtar Auezov, as critical of the Kazakh nation and supportive of efforts toward their further Russification. More recent attempts have been made by Kazakh historians to present Abai as a champion of the Kazakh nation. Regardless, Kunanbaev was supportive of modernization for the Kazakhs and is recognized as one of the first and most influential modern Kazakh intellectuals. His writings were often philosophical. In Kunanbaev's *Book of Words*, he struggles to come to terms with the economic, social, and political transitions of the Kazakh nation in the late nineteenth century. He was educated both in a Russian school and in a madrasa. *See also* Russian Empire.

FURTHER READING: Auezov, Mukhtar. *Abai: A Novel*. Moscow: Foreign Languages Publishing House, n.d.; Kunanbaev, Abai. *Book of Words*. Translated by David Aitkyn and Richard McKane. Almaty: EL Bureau, 1995.

SCOTT C. BAILEY

## Kwang-chow Wan

Kwang-chow Wan was a port and coaling station in China's south Kwantung province just north of Hainan Island. In 1898, France obtained a 99-year lease on the territory from the Chinese government on the same terms as Liaochow was held by Germany, **Port Arthur** by Russia, and **Weihaiwei** by Britain. The cession provided for full extraterritorial control of the jurisdiction for the duration of the lease, as well as a *de facto* acknowledgment of a French sphere of influence in the southern provinces of Kwantung, Kwangsi, and Yunnan. In 1900, Kwang-chow Wan was placed under the jurisdiction of the governor-general of **Indochina,** who appointed a civil administrator for the territory. *See also* Boxer Insurrection; French Empire.

FURTHER READING: Brötel, D. *Frankreich im Fernen Osten: Imperialistische Expansion Aspiration in Siam und Malaya, Laos und China, 1880–1904.* Stuttgart: Steiner, 1996.

ADRIAN U-JIN ANG